British Political History 1867–1990

How and why has Britain changed over the last 125 years? In a single text, this book examines the key elements in the evolution of today's society.

Illustrated with original cartoons and documents, and making good use of contemporary quotes, it is written in a coherent and accessible style intended both to inform and to stimulate discussion. Each chapter provides an in-depth survey which explores key issues within the topic and includes a section outlining recent trends and debates in historical interpretation.

British Political History 1867–1990 is not afraid to approach broad themes and take a fresh view of British history, setting politics within wider cultural, economic and social contexts. Up to date both in content and approach, this is a thought-provoking text which successfully bridges the gap between A-level and higher education.

Malcolm Pearce is Head of Politics and **Geoffrey Stewart** is Head of History at York Sixth Form College. They are both experienced A-level teachers and examiners, and their previously published books include the successful *Sources in History* series.

British Political History 1867–1990

Democracy and Decline

Malcolm Pearce and Geoffrey Stewart

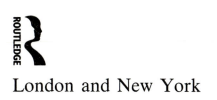

London and New York

First published 1992
by Routledge
11 New Fetter Lane, London EC4P 4EE

Simultaneously published in the USA and Canada
by Routledge
29 West 35th Street, New York, NY 10001

Reprinted 1994

Typeset in 10/12 pt Times by
Intype Ltd, London
Printed in Great Britain by
T J Press (Padstow) Ltd, Padstow, Cornwall

British Library Cataloguing in Publication Data
Pearce, Malcolm L.
  British political history 1867–1990: Democracy and decline.
  I. Title   II. Stewart, Geoffrey
  941.08

Library of Congress Cataloging in Publication Data
Pearce, Malcolm
    British political history 1867–1990: Democracy and decline
  Malcolm Pearce and Geoffrey Stewart.
      p. cm.
    Includes bibliographical references and index.
    1. Great Britain—History—20th century. 2. Great
  Britain—History—Victoria, 1837–1901. I. Stewart, Geoffrey.
  II. Title.
  DA566.P43 1992
  941.08–dc20   91–33613

ISBN 0–415–07246–8 (hbk)
ISBN 0–415–07247–6 (pbk)

FOR DIANA
(M.L.P.)

TO ALL MY FAMILY
AND THE MEMORY
OF THE THREE 'Bs'
(G.S.)

Contents

Illustrations

Maps

Preface

This is clearly not a work of original scholarship but the offering of two practising and busy A-level teachers. It is intended to present, in a form as simple as is possible with minimal distortion, a complex mass of events upon which students will then be encouraged to form their own opinions and judgements. The text is complemented by relevant, and we hope enlightening, visual sources and an arbitrary selection of some of the primary written sources that historians use in constructing their narratives and analyses. In a work which attempts to cover over a hundred and twenty years of history it is inevitable that certain events have had to be omitted which some scholars and teachers would consider vital. The division of this period into fourteen chapters must also be thought by some to be idiosyncratic. The choices were made on the grounds of clarity of theme for the reader as well as association with possible examination topics. The book therefore follows the pattern that many teachers might choose to adopt in their lessons.

At the end of each chapter are two important additional sections. The first is headed 'Controversy'. These controversies are not intended to be definitive historiographies of the topic covered but introductions to historiography, making the student aware of one area of historical debate relevant to individual chapters. These controversies vary enormously in range and emphasis from the extensive one on Victorian imperialism at the end of chapter 5 to a straightforward survey of the perceptions of the inter-war years at the end of chapter 9. The simple example given at the end of chapter 14 of how different primary sources can be used to construct a narrative and analysis of one narrowly focused issue is a third variant. The second section at the end of each chapter is a bibliography. Once again, these are not intended to be in any way exhaustive. Where possible, recent and readily available texts are included. These lists of books are there not for appearance's sake but to guide students to further reading, graded according to a simple scale. In general terms '1' denotes a text that is both short and aimed specifically at sixth-form students. No-one attempting to secure an A-level pass should find such texts beyond them. A '2' suggests a slightly longer book which more often than not has been written for the general reader and is either simply constructed or in a narrative style that makes it easily accessible to most students. The designation '3' suggests a 'major read' but not one beyond a good A-level student who is prepared to put in extra effort. Those texts denoted with '4' are either works of high scholarship or very long indeed which could be off-putting to many A-level students. They can, however, still be used selectively, with careful guidance. Any rating system is by its nature subjective, after all one man's difficult read can be another woman's literary jaunt and vice versa, but the grading in terms of length and difficulty will, we hope, be generally useful.

Finally, the sources for coursework sections at the end of chapters again can be no more than simple pointers, suggesting a few lines of fruitful enquiry. All students should, of course, familiarize themselves with their local lending and reference libraries in order to locate the information they need or identify suitable alternative sources. There is access to virtually every book in print via the inter-library loan service (a small charge may be made) although students must be aware of the need to order certain texts, in some cases months in advance, when using this overstretched resource.

Geoffrey Stewart and
Malcolm Pearce
York Sixth Form College

Acknowledgements

The authors and publisher gratefully acknowledge permission to reproduce the illustrations. Copyright holders are credited in the list of illustrations on p. xii.

The extracts from manifestos in chapter 12 are reprinted by permission of the Labour Party and the Conservative Party.

The authors are grateful to Andrew Hicks of York Sixth Form College, who drew the maps.

1 Introduction: Britain in 1867

INTRODUCTION

The toilet roll lay four years in the future. To the 1870s also belonged the appearance of chewing-gum, jeans and milk chocolate. The men and women of 1867 were without all these everyday articles which ease our path through life in the twentieth century. They would have to wait 19 years for Coca-Cola, 26 for breakfast cereals and 30 years for arguably the greatest of all medicines: the humble aspirin. Milk bottles, bras and soap powder would not offer their welcome presence until the early years of the present century. It was a world, in various important aspects, very different from our own.

What events distinguished 1867, the thirtieth year of Queen Victoria's reign, from those that followed it and preceded it? On the eastern borders of Europe, Count Leo Tolstoy was writing *War and Peace*. In far away Japan perhaps the most momentous events of the year were taking place as Emperor Meiji revoked the powers of the shogunate and launched Japan on its revolutionary course of modernization. In central Europe the North German Confederation came into existence, a major step towards the eventual unification of Germany under Prussian, and more particularly Bismarck's, leadership. In Paris the emperor Napoleon III enjoyed the Paris exhibition which drew vast crowds, and Verdi's new opera 'Don Carlos' had its opening. Manet, Degas and other Impressionist painters were rocking the art establishment of France – and establishing their reputations.

In Britain the Second Reform Act became law in August, giving the vote to one in three males. Women were, of course, excluded. However, for the first time the working classes formed a majority of the electorate and for many Conservatives the nightmare concept of democracy had apparently become a reality. The new iron-clad HMS *Hercules* was launched, emphasizing Britain's technological pre-eminence and the fact that Britannia really did rule the waves. Darker deeds marked the ending of the year when Fenians in their fight for an independent Ireland blew up the outer wall of London's Clerkenwell prison. Over-generous with their quantities of explosives they killed twelve people, injured 120, and demolished several houses. The Fenians had used gun-powder but the year also saw the invention of dynamite. From now on bigger explosions would be possible.

PEOPLE AND PLACES

There were considerably fewer Britons in 1867 than there are in the late twentieth century. England and Wales contained 21.5 million people, compared to the present 50 million, and Scotland had just over 3 million, compared to today's figure of a little over 5 million. In Ireland the position was reversed with at least 1 million more Irish men and women in the 1860s than in the 1980s. It was the Celtic fringes which provided the largest percentage of migrants to all parts of the globe in the last quarter of the nineteenth century. In the United Kingdom as a whole there were 800,000 more women than there were men, and children formed a greater percentage of the population. There were many fewer old folk, especially those over 70.

The population had been rising rapidly throughout the nineteenth century. The birth rate per thousand was three times that of the late twentieth century. The death rate was twice as great and causes of death changed with seasons – the cold carrying most off in the winter months and water-borne diseases taking their toll in the summer. In the 1860s the already high mortality rates actually increased, at least for the first part of the decade, and there had been no significant improvement compared with the early years of the century. Many people were under-nourished but then a large proportion of the population had always gone hungry. Despite all the efforts of the Public Health reformers of the 1830s and 1840s much remained to be done. It was in the overcrowded cities that mortality rates were highest. Cholera, the new curse of the nineteenth century, had its last great outbreak in 1866–7, killing over 2,000 people in Liverpool alone. Smallpox, the 'grim reaper' of the eighteenth century, was still rampant and the last swipe of this disease in the early 1870s took the lives of nearly one thousand people. However, the chief killers remained the more mundane diarrhoea and dysentery that succeeded in carrying off 50,000 in Liverpool in the 1860s. In the same decade whooping cough killed another 32,000 in that city. Many of the victims were children, and infant mortality remained stubbornly high at around 150 per 1,000 live births up until the First World War.

In the last quarter of the nineteenth century market forces and state and municipal action combined to produce a dramatic improvement in life expectancy. The state finally grasped the nettle of public health by legislating on such fundamental issues as sewage disposal and water supply. It is significant that the last cholera outbreak in Britain only really affected those parts of the East End untouched by the new improved water system of London. Birmingham was much worse affected than Manchester but then half of Birmingham's water came from wells some of which filled with seepage from the city's largest graveyard. Manchester's water supply, on the other hand, was a model for the rest of the country.

Market forces provided a vast improvement in food supplies and consequently in living standards. From the late 1870s the price of wheat tumbled as foreign imports flooded in. Canned meat from the Americas and refrigerated lamb from the Antipodes combined to boost the diet of Britons to hitherto unknown heights, even higher than the previous zenith of the 1450s when plague and population loss had left the survivors with ample food supplies. In the late nineteenth century the food production of the newly settled regions of the world, many of them populated by British migrants, gave the British Isles not just a temporary feast but a steadily improving diet. By 1900 life expectancy was over 50, an improvement of some twenty years on what it had been in 1800. The New World had come to the rescue of the Old.

There was a price to be paid for this dietary bonanza, which was met by rural Britain and even more so by rural Ireland. The collapse of grain prices had a devastating effect on British agriculture. In the 1860s however this lay in the future. The protective Corn Laws had been repealed in 1846 and despite dire warnings of the flood of foreign grain English agriculture had prospered in the 1850s and 1860s in what has been described as its 'Golden Age'. The largest occupation category of the 1861 Census was 'Agricultural labourer, farm servant and shepherd', of which 1,188,789 were recorded. A further quarter of a million were described as 'Farmers or graziers'. Agriculture remained overwhelmingly the largest employer with three times as many workers as the second largest, the textile industry. Blacksmiths numbered 100,000 and there were 32,000 millers. Yet the same census records a momentous change in its report of 1863:

> 781 towns . . . contained 10,960,998 inhabitants; while the villages and country parishes contained 9,105,226, a large population in itself, and exceeding indeed in number the whole population of England and Wales in 1801, but less by 1,855,772 than the population of the towns in 1861.
>
> The English nation then, without losing its hold on the country, and still largely diffused over 37 million acres of territory, has assumed the character of a preponderating city population.
>
> (*Parliamentary Papers*, 1863, vol. LIII/I, p. 11)

Many of these 781 towns were, in fact, small country towns, essentially rural rather than urban in character. Only 28.8 per cent lived in cities containing over 100,000 inhabitants. Even so Britain was unique in the world and the world's history. It had become, by this time, a predominantly urban society and the implications of this were enormous.

London was a world phenomenon. The greater London conurbation contained some 3.5 million people by 1867. The capital of the 1860s caught the attention of various writers, each giving different insights and impressions and emphasizing different aspects. As Henry James wrote in 1868, 'Its immensity was the great fact, and that was a charm; the miles of housetops and viaducts, the complications of junctions and signals through which the train made its way to the station had already given me the scale.' Large as it was, great tracts of what we think of today as Greater London were fields and villages. Hampstead retained its separate village identity and Harrow lay far out through fields and country from the newly urbanized area of Paddington.

The capital was a city of many extremes and contrasts. The rush hour was already established, and the traffic jam clearly existed too, especially at the bottle necks at crossing points of the river. Dickens, in his last great novel, *Our Mutual Friend*, published in 1865, shows us the low-life London of the river and also scenes from the more affluent London of the rich Boffins. Trollope's political novels of the late 1860s and the 1870s describe the high political world which was also sketched from time to time in the *London Illustrated News*. The world of the Mall with its male swells and shapely, well-tailored females is not far from the Haymarket with its army of prostitutes and dolly mops – part-time prostitutes which some authorities have estimated numbered 80,000 throughout London as a whole.

In one sense there was nothing new about the relative size and dominance of nineteenth-century London. In Elizabethan times its crowded streets and teeming population had stood in stark contrast to the villages of Tudor England. Now in the reign of Victoria other great manufacturing centres rose to rival the capital and grew with astonishing speed. Liverpool, already mentioned for its appalling health record, was the second city of England. Manchester, capital of the 'Cotton Kingdom' of Lancashire, ranked third with a population of 357,979 in 1861. These and other northern and Midland cities were the new urban England of the nineteenth century, the product of the Industrial Revolution, enriched by their trade and industry and proud of their achievements, as their new town halls and libraries still proclaim to the twentieth century. Manchester seemed to embody this new England in the early nineteenth century, and Birmingham in later decades. There is a danger of stereotyping these throbbing industrial centres of steam, smoke and squalor. Dickens himself was guilty of this in his 1850s creation of Coketown in *Hard Times*. Perhaps Mrs Gaskell's Milton – surely her own Manchester – is more balanced: 'the chimneys smoked the ceaseless roar and mighty beat and dazzling whirl of machinery struggled and strove perpetually.'

Glossop in the 1850s

Here also was real poverty and suffering to set against the image of the prosperous thrifty skilled worker.

Besides the great cities of Leeds, Bradford, Manchester, among others, were the new little industrial centres – hamlets and villages in the eighteenth century but now bustling communities with their factories lining the banks of rivers and their rows of workers' cottages filling the fields. Glossop in north-west Derbyshire had swelled its numbers from a mere 2,759 in 1801 to 19,126 by 1861. Its new town centre covered an area of former marsh ground, and bricks and mortar rolled down the valley bottom alongside the great cotton factories of Wood and Sumner. The Glossop gas company had been established in 1845 and eight years later piped water was available for mill and cottage. Churches and chapels multiplied along with the public houses and in 1866 came the crowning glory: borough status. The growth of Manchester, Liverpool and Glossop all reflected the growing importance of cotton textile manufacture, a vital component in the national wealth – contributing as it did 8 per cent to Great Britain's national income in 1850 (agriculture contributed 20 per cent). A large proportion of the cloth produced, perhaps 67 per cent in the late 1860s, was exported. By the 1860s the steam engine was everywhere triumphant. The handloom weaver whose cries of despair echoed in the 1830s and 1840s was now largely extinct. The factory system and factory life was the norm.

Across the Pennines the older woollen industry grew and likewise adopted factory production methods but it never equalled in the late nineteenth century the size and importance of its Lancastrian rival. Coal-mining, iron-production and ship-building were the other great industries which made Britain foremost in the world in 1867. In each case Britain had out-produced all other countries. Coal-mining still had a long way to go before its output peaked in 1914 but it was already a large and very visible industry, making an immediate impact on the landscape of north-east England, South Wales and other coal-mining regions. In 1870 Britain produced 50 per cent of the world's pig-iron and 40 per cent of the world's steel, much of the latter produced by the new mass production techniques pioneered by the English inventor Henry Bessemer in the 1850s. In ship-building sail still outstripped steam and in 1860 there was still ten times the tonnage under sail as under steam. The position was changing rapidly, though, and British shipyards, which had been struggling against American and Scandinavian rivals in wooden construction, now consolidated a world-commanding lead in ship-building using iron which was maintained until 1914. The railway was the other vital component of the British economic scene. Invented and developed first in the British Isles, a sophisticated rail network covered the country by the late 1860s and helped to create a new life-style. Two hundred and fifty million passengers travelled by rail in 1867 and journey times had been slashed: in 1830 York to London took twenty hours – by the 1860s the journey by rail took under four hours. The Kingdom was united in more than just a political sense. Newspapers and people could now reach every corner of the island in twenty-four hours.

What has been described in bare outline is the economy of the richest country in the world. In 1870 perhaps one-third of all the articles manufactured on earth came from Britain. She was responsible in the preceding decade for 30 per cent of all Europe's commerce with the rest of the world and for 43 per cent of all Europe's manufactured exports. She appeared to have left all her rivals behind and established a staggering economic lead. In fact this lead had been built up since the end of the seventeenth century, for by modern standards the economic growth of the British Isles in the nineteenth century was not great – on average just over 2 per cent per annum. In the second half of the century other countries began to catch up and grow markedly faster. In 1880 the USA's GNP (gross national product), the measure used to indicate the wealth of a nation, was greater than that of Britain, and by 1914 Germany had also just about passed her as well. Nevertheless, throughout the whole of the nineteenth century Britain's GNP per head of population was considerably higher than her continental neighbours as the figures in Table 1.1 indicate.

The so-called 'average Briton' was considerably richer than the 'average Continental', but both of them were massively poorer than their

Table 1.1 Per capita GNP of the European great powers, 1830–90 (in 1960 US dollars and prices)

	1830	1840	1850	1860	1870	1880	1890
Britain	346	394	458	558	628	680	785
Italy	265	270	277	301	312	311	311
France	264	302	333	365	437	464	515
Germany	245	267	308	354	426	443	537
Habsburg Empire	250	266	283	288	305	315	361
Russia	170	170	175	178	250	224	182

Source: P. Kennedy, *The Rise and Fall of Great Powers*, London, Unwin Hyman, 1988, p. 171.

twentieth-century descendants. Even the richest country in the world contained hideous poverty. This arose not from man's wickedness nor even the maldistribution of wealth but mostly from the low level of production when compared with the twentieth-century norms of developed countries. However, it is true to say that what wealth there was in the Britain of 1867 was very unevenly distributed.

But even if all the wealth in Britain had been more evenly shared the result would still have been misery and deprivation on a massive scale. The most advanced state in the world in 1867 was what we would call

Table 1.2 Distribution of the national income between families, England and Wales, 1867

	Families		Income	
	Number 000	Percentage	Amount £000	Percentage
I Upper class				
(1) £5,000+	4.5	0.07	111,104	16.2
(2) £1,000–£5,000	25.2	0.41	69,440	10.1
II Middle class				
£300–£1,000	90.0	1.46	72,912	10.6
III Lower middle				
(1) £100–£300	510.3	8.29	93,744	13.7
(2) Under £100	946.0	15.37	70,958	10.3
Upper and middle classes	1,576.0	25.6	418,158	60.9
IV Higher skilled	840.8	13.8	72,028	10.5
V Lower skilled	1,610.0	26.1	112,042	16.3
VI Unskilled and agricultural	1,516.8	24.6	70,659	10.3
VII Wageless families	610.4	9.9	13,466	2.0
Manual labour classes	4,578.0	74.4	268,195	39.1
All classes	6,154.0	100.0	686,353	100.0

Source: H. Perkin, *The Origins of Modern English Society*, London, Routledge & Kegan Paul, 1969, p. 420.

a developing country, on a par with those of South America in the late twentieth century. What can be said of our Victorian ancestors is that they made great strides and provided a worthy example of how man could begin to conquer the curse of poverty. Their tools were their ingenuity, capacity for hard work and, it must be admitted, greed.

THOUGHT AND FEELING

The physical world of 1867 can be re-created today using photographs, statistics and the vast welter of sources available to students of history in the twentieth century as evidence for their enquiry. The mental world is more elusive and the risk of over-simplification and stereotyping is always present in any attempted generalization. We have included some cartoons from *Punch* for 1867, not necessarily for political comment but for what they can tell us about the values of some Victorians. These values can be found in two senses – those that the cartoonist hoped to get across to his audience and those that sharp-witted observers can discern for themselves at a distance of time.

Charles Dickens, Anthony Trollope, George Eliot and Alfred, Lord Tennyson were all literary figures of the 1860s and reading their works is invaluable for the insights it can give into their society, provided we realize that each one was an individual and may have possessed particularly idiosyncratic or, at least, distinctly minority opinions. Trollope was scathing in his view of Dickens as 'Mr. Popular Sentiment', yet it is Dickens's very widespread popularity in mid-Victorian Britain that makes him so useful in our quest for knowledge about the period.

Religion figured more deeply in the lives of our forefathers than it does in late twentieth-century Britain although the religious returns of the census of 1851 are useful in indicating that there were large numbers, particularly in the cities, who were *not* regular church- or chapel-goers. Within the Church of England at the time there was fierce controversy over the spread of ritualism, a fear on the part of many Protestant Anglicans that their Church was drifting towards Rome. There was indeed widespread hatred of the Roman Catholic Church. Early in his life, the future Prime Minister William Gladstone had demanded that his father throw out his sister when she became a Catholic. One young lady is reported to have called the guard when she discovered that the gentleman sharing her train compartment was a Catholic. Non-Conformist Englishmen and women might have shared the Anglican detestation of Rome and the Pope but they also felt bitterly hostile to the privileged Anglican Church which demanded church rates to be paid and which had a firm grip on education, from village church schools to the ancient universities of Oxford and Cambridge. Whatever the causes of sectarian hatred, which the twentieth-century commentators usually interpret in terms of class or some material interest, more of our ancestors believed

PUNCH, OR THE LONDON CHARIVARI. [SEPTEMBER 14, 1867.

WHAT NEXT!

Mistress. "FOR GOODNESS GRACIOUS SAKE, MARTHA, GO AND TAKE THAT RIDICULOUS THING OFF, DO!"

Martha. ("*which I were well aware it were my New Bonnet she were eluding to*"). "WELL, THERE, MUM, I DECLARE, MUM, I GIVE MY MILLINER HORDERS TO MAKE IT PERCISELY SIMILAR TO YOURN, MUM!!"

in God and read their Bible. No twentieth-century Prime Minister could have written, as Gladstone did in December 1868:

> It has been a special joy of this December that our son Stephen is given to the Church: 'whose shoe's latchet I am not worthy to unloose['].

PUNCH, OR THE LONDON CHARIVARI.—August 10, 1867.

THE ABYSSINIAN QUESTION.

Britannia. "NOW, THEN, KING THEODORE! ¡HOW ABOUT THOSE PRISONERS?"

Yet even I may be forgiven and ultimus ultimorum may yet come to be as a doorkeeper in the house of my God.

Farewell great year of opening, not of alarming, change: and welcome new year laden with promise and with care.

(*Gladstone Diaries*, ed. H. C. G. Mathews, vols 5–6, Oxford, Oxford University Press, 1978, p. 656)

Gladstone's concluding of the year on a note of optimism would also seem to mark a common attribute of mid-Victorian thought. Even Gladstone's arch-rival, the Conservative Benjamin Disraeli, admitted in November 1867 that 'in a progressive country change is constant'.

The whole concept of improvement and change for the better appears a popular notion in the 1860s. The rise in hygiene and living standards, improved communications in the form of telegraph lines, railways and the increase and spread of newspapers, all seemed part of the huge advance by mankind, spearheaded by the British. Tennyson had expressed it beautifully in a poem of 1838, 'Locksley Hall':

Men my brothers, men the workers, ever reaping something new;
That which they have done but earnest of the things that they shall
    do.
For I dipt into the future, far as human eye could see,
Saw the Vision of the world and all the wonder that would be;

Not in vain the distance beacons. Forward, forward let us range.
Let the great world spin forever down the ringing grooves of change.
Thro the shadow of the globe we sweep into the younger day;
Better fifty years of Europe than a cycle of Cathay.

Surveying not just his own country but the world in 1867, an Englishman could be forgiven for believing not just in material progress but also in a moral progress. Slavery had just been abolished in the United States where the North had triumphed over the South. Serfdom had been abolished in Russia at the beginning of the decade. Freedom, toleration and the 'Liberal' values seemed everywhere to be victorious. In France the Bonapartist dictatorship was crumbling and transforming itself into a constitutional monarchy. Even the Turkish Sultan was promising reform and to behave somewhat better towards his subjects than he had done in the past. The fez would inevitably give way to the top hat.

Man had steadily been making sense of the natural world: discovering, classifying and explaining. Charles Darwin's *Origin of the Species*, published in 1859, might raise fierce controversies with those who held to Archbishop Usher's chronology of the earth but Darwin's ideas slowly eroded the opposition with the inevitability of an in-coming tide. The Newtonian view of the universe seemed everywhere triumphant as modern technology made possible the verification of predictions based on Newton's laws of motion published in 1687. The planet Neptune had been discovered in 1849 as a result of the advance of telescope design and calculations based on the perturbations of the planet Uranus. Nineteenth-century technology had provided yet further proof of the genius of that great seventeenth-century Englishman and his explanations of creation. Even England's own past seemed to be yielding its secrets and the mist of the Middle Ages cleared as the nation's archives were sorted, classified and published in the rolls series. As the President of the British Academy was to put it: 'The acquisition of truth can alone satisfy the human mind and slowly and surely each succeeding generation comes nearer to the object of its quest.'

Yet there remained doubters. The poet and critic Matthew Arnold in *Culture and Anarchy* in 1869 expressed reservations and concern at certain tendencies in the new world. Robert Cecil, the future Prime Minister, was more forthright in a passage penned in 1862:

A few years ago a delusive optimism was creeping over the minds of men. There was a tendency to push the belief in the moral victories of civilization to an excess which now seems incredible. It was esteemed heresy to distrust anybody, or to act as if any evil still remained in human nature. At home we were exhorted to show our confidence in our countrymen, by confiding the guidance of our policy to the ignorant and expenditure of our wealth to the needy. Abroad we were invited to believe that commerce had triumphed where Christianity had failed, and that exports and imports had banished war from the earth. And generally we were encouraged to congratulate ourselves that we were permanently lifted from the mire of passion and prejudice in which our forefathers had wallowed. The last fifteen years has been one long disenchantment; and the American Civil War is the culmination of the process.

(Quoted in R. Taylor, *Lord Salisbury*, London, Allen Lane, 1975, p. 21)

Thus, even in the age of the optimists whose religion was progress there were those who rejected the new orthodoxy. The optimists believed that freedom was the key to human progress and certainly by our standards mid-Victorian England had an extraordinary faith in freedom and individual effort. Samuel Smiles is often described as the spokesman of this age, with self-help its gospel, *laissez-faire* its creed. In the best-seller *Self-Help* published in 1859, he expressed this doctrine:

All life is a struggle. Amongst workmen, competition is a struggle to advance towards high wages. Amongst masters, to make the highest profits. . . . Stop competition, and you stop the struggle of individualism. . . . Under competition, the lazy man is put under the necessity of exerting himself; and if he will not exert himself he must fall behind. If he does not work neither shall he eat. . . . There is enough for all but do your own share of work you must.

Whatever is done for men and classes to a certain extent takes away the stimulus of doing for themselves. . . . No laws, however stringent can make the idle industrious, the thriftless provident or the drunken sober. Such reforms can only be effected by means of individual action, economy and self-denial, by better habits than by greater rights.

(Quoted in A. Briggs, *Victorian People*, Harmondsworth, Penguin, 1965, p. 141)

Certainly the state's role was much more confined than it was to be a hundred years later and its agents were viewed with more suspicion. Taxation was clearly considered an evil and even the slightest rise provoked hostile reaction.

The police, who were not established as a national force until 1856, were still viewed as essentially continental in origin and, as such, tainted as the agents of despotism even though in England they were deliberately not armed. The state did not seek to regulate life except with the deepest reluctance. The Disraeli Government of 1874–80, often associated with social reform because of such milestones as the Public Health Act of 1875, could not bring itself to end the acknowledged evil of child murder for insurance gain by the simple banning of the insurance of small children. The most it could bring itself to do was to limit the amount parents could insure their children for. Where a government did act it often passed the buck to local authorities who themselves then failed to take effective action. The Public Health Act of 1866 gave extensive powers to local authorities but ten years later only 7 out of 38 London parishes had made, and enforced, regulations under the Act. There can be little doubt that there was an idealization of individual effort and a hostility to all that might impede such effort and undermine individual responsibility. Employers and employees showed a lamentable ignorance and indifference when it came to safety at work and regulation by the state was resented and only reluctantly accepted. Horrific accidents were taken as a price of progress. In a mining disaster in 1867 178 lives were lost in the Rhondda, but in December 1866 420 died in similar circumstances. In both cases colliery workmen were responsible as a result of the use of naked lights.

Yet despite the widespread proclamation of the gospel of self-help the mid-Victorian age was marked by a large-scale advance in regulation. The needs of an increasingly complex society forced people and governments to act. Public health acts, police acts, acts to ensure parents had their children vaccinated, acts to stop the sale of obscene publications, others to control and inspect prostitutes in certain areas, all marched onto the statute book. A belief in the individual and suspicion of the

Beata Beatrix by Dante Gabriel Rossetti, 1864

state lived side-by-side with a growing acknowledgement that overwhelming evils had to be tackled by government action.

Contradictions such as this abound in every society and many others stand out in the Britain of 1867. The idealization of the family and the home was very marked, yet child murder and child prostitution abounded. If women were placed upon a pedestal for worship they were also battered, frequently denied property rights and denied the right to vote. This paradox is illustrated by the 1864 painting by Rossetti entitled 'The Blessed Beatrix'. This beautiful image of his wife, Lizzy Siddal, contrasts harshly with Rossetti's treatment of her, a woman whom he had betrayed through numerous affairs and who had poisoned herself the year before. The reality for Victorian women and especially wives is well expressed in the other illustration which portrays the lives of many at this time.

Along with the romanticized and idealized view of women in Rossetti's painting one can also sense a feeling of looking back to the past in a

"WOMAN'S WRONGS."

BRUTAL HUSBAND. "AH! YOU'D BETTER GO SNIVELLIN' TO THE 'OUSE O' COMMONS, *YOU* HAD! MUCH THEY'RE LIKELY TO DO FOR YER! YAH! READ THAT!"

"MR. DISRAELI.—There can be but one feeling in the House on the subject of these dastardly attacks—not upon the weaker but the fairer sex. (*A laugh.*) I am sure the House shares the indignation of my hon. friend who will, I hope, consider he has secured the object he had in view by raising, the question. * * * Assuring my hon. friend that Her Majesty's Government will not lose sight of the question, I must ask him not to press his Motion further on the present occasion."—*Parliamentary Report, Monday, May 18.*

singular fashion – through rose-tinted spectacles. It is true to say that the past and tradition were revered but it was very much a view of the past that the Victorians wanted to see. Historic scenes decorated the new House of Commons and Manchester Town Hall. There was a fascination with things medieval. All this at a time when the real products of the Middle Ages were being torn down and much of the English heritage was being eradicated, or at least obscured, by the new dynamic industrial world.

POWER AND THE CONSTITUTION

Britain in 1867 was not a democracy. In January one in five adult males could vote and by December the proportion had risen to one in three. While this limited franchise fell short of true democracy, it can be argued that the British political system was successful in providing certain elements of a modern political system: stability without stasis, dynamism without destruction. There was security for property-owners yet hope of betterment for the poor, and pride for all in belonging to what was acknowledged to be the world's most successful community. A west Briton from Ireland might see things differently but Englishmen, Welshmen and Scotsmen, whether they had the vote or not, had sound reasons for accepting the system as they found it: it worked.

In theory Britain was a monarchy like most of the countries of Europe, but as the English journalist Walter Bagehot pointed out in his classic work on the British constitution, first published in full in 1867, the monarchy belonged to what he termed the 'dignified' part of the constitution. It was decorative and induced respect but did very little compared to the European kings and queens who really did exercise political power. Queen Victoria in theory appointed the Prime Minister and, on his advice, her other ministers. In practice she had to accept the man who could command a majority in Parliament and he could force upon her completely distasteful ministerial colleagues, if he chose. In 1880, despite all her protestations, Victoria took Gladstone back as Prime Minister and two years later she had to accept the republican Sir Charles Dilke into the Cabinet. She could advise and irritate; her contacts with her European relatives could be useful in foreign policy, but it is easy to understand the opinion of the French King Charles X who earlier in the century had expressed the view that he would rather chop wood than rule as the King of England.

At the heart of the British government lay the Cabinet, the policy-making body of ministers, usually about fifteen in all, who were responsible for all major decisions. All cabinet ministers were men and the vast majority were landowners. Of 68 ministers between 1851 and 1868 only 14 were born outside the ranks of the aristocracy or greater gentry (that is, owning more than 3,000 acres of land). No Prime Minister before

1908 was without a landed estate, even if in Disraeli's case it had been given to him by a devoted aristocratic admirer. This is the world so brilliantly described in Trollope's Palliser novels. His Duke of Omnium was a literary reflection of the real landed magnates like the seventh Duke of Devonshire who owned 198,667 acres in fourteen different English and Irish counties. Cabinet ministers of the 1860s not only governed the country, they tended to own a large chunk of it as well. Yet wealth alone was not sufficient, nor was it the richest man who became Prime Minister. The capacity for extreme hard work marked both Palmerston and Gladstone. Political cunning, powers of oratory and sheer ambition, then as now, were required. Talent was respected by the British aristocracy even if at times it was fashionable to conceal it. The Prime Minister in the nineteenth century was less powerful than his twentieth-century counterpart. Lack of media attention and equally an absence of cabinet committees (membership of which the Prime Minister controls carefully today), meant that the Prime Minister was just a first amongst equals. Ministers were allowed to get on and run their departmental empires sometimes with no interest at all shown by their nominal chief. A really energetic Prime Minister like Gladstone might take on a department as well as the office of Prime Minister. Gladstone twice served in the dual capacity of Prime Minister and Chancellor of the Exchequer – in 1873–4 and 1880–2. The sheer volume and pressure of government activity and business in the twentieth century would make this very difficult to contemplate today.

The scale of government and its activity is usually indicated by its expenditure – some £65–70 million per annum in the 1860s which amounted to perhaps 8 per cent of GNP. This should be compared with the £200 billion spent by the government in 1990 – 40 per cent of a much larger GNP. Not surprisingly, the number of government departments in the 1860s was far fewer than at present, reflecting the important fact that the range of government activity was narrower. The senior positions were the Foreign Office, the Home Office (dealing essentially with law and order but increasingly burdened with newer tasks such as factory inspection) and the Exchequer. The War Office and the Admiralty accounted for the largest slice of government spending and the Lord Chancellor enjoyed great prestige as the head of the legal system. The Board of Trade was a junior position, often the first cabinet office held by an aspiring minister. The India Office and one or two non-departmental titles such as Lord Privy Seal or Chancellor of the Duchy of Lancaster usually completed the tally. New areas of government activity such as health and education were supervised under the general umbrella of the Privy Council and out of these, later in the century, new ministries were to emerge. Ministers then as now operated through a civil service but it was a civil service far smaller and less professional than its modern equivalent. Stars like John Simon with the Health Department of the

Privy Council, or Trollope with the Post Office, might shine as examples of competence and ability. No qualifications were laid down and family influence and personal acquaintance determined appointments – a system brilliantly, albeit with some exaggeration, described by Dickens in *Little Dorrit*:

> The Barnacle family had for some time helped to administer the Circumlocution Office. The Tite Barnacle Branch, indeed, considered themselves in a general way as having vested rights in that direction, and took it ill if any other family had much to say to it. The Barnacles were a very high family, and a very large family. They were dispersed all over the public offices, and held all sorts of public places. Either the nation was under a load of obligation to the Barnacles, or the Barnacles were under a load of obligation to the nation. It was not quite unanimously settled which; the Barnacles having their opinion, the nation theirs.

The army, with its system of purchase of commission, displayed an even more flagrant disregard for the principle of meritorious promotion.

The jewel in the crown of the constitution was Parliament to which cabinet ministers were answerable for their decisions and the mistakes of their civil servants. In many ways the 1860s represent the high point of parliamentary power and prestige for the individual member of Parliament. The House of Lords was composed entirely of hereditary peers and bishops, and enjoyed great social respect. In theory this Upper Chamber was the equal of the Commons but in practice it was the Lower Chamber that exercised greater power and influence. The Lords had tried to stand up to the Commons over the Great Reform Act in 1832 and had failed, and Gladstone emphasized this subservience in 1861 when he forced through his reduction of paper duty despite widespread lordly opposition. As W. S. Gilbert expressed it in 1882 in 'Iolanthe':

> And whilst the House of Peers withholds its legislative hand,
> And Noble statesmen
> Do not itch
> To interfere in matters which
> They do not understand.
> Then bright will shine Great Britain's rays
> As in King George's glorious days.

The House of Commons was the ultimate club to which a gentleman might aspire to belong. Like all good clubs it was costly and difficult to join. It imposed obligations but less weighty than those on its twentieth-century counterparts. It met for less time in the year, seldom at all from August to January, and if an MP chose to absent himself for a lengthy vacation on the Continent that was his affair. Parliament's chief function was to approve taxation, to act as a forum for national debate and to keep in check the activities of ministers. Far down its list of priorities was the creation of new laws, a new-fangled development somewhat distressing to Palmerston, for instance, who felt an impatience with men like Gladstone and their desire to be forever enacting legislation.

In 1867 all MPs were either Liberals or Conservatives, but they were MPs first and foremost. The party machine had not developed so far as to grind the independence out of individual MPs. Governments were regularly defeated on votes in the Commons despite having theoretical majorities, and members had to be persuaded by oratory or team loyalty to support their nominal leaders. Most MPs were only in politics because of their own wealth and/or local influence so they were beholden to no machine for their position. (MPs were not of course paid and wealth was essential therefore to survive, let alone cover the huge cost of being elected.) Socially there was no great difference between Liberals and Conservatives, although the Conservatives were traditionally the party of land. In 1868 46 per cent of Conservative MPs were great landowners compared to only 26 per cent of the Liberals. Only 31 per cent of Conservatives were associated with trade and industry compared to 50 per cent in the Liberal party. Lawyers figured in both groups.

In geographical terms there were wide discrepancies in representation. The new urban England was massively under-represented in Parliament. Manchester and Leeds returned two MPs each but so did such tiny boroughs as Malton and Beverley. Cornwall, a Duchy of the Crown with less than half a million inhabitants, returned far more MPs than urban-ized Lancashire. The south in general was thoroughly over-represented and, with the exception of London, the north could rightly feel aggrieved that its economic importance was not reflected in the number of its members at Westminster. The Great Reform Act of 1832 had corrected many abuses and re-allocated some MPs to the new industrial centres, but the south remained very much over-represented and the continuing growth of industry in the Midlands and the north made the maldistribu-tion more intolerable by the 1860s. Under the terms of the 1832 Act the right to vote was based on property ownership. Owners of property worth £10 per annum could vote in seats designated to the boroughs but in the county seats a more varied franchise prevailed from property owners worth £2 per annum to those who leased property at £50 per annum. What could be said is that the million or so males who had the right to vote in 1867 were essentially middle class, although high house prices in London led to certain categories of skilled manual workers being included in the franchise. The theory of one man:one vote was clearly not the basis of the system; indeed there was a widely held belief that the system did or should represent the differing interests in the country. If women could not vote, it was because they were generally held to be emotionally and intellectually unsuited to the task. It was also held that their husbands and fathers could effectively exercise the vote for them. And, if particular workers were excluded, it was felt that their employers, whether landlord or industrialist, could speak and vote for them. The political system for all its obvious imperfections was widely believed to be sensitive to the country's needs and opinions.

Local government was no less at variance with democratic principles. In the counties or 'shires', as they were often still called, there were no elected bodies, merely the Commission of the Peace, a body of men selected from the owners of substantial amounts of land. These men administered the new police force and had other central government tasks allotted to them. In the growing boroughs, elected town councils existed but even here the principle of deference prevailed. In the newly chartered borough of Glossop, for example, the new council of eighteen contained twelve mill-owners and a manager, and in the next forty-three years all but three of the mayors were mill-owners. A 'millocracy' rather than an aristocracy governed in this area.

As with all human institutions the government of Great Britain in the 1860s was not perfect, but it did not only consider the male interest. A Parliament of men still passed the Criminal Law Procedure Act in 1853 to try to end the evil practice of wife beating and in 1878 the Matrimonial Clauses Act facilitated divorce for ill-used wives. Successive Married Women's Property Acts were to be passed to give married women the right to own property themselves even if they still had no vote. And although the landowning aristocracy appeared to dominate the system, this had not prevented the repeal of the Corn Laws in 1846 which had seemed to many to be a blow to agricultural interests. Landowners were unable to protect themselves in the 1870s and 1880s by imposing duties on foreign imports of food as were imposed in France and Germany. Cheap food flooded into Britain to the relief of the urban masses and to the ruin of many estates. The British system provided no *liebesgaben* (financial perks) which had filled the pockets of the German ruling elite at the expense of the poor. The burden of taxation in Britain was largely borne by the rich, and thus while they governed the country they also paid for its government. On most of the Continent possession of political power led to attempts to shift the tax burden to less privileged classes. The basic contentment with the British system was revealed in the failure of radical reformers to excite popular passions to push through a reform of Parliament itself.

THE REFORM CRISIS 1866–7

In the 1840s the Chartists had declared two major political objectives: extension of the franchise and the reform of Parliament. They failed to convince the men who could make reform a reality – the MPs themselves. Throughout the 1850s and the early 1860s various individuals had introduced Reform Bills but failed to enact them, and outside Parliament there appeared to be widespread apathy. Henry Viscount Palmerston, the Prime Minister from 1859 to 1865, was hoping to let the matter rest. He felt a personal distaste for further reform, he had had little enthusiasm in 1832, and in any case reform bills were notoriously difficult to pilot through the Commons. The existing system seemed to work and as working-men's houses rose in value to the £10 per annum fixed in the 1832 Act so they would secure the vote. John Bright, the radical MP for Birmingham, might proclaim his faith in reform and Palmerston's cabinet colleagues Lord John Russell and W. E. Gladstone might express sympathy, but in the circumstances it seemed wiser to let well alone.

Of course, on the one hand everyone would agree that the distribution of seats was unfair and Gladstone, like many other Liberals, was increasingly convinced that the growing number of skilled workers were underrepresented in the existing system, but on the other it could be argued that to extend the franchise would lower the whole tone of politics and help strengthen venality and corruption. The two most democratic countries, the USA and Australia, were hardly models of good government. Give the masses the vote and instead of serious political debate one saw increased alcohol consumption, corruption and cheap slogans that would swing elections. In the USA in 1836 the winning vice-presidential candidate had campaigned with the mind-shattering slogan of

Rumpsey dumpsey, rumpsey dumpsey,
Colonel Johnson killed Tecumseh.

In the general election of 1865, reform of Parliament had not figured highly and Palmerston was returned with a safe majority of 70. The old man then died, the last Prime Minister to do so in office. He was succeeded by Lord John Russell, with Gladstone continuing as Chancellor of the Exchequer, but now also viewed as heir-apparent. Russell wished to exit on a political high-note and what better testimonial to end a long political career than another Reform Act? Gladstone had been convinced the previous year of the virtue of reform. The two men were in no hurry but they were pitch-forked into action in 1866 by a speech by the radical MP for Bradford, W. E. Foster. Already there was some stirring of extra-parliamentary pressure for reform. In April 1864 the National Reform Union had been founded, drawing its support from northern manufacturers and Non-Conformist clergy. It demanded fairer distribution of seats and a franchise for all rate-payers. In February 1865 a more potent organization, the Reform League, had its first meeting. Although its president was a middle-class barrister, Edmund Beales, it attracted widespread working-class support. George Howell, a former bricklayer, was its Secretary and Robert Applegarth of the Joiners' and Carpenters' Union was a founder member. It demanded manhood suffrage.

Far short of this demand, and even that of the Reform Union, Russell's and Gladstone's Bill of February 1866 was very modest. It was carefully calculated to increase the number of working-class voters in the boroughs and yet avoid giving the working classes a majority amongst the electorate. The franchise in the boroughs would be extended to include all those in rented housing paying over £7 per annum and to lodgers paying £10 per annum. In the counties the franchise would be lowered from £50 to £14 for lease holders, a change that was felt would help the Liberals. In all, an extra 400,000 voters would be added to the electorate. One in four males would now be able to vote instead of one in five. Gladstone and Russell were anxious not to offend their own moderates. They did just this. A group of rebel Liberals, led by Lord Elcho and, most formidably, Robert Lowe, determined to wreck the bill which they saw as a slippery slope to democracy, something Lowe had experienced with horror in Australia. The Conservatives in the Commons under Disraeli co-operated with the Liberal 'cave of Adullam', as Bright christened the rebels. In June the Liberal Government suffered a major defeat on an amendment and Russell resigned. Reform had once again failed.

The Queen quite properly invited Lord Derby, leader of the Conservatives, to form a government. He had no majority but the splits in the Liberals gave hopes of a period of parliamentary success. Benjamin Disraeli at 64 became the Chancellor of the Exchequer and Leader of the House of Commons for the third time in his career. As on the two previous occasions this was only possible as a result of a Liberal split. Although the Conservatives were the party of resistance, as the French would express it, and the Liberals the party of movement, they were not totally averse to reform of Parliament if it was to be very modest and served the Conservative Party's interests. In 1859 Disraeli had tried to secure the passage of such a reform bill much to the horror of the extreme resisters in his own party. It had failed and in 1866 Disraeli did not feel inclined to try again. However, public pressure for reform was growing. The membership and the number of branches of the Reform League grew so that by 1867 the figures stood at 65,000 and 600 respectively. Robert Lowe, the Liberal critic of reform, had ironically proved to be one of the League's best recruiting sergeants. His vitriolic attacks on the working class and their inability to use the vote sensibly stung them into demanding the vote. The whole nation's attention and coverage in the press created an interest in the reform issue that had previously been missing, and the banking crisis of 1866 followed by a short, sharp slump with wages falling and unemployment rising to 8 per cent combined to fuel a popular outburst which any government would have found hard to ignore. The freshly installed Conservative Government faced a challenge almost immediately. The Reform League proposed to hold a rally in Hyde Park in July. The Home Secretary banned it and troops were drafted in, ready for action. In the event the government backed down. The railings of Hyde Park were pushed aside and the demonstration went ahead. In 1848 the government had called the bluff of the Chartists and won. This time it was the government who climbed down.

If these famous Hyde Park riots of July 1866 did not force the government to take action, the continuing and growing unrest later in the summer and autumn did. Bright addressed mass meetings in the Midlands and the north and on 16 September Derby wrote to Disraeli claiming that he was 'reluctantly coming to the conclusion that we shall have to deal with the question of Reform'. At the end of the month the Queen voiced her concern, expressing the hope that the issue of reform could be settled. Derby finally persuaded Disraeli to proceed cautiously, first, by drawing up outline resolutions to be followed by a Royal Commission which they hoped would bury the question until 1868. The Cabinet duly agreed in November to the outline proposals, the most important of which was that the working-class voters should not end up as the majority. Between November and February 1867, after much discussion and attempts at statistical research, Disraeli seemed to have settled on household suffrage with safeguards such as a three-year residence qualification, personal payment of rates by house-holders, and extra votes for the middle class on the grounds of education, extra property, etc. The whole was designed to settle the question yet prevent a working-class majority emerging. The latter appears to have been the only fixed principle but Disraeli chopped and changed the details. The most notorious example of this came on 23 February when he tried to bounce his proposals for household suffrage with safeguards through the Cabinet. He claimed he had another engagement and was in a hurry, so he quickly rattled off some figures and closed the meeting with little discussion. Lord Cranborne, a sworn enemy of democracy, had taken the figures down and spent the rest of the day working on them. He consulted two other opponents within the Cabinet, Carnarvon and General Peel, a 'man whose eyes lit up with insanity at the mention of household franchise'. All three threatened to resign if Disraeli pushed ahead. The following day, just before introducing his measure to a Tory delegation of MPs, Disraeli altered it to a £6 rating franchise and a two-year residence qualification, not very unlike the Gladstone Bill of 1866. The change kept Cranborne in the Cabinet for the time being and the new measure became known as the 'Ten-minute' Bill. Its reception in the Commons was lukewarm even amongst Conservatives and at the end of the month Disraeli reverted to his original proposal. The three opponents resigned on 2 March but Disraeli pushed ahead, also having changed his mind on timing. He decided not to wait until 1868 but introduced his Bill on 18 March.

The passage of the Bill was a triumph of parliamentary fast footwork. Disraeli consistently out-manoeuvred Gladstone, largely by doing a deal with a group of Liberal radicals through James Clay, a Liberal but also a friend of Disraeli's. A wrecking amendment by Gladstone was defeated in April. Disraeli now had his own pack of Conservatives behind him, hollering for victory – the details no longer mattered: smashing Gladstone was all. By this time many Liberals simply wanted the question settled and Disraeli appealed to their sense of fair play by declaring in the House that Gladstone had had his innings already. After his triumph over Gladstone on 13 April Disraeli was toasted in the Carlton Club and returned home to his wife, Mary Anne, who thoughtfully provided a game pie and a bottle of champagne. 'Well, my dear you are more like a mistress than a wife' was Disraeli's famous compliment.

The pay-off to the rebel Liberals came in May when amendments were accepted by Disraeli which radicalized the Bill by extending the franchise and removing safeguards. The two-year residence qualification was dropped to one on 2 May. Lodgers who paid more than £10 a year received the vote by the Torrens amendment of 9 May and on 17 May Disraeli accepted the amendment of Grosvenor Hodgkinson, Liberal MP for Newark. Hodgkinson proposed that every rate-payer should have to pay his rates personally rather than through the landlord. Disraeli, to everyone's astonishment, accepted this without consultation with any of his Cabinet colleagues. At a stroke he had added up to half a million extra voters and removed the most important of his safeguards. It seems he was more worried about an alternative but similar amendment to be proposed by Gladstone's close associate, Hugh Childers. Disraeli was determined to avoid giving any credit to Gladstone, so he accepted Hodgkinson's proposal. Other safeguards, including dual voting for some property-owners, also disappeared and the county franchise was reduced from Disraeli's proposal of £15 to £12. Some amendments were resisted, for example the proposal by John Stuart Mill to give votes to women was defeated by 196 to 73. The final measure enfranchised just over one million new voters – 830,000 in the boroughs and 290,000 in the counties. Perhaps half of all adult males could now vote in the towns but in the rural shires the franchise remained essentially middle class. A Redistribution Bill was also passed in August of distinctly modest extent. Fifty-three seats were redistributed from small boroughs and the merger of two Scottish counties. Twenty-eight of these went to the counties: twenty-five in England and three in Scotland. Four new cities – Manchester, Liverpool, Birmingham and Leeds – had their representation raised from two to three members each. However, these, like all cities, were still very much under-represented. Nine new boroughs and London University gained one MP each, four towns in England and Wales were raised from one MP to two, and five towns in Scotland received similar treatment. Southern and rural England remained very much over-represented at the expense of northern and industrial England. To strengthen the Conservative hold on rural areas, boundaries were re-drawn which transferred 100,000 voters from county seats to the towns. The Bill became law on 15 August 1867 after an easy passage through the House of Lords. Disraeli had secured a great political triumph. Was it a 'leap in the dark' as Derby described it or had Disraeli, as he told a meeting in Edinburgh later in 1867, 'educated his party' on the question of Reform?

CONTROVERSY: HISTORIANS AND THE REFORM CRISIS

There has been much controversy amongst twentieth-century historians as to how the Reform Act of 1867 came about. The centenary of the passing of the Act produced a wealth of argument. The central problem was how to explain a minority Conservative Government getting an apparently radical reform measure through the Commons when a majority Liberal Government had failed with a modest bill. Traditional Liberal historians like G. M. Trevelyan tended to see the whole episode as one produced by an unprincipled Conservative Government determined to stay in office and forced by the Liberals into accepting amendments. In a spirited essay in the book *Before the Socialists* (1965) Dr Royden Harrison argued strongly that it was response to Reform League pressure that forced the government to surrender. An American, Gertrude Himmelfarb, is one twentieth-century historian to take Disraeli at his word. She argued in an essay published in 1968 that Disraeli embraced democracy and educated his party to accept something which instinctively it disliked, and she went on to say that Disraeli in his novels and some of his speeches shows a faith in the people and their natural inclination to vote for their 'betters'. She accepts that Disraeli believed democracy would create a popular conservatism which would rescue the Tory party from thirty years of Liberal dominance. Two very detailed studies of the whole reform crisis, *The Making of the Second Reform Act*, by F. B. Smith (1966) and *Disraeli, Gladstone and Revolution* by Maurice Cowling (1967), take rather different lines. Both point out the element of party political manoeuvring and could perhaps be said to illustrate the truth of Oliver Cromwell's famous dictum 'No man goes so far as he who knoweth not whither he goeth'. Both see party advantage as being a decisive influence although Dr Smith would concede something to the notion of external pressure.

BIBLIOGRAPHY

For an explanation of the grading system, see the preface p. xiii.

The economy

4　Crouzet, F., *The Victorian Economy*, London, Methuen, 1982
3　Hobsbawm, E., *Industry and Empire*, Harmondsworth, Penguin, 1968
4　Landes, D., *The Unbound Prometheus – Technological Change*, Cambridge, Cambridge University Press, 1969
3　Mathias, P., *The First Industrial Nation*, London, Methuen, 1969

Social life

2/3　Best, G., *Mid-Victorian Britain*, St Albans, Panther, 1973
2/3　Briggs, A., *Victorian Cities*, London, Penguin, 1968
2/3　Briggs, A., *Victorian Things*, Harmondsworth, Penguin, 1990
3　Burn, W. L., *The Age of Equipoise*, London, Allen & Unwin, 1968
3/4　Chadwick, O., *The Victorian Church*, London, A. & C. Black, 1969
3　Checkland, S. G., *The Rise of Industrial Society in England*, London, Longman, 1964
3/4　Dyos, H. J. and Wolff, M. (eds), *The Victorian City*, two vols, London, Routledge & Kegan Paul, 1973
3　Horn, P., *Labouring Life in the Victorian Countryside*, Gloucester, Alan Sutton, 1976
3/4　Mingay, G. (ed.), *The Victorian Countryside*, two vols, London, Routledge & Kegan Paul, 1981
3　Perkin, H., *The Origins of Modern English Society*, London, Routledge & Kegan Paul, 1969
3/4　Thompson, F. M. L., *English Landed Society in the Nineteenth Century*, London, Routledge & Kegan Paul, 1963

Ideas and intellectual life

3　Chapman, R., *The Victorian Debate – English Literature and Society 1832–1901*, London, Weidenfeld & Nicolson, 1968
4　Himmelfarb, G., *Victorian Minds*, London, Weidenfeld & Nicolson, 1952, rev. 1968
4　Williams, R., *Culture and Society 1780–1950*, London, Penguin, 1961

Politics and the reform crisis

3　Burn, W. L. (1968) and Checkland, S. G. (1964), both referred to above, have useful introductions to the political system, as does the first chapter of Pugh, M., *The Making of Modern British Politics*, Oxford, Blackwell, 1982
2/3　Briggs, A., *Victorian People*, London, Penguin, 1954
4　Cowling, M., *Disraeli, Gladstone and Revolution*, Cambridge, Cambridge University Press, 1967
3　Harrison, R., *Before the Socialists: Studies in Labour and Politics, 1861–1881*, London, Routledge & Kegan Paul, 1965

4   Seymour, C., *Electoral Reform in England and Wales*, Newton Abbot, David & Charles, 1970

3   Smith, F. B., *The Making of the Second Reform Act*, Cambridge, Cambridge University Press, 1966

1   Walton, J. K., *The Second Reform Act*, London, Methuen, 1987

1   Wright, D. G., *Democracy and Reform*, London, Longman, 1970

Sources for coursework

There are many useful compilations of documents available. Penguin have published *Useful Toil* by John Burnett, a collection of autobiographies of working people of the nineteenth century. Allen & Unwin have the excellent 'Human Documents' series, including *Victorian Golden Age* by E. Royston Pike. Selections from Henry Mayhew's *London Labour* and the *London Poor* have been edited by Peter Quennell and published in three volumes by Constable (1968) and by Penguin in 1985. These can be compared with Charles Booth's *London 1875–1903*, from which a selection was published by Penguin in 1971. B. R. Mitchell and P. Deanes's *Abstract of British Historical Statistics* (1962) is indispensable.

Particular aspects of the rural Victorian world can be explored through texts such as Flora Thompson's *Lark Rise to Candleford* (Penguin edition 1973), which records events of the 1880s, and reminiscences of a Victorian childhood. *Kilvert's Diary* (abridged edition published by Cape in 1976) is the work of Reverend Francis Kilvert and gives a view from the parsonage in the 1870s. Clearly the literature of the period can be read for insight and entertainment. Dickens's *Great Expectations* (1861) and *Our Mutual Friend* (1865) both date from the 1860s as does Mrs Gaskell's *Wives and Daughters* (1865) and George Eliot's *Silas Marner* (1861). Photographs from the Victorian era are collected together in publications such as Gordon Winter's *A Country Camera 1844–1914* (Harmondsworth, Penguin, 1973), and William Sansom's *Victorian Life in Photographs*. In addition there are a growing number of village and town collections being published by individuals and local history groups.

Political life can be investigated in compilations of documents like H. J. Hanham's *Nineteenth Century Constitution* (Cambridge, Cambridge University Press, 1969) or Walter Bagehot's classic work, *The English Constitution* (1867). Anthony Trollope is a literary figure with the most overt interest in, and knowledge of politics in the 1860s, and his Palliser novels, begun in 1864, with *Can You Forgive Her*, provide a leisurely perambulation through the Victorian political milieu.

2 The Gladstonian Liberal Party 1868–95

INTRODUCTION: LIBERALISM AND THE POLITICAL AGENDA IN THE LATE NINETEENTH CENTURY

The Liberal Party's election victory in 1868 was even more convincing than in 1865, despite Disraeli's triumph of the previous year. Only the extent of the victory was surprising. The Conservatives had not won a majority since 1841 and only held office when the Liberals fell out. In other words the prevailing mid-Victorian pattern of Liberal dominance was continuing. Every boy and every gal might be a little Liberal or a little Conservative, as W. S. Gilbert put it in 'Iolanthe', but more were little Liberals.

As with most '-isms' there exists no clear-cut dictionary definition of Liberalism which will satisfy. There is no one writer who can be said to expound Liberal thinking. Like all great packages of ideas it was not static but evolved and changed with society. The philosophers John Stuart Mill, Herbert Spencer and T. H. Green all made important contributions to Liberal thought between 1850 and 1890, but they owed a debt to their intellectual ancestors Jeremy Bentham, Adam Smith and even John Locke, whose great works had been published at the end of the seventeenth century. A few basic strands in the complex web of Liberal thought should perhaps be highlighted. The word itself clearly relates to freedom and all Liberals espoused this as a good – the freedom of the individual. Gladstone, the greatest of Liberal leaders, was to express it simply in a letter written in 1890:

> But the basis of my liberalism is this. It is the lesson which I have been learning ever since I was young. I am a lover of liberty; and that liberty which I value for myself, I value for every human being in proportion to his means and opportunities.

John Stuart Mill concluded his important philosophical work, *On Liberty*, published in 1859, with the following:

The worth of a state, in the long run, is the worth of the individuals composing it . . . a state which dwarfs its men, in order that they may be more docile instruments in its hands even for beneficial purposes – will find that with small men no great thing can really be accomplished; and that the perfection of machinery to which it has sacrificed everything will in the end avail it nothing, for want of the vital power which, in order that the machine might work more smoothly, it has preferred to banish.

Most Liberals felt that the free interplay of forces would produce harmony not discord. Economic freedom, in the form of free enterprise at home and free trade in international relations would result in economic growth and benefit to all. Greater individual freedom would lead to a better society and better human beings. Freedom, in short, would be the agent of progress. Thus, optimism was also a vital strand in the web: unfair privilege was the enemy. Merit and effort, not birth, should determine a man's place in society. The appeal of Liberalism to a large segment of Victorian England lay in the widespread awareness of beneficial change and a growing impatience with privilege in all its forms.

By 1868, it seemed to many Liberals, including Gladstone, that the essential framework of a Liberal state had been created. Free trade seemed firmly established, with only minimal revenue duties remaining – 48 instead of the 1,000 plus of 1840. Taxation was again minimal, allowing, in Gladstone's famous words, 'money to fructify in the pockets of the people'. There was a free press, freedom of speech and religion, and, if not a democracy, a balanced constitutional government far removed from the tyrannies of Eastern Europe. Liberals took different views on how much had to be done depending on their position within the political spectrum of the Liberal Party. Radicals like Joseph Chamberlain or Sir Charles Dilke, the republican MP for Chelsea, felt the Liberal edifice was far from complete. Chamberlain and the National Education League wanted a secular state education system freed from the grip of the Established Church. Other radicals, among them W. S. Caine and Sir Wilfred Lawson, were devout opponents of the demon drink and were spokesmen of the powerful temperance lobby. John Stuart Mill, briefly an MP in the 1860s, could espouse the eccentric position of votes for women. John Bright, MP for Birmingham and the grand old man of radicalism, could proclaim his faith in manhood suffrage. All these radicals had in common a driving urge to change some aspects of British society. Most, like Bright, would have looked to the USA for their ideal: a meritocratic, not aristocratic, society where no one religion was established and hard work and brains gave a man his place. Other Liberals were less convinced of the need for wholesale changes although a secret ballot voting system, firmly on the political agenda since its proposal in 1831, was a shared party objective. Most would accept the need to do something about education, fought over for so long by church and chapel to the detriment of British children.

The majority, who were not radicals but decent landowners, business-men and lawyers, felt freedom and progress and the national interest were best served by the Liberal Party. They might be tempted, like Trollope, to say to the radicals, 'Go home sir, take a dose of salts and work it all out of you', but for all their differences they saw the Conserva-tives as a party which spoke for a sectional interest, the land, and essentially a set of outmoded values. Liberal governments tended to be dominated by two other groups within the party, the Whigs and Peelite ex-Conservatives. Neither of these groups was big, certainly fewer than fifty MPs in each, and yet they tended to predominate in most of Glad-stone's cabinets. The Whigs were Liberals by family connection rather than conviction. Such were the Cavendishes, Dukes of Devonshire, and the Russells, Dukes of Bedford. They brought to any government great prestige and the habit of ruling almost by hereditary right. Most of them were of course suspicious of radicalism and often irritated by radical pressure.

Whig families had accepted the name in the struggles of the seven-teenth century and were still proud to bear the Whig title as much as they were proud of their domination of the party. The Peelites were another element in Liberal cabinets, being those progressive Conserva-tives who had supported Sir Robert Peel when he repealed the Corn Laws in 1846 and thus fractured his own party. Gladstone and Edward Cardwell, War Minister 1868–74, were the most notable of those left by 1868. They were not Whig grandees but men of office, committed to good government and contemptuous of what they saw as the stupidity of those Conservatives who had rebelled against their old leader twenty years before. The Liberal Party at Westminster was thus an alliance of disparate groups unified by only a vague ideology and a dislike of the other 'team', the Conservatives, and in particular its leader Disraeli.

Liberal support throughout the country made it seem a national party in the sense that it appealed to all classes and sections. The Howards, Dukes of Norfolk, were traditionally Liberal and so, in 1868, were most trade unionists. George Howell of the Reform League threw himself into the Liberal election campaign of 1868 and it seems a majority of the newly enfranchised working classes were to identify with the Liberal Party. As Howell put it: 'I want a government of the entire people where wealth and intellect will have its fair share of power – no more.' Respectable artisans could join in an assault on the landed elite and their privileges.

Perhaps the single most important interest group which identified with the Liberal Party were the Non-Conformists. As Gladstone was to express in 1877 they formed the backbone of British Liberalism. Amount-ing to over half the church-going population, Non-Conformists of all shades – Methodists, Baptists and Congregationalists – looked to the Liberal Party for the redress of their particular grievances. Ultimately they hoped for 'free religion' to parallel free trade. This would involve the disestablishment of the Anglican Church, the ultimate aim of the pressure group the Liberation Society. If this long-term goal was not immediately attainable then at least reforms in education or curbing alcohol abuse could proceed through the agency of Liberal governments. Non-Conformists often supplied the infantry of the Liberal army. Only 14 per cent of Liberal MPs in 1868 were Non-Conformists but their numbers grew: by 1880 they totalled 24 per cent. The first Non-Conformist, John Bright, entered the Cabinet in 1868. They also supplied much-needed organization in the constituencies. The Liberation Society paid for thirteen electoral agents in 1871, at a time when the national party had no regional organization at all. The success of the Liberals in Wales in 1868 may in part be ascribed to the efforts of militant Non-Conformist campaigners.

The Liberal Party also enjoyed the support of the bulk of the press. Helped by Gladstone's abolition of the paper duties in 1861, and his earlier abolition of stamp duties on advertisements, the press had blossomed. Undoubtedly the most important of these was the new *Daily Telegraph*, founded in 1855 as a penny daily. As the journalist W. T. Stead put it, 'The Daily Telegraph created the People's William', as Gladstone became affectionately known. By judicious leaks and advance notice of speeches he skilfully used the *Telegraph* in the 1860s when, as Chancellor of the Exchequer, he was the most dynamic and creative of Palmerston's ministers. He became a popular folk-hero in a way no previous minister of the crown could or would have deemed it proper to be.

Gladstone succeeded Russell as Liberal leader in December 1867. He was 58 on the 29th of that month. Already his work as Chancellor of the Exchequer had ensured he was the only possible heir to Russell. He was a complex man and in many respects an unlikely leader of the Liberal Party. He was a devout High Anglican and yet so many of his followers were Non-Conformists. He had started his parliamentary career in 1832 as a thorough-going Tory, both by conviction and family tradition. Only slowly had he embraced Liberal ideas, first free trade and then, in the 1860s, parliamentary reform. His battle with the Lords over paper duties had endeared him to the radicals and although he felt little enthusiasm for educational reform, the Non-Conformist Liberals could identify with a man who saw politics essentially as a field of moral activity. To be Prime Minister was not simply to get to the top of the greasy pole, as Disraeli was to put it.

The secret of Gladstone's success lay in his clear logical mind and his incredible energy and aptitude for work. Later in life one of his secretaries rated his 'horse-power' as ten times that of ordinary men. His extensive diary bears witness to this energy and his fanatical belief in

William Gladstone by J. E. Millais, 1879

the God-given duty not to waste a precious moment. He was excessively orderly and punctilious and clung to formalities. Queen Victoria was later to lament that her Prime Minister always addressed her as if she were a public meeting, not as a woman. Even his most relaxed letters to his wife Catherine, whom he married in 1839, were always signed W. E. Gladstone or, in the very rare moments of informality, W. E. G. Most people agreed he lacked the capacity for empathy. He was a good listener when there was information to be learned but conversations were apt to be debates for his own intellectual edification.

At the root of the man was religion and the quest for the correct moral course. It was this that enabled his opponents to create the image of the humourless religious fanatic. Lady Palmerston was to declare that 'if you boiled Gladstone I don't believe you would extract an ounce of fun from him'. This judgement was quite unfair, as the happy and jolly family atmosphere of the Gladstone household showed. It is true that

Gladstone took life very seriously. Even his devoted wife was once moved to complain that 'if you were not such a great man you would be a great bore'.

Gladstone saw himself as chosen and protected by God to do God's work, as evidenced by his diary entry for 29 December 1878:

> Why has my health and strength been so peculiarly sustained? All this year, and more, I think, I have not been confined to bed for a single day . . . I have been upheld in an unusual manner and the free and effective use of my voice has been given to me and to my own astonishment. Was not all this for a purpose? And has it not all come in connexion with a process to which I have given myself.
>
> (*Gladstone Diaries*, ed. H. C. G. Mathews, vol. 9, Oxford, Oxford University Press, 1982, p. 374)

Aligning himself with God laid him open to charges of using his religion as a cloak for his political ambition and monstrous vanity. Even a Liberal supporter like Henry Labouchère could complain 'I don't object to Gladstone always having the ace of trumps up his sleeve but merely to his belief that God almighty put it there.'

GLADSTONE'S FIRST MINISTRY 1868–74

Disraeli had succeeded Derby as Prime Minister in February 1868 but his government could not be expected to last long. It relied on the continuing fragmentation of the Liberals. This Gladstone proceeded to end. Despite being leader of the opposition he acted more like Prime Minister in determining the agenda of Parliament. He pushed through the abolition of church rates, to the great joy of the Non-Conformists, and in March successfully moved a resolution for the disestablishment of the Irish church. By this means he united his own party and forced Disraeli onto the defensive. The Church of Ireland, which Gladstone proposed to disestablish, was the perfect symbol of illicit privilege that Liberals of all shades could rally against. It was the rich official Church of Ireland serving a minority of the population that was largely Catholic. By choosing the Irish church as the battleground Gladstone could hope to attract the support of Roman Catholics in Ireland and Non-Conformists in Britain who would see this as the first step on the road to free religion. Disraeli could not concede church reform as he had done with the church rates, and the resulting equation of the Conservative Party with privilege and the Liberal Party with freedom and justice was a recipe for Liberal success.

The Liberals were also helped by a certain degree of ill luck that befell the Tories. A short and sharp trade recession with unemployment touching 8 per cent and a rise in corn prices due to poor harvests brought unpopularity to the government. The Tories added to their problems by increasing income tax to pay for an expedition to rescue prisoners held in Abyssinia. The electorate gave the Liberals a majority of 112 in December and Disraeli resumed his accustomed place on the opposition benches. Gladstone assumed the title of First Lord of the Treasury for the first, but not the last, time.

In his diary Gladstone drew up a list of significant events that had occurred in the month, confessing the triviality of the exercise but unable to resist the temptation. On the first of the month he had been at Hawarden, his country home, chopping down a tree, when the first intimation of his new appointment came. He read the telegram. 'Very significant' were his only words. After several more blows at the unfortunate tree he paused and uttered the famous sentence 'My mission is to pacify Ireland.'

Ireland was to be one of his major personal concerns during this first ministry. He took a prominent part even in the drafting of legislation, a skill of which he was rightly proud. The settling of the Irish question, he felt, was an essential task. The Fenian bomb outrages of 1867 drew the attention of the British public to Ireland. Gladstone had long held that England's relations with her sister island were unsatisfactory and a blot on a country which rightly claimed to be the moral leader of Europe and the highest example of human progress. It was essential, the new Prime Minister felt, to divide the Fenian extremists from the bulk of the population and this meant justice for Ireland, the remedying of her legitimate grievances. The first of these was to destroy the privileges of the Anglican Church of Ireland. This incidentally had had the beneficial side-effect of rallying the disunited forces of English Liberalism in the election campaign. Political calculation and morality could walk hand in hand.

Gladstone introduced an Irish Church Bill within two months of taking office and was able to push it through both the Commons and the Lords. The Irish church's connection with the state was ended and it lost a quarter of its revenue which was used for a variety of charitable purposes. It still remained relatively wealthy if no longer the official church of Ireland. Urged on by the radical John Bright, whom Gladstone had included in his Cabinet and whom he always treated with kid gloves, he turned next to the complex question of land and tenant rights in Ireland. The Irish Land Act of 1870 was a modest measure in many respects. It did little to interfere with the contractual relationship between landlord and tenant, but contented itself with extending to the whole of Ireland the so-called 'Custom of Ulster', whereby evicted tenants were entitled to receive compensation for any improvements they had made to the land as well as compensation for unfair eviction (see chapter 4). The Act failed to give the tenants what they wanted, control of rents and fixity of tenure. The Roman Catholic bishops declared in favour of these, in March 1870, and the Act was seen by most Irish as a bitter disappointment. Tenants could still be evicted for non-payment of rent and in the mid-1870s, with the onset of the great agricultural depression, rural misery in Ireland became worse than ever. Gladstone had made a gesture of goodwill and for the first time an English government had recognized that Ireland was different from England with its large-scale capitalist farming, and more akin to the rest of Europe whose future lay with small-scale peasant holdings.

Other gestures of goodwill accompanied these legislative measures. Political prisoners were released against strong Whig opposition in the Cabinet and Gladstone struggled manfully to persuade the Queen to allow her son to go to Dublin as Viceroy. Victoria refused. A third major piece of legislation to appease Ireland was introduced in 1873, the Irish Universities Bill. This was designed to provide Roman Catholics with a university which they could in conscience attend. It was a disastrous proposal. Protestant sentiment in England would not allow a Roman Catholic University supported by the state, and the Roman Catholic bishops could not accept secular institutions. The Roman Catholic primate Archbishop Collins' denunciation of it ended Liberal Ireland, it has been said. Thirty-five Irish Liberals voted against it and twenty-two others abstained. The measure was lost.

Gladstone had failed to pacify Ireland. He had done worse than this. By raising expectations and then disappointing them, he virtually destroyed the Liberal Party in Ireland. The result was the birth and growth of the Home Rule Movement. The election results tell the story of his failure. In 1868 the Liberals had secured 65 out of the 105 Irish seats, 9 more than in 1865. In 1874 only 12 Liberal MPs for Ireland were returned to Westminster and in their place were 57 Irish Nationalists.

If Ireland occupied pride of place with Gladstone, it was by no means the sole concern of his government. Few ministries of the nineteenth century could equal its legislative achievements. This on the whole did not stem from the Prime Minister who, in many respects, saw the edifice of Liberal England as all but complete. It was the expectations of his followers in and out of the Commons, that forced the government on. Only through legislative titbits could the Liberal Party be held together.

Gladstone felt little enthusiasm for educational reform although he recognized it as essential for the party to respond to pressure groups, such as Joseph Chamberlain's National Education League. The Prime Minister took a major part in getting the measure through the Commons, although such details as the Cowper-Temple clause, allowing for non-denominational religious teaching, were repugnant to him.

W. E. Forster, MP for Bradford, had been appointed to the position of Vice-President of the Privy Council, initially outside the Cabinet but he was admitted in 1870. He was in effect minister for education but as yet no such title existed. He presented his schemes to the Cabinet in 1869 and the Education Reform Bill went through in 1870. Its object was to supplement the existing voluntary system or in Forster's own words, 'to fill up its gaps at the least costs of public money'. It therefore fell short of the Education League's objective of a national non-sectarian system and Chamberlain together with a mass delegation in March 1870 made known the League's disappointment with the government.

The Act in its final form allowed for the Education Department of the Council to set up school boards in any district where the provision of education was not efficient and suitable. These boards were to be elected by rate-payers and were given powers to set up schools, raise a rate to support them and compel attendance if they wished. Various concessions were made to Non-Conformists' complaints, the most notable being the inclusion of the Cowper-Temple clause Gladstone so disliked. This clause made it easier to withdraw children from religious lessons if parents wished, and grants to existing voluntary schools, largely Anglican but also some Roman Catholic, would come from central government not the rates. This concession however was largely cancelled out by what became the chief Non-Conformist grievance, Clause 25, which allowed the fees of poor children attending church schools to be paid out of the rates. Although the Act was a major step forward to a national education system it fell far short of this and many Non-Conformist activists were bitterly disappointed with Forster and Gladstone.

Another major reform of 1870 was produced not by Act of Parliament but by an Order in Council which established competitive examinations as the normal method of entry to the civil service. It applied to all departments except the Foreign and Home Offices, but when Robert Lowe, the author of the change, moved to the Home Office in 1873 the principle of appointment by merit was established there as well. It was Lowe's enthusiasm which carried this change which had been in the pipeline for fifteen years. The civil service was rigidly divided into two classes, an upper grade recruiting from the universities, largely Oxford and Cambridge, and a lower clerical grade drawn from the middle and even working classes. No amount of merit, however, was likely to move an energetic and talented civil servant from the humble ranks of the clerks to the exalted plateaus of power where the new Whitehall 'mandarins' operated.

Edward Cardwell at the War Office carried through an important reorganizing programme which well illustrates the principles of merit, efficiency and economy. The Crimean War had revealed a multitude of deficiencies in the British army which were again highlighted in August and September 1870 when the victories of the Prussian army displayed the virtues of military efficiency. Gladstone himself wrote an anonymous article to the *Edinburgh Review* in October on this subject. In a whole series of Acts and Orders in Council, Cardwell sought to improve the army. Peacetime flogging was abolished, the War Office was reorganized and the Commander-in-Chief was placed firmly under the Secretary of

War. The Crown's control of the army was now only through a politician answerable to Parliament. The part-time militia in the counties was removed from the control of the Lord Lieutenants, usually great land-owners, and transferred to the War Office. The length of service in the army was reduced from twelve years to six and an attempt made to raise the general tone by discharging bad characters. New breech-loading rifles were issued and a linked battalion system was organized on a territorial basis. Regiments of infantry were attached to particular regions to foster local spirit and also enhance recruitment. Each regiment was to be composed of two battalions, one based at home and one serving abroad on a rotation basis. Unnecessary garrisons were at the same time with-drawn from the Empire to create an effective reserve force at home. All of this was achieved with a reduction in costs. The most controversial aspect of Cardwell's work was the abolition of the purchase of com-missions in 1871 – another blow to the aristocracy – and Cardwell and Gladstone eventually had to circumvent considerable opposition in the House of Lords by simply using a royal warrant on the grounds that an existing law had outlawed purchase in 1809, except where royal warrant permitted. It was a clever device but much hated by both Tories and radicals.

All in all Cardwell's achievements were remarkable but inevitably limited by resistance to change. No General Staff was appointed to plan future campaigns despite the enormous contribution of the Prussian General Staff in the victory of 1870. The British generals refused to switch to breech-loading artillery and, despite the creation of a reserve force of 35,000, Britain could not seriously take part in a European conflict. Prussia could mobilize her one million men and sweep across Europe; Cardwell's army could cope with Zulus and Egyptians.

Other important Liberal measures marked Gladstone's first ministry. The long overdue Ballot Act of 1872 finally ended the old-fashioned, disorderly hustings, while striking a blow against bribery and intimi-dation. The Judicature Act of 1873 enabled a massive tidying-up of the British legal system. This too was long overdue. Largely the work of Lord Selborne, the Lord Chancellor, it fused the two legal systems of equity and common law and united seven ancient courts into a supreme Court of Judicature. It swept away a good deal of inefficiency as well as removing the judicial function of the House of Lords.

The establishment of the Local Government Board in 1871 to supervise the Poor Law was also in the cause of efficiency, and led to dramatic reductions in expenditure on outdoor relief for the poor. There was, however, no wholesale reorganization of local government. The counties remained without elected bodies. Local government remained a hotch-potch of authorities with elected town councils, elected poor-law and now school boards, and nominated Justices of the Peace.

The state thus slowly expanded its tentacles but with maximum reluctance, and at the same time exercised great resistance to increased expenditure. Non-Conformists might have been disappointed with the Education Act but they received a concession in 1871 when Parliament ended the Anglican Church's monopoly of teaching posts at Oxford and Cambridge universities by the University Tests Act. Roman Catholics received a titbit with the repeal of the 1871 Ecclesiastical Titles Act which had forbade their bishops from accepting territorial titles.

Gladstone was later to speak of his first ministry with nostalgic affection as an 'era of liberation'. Yet it was also an era of increased regulation and these two aspects of Liberalism sat uneasily together. No measures illustrate this more clearly than two acts of 1871 affecting trade unions. The newly formed Trade Unions Congress pressed for clearly defined legal protection for unions after court cases in the 1860s had weakened their official status. Union violence was sparked in Sheffield in 1866 when a 'black-leg' had been shot and gunpowder dropped down the chimneys of workers deemed insufficiently enthusiastic for the union cause, which led to the setting up of a Royal Commission in 1867. It reported in 1869. The government promised legislation to head off a private member's bill and eventually in 1871 the Home Secretary, H. A. Bruce, who was less than friendly towards unions, produced two bills which were passed. The Trade Union Act gave unions their legal recognition and enabled them to register as Friendly Societies. The Criminal Law Amendment Act of 1871 attempted to cover the thorny issue of picketing, but failed to give protection to peaceful picketing as intended and the courts interpreted it in a very anti-union fashion. Trade Unionists were outraged and the government's hesitant steps to introduce fresh legislation had not been productive by the time of the next election. Bruce's other measure, the Licensing Act, was similarly disastrous in electoral terms. Non-Conformist pressure groups like the United Kingdom's Alliance pressed for temperance reform and in 1872 Bruce's Act restricting opening hours came into force, although it was accompanied by prolonged rioting in some cities in protest at this curtailment of a Briton's rights. As one bishop in the House of Lords observed, he preferred an England free to an England sober. Gladstone probably exaggerated in 1874 when he explained the Liberal defeat with the well-known phrase 'we have been borne away in a torrent of gin and beer', but the measure certainly hurt the Liberals with many working-class voters annoyed and, on the other side of the fence, temperance reformers disappointed at not getting all they demanded.

By 1873 the Prime Minister was exhausted and his government running out of steam. On its defeat over the Irish Universities Bill Gladstone tried to resign and install another minority Conservative government to enable Liberal recovery to take place. Disraeli was not going to fall for this and Gladstone and the other exhausted 'volcanoes', to use Disraeli's expression, had to smoulder on. Troubles multiplied, as Disraeli anticipated. After a minor irregularity at the Exchequer Lowe had to resign and Gladstone took over the burdens of this office as well. The Liberal Party appeared to be fragmenting into its component parts: the Non-Conformists were bitterly disappointed with the Education Act; trade unionists resented the Trade Union legislation of 1871; and Whig magnates were unhappy with such measures as the Land Act and the abolition of the purchase of army commissions, both of which could be interpreted as attacks on property. In addition there was widespread discontent with the government's handling of foreign policy. Many voters felt nostalgia for Palmerston's firmness. The government's 'strange mania for eating dirt', and its 'living in a blaze of apology', as Disraeli termed its peaceful foreign policy, were not popular. There was growing agitation against the Contagious Diseases Acts, the last of which had been passed in 1869. These were intended to control the spread of venereal disease by licensing prostitutes and insisting on examination, sometimes forced and often painful. A powerful moral and feminist lobby led by the redoubtable Josephine Butler sought repeal, and if women had not the vote themselves they could influence others who did.

Gladstone cast around for a solution to the problems. The great economic boom of 1873 had boosted government revenue and provided him with a surplus of £5 million. His mind returned to his great budgets of 1853 and 1860 and he saw some similar large scheme as a means of rescuing Liberalism. He came up with a proposed plan of massive tax cuts, most important of which was the abolition of income tax. To achieve this he had to get Cardwell at the War Office to agree to more cuts. Cardwell refused. The Cabinet seemed threatened by splits. There was no agreement on a reform of local government in the counties and in Gladstone's words there was 'No great public object on which the Liberal Party are agreed and combined'. This explains Gladstone's extraordinary conduct in calling a snap election to be held in February 1874. He seems to have intended to strengthen his hands with his colleagues. It took the party by surprise. He had never devoted much time to organizational matters nor acquired, like Disraeli, an organizational genius such as John Gorst. Arthur Peel, the Liberal Chief Whip in charge of party organization, was ill and did not have time to sort out the multitude of contending candidates in some constituencies. Gladstone's great tax plan was a 'damp squib'. E. S. Beesly spoke for the working-class voter when he wrote in *The Beehive* in January 1874 'Mr. Gladstone has sacrificed the lower classes who worshipped him to the richer classes who disliked him.' The abolition of income tax, standing at 3d in the pound, had no great emotional appeal. In Chamberlain's phrase: 'It was the meanest public document that has ever in like circumstances proceeded from a statesman of the first rank.'

The election was a disaster. Ireland was lost. The Tories strengthened their hold on the counties through the apathy of Whig landowners.

Lancashire and Cheshire, which had notably swung to the Conservatives in 1868, remained solidly in the same position, possibly as a result of anti-Irish feeling. Most ominously, London suburbia swung to the right with ten out of twenty-two seats going Tory, whereas in 1859 there had been no Conservatives returned. Gladstone himself had a close-run fight at Greenwich. He resigned on 17 February and the Queen sent for Disraeli.

So ended the first and greatest of Gladstone's four governments. He assumed it to be his last, for within twelve months he had retired from the leadership of the Liberal Party.

In many ways Gladstone's first ministry had been the zenith of English Liberalism, if we define Liberalism as a belief in the desirability of freeing the individual from unnecessary restraint and that the consequences of this liberation would be progress and social harmony. It was the last occasion on which Liberalism, so defined, had clear objectives which commanded widespread agreement amongst those calling themselves Liberals. Over the next twenty-five years, the Liberal Party was to be wracked with division and dissent as to what it was and where it was going. To many the work was complete but to the followers of the New Liberalism of the 1880s with its emphasis on social reform, there was much to be done, but even they lacked the heady optimism which marked the 1860s.

Gladstone certainly felt his work was over in 1874 and looked forward to a peaceful interval between high office and the grave.

OUT OF OFFICE: BULGARIA AND THE CAUCUS

'We have no public object on which we are agreed', Gladstone wrote to Earl Granville in December 1874. Shortly afterwards he resigned the leadership of the party. Granville, who was Foreign Secretary 1870–4, became leader in the Lords, and the Marquis of Hartington (the eldest son of the Duke of Devonshire – the title Marquis was a courtesy one and did not prevent membership of the House of Commons) became leader of the Liberals. The party of action passed to the control of the sound, somnolent Whigs. It was said of Hartington that he dreamt he was making a speech in the House of Commons and woke to find that he was. His relaxed, easy-going style was in complete contrast to the frenetic Gladstone.

However, a new radical star was about to blaze in the parliamentary firmament. Joseph Chamberlain was elected unopposed as MP for Birmingham in a by-election in 1876. He was thirty years younger than Gladstone and of a very different background. He had left school at sixteen and had not attended Oxford or Cambridge. His family were Unitarian small businessmen from south London, but at 18 Joseph had been sent by his father to Birmingham – the city with which he was always, henceforth, to be associated. He was to represent his father's interest in the firm of Chamberlain & Nettlefold. He was a commercial success yet by the late 1860s he showed himself increasingly inclined to abandon business for politics, becoming a leading light in the National Education League and a local Liberal councillor. In 1873 he was made Lord Mayor of Birmingham and over the next three years he worked to transform that city into a model for the country, behaving in the process more like an executive American-style mayor than the usual honorific English counterpart. The city benefited from his energy and vision. The gas company was municipalized and its profits ploughed into improvement schemes. The water company was bought out and the city's supplies improved. The centre was rebuilt – Corporation Street is probably Chamberlain's finest surviving monument. Slums were torn down and new houses constructed, together with an art gallery and museum. Here was action and what the party of action did in Birmingham the party of action could, and should, do in Britain as a whole.

Chamberlain differed from many of the older radicals. He was a new breed of politician, a programme rather than a single-issue campaigner. On these grounds he favoured dissolving the National Education League and transforming it into a broader National Liberal Federation. The machinery and the headquarters of the League were placed at the disposal of the new organization of which Chamberlain became president. Here was an instrument with which Chamberlain hoped to unify radicalism, transform the Liberal Party and provide a launch-pad for his own race to Number 10.

Birmingham itself had led the way in evolving a new democratic and highly effective method of political organization. In 1865 the Birmingham Liberal Association had been founded. From the start it enjoyed a popular basis in contrast to most Liberal associations which were narrowly oligarchical. William Harris, the Association's first secretary, created a powerful structure with elected ward committees at the bottom level, a central committee of 600, and the Council of Ten at the top – nicknamed the 'Caucus'. It was these ten who took the vital decisions, much like the parliamentary Cabinet, but the overall democratic nature combined with a centralized leadership proved highly effective in winning elections, much to the horror of the local Conservatives. The Liberals swept the school board and city council elections and gained all three parliamentary seats in 1874. Other cities copied Birmingham for there was no doubt as Chamberlain was to point out in a letter to *The Times* on 13 April 1880, although with some exaggeration, the model he had helped to create was remarkably successful:

Popular representative organizations on the Birmingham model, sometimes called 'The Caucus' by those who do not know what a caucus really is, and have not taken the trouble to acquaint themselves with the details of the Birmingham system, exist in 67 of the Parliamentary boroughs in which contests have just taken place. In 60 of these Liberal seats were gained or retained. In seven only the Liberals were defeated, but in three at least of these cases a petition will be presented against the return on the ground of bribery.

This remarkable success is a proof that the new organization has succeeded in uniting all sections of the party, and it is a conclusive answer to the fears which some timid Liberals entertained that the system would be manipulated in the interest of particular crotchets. It has, on the contrary, deepened and extended the interest felt in the contest; it has fastened a sense of personal responsibility on the electors; and it has secured the active support, for the most part voluntary and unpaid, of thousands and tens of thousands of voters, who have been willing to work hard for the candidates in whose selection they have for the first time had an influential voice.

The caucus system ideally suited Chamberlain's conception of radical programme politics, consisting as it did of democracy with powerful executive action. The National Liberal Federation represented an effective coming together of different local organizations and would, Chamberlain hoped, breathe democratic life into the musty Whig-dominated recesses of the Liberal headquarters in London. The Federation held its first conference on 31 May 1877 at the Bingley Hall, Birmingham. Hartington refused to attend but Gladstone had his own reasons for accepting the invitation to address the first of the modern party conferences. Chamberlain and his radical friends were hoping to use the ex-Prime Minister, for as he had written to Dilke in 1876, Gladstone was their best card – 'if he were to come back for a few years (he can't continue in public life for very much longer) he would probably do much for us and pave the way for more'. Little did Chamberlain appreciate that it was Gladstone who was to hijack the National Liberal Federation rather than vice versa.

Gladstone's interval between retirement and the grave was not to be in the 1870s – for that he had to wait another twenty years. In the autumn of 1876 he reappeared upon the political scene in dramatic fashion. Outraged at the Conservative Government's support for the Turkish regime, despite Turkish atrocities in Bulgaria, Gladstone first urged the official Liberal leadership to condemn Disraeli but eventually, frustrated by Hartington and Granville's lack of action, he denounced both Turks and Disraeli in a celebrated pamphlet of September 1876: 'The Bulgarian Horrors and the Question of the East'. Forty thousand copies were sold in a few days. Its ringing conclusion still resounds down the years:

But I return to, and end with, that which is the omega as well as the alpha of this great and most mournful case. An old servant of the crown and state, I entreat my countrymen, upon whom far more than perhaps any other people of Europe it depends, to require and to insist that our government which has been working in one direction shall work in the other, and shall apply all its vigour to concur with the other states of Europe in obtaining the extinction of the Turkish executive power in Bulgaria. Let the Turks now carry away their abuses in the only possible manner, namely by carrying off themselves. Their Zaptiehs and their Mudirs, their Bimbashis and their Yuzbashis, their Kaimakams and their Pashas, one and all, bag and baggage, shall I hope clear out from the province they have desolated and profaned.

Never before, or since, has there been such a noble outburst of popular moral indignation at human wickedness. Turkish troops had committed appalling atrocities upon innocent men, women and children – babies speared, men and women left impaled on posts, writhing in agony. The news was quickly spread by telegraph, and at a time of heightened moral sensibility it produced outrage in many parts of Britain.

Gladstone saw the issue as a crusade and became more than ever convinced that Disraeli was virtually the Devil incarnate, so indifferent was he to the sufferings of the Bulgarians, news of which he dismissed as 'coffee-house babble'. Gladstone campaigned inside and outside Parliament, seizing every opportunity to mobilize opinion against the government. He became the reluctant leader of a movement rooted in the Non-Conformist congregations of the north and the Anglo-Catholic intellectuals of Oxford. Chamberlain threw himself into the fight on Gladstone's side and Gladstone used the opportunity of the first National Liberal Federation meeting to spread his gospel. The official Liberal leadership was embarrassed and even devoted followers in the parliamentary party shook their heads over Gladstone's seeming lack of balance. As Henry Lucy, lobby correspondent, was to write,

If he had only a tenth part of the imperturbability of Hartington. . . . But as he is pretty constant in his attendance, never sleeps on the front Opposition bench, and is able to follow a debate even whilst he is writing letters, the consequences are disastrous. There is not a dull-witted or malicious man on either side of the House who is not able to stir him up, and set him either excitedly shaking his head or bring him to his feet with a contradiction or an explanation.
(*A Diary of Two Parliaments*, vol. I, London, Cassell, 1885, p. 236)

When Russia declared war on Turkey in 1877 and eventually seemed to threaten Constantinople itself in 1878, public opinion swung round to support Disraeli and the windows of Gladstone's house were broken by an anti-Russian mob. Disraeli's great triumph at Berlin in June was gall and wormwood to Gladstone but by 1879 the tide had turned in his favour. Two unpopular expeditions to, and badly conducted wars in, South Africa and Afghanistan gave Gladstone his chance to denounce afresh the foreign policy of the Disraeli Government. Gladstone decided to offer himself as candidate for a new constituency, Midlothian, south of Edinburgh, in January 1879. In November of that year he began his Midlothian campaign in preparation for a general election. He addressed great crowds and rallied and excited the forces of Liberalism in the country. The Liberal Party now had an issue, a moral crusade as in 1868, to pull together the disparate groups. All shades of Liberal could agree in disliking Beaconsfieldism (Disraeli had become Earl of Beaconsfield in 1876), as Gladstone christened Disraeli's policy. The Queen was outraged by Gladstone's behaviour and informed Lady Ely, a close confidante, that nothing would induce her to accept him as her Prime Minister again.

Disraeli decided to dissolve Parliament in March 1880 after a Conservative by-election victory at Southwark. It was a costly mistake. The country was depressed with agriculture struggling under foreign competition and bad harvests, and trade and industry suffering from a short, sharp slump. The Liberals had the edge in party organization and Gladstone had found a moral issue on which to campaign. The Liberals won a convincing victory with 347 seats to 240 Conservatives and 65 Irish Nationalists. The dark days of 1874 seemed like an unpleasant dream, an aberration in the pattern of Liberal dominance. As Gladstone was to put it in a letter to the Duke of Argyll, the downfall of Beaconsfieldism was like 'the vanishing of some vast magnificent castle of Italian romance'.

GLADSTONE'S SECOND MINISTRY 1880–5

The Queen accepted Disraeli's resignation on 21 April 1880 and the next day she sent for Hartington to form a government. He explained that this was impossible without Gladstone accepting to serve under him, as Gladstone had played the role of leader during the election campaign. The former Prime Minister had also made it clear to Hartington and Granville that he would accept no such position. It seems that he had become convinced that he alone embodied the natural will to banish Beaconsfieldism for ever. With much reluctance the Queen eventually accepted this 71-year-old man back as her premier. She, like many others, was amazed at his decision to combine the post of Prime Minister with that of the Exchequer. The Cabinet that Gladstone proceeded to construct was heavily dominated by the Whiggish right of the party. This partly reflected Gladstone's personal predilection for Whig grandees but also a feeling that the radicalism of the Midlothian campaign and the National Liberal Federation needed counter-balancing. Only after some resistance did he agree to admit Chamberlain to the Cabinet as President of the Board of Trade. The aged Bright was also included, as was Forster, but both had lost much of their radical fire, which meant Chamberlain was very isolated. His close associate Sir Charles Dilke had to be content with a junior position at the Foreign Office. Gladstone's obsession with the minutiae of the Exchequer and the failure of the Cabinet to reflect the dynamic forces of the National Liberal Federation augured ill for active government.

The Liberal Party had no clear idea of what it wanted to do except to exorcise the Disraelian poltergeist. The new Home Secretary, Sir William Harcourt, had summed the party's problem the previous year: 'It is much easier to persuade the public that the government [Disraeli's] are duffers than that we are conjurors.' Gladstone seems to have seen his role negatively and looked forward to an early retirement after undoing evil. He became obsessed first with the details of budget strategy and then with Ireland. There was no largeness of vision and no reforms that commanded a broad spectrum of support, as in his first ministry.

This lack of a clear programme reflected the intellectual disarray of Liberalism. On the one hand the Oxford don, T. H. Green, could argue in his 'Lectures on the Principles of Political Obligation' (1879–80) that the state had a more positive role to play in the improvement of mankind. It was not enough to remove restraint and allow the free interplay of market forces for good to triumph. The state had a moral obligation to promote 'goodness' of life. This view was still firmly Liberal, in that concern for the individual was paramount but Green's vision was of a more assertive state. In direct contrast, a classic work on Liberalism, Herbert Spencer's 'Man versus the State', written in the early 1880s, was a vengeful denunciation of the enlarged role of the government. His concluding words were:

> The function of Liberalism in the past was that of putting a limit to the powers of kings. The function of true Liberalism in the future will be that of putting a limit to the powers of Parliaments.

Both Green and Spencer spoke and wrote as Liberals, but drew opposite conclusions after reflecting on their society. Liberalism's tendency to liberate and regulate seemed to be reaching a point of irreconcilable conflict.

At the same time the high tide of Liberal economics had passed. Free trade and *laissez-faire* no longer seemed to produce a British economy which could dominate the world. The USA had already overtaken Britain's lead, and Germany was not far behind. British farming was now exposed to the full implications of free trade in food and there was in consequence a growing demand from farmers for a return to protection. The confidence of youth was over: Britain's economic joints were beginning to creak. Only a few Liberals such as Forster and Dilke recognized the problem and looked to the Empire to solve it. Gladstone saw the answer in yet more rigid retrenchment and the banishment of Disraelian extravagance from national life.

The lack of a coherent programme in part accounts for the legislative shortcomings of the second Gladstone government but the condition of the new House of Commons along with external pressures added to this ministry's problems. The sixty-five Irish Nationalist MPs set out to be deliberately obstructive to all business of the House. Now that Charles Stewart Parnell had replaced Isaac Butt as leader of the Irish Nationalist Party there was official sanction for the policy of obstruction initially pioneered by another MP, J. G. Biggar, a Belfast Catholic convert. If Ireland could not have her own parliament then the British parliament should be rendered useless. The free and easy rules of debate allowed filibusters to work and in January 1881 it required a 41-hour sitting to get a Coercion Bill for Ireland through. Four young Conservative MPs added to the chaos quite deliberately and this 'Fourth Party', as it was nicknamed, specialized in attention-seeking tactics. Lord Randolph Churchill, its most noisy member, was particularly adept at insulting Gladstone. Lord Randolph was hardly the embodiment of religious virtue yet he and the other three chose to exploit the case of Charles Bradlaugh to embarrass the government. Bradlaugh was a serious-minded radical and MP for Northampton. He offended traditional Victorian values on two counts. He was a self-proclaimed atheist and an advocate of birth control (seen by many as a filthy and loathsome practice). His promulgation of his views on birth control had caused him to spend several months in prison. Bradlaugh had originally refused to take the traditional oath as a new MP and declared his desire to affirm instead. When he was refused this he agreed to take the oath but wrote a letter to *The Times* stating that this was meaningless. Sir Henry Drummond Wolf, one of the 'Fourth Party', objected to him swearing the oath in these circumstances and so set off a massive parliamentary diversion which threatened to split the Liberal Party. Many Liberal MPs were appalled by Bradlaugh and it gave Churchill great pleasure to make the devout Gladstone defend the atheist. The Commons refused to allow him to take his seat. At times the situation became high farce with ten policemen dragging Bradlaugh from the chamber. He was loyally returned twice by his constituency, Northampton, in 1881 and 1884. He was re-elected in 1885 and the new Speaker of the 1886 Parliament finally allowed him to affirm before taking his seat.

Imperial adventures added to the Cabinet's woes and the unscrambling of Disraeli's imperialism proved more difficult than Gladstone had anticipated. Finally the Queen posed innumerable difficulties. She found it impossible to hide her dislike of him and proved troublesome in her criticism and advice. Moreover, she was frequently absent from London which necessitated lengthy journeys to see her. As Gladstone was to inform Lord Rosebery in 1883, 'The Queen alone is enough to kill any man.' Small wonder that the Prime Minister frequently expressed the desire to retire.

Under the circumstances the legislative achievements of the second Gladstone ministry should not be underestimated. True, there was no local government reform, as many had hoped for, and the counties remained without democratic government. The anti-drink lobby was disappointed as was the contagious diseases pressure group. However, two major measures of great importance were passed: the Irish Land Act of 1881 and the Franchise and Redistribution Acts of 1884–5. A crop of minor measures introduced in 1880 in many ways illustrates the coalition that the Liberal Party really was. A Burials Act remedied a long-standing Non-Conformist grievance by allowing them to hold burial services in parish churchyards. Chamberlain at the Board of Trade attempted to continue Samuel Plimsoll's work with two measures relating to merchant shipping and an Employers' Liability Act which began the process by which employers were increasingly held responsible for injury on their premises (see chapter 3). It was a small start with many loopholes, yet it has been seen by many as an important departure by the state in interfering in the law of contract between employer and employee. Tenant farmers received a minor boon in the Ground Game Act which gave tenants the right to take hares and rabbits from their rented land. This proved a thorn in the privileged side of landlords since previously all game belonged to the landowner. The great measure of 1881 was a real blow for the landed interests. Ireland forced itself upon the attention of the government through the antics of the Irish MPs and the violence endemic in Ireland. The response from Forster, the Irish Secretary, was a Coercion Act which basically gave the Lord Lieutenant powers to lock up almost anyone he chose. But the Liberal Government was not satisfied that the Coercion Act could provide a solution, and the Second Irish Land Act of 1881 went a long way towards removing the central Irish grievance concerning land. It gave tenants the much desired '3 Fs' of fair rent, free sale of leases and fixity of tenure. In so doing it amounted to a major assault on the rights of property, establishing what has been described as dual ownership. Little wonder that this made many Whig aristocrats deeply unhappy. Lord Lansdowne had resigned over a minor land measure in 1880 and now Gladstone's close friend the Duke of Argyll departed from the government. It was an ominous sign of that flow of 'blue blood' from the Liberal Party which became a gush in 1886.

At the Board of Trade, Chamberlain's hope that 1882 'might see the government able to devote ourselves absolutely to home legislation and reform' was to be disappointed. Foreign policy and Ireland continued to darken the scene and frustrate. The release of Parnell from Kilmainham gaol in 1882 led to Forster's resignation, and the promise of a new dawn in Parnell–Liberal relations was then aborted by the murder of the Irish Secretary, Lord Frederick Cavendish, in Dublin's Phoenix Park in May.

The resignations continued. John Bright resigned in July in protest at British military action in Egypt, which he viewed as aggressive and unjustified. Gladstone's retirement in these circumstances was impossible and he soldiered on and reconstructed the Cabinet. He gave up the Exchequer to ease his burden and at the same time brought Dilke into the Cabinet as President of the Local Government Board. This did not mean a swing to the left as it was balanced by the arrival of the ex-Conservative Lord Derby as Colonial Secretary. Radical frustration was to continue. Liberalism had only advanced slightly this year with the Married Women's Property Act which greatly extended a previous Act of 1870 to enable married women to own property in their own right.

The following year was little better. Reform of local government, and London in particular, was contemplated and much work was done by Dilke and Harcourt. In July the Cabinet decided to drop eight bills and push on with six. Only three became law. Harcourt, the Home Secretary, complained in January about a want of a programme. His fears were being frustratingly realized. The only important measure of 1883 was the Corrupt Practices Act put through the Commons by the Attorney General. It attempted to reduce bribery at elections by laying down limits on election spending and tough penalties for non-compliance. It grew out of the complaints of corruption in the 1880 election and also the growing disparity in wealth between the Liberal and Tory party 'machines'. Elections could still be very expensive for the candidates and highly entertaining for the voters. In 1868 in Bradford the Independent Liberal candidate spent £7,212 hiring rooms in public houses and his opponents W. E. Forster and Edward Miall spent £3,397 and hired 127 rooms in public houses. This added up to a lot of beer for the largely Irish population of the central district of the city. The Corrupt Practices Act, together with the Ballot Act of 1872, went a long way in transforming elections from the violent drunken hustings to the sedate affairs of the twentieth century.

No major reforms had been passed and Chamberlain and his associates had to content themselves with rhetoric such as the famous assault on Lord Salisbury who was 'the spokesman of a class – which toil not neither do they spin'. The Queen was irritated in June by digs at royalty in a Birmingham meeting of the radicals.

To rouse and rally the disparate forces of the Liberal Party, the Cabinet decided in 1884 to go for one of the major political issues of the day, the reform of Parliament itself. Such a measure would rally the radicals and persuade special-interest groups like Wilfred Lawson's for temperance reform and James Stansfield's contagious diseases lobby to forego their fads for the greater good. Many Whigs were dubious but Hartington reluctantly accepted that a Franchise Bill was inevitable and the prospect of succeeding Gladstone kept him within the Cabinet. The case for further parliamentary reform was undeniable. All male house-holders could vote in boroughs but in the counties property worth £12 was necessary to qualify men for the franchise. Radicals saw the equalization of the franchise as a great political boost to themselves and a blow not only to the enemy Tories but also the Whigs. It was decided to postpone the potentially difficult issue of redistribution. Gladstone introduced a Franchise Bill in February 1884 which would have established a uniform householder and lodger franchise for every borough and county. It was also to apply to Scotland and Ireland. Amendments for proportional representation and a women's franchise were easily defeated and by the summer the Bill faced the large Tory majority in the Lords. Like the Whigs many Tories feared the implications, but could see the dangers of open opposition to such a sensible rationalization. The Lords decided to stall. They rejected the Bill in July by 59 votes and demanded that a Redistribution Bill be introduced. To some Conservatives this was a simple device to put off an unpalatable measure. To others it made franchise reform more acceptable.

Many radicals were delighted by the Lords' actions which enabled them to raise the cry of 'peers against the people' and the new MP for Newcastle, John Morley, hitherto Chamberlain's guru, coined the phrase 'mend them or end them'. Neither Salisbury nor Gladstone wanted a constitutional crisis and an assault on the Lords, and long and complex discussions involving both party leaders settled the question satisfactorily. The Franchise Bill went through and a Redistribution Bill was introduced to become law in 1885. Salisbury had realized that if single-member constituencies could be established in the big cities then the increasingly Conservative middle class or 'villa vote' as he termed it, might elect Conservative MPs in suburbia. The Conservative Party might survive democracy. The result was a sweeping Redistribution Act which established the single-member constituencies throughout almost the entire country. A total of 159 existing seats across the country were lost and 175 new ones appeared. For the first time in the history of seat distribution there was something approaching fair parliamentary representation. London gained forty seats while in the counties Lancashire gained and Cornwall lost heavily.

The implications of the measure were vast and not quite as the radicals had anticipated. It was certainly a blow to the landed interests and the Whigs within the Liberal Party lost out, but it accelerated the transformation of the Conservative Party from the party of landed property simply to the party of property – no longer the party solely of the shires but now equally strong in the leafy suburbs. Two million, three hundred thousand new adult male voters were added taking the electorate by 1886 to some 5.5 million throughout the United Kingdom as a whole, compared to just 3 million in 1883.

Electoral reform was a great achievement but by 1885 the old problem of division inside the Liberal Party returned. There was a need for

another umbrella issue under which the Liberals could shelter their differences. Chamberlain returned to his programme politics. He was anxious
to get away from the fads and single-issue approach of the past.
Chamberlain opened the year with speeches demanding reform of local
government, free education and attention to the land question. Like
many urban politicians he was concerned at the growing flood of labourers to the towns as the agricultural depression took hold. He was also
staking out his position in the fight for succession to Gladstone either in
his own right or, as was more likely, in a senior position under Hartington. Gladstone was ill and embarrassed by the problems presented by
Egypt and the Sudan (see chapter 5). Ireland also threatened the break-
up of the government. Chamberlain was negotiating with Parnell. He
hoped to win him over with a scheme of devolution giving Ireland a
glorified 'county council' generally known as a Central Board Scheme.
The Whigs in the Cabinet, and particularly Lord Spencer, the Irish
viceroy, resisted. Chamberlain and Dilke had both threatened resignation
in May 1885 but were overtaken by events, for Parnell had also been
negotiating with the Tories and on 8 June he voted with them to defeat
a budget proposal. Seventy Liberals were absent or abstained and the
government was defeated by twelve votes. Gladstone chose to resign;
almost delighted to be rid of a difficult position.

THE CRISIS: JUNE 1885 to AUGUST 1886

The fourteen months from 8 June 1885 to August 1886 were amongst
the most momentous in recent British history. The country underwent
two crises, one economic, the other political, and yet it is difficult to
show any connection between the two. Agriculture was in deepening
trouble with food and land prices falling but now trade and industry
followed suit. Unemployment in the cities rose alarmingly and widespread rioting followed. Troops were sent in against Welsh quarrymen
in January. In February there were riots in Birmingham and Leicester,
and a great socialist demonstration in Manchester at the end of the
month. There were 50,000 Socialists at a meeting in London's Hyde Park
on 21 February, and two weeks earlier there had been considerable
disturbances in Trafalgar Square and surrounding areas of the West End.
   Yet all of this was but noise off-stage from the main political drama
conducted at Westminster, Hawarden and other places where great political decisions were taken. On Gladstone's resignation Salisbury's decision
to form a Conservative Government was in part an effort to consolidate
his own leadership of the party, which was far from secure. An election
was inevitable – as soon as the new boundaries had been finalized – and
in effect an extended election campaign began. Chamberlain within the
Liberal Party appeared to make much of the running with his so-called
'unauthorized' programme. Free education, local government and land

reform formed the bedrock of Chamberlain's position, but he and his followers made embarrassing references to the disestablishment of the Anglican Church from time to time. Chamberlain privately acknowledged that this was not an immediate possibility. In August he visited Hull as the 'crown prince' of the party, and over the next two months he displayed a remarkable self-confidence in the strength of his position. Gladstone played the election campaign quietly. It had not been clear until August that he would continue as leader. His manifesto of 17 September was vague and unexciting but contained reforms of local government and amendment of the land laws. He appeared to be trying to keep the different strands of Liberalism together and was irritated by Chamberlain's determination to drag the party in a more radical direction. He censored the younger man for his attacks on the right-wing Liberal, George Goschen, who had gone further than his Whig associates in criticizing Chamberlain.

Ireland had been prominent in Chamberlain's plans earlier in the year but Parnell's dalliance with the Conservatives and the Catholic Church's opposition to free schools led to this issue being played down. Chamberlain, it seems, felt betrayed and conned by Parnell and never forgave him. Parnell declared for 'National Independence' in August, but on 8 September, campaigning at Warrington, Chamberlain made it quite clear that whilst he favoured devolution, five million Irish had no more right to self-government than five million Londoners. Gladstone at the same time was ruminating on what issue was ripe. He felt Chamberlain's programme had much in it that was not ripe. Ireland, as in 1868, could perhaps provide the focus for Liberal Party unity, and an escape from the more embarrassing aspects of Chamberlain's programme. Single-issue politics, morality and Gladstone would triumph over programme politics, liberal schism and Chamberlain. He made no public pronouncement on the subject and certainly failed to take Chamberlain into his confidence when the latter visited Hawarden in October, although he dropped heavy hints about how Ireland 'might elbow out all others'. Gladstone appears to have hoped that the Irish alliance with the Conservatives would produce a solution, and Parnell gave some substance to this by urging Irish voters in England to vote Tory thereby costing the Liberals perhaps twenty seats.

Whilst the election results were still coming in, the newspapers on 17 December carried news of the famous 'Hawarden kite'. Herbert Gladstone, the Liberal leader's son, had decided to brief the press on his father's conversion to Home Rule. Wemyss Reid, the editor of the *Leeds Mercury*, and a bitter anti-Chamberlainite, was behind the leak. He and Herbert were determined to strike first at Chamberlain who appeared to be planning to ditch Gladstone and the Irish question by allowing the Tories to continue in office for a short time. Chamberlain seems to have had enough of the 'Grand Old Man', and even if the glittering prize of the premiership was not yet within his grasp, he appears to have decided that a deal with Hartington was preferable to dancing attendance on Gladstone's political whims. By striking first, Herbert pushed his father to the centre of the Liberal stage with Home Rule as the great issue around which the Liberal Party would coalesce.

The election was a disappointment for the Liberals and a dream result for the Irish Nationalists who held the balance exactly between 335 Liberals and 249 Conservatives. Gladstone placed the blame on the fair trade movement (a group of Conservatives demanding protection for British manufacturing and agriculture in answer to the slump), Parnell and Chamberlain – the latter because he feared Chamberlain had frightened many voters in the boroughs. Whether Chamberlain's programme of land reform, which was quickly dubbed 'three acres and a cow', won over the new agricultural voter is open to speculation. Gladstone still refused to reveal his hand hoping that Salisbury might be inclined to deal with Ireland. In fact he had decided not to, preferring coercion and resolute government to Home Rule. The Queen's Speech on 21 January made absolutely clear the Tories' rejection of the Parnellite alliance. Salisbury was brought down five days later by the famous amendment to the address moved by Jesse Collings on the subject of smallholdings and allotments (three acres and a cow). Ominously Hartington voted with the Tories as did seventeen other Liberals.

GLADSTONE'S THIRD MINISTRY 1886

Gladstone now formed his third administration, with Ireland clearly the major preoccupation. Hartington refused to join and Chamberlain was handled by Gladstone with consummate rudeness. He was refused the Colonial Office, which he wanted, but agreed to accept the Local Government Board. In turn Gladstone agreed to appoint his associate Collings to a junior position with Chamberlain but insisted on the office taking a salary cut. Two months later when Gladstone presented his Home Rule Bill to the Cabinet Chamberlain resigned. His motives were mixed. The Bill proposed to remove all Irish MPs from Westminster which appeared to Chamberlain a first step to inevitable separation, an outcome he had always opposed. But in addition to principle there was the frustration and anger of an ambitious man who had come to resent Gladstone and his hold on the Liberal Party.

The Bill itself was moderate with the exclusion of defence, foreign affairs and international trade from the control of the new Irish legislative body. Safeguards for minorities and landowners were plentiful, and Gladstone did well to get Parnell and the Irish parliamentary party's support for the measure. There were riots in Belfast and patriotic anti-Home Rule meetings in Britain. Salisbury happily banged the patriotic drum with reactionary relish suggesting that the Irish were no more fit for self-government than the Hottentots. Firm government and the emigration of surplus Irish to Canada was the answer, a policy christened 'manacles and Manitoba' by John Morley, Gladstone's chosen lieutenant. The political temperature rose and British party politics defined themselves around this one issue of Ireland, just as Gladstone had foreseen. He introduced the Bill into the Commons on 8 April, and spoke for three and a half hours. It was one of the great parliamentary occasions. Chamberlain, Hartington and Churchill were all notable assailants of the measure.

On 8 June when the vote on the second reading was taken – 343 'noes' and 313 'ayes' – 93 Liberals voted against. Hartington and some seventy right-wing Liberals, including Goschen, long worried by the steady radicalization of the party, were no surprise, but Chamberlain and about twenty radicals had also opposed the Bill including the aged John Bright. Clearly the Liberal Party had suffered a major split. This time Gladstone decided to go to the country rather than resign. The subsequent election campaign which saw a pact between the Liberal Unionists and the Conservatives hardened the fissures.

A UNITED MINORITY 1886–92

'The Liberals are no longer a flabby disconnected majority but a compact minority united by principle.' So wrote Lord Rosebery in 1887, one of the few Whigs to remain within the Gladstone fold. Commitment to Home Rule now provided a focus for Liberal loyalty and indeed defined English politics to the benefit of Gladstone within the Liberal Party and Salisbury in the country at large. Some traditional Liberal families had been lost and Chamberlain had taken Birmingham with him, but the Gladstonians rapidly captured most of the Liberal organization including the National Liberal Federation. Numerous pressure groups like the Liberation Society and the UK Alliance aligned themselves with Gladstone and even accepted the primacy of Home Rule over all other issues. The slogan 'Ireland blocks the way' was often heard, and there was a new-found unity in accepting this. Single-issue politics had triumphed over programme politics. Gladstone's own position seemed stronger than ever. 'Talk of the Liberal Party', said John Morley in 1891, 'Why it consists of Mr. Gladstone – after him it will disappear and all will be chaos.'

Many of the radicals who had left with Chamberlain were increasingly unhappy in Salisbury's reactionary grip and some, like George Trevelyan, drifted back. A major conference on reunion was held in 1887, but Gladstone's terms were too harsh for 'Birmingham Joe' – Chamberlain was not prepared to crawl on his belly to the 'Grand Old Man'. By-elections began to go in favour of the Liberal Party and even Chamberlain's Birmingham base was threatened. The tide flowing in favour of

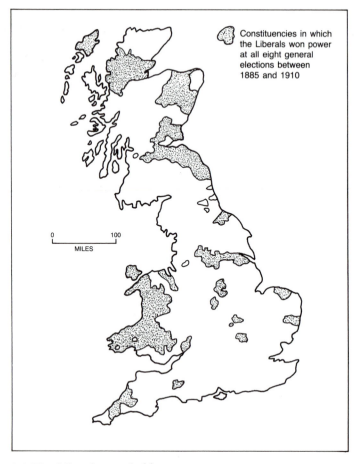

Constituencies in which
the Liberals won power
at all eight general
elections between
1885 and 1910

0   100
MILES

2.1 The Liberal strongholds

Gladstone and Home Rule seemed unstoppable, when the Pigott forgeries were exposed (see chapter 4), and for the first time in his career
Parnell, the Irish leader, found himself popular in England. He was even
received at Hawarden in December 1889.

Yet the concentration on Home Rule concealed rather than solved the
problems of the Liberal Party. Increasingly it was a party of the Celtic
fringe, as Map 2.1 indicates, and therefore increasingly wedded to politics
with little relevance outside Wales and Scotland. Disestablishment of the
Anglican Church in Wales might cause a waving of flags in the valleys
and chapels of the Principality, but in Huddersfield, Newcastle and the
East End of London it meant very little. The central problem was the
working-class vote in the big cities of England. Without this support the
Liberal Party would die. Gladstone, like many others, recognized this.
He appointed a working man and trade unionist as Home Office Under-

Secretary in 1886 – Henry Broadhurst – and in 1891 at the famous party conference in Newcastle he urged the party to adopt working-class candidates. In mining areas where working men were grouped and were effectively organized by their unions this was possible, but all too frequently small Non-Conformist and middle-class cliques dominated local Liberal parties and working men were rejected. Keir Hardie, Ramsay MacDonald and Arthur Henderson, who became founding fathers of the Labour Party, were all rejected as candidates in this period by their local Liberal associations. Shortage of money contributed to the problem. The split of 1886 brought a haemorrhage of money. Standing as a candidate was still expensive and, even if successful, MPs still had to support themselves. There was a lack of money either to fund working-class candidates or to mount an effective organization that democratic politics necessitated. The number of unopposed Tory candidates grew alarmingly. On matters of policy that touched the working class, Liberals found themselves in an awkward corner. Issues like the eight-hour day exposed dangerous class fissures within the party. Sir James Kitson, a wealthy Leeds businessman and President of the National Liberal Federation from 1883 to 1890, was bitterly opposed to such a demand as was Morley who felt unhappy at such an extension of state power. Gladstone himself expressed his deep suspicion of state activity in 1889: 'If government takes into its hands that which man ought to do for himself it will inflict upon him greater mischiefs than all the benefits he will have received or all the advantages that would accrue from them.'

The 'Grand Old Man' showed little interest in any issue other than Ireland, but even he agreed to endorse a programme of reforms at the conference in Newcastle in 1891 in the hope of tempting the electorate. It was very much a case of something for everyone in the party, but the emphasis on disestablishment in Wales and Scotland and the local veto on alcohol sales, emphasized the grip in which the Non-Conformist faddists held the party. Land reform, elected parish councils and extensions of employers' liability were promised but as the leader made clear in 1892 Ireland maintained its primacy of place. 'I am fast bound to Ireland as Ulysses was to his mast', Gladstone told Lord Ripon.

Salisbury dissolved Parliament in July 1892. Home Rule was less popular than it had been in 1889. Since then Parnell's affair with Mrs O'Shea had split the Irish party and embarrassed the Liberals. The results of the election were a disappointment for everyone. The electorate appeared bored with Home Rule. In the House 273 Liberals and 81 Irish Nationalists faced 268 Conservatives and 47 Liberal Unionists. There was one Independent Labour member, an ominous portent for the future.

THE LAST GLADSTONE GOVERNMENT 1892–4

The government which took office in August 1892 was not lacking in ability. It blended seasoned campaigners like Earl Spencer at the Admiralty with new blood like the brilliant young barrister H. H. Asquith at the Home Office. The junior ministers were rich in talent: Sir Edward Grey, for instance, was at the Foreign Office. Yet despite this, the problems were enormous. An 83-year-old man led a Cabinet which exuded more bad blood and personal rivalry than most. Harcourt, the Chancellor of the Exchequer, did not speak to the Foreign Secretary, Lord Rosebery, and Morley, Chief Secretary for Ireland, treated Harcourt with chilly disdain. The personal bickering of the Cabinet mirrored the rag-bag of Liberal fads which permeated the parliamentary party. Each interest group jostled for its place. An 1893 *Punch* cartoon captured the mood.

In Parliament the government lacked a reliable majority, depending as it did on the Irish who were themselves split into factions. The Liberal army of backbenchers was difficult to discipline. David Lloyd George, the new young member for Carnarvon Boroughs resigned the whip in 1894 when Welsh disestablishment was not given priority. There was a bitter unionist opposition intent on obstructing business in the Commons and in the Lords an overwhelming majority determined to maim and mangle any measure that reached them. All things considered the achievements of the fourth ministry are perhaps remarkable.

Home Rule dominated the first year of the government and the extent of Gladstone's skill and stamina was extraordinary in piloting it through eighty-five sessions to receive its third reading in September 1893. The major difference between the second Home Rule Bill and that of 1886 was the retention of a reduced Irish cohort at Westminster with a rather complex and contradictory set of rules for their participation. The Prime Minister's skill was in vain. A week later, passing from the Commons to the Lords, the Bill was butchered by a massive 419 to 41. Other measures were either abandoned or amended. Asquith's Employers' Liability Bill was one such victim, dropped in February 1894. Bills on a local veto, on the Welsh Church, labour disputes and registration of voters all had to be abandoned in September 1893, pushed aside by the titanic struggles over Home Rule. (There was one exception, the Parish Council Bill which did eventually become law in 1894 and established elected parish councils for which women could vote and stand. The powers however of these new democratic bodies had been much curtailed by the Lords and they began life as much feebler institutions than their designer A. H. Fowler had intended.)

Gladstone now saw a new single issue to revive Liberalism, a fresh 'block on the line' to progress: the House of Lords. He tried to interest his Cabinet colleagues in a dissolution and assault on the monster but

the Cabinet would not have it. The party organizers pointed to the perilous state of Liberal finances and the poor shape of the organization throughout the country as a whole. Many leading Liberals suspected that the Lords' rejection of the Home Rule Bill had been popular. Before Gladstone could bring the issue to fruition a bitter quarrel developed between himself and the rest of his colleagues over increased spending on the navy. He had already been put out by Harcourt's attitude to the Irish Bill the previous year and his quarrels with Rosebery at the Foreign Office are detailed in chapter 5. His eyesight was failing and deafness was creeping upon him. His resignation was finally offered in March 1894 and was gratefully received by his sovereign Queen Victoria. Gladstone was irritated by the blubbering farewell speeches of cabinet colleagues.

The Queen did not consult Gladstone on his successor. She chose Lord Rosebery who was probably the Cabinet's choice although certainly not Harcourt's. The next fifteen months formed an unhappy postscript to the Gladstone era. Archibald Primrose, Earl of Rosebery, was a very rich man. He was born rich and married a Rothschild. He was clever and eloquent and yet also moody and petulant. Political success had come too easily to him and he lacked Gladstone's inner steel. The divisions within his Cabinet and party produced a pessimistic desire for resignation and retreat. Harcourt produced the only real substantial achievement in his budget of 1894 introducing for the first time consolidated death duties and establishing the principle that the state could tax capital. The highest rate of 8 per cent on estates valued at over a million pounds was not perhaps excessive but it sent a shudder through the propertied classes. Neither Gladstone nor Rosebery were happy with the proposals but the radical troops were delighted, and as the Lords could not interfere with a budget, it was a way of cocking a snook at the enemy.

If the government could not legislate for progress because of the Tory opposition then administrative measures could be used. Morley in Ireland promoted Roman Catholics to the bench of magistrates and Asquith made important advances in standards of safety and conditions at work with the factory inspectorate. The government itself made a gesture of friendship to labour by substantially raising government employees' salaries and A. H. D. Acland, the Education Minister, carried through a series of departmental reforms.

The major legislative proposals of 1895 were, once again, a local veto on alcohol sales and Welsh disestablishment. Rosebery tried to raise reform of the Lords as a unifying issue, but only produced more dissent as many of his colleagues preferred ending to mending the Lords. On 21 June 1895 Rosebery found an excuse to call it a day. The government was defeated on a snap vote in the House of Commons on a marginal issue of army stocks of cordite explosives. Had he wished Rosebery could have soldiered on, as the Whigs and Robert Hudson, the Secretary of the Liberal Central Office, advised. But he had had enough of Harcourt, his colleague, and of Number 10. He resigned and handed over to Salisbury who called an election and trounced the Liberals with a huge majority. The result was not surprising given the limp performance of Rosebery's government and the Liberal election campaign. Morley campaigned for Home Rule, Harcourt for local veto and Rosebery for reform of the House of Lords. Gladstone was gone and ten years of Conservative rule ensued.

ASSESSMENT

Gladstone died on Ascension Day, 19 May 1898. He was accorded a state funeral and, much to the Queen's displeasure, the Prince of Wales and his son, the future George V, were among the pall bearers. The man who started life as a high Tory and remained a devout High Anglican to the end was a model Liberal statesman of Britain and Europe. Yet a vital streak of Conservatism never left him. He revered monarchy and felt an affinity for Whig aristocrats and their world whilst showing distaste for such pushy *nouveaux-riches* as Chamberlain. Perhaps it was Gladstone's innate Conservatism that partially accounts for the very limited transformation of Britain that the Liberal Party achieved in his years of leadership. A hereditary House of Lords survived – a mockery of the principle of merit. There was to be no disestablishment of the Anglican Church, and alone amongst western democratic states compulsory religious services in schools live on in the secular society of the 1990s. Elected local government in the shires only came in 1889, and that from a Conservative government, and the gentry domination of the bench of magistrates was only slowly eroded in the twentieth century. *Ancien régime* England lived on with its hold on the ancient universities, the law and the army only partially modified. The greatest injury to the power of the landed elite came from the flood of foreign food from the New World. American wheat did more damage than Liberal majorities. Land values and rent rolls fell. In addition to the failure to destroy privilege there was a failure to recognize many of the needs of the new industrial England. The British education system remained patently inferior to that of Germany with serious long-term economic consequences.

Gladstone, it has been argued, prevented the evolution of a genuinely radical programme-oriented Liberal Party which could transform Britain and enthuse the new working-class voter. His embrace of radicalism in 1876–8 smothered it and, according to Chamberlain, in 1886 Home Rule diverted Liberalism from radical channels. Gladstone's concern with retrenchment and his suspicion of collectivism prolonged the minimalist state with government spending reaching its all-time low as a percentage of GNP in the 1880s.

Yet a politician's greatness or a party's utility is not to be judged by its ability to reform society, although that can be one aspect of political success. Gladstone and the Liberal Party in these years performed an inestimable political service in integrating the new working-class voters into the political system. The 'People's William' was the first Prime Minister the masses could identify with and adore. Perhaps this was one of Gladstone's and Liberalism's more conservative achievements. There was no mass revolutionary socialist movement as developed in Germany, committed to the overthrow of the state. Instead British politics became more settled and sedate. The old world was not totally overthrown yet room was made peacefully for the new. The thorough-going triumph of free trade ensured cheap food and rising living standards, which, for most ordinary Britons in the 1880s and 1890s, was the greatest of boons. There was no return to protectionism as happened in France and Germany.

Finally, Gladstone implanted in the Liberal Party and bequeathed to the political left in general a moral dimension to British politics. He showed that the language and rhetoric of morality was a potent political weapon when wielded by a master.

CONTROVERSY: HISTORIANS AND THE HOME RULE CRISIS

John Morley produced a great work of literature in 1903. His multi-volume life of his dead chief was fitting tribute and it has been extremely influential in shaping popular views of Gladstone and the Home Rule crisis. Essentially Morley saw Gladstone's behaviour as part of a heroic struggle for justice. The Home Rule Bill sprang as much from Gladstone's personality as from the situation in Ireland. His language indicates his admiration:

> Mr. Gladstone had pondered the matter more deeply. His gift of political imagination, his wider experience, and his personal share in some chapters of the modern history of Europe and its changes, planted him on a height whence he commanded a view of possibilities and necessities, of hopes and of risks, that were unseen by politicians of the beaten track. Like a pilot amid wandering icebergs, or in waters where familiar buoys had been taken up and immemorial beacons put out, he scanned the scene with keen eyes and a glass sweeping the horizon in every direction.
>
> (J. Morley, *The Life of William Ewart Gladstone*, London, Macmillan, 1903, p. 475)

He continues in the same paragraph to mention such heroic contemporaries as Bismarck, Cavour and Lincoln. J. L. Hammond in another literary masterpiece, *Gladstone and the Irish Nation*, published in 1938, placed Gladstone on an even higher pedestal. For Hammond the defeat of the Home Rule Bill was the great lost opportunity. The great man was defeated by selfish factions within and without the Liberal Party:

> For five years the strain wore him down; those were the five years of his second Government when his duty was often obscure to him, and the struggle itself was, not a pitched battle, but a series of manoeuvres within the Cabinet and a series of experiments within his conscience. His mistakes and his misfortunes aged him fast, and doubt and sorrow cast their gloom over his spirit. In 1886 as in 1877, the battle was open, his course was clear, and strength and youth returned to him. It was now a battle between men moving within the circle of an island mind and a man who lived in the wisdom of the ages, among
> 'The mighty ones who have made eternal day
> For Greece and England.'
> (J. L. Hammond, *Gladstone and the Irish Nation*, London, Cass, 1964,
> p. 739)

Philip Magnus in his popular biography written in 1954 essentially follows the same line

> He finally made up his mind to fight the cause of Home Rule during a brief holiday which he took in the Norwegian fiords on Sir Thomas Brassey's yacht, the *Sunbeam*, from 8 August to 1 September, 1885. Gladstone found in Norway a small people living happily in a spirit of democracy, and the effect upon his mind was comparable with that of his visit to Naples in the winter of 1850–1. He loved what he found in Norway, for it touched one of the deepest chords in his nature.
> To Gladstone the cause of Home Rule was an end in itself. He made it clear to his sons that he was not willing merely to continue to fight the battle of Liberalism versus Conservatism. If that were all, he would prefer to retire.
> (P. Magnus, *Gladstone*, London, John Murray, 1954, p. 352)

The pages of *Punch* in 1886 often reflected this same view of events, Gladstone the tragic hero brought down by lesser men.

Since 1970 there has been a change of perspective with more emphasis on the British rather than Irish dimension and attention drawn to Gladstone the consummate politician rather than the moral hero. D. A. Hamer, in a book published in 1972, sees the crisis as growing out of the need to restructure the Liberal Party:

> And in Gladstone's thinking on the political situation it was Ireland that began to emerge as the great cause that might control and subordinate all other political questions and thus create order out of the

ACTÆON AND HIS HOUNDS.

prevailing chaos. Gladstone saw Irish Home Rule as a 'ripening' issue, assessed its significance as such in relation to the condition of Liberal politics, and began to shape his concern with it accordingly. Gradually there was impressed on him the possibility that it might be such a question as he had craved in 1873, one that, if worked into certain shapes, might serve for a time 'to mould the rest'.

(D. A. Hamer, *Liberal Politics in the Age of Gladstone and Rosebery*, Oxford, Oxford University Press, 1972, p. 110)

In 1974 a highly influential and very detailed study of the crisis, *The Governing Passion*, by A. B. Cooke and J. R. Vincent, was published. Here Gladstone is seen as a skilled politician reacting to pressures and situations which he did not control any more than any other politician controlled them. He was playing the game of high politics.

> Gladstone did not in fact enter upon home rule in a state of incandescence. He did not have Parnellites to dinner: indeed, with one or two possible secret exceptions, he refused point blank to meet them socially or politically. His recorded conversation at the time shows no trace of good feeling towards them, and suspicion of their motives which readily turned to disparagement. He barely preferred them, politically or personally, to Chamberlain. His entry towards home rule had no happy or generous note about it. He was not buoyed up and in high spirits, as Peel had been in December 1845, by the knowledge there was great work to be shaped. There was, in 1886, no union of hearts. From Gladstone's own point of view, the home rule fiasco is to be seen not as a tragic failure to achieve a potentially excellent settlement in Ireland, but as a not at all ineffective means of preventing that dire worsening of the situation over there which he had half convinced himself was imminent in January 1886.
>
> In a pleasanter way, it is important that Gladstone was less obsessed than on some previous occasions by his 'cause' of the moment, at least until the election campaign of June 1886. Seldom can a premier have had a more enjoyable short ministry. Absorbed only in problems which stimulated him, he dined out almost continuously, far more than in previous years. At the dinner table, he was almost always in capital form, and he chose his company more with a view to pleasure than to political effect. His conversation frequently centred on the trivial and anecdotal. Conventional accounts written in the shadow of party warfare entirely fail to convey how much Gladstone in 1886 was a sane, balanced, goodhumoured but old-fashioned old gentleman whose life contained much more private pleasure than public anguish.
>
> (A. B. Cooke and J. R. Vincent, *The Governing Passion*, Brighton, Harvester, 1974, pp. 53–4)

The year after Cooke and Vincent's work was published Michael Barker returned to a more traditional view. He gives Gladstone credit for being more sympathetic to radical ideas.

> In 1885 Gladstone retained his faith in the people but had lost confidence in the aristocracy. . . . His marked dissatisfaction with the state of inertia, even indifference, with which Hartington was identified guaranteed that were the party to break up he would not willingly be found in association with the Whig rump. As early as 1877 Gladstone had become convinced that 'the vital principle of the Liberal

party . . . is *action*, and that nothing but action will ever make it worthy of the name of a party'. By 1885 the forces ready and eager for 'action' were amassed in the camp of Chamberlain.

(M. Barker, *Gladstone and Radicalism 1885–1894*, Hassocks, Harvester, 1975, p. 17)

There is of course no resolution of the debate but it is perhaps worth returning to Morley who in 1903 stressed the duality of dimensions in the crisis:

What were 'the anxious and doubtful matters,' what 'the coming political issues,' of which Mr. Gladstone had written to Lord Hartington? They were, in a word, twofold: to prevent the right wing from breaking with the left; and second, to make ready for an Irish crisis, which as he knew could not be averted. These were the two keys to all his thoughts, words, and deeds during the important autumn of 1885 – an Irish crisis, a solid party. He was not the first great parliamentary leader whose course lay between two impossibilities.

(Morley, op. cit., p. 460)

BIBLIOGRAPHY

For an explanation of the grading system, see the preface p. xiii.

Biographies

W. E. Gladstone

There have been many excellent books on the 'grand old man', starting with John Morley's in 1903 (see below). Of more recent works the following are recommended:

3   Feuchtwanger, E. J., London, Allen Lane, 1975
4   Hammond, J. L., London, Cass, 1964
2   Mathews, H. C. G., Oxford, Oxford University Press, 1986 (only to 1874)
4   Morley, J., London, Macmillan, 1903
4   Shannon, R., London, Hamish Hamilton, 1982 (to 1865; Volume 2 forth-coming)
1   Winstanley, M. J., London, Routledge, 1989

J. Bright

3   Ausubel, H., New York, Wiley, 1966
2   Robbins, K., London, Routledge & Kegan Paul, 1979

J. Chamberlain

4   Jay, R., Oxford, Oxford University Press, 1981
2   Judd, D., London, Hamish Hamilton, 1977

1   Powell, E., London, Thames & Hudson, 1977

C. Dilke

2   Jenkins, R., London, Collins, 1958

J. Morley

3   Hamer, D., Oxford, Oxford University Press, 1968

Lord Rosebery

2   James, R. R., London, Weidenfeld & Nicolson, 1963

Queen Victoria

4   Hardie, F., London, Cass, 1963
2/3   Longford, E., London, Weidenfeld & Nicolson, 1964

Secondary works

1   Adelman, P., *Gladstone, Disraeli and Later Victorian Politics*, London, Longman, 1970
4   Barker, M., *Gladstone and Radicalism 1885–1894*, Hassocks, Harvester, 1975
3   Bentley, M., *The Climax of Liberal Politics, 1868–1918*, London, Arnold, 1987
3   Briggs, A., *A History of Birmingham*, vol. 2, Oxford, Oxford University Press, 1952
4   Cooke, A. B. and Vincent, J. R., *The Governing Passion: Cabinet Government and Party Politics in Britain 1885–1886*, Brighton, Harvester, 1974
3   Hamer, D. A., *Liberal Politics in the Age of Gladstone and Rosebery*, Oxford, Oxford University Press, 1972
4   Hanham, H. J., *Elections and Party Management: Politics in the Time of Disraeli and Gladstone*, London, Longman, 1959
4   Harvie, C., *The Lights of Liberalism? University Liberals*, London, Allen Lane, 1976
3   Mathews, H. C. G., Introduction to Vol. 7 of the *Gladstone Diaries*, Oxford, Oxford University Press, 1982, is probably the best introduction to Gladstone's first ministry
4   Pelling, H., *The Social Geography of British Elections 1885–1910*, London, Macmillan, 1967
4   Shannon, R. T., *Gladstone and the Bulgarian Agitation*, Hassocks, Harvester, 1975
3   Southgate, D., *The Passing of the Whigs 1832–1886*, London, Macmillan, 1965
3   Vincent, J. R., *The Formation of the Liberal Party 1857–1868*, London, Constable, 1966

Sources for coursework

There are many readily available printed primary sources of which the most notable must be the *Gladstone Diaries 1868–1880* (Oxford, Oxford University Press, 1982). John Morley's *Life of Gladstone* (1903) contains many useful primary extracts, particularly letters. *The Political Correspondence of Mr. Gladstone and Lord Granville 1868–1886*, edited by Agatha Ramm (Oxford, Oxford University Press, 1960), is of great importance. Many other collections of correspondence and diaries have been published and are available in the bigger reference libraries. Just two examples are: *Letters of Queen Victoria 1861–1901*, 2nd–3rd series, 6 vols, London, John Murray, 1926–32 and *Lord Carlingford's Journal 1885*, eds Vincent and Cooke, Cassell & Co., 1971. The 'Diaries' of various parliaments written by Henry Lucy are very entertaining accounts by a lobby correspondent and worth seeking out. There are endless possibilities for research using newspapers and journals. *Punch* and *The London Illustrated News* provide ample illustrative material and local and national newspapers can be consulted. Elections can be studied in a local context and the impact of particular pieces of legislation, for example the Licensing Act of 1872 or the impact of the Ballot Act of 1872 on the conduct of election can be assessed.

Election results

Dec. 1868	Feb. 1874	April 1880	Nov. 1885
C 271	C 342	C 238	C 249
L 387	L 251	L 353	L 335
	IN 59	IN 61	IN 86

July 1886	July 1892	July 1895
C 317	C 268	C 340
LU 77	LU 46	LU 71
L 191	L 272	L 177
IN 85	IN 80	IN 82
	O 4	

C = Conservative, L = Liberal, IN = Irish Nationalist, LU = Liberal Unionist, O = Other

3 The Conservative Party 1868–1905: the regaining of power

INTRODUCTION

In February 1858 Gladstone had received a letter from John Bright, who feared he was about to join a Derby Conservative Government, saying 'If you join Lord Derby you link your fortunes with a constant minority and with a party in the country which is every day lessening in numbers and power.' Bright's fears were groundless and Gladstone, as we have seen, became the dominant Liberal of the late nineteenth century. Bright's other assessment was equally wrong-headed. When the old Quaker died in 1889, far from lessening in numbers and power the Conservative Party had undergone a revival and was enjoying the fruits of office with a large majority. It was the Liberals who were the minority in England and they were to remain in that position for another sixteen years. This transformation of party fortunes was remarkable. In election after election in the 1850s and 1860s the Conservatives failed to achieve a majority and this under a grossly unfair electoral system. After the break-up of Peel's Government in 1846 they enjoyed only four years of minority office. Between 1874 and 1905 the position was transformed with twenty-two years of majority government. In particular regions of England this revival becomes even more pronounced.

The Conservatives had always won a majority of seats in rural England, a position only threatened in 1885. As Table 3.1 indicates it is the upsurge of Conservatism in urbanized Lancashire and the capital that lies at the heart of the revival. With the defection of the West Midlands under Joseph Chamberlain, from the Liberal Party after 1886, the Tory dominance in England was consolidated.

Conservatism is even harder to define than that package of ideas that went by the name of Liberalism. Many Conservative writers, particularly on the Continent, would stress the organic or natural state of society. They would argue that forms of government are not created by men from abstract principles of good and evil, but evolve with a natural order which some would have said was 'God given'. The individual member

Table 3.1 The Conservative breakthrough 1859–95

	1865	1868	1874	1880	1885	1886	1892	1895
London	0(18)	3(22)	10(22)	8(22)	35(59)	47(59)	36(59)	51(59)
Lancashire and Cheshire	18(38)	31(46)	34(46)	19(46)	46(69)	58(69)	45(69)	60(69)

Note: The total seats for each area are given in brackets. Figures taken from various sources.

of the society has meaning only in his or her relations to the whole. Communities like the family and the nation give meaning and significance to the individual man or woman. Where the individual asserts his or her individuality at the expense of the whole, then anarchy and chaos are the likely result. Perhaps modern British Conservatism goes back to Edmund Burke and his tirades of the 1790s against the French Revolution. Here was a society, according to Burke, seeking to redesign itself using reason and abstract principles, destroying monarchy, church and nobility in the process. The French made nature conform to human reason and the new calendar was decimalized with ten not twelve months, and ten not seven days. To Burke such reforms were chaotic folly. Men were governed by habit and custom not by reason. Reason was not a strong enough barrier to human wickedness. Destroy habits and anarchy would surely follow. Most Conservatives of the nineteenth century tended to define themselves in terms of opposing Liberalism and condemning the French Revolution of 1789. In so far as English Liberals were more moderate than their Continental equivalents so the English Conservatives were less bloodthirsty in their defence of the status quo.

Throughout the period in question British Conservatism saw itself as preserver of society against threatening forces. Salisbury, one of the few British political leaders to take political theory seriously, outlined the basis of Conservative Party support in an article of October 1869:

> Social stability is ensured, not by the cessation of the demand for change, for the needy and restless will never cease to cry for it, but by the fact that change in its progress must at last hurt some class of men who are strong enough to arrest it. The army of so-called reform in every stage of its advance necessarily converts a detachment of its force into opponents. The more rapid the advance the more formidable will the desertion become, till at last a point will be reached when the balance of the forces of conservation and destruction will be redressed and the political equilibrium will be restored.
>
> (Quoted in R. Taylor, *Lord Salisbury*, London, Allen Lane, 1975, p. 35)

By the 1880s the Conservatives' two main enemies had become disorder and division in Ireland and the growth of socialism in mainland Britain.

It was against these twin threats that unionism rallied in the defence of property and national cohesion. In this struggle the appeal to patriotism proved a valuable weapon. As the Conservative Party broadened its base with the accretion of middle-class converts so the Conservative ideology evolved. The Tory Party of the twentieth century, with its emphasis on the entrepreneurs' role in enriching society, emerged from these Liberal Conservatives. W. H. Mallock's book, *Aristocracy and Evolution*, published in London in 1898, expressed this new strand of Conservatism perfectly and could be taken as the handbook for what the late twentieth century has christened 'Thatcherism'.

THE BASIS OF CONSERVATIVE SUPPORT

A Liberal MP in 1867 spoke of the two great parties, 'the one which represented the agricultural, and the other, the manufacturing and commercial interests of our vast community'. This identification of the Conservative Party with agriculture was a pardonable exaggeration. Before the Reform Act the Conservatives took 67 per cent of agricultural seats, and after 1867 77 per cent. H. J. Hanham, in his impressive study of politics between 1868 and 1880, hardly disagrees with this comment:

> The roots of the Conservative strength in the counties lay in the kinship of outlook and interests between landlord, farmer, and villager at the level of half-formed ideas and instinctive reactions. It was an alliance of the hunting-field and the cattle-market rather than of the political meeting, or even the agricultural society. And the Conservatives came, therefore, to be more than a party of squires and parsons. They were as near as possible to being the party of the 'agricultural interest', the party of those who cultivated the land.
> (H. J. Hanham, *Elections and Party Management: Politics in the Time of Disraeli and Gladstone*, London, Longman, 1959, p. 32)

The Tory Party of the mid-nineteenth century owed its essential character to the defence of agricultural interests. The followers of Disraeli and Derby were those Conservative MPs who rallied to the defence of the Corn Laws in 1846 and rejected their leader (Peel) as a traitor.

If the Liberal Party drew its strength from pressure groups like the Liberation Society, the Conservatives had the Central Chamber of Agriculture, established in 1866. It campaigned vigorously for farming interests and one of Disraeli's first actions on taking office in 1874 was to receive a delegation from the Chamber and express sympathy and support for their views. His government took a great deal of notice of their groans about local taxation and made valiant efforts to relieve rural rate-payers.

Agriculture, as indicated in chapter 1, was the single most powerful economic interest group in the 1860s but it was still not big enough to be the sole basis of the Conservative Party. The Tories also spoke as the party of the Established Church and enjoyed the support of the majority of Anglican parsons. It also drew to itself an increasing number of middle-class supporters of diverse economic interests. In Glossop, the Wood family, owners of the biggest weaving shed in the world, were devout Anglicans and Tories. They built churches and, along with their relatives, the Sidebottoms, controlled local politics in the Conservative interest. Two Sidebottom brothers sat as neighbouring MPs for Staly-bridge in Cheshire and High Peak in Derbyshire. Elsewhere in the north-west there was a powerful fraternity of Conservative manufacturers. John Laird, of the great ship-building firm of Birkenhead, represented that town as a Tory from 1861. In London there was a drift of middle-class support towards Conservatism from the 1860s. W. H. Smith, the bookseller, abandoned the Liberals and won Westminster for the Conservatives in 1868, defeating the philosopher J. S. Mill. Over the next twenty years the trickle of middle-class support was to swell and trans-form the Conservative Party.

Support lower down the social order was to be found as well. Butchers were traditional Tories and the identification of the temperance move-ment with Liberalism drove the licensed trade into the opposite camp. Chimney-sweeps were also traditionally Conservative. In Lancashire there was a strong and growing current of working-class Conservatism, a force that was to defeat Gladstone in south Lancashire in 1874. Perhaps the anti-Irish feeling fuelled the Anglican and Tory revival that occurred here.

Under Disraeli's leadership the party's organization was transformed. Money was the one big advantage they enjoyed over the Liberals and the bulk of it came from traditional supporters such as the landed gentry. In 1867 the National Union was organized. Unlike the National Liberal Federation the impetus for this came from the top and it had as its objective the winning over of the working classes. In 1871 John Gorst became its Secretary and as he was already National Agent and the chief figure at the new Central Office, established in 1870, the National Union became the servant of the Central Party Organization. Gorst was an important driving force in mobilizing the new Conservative middle-class voters into urban Conservative Associations. By 1873 there were 400 of them, many in the big cities. This revolution in party organization was not only in response to the new electoral changes but also to Disraeli's own insecure position as leader. There were tensions between him and the Chief Whip, Colonel Taylor, and the Whips' Office had until then been responsible for the party's organization.

Disraeli had become party leader and Prime Minister in February 1868 as reward for his success the previous year. If Gladstone was in some ways an unlikely leader of the Liberals, his opponent Disraeli, Jewish, novelist, and landowner only by the charity of his friends, was an even more unlikely leader of the Conservatives. He was born in 1804 into

Benjamin Disraeli, Earl of Beaconsfield by J. E. Millais, 1881

upper-middle-class literary circles, and his father having quarrelled with the local synagogue had young Benjamin baptised an Anglican. He was privately educated and made none of those useful contacts at the public schools or Oxford that served Gladstone so well. In this sense he was an outsider and remained one always. His salient characteristics were ambition, brains, courage and an amoral lack of scruples. By his twenties he was £20,000 in debt (perhaps half a million pounds in modern terms). He sponged mercilessly on all who presented themselves for exploitation. He gained his entry into politics via the bed of his mistress whom he shared with Lord Lyndhurst, an ex-Lord Chancellor.

Disraeli was convinced of his own genius. He resented his mother for not sharing his certainty on this point. He had a romantic attachment to England and a nostalgic love of its aristocracy with whom he identified himself. But there was always a hint of radicalism, a willingness to try something different and to shock. He married a widow with an income of £4,000 per annum and a London house, and by all accounts the marriage was a perfectly happy one resting as it did on Mary Anne's acceptance of his genius. His brilliance and courage in challenging Peel in 1846 transformed him from an eccentric backbencher to a leader of the Tory rebels defending the Corn Laws. In the resulting Conservative rump his brain and mastery of parliamentary tactics made him Lord Derby's lieutenant, a position he was to hold for twenty years. He was not loved but accepted for his cleverness, a commodity in rather short supply in the mid-Victorian Tory Party. His skill and flexibility was demonstrated during the months of the Reform Crisis 1866–7 (see pp. 20–4). His triumph made his succession to Derby in 1868 inevitable. On gaining the premiership, there was no weighty pronouncement on mission as in Gladstone's case, merely the flippant remark 'Well I've climbed to the top of the greasy pole.' Many Tories distrusted him, few as much as Viscount Cranborne, who became the Marquis of Salisbury in 1868. To Cranborne, Disraeli was 'a mere political gamester' or, as he put it in a letter shortly before he went to the Lords:

> If I had a firm confidence in his principles or his honesty, or even if he were identified by birth or property with the Conservative classes in the country – I might in the absence of any definite professions work to maintain him in power. But he is an adventurer: & as I have too good cause to know, he is without principles and honesty.
> (Quoted in R. Blake, *Disraeli*, London, Eyre & Spottiswoode, 1966, p. 499)

What Disraeli's beliefs were is difficult to ascertain. He wrote and talked much of patriotism and one nation. Certainly he had a disdain for much of the intellectual baggage of Liberalism. He was sceptical of reason, and once said 'Man is only truly great when he acts from the passions, never irresistible, but when he appeals to the imagination, Man is made to adore and obey.' In his novels of the 1840s, Disraeli had written of the 'two nations', the rich and the poor, and expressed sympathy for the poor and their plight. Yet in 1850 at the request of Lord Londonderry, a notoriously harsh mineowner, he opposed a Mines Bill providing for the inspection of mines. In his speech of 1872, he extolled the Empire, yet twenty years earlier he had expressed the opinion that our colonies were 'mill-stones around our neck'. Well might Salisbury call him a 'mere political gamester'. As Disraeli told Bright, 'We came here for fame', and this was probably his driving passion. He was a performer; a surface without an interior. *Punch*'s favourite portrayals of him were as the 'tight-rope walker', 'juggler', 'sword swallower' or a stage personality whose act was designed to amuse, excite and deceive. He was, in Thomas Carlyle's famous phrase, the 'Hebrew Conjuror'.

The loss of the 1868 election by such a convincing margin was a disappointment and 'Dizzy' returned to the opposition benches he knew so well. His wife was old and sick and the large Liberal majority gave little prospect of success in the immediate future. He maintained a low political profile and wrote a novel, *Lothair*. Discontent with his leadership grew. Had Salisbury been elected to the leadership of the party in the Lords, Disraeli's position would have been impossible as the two were not on speaking terms. The party, however, contented itself with a non-entity, the Duke of Richmond. By 1872, however, plots were afoot to topple Disraeli and substitute Derby's son. In self-defence Disraeli emerged from seclusion with brilliant timing to reassert his leadership. He chose to address the Lancashire branches of the National Union at the Free Trade Hall in Manchester on 3 April 1872. He spoke for three hours, refreshing himself with two bottles of white brandy, which to the audience was indistinguishable from water. Whatever Disraeli's state by the end, he impressed the Lancashire faithful with his message. Most commentators in the twentieth century have picked on his passing reference to the need for social not political reform. 'The first consideration of a minister should be the health of the people.' Most of the speech however was taken up with attacking the Liberals for their excessive radicalism and feeble foreign policy, and it contains one of his most memorable passages:

> As time advanced it was not difficult to perceive that extravagance was being substituted for energy by the Government. The unnatural stimulus was subsiding. Their paroxysms ended in prostration. Some took refuge in melancholy, and their eminent chief alternated between a menace and a sigh. As I sat opposite the Treasury Bench the Ministers reminded me of one of those marine landscapes not very unusual on the coasts of South America. You behold a range of exhausted volcanoes. Not a flame flickers on a single pallid crest. But the situation is still dangerous. There are occasional earthquakes, and ever and anon the dark rumbling of the sea.

On 24 June he made another major speech to the National Union, this time at the Crystal Palace in London. He returned to the theme of social reform:

> I ventured to say a short time ago, speaking in one of the great cities of this country, that the health of the people was the most important question for a statesman. . . . It involves the state of the dwellings of the people, the moral consequences of which are not less considerable than the physical. It involves their enjoyment of some of the chief elements of nature – air, light and water. It involves the regulation of their industry, the inspection of their toil. It involves the purity of their provisions, and it touches upon all the means by which you may wean them from habits of excess and brutality.

He also enunciated the image of the Conservative Party as the party of Empire and national greatness. It had according to Disraeli three clear objectives: 'to maintain the institutions of the country . . . to uphold the Empire of England and the elevation of the condition of the people'.

The rhetoric in April and June was effective in safeguarding Disraeli's leadership and some historians can see here a forthright statement of Disraelian Conservatism – the Empire and social reform. In fact he seems to have had few concrete ideas for, as his colleague the Earl of Carnarvon observed, 'he detests details'. Social reform occupied only five minutes of the three hours at Manchester but favourable press comments encouraged him to return to it at Crystal Palace. Whether these speeches amounted to anything more than well-constructed phrases is difficult to know. From 1872 the tide appeared to be flowing strongly in Disraeli's favour. 'Dizzy' refused to take office in 1873 with a minority government following Gladstone's defeat over his Irish Universities Bill. The election results of 1874 proved Disraeli right. An essentially negative campaign playing up the mistakes of the Liberals – their 'incessant, harassing legislation' and their ineffective foreign policy, 'their strange mania for eating dirt' – proved to be the correct strategy. The Palmerstonian formula of inactivity at home and energy abroad appeared to be a promising one. The Conservatives had won their first majority in thirty-three years.

IN POWER 1874–80

The 351 Conservative MPs in the Commons certainly represented a broader social base of support than those of 1868. There had been significant gains in the big towns (over 50,000 population). Forty-four such seats were held, including some in Leeds, Newcastle and Glasgow, but it was Lancashire, where 26 out of 33 seats went to the Conservatives, where the trend was most rewarding. Perhaps equally significant was the change in London where many middle-class voters had switched parties, a development explained by contemporaries as arising largely from fear, as one Whig peer, Lord Halifax, put it to Gladstone:

> As far as I can make out people are frightened – the masters were afraid of their workmen, manufacturers afraid of strikes, churchmen afraid of the nonconformists, many afraid of what is going on in France and Spain – and in very unreasoning fear have all taken refuge in conservatism. Ballot enabled them to do this without apparently deserting their principles and party.
> (Quoted in J. Morley, *Life of William Ewart Gladstone*, vol. II,
> London, Macmillan, 1903, p. 102)

Despite these new areas of support the rock solid rural foundation remained the same and should not be forgotten. The big towns provided 17.5 per cent of Tory MPs, the English and Welsh counties and small market boroughs 60 per cent. If the number of Tory MPs who were brewers went up from 7 to 14 per cent, 73 per cent of Tory MPs were still landowners. Disraeli's Cabinet was likewise traditional in its composition. Eleven of the twelve ministers had served in the 1866–8 government. All except one were peers and country gentlemen. A duke, the son of a duke, one marquis, three earls and a baron made it the sort of cabinet that would not have shocked the House of Commons in the eighteenth century. Disraeli's arch-enemy, Salisbury, was offered and accepted the India Office and with his High Anglican friend, Carnarvon, he kept a wary eye on the new Prime Minister. The one surprise appointment was Richard Assheton Cross as Home Secretary. A Lancastrian of upper-middle-class background he was Disraeli's gesture of thanks to the north-west. He proved to be the most creative member of the Cabinet but his appointment appears to have been an afterthought. Two ministries included by Gladstone in his Cabinet were relegated by Disraeli. The Board of Trade was given to the incompetent Sir Charles Adderley and the new Local Government Board was given to George Sclater-Booth. The exclusion of these two offices hardly indicated a high priority for social reform. Adderley complained to his leader that he knew nothing of the Board of Trade's work. 'Dizzy' airily dismissed this unnecessary concern with the words 'You know as much about it as Ward Hunt [the new head of the Admiralty] knows about the Navy.' The whole team certainly did not appear a recipe for active government.

Disraeli was to bemoan the fact that power had come to him too late. He was 70 and lacked vigour. He had no programme and Cross was later to describe his surprise at finding Disraeli's head devoid of schemes. He looked around at his cabinet colleagues for something to put in the Queen's Speech. When in October 1874 Cross suggested a reform of London's government Disraeli discouraged him: 'we came in on the principle of not harassing the country'. It has been said that Disraeli relished the trappings of power not the reality. Playing the great game was enjoying contact with royalty, dispensing of titles and honours and basking in the limelight. Foreign policy was later to absorb all Disraeli's failing energies but even here details were not his forte. Privately he was dismissive of the bourgeois manners of the constructive Cross, but he had the political perspicacity to back Cross at times against a hostile cabinet when he thought that electoral advantage could be gained.

The reputation of Disraeli's ministry rests largely on its social reforms. It would be wrong to term it a programme as that could imply coherent planning. There was a series of haphazard responses to pressure which produced eleven major acts of Parliament, and various minor ones. In 1874 the government put through two pieces of social legislation. The first, introduced in April, was an amendment to the Liberal Licensing Act of 1872. Cross was repaying their debt to the electorate, as *The Times* put it: 'Beer, one of the greatest powers in the country has pronounced unequivocally in their favour. The public house windows in

London everywhere displayed the placards of the Conservative candidate.' Cross's Bill extended opening hours by half an hour, removed the adulteration clauses (against the watering of beer) of the 1872 Act and much reduced the police's rights of entry. It was almost wholly reactionary and ran contrary to all the evidence available to the Home Office which emphasized the beneficial effects of the 1872 Act. Afer much chopping and changing in response to different pressure groups, the Bill became law and gave the brewers most of what they wanted. Cross's own comment was 'I have not much to be proud of in this matter.'

The other major measure of the year was a Factory Act which was again in part a debt-paying exercise – this time to the working-class voters of Lancashire. As one of the Tory MPs for Manchester told Disraeli's secretary,

> The elections in Lancashire have largely hinged upon 2 questions – the 9 Hours bill & the demands of the Trades Unionists. On both these points – every candidate for a borough constituency has had to promise compliance.
> (Quoted in P. Smith, *Disraelian Conservatism and Social Reform*, London, Routledge & Kegan Paul, 1967, p. 188)

Cross's Bill was largely non-controversial. A Local Government Board Inquiry had recommended a reduction in hours and there appeared little counter-pressure from textile employers. A Liberal private member's bill was introduced which Cross took over. The Act reduced the maximum working hours for women and children to 56.5 a week, and raised the legal age of half-time employment to 10, and full-time to 14. Men's hours were not in theory regulated, as this was feared to be a breach of the principle of free contract. In effect men's hours were reduced as well and the 'week-end' with its Saturday afternoon football match became an integral part of the English way of life. Cross was deservedly popular in his native Lancashire:

> For he's a jolly good fellow whatever the radi(cal)s may think,
> He's shortened the hours of work and lengthened the hours of drink.

The most productive year of the ministry was 1875, although not all the bills were progressive or to do with social reform. It did, however, produce two genuinely radical measures. Probably the greatest achievement of the year was in the form of two Trades Union Acts which satisfied the TUC and Labour movement. Much more than the hours question, it was Henry Bruce's Criminal Law Amendment Act of 1871 that had most concerned organized labour at the election. There was considerable pressure for change. Cross resorted to the standard delaying tactic of a Royal Commission in 1874. Its report offered little comfort to trade unionists and Cross surprisingly ignored it. He and Disraeli forced through the Cabinet a radical solution to the complex problem of trade union rights. This solution took the form of two bills. The Employers' and Workmen's Act replaced the old Master and Servant Act. It placed employer and employee on an equal footing before the law by withdrawing recourse to the criminal law for breakers of contract. Cross's second measure – the 1875 Conspiracy and Protection of Property Act – altered the law of conspiracy and thereby freed the trade unions from a very potent threat. Henceforth a group of men could do anything that one man was legally allowed to do. Striking could no longer be classed as a conspiracy and therefore liable for legal action. Under pressure in the Commons Cross finally conceded to all the working-class demands and repealed the Criminal Law Amendment Act of 1871. Peaceful picketing was now legalized. Disraeli showed more interest in this legislation than most and was delighted with the outcome. His motives were explained in a letter written to the two sisters to whom he was romantically attached. To Lady Bradford he wrote on 29 June:

> I cannot express to you the importance of last night. It is one of those measures, that root and consolidate a party. We have settled the long and vexatious contest bet[wee]n capital and labor.
>
> (Quoted in Smith, op. cit., p. 217)

and to her sister, Lady Chesterfield, on the same day:

> This is the greatest measure since the Short Time Act and will gain and retain for the Tories the lasting affection of the working classes.
>
> (ibid.)

Clearly Disraeli wanted to consolidate a working-class Conservatism.

Cross produced another major act in 1875 which attempted to deal with the issue of working-class housing and became known as the Artisans' Dwelling Act. The last great cholera outbreak of 1866–7 had once again shown how poor housing areas could suffer. An important report on the subject, 'The Dwellings of the Poor', had been produced by the Charity Organizations Society. Four members of the government had assisted in drafting the report, and the government was therefore likely to view favourably its recommendations for action. It was a thorny issue on two counts – funding and the principle of state interference which clashed with property rights. Cross also had his doubts but was urged on by a report from the chief medical officer of health for London. Disraeli appears also to have given encouragement. The measure Cross introduced into the Commons in February 1875 empowered local authorities to purchase land compulsorily and to build and rehouse where necessary. Central government would supply cheap loans to assist the authorities, despite the misgivings of the Chancellor of the Exchequer. The Act was important as it recognized the problem but did not offer a solution, as it was purely permissive and the overwhelming majority of local city councils chose to ignore it.

Disraeli in 1872 had made reference to the masses' 'enjoyment of air, light and water', and 'the purity of their provisions'. As indicated, he had no clear ideas on these issues, and the department that might have been expected to deal with them, the Local Government Board, had lost its cabinet status. Sclater-Booth, at the head of the Local Government Board, was responsible for the three measures in 1875 which appeared to put Disraeli's vague ideas into reality. The most famous of these measures was the Public Health Act which has attracted more praise than it probably deserves. It simply completed twenty-five years of steady improvement and built on two major acts of 1866 and 1872. It consolidated existing sanitary legislation by laying down national minima on such matters as sewage disposal, noxious trades and notification of contagious diseases. It broke no new ground and simply carried out the recommendations of the Sanitary Commission of Inquiry. Similarly, Sclater-Booth's Sale of Food and Drugs Act stemmed from a Select Committee which had considered the effectiveness of existing legislation on the notorious practices of adulteration. Chalk in flour was one of the less dangerous mixes; lead in bread a more lethal diet. Despite the Select Committee's recommendations of tough compulsory action, the Act failed to make it compulsory for local authorities to appoint food analysts and without this official watchdog the excellent list of provisions in the Act was ineffective. In fact many local councillors were also the adulterating local tradesmen, and those who were not hated spending rate-payers' money, so the measure was less of a landmark than it might appear. The third measure, this time to tackle river pollution, was based on another Royal Commission, which had reported in 1874. Britain's rivers at the time were in a truly horrific condition, containing every kind of effluent and noxious waste. The government introduced a Bill in 1875 under the terms of which polluters were given twelve years in which to correct their practices. This was seen as too harsh and after much argument it was dropped. A milder Bill was carried and became the River Pollutions Act in 1876 and prosecutions were only possible with the permission of the Local Government Board in London. It was not notably successful in cleaning up the nation's rivers. The Disraeli Government's commitment to 'air, light and water' and 'purity of provisions' should perhaps be weighed in the light of the resignation in May 1876 of Dr Simon, the Chief Medical Adviser. Clearly Simon doubted the seriousness of his political masters' intentions.

Unwillingness to make inroads into freedom also marked the other two social reforms of 1875. This time the minister was Sir Stafford Northcote, Chancellor of the Exchequer, and the issue was Friendly Societies. These societies were the great foundations of working-class self-help. They had some four million members and often took strange names like the 'Odd Fellows'. They played an important role now played by the welfare state. Many of the societies were felt by the previous government to be unsound and a Royal Commission had been set up in 1870. It fell to Northcote to translate the Commission's recommendations into law. It recommended the issue of guidelines or model tables of premiums and benefits for use by the societies, and prohibited the insuring of infant children, which it was known had led to infanticide. Northcote's measure was cautious and tentative. Model tables were provided but were purely advisory and the registration of the societies was purely voluntary. Perhaps worst of all the insurance of infants was not prohibited, merely the amount limited. The reluctance to regulate proved greater with the Conservatives than with the Liberals.

Another noted evil of mid-Victorian England, the overloading and undermanning of ships, which worked to the advantage of their owners but to the detriment of their crews, was half-heartedly tackled. The driving force in the campaign for safer shipping was the Liberal member for Derby, Samuel Plimsoll. Sir Charles Adderley was reluctant to see any increases in state responsibility for safety at sea. Adderley was also simply incompetent. A modest government measure was piloted through various stages in 1875 but then dropped. Following an outburst from Plimsoll and, more significantly, unrest on the Tory back benches, many of whom had port-town constituencies, a stop-gap measure was pushed through with the promise of more in 1876. When this was finally passed it did include a load-line but one at the discretion of the owner. The government tried to discourage deck-loading but in Dr Paul Smith's words: 'the measure was far from ensuring the safety of the merchant seaman and did very little to promote his general welfare.' Significantly the government ignored totally the seamen's demands for regulation of diet and speedier payment of wages.

The final measure of 1875 which in fact had elbowed the merchant shipping legislation out of the way was an Agricultural Holdings Act. This was very dear to the Prime Minister and through it he attempted to do something for tenant farmers on the lines of Gladstone's Irish Bill of 1870. In practice the measure was tentative and permissive allowing landlord and tenant to adopt its provisions if they wished.

The pace of reform slackened in 1876, apart from the Merchant Shipping Act and the River Pollution Act which were simply carried over from 1875. The only measure of 1876 that stands out was the Education Act. Here Viscount Sandon, vice-President of the Privy Council in charge of education, introduced a measure which cleverly seemed to serve the forces of progress and maintain the bond between the Tory Party and the Church of England. The basic problem was the success of the board schools set up under Forster's Act and nearly all Conservatives could agree to wanting to preserve as large an Anglican share of the education institutions as possible. The voluntary Anglican schools, relying on a mixture of charity and small parental contributions plus a grant from the state, found it hard to compete with the board schools funded from the rates. Sandon's measure aimed to boost revenue to rural voluntary schools by increasing their pupil numbers. His political motives were clearly expressed in a cabinet memo of November 1875.

> It cannot be too often repeated that School Boards, though politically harmless and often highly necessary in large towns, are of the worst political effect in small communities, where they afford the platform and the notoriety specially needed by the political Dissenting Ministers (many of them, to my mind, the most active and effective revolutionary agents of the day), and also provide a ready machinery for lowering the legitimate and useful influence of the leading personages of the place.
>
> (ibid., p. 249)

The Bill introduced in May 1876 forbade the employment of children under 10 and made part-time employment between 10 and 14 conditional on holding an educational certificate of attendance. In other words attendance at school was compulsory but the method used was indirect. A back-bench amendment to dissolve unnecessary rural school boards was reluctantly accepted by Disraeli. The whole measure under the guise of progressiveness was an attempt to bolster the church's weakening grip on the country's children.

From 1876 to 1880 little else was done in the way of social reform. Cross carried another Factory Act in 1878 which consolidated existing legislation relating to safety and went some way towards removing a distinction between factories and workshops. Further attempts at legislation on merchant shipping came to nothing. The Home Office was under pressure to do something about employers' liability for the injury of an employee. A measure was promised in 1878 but nothing came until 1879 and then it failed to get through by the time of the dissolution in 1880. The government's legislative efforts whimpered to a close with another failed measure relating to London's water supply. Reluctantly, under much prodding and the recommendations of a Royal Commission, a scheme was proposed to disband the eight private water companies supplying the capital. The scheme was badly handled and the terms of compensation were over-generous. The Bill was dropped and the whole episode gave rise to the witticism that the government had come in on beer and gone out on water.

The failing legislative vigour at the end of the Conservatives' term was a product of many developments. Disraeli and his Cabinet were increasingly absorbed in questions of foreign policy. The Cabinet crisis of 1878 over the Eastern Question strengthened the hold of the traditionalists when Salisbury replaced the more liberal Derby as Foreign Secretary in March. More important was the worsening financial situation. The surplus of 1875 had given way to a deficit under the impact of an economic recession and increased military expenditure. Northcote wrestled with ways of cutting government spending. He tried to cut loans to local authorities. There was also pressure from the squirearchy to reduce the burden of the poor-rate which was becoming increasingly intolerable as bad harvests and low prices reduced their income at the same time as distress boosted demands. In the circumstances the failure to proceed with reforms becomes obvious and yet this misses the main point which is there never was an intention to proceed with reforms as the halting tentative measures detailed above indicate. Measures in the pipeline were dealt with but that pipeline now only contained an intermittent dribble.

The whole concentration on legislation is in many ways a distortion of perspective. Law-making was not what really mattered at the time to Disraeli or to anyone else. The downgrading of the Board of Trade and the Local Government Board indicates Disraeli's priorities. The important business of the government lay in the use of the budget to relieve expenditure at local levels. Northcote tried to placate the shires by diverting £1.25 million in 1874 to relieve them of some of the cost of policing and maintaining lunatic asylums. Disraeli showed far more interest in the exercise of patronage than legislation. Power meant the ability to reward friends with positions in the church and on the judicial bench. It also gave Dizzy great delight in distributing honours and titles. The social legislation that history books make so much of did not figure in the 1880 election campaign. It was, in short, the sort of non-controversial things all governments did. There was little that a Liberal government would not have done, and in fact much arose from Royal Commissions set up under the previous Gladstone Government. Only the trade union legislation was radical. The Education and Licensing Acts can be seen as reactionary. As to the rest they were, as one Tory MP put it, 'suet pudding legislation, wholesome but not very interesting'.

If the government's social reform was unadventurous – 'pragmatism tempered by prejudice' as it has been termed – its attitude towards political reform was positively hostile. There were to be no more 'leaps in the dark', as in 1867. Disraeli's conduct reassured such die-hards as Salisbury of his essential belief in the status quo. The government firmly rejected radical demands for the extension of the urban franchise to the counties. A Corrupt Practices Act affecting the conduct of elections was passed just before the government expired and has been described as the only truly reactionary electoral measure passed in the nineteenth century. It allowed borough candidates to pay for electoral conveyances. It stoutly defended property qualifications for membership of town councils and even refused to consider an extension of polling hours to facilitate voting for workers, many of whom found it difficult to reach the polls in time. Disraeli, like most of his party, had little faith in the virtues of real democracy.

In these circumstances it comes as no surprise to realize that Disraeli's defeat in 1880 arose not from an excess of legislative fervour as

Gladstone's had in 1874. 'Hard times . . . has been our foe', was Disraeli's own explanation. Industry underwent a very short sharp slump in 1879 with the percentage of trade union members faced with unemployment rising to an alarming level of 11.4. This came after a period of declining real wages from the boom year of 1873. Poor relief statistics tell the tale of increased misery in the industrial districts. One Liberal election leaflet simply presented the following:

FACTS ARE STUBBORN THINGS
SALFORD WORKHOUSE

When Gladstone took				
office there were	901 Inmates		3375 Receiving Out-Door Relief	
When he retired there				
were	851	,,	1922	,,	,,
DECREASE	50	do.	1453	do.	do.
When Lord Beaconsfield				
took office	851	,,	1922	,,	,,
And on 1st of January,				
1880	1718	,,	4760	,,	,,
INCREASE	867	do.	2838	do.	do.

So much for TORY RULE, with its Bad Trade, Heavy Rates & Taxes.

IF YOU HAVE NOT HAD ENOUGH OF THESE, VOTE FOR THE TORIES.

(Hanham, op. cit., p. 230)

The urban misery alone is enough to explain the Conservative defeats in the large towns (over 50,000 population). They won only 24 out of 114 seats compared with 44 in 1874.

Perhaps more serious was the state of agriculture. A series of bad harvests culminated in 1879 when appalling weather brought disaster. Normally farmers then at least benefited from rising prices. Now, however, foreign imports kept prices well below their 1873 level. The situation became so bad that a tenant farmers' pressure group, the Farmers' Alliance, put up candidates and hurt the Conservative cause in many of its previously safe areas. The government had no answer to the crisis in agriculture other than the setting-up of a Royal Commission. Disraeli, once the protagonist of the Corn Laws, saw little electoral mileage in copying Bismarck and introducing tariffs. Clearly the government was not to blame for the cyclical downturn in industry nor for the more permanent crisis affecting agriculture, but the Liberals, like all opposition parties, held the incumbent ministry responsible. Gladstone equated depression with increased income tax, itself due to a more adventurous, and in Gladstone's eyes more wicked, foreign policy.

Bad luck also dogged the government with regard to the personal health of its members. Disraeli was no match in vigour for Gladstone, five years his junior. Henry Lucy, a lobby correspondent, recorded the last speeches of the two leaders before the election. Dizzy spoke in the Lords and Gladstone in the Commons but Lucy's comments are instructive all the same:

1880 Mar. 18 – Historical last words.

> On Monday night, by an unpremeditated coincidence, an event happened in Parliament to which the newspapers have not called attention, though history will doubtless not find it unworthy of notice. On that night Gladstone in one House, and Beaconsfield in the other, for the last time addressed the Parliament which has proved such a memorable turning-point in the career of both.
>
> The physical energy with which this election speech was delivered was certainly very remarkable for a man in his seventy-fourth year. There is, however, unmistakable evidence of pumping up in the Premier's latest oratorical feats. The vigour is spasmodic, the strength artificial, and the listener has a feeling that at any moment a spring may break, a screw grow loose, and the whole machinery come to a sudden stop.
>
> Gladstone's *tours de force* are perfectly natural. When after one of his great speeches he resumes his seat, he is, and often proves himself to be, ready to start again. With the Premier, the excitement of the moment over and the appointed task achieved, he falls into a state of prostration painful to witness. His eyes seem to lose all expression, his cheeks fall in, and his face takes on a ghastly hue. Physically he is at least ten years older than Gladstone.
>
> (*A Diary of Two Parliaments*, vol. I, London, Cassell, 1885, p. 151)

Six weeks earlier Disraeli had recorded in a letter the general ill-health afflicting his Cabinet:

> I am unable to move, Salisbury is confined to his room at Hatfield & must do no work, the Lord Chancellor attacked by asthma for the first time was so frightened that he rushed to Bournemouth, where he found the fog blacker than here. The Chancellor of the Exchequer is in bed with influenza. Sandon is at Liverpool. Where John Manners's broken bones are I hardly know – but if there had been a Cabinet today *six* would have been absent.
>
> (*Letters of Disraeli to Lady Bradford and Lady Chesterfield*, ed. Marquis of Zetland, London, John Murray, 1929, p. 261)

In these circumstances the decision to call an election which took all by surprise is somewhat remarkable. The Conservative Party machinery had been neglected after John Gorst's resignation as election agent in 1877. As indicated in chapter 2 the Liberals had much improved their political organization in the big towns. Disraeli appears to have been misled in his decision by a successful by-election result in Southwark and decided to avoid further embarrassment on the Metropolitan Water Bill by a dissolution. It was a serious miscalculation and the extent of the defeat hit him hard. The Conservatives returned to the opposition benches they knew so well.

OUT OF OFFICE 1880–5

Despite old age and ill health, Disraeli performed one last service to his party before his death in April 1881. He showed them that they could fight from the House of Lords a large Liberal majority in the Commons. What Disraeli could not show to his party was a future bright with electoral promise. Since the onset of popular politics in 1867 the Conservatives had lost two elections by substantial majorities; an extension of the household franchise in the shires would reinforce a Liberal preponderance and such a move the new government would surely make before the end of this parliament. On the old man's death the prospects became bleaker still because 'Elijah's mantle was rent in twain', and the dual leadership of Sir Stafford Northcote and Robert Gascoigne Cecil, third Marquis of Salisbury in the Lords, did not look to be a winning combination against the Grand Old Man.

Northcote had served Disraeli as Leader of the House of Commons when Dizzy had ascended to the Lords. The Queen in 1881 clearly regarded Sir Stafford as the man she would select as Prime Minister should the Conservatives be called to power. A competent administrator he was ill-adapted to the new age of popular politics. His good speeches were merely dull; his bad ones tedious. He was tentative and cautious in his approach. He hoped by the moderation of his party to attract dissident Whigs and thereby resist the radicals. His worst failing in the eyes of his followers was his deference to Gladstone whose private secretary he had been forty years before in Peel's government. To his sterner critics he became 'The Grand Old Woman'.

Northcote's partner and eventual victorious rival was on the surface an even less promising leader in an age of fledgling democracy. Robert Cecil was a self-proclaimed enemy of democracy. Descended from the two great Elizabethan and Jacobean statesmen, William and Robert Cecil, this latest Robert saw little that was hopeful in the nineteenth century. He had a wretched and unhappy childhood, and nerves to the point of mental breakdown marred his passage through Oxford University. Only a blissfully happy marriage and a close family life brought an increasing stability and kept the black depression at bay as he matured. Family and religion were the loadstones of his life and in this he had more in common with Gladstone than the man who had been his political leader since 1868, the year he had left the Commons and become Lord Salisbury. Physically he was an imposing figure, six feet four inches in height with an impressive beard and, with age, a rotund bulk to accompany his frame. He remained an eccentric to the end. Shy and retiring outside his family circle, whenever he could he fled London to his beloved Hatfield and his science laboratory where explosions and electrical devices amused or terrified visitors. He was impatient of garrulous company and kept a small paper knife to jab into his leg to keep

Robert Gascoyne Cecil by H. Furniss, *c.* 1880

himself awake on such occasions. He was notoriously short-sighted, mistaking a servant in a fez for the Shah of Persia at one diplomatic encounter. His dress was scruffy: on this account he was refused entry to the casino at Monte Carlo, and horrified the future Edward VII, a stickler for uniform, by wearing the trousers of one official outfit with the inappropriate jacket of another. Physical peculiarities apart he possessed a first-rate mind. He wrote and spoke succinctly and had at his disposal a lively and mischievous wit. Reference has already been made to his political beliefs and his distrust of adventurers like Disraeli. He had little doubt but that the barbarians clamouring at the gate of civilization would eventually overwhelm society as he knew it. 'Looters', as he called Socialists, would grow and flourish as the tide of democracy flowed ever stronger. Elections would become auctions with victory to the party that promised most to the masses. Yet his response to this was not crushing despair. He was a fighter who strove to preserve the best of the old world. He saw his role in politics as being one of defence and yet not a blind unreasoning defence. In one of the last articles he wrote for the *Quarterly Review* in 1883, suitably entitled 'Disintegration', he expressed his political aims:

> The object of our party is not and ought not to be simply to keep things as they are. In the first place, the enterprise is impossible. In the next place there is much in our present mode of thought and action which it is highly undesirable to conserve. What we require is the administration of public affairs . . . in that spirit of the old constitution which held the nation together as a whole, and levelled its united force at objects of national import, instead of splitting it.
>
> (Quoted in D. Southgate (ed.), *The Conservative Leadership 1832–1932*, London, Macmillan, 1974, p. 105)

Unlike Northcote, Salisbury did not believe in moderation in order to attract the Whigs. In his view they would inevitably come over as the wildness of the radicals made the Liberal Party too uncomfortable for them. The Tory Party must be seen to be fighting in defence of something. In this sense he felt that style and image were as important in politics as reality. The party must not jump at every opportunity to gain power as Disraeli seemed to do. The Conservative ethos was shared by a great section of the British people, as Salisbury indicated in a letter to Alfred Milner, the British High Commissioner in South Africa:

> It is a party shackled by tradition; all the cautious people, all the timid, all the unimaginative, belong to it. It stumbles slowly and painfully from precedent to precedent with its eyes fixed on the ground. Yet the Conservative Party is the Imperial Party. I must work with it – who indeed am just such an one myself.
>
> (Quoted in P. Adelman, *Gladstone, Disraeli and Later Victorian Politics*, London, Longman, 1970, p. 71)

Salisbury's initial period of leadership in the Lords was not auspicious. There were serious divisions as to how far resistance to the Commons should be pushed. In 1882, he was deserted by the bulk of the peerage who allowed the Liberal Arrears Bill through, against his advice.

A third figure was also bidding to lead the Tory Party during this period of opposition. Lord Randolph Churchill was young, talented and not unduly troubled by principles. He was the younger son of the Duke of Marlborough. Despite an addiction to sport, social occasions and breaking windows he was placed top of the second class at Oxford. He was lazy yet quick-witted but with a streak of mental unbalance, a capacity to carry things to extremes regardless of the consequences. A clash with the Prince of Wales led to talk of a duel and the Prince let it be known he would enter no house in which Lord Randolph was welcome. The result was a period of ostracism from London society. Despite being elected MP for the family borough of Woodstock in 1874 he decided to spend three years in Ireland as the unpaid secretary of his father, the Viceroy. In the 1880 elections he had an uphill fight against the Liberal candidate but family influence prevailed and this time the 31-year-old decided to make his mark in Parliament. His wit and courage quickly gained him a reputation in Parliament. His speciality was taunting Gladstone. The Bradlaugh affair (see p. 46) was a gift from the gods and Churchill, with three other Conservatives, Arthur Balfour, Sir Henry Drummond Wolff and John Gorst, decided to make the most of it. The four became known as the 'Fourth Party' and amused themselves and the Tory backbenchers, who had little else to cheer about. Their real target was Northcote, whose cautious moderation infuriated them. Churchill loved to laugh – it was said to resemble the neigh of a horse – just behind Northcote's back as the Tory leader strove for the attention of the House. It was Churchill who coined the phrase 'Grand Old Woman'.

Churchill's beliefs are difficult to isolate. He flirted with protection but latterly espoused free trade. He condemned extension of the franchise in a speech in Edinburgh and later switched to demanding extensive reform. He spoke as a die-hard aristocrat and in so far as he believed in anything, it was probably in the rights of the old ruling elite to rule. He spoke with sneering snobbery of the two leading middle-class Tories, W. H. Smith and Richard Cross. They were contemptuously dismissed by Churchill as 'Marshall and Snellgrove'. Yet he found it convenient in 1882 to invent and popularize 'Tory democracy'. He cast himself, with Gorst's help, as the true heir of Disraeli broadening the appeal of Conservatism to the masses. Churchill himself was a populist in a way that neither Northcote could, nor Salisbury would be. He loved the fun of the public platform and the mass electorate loved him. He was clearly the Tories' answer to Chamberlain, Bright and the Grand Old Man.

In 1883 and 1884 Churchill launched an assault on the leadership as the ostensible champion of the National Union and greater democracy in the party. With his usual vigour he denounced the old gang in a speech at Birmingham in October:

> Some of our friends in the party have a lesson to learn which they do not seem disposed to learn. The Conservative party will never exercise power until it has gained the confidence of the working classes; and the working classes are quite determined to govern themselves, and will not be either driven or hoodwinked by any class or class interests. Our interests are perfectly safe if we trust them fully, frankly and freely; but if we oppose them and endeavour to drive them and hoodwink them, our interests, our Constitution and all we love and revere will go down. If you want to gain the confidence of the working classes, let them have a share and a large share – *a real*

share and not a sham share – in your party Councils and in your party government.

(Quoted in R. R. James, *Lord Randolph Churchill*, London, Hamish Hamilton, 1959, p. 133)

Churchill was climbing on a band-wagon which he hoped would carry him to Downing Street. Discontent with party organization had grown since the débâcle of 1880 and the National Union with its middle-class membership demanded greater effectiveness and a larger say in the running of the party. Churchill threw all his platform skills into the struggle. He shouldered aside the tame chairman of the National Union and boldly confronted Salisbury with demands. Salisbury initially took a firm stand in 1884 and threatened to evict the National Union from the Central Office. Churchill also urged on Salisbury the setting up of a mass movement of supporters – 'the Primrose League' – originally the idea of Drummond Wolff. The conflict between Churchill and Gorst on the one hand, and Salisbury and the old gang on the other reached a climax at the National Union conference in Sheffield in July 1884. The split was damaging and the menace of the Liberal Reform Bill concentrated the minds of all parties. An eventual compromise was reached. Churchill resigned as chairman of the National Union and was promised consideration worthy of a leading figure in the party. The Primrose League was recognized and various organizational changes were agreed upon. To Gorst it was surrender, to Churchill a leg-up the party ladder, and to Salisbury a victory. Northcote had played hardly any part in the negotiations. Salisbury's opinions of the new member of the party hierarchy are worth repeating: 'Randolph and the Mahdi have occupied my thoughts about equally. The Mahdi pretends to be half mad, but is very sane in reality; Randolph occupies exactly the converse position.'

The struggle with the Liberals over the Reform Bill also enhanced Salisbury's standing. It was his firm use of the Lords to resist the Franchise Reform Bill that forced Gladstone to compromise and to agree to introduce a Redistribution Bill. Salisbury himself negotiated the basis of redistribution with Gladstone and Dilke at his Arlington Street house. Maps were strewn around the floor as deals were rapidly struck. Boundaries were drawn to match as closely as possible class and occupational interests and in the large towns minority middle-class voters would not now be swamped by a working-class majority in multi-member constituencies. Very cleverly Salisbury preserved as much of the old system as he could, despite the latest surge of the democratic tide.

The struggle for the leadership within the Tory party in the years 1880–5 is often seen as the struggle for the soul of the party between the Peelite moderation of Northcote, the Tory democracy of Churchill and the Tory resistance of Salisbury. It is an excellent illustration of the impossibility of separating policy and personality. In a sense, it was a struggle for a style. All three would acknowledge the need to adjust to the new 'villa Toryism', all felt an instinctive loyalty to the old aristocratic backbone of the party to which they owed their position. Churchill was prepared to go further in embracing platform oratory and all the tricks of popular politics but then he had more to gain by doing so. His Primrose League proved an excellent vehicle for merging the old and new Conservatism. By 1891 it had one million members and it was particularly successful in utilizing the energies and enthusiasm of women. Privately Salisbury might disdain its phoney medieval flummery but it enabled villa and country-house Conservatism to mix and it gave assistance to that process of social integration that Conservatism espoused.

THE CARETAKER GOVERNMENT AND THE HOME RULE CRISIS

Salisbury had a double motive for wishing to take office in June 1885 when Gladstone resigned. It would confirm his, as yet unofficial, primacy in the party if and when the Queen sent for him to be Prime Minister, and it would enable him to extricate the country from the unfortunate mess in international relations that the Gladstone Government had landed it in. He took part in no negotiations with the Irish which led to thirty-nine of them voting with the Conservatives, thereby precipitating the fall of the government. It was Churchill who led Parnell to believe that the Conservatives would drop coercion in return for support.

Salisbury found great difficulty in constructing his government. He himself decided to take the Foreign Office. He assumed Northcote would be leader in the Commons but Lord Randolph and the rest of the Tories pointed out his inadequacies. Northcote was compensated with a peerage and the office normally associated with the premiership, First Lord of the Treasury. Churchill gave ample proof of his potential for trouble by deliberately leaking his opposition to Northcote and giving the impression that he had forced Salisbury's hand.

Churchill was given the India Office and Sir Michael Hicks Beach became leader of the Commons. If foreign policy was Salisbury's main concern Ireland was clearly the prime domestic consideration. The Conservative response was unclear and deliberately ambiguous. Salisbury was personally opposed to Home Rule – such a concession smacked too much of the two previous Conservative surrenders, in 1829 and 1846, both over Ireland, and each time had brought disaster on the Tories. Churchill and Hicks Beach were sympathetic to Irish grievances and the man Salisbury appointed Viceroy, Lord Carnarvon, believed that limited self-government might answer the problem. Carnarvon spoke publicly of the need to 'trust' the Irish and, with the knowledge only of Salisbury, he had a private meeting with Parnell in an empty house. At Westminster the Irish agreed to support the Tory Government in return for two measures, a Labourers' Bill, to improve conditions for farm workers, and a Land Purchase Bill to help tenants buy the land they farmed. In return for these, and the prospect of more, Parnell also used his influence amongst Catholic voters in Britain on behalf of the Conservatives. Salisbury himself kept quiet and it has been said he thereby 'deceived Gladstone and beguiled Parnell'.

The election of November 1885 was a defeat for the Conservatives with an improvement of only ten seats on their defeat of 1880. On the other hand they secured 49.5 per cent of the votes and half the seats in the English boroughs. Only the slump in their normally safe agricultural base denied them a much closer finish. As it was they only had eighty-six fewer seats than the Liberals: Parnell with eighty-six seats held the balance.

What followed was a complex game of political poker with neither Gladstone nor Salisbury anxious to reveal their hand. Both sought to preserve their party unity and circled warily around the poisoned chalice of Home Rule. Salisbury had the stronger hand but lacked Gladstone's experience and skill as indicated by the manner in which the government of January 1886 was turned out. Once Gladstone had decided to go for Home Rule, Salisbury's position became much easier. He could carry his party into whole-hearted opposition and sit back and watch the Liberals disintegrate. There were to be no more ambiguities, no false moderation with which to ensnare the Whigs. Salisbury nailed up the Union Jack and let opponents of Home Rule rally to him. His speech to the National Union in St James's Hall in May left no doubt as to his opinions:

> Confidence where it carries with it the grant of representative institutions is only fitly bestowed upon a homogeneous people. It is only a people who in the main are agreed – who upon deep questions that concern a community think with each other, who have sympathy with each other, and have common interests, and look back on common traditions and are proud of common memories – it is only people who have these conditions of united action who can be, with any prospect of prosperity and success, entrusted with the tremendous powers which have been granted in the past and – let us thank God for it – granted safely and with great and prosperous results to the British people.
> (Quoted in P. Marsh, *The Discipline of Popular Government*, Hassocks, Harvester, 1978, p. 92)

Churchill with less consistency but even greater enthusiasm threw himself into destroying the Bill. He stirred up the 'orange' passion of Ulster and took a leading role in defeating Gladstone in the Commons. We described in chapter 2 how the Liberals split and the Conservative Party was able to fight an election on the congenial platform of resistance. Salisbury emerged from the crisis with 316 MPs – only twenty short of an overall majority but with the sympathies and slippery support of seventy-eight Liberal Unionists. Home Rule had transformed British politics and now ushered in the age of Lord Salisbury.

SALISBURY'S SECOND MINISTRY 1886–92

The election so soon after the defeat of Home Rule was vital in making the Liberal split permanent. Divisions in Parliament could be healed much more readily than gaping wounds left by a bitter election campaign. Salisbury offered the rebel Liberal Unionists generous terms when constructing the election pact which dated back to April. As far as local conditions would allow Liberal Unionists were freed from Conservative opponents. In return Liberal Unionists merely promised to use their influence in the Conservative cause elsewhere. The government that emerged from the election was no coalition but wholly a Conservative one. Hartington was in fact offered the premiership but on terms he could not accept. Instead of coalition, the dissident Liberals promised to preserve the new Conservative Government as the only safeguard against Home Rule.

Salisbury had played his cards with masterly skill since March but even so his position was insecure. He depended on seventy-eight Liberal Unionists with whose two leading figures he felt personally uncomfortable. Hartington might be a fellow aristocrat but his lifestyle was totally alien to that of Salisbury. As Lady Salisbury reported years later to Balfour after a visit to Chatsworth, Hartington's palace:

> The minute we arrived here every one sat down to poker & bezique – before we took our bonnets off! & played till dinner. Afterwards we played till 12 & then went to bed. . . . No one . . . has the slightest knowledge of, or interest in [Chatsworth's] great treasures of books pictures &c.
> . . . I am glad that your uncle goes tomorrow, or he might be guilty of some act of violence which he would regret.
>
> (ibid., p. 109)

Hartington's long-standing liaison with the Duchess of Manchester cannot have endeared him socially to the Salisburys for their home at Hatfield was one of the few great houses where not even the Prince of Wales was received with his mistress. Chamberlain was even less acceptable to the Tory leader. They had exchanged insults by letter in the past and looked very unlikely colleagues now. Within his own party Salisbury's position was uneasy. Directing operations from the Lords posed great problems and he had need of a trustworthy team in the Commons. Here he was short on talent. The two vital figures were Hicks Beach, who was given what had become the major post of Irish Secretary, and Lord Randolph who gained all the trappings of 'crown prince', holding the Exchequer and leadership of the Commons. The rest of the frontbenchers were cast into shadow by the brilliance of Churchill. Under pressure from these colleagues Salisbury agreed to hand over the Foreign Office to Northcote so that he could direct operations more firmly, particularly the new Irish Affairs Committee of the Cabinet.

A crisis with Churchill quickly followed. He proved an impossible colleague. He attempted to map out the direction of the government in a well-publicized speech to 14,000 at Dartford, Kent, in 1886. He advocated a stream of reforms and even seemed to be dictating the foreign policy. Salisbury objected to the tone rather than the substance of the projected reforms. It was Churchill's high-handed treatment of colleagues over budget details that finally precipitated the crisis. He outraged the easygoing W. H. Smith, now war minister. Smith, after receiving one insulting message from Churchill, wrote to Salisbury: 'It comes to this – is he to be the government?' Salisbury ditched Churchill with great skill in choosing to interpret an intemperate letter from Churchill in December as a letter of resignation, ensuring at the same time that Hicks Beach and the rest of the Cabinet stayed. Churchill 'fell like Lucifer'. His political career was finished. He was seen as a man who had abandoned the team in its hour of need and the backbenchers and his cabinet colleagues never forgave him. Salisbury would not have him back, likening him to a 'boil on the neck'. His capacity for mischief remained, but in the course of the next decade tragedy ensued. The man whose wit and brilliance had brought MPs flooding in from the bars and terraces to listen to his latest assault on Gladstone began to suffer from a brain disease whose cause was either syphilitic or tumorous. Now in the 1890s when he spoke the House emptied in embarrassment, apart from Gladstone who answered him with all the attention he had deserved in better days. The government survived Churchill's departure better than anyone could have guessed. A leading Liberal Unionist, George Goschen, was brought in as Chancellor of the Exchequer, which had the double benefit of strengthening the alliance and bringing an able and competent debater to the front bench. As a temporary measure W. H. Smith took over as leader of the House of Commons. Salisbury also handed over to him Number 10 and the title First Lord of the Treasury. Smith, to everyone's surprise, including his own, proved an excellent leader. What he lacked in brilliance he made up for in simple decency. 'Old Morality' was too nice a man to flay with any degree of satisfaction. Salisbury also replaced Northcote as Foreign Secretary, who unfortunately suffered a heart-attack in an ante-room of Number 10 while waiting to be told of his dismissal. One more change completed the metamorphosis of Salisbury's government. In March ill-health forced Hicks Beach to resign as Irish Secretary and he was replaced by Salisbury's languid but brilliant nephew, Arthur J. Balfour.

Ireland was the most urgent and likely to be the most intractable problem. If Home Rule was not to be granted then coercion seemed to be the only alternative. Salisbury welcomed this. Here was his recipe for firm government. Hicks Beach had hoped to avoid coercion if possible but the success of the Plan of Campaign and the National League led the government to force through a new Crimes Bill giving wide powers to the executive in Dublin. Hicks Beach's resignation led to a tougher measure being presented than he would have supported and Balfour showed a steel few thought him capable of – both at Westminster and in Ireland. It was said that he looked at the frantic antics of the Irish Nationalists, who at times threatened him with violence, as though he were inspecting some rare species of insect life. In Ireland police and troops fought a successful war to restore order. Balfour became 'Bloody Balfour' to the Irish, but he won. Side by side with coercion stood conciliation in the form of a new Land Act in 1887 which reduced rents further. Later, measures of reconstruction were introduced to stimulate the Irish economy. A Light Railways Act in 1889 was followed by the setting up of a Congested Districts Board to spend public money on relief and recovery. Home Rule was to be killed by kindness as well as firmness.

In England as in Ireland resistance to change was not enough. The consequence of democracy as Salisbury feared was pressure for reform. Joseph Chamberlain and his radical Unionists were anxious to uphold their radical credentials with their own constituency parties. Even Conservative county members were conscious of the new labouring electorate and now backed an Allotment Bill to make available land for labourers. Decent middle-of-the-road Whigs like Hartington pressed for modest measures. The net result was a steady stream of remedial legislation and increased spending, mainly via local government. The most important measure was the Local Government Act of 1888. Under its terms, sixty-two elected county councils were established. George Goschen and C. T. Ritchie of the Local Government Board were behind the measure. The extension of the franchise in 1884 made democratic shire government essential and it was better for it to come from Conservative rather than from Liberal hands. Salisbury had many misgivings and tried to prevent it by taking a stand against what he saw as a move towards strong centralized government. The new authorities took over roads, bridges and lunatic asylums and were to share in the overseeing of the police force as well as the bench of magistrates whose powers they had diminished. The new authorities were not given responsibility for poor relief for fear of profligacy – that remained with the boards of guardians elected by rate-payers. On the insistence of Goschen, London was included in the scheme, and the London County Council emerged in 1889. It promptly passed under the control of 'Progressives' which outraged entrenched Conservative opinion. The police in the capital were kept firmly under the control of the Home Office and have remained so until this day.

Education was not neglected. In 1889 the new county councils were made the agents of the Technical Instruction Act. This was the first recognition of Britain's lamentable failure to match Germany in this area. The first government grants to universities were made and the Board of Education set up. The system begun by Robert Lowe in the 1860s of payment by results was slowly unscrambled over the next few years, and in 1891 free elementary education was established.

Various minor social reforms were enacted. In 1890 a Housing of the Working Classes Act granted councils the powers to close insanitary dwellings and build council houses, and in the same year another Public Health Act was passed along with a Factories Act to improve conditions and raise the minimum age for child labour. Shop workers received some protection from an act in 1892. The new rural voters received an Allotment Act and tenants were relieved of the payment of tithes to the church, the upkeep of which was placed firmly at the feet of the landowner.

Goschen proved a competent and progressive Chancellor. Like all the successful ones he was lucky in enjoying a revival of trade. In 1892 income tax was reduced to 2.5 per cent and tea and tobacco duties were also reduced to appease the poor. More grants were provided to local authorities and £2 million given for free education. The new technical education duties of local authorities were to be financed by whisky profits by means of an increased duty on spirits. The Chancellor also introduced a small estate duty of 1 per cent which Sir William Harcourt was later to expand in 1894.

All in all the government of this Conservative 'die-hard' was not as reactionary as some might have feared. Salisbury was certainly over-cautious about the reaction of his right-wing but the logic of democracy and his parliamentary party drove him on. Only in its readiness to use force did the Salisbury ministry perhaps fulfil the fears of its opponents. In Ireland violence was answered with violence and in Wales troops were sent in to deal with the anti-tithe rioting. Even in London troops with fixed bayonets and live ammunition confronted socialist demonstrators in Trafalgar Square on what became known as Bloody Sunday.

Salisbury certainly guided with loose reins leaving departmental ministers the same freedom he expected and enjoyed at the Foreign Office. He was a distant figure to most MPs, glimpsed occasionally slipping from the Foreign Office to the Lords. It was not just short-sightedness that caused him not to recognize ministers. Many of the junior ones he simply did not know. The system worked while Smith was prepared to put heart and soul into making it work but by 1890 he was a sick man. In October 1891 'Old Morality' died and the Conservatives would not accept Goschen. Balfour was drafted in to replace Smith. At the same time Hartington succeeded to his father as Duke of Devonshire, leaving Joseph Chamberlain to become leader of the Unionists in the Commons. His influence with Balfour was much greater than it had been with Smith and 'Birmingham Joe' was clearly going to play a greater part in the future of the alliance.

By 1892 the government had run a six-year course and an election was due in the next twelve months. Deferring to the advice of others Salisbury agreed to a summer dissolution. The Conservative coffers were full and R. W. E. Middleton's organization in excellent form (see p. 99). The onset of the recession may have hurt the government but the timing of the election, on Middleton's advice, was a ploy to keep down the number of rural voters who, it was hoped, would be fully occupied with the harvest. The result was cheering to the government. Despite the string of by-election defeats 268 Conservatives faced 270 Liberals. Gladstone would be dependent on the fragmented Irish Nationalists to give him an unstable parliamentary majority. Salisbury was delighted. He could sleep and recover his energies secure in the knowledge that he wielded a massive majority in the Lords and that Gladstonian radicalism would be largely ineffective.

'THEIR LORDSHIPS DO ITCH TO INTERFERE' 1892–5

Although the Unionists as a whole were cut down to forty-six members, Chamberlain gained an extra three seats in his Midland 'duchy' and enhanced his reputation with the Conservatives as an electoral asset. In the Commons his abilities showed in his vitriolic assaults on the Liberals. At times they were so effective that many Conservatives felt that the force of Chamberlain's assault was preventing fracture and dissolution amongst the Gladstonian party. For all Chamberlain's debating skills it was in the Lords that the greatest damage was done.

Salisbury rallied his forces to inflict a terrible ten to one defeat on the Home Rule Bill and followed this with opposition to Asquith's Employers' Liability Bill which forced its withdrawal. And if the alterations to the Parish Councils Act were not as sweeping as Salisbury wanted the final measure still bore the imprints of the Lords' amendments. Blocked by the Upper House the Liberals were driven to ploughing the sands and to using Harcourt's budget to raise morale. Salisbury did not want to force a constitutional crisis by defeating the budget; not because he felt such an action by the Lords was unconstitutional, but that it might give the government an undeserved popularity. When Rosebery, the new Liberal leader, looked like taking up the issue of Reform of the House of Lords Salisbury behaved quite improperly in advising the Queen to exercise her rights to dissolve Parliament. Her sympathies were completely Conservative by this time and it was lucky for the survival of the monarchy that she also consulted the leading Liberal Unionist lawyer, Sir Henry James, who advised against such a step. In the event it was unnecessary as shown by the unseemly collapse of the

Liberals in 1895. Rosebery handed over to Salisbury after the vote of censure on the Liberal war minister. Salisbury accepted office with haste but made it known to the Queen that he would seek an election immediately.

Salisbury's government was formed before the election and the Liberal Unionists were this time to be included. Many Conservatives felt that Chamberlain could be better controlled inside rather than outside a cabinet, and that his debating skills would massively strengthen the Tory front bench. Salisbury insisted on the leadership of the Commons, with Number 10, for his nephew Balfour, but offered the Liberal Unionists the pick of four offices. Devonshire became Lord President with a general responsibility for the armed services and, much to Salisbury's surprise, Chamberlain asked for the Colonial Office instead of the Home Office or even the Exchequer. Salisbury eventually agreed, unsure how the man's radical energies would affect the Empire. He had carefully moderated Chamberlain's demands for a thorough programme of measures and the Conservatives went to the election with a markedly slim agenda and on few items were they committed. The Liberals performed far worse than anyone expected: they left 130 seats uncontested and in many others Liberal candidates were selected too late to have much impact. (See chapter 2 for an account of the divisions within the Liberal Party.) When the results came in the Conservatives had 341 seats and, with the 80 Unionists, commanded a massive majority of 259. The victory almost overcame Salisbury's natural pessimism and gave him faith in democracy.

SALISBURY'S THIRD MINISTRY 1895–1902

With Balfour, Chamberlain, Goschen, Hicks Beach and Ritchie on the front benches, Salisbury's government was not lacking in talent. A major economic recovery ensured expanding revenues, an impressive parliamentary majority was to hand, and control in the House of Lords was assured by the presence of Devonshire and Salisbury. Yet no government produced so little in the way of constructive legislation as that between the two general elections of 1895 and 1900. The failure of the dynamic Chamberlain to capitalize on these favourable circumstances can be attributed to several reasons, not least Lord Salisbury himself.

Salisbury remained suspicious of Chamberlain's enthusiasm and, if not in firm control of the Cabinet, he was little inclined to push against Conservative prejudices in both the Lords and the Commons. Ministerial talent tended to be distributed away from home affairs. Chamberlain, the most restless and constructive member, seized the Colonial Office by the scruff of the neck and pitch-forked it into the twentieth century. The Empire was big enough to absorb most of his energies. Goschen took the Admiralty, and Hicks Beach at the Exchequer was concerned with thwarting Chamberlain's old age pension schemes by seeing that due economy was observed. Two vital offices were held by incompetents. Henry Chaplin, the farmers' friend, had the Local Government Board and the Home Office lay under the dead hand of Sir Matthew White Ridley. The Duke of Devonshire, old and increasingly deaf, had education under his charge – about which he knew little. There was no central guiding hand: Salisbury, Devonshire, Balfour and Chamberlain shared the leadership. The problems that could arise from this are well illustrated by the request for guidance from the four as to whether the news of the signing of the peace with the Boers should be released:

> Lord Salisbury deprecated haste, urging that such communications were often erroneous. 'Wait till Monday.' A. J. B. [alfour]. said: 'Decide as you think best.' Chamberlain asked: 'Why have you not published it at once?' No reply from the Duke of Devonshire.

From 1899 and the outbreak of the Boer War lack of progress on the domestic front became readily intelligible with the South African conflict absorbing energy and finance. Before this the legislative paralysis is remarkable. Perhaps the very real improvement in the economy and living standards accounts for the torpor. Wheat prices were half what they had been in the 1870s and real wages increased rapidly as industry recovered from the slump of the early 1890s. What need was there for government action in these circumstances?

In Ireland Gerald Balfour continued his brother's policy of coercion and conciliation. To the irritation of Lord Salisbury another Land Act was produced in 1896 to assist the sale of land to tenants. A Local Government Act in 1898 brought genuine democracy with elected county councils throughout Ireland. Salisbury was concerned at the effects of both Acts on the traditional Anglo-Irish elite.

In legislative terms 1896 was almost sterile as a parliamentary session. Two measures were pushed through to help agriculture which was still suffering from a depression as a result of vast foreign imports. Wheat prices had reached an all-time low in 1894 and showed little sign of recovery. Salisbury, no more than Disraeli, thought to offer protection. The farmers received two palliatives, an Agricultural Ratings Bill which reduced the burden of rates on agriculture, and a very minor measure of protection under the guise of a Diseases of Animals Act which stiffened the regulations for the import of foreign cattle. The major measure of 1896 – an Educational Bill to aid denominational schools – was defeated. Once again the religious issue bedevilled British education. Over one thousand amendments were made, and in five days the government succeeded in carrying thirteen words of the first clause. To Salisbury's fury the Bill was withdrawn and a temporary support given in a measure pushed through in 1897. Chamberlain's chief hopes for constructive reform at home centred on a Workmen's Compensation Act and Old Age Pension. He succeeded in getting a sweeping measure relating to employers' liability through the Commons, and after much opposition through the Lords too, but the difficulties he encountered indicated the very tight limits the Conservative majority could impose on 'Joe's' radical initiatives. His desire for an old age pension scheme was blocked by Hicks Beach and then overtaken by the Boer War. Apart from the Workmen's Compensation Act Chamberlain had to content himself with attempting to transform the Empire. Even here he encountered extensive resistance to increased spending. The Colonial Office was refitted with electric lighting, hospitals for tropical diseases were established in London and Liverpool, and colonies in West Africa and the West Indies benefited from development schemes. Lack of funding and the war in South Africa prevented any further measures from getting underway.

Apparent victory in South Africa in the summer of 1900 laid the basis for a great election victory. Reluctantly Salisbury allowed himself to be persuaded to go to the country. He distrusted the euphoric jingoism of Mafeking Night (see chapter 5). He took little part in the election and initially proposed not to issue a manifesto. When the Duke of Devonshire insisted Salisbury claimed he had 'nothing to say'. Chamberlain, however, had plenty to say: 'A vote against the government is a vote for the Boers.' The electorate appeared strongly apathetic and the overall turnout of voters was one million less than in 1895. The Liberals were as divided as ever, the Middleton party machine was still in fine form and 153 Unionists were unopposed in mainland Britain. Against all his expectations Salisbury romped home with another massive majority – just eighteen seats fewer than in 1895.

It was now only a question of waiting until the end of the Boer War before Salisbury retired. He was old and increasingly ill. His wife had died in 1899 leaving him heartbroken and prey to his old pessimism. Under pressure from his Cabinet he surrendered the Foreign Office in 1900 to Lord Lansdowne and became increasingly marginalized. Despite his opinions the Alliance with Japan was signed in 1902 (see chapter 5) and work proceeded on an education measure, which he feared would cause more trouble than it was worth. He retired after the succession of the new king, laying down the seals of office as quietly and unobtrusively as he had governed in July 1902. As so often before he slipped off to Hatfield with great relief. He asked to be excused from attending the Coronation.

Salisbury's achievements as a politician lie mainly in the realm of foreign policy. At home he left no legislative memorials to himself. Disraeli had his 1867 Reform Act and Gladstone his work as Chancellor along with the vast array of reforms his ministries had produced. Salisbury had blocked rather than facilitated reform. He had failed to stem the tide of democracy but he had done something to slow its headlong progress and, as he saw it, moderate its potential for destruction of the *ancien régime*. The basis of his political success is difficult to analyse, compounded as much by luck as skill. The Home Rule Crisis of 1886 and the later self-inflicted wounds of the Liberals played a major part. The slow but steady drift of the middle classes to the party of resistance was vital. There were no Conservatives returned for London in 1859 and 1865 yet in 1900 they won sixty-seven out of seventy-five seats in London and its suburbs. The hold on Lancashire established in the 1860s through the identification of Liberalism with the Irish cause was maintained in all except the 1880 election. In 1900 Conservatives were able to retain fifty-one out of the sixty-two seats in that county. How far patriotism helped the Tory party is impossible to tell. What is beyond dispute is the superiority of the Conservative party machine under Lord Salisbury. For a man with such a contempt for democracy he paid it the great compliment of taking it very seriously. The key figure in this area was Captain R. W. E. Middleton who ran the machine for Salisbury from 1885 until his retirement in 1903. Middleton was a true professional. After a brief career in the navy he served as a constituency agent and then as an organizer in West Kent. He became national agent in 1885 and was also secretary of the National Union. He was Salisbury's eyes and ears, and his advice on patronage and election timing was always treated with the greatest respect. The Conservatives had the advantage of money which Middleton exploited to the full. By 1900 half the constituencies had full-time agents and above them lay a tier of regional organizers. In London alone there were thirty full-time Conservative workers to the Liberals' three. A National Society of Conservative Agents was founded in 1891 and a journal, *The Tory*, was published for them with necessary information on registration law.

Registration of voters was particularly vital in exploiting to the full the system of plural voting (according to property qualifications, some individuals had the right to more than one vote). The National Union was reorganized by Middleton in 1886 into nine subordinate regions. Its role was largely propagandist and full use was made of magic lantern slides and pamphleteering. Workingmen's Conservative Clubs flourished, particularly in Lancashire, with Middleton's encouragement. The work of the National Union was complemented by the Primrose League (see pp. 88–9). The new craze for cycling was enrolled in the cause with Conservative cycle clubs springing up everywhere. These clubs provided dispatch riders at election times. Middleton's work was recognized fully at the time by the presentation to him in 1895 of a casket containing £10,000. This handsome gesture was repeated in 1900. His retirement in 1903 was a sad blow to Salisbury's successor.

A. J. BALFOUR – THE DECLINE AND FALL OF THE CONSERVATIVE ASCENDANCY 1902–5

Arthur Balfour had brains, courage and vision. He had served a long political apprenticeship since he entered the Commons for a Cecil family borough, Hertford, in 1874. He inherited great wealth from his Scottish father and very useful family connections from his mother who was Salisbury's sister. Like his uncle he was an intellectual, and published in 1879 a minor work of philosophy, *A Defence of Philosophic Doubt*. He served Salisbury as private secretary from 1878 to 1880 and was brought into the Cabinet in 1886. His initial reception in the Commons was not favourable. He was languid and bored, treating the whole business as a game, sometimes amusing and sometimes not. His delicacy of appearance and manners earned him the nickname 'pretty Fanny'. His appointment as Irish Secretary in 1887 revealed a steel that few had suspected he possessed. He was ruthlessly efficient and quite undismayed by demonstrations in the Commons or Dublin. Ever after he retained a distaste for the Irish which was reciprocated. Distaste was perhaps as strong an emotion as he was capable of feeling. He never married and, apart from an adoring circle of female relatives, formed few attachments. He was a sleek, feline character disdainfully immaculate in the direst of situations. His cold detachment was his strength and weakness. It made him an excellent administrator and a formidable debater but he lacked a vital commodity as a popular politician. In common with his uncle, Balfour disliked democracy but he also differed from Salisbury in that he never took it seriously. He never mastered the arts of platform oratory like Chamberlain nor does he seem to have appreciated the manipulative arts of Middleton's machine. Salisbury feared the masses and respected his backbenchers' prejudices. Balfour did neither. He was too cerebral, too uninvolved. As far as he was concerned the Tory Party was an instrument for solving the nation's problems.

Like many other politically aware individuals of his time Balfour was conscious of national decline and in consequence became one of the leading proponents of what was termed 'national efficiency', a drive for national regeneration. The decline of Britain was rooted in many causes, but was plain to see. A league table of the twelve most advanced countries placed her ninth in terms of economic growth and tenth in terms of productivity. That she still remained the richest country in Europe was due to her early lead in industrialization, but the writing was on the wall. Britain was no longer the workshop of the world, only one of the three leading industrial nations – and the least dynamic of the three at that. Action was needed on two fronts: to defend the overstretched Empire and to make the British Isles more competitive. Chamberlain, like Balfour, could read the ominous signs, and true to his radical nature he produced his own sweeping response. Between them they brought ruin to the party Lord Salisbury so cherished.

One of Balfour's greatest achievements was the Education Act of 1902. It was also a political disaster. By 1900 various educational problems had become acute. Education was a vital issue in the promotion of national efficiency. As the Duke of Devonshire said in the Lords that year 'Unless secondary education receives some assistance from the rates, I am afraid that we shall remain permanently behind other countries.' Such help from the rates was pronounced illegal under existing law by an auditor, Cockerton. His judgement in 1901 related to London but it had national implications. Clearly it was necessary to expand and fund secondary education. There was also the old conflict between Board and denominational schools. The temporary increase in grants under the 1897 measure was exhausted by 1900 and denominational schools began to close at an alarming rate. Finally, additional pressure was brought to bear by the new civil service supremo at the Board of Education, Robert Morant, a formidable, creative individual who was anxious to tackle the two problems head-on. The result was a bold piece of legislation and one of the legal masterpieces of the twentieth century. Against the advice of Salisbury and Chamberlain, Balfour and Devonshire pushed through a bill which proposed major changes. The school boards set up under the 1870 Act were abolished and all education placed under the county and county borough councils. Various compromise attempts to avoid rate-funding of denominational schools were swept aside and much to Chamberlain's horror, owing to his Non-Conformist background and Non-Conformist support, rate support for denominational schools was at last allowed. Chamberlain was incapacitated by a serious cab accident and unable to defend his corner effectively. The result was an enormous boost to education and a blow to the government's popularity. Non-Conformists up and down the country were outraged at 'Rome on the rates'. A London Baptist minister, Dr Clifford, attempted to orchestrate a campaign against it and in Wales the conflict became long and bitter. Whether this measure contributed to the disaster of 1906 is difficult to evaluate but until the summer of 1902 the government had fought ten by-elections and won nine of them. Then, just after Balfour's succession, it lost North Leeds. In September 1902 a Tory majority of 5,000 in Sevenoaks was cut to less than 1,000. The Non-Conformist revolt had begun.

The following year produced another major legislative landmark. George Wyndham had succeeded Gerald Balfour as Irish Secretary in 1900. Three years later he produced a Land Purchase Act of massive proportions. This Act would cover whole estates not single holdings and the state provided long-term, low-interest loans to enable tenants to buy. It pleased landlords and tenants alike, and, coupled with the previous Land Purchase Act it seemed to have solved the land question in Ireland.

Another national boil was lanced by the government in 1904 by a Licensing Act which made provision for closure of supernumerary public houses but also compensated those who lost trade by a levy on those remaining. The temperance lobby was disappointed and complained bitterly at the compensation. Once again Non-Conformity was irritated by government policy.

In two areas Balfour showed a political insensitivity to public opinion. First, the damage caused by the war in South Africa led Alfred Milner, the British High Commissioner, to ask for the right to import bonded Chinese labourers to work in the gold-mines of the Rand. Chamberlain was aware of a possible hostile public response and vetoed the idea but after his departure from the Colonial Office in 1903 the Cabinet sanctioned Milner's request. It produced a storm of protest in Britain; Chinese slavery became a moral issue. To working men it seemed to belittle labour but also threaten white jobs. To the sensitive consciences it was inhuman and there was also the problem that large numbers of men in close confinement might be given to nameless practices. Such arguments were of no avail. To Balfour it was a simple solution to a problem and the Chinese earned fifteen times more in South Africa than in China. Second, he also showed himself to be totally uncomprehending over the trades union agitation that arose from a series of legal judgments in the late 1890s most notably Quinn *v*. Leatham and Taff Vale (see chapter 7). In contrast to Cross and Disraeli in the 1870s he made no move to placate this most powerful pressure group. Balfour's concerns were increasingly with foreign policy and defence. Here there was no high drama and the public was indifferent to the benefits of the Anglo-French Entente, the setting-up of the Committee of Imperial Defence, and projected army reforms.

If Balfour attempted to tackle British regeneration piecemeal-fashion Joseph Chamberlain produced a sweeping panacea, a radical bombshell which was to split the Tory Party and irretrievably halt the Conservative ascendancy. On 15 May 1903, Chamberlain declared his faith in 'imperial preference' in a justly famous speech at Birmingham. He proposed to abandon free trade, a canon of British political life for fifty years. A system of duties, lower for goods within the Empire, would tie the Empire together, raise revenue for social reform and protect British industry. The tariff reform campaign had been launched. Here was problem-solving with a vengeance. It also had the added advantage of shifting the limelight back to Chamberlain whose role after the Boer War had been less than prominent.

Chamberlain had long been concerned with the issue of imperial unity. Like many others, including his old Liberal associate Dilke, he felt that only through the Empire could Britain survive in the twentieth century as a world superpower. In 1897 he had proposed to the Empire's Prime Ministers an imperial *Zollverein* (literally 'customs union') or free trade area. They resisted this but pressed for 'imperial preference'. The emotional bonds of unity fostered by the Boer War led Chamberlain to believe that the opportunity for strengthening these links had to be seized. Hicks Beach was succeeded as Chancellor by a convinced free trader, Ritchie, in 1902 but a clash with Chamberlain was put off when the latter made a long winter tour to South Africa. On his return he found Ritchie planned to drop the corn duty. Chamberlain's May 1903 speech was a challenge which rapidly escalated into a massive political crisis. In the Commons he allowed himself to be drawn by Lloyd George into advocating food taxes to pay for social reform, notably pensions.

A group of Unionists formed a Free Food League in July 1903 and Balfour faced disaster. He tried to regain control of the situation in September by sacking Ritchie and the most outspoken free traders and encouraging 'Joe' to leave the Cabinet to lead a crusade to convert public opinion. As a token of his secret support he promoted 'Joe's' son, Austen, to replace Ritchie. He hoped to retain that supine symbol of rectitude the Duke of Devonshire but, prodded by his wife, the Duke resigned at the beginning of October, thereby lending his weight to Chamberlain's opponents. Bitter quarrels developed between tariff reformers and those who supported free trade. Salisbury's son, Lord Hugh Cecil, became the centre of a free-trade group nicknamed the 'Hughligans'. Winston Churchill, Randolph's son, crossed the floor of the Commons to join the Liberals. Balfour used all his genius to conceal the real differences amongst his followers yet Chamberlain made great headway amongst the Conservative faithful. Tariff reform became the party's albatross. Just as Gladstone had hung Home Rule round the necks of the Liberals and Clause Four (see chapter 7) was to weigh down the Labour Party in the years after 1945, so tariff reform became a rallying cry for Conservatives and an electoral liability.

Protection had appeal to some manufacturers facing German competition and this was particularly true of Chamberlain's own Midland heartland. Many farmers, of course, followed Squire Chaplin in backing protection but to most Englishmen and women free trade meant prosperity and cheap food. Protection meant smaller loaves. Chamberlain was unlucky that his campaign coincided with a considerable economic revival, particularly in Lancashire where the biggest export industry was situated. Fears of dear food and retaliation in the county produced a swing against the Conservatives of devastating proportions. By-elections began to run steadily against the government. The party machinery seemed unable to cope. Middleton's successor, Percival Hughes, was inadequate, and complacency with years of victory left its mark on the Conservatives, but so too did the split. Chamberlain's supporters rapidly captured the National Union but the Central Office remained under Balfour's control. Hughes, as national agent, made the mistake of not taking the dual function of Honorary Secretary of the National Union, thus a policy split was mirrored in an organizational divide.

Balfour clung to office hoping to complete his defence reorganization but by 1905 papering over the gaping cracks was becoming more and more difficult. Following fresh signs of differences within the Liberal Party on the issue of Home Rule, Rosebery made a speech condemning the issue on 25 November, and Balfour decided to resign. He handed over the seals of office on 4 December fully expecting that the Liberals would engage in damaging inter-party conflict and thereby enhance Unionist prospects at the inevitable general election. Balfour miscalculated and went down with a landslide defeat in 1906.

CONTROVERSY: DISRAELIAN CONSERVATISM

The past is frequently cannibalized to serve the present. Visions of the past become weapons to sanctify some present cause or to blast enemies. Ever since Lord Randolph Churchill chose to use the dead Disraeli in the furtherance of his own career and invented 'Tory democracy', the Disraelian legacy has been the subject of argument and reinterpretation. In the 1980s various Conservatives have chosen to appeal to Disraelian tradition as a covert form of attacking Margaret Thatcher's controversial style. In 1981 Norman St John Stevas, a critic of Thatcherism although a member of her government, gave a talk on television on the subject of Disraeli:

> Disraeli's Toryism, with its national principles, its profound sense of the organic nature of society, its compassion for those in need – as evidenced by his almost lone championship of the Chartists – was sharply opposed to what he called 'the brutalitarians', 'the school of Manchester' (an original and intentionally uncomplimentary phrase), the Benthamites who would re-fashion England with their harsh logic and their pitiless economic doctrines, careless and possibly ignorant of basic human instincts and feelings. Disraeli knew about and therefore sympathised with the lot of the poor: his knowledge of their actual life was greatly superior to that of Dickens. He saw society in terms of a trust, drawing its cohesion from the observance of mutual obligation, and its rulers ready to employ where necessary the huge engine of government to promote the wellbeing of the people.
>
> (*The Listener*, 16 April 1981, p. 495)

He continues and the contemporary message was plain:

> He had experienced for himself what happened to the Conservative Party when it identified itself with a single interest, and that a declining one – land. . . . He was determined that this would not occur again

as were many of his successors, Baldwin, Chamberlain, Churchill, Butler and Macmillan, who had read the signs of the time aright.

(ibid.)

The omission of Mrs Thatcher's name was surely significant.

Out of the various academic studies of the period, an essay by J. T. Ward published in a volume entitled *The Conservative Leadership*, comes closest to this view of Disraeli, the apostle of a one-nation Conservatism:

> Disraeli had tried, in different ways, to 'move' Britain. He had taught a party of haughty patricians and apoplectic squires to face unpleasant realities. He had regularly demonstrated that the defence of ancient institutions could be allied with 'radical' social policies: he had shown that Toryism need not fear an extension of the suffrage beyond the dreams of Radicals; that Toryism cared about health, industrial labour and urban housing; that Toryism would correct the unfairnesses of Gladstone's trade union legislation. But he also taught his party that politics was conditioned by possibility and that conservation involved knowing precisely what was most worth conserving at any period. He followed Palmerston in encouraging Britons to believe in an imperial mission and in their importance in European affairs. He largely invented that combination of respect for ancient things, British (or, from his viewpoint, English) nationalism and a reaction against the harshness of *laissez-faire* which restored his party to major status. And despite many vicissitudes and many alternative formulae, the Disraelian ethic still survives. It may well be true that Tory cabinets tend to be Peelite; but Tory supporters remain largely Disraelian.
>
> (J. T. Ward, *The Conservative Leadership*, London, Macmillan, 1974, p. 100)

Dr Paul Smith in an important detailed study of Disraelian Conservatism published in 1967 agrees that Disraeli 'had conceived the vision of national Toryism, rooted in the affection of the people and ministering to their needs', but he continues with a major reservation on the limitations of Disraeli in practice:

> In short, the government of 1874–80 did not possess and never attempted to develop a domestic 'policy'. Disraelian Conservatism in office was found to mean much the same as other Conservatism: empiricism tempered by prejudice. Those who, like Cross, had expected their leader to unlock from the recesses of his mind a Conservative programme were forced to realise that there was no programme there. What the ministry would do in the field of social improvement would depend almost entirely on what the ministers most concerned found readiest to hand.
>
> (P. Smith, *Disraelian Conservatism and Social Reform*, London, Routledge & Kegan Paul, 1967, p. 100)

A more recent study by Bruce Coleman is even more dubious about the legacy of Disraeli:

> In so many respects it is the continuity and traditionalism of the Disraeli ministry that stands out, not any new departure. Certainly the party had become more self-consciously patriotic in its appeal by 1880 than at the time of Palmerston's death, but this was a reversion to an earlier role, was entirely compatible with the party's existing composition and instinct and was supporting a firmly conservative line of domestic policy. The experience of office with a majority had confirmed the essential conservatism of the still predominantly aristocratic parliamentary party with which Disraeli instinctively identified.
>
> This conclusion will disappoint romantics who wish to find profound creativity in Disraeli's leadership. If there is anything which can properly be called Disraelian Conservatism (and it is doubtful), then the emphasis should be on the second word. The party was simply adjusting naturally to the post-Palmerstonian situation and reasserting its traditional commitment to stability and security both at home and abroad in contradistinction to what the Liberals and the Home Rulers seemed to offer. In essentials Disraeli left his party much as he had inherited it from the elder Derby; the changes had come mainly in the circumstances in which it operated.
>
> (B. Coleman, *Conservatism and the Conservative Party in Nineteenth Century Britain*, London, Arnold, 1988, p. 161)

Perhaps in the end we should resort to the conclusion of the best recent biography to date, that by Lord Blake, published in 1966. Whatever the arguments over Disraeli's serious contribution to politics perhaps we can agree on his amusement value:

> Moreover, Englishmen instinctively distrust wits and cynics, and are uneasy if they encounter irony or fancy – anyway in politics. If Disraeli had simply been a romantic worshipper of England's traditions, institutions and grandeur, he would have had an easier passage. One side of him was indeed that, but another was a slightly mocking observer surveying with sceptical amusement the very stage upon which he himself played a principal part. When Archbishop Tait finished *Endymion* 'with a painful feeling that the writer considers all political life as mere play and gambling' he hit on a half-truth which was widely held. Disraeli's inner pessimism about the ultimate ends of politics did often lead him to use just that sort of language. To him, more than to most, politics avowedly was 'the great game'. But the British – and this was particularly true of the Victorian era – prefer public men to be serious figures assuming their load of responsibility with conscientious reluctance and sedate demeanour. As Disraeli himself wrote, 'The British People being subject to fogs and possessing a

powerful Middle Class require grave statesmen'. Perhaps this was why he was so often in opposition and so seldom in power. Disraeli never was a grave statesman.

(R. Blake, *Disraeli*, London, Eyre & Spottiswoode, 1966, p. 766)

BIBLIOGRAPHY

For an explanation of the grading system, see the preface p. xiii.

Biographies

A. J. Balfour

3   Mackay, B. F., Oxford, Oxford University Press, 1985
2   Egremont, M., London, Collins, 1980

J. Chamberlain

See bibliography on p. 64.

Lord R. Churchill

2   James, R. R., London, Hamish Hamilton, (1959) 1986
4   Foster, R. F., Oxford, Oxford University Press, 1981

B. Disraeli

2/3   Blake, R., London, Eyre & Spottiswoode, 1966
1   Bradford, S., London, Weidenfeld & Nicolson, 1985
2   Davies, R. W., London, Hutchinson, 1976
1   Walton, J. K., London, Routledge, 1990

Salisbury

3   Blake, R. and Cecil, H. (eds), London, Macmillan, 1987
3/4   Gascoigne-Cecil, G., 4 vols, London, Hodder & Stoughton, 1921–32
2   Taylor, R., London, Allen Lane, 1975

Secondary works

1   Adelman, P., *Gladstone, Disraeli and Later Victorian Politics*, London, Longman, 1970
2   Blake, R., *The Conservative Party: Peel to Churchill*, London, Fontana, 1970; updated to Thatcher in 1985
2   Coleman, B., *Conservatism and the Conservative Party in the Nineteenth Century*, London, Arnold, 1988
3   Hanham, H. J., *Elections and Party Management: Politics in the Time of Disraeli and Gladstone*, London, Longman, 1959

4   McKensie, R. and Silver, A., *Angels in Marble: Working-class Conservatives in Urban England*, London, Heinemann, 1968

3   Marsh, P., *The Discipline of Popular Government: Lord Salisbury's Domestic Statecraft 1881–1902*, Hassocks, Harvester, 1978

4   Pelling, H. M., *Social Geography of British Elections 1885–1910*, London, Macmillan, 1967

4   Pugh, M., *The Tories and the People*, Oxford, Blackwell, 1985

3   Smith, P., *Disraelian Conservatism and Social Reform*, London, Routledge & Kegan Paul, 1967

2   Southgate, D. (ed.), *The Conservative Leadership 1832–1932*, London, Macmillan, 1974

Sources for coursework

The section at the end of chapter 2 will be particularly useful. In addition the multi-volumed biography of Disraeli by Moneypenny and Buckle 1910–20 (revised edition London, John Murray, 1929) contains much documentary material. *The Letters of Disraeli to Lady Bradford and Lady Chesterfield*, edited by the Marquis of Zetland (London, John Murray, 1929) is a useful supplement to the material to be found in Moneypenny and Buckle.

Lord Salisbury on Politics, a selection of his articles in the *Quarterly Review* 1860–83, published in Cambridge in 1972, has not only a fine selection of Cecil's journalism but an excellent introduction by Dr P. Smith.

The Diary of Gathorne Hardy, later Lord Cranbrook, 1800–1892, edited by N. F. Johnson was published by Oxford University Press in 1981 and provides insights from a prominent Conservative cabinet minister. In addition to these products of 'high politicians' there are endless possibilities from local sources for the study of Conservatism outside Whitehall and Westminster.

4 Ireland 1868–1922: province or nation?

Dear Sir,

I am not surprised at your friend's anger but he and you should know that to denounce the murders was the only course open to us. To do that promptly was plainly our best policy.

But you can tell him and all others concerned that though I regret the accident of Lord F Cavendish's death I cannot refuse to admit that Burke got no more than his deserts.

You are at liberty to show him this, and others whom you can trust also, but let not my address be known. He can write to House of Commons.

Yours very truly,
Chas. S Parnell.

This letter was published in *The Times* on 18 April 1887 and contained references to past events that were considered to be political dynamite. The letter was signed by Charles Stewart Parnell, leader of the Irish Nationalists (the Home Rule Party) in the English House of Commons. It hinted at if not his direct involvement in the Phoenix Park murders then at least a sympathy with and knowledge of this event. The words 'Burke got no more than his deserts', referred to T. H. Burke the Under-Secretary for Ireland. On 6 May 1882 Burke, along with Lord Frederick Cavendish, was slashed with surgical knives by a band of assassins calling themselves 'The Invincibles'. But what were these events? Why was

Parnell being linked to them five years later? And, what importance did the letter have for Anglo-Irish relations at this time and later? In order to answer these questions it is necessary to look back at the fascinating, yet often violent and exasperating, relationship between Ireland and England in the years from 1868 to 1887.

INTRODUCTION: ATTITUDES AND ANTECEDENTS

It is not an exaggeration to claim that Ireland was seen from the English standpoint as a 'problem' to be solved, if only the key could be found. It was in part Ireland's fault that concession, reform, coercion and repression, either separately or together, had no lasting effect on the stormy relationship between the two countries. From the Irish side the 'problem' was even simpler: it was England's desire to remain an imperial power and to deny Ireland's once proud and rightful heritage as an independent nation. Even this straightforward division could not last long, and the question was soon complicated by the emergence of a group of Irishmen, in the north of the country centred in Ulster, who wanted a different form of relationship with England and therefore a different solution to Anglo-Irish affairs.

There is no doubt that English attitudes to Ireland were 'problem'-centred. After all it was Ireland that drew the attention of Elizabeth I in the sixteenth century and Oliver Cromwell in the seventeenth century. It was Ireland that had 'threatened' England in the eighteenth century with its connivance at French plans to invade the English mainland from Ireland – although this came to nought in the end. It was the Irish in 1798 who rebelled and forced the English Parliament to bring the 'problem child' into its closer embrace by the Act of Union in 1801 that denied Ireland the right to its own Parliament and made its representatives sit as a minority in the English Parliament. What is too easily forgotten is that viewed from the other direction the 'problem' was one of the unwelcome imposition of English social, economic, political and even religious control on a subject nation that denied its patriotic and nationalistic populace its true identity. Looked at from this perspective, English actions take on a different character. The events of the sixteenth and the seventeenth centuries could be portrayed as very violent and catastrophic imperialist jaunts with England intent on creating a colony out of Ireland. In the eighteenth century the same imperial power violently over-reacted to an Irish nationalistic outburst in 1798 by denying political representation in 1801, and continued to do so throughout the nineteenth century. Expressed in these terms, as biased as the English view, then Ireland's history could become, as some today would like to portray it, a 'struggle for freedom'. There are many different viewpoints of any event in history. The tragedy with Ireland's case was that the blinkered views adopted by most politicians on both sides merely reinforced their inability to settle on what was the key issue at stake, let alone try to proceed and solve it. There were too many solutions for the problems that existed.

One additional complicating factor was the question of attitudes. National stereotypes help to colour political issues and events, and unfortunately for Anglo-Irish relations such attitudes had long traditions and appeared to be reinforced throughout this era. Add to this the strongly held Irish belief, not entirely unsubstantiated, that England deserted Ireland in her hour of direst need during the catastrophic potato famine years of 1845–9, in which a quarter of the Irish population was lost through death or emigration. Inevitably such attitudes, and their reinforcement and perpetuation, did little to help the often strained relations between Britannia and Hibernia.

Gladstone's fateful words, 'My mission is to pacify Ireland', spoken in celebration of his election victory in 1868, revealed the crusading nature of the Liberal leader's approach to the Irish. His stress on the word pacify would allow for a pursuit of both coercion and conciliation ('kicks and kindness'), and his self-appointed task would necessitate a thoroughgoing revision of England's policy as far as the key issues of Ireland were concerned. These issues were: the position of the Irish Church; the regularization of land ownership, tenancy rights and compensation; and the future political identity of England's close neighbour across the Irish Sea.

THE CHURCH

Gladstone needed no help in the arena of ecclesiastical affairs as he was an accomplished theologian, church historian and moralist. His own personal religious fervour and commitment meant that his first actions concentrated on the question of the Irish Church. For the nine out of every ten Irishmen who were Catholics the imposition of a foreign English Church as the nation's established church was a bitter pill to swallow. Gladstone had come to the conclusion that a recognition of the Catholic Church's rights and position in Ireland would go some way to alleviating the tension which existed in Ireland. Hardly surprisingly people resented giving tithes to a church that did not look after their physical and spiritual well-being. Perhaps it is a comment on Gladstone's approach to Ireland, or the intractability of the relations between the two countries, that whatever he might do for the Church it would have little effect on the 'men of violence' – the committed Fenian Brotherhood. The Fenians appeared in the United States and Ireland in 1857–8 and had already hit the headlines and lived up to their reputations with the bombing at Clerkenwell Prison in 1867. Nevertheless, the Fenian violence served a purpose in that it would make English politicians more amenable to allowing Gladstone's Bill to pass through.

Thus, the Irish Church was disestablished by an Act of the English

Parliament in 1869. The Act severed all legal connections between the church and the state to take effect from 1 January 1871 thus making the church a purely voluntary body from which property would be taken en masse. In all the church lost half its property valued at about £16 million and the other half was administered for it by Commissioners and was to be used for the relief of poverty of which there was no shortage in Ireland. The optimism of many was based on a short-lived hope that the disestablishment act could alleviate the problems of Ireland. No single piece of legislation could do this and Gladstone needed to turn his attention quickly towards land.

THE LAND QUESTION

If Gladstone had not needed guidance on the church question he was quick to seek advice on the land question, both at home and abroad. He needed all the statistical information and detail he could get in order to be as persuasive as possible in Parliament to overcome the entrenched belief in *laissez-faire* and landlord rights.

With a predominantly Catholic population Ireland was ruled by a predominantly Protestant landlord class. Many landlords were absentees and took money out of Ireland without ever giving anything back and in some cases without ever setting foot on Irish soil. For the most part Irish tenants never saw their 'foreign' landlords, and yet few of them were secure in their tenancy or enjoyed the 'privilege' of receiving compensation for improvements they made to property. Only those in Ulster enjoyed the local custom of protection and compensation payments – the so-called 'Ulster Custom'. For the vast majority it was a case of being turned out at a moment's notice and with no compensation for the work, time or money put into improvements. This practice simply meant that the next tenant could be charged more by the landlord's agent for an improved property. This inimical situation needed quick attention as its obvious unfairness was becoming a weapon in the hands of the Irish. Gladstone tried to tackle the issue head-on with the 1870 Land Act which guaranteed in law the 'Ulster Custom' where it already existed and established elsewhere the principle of compensation if tenants were uprooted by landlords. The clear intention was to give tenants more security. Although in theory the onus was moved from tenant to landlord to disprove claims of improvement, and eviction was made more expensive – from one to seven years' rent with a maximum of £250 – the Act failed to define adequately the 'Ulster Custom', did not attempt to extend it, made the procedures very complicated and excluded leaseholders of more than 31-year-old leases. In addition nothing was done to prevent landlords from simply increasing rents at will. A further concession of providing funds for tenants to purchase their land brought only 877 takers as the one-third deposit proved far too large. Although the Act was a step in the right direction, as with much of Irish history in this period it seemed more of a half-hearted attempt to placate the worst grievances of the Irish rather than to adopt a thorough-going reform. Certainly the Irish saw the Act in this light and Gladstone's high hopes for the pacification of Ireland in 1868 had not borne fruit by 1871. So vociferous and violent was the storm of protest that met the Gladstonian legislation that the Liberals were forced to resort to the imposition of a Coercion Act in 1871. This piece of legislation was a renewable law that allowed for the summary arrest of suspected trouble-makers and their detention without them having access to the normal legal processes. Seen by the Irish as yet another infringement of their rights, the English considered it was an absolute necessity for the protection of landlords, because Ireland had become a lawless society.

TOWARDS A NEW DEPARTURE

At the same time that English politicians were reviving their interests in Irish affairs the Irish themselves were making their own efforts to enter the constitutional arena to try to affect decisions about their homeland. In 1868 there were sixty-five Liberal Irish members and forty Conservative Irish members, but by 1885 the two great English political parties could only muster eighteen members between them, the rest, eighty-five in all, were Home Rule members. No doubt the Secret Ballot Act of 1872 did much to relieve the Irish voter of his fear of landlord reprisals in elections. Certainly, the Irish voted with their hearts in the successive elections and in favour of an Irish party committed to constitutional reform. At first the Irish Home Government Association had called for a separate Irish Parliament shared by Protestants and Catholics but the appeal of this idea proved too narrow. It was not until 1873 that the Association gained the support of the Catholic Church and decided to call itself the Home Rule League. The Church was reacting against Gladstone's failure to provide money for Irish universities and hence subsidies, in part, for Catholic higher education. In 1874 fifty-nine Home Rulers were elected – mainly at the expense of Gladstonian Liberals – and Ireland had its voice in the House of Commons: all it needed now was a leader. Unfortunately, it had to wait. Isaac Butt, the leading light of the day was no political tiger. His belief in persuasion and force of argument made him a gentlemanly negotiator for constitutional reform but he was essentially ineffective as leader in the House of the Home Rule movement. Butt remained the Irish leader until 1879, although by this date another politician, a real political firebrand, had appeared on the scene.

   Charles Stewart Parnell was born in 1845 in Avondale, County Wicklow, a product of the landed elite Protestant ascendancy who was half-American. He was a fiery young man and was expelled from Cambridge for brawling outside the city station. His background, however, did him little harm in the more rarified social circles of Parliament when he was elected for Meath in 1875. His early tendency to fly off the handle mellowed into an effective combination of prudence, firmness, political acumen and good tactical sense. However, his fiery nature would show through in the vehemence of his language. He certainly pulled no punches and latched very quickly onto J. G. Biggar's ploy of obstructionism in Parliament.

In 1877 Parnell replaced Butt as President of the Home Rule Confederation of Great Britain but he needed a further two years, and some help, before replacing Butt as Irish leader in the House of Commons. By 1879 Parnell had caught the eye of the Fenians who were keen to push for land reform at a time when Ireland was facing an acute agricultural depression which had cut incomes but had also seen an increase in rents, a combination particularly disastrous for Ireland. The two sides of the national movement, the constitutional and the revolutionary, joined forces. Parnell negotiated with Michael Davitt, the adventurous Fenian just released from fifteen years in gaol who had experienced eviction at the age of 4. This so-called 'new departure' saw a formalization of the relationship with Davitt's Land League, established in October 1869, gaining Parnell as its President. With his high profile Parnell also had the good fortune to see the constitutional wing of the Nationalists without a leader. Butt died in May 1879 and thus cleared the way for Parnell to dominate affairs, although not before he had seen off William Shaw, the Home Rule party chairman, in a competitive election held by new Home Rule MPs in Dublin in 1880.

LAND AGAIN

It was in the same year, 1880, that the two protagonists in the Irish struggle locked antlers again. Gladstone was once more Prime Minister and led a Liberal Government already aware of the relevance of the land question and waiting for the Richmond Committee to report on agriculture in general in Britain, and the Bessborough Committee to report specifically on Ireland. The Liberal proposal for a Compensation for Disturbance Act in 1880 fell at the House of Lords because a more thorough-going reform measure would be necessary to overcome the feelings already prevalent in Ireland. Gladstone was hampered by hanging onto the rapidly outmoded idea that Ireland's problems could be solved by simply passing 'good' legislation and crushing violence. Parnell's response to this token remedial action was to urge for the most openly damaging protest against the government and the landlord class that had been seen to date. It consisted of rent strikes, harvests withheld and the boycotting of landlords and their sympathizers in the Irish countryside, in association with an organized campaign of obstructionism in the House of Commons. Parnell's sister, Fanny, set the mood in her poetry:

Hold the rents and hold the crops boys,
Pass the word from town to town,
Pull away the props boys,
So you'll pull coercion down

While Fanny Parnell wrote poetry, her brother was busy following what he called 'The Four Gospels According to Biggar', or obstructionism. Of the 14,836 speeches in the House of Commons in 1880 over 6,300 of them were by Irish members, although only a small portion of these were by Parnellites. Nevertheless, it was a very successful campaign and sufficient to get the Speaker to admit that 'with his [Parnell's] minority of twenty-four, [he] dominates the House'. Parnell ran debates into interminably long sessions, and eventually sessions into next day's business and next day's business into postponements; simply he drove a coach and horses through parliamentary procedures. In January 1881 after a session lasting over forty hours the Speaker was forced to adopt the measure of closing the debate which then became known as the 'closure' – a general rule of the House of Commons since 1887.

While Parnell did his bit in London the Irish people tried their best too. The ploy of boycotting became common after its first use against a certain Captain Boycott, a farmer and Lord Erne's agent in County Mayo. So ostracized ('sent to Coventry' or 'boycotted') was he that the government was forced to come to his aid before his crops rotted in the field because he could find no labourer or tenant willing to help him, or even talk to him. Davitt reckoned that this exercise, with the Boycott Relief Expedition, cost £3,500 to take in a £350 harvest. Boycott was just the first and soon many like him found themselves entirely cut off from the local communities, powerless to carry on their normal activities. As long as evictions continued which could see honest Irish families thrown out of their homes often for no good reason, apart from a landlord's desire to raise the rent, then violence and boycotting inevitably followed. In 1877 there had been 963 evictions in Ireland and 236 'outrages', but by 1880 2,000 evictions had seen 2,500 'outrages' committed. 'Outrages' were acts of violence against the person and property, physical assault, arson, harassment, etc. and most of these happened at night by the light of the moon – hence the term 'moonlighting' and the mysterious and frightening antics of 'Captain Moonlight'. The net result was chaos, which brought with it the slow realization that on the back of the land agitation problem Irish politicians were successfully denying the English Parliament's authority in Ireland – a situation that could not continue for long. The government felt it necessary to impose yet another Coercion Act in February 1881. Although this enhanced the authorities' powers to deal with the violence it did nothing to tackle the cause of the grievances.

More importantly, at the beginning of 1881 the Bessborough Commission had reported and it recommended a complete revamping of the 1870 Land Act and called for the 'three F's' – fair rents, freedom of sale and fixity of tenure. These demands inevitably became the central themes of Gladstone's 1881 Land Act which was the 'good' piece of reform with which he hoped to temper coercion. The Act gave the 'Ulster Custom' full legal force throughout Ireland and set up land courts to fix judicial rents to which both parties agreed and which stood for fifteen years. This was as close to a system of dual ownership, tenant and landlord, as one could hope for in the circumstances. While paying his rent the tenant enjoyed fixity of tenure and could freely sell his right of occupancy to the highest bidder. The long rent guarantee persuaded many landlords to sell some of their property, and the government offered financial help by means of low-cost loans of between two-thirds and three-quarters of the purchase price over thirty-five years. However, since the majority of tenants could not afford the balance as down-payments, the number of properties purchased was very low indeed. Apart from success in Ulster the Act was received with much indifference and campaigns of violence continued in many areas. Most Irishmen were waiting to see what Parnell thought, but their leader was in a dilemma. The land-tenure issue was only one step towards a greater political goal: Irish independence. Secretly Parnell was not too disappointed by the measure but he had to be careful. If he was seen to accept the Act too wholeheartedly he would alienate some supporters who had hoped for more, and it might take the force out of the Irish movement by dampening down spirits. However, if he was too critical the extremists and hotheads might hijack the movement and take it into areas that Parnell felt were not at all safe, and thus risk destroying Home Rule before it had even been given a chance. Parnell decided to be ambivalent and play for time. He refused to denounce the Act completely but he warned tenants not to accept the new land courts too readily. While Parnell waited, Gladstone hoped that the Act would be a success and provide a foundation on which to build some measure of political reform, perhaps along the lines he suggested in the Commons in February when he said 'the local affairs of Ireland could be . . . separated from the Imperial affairs of Ireland'. However, as violence continued in Ireland all thoughts of further reform vanished. This continuing violence placed Parnell in an exposed position because the blame laid at the feet of the Land League would eventually also lie at his feet. In October 1881 Parnell was arrested, taken to Kilmainham gaol and there detained at the government's pleasure, although he was allowed some measure of comfort and visits from friends and family. It is possible that Parnell was privately not a little relieved by his experience. It distanced him from the ongoing Land League violence but he had not been forced publicly to denounce the League itself. Parnell was not content simply to rest – in fact he was organizing the 'No Rent Manifesto' – but he promised restraint on his release. His ploy worked and Gladstone was forced to discuss, through intermediaries, the so-called Kilmainham Treaty of April 1882 in which Parnell promised 'to co-operaté cordially with the Liberal Party' and come down on the side of 'moderation' if Irish tenants' rent arrears were forgotten. 'Moderation' may well have been Parnell's natural inclination but a decision to pursue 'moderation' placed him in a delicate position. The Land League was far from moderate but Parnell would have to denounce any immoderate actions and eventually this would mean denouncing the Land League itself. He was lucky – fate played her hand and a way out presented itself.

While Parnell had been in Kilmainham several organizations had pledged themselves to revenge and in the words of one such organization, 'The Invincibles', revenge could come in the form of the 'removal of obnoxious political personages'. These political targets, discussed at the beginning of this chapter, were the new Chief Secretary for Ireland Lord Frederick Cavendish and especially his Under-Secretary Thomas Burke. The mutilation of these two men was a despicable deed as far as English politicians were concerned but, importantly, the murders gave Parnell his opportunity to distance himself from violence in all forms, which of course included the Land League too. He immediately took the opportunity to establish a new organization, which grew out of a meeting at his own property at Avondale in September 1881. The so-called 'Avondale Treaty' created the National League in October, but any personal gains out of these events were greatly outweighed by larger political losses. The government had already moved to coercion and passed a Prevention of Crimes Bill which allowed trial by three judges, without a jury, for suspects. Parnell was heard to comment in the Commons 'we have got to begin all over again'. By 1882 though Parnell was not thinking of starting a new campaign for land reform but for Home Rule itself – the right for Ireland to have some measure of political independence. While Parnell organized the authorities did not rest and the 'Invincibles' were brought to trial in 1883 on the evidence of an informer, James Carey, who was vilified by the Irish Nationalist press.

THE MOVE TO HOME RULE

Parnell was not simply overworked with the organization of the newly created National League, and his struggle with the likes of Davitt who still favoured giving priority to a land nationalization programme. The relatively 'peaceful' interlude between 1882–4 was also explained by other pressing and more personal concerns. Parnell's financial position was not good and worries about his debts constantly preoccupied him. More importantly Parnell was in love with Mrs Katherine O'Shea whom he had met in 1880. Unfortunately she was still married, although she and her husband were 'separated' but, importantly, not divorced. 'Kitty' had children by Parnell, and the couple started to live together quite openly, which in the moral age of Victoria was a very dangerous practice. (In 1886 Sir Charles Dilke would have his political career ruined when he was cited as co-respondent in a divorce case.) Parnell was playing with a political timebomb, especially as Captain O'Shea was also a member of the Irish political movement and possibly not averse to using his position as the 'wronged' husband to obtain personal, political and financial advantages. At this time though the scandal was being kept under cover, but it would raise its head with disastrous consequences later.

While Parnell wrestled with family matters English politicians wrestled with their consciences and the practicalities of doing something about Ireland's position. A major debate centred on the 'pluralist' versus 'organic' approach to the governing of the British Isles. Those favouring the organic approach saw Britain and the whole problem of the 'Celtic fringe' in these terms. To recognize separateness would be to create 'states within a state' which would eventually lead to a weakening of Britain and perhaps the Empire. On the other side the pluralists argued that Ireland, along with Wales and Scotland possibly, were distinct communities which demanded their own distinct institutions, not ones imposed by England. It is fair to say that Gladstone had moved progressively from the organic to the pluralist position as the years and events passed. It was not entirely an intellectual conversion persuaded by mere power of argument. Gladstone was acutely aware of divisions within his party, notably the old landed Whigs in the Lords and the new 'radical' liberals led by Joseph Chamberlain. After all, these divisions had caused the fall of the Liberals in June 1885. They had been brought down by Salisbury's Conservatives and, ironically, Parnell, who now wielded considerable political power, and had returned to the political fray with renewed vigour. This heightened power had come from the Parliamentary Reform Act of 1884 which had seen a further extension of the franchise, increasing the Irish electorate from 4.4 per cent of the Irish population to 16 per cent. This massive rise, coupled with a reduction in the boroughs' representation had resulted in Parnell leading eighty-five Irish members in the Commons after the 1885 election. Such a victory, which included seventeen seats in Ulster itself, was a worrying new factor in the increasingly complex Irish political equation.

Back in office, naturally the Conservative Government turned its attention towards Ireland, and Lord Ashbourne's Act of 1885 extended the land purchase scheme enshrined in the Liberals' 1881 Act. The land-commissioners were now empowered to advance tenants four-fifths of the purchase price, a measure which proved to be very successful, and enabled many Irish tenants to contemplate the purchase of their holdings in all parts of Ireland. This fine piece of legislation was not enough, however, to save the Conservative Government that found its minority position untenable and it fell. Oddly enough this was a blow to Gladstone who felt that the Conservatives had a better chance of negotiating Irish legislation through Parliament than the Liberals. After all Salisbury had led from the Lords and Lord Carnarvon was Lord Lieutenant of Ireland. However, it was not to be and Gladstone would have to do the job himself. The wave of enthusiasm from the electorate that had carried Parnell to victory was bound to press its leader to make use of all English politicians, no matter what their party colours, to further the Home Rule cause.

Gladstone *had* come round to Home Rule but in truth he needed time to convince members of his party and cover the inevitable gaps that would appear as those who would not be convinced fled the party ranks. Gladstone's conversion had grown out of his long familiarity with the question, recognition that coercion had failed, and a readiness to adopt a new perspective on Ireland. He came round to see the question through Irish eyes and to treat it as a moral issue. In these circumstances Home Rule became a necessity. One might add that Gladstone had become a little tired of being beaten by opponents with the stick of his own failure. There was also the need to do something about the debilitating splits between the Whigs and the radicals within his own party. In truth though it is fair to say that Home Rule was more the vehicle rather than the cause of the opposition he experienced inside the party. Nevertheless, Home Rule provided him with an opportunity, given time, to realign the party to his own benefit. In the event it was time he was denied. His conversion to Home Rule was quickly publicized by his own conversations in Parliament and his son's injudicious leak of the fact to the *Leeds Mercury* and via this newspaper to *The Standard* in London in December 1885. The news moved too quickly and the election, whilst giving Gladstone a majority with 335 seats to 249 Conservatives also gave Parnell the balance of power with his 85 Irish members pledged to unified action, and the support of T. P. O'Connor returned for the Irish Catholic-dominated Scotland Road area of Liverpool. Hence the election victory was not a triumph but a badly timed tragedy: Gladstone, only recently committed in public to Home Rule, faced a growing Liberal Party revolt and the domination of Parnell in the Commons – the worst possible combination of parliamentary circumstances. It was in this situation that Home Rule made its first appearance as a full-blown legislative proposal in 1886.

UNIONISM AND THE FAILURE OF THE FIRST HOME RULE BILL

Gladstone was now being seen in a familiar role, as the champion of a cause, and this time the cause was Home Rule. However, his personal and political convictions were not necessarily matched by those of his party which could only see Ireland and its nationalist cause in the worst possible light. In fact, many members felt their suspicions were confirmed as Ireland once again succumbed to sectarian violence in 1886. Not all of the Liberal opponents considered the problem dispassionately. Lord Hartington, leader of the Whigs, was the brother of the murdered Lord Cavendish. Joseph Chamberlain and some of the radicals were bitter about not being consulted by Gladstone over his publicized change of heart on the Irish issue. But, without doubt, the greatest opposition came from those in the Liberal Party who saw Gladstone's conversion as a betrayal of England and Ireland, and more particularly the Union of 1801 that bound the two nations together for better or worse. These Unionists found their champion in Lord Randolph Churchill whose belligerent cry of 'Ulster will fight and Ulster will be right' became the rallying point for all Unionists.

Churchill's playing of the 'orange' card was something of a trump. He found ready support in the Liberal Party and excited much sectarian unrest in Ireland with the southern nationalists in particular seeing in Churchill a return to Protestant dominance at the head of an Irish province subjected to an English Parliament and a Protestant Church. Such fears, born of old, and revived in the present climate can be seen in the nationalist response to the Unionist call. Churchill visited Ireland in 1886 to galvanize Northern Irish Protestant Unionist feelings with all that implied – 'No Surrender', 'No Popery', and violence. While the Nationalists were caricatured in the Unionist and English press, the Unionists too were caricatured in the Nationalist press, baying for blood in a senseless outburst of sectarian feeling. It was in these difficult circumstances that Gladstone rose in the Commons on 8 April 1886 to introduce the Home Rule Bill. He was acutely aware of the difficulties before him and at pains to portray the measure as some kind of modification of the Act of Union rather than its abolition, simply to make the measure more palatable to the Commons. There was no doubt that Gladstone was handling political dynamite not only in terms of Anglo-Irish relations but also in party political and career terms. Equally so, Parnell was faced with difficulties. He had to placate the Nationalist sentiment, contend with Unionist criticism, and all at a time when the ordinary Irishman was faced with intense agricultural distress that would last two years and that would soon give power back to the Land League and an orchestrated campaign of disturbance and violence. Finally, Parnell needed to be wary of clutching at any measure offered by the Liberals and ensure that Home Rule did not result in a political cover-up which gave Ireland independence in name only.

The Bill was wide ranging. It proposed to establish an Irish legislature in Dublin which would be formed of two 'orders'. The upper chamber would number twenty-five peers plus seventy-five others elected for ten years on a £25 per annum land-owning franchise. The lower chamber would be Ireland's 103 members of Parliament plus a further 101. The upper assembly could veto for three years maximum. The Lord Lieutenant was the nominal executive responsible to the Irish Parliament. Westminster reserved a long list of rights over the Crown and the succession, peace and war, defence forces, treaties, titles, honours, treason, trade, navigation, posts and telegraphs, lighthouses, coinage, weights and measures, and copyright and patents. It was not this list however, that proved to be the stumbling block on the Irish side. Written into the Bill was the exclusion from Westminster of Irish peers and members of Parliament. This was rejected by Irish members because the Bill also included the vexed question of 'imperial dues' which were charges made on the Irish by Westminster. In addition the Irish also raised the famous cry of 'no taxation without representation'. The Bill seemed to ignore the right of those who paid to have a say in how the money was to be spent. Wranglings about the 'imperial dues' caused the sum to be lowered from two-seventeenths to one-fifteenth of the costs of the Royal Irish Constabulary, the Civil Service, debt repayments, etc., which would total £8.5 million. Such a burden would leave the Irish Parliament with a paltry £400,000 per annum to spend. It was too little for effective government and Parnell's plea for a 'due' of one-twentieth was ignored. If Home Rule went through it would be a travesty of independence and Ireland would become the even poorer relation. Although in favour of Home Rule and the measure, which Parnell 'applauded' in spirit, the Bill itself was blemished by great 'faults and blots'. The opposition from the Nationalists was matched by the cries from the Unionists, Ulster, Gladstone's Liberal opponents and the Conservatives. Some objected simply on Unionist grounds, others thought that the particular measure was at fault, and yet more saw the Bill as an unwelcomed test case for the British Empire clearing the way for India to become the next territory to break away from the imperial hold. The debates raged throughout the spring and early summer but defeat became inevitable and the Bill fell by a surprisingly close 343 against to 313 for. Ninety-three Liberals had voted against the measure and an election was called. The result gave the Liberals a much smaller return of 191 seats, the Conservative and Unionist group 314 and Parnell 86.

The defeat of Home Rule did not bring to an end the arguments about Ireland's future. Gladstone may well have been, in Churchill's words, 'an old man in a hurry' but his opponents knew that time was on their side. With renewed agitation for land reform under the so-called 'plan of campaign' launched in October 1886, all the poison released by Home Rule could air itself again. The violence was met by stern government, this time administered by the new Conservative Chief Secretary for Ireland, Arthur Balfour. His initial reaction to outlaw the 'plan of campaign' in December 1886 and pass a Criminal Law Amendment Act in

July 1887 helped to earn him the name 'Bloody Balfour'. However, as before 'kicks' were followed by 'kindness', and he relaxed the Coercion Act in 1890, helped to relieve distress with Public Works in the winter of 1890–1, and then unveiled his own Land Purchase Bill in 1890. It provided for total financial assistance spread over forty-nine years, the establishing of a central department to deal with land, and, in those areas where tenant holdings were too small to make purchase viable, Balfour allowed for the promotion of industry, assisted migration, and the combination of smaller holdings into larger ones. It was however, amidst all this that Parnell's career and life suddenly came to an end.

Whilst agrarian crimes and violence once more adorned the pages of English newspapers *The Times* prepared to scoop them all. On 18 April 1887 it published a series of letters on Parnell and crime in which it tried to establish the connection between the leader of the Nationalist cause and the Phoenix Park murders in 1882. The same letter is reproduced at the beginning of this chapter in which it was claimed that Burke 'got no more than his deserts'. There was an outcry and an immediate call for explanations. Parnell knew the letters to be forgeries, but such was the feeling against him that all too many people, leading politicians amongst them, were keen to believe in his guilt. It was noticeable that Gladstone remained quiet for the most part on the question of Parnell's complicity. Parliament established a Parnell Commission to investigate the allegations and the case finally went to open court in 1889. It was here that Richard Pigott, a forger and fraud, under Sir Charles Russell's cross examination, admitted to forging the letters. Parnell's reputation had been saved; Pigott absconded and committed suicide in Madrid on 1 March 1889. However, the Parnell Commission reported in 1890 that, although the letters were forgeries and Parnell had not approved of murder, the Irish members, including their leader, had entered into a conspiracy against the payment of agricultural rent and had incited Irish people to the crime of intimidation. Where the forgery plot had emanated from never became clear, although some have suggested that it was an ill-conceived attempt by English politicians to discredit Parnell. As Boyce has suggested:

> The Unionists could offer firmness [and] use state coercion when appropriate, and indeed connive at, or encourage, the attempt made in 1887 to blacken Parnell's name by associating it with the Phoenix Park murders.
>
> (D.G. Boyce, *The Irish Question and British Politics 1868–1986*, London, Macmillan, 1988, p. 34)

In this context, 'Unionists' refers to those who broke away from the Conservative Party over Home Rule. If so, they failed miserably and it is interesting to speculate how much Parnell might have gained from this farce had it not been for another more telling scandal. Perhaps having failed to get their man one way those involved finally prevailed upon the obvious candidate who could get at Parnell another way – Captain O'Shea. The bombshell dropped in November 1890 when Parnell was cited as co-respondent in the divorce proceedings of Captain and Mrs O'Shea. Gladstone's open mind over the forged letters could not remain so over the question of divorce. His own moral and religious upbringing could not allow him to accept Parnell's actions. His own beliefs were reinforced by the outbursts amongst English Non-Conformists. Gladstone summed up the inevitable when he privately said: 'I fear a thunder-cloud is about to burst over Parnell's head, and I suppose it will end the career of a man in many respects invaluable.' Perhaps Gladstone's last words need amplification for it is true to say that he had some respect for Parnell as a politician, and more importantly as a 'restraining influence'. In public Gladstone could not afford to be so charitable and was forced to accept the moral condemnation of the Irish leader by the likes of the Welsh Non-Conformist minister Hugh Price Hughes who claimed that 'it would be an infamous thing for any Englishman to compel his chaste and virtuous Queen to receive as her first Irish Prime Minister an adulterer of this type'. Parnell wanted to meet criticism face on but the mass of public opinion, allied to public morality and bigotry, was against him. His stubbornness saw the split and breaking up of his party as the majority accepted the leadership of Justin McCarthy and the few remaining Parnellites turned to John Redmond. The whole sorry and disappointing tale came to a close shortly afterwards when the man who had been 'the pride of Erin's Isle' died on 6 October 1891, isolated, rejected and ostracized.

Although Parnell headed the drive towards Irish Home Rule and led his party, and country, into the fray his role in the overall context of Irish history may well have been ambivalent. The decision to ally with the Liberals in 1881–2 and to nail his colours to the Gladstonian Home Rule mast in 1885–6 could have denied the possibility of a peculiarly Irish 'revolution' in government. Instead he helped to create the conditions for an English-led 'revolution' in Irish politics which inevitably complicated matters, eventually ushering in an era of division and hatred. At the same time he helped to preside over an equally important 'revolution' in British politics that saw Liberalism lie down with Irish Nationalism, and Unionism take the side of Conservatism, thus drawing up the lines for an even more intense struggle over Irish affairs in the future. But, if Parnell was no more, the issue would not die, nor, so it seemed to many people, would Gladstone. He returned to government in 1892 and was in even more of a hurry than on the previous occasion. Home Rule for Ireland had become his sole ambition in the years that were left to him. His chances of success were small. Even if his massed forces of Liberals, Irish Nationalists and one Independent Labour member gave him 355 votes against the Conservative and Unionists' 315 it would not be in the Commons that the Bill would stand or fall, but in the Lords.

The Second Home Rule Bill was little different to the first, but those little differences made for very big political arguments. Irish members were to be reduced to eighty-one but allowed to sit at Westminster. However, it was felt unfair that they should be allowed to vote on all issues especially those that concerned only England, or Wales or Scotland. An argument raged about 'inclusion' which created the anomaly of Ireland influencing issues other than those that concerned her, or 'exclusion' which threatened to revive the old complaint of 'no taxation without representation'. The 'in-and-out' clauses provided for endless debate and needed the use of the guillotine for the Bill to achieve its Commons final vote and produce a majority of thirty-four in September 1893. However, the fledgling Bill stood no chance in the Lords and it suffered a 419 to 41 defeat in the following year. The Second Home Rule Bill had failed and Gladstone, who died four years later, gave way to Lord Rosebery. The new Prime Minister, no natural enemy of Home Rule, believed that it would languish and that 'England will have to be convinced of its justice' before it was finally granted. At least as pertinently, Home Rule, which had dominated parliamentary affairs for the past generation, would give way to other pressing concerns as the new century approached.

FROM HOME RULE TO REBELLION

Although imperial defence, budgetary concerns, European diplomacy and a welter of social and political issues would force the Ireland question off the centre stage it waited patiently in the wings for another entrance. The Conservative and Unionist ploy of trying to 'kill Home Rule by kindness' continued. Typical of this policy was the 1903 Land Act in which the Chief Secretary George Wyndham provided for an extension of the Irish tenants' right to buy, and backed this up with additional government help in the form of reduced interest charges and purchase costs met from public funds. In 1903 there were 500,000 tenant farmers in Ireland but by 1909 270,000 had negotiated purchases and a further 46,000 were pending. By the 1920s, as Professor Beckett has commented, 'Landlordism in rural Ireland had become a thing of the past.' Many could have sympathy with the words of Walter Long who in 1903 claimed that 'what the country wants now is rest and peace; steady, quiet, but firm administration, wholesome food and drink; she has had too much medicine lately.' It looked at first as though Long might get his wish but the devolution conference in 1904 revived Unionist fears and demonstrated that the Conservatives had not forgotten Ireland. Their tenure of office was about to end, and in the most dramatic of ways, allowing for the return of the Liberals astride a massive majority and with a crusading spirit glinting in their eyes. But this did not mean an immediate and automatic revival of Home Rule.

If this was the situation in 1906 when the Liberals were returned to government why was a Home Rule Bill finally passed in 1914? Several factors need exploring in order to piece together the puzzle and explain this turnaround in the fate of the Irish. First, there had been a deliberate and successful buildup of Irish nationalism. In the first instance this had been a cultural movement and grew out of a desire amongst men like Douglas Hyde, founder of the Gaelic League in 1893, to de-anglicize Ireland. With only 64,000 Gaelic speakers left in 1880 Ireland, it was felt, was in danger of losing its identity and heritage. New publications like the *Gaelic Journal* soon sprang up, as did the Gaelic Athletics Association, which promoted Irish sports and pursuits and not, in the words of Archbishop Croke of Cashel, 'such foreign and fantastic field-sports as lawn tennis, polo, croquet, cricket and the like'. Spurred on by the centenary of the great rebellion of 1798 such associations and clubs, despite the best efforts of their founders, did take on a greater significance. It is known that many sporting activities were organized by Sinn Feiners who were on the lookout for committed and fit young Irishmen, proud of their country's heritage. It is a short jump from asserting a separate cultural identity to asserting a separate political identity. More importantly the emergence of an aggressive nationalism provided an opportunity for Ireland to move away from Home Rule towards an even more radical concept of total political independence and the call for an Irish Republic. Typical of this trend was Arthur Griffiths, a Dublin printer, who founded the *United Irishman* in 1898 in which he preached the idea of 'Sinn Fein' ('Ourselves'). A few years later, in 1907, the Irish Republican Brotherhood was to appear and their message would spread through the pages of their own journal, *Irish Freedom*, established in 1910.

Second, as more extreme Irish nationalism appeared so too did a fresh wave of political interest that would ensure a warm welcome for any moves to revive Home Rule – Irish unionism, both of the North and the South. The starting point for the Ulster Unionists was expressed well enough by the Belfast Chamber of Commerce when it stated 'All our progress has been under the Union.' Certainly the prosperous north was a stark contrast to the relative economic decline of the predominantly agricultural south. The fear in the factories, the shipyards and the bust-ling prosperity of Belfast was that if Home Rule should finally come about, the influence of the depressed agricultural south would spread to all parts of Ireland. The contrast was cruelly drawn in Unionist propa-ganda with the usual implication on the one side that southern Ireland was populated by rough untutored thugs whose ways would soon destroy the grandeur of the north, if Ireland ever had to suffer the inequalities imposed by Home Rule. However, unionism was more complex than

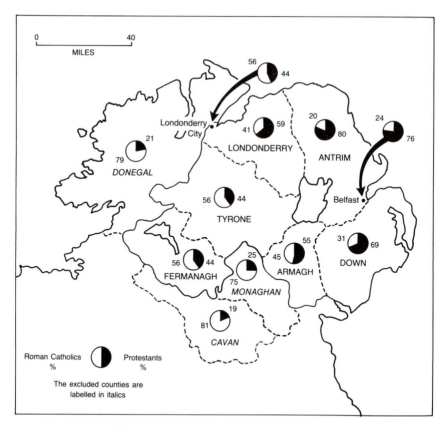

4.1 Northern Ireland – The Protestant and Catholic divide in 1911

just north versus south. In the north as the map of Ulster shows, the Protestant majority in some counties allowed for a far more broadly based unionism to appear, which cut across the social strata. By contrast in the south the population was 90 per cent Catholic and although unionism existed it was concentrated into very small unrepresentative groups formed of the older Anglo-Irish nobility, such as the Kavanaghs, wealthy industrialists including the Guinness family, and some academics at Trinity College, Dublin. Both sides of unionism saw the sense of a combined front and this led to the formation of the Irish Loyalist and Patriotic Union in 1885 which gave way in 1891 to the Irish Unionist Association, centred in Dublin. A broadly based organization with countywide branches, good finances and a centralized control complemented the Ulster equivalent and allowed unionism to present a solid front in the twentieth century. However, although both sides could agree on the desirability of maintaining the Anglo-Irish connection their approaches often diverged on specific issues. The greater problem, however, was that if the Home Rulers pushed their measure through the Ulster Unionists might have to be prepared to sacrifice the southern Unionists to ensure their own survival – in the event they moved with alacrity when the opportunity offered itself.

The third part of the puzzle came with the Liberals' programme of social reform. This had already been sweeping enough with the provision of pensions in 1908 and the financing of such a measure inevitably raised the question of who would pay. More worrying for many in the House of Lords was the fundamental question of who would rule Britain in the future. It was at this point that the Lords dug their feet in and the Liberals had to turn their attention towards the Lords themselves before any further progress could be made on their programme of legislation. It was in the midst of this protracted quarrel that the 1910 election saw the Liberals' massive 400-seat landslide of 1906 fall to 275, only two more than the Conservatives and Unionists. Even with the possible support of forty Labour Party members it was obvious that Redmond's Irish Parliamentary Party, which numbered eighty-two, would hold the balance of power. The political realities outweighed the political interest in Ireland. As in 1906 the question of Ireland had not predominated in the campaigns, speeches or pamphlets of this election but it was soon to be back on the political stage. Redmond, knowing the value of his Parliamentary Party to the Liberals' attempt to reduce the power of the Lords, could use this as a lever to lead the Liberals towards Home Rule.

The logic of events now took over with the Liberals successfully passing their 1911 Parliament Act which reduced the powers of the Lords permitting them merely to delay the passage of a bill for up to three sessions, or two years. The warning sirens had already been sounding in Ulster and the Unionists there were quick to respond. They knew full well that the Conservative majority of 257 in the Lords that had been their great safety cushion in the past could not protect them much longer. Moreover, there was the additional worry that with Home Rule a foregone conclusion the Lords might bend to the 144 peers with Irish interests, 116 of whom had connections in the South. With this in mind the Union needed defending as never before and the work started in earnest. If any further spur was needed, it came when the Liberals acknowledged Redmond's help in reducing the Lords' power by the presentation to Parliament of the third Home Rule Bill.

The Unionist attack on what was in reality a measure little different to those that had been proposed on the first and second occasions of Home Rule, was both broad and intense. The usual objections were raised. Home Rule would aid the break-up of the United Kingdom and leave Ireland with a say in English affairs while England had no reciprocal rights. This was graphically expressed in the Lords by Lord Oranmore and Browne who commented 'not only do they take the outer works but leave forty-two spies within the fortress'. The economic consequences of Home Rule also exercised the minds of the Unionist propagandists with its emphasis on Ulster as 'prosperity province'. The vexed question of safeguards also was raised and especially so for those 250,000 Unionists outside Ulster. In Munster, for instance, only 2 out of 223 councillors were Unionists but the latter, as a group, paid half the rates and taxes in Munster. Ideas, like that of Walter Guinness for proportional representation, were floated but rejected. Moral objections were raised on the grounds that it was wrong to compel a substantial minority to accede to a larger majority. Others feared for the Empire and what the passage of Home Rule might mean for India and other imperial territories.

In Ulster the movement against Home Rule was obvious and strong. Since 1910, under the leadership of Sir Edward Carson, Unionists had been marshalling their forces. His great standing and popularity in Ulster was clear for all to see. It was Carson who organized the Ulster Unionists on Covenant Day, on 28 September 1912. The Covenant was an impassioned and emotional statement and appeal signed by 200,000 Ulstermen on that September day.

While Carson was ordering the ranks of the Ulster Unionists the Unionists of the south were using their considerable influence to very good effect in the Conservative Party ranks and the House of Lords. This southern Unionist influence was all the more important at a time when Conservatives, after terrible squabbles over tariff reform, were looking for a major issue to unite the remnants of a disparate and dispirited party. Home Rule proved to be the issue and the Unionists made as much of it as they could. Ably fought by the Unionist Andrew Bonar Law the Home Rule Bill although it passed through the Commons met the Lords head on. An orchestrated Unionist campaign in the Lords kept the issue of Home Rule off the statute book for as long as possible.

With Ulster rapidly arming itself under Carson, and his Ulster Volunteers being matched by the Nationalist equivalent, the Irish Volunteers, there was a need for strong leadership and decisive action. Asquith, Liberal Prime Minister, provided neither. He did not prevent either side from arming itself, he did not pursue the policy of Ulster's inclusion or exclusion beyond an unsatisfactory compromise which Carson described as 'a sentence of death with a stay of execution for six years', and he did not negotiate fully with Redmond. It was hardly surprising that, given the emotions raised, there was real fear of civil war in Ireland. The two sides were prepared for it with each receiving large shipments of arms and the injection of substantial sums of money, from both Germany and the United States. The final straw was the government's realization that if it had hoped to control the situation by force, then it could not rely on the armed forces. The so-called Curragh incident, when fifty-eight cavalry men at the Curragh made it plain that they would prefer to be dismissed rather than take up arms against Irishmen, put an end to any ideas of forcing the sides to submit. One last desperate attempt was made by the King's personal intervention and the calling of the Buckingham Palace Conference on 21 July 1914, but it broke up after three days with no conclusions drawn on either side. What might have happened next is open to some debate given the level of emotional feeling and military preparedness.

In the end an even greater disaster befell the British government but it at least served to postpone potential civil war in Ireland, but at the cost of European conflagration – for within days Britain was at war with Germany.

An Act of Parliament, granting Home Rule, no matter how much it was criticized, seemed to many to be a final enough measure. Even if the Bill was to be delayed until the war was over it would nevertheless become law at some time in the future. This was the view of many, but not all, and one group in particular reacted against the measure. While the majority of Irish Nationalists rallied to the English flag in the years of war some extreme elements used this co-operation as an excuse to further their own ends and increase support. Redmond backed Britain and 169,000 of the Irish Volunteers joined him, many joining the forces to fight against Germany, but a small minority of 11,000 rejected Redmond's call, just as they rejected Home Rule rather than full independence, and constitutional tactics only. It seemed to these extremists that a symbolic show of force and determination was necessary. The end result of such an event may well be death and failure but perhaps it would be sufficient to stimulate the Irish appetite for a fully independent Irish state and not the vague promises of the suspended Home Rule Bill. On this basis, members of the Irish Republican Brotherhood, including Pearse, Plunkett, Ceannt, MacDonagh, Clarke, MacDermott and Connolly, made preparations for a rising in Dublin in 1916. The plan was to organize parades and manoeuvres for Easter Sunday, 23 April 1916, but this was to be a front for a real rising. These plans were kept from Eoin MacNeill, leader of the renegade minority Irish Volunteers until 20 April at which point, fearing the worst and knowing that plans and arms shipments had gone astray, MacNeill ordered all units to ignore the instructions for 23 April. His note to this effect was brief and clear but the story did not end here because MacNeill was persuaded to countermand the order and the Irish Republican Brotherhood met and voted in favour of continuing the rising even though the chances of success were now nil.

On the Easter Sunday a small force seized key locations including the Dublin Post Office which became the headquarters for the self-styled leaders of the new Irish Republic. One of them, Pearse, in his proclamation, said they were acting 'in the name of God and of the dead generations from which she receives her old traditions of nationhood'. The 1,600 or so insurgents stood no chance against the British army and were soon overwhelmed. They surrendered in order to save lives, but not before 450 dead, 2,600 wounded, £2.5 million worth of damage was caused and 100,000 of Dublin's population were in receipt of relief. After the surrender, on 29 April 1916, the government still had to impose martial law, but the leaders were rounded up and fifteen of them were executed between 3 and 12 May. It was as if, according to Bernard Shaw, 'the British were canonising their prisoners'. The failures of 1916 suddenly became the martyrs of another great and glorious rebellion in the best Irish traditions. Not only were the martyrs elevated but they ensured the deflation of the nationalist cause in the hands of the bland, complacent and seemingly ineffective Redmond.

The rebellion was a spur to political leaders to find a solution to Ireland's problems. But even Lloyd George found the Redmond call for immediate Home Rule balanced by the Carson claims on Ulster's behalf. The southern Unionists were yet another complicating factor as was cabinet opposition to Lloyd George's high-handed tactics of trying to present the Cabinet with a *fait accompli*. However, where British politicians failed the 1916 rebellion succeeded and in 1917, trading on the rising, Sinn Fein took Roscommon in February and Longford in May. Both election successes relied not only on the emotional response of 1916 but improved organization of the extreme Nationalists. A further spur was provided in 1918 when the government's ineptitude over the 1916 rising was matched by the conscription crisis. With another large German offensive in 1918 troops were in short supply. The levy of 1916 was badly depleted and another was needed but this time it was intended that Irishmen should not escape – forgetting the many tens of thousands who had joined willingly in 1914. The new call-up excited even more nationalistic passions.

It was hardly surprising then that in the immediate post-war election the Nationalists did particularly well. The December returns gave Éamon de Valera, the new leader of the Sinn Fein group who took over from Arthur Griffiths in October 1917, seventy-three seats. The former Parliamentary Party managed just six, and the Unionists twenty-six. It was symptomatic of the new breed of Irish Nationalists that thirty-four of those elected were serving terms in gaol at the time of their election. So too was the tactic of refusing to take their seats, preferring a meeting in Dublin in January 1919 to the opening of Parliament.

Hopes for an easy post-war settlement disappeared with the re-forming of the Irish Volunteers who were reconstituted in 1919 as the Irish Republican Army (IRA). The government's response was to answer force with force and it relied on ex-army personnel (who became known as the Black and Tans because of their dress) and on a number of auxiliary divisions. As Professor Beckett has claimed what happened next was a struggle

fought between two largely irresponsible military organisations, in circumstances where the normal laws of war could hardly be said to apply and the main object of each side was to break the morale of the other by a system of terrorism.

(*The Making of Modern Ireland, 1803–1923*, London, Faber, 1966, p. 448)

The IRA 'flying columns' and the 'squad' of Michael Collins, a leading figure in IRA military operations, started to put pressure on the authorities. In 1919 seventeen policemen were killed. By 1920 the number had risen to 165 with a further 251 wounded, and 89 civilians losing their lives. Despite the government reprisals that matched the IRA in savagery and senselessness the condition of Ireland was deteriorating fast. There was insecurity of life and property, the breakdown of normal behaviour and the imposition of martial law in most areas. In fact by January 1921 eight out of twenty-six southern counties were constrained under this system.

The government tried to legislate its way out of 'the Troubles' but the measure they proposed in September 1920, which became law in December of that year, was far from satisfactory. It was a Home Rule Bill that provided for the division of Ireland into two. Northern Ireland comprised the six Ulster Protestant counties and Southern Ireland comprised twenty-six counties, each part having its own upper and lower house and responsible ministry. However, imperial parliamentary rights were totally preserved and England could be accused of trying to solve an Irish situation of 1920 with the methods of 1914. Certainly both sides made their views plain in the elections of 1921. In the North the Unionists returned forty of the fifty-two seats in the Commons. In the South Sinn Fein swept the board with 124 of 128 seats but, true to tactics, refused to take up any of them. In fact, Sinn Fein had only agreed to the election in order to demonstrate the strength of feeling behind them. Obviously, the new act, known as the Government of Ireland Act, simply was not going to live up to its name. Long before the early summer elections of 1921 it had failed. In Ireland the Nationalists were already establishing and working their own government and legal system. It was only Lloyd George's willingness to negotiate with Sinn Fein and through the good offices of the King that talks continued throughout the second half of 1921, resulting in a treaty of agreement on Tuesday 6 December. The Irish Free State (the counties of Southern Ireland) would become a self-governing dominion within the Empire, a status akin to that of Canada. Britain would be responsible for coastal defences and have the right to maintain naval bases. A separate Parliament would come into being but an oath of loyalty would be demanded. As for Ulster she could secede at any time by formal demand to the imperial Parliament and would revert to her position under the original act of 1920 but this applied only to the six counties. The key vote was that of the Nationalists and they just passed the proposal by sixty-four votes to fifty-seven with de Valera resigning. De Valera's so-called wild-men started a campaign of violence that was met by the moderates and civil war raged between those in favour and those against the treaty. It lasted from early 1922 through to 1923, and was very bloody as private vendettas, ambush, murder and destruction were waged by 'regular' and 'irregular' sections of the IRA. The new Free State government continued its work in spite of the violence and agreed to a constitution in June 1922. It was forced to imprison and execute many Irishmen to bring peace to the new state but bring peace it did. The constitution came into force on 6 December 1922 and a day later the North exercised its right to secede, which it did in the spring of 1923.

CONTROVERSY: EASTER 1916

There is no doubt that the Irish question or problem was a multi-faceted historical phenomenon, and of course for the contemporary historian it still is. The complex nexus of issues and competing groups have complicated the events that have taken place in Ireland. As one would expect these different and competing groups have taken their own stance on the issue of Ireland and likely solutions to its problems. Indeed the question of Ireland depends upon one's standpoint and assumptions. A Nationalist has a rather different perception of Ireland and its future than a Unionist. More often than not English politicians are caught in the middle, uncertain about which path to follow, and by doing nothing or presenting a broad compromise they often exacerbate the whole issue. Thus the intractable nature of the Irish question can be seen. Easter 1916 and the attempted rising in Dublin can be used as a precise example of these difficulties and the nature of the Irish problem.

Eoin Neeson has given a nationalistic and positive assessment of both the organization and the ideas behind the rising. This is complemented by a genuine belief that the rising would be a lead to others who would take the struggle for independence on to another plane.

> In the context of the period the Rising was initiated by a small group of men whose vision was *both* social and political reform *and both of* which were contrary to the inclinations of the majority of the people of the country in 1916. Their ideals were, as it were, radical and ahead of their time and were not consonant with the more conservative pattern of recent (but now halted) progress in Irish political affairs. The men who planned the Rising were well aware of this, and, indeed suspected that their action could hardly, of itself, produce the reforms which they desired: it might, they hoped, induce them.
>
> (E. Neeson, *The Life and Death of Michael Collins*, Cork, Mercier Paperbacks, 1968, p. 22)

However, Neeson goes on to explain that not all was success and cites Michael Collins, the leader of the reformed Irish Volunteers, who was amongst those arrested and a self-confessed man of violence:

> He was now a man of mature judgement, whose opinions were the result of personal deliberation rather than emotive historical tradition, and who would write:
> 'On the whole I think the Rising was bungled terribly, costing many a good life. It seemed at first to be well organised, but afterwards became subject to panic decisions and a great lack of very essential organisation and co-operation.'
>
> (ibid., p. 24)

As one might expect the rising was seen in a different light by those in Ulster and Steve Bruce encapsulates some of the province's feeling about the events of 1916:

> However, Protestant opposition to 'Rome rule' was not eradicated. If anything, it had been reinforced by the republican 'Easter Rising' in Dublin in 1916 and the violent struggles which followed it. For the Protestants, the rising was proof positive of the treachery of the Catholics who had waited until Britain was occupied in a bloody struggle for democracy and freedom, and then attacked from the rear.
> (S. Bruce, *The Religion and Politics of Paisleyism: God Save Ulster*, Oxford, Oxford University Press, 1986, pp. 14–15)

Other similar loyalist attitudes can be found and the next extract deals with the events in a purely matter of fact way but the disdainful final line in the extract belies the real concern at the time which was shown by both sides in Ireland itself:

> Irish units for the main part contained the rebellion at the outbreak. The Dublin populace, many of whom had dear ones in the trenches or their wartime dead to mourn, jeered the rebels as they passed between their captors. Not many of the prisoners suffered death or even lengthy imprisonment.
> (J. Biggs Davidson, *The Hand is Red*, London, Johnson, 1973, p. 90)

Even the Nationalists were divided amongst themselves. Some groups were highly critical of the party's leadership as suggested by the writer James Stephens who took Redmond to task:

> Why it happened is a question that may be answered more particularly. It happened because the leader of the Irish Party misrepresented his people in the English House of Parliament. On the day of the declaration of war between England and Germany he took the Irish case, weighty with eight centuries of history and tradition, and he threw it out of the window. He pledged Ireland to a particular course of action,

and he had no authority to give this pledge and he had no guarantee
that it would be met.

> (L. de Paor, *The Peoples of Ireland*, London, Hutchinson, 1986,
> pp. 286–7)

However, Redmond was concerned with the broader issues, too, but
also the political realities of work in Westminster as the extract from
one of his letters shows:

> You should urge strongly on the government the *extreme* unwisdom
> of any wholesale shootings of prisoners. The wisest course is to execute
> *no one* for the present. This is *the most urgent* matter for the moment.
> If there were shootings of prisoners on a large scale the effect on
> public opinion might be disastrous in the extreme.
>
> *So far* feeling of the population in Dublin is *against* the Sinn Feiners.
> But a reaction might very easily be created. . . . Do not fail to urge
> the government not to *execute any* of the prisoners.
>
> I have no doubt if any of the well-known leaders are taken alive
> they will be shot. But, except the leaders, there should be no court-
> martial executions.
>
> (Quoted in F. S. L. Lyons, *John Dillon*, London, Routledge & Kegan
> Paul, 1968, p. 373)

It was not simply a matter of reacting to events. Some politicians needed
to be made aware of the wider implications as Redmond obviously was.
Others and especially those on the fringes could afford the luxury of
criticism. And yet others chose to widen the arguments even further such
as George Bernard Shaw, who noted that Britain's defence in August
1914 of the rights of a small nation, Belgium, seemed to place her in a
difficult position over another small nation, Ireland, in 1916:

> Be very careful what political doctrine you preach. You may be taken
> at your word in the most unexpected directions.
>
> I wonder how many of those who have made such resounding
> propaganda of Sinn Fein for small nationalities for twenty months past
> would have died heroically for their principles in the burning ruins of
> the General Post Office in Sackville Street.
>
> (*New Statesman*, 6 May 1916)

The multiplicity of concerns and conflicting interpretations surrounding
Dublin in 1916 can be gleaned from the extract below:

> But as often myth extinguished fact. The blood of the Easter sacrifice
> proved the seed of a republican harvest. The Government veered over
> to conciliation. Asquith devised a new Home Rule Bill. The rising
> also had the effect of reinvigorating Northern resistance to Home Rule
> and of dashing the hopes of some who dreamed that an autonomous

Ireland connected with Britain could bury the differences of Orange and Green in the graves of France and Flanders.

(J. Biggs Davidson, op. cit., p. 91)

It is hardly surprising that the Irish question remains intractable both for historians and politicians.

BIBLIOGRAPHY

For an explanation of the grading system, see the preface p. xiii.

Biographies

H. H. Asquith

3   Jenkins, R., *Asquith*, London, Collins, 1964
3   Koss, S., *Asquith*, London, Allen Lane, 1976

A. J. Balfour

See bibliography on p. 107.

I. Butt

3   Thornley, D., *Isaac Butt and Home Rule*, London, MacGibbon & Kee, 1964

E. Carson

3   Hyde, H. M., *Carson: The Life of Sir Edward Carson, Lord Carson of Duncairn*, np, 1953

Lord R. Churchill

See bibliography on p. 107.

M. Davitt

3   Sheehy-Skeffington, F., *Michael Davitt: Revolutionary, Agitator and Labour Leader*, London, MacGibbon & Kee, repr. 1967

J. Dillon

3   Lyons, F. S. L., *John Dillon: A Biography*, London, Routledge & Kegan Paul, 1968

W. E. Gladstone

See bibliography on p. 64.

C. S. Parnell

2   Bew, P., *C. S. Parnell*, Dublin, Gill & Macmillan, 1980
3   Cruise O'Brien, C., *Parnell and his Party, 1880–90*, Oxford, Oxford University Press, 1957
3   Lyons, F. S. L., *The Fall of Parnell, 1890–91*, London, Routledge & Kegan Paul, 1960
3   Lyons, F. S. L., *Parnell*, Dundalk, W. Tempest for the Dublin Historical Association, 1813
2/3   Lyons, F. S. L., *Charles Stewart Parnell*, London, Collins, 1977

J. Redmond

3   Gwynn, D., *The Life of John Redmond*, np, 1932

Secondary works

2/3   Beckett, J. C., *The Making of Modern Ireland, 1803–1923*, London, Faber, 1966
2/3   Boyce, D. G., *The Irish Question and British Politics 1868–1986*, London, Macmillan, 1983
3/4   Buckland, P. J., *Irish Unionism*, in two vols, Dublin, Gill & Macmillan, 1972–3
1   Buckland, P. J., *Irish Unionism*, HA pamphlet, HA, 1973
3   Corfe, T. H., *The Phoenix Park Murders: Conflict, Compromise and Tragedy in Ireland 1879–1882*, London, Hodder & Stoughton, 1968
2/3   Kee, R., *The Green Flag: A History of Irish Nationalism*, London, Weidenfeld & Nicolson, 1972
3   Lyons, F. S. L., *The Irish Parliamentary Party 1890–1910*, London, Faber, 1951
2/3   Lyons, F. S. L., *Ireland Since the Famine*, London, Weidenfeld & Nicolson, 1973
2/3   Mansergh, N., *The Irish Question 1840–1921*, London, Allen & Unwin, 1965
1/2   Morton, G., *Home Rule and the Irish Question*, London, Longman, 1980
2   Nowlan, K. B., *The Making of 1916*, Dublin, Stationery Office, 1969
1   Winstanley, M. J., *Ireland and the Land Question 1800–1922*, London, Methuen, 1984

Sources for coursework

The various biographies mentioned above contain a certain amount of primary material in the form of correspondence and excerpts from diaries and speeches. Parnell is probably the best served from this point of view. Obviously the *Gladstone Diaries* contain much useful information and revealing insights into the Gladstonian side of the story. The BBC publication, *Ireland: Some Episodes from her Past* (by H. Smith, London, BBC, 1974), is particularly useful as a source of material both written and visual, as is L. P. Curtis's *Apes and Angels: Irishman and Victorian Caricature*, London, David & Charles, 1971.

G. D. Zimmermann's compilation of *Songs of the Irish Rebellions 1780–1900: Political Street Ballads and Rebel Songs* (Hatboro', Pa, Folklore Assoc., 1967) will provide a useful artistic and emotional insight into the Irish feeling as does, of course, W. B. Yeats, *Collected Poems* (1950).

Other material of a primary nature will be less easy to find as most of it is kept in the national repositories in Belfast and Dublin. However, the new Centre for Irish Studies based at Liverpool University provides useful information about the location of materials for the study of Irish history.

5 Britain and the world 1867–1905: the onset of decline

INTRODUCTION

On 26 June 1897 thirty miles of ships were stretched out in six great lines off the coast at Portsmouth for the Spithead review, marking Queen Victoria's Diamond Jubilee. As *The Times* pointed out it was the greatest naval force the world had ever seen. It symbolized British world pre-eminence. A popular music-hall song of the decade celebrated this power with pardonable exaggeration:

> We are getting it by degrees, we are getting it by degrees,
> We get a bit here, we get a bit there,
> The Union Jack is everywhere,
> And now and then we give it a gentle squeeze.
> We haven't got quite the whole world yet – but we're getting it by
>   degrees.
>
> (Quoted in E. Chatfield, *The Navy and Defence*, London,
>   Heinemann, 1942)

Britain was the possessor of the world's greatest empire: a quarter of the world's surface and a fifth of humanity lay under the union flag. She was the single genuine world power. Only Britain through the agency of her fleet could project force to all corners of the globe. Yet 1897 was also the year when Germany outproduced Britain in steel. It was the year of Kipling's 'Recessional':

> Far-called, our navies melt away;
>   On dune and headland sinks the fire:
> Lo, all our pomp of yesterday
>   Is one with Nineveh and Tyre!
> Judge of the Nations, spare us yet,
> Lest we forget – lest we forget!
>
> (lines 13–18)

It is the image of power and expanding Empire that colours most people's perceptions of the years 1867–1905, yet it is also the period when the

Foreign Office began seriously to confront the problems of relative decline.

At the heart of this decline lay the performance of the British economy. Her outstanding world economic position in the 1860s has been briefly sketched in chapter 1. Perhaps two-thirds of world coal and half the world's cotton, cloth and iron were produced in this small damp island off the coast of Europe in that decade. Over the next forty years this economic pre-eminence disappeared. The growth in industrial production which had been 4 per cent in the 1820s and 1830s slowed to 1.5 per cent between 1875 and 1894. First the USA in the 1870s and then the new German Empire in the early twentieth century, overtook her as a centre of manufacture. In 1870 Britain had 32 per cent of the world's manufacturing capacity. By 1910 it was 15 per cent. Her share of world trade fell in the same period from 25 to 14 per cent. The roots of world power were withering even if the visible foliage seemed more impressive than ever.

The explanations of this decline are many and hotly debated. It was, in one sense, inevitable that such a tiny portion of the globe should fail to retain its outstanding position. As Disraeli put it in 1838 'The continent will not suffer England to be workshop of the world.' The greater resources of the USA, Germany and Russia would sooner or later dethrone Britain. This was only a partial explanation, as the success of Japan in the late twentieth century indicates. A small group of islands similar to Britain with even less resources has overtaken the United States as a centre of manufacture. Britain's neglect of education as one cause has already been referred to and has attracted the attention of contemporaries. The growth of trade unions in Britain hardened the economic arteries by imposing a barrier to change in work practices. There was an increasing tendency for Britain and British institutions to invest abroad where returns on capital were greater than at home. By 1914 there was a huge portfolio of investment overseas, totalling perhaps $20 billion. Four and a half billion of this was in the USA. British industries increasingly made do with obsolete machines and techniques.

More difficult to quantify and assess is the question of values and entrepreneurial spirit. It has been suggested that although Britain was the first industrial nation, a number of the pre-industrial values of her ruling elite survived to impair innovative and creative attitudes. Many manufacturers sought to forget the smell of oil and the clink of counting-houses and fled as soon as possible to rural retreats. The greatest social prestige belonged not to the engineer but to the lawyer, politician and academic, and most of all to the country gentleman. Oxford and Cambridge retained their educational prestige and with them the cult of the gentleman-amateur. The growth of the Empire reinforced these pre-industrial values. Clever young Britons could go out to Africa or India and rule millions instead of contributing to their country's GNP. Empire gave a new lease of life to a hierarchical society which might otherwise have died during industrialization. Whatever the predominating cause, national economic decline was a reality undermining Britain's world position at the turn of the century.

This world status was also threatened by other developments. The growth of the railways shifted the military balance of power away from navies and towards land forces. In the Crimean War of the 1850s, Britain had found it easier by using sea instead of land routes to supply and reinforce her armies than had Russia. In the early nineteenth century, the fire power of a warship was unmatched by any land-based artillery. A single first-rate man-of-war in 1815 had by weight more shot than all Napoleon's army at Waterloo. Railways and technical developments like the mine reduced the impact of Britain's premier instrument of force. Other nations also sought to build up their fleets and world domination so easily maintained at mid-century was now threatened. Britain might still have the largest fleet (which remained the case until 1944), but it was spread thinly and a nation such as Japan, which had a formidable naval force by 1900, could achieve a local superiority which Britain could only challenge by putting her interests at great risk elsewhere. The defence of the huge sprawling Empire became increasingly difficult and expensive. The naval estimates tripled between 1870 and 1900.

Britain found herself involved in disputes with several powers simultaneously. In 1897 there was an unresolved clash with the USA over Venezuela, a worsening situation in South Africa, disputes with France in West Africa and in the Nile Valley and a growing Russian challenge in northern China. In Europe the Russian threat to Constantinople was still taken seriously and unbeknown to the British government at the time, the German high command was examining the possibility of a lightning invasion of the British Isles via Holland in the event of war. The plan was rejected as impractical but in the following year the most deadly of threats to Britain began to take shape with the passing of the First German Navy Law. Germany was preparing to have a large fleet within striking distance of Britain. In addition to this multitude of problems there was the growing headache of how to protect British commerce from raiders on the high seas. The increasing dependency on foreign imports of food made Britain more vulnerable than at any time in her history to a '*guerre des courses*', and indeed this was the plan being formulated by the French navy. The splendour of British sea power was matched by the scale of the problems to which it might have to respond.

Despite these ominous signs British assets were enormous and growing. In the last thirty years of the nineteenth century an extra 60 million people and 4.5 million square miles were added to the Empire. Almost every vital strategic point on the globe was under British control, as Map 5.1 indicates. Gibraltar, acquired in 1703, guarded the entrance to the Mediterranean, and Malta (1815) its centre, while Cyprus (1878) and

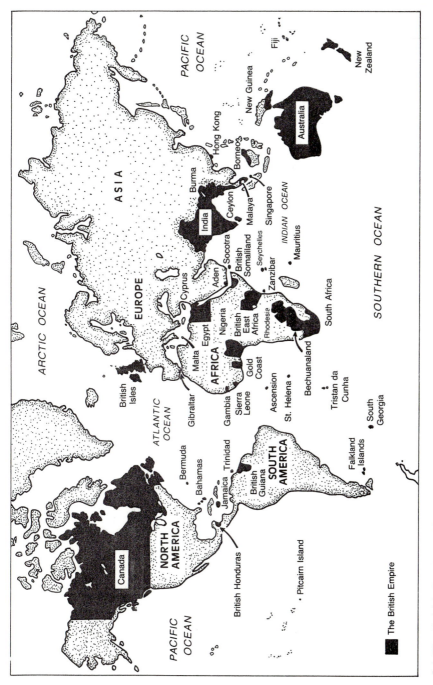

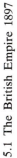

5.1 The British Empire 1897

Alexandria (1882) provided bases in the eastern Mediterranean. The Suez Canal was under British control as was the mouth of the Red Sea – Aden (1839). Kuwait passed to Britain in 1899 and other bases ringed the Indian Ocean. Singapore (1819) and Hong Kong (1842) gave bases in the Far East. British islands were liberally sprinkled across the Pacific. The Atlantic could be patrolled from the West Indies, Canada, West Africa or islands like St Helena. Cape Town (1815) and the Falklands (1834) guarded the tips of South Africa and South America respectively. The world's submarine telegraph cables were under British control. Much of the world's mineral wealth was either within the Empire – the tin of Malaya and the diamonds of Cape Province – or indirectly controlled by British companies, for example in South America. The British merchant marine was overwhelmingly the biggest, carrying 50 per cent of the world's trade. London was the world's financial capital and Britain's $20 billion of overseas investment comprised 40 per cent of the world total. Decline and weakness was not obvious to foreign observers. As E. Marcks, a German historian, has written:

> There had taken place, in the half-century or so before the [1914] war, a tremendous expansion of British power, accompanied by a pronounced lack of sympathy for any similar ambition on the part of other nations. . . . If any nation had truly made a bid for world power, it was Great Britain. In fact, it had more than made a bid for it. It had achieved it. The Germans were merely talking about building a railway to Bagdad. The Queen of England was Empress of India. If any nation had upset the world's balance of power, it was Great Britain.
>
> (Quoted in P. Kennedy, *The Realities Behind Diplomacy*, London, Fontana, 1981, p. 223)

'Whatever happens will be for the worse and therefore it is in our interests that as little should happen as possible.' Lord Salisbury in 1887 was expressing the basic truism that Britain was a satiated power and therefore conservative in world affairs. She sought no major transformation in the relationship of states. Winston Churchill, a quarter of a century later, made the same point but with greater cynicism: 'We have got all we want in territory and our claim to be left in unmolested enjoyment of vast and splendid possessions mainly acquired by violence, largely maintained by force, often seems less reasonable to others than to us.' With the possible exception of Disraeli in the 1870s and Chamberlain in the 1890s, there was widespread agreement with these sentiments. Britain sought peace and tranquillity, first, because she already had much and second, because the trade and growing financial service sectors in the City demanded it.

As with all states in all ages the security of their homeland was the prime concern. Every shade of political opinion would agree that this was best maintained by Britain's naval dominance. How far this naval supremacy needed to be taken was less obvious and more open to debate. The Liberal journalist W. T. Stead claimed that French naval spending was nearly as high as Britain's in 1884–5 and that the challenge to supremacy demanded action. Gladstone resigned in 1894 over his Cabinet's unanimous decision to back the Admiralty's demands for more ships but even he did not deny that British maritime supremacy was a fundamental interest. Luckily, throughout most of this period, and Stead's assertions notwithstanding, Britain was not really threatened until Germany began to construct a vast fleet. Nelson had destroyed the last great challenge in 1805 and it was not until exactly one hundred years later that a new deadly threat emerged.

Security might also lie in other courses of action. Traditionally it was felt that the independence of Belgium was a vital interest, ensuring that no single power should occupy the coastline opposite to Britain and thereby make invasion easier. Certainly Britain had guaranteed Belgium's neutrality in 1839 and sought to uphold it vigorously in the 1860s and again in 1914. More open to debate was the pursuit of a balance of power – the attempt by Britain to ensure that no one European state so dominated the continent that it might threaten the British Isles. Spain had been resisted in the late sixteenth century and France in the seventeenth and eighteenth centuries on these grounds. Within the Foreign Office and 'the official mind' there was an acceptance of this argument. Unofficial minds disagreed. John Bright in a speech at Birmingham in 1865 claimed:

> I think I am not much mistaken in pronouncing the theory of the balance of power to be pretty nearly dead and buried. You cannot comprehend at a thought what is meant by that balance of power. If the record could be brought before you – but it is not possible to the eye of humanity to scan the scroll upon which are recorded the sufferings which the theory of the balance of power has entailed upon this country.
>
> (Quoted in K. Bourne, *The Foreign Policy of Victorian England*, Oxford, Clarendon Press, 1970, p. 380)

Luckily for nineteenth-century Britain, Belgium was not seriously threatened and a balance of power seemed to exist without too much exertion by Her Majesty's Government. There was a happy interlude between the eighteenth-century menace of France and the threats posed in the twentieth century by the dynamic new German Empire. British foreign policy could at a pinch consist, as Salisbury put it, of 'floating lazily downstream occasionally putting out a boat-hook to avoid a collision'.

If Britain was secure other vital interests were not. Almost all agreed that the possession of India was essential. As Lord Curzon, Viceroy from

RIVAL SPORTSMEN.

" I say now, as I have said before, that there is room enough in Asia for both England and Russia."—Lord Beaconsfield.

1898 to 1905 was to put it: 'As long as we rule India we are the greatest power in the world. If we lose it we shall drop straight away to a third rate power.' Russia was seen as the enemy and sparring partner in the great game for control in Asia. Afghanistan offered an invasion route, and was a key pawn between the two contestants as the 1878 cartoon illustrated. The cartoon's presentation of a hunting competition fails to highlight the very real British interests involved. India was a major market for British cottons, but whether Curzon referred to this is doubtful. It was the romantic illusions of power that India gave which seduced both Curzon and Disraeli. Curzon failed to understand that British power rested not on her Empire, which was a consequence of power, but on her industrial pre-eminence. Britain lost India when she became a second-rate state in the late 1940s and could no longer afford the luxury of ruling the Raj. Whether India was, or was not, a vital interest is not what in the end matters. It is that most Britons in these years *felt* that it was and perception is sometimes of more consequence than reality.

The security of routes to India were likewise deemed 'vital' interests for which blood would be shed and treasure lost. The Cape of South Africa and Egypt in the north of the continent with the new Suez Canal provided the two alternatives and both were felt to be worthy of wars to secure these routes. By the 1890s control of Suez, the windpipe of the British Empire as it was later to be described, was felt to entail control of the whole Nile Valley and war with France was risked in 1898 to assure British possession. Thus new vital interests could arise. Likewise, interests could cease to be vital. Control of a Central American canal, mooted in the 1850s, was assumed to be of prime importance to Britain but in the early twentieth century when such a canal became a reality in Panama, Britain surrendered control of it to the USA. For much of the period in question most countries and informed opinion at home generally agreed that Britain would fight to keep Russia out of Constantinople and thereby deny her control of the Bosporus and Dardanelles Straits linking the Black Sea and the Mediterranean. Yet by 1897 Lord Salisbury had resigned himself to ultimate Russian possession of the city and merely hoped that the evil day could be put off.

A nation's foreign policy and international relations can, of course, be influenced by considerations other than security or hard-headed perceptions of economic interest. Many states have sought to spread ideological interests. Britain, as the world's most advanced state, saw herself as the vanguard of Liberalism and, other interests being absent, sought to advance freedom and constitutional government. As Lord Granville put it in 1852:

> In the opinion of the present Cabinet, it is the duty and the interest of this country, having possessions scattered over the whole globe, and priding itself on its advanced state of civilization, to encourage moral, intellectual and physical progress among all other nations.
>
> (ibid., p. 310)

Public pressure or genuine conviction on the part of politicians might lead to support for humanitarian causes such as anti-slavery. Public opinion could also force governments to consider national prestige. Disraeli embraced this notion with great enthusiasm but even the calculating mind of Lord Salisbury felt that public opinion must be respected on this issue.

'FLOATING LAZILY DOWNSTREAM' 1867–74

When Edward Stanley took over the Foreign Office from Lord Clarendon in June 1866, Clarendon's advice was 'Not to proclaim our determined inaction on every opportunity that arises – the policy of not meddling is of course the right one but it is not necessary that all mankind should be let into the secret twice a day.' Stanley made Great Britain's inaction perfectly clear and constantly let Europe know once a week if not 'twice a day'. Under successive Liberal and Conservative Foreign Ministers, Britain's influence on European affairs was negligible in the ten years after 1864. This arose from a combination of circumstances. The great upheavals of the Continent which involved three wars and the unification of Germany had Britain as a passive spectator. Public opinion in Britain had swung violently round from the strident nationalism of the Crimean War (1853–6) to an anti-war sentiment which seemed so well expressed by the two northern radicals – Richard Cobden and John Bright. Bright's views on the balance of power have already been quoted. To him, the whole diplomatic service was merely outdoor relief for the aristocracy. There was a widespread unwillingness to repeat the Crimean experience with its waste of blood and money. Britain had no continental force with which to assert her wishes, for public opinion would not tolerate conscription. The small professional British army was scattered throughout the world with the largest contingent kept in India since the Indian Mutiny of 1857. How could Britain face the massive armies of Prussia or Russia? As Bismarck had retorted in 1864 when it was put to him that Britain might intervene on Denmark's side against Prussia, 'We should send the police force to arrest them.' The country's humiliation over Denmark confirmed the Foreign Office in the essential rightness of non-intervention. After all, no real British interests were at stake. Prussia defeated Denmark, Austria and France without Britain feeling any heightened threat or concern. A strong Germany was, on the contrary, a useful check to the ambitions of Russia or France.

Clarendon resumed the Foreign Office in 1868 much to Queen Victoria's irritation. She found his sense of humour and lack of tact far from attractive. To Clarendon the Queen was always 'the missus' and his Prime Minister 'Merrypebble'.

Clarendon's chief problem was the growing tension between Prussia and France. He failed to produce an agreement on disarmament but helped to defuse at least one crisis. Bismarck later told Clarendon's daughter that had her father lived, there would have been no Franco-Prussian war. He died in June 1870 and his successor, Lord Granville, whilst his superior in tactful handling of the Queen rivalled Stanley in supine inactivity. The crisis over the Spanish throne which precipitated the war between France and Prussia blew up shortly after Granville took over. He let it develop without involvement. Possibly a firm warning from Britain could have produced a peaceful solution but Granville and firmness did not mix. He was not out of step with British public opinion, as one British diplomat was to put it, 'the war could have been prevented if for twenty-four hours the British people could have been furnished with a backbone'. Granville and the Cabinet contented themselves with seeking promises from the two countries that they would respect Belgian neutrality. These promises having been received on 16 and 19 July, the Foreign Office like the British people sat back to watch. Initially there was probably more sympathy with Prussia but reports of the suffering and heroism of the besieged Parisians later in the year swung opinion round to the French underdog.

Gladstone was far less inclined to passivity than his Cabinet. He disliked the Palmerstonian tradition of abrasive national self-assertion but he was heir, through his mentor the Earl of Aberdeen, to a policy of European involvement that went back to Lord Castlereagh (Foreign Secretary 1812–22). He believed in 'the pursuit of objects, which are European, by means which are European, in concert with the mind of the rest of Europe and supported by its authority'. He saw Britain as Europe's moral leader and Bismarck's attempts to rearrange Europe without reference to other powers was in clear breach of the 'concert' of Europe tradition. Gladstone's Liberal principles of belief in national self-determination were also outraged by the proposed transfer of Alsace and Lorraine from France to the new German Empire. As he presciently put it, 'this violent laceration and transfer is to lead us from bad to worse and to the beginning of a new series of European complications'. The Cabinet disagreed and inactivity continued to be the order of the day. A diplomatic initiative in 1871 might have enabled Bismarck to resist the pressure he was under from the army and the Kaiser to take Alsace and Lorraine. Nothing, however, was done and a major revolution in European affairs had taken place without British participation.

Gladstone's commitment to the 'concert of Europe' showed itself on another issue that arose out of the Franco-Prussian War. On 9 November 1870 London received news that the Russian government no longer felt bound by the Black Sea clauses of the Treaty of Paris that had ended the Crimean War in 1856. By these clauses Russia was forbidden to fortify naval bases or keep warships in the Black Sea. Turkey would thereby be partially protected from further Russian assault. The Russians were bluffed into thinking that Britain might go to war and agreed to attend a conference in London (December 1870–13 March 1871), on the understanding that they would get what they wanted. The Black Sea treaty clauses were abrogated but Gladstone felt he had upheld the principle that international treaties could not be broken unilaterally. To the Conservatives it was simply shutting the stable door after the horse had bolted – Britain had climbed down to Russia. In fairness to Gladstone he had exacted a major concession in getting the Russians to agree to accept modifications of the Straits Convention which regulated the passage of warships from the Mediterranean to the Black Sea. Russian ships were banned but with Turkish permission British ships could pass the Straits to threaten Russia.

Gladstone and Granville's commitment to international law is also well illustrated by their settlement of the long-running dispute over the commerce-raider *Alabama* sold by a British Merseyside firm to the Confederacy during the Civil War in America. After leaving Liverpool in 1862 the ship did enormous damage to shipping of the Northern states and the victorious North claimed compensation from Britain for her breach of neutrality. The issue dragged on due to the intransigence of Earl Russell and the extent of the US claims. In 1869 there was talk in the Senate of seizing Canada in compensation. The dispute with Britain's chief trading partner was clearly in nobody's interests and Gladstone rightly accepted that the USA had grounds for complaint. Eventually, by the Treaty of Washington of May 1871 Britain and the USA agreed to take their case to international arbitration. The USA was awarded $15.5 million against Britain, and Canada was to receive $7.5 million from the USA for damage to her economic interests caused by the war. The settlement was a sensible one and both Gladstone and Granville had shown great patience and determination. To the British public and the Conservative opposition it showed the government's 'strange mania for eating dirt', as Disraeli was to put it. Clearly it was not a glorious result and far from the eye-balling tactics of Palmerston, used in the past, yet it defended British economic interests and international law and in the long term it laid the foundations of British and American friendship.

The foreign policy of Gladstone's first ministry was clearly not exciting yet it is hard to argue that any essential British interests had been sacrificed. With the setting up of the *Dreikaiserbund* (literally 'three emperors league') in 1872, composed of Russia, Germany and Austria, Britain was more excluded than ever before from continental affairs, but this hardly bothered most Britons. Fog in the Channel meant 'Europe cut off'. Perhaps Granville and Gladstone did not see as clearly as Disraeli did the harm that might come to Britain from the *Dreikaiserbund*. A Russia that was secure in Europe with its western frontiers unthreatened could afford to risk antagonizing Britain in Asia by expansion towards the Indian frontier. The Russian seizure of Khiva, a key strategic point to the north of Afghanistan in 1873 caused concern in Whitehall.

DISRAELI'S GOVERNMENT 1874–80: 'PEACE WITH HONOUR'

'He believes thoroughly in prestige and would think it quite sincerely in the interests of the country to spend 200 millions on a war if the result

was to make foreign states think more highly of us as a military power.'
So wrote Stanley, Fifteenth Earl of Derby of his chief, Disraeli. Two
more ill-matched managers of foreign policy it would be hard to envisage.
Disraeli was an activist intent on recapturing Palmerstonian glories. He
wanted to re-establish British influence in Europe and correctly saw the
Dreikaiserbund as an obstacle to this. He was romantically attached to
the concept of India and the Indian Empire and also to the notion of
Britain as an Asiatic power. If all politics was a game to Disraeli then
foreign affairs presented it in its most exciting and challenging form. As
he had shown in his speeches in 1872 he believed that an appeal to
patriotism could also offer electoral rewards. The cult of Empire and
national greatness could win votes. His choice of Derby, Foreign Secretary as Stanley in 1866–8 before he inherited the title, is extraordinary
in view of his desire for activity. Stanley had lost none of his caution
and the relationship between Foreign Secretary and Prime Minister was
not going to be a happy one. It is surprising that Derby's resignation
was put off for four years.

The first real chance for a return to Europe came in May 1875. The
possibility of breaking the mould shaped by the *Dreikaiserbund* was very
real and excited 'Dizzy', if not Derby. The so-called 'war in sight' crisis,
is something of a mystery to this day. It appeared that Bismarck was
threatening another assault on France and Britain followed Russia's lead
in applying pressure on Bismarck to desist. Bismarck, of course, claimed
no such threat existed but it was enough that he backed off. Disraeli
was overjoyed at what he saw as a triumphant return to the European
league of big diplomatic players. As he wrote to Lady Bradford: 'I
believe since Pam [a reference to Palmerston] we have never been so
energetic and in a year's time we shall be more.' Derby appreciated the
reality of the situation and put it bluntly to Disraeli in a letter of 20
May 1875: 'We have been lucky in our foreign policy. What we did
involved no risk and cost no trouble, while it has given the appearance
of doing more than we really did to bring about the result.'

Later the same year the opportunity arose for the sort of bold dramatic
stroke that Disraeli so loved. The khedive (king) in Egypt was in financial
difficulties and had to raise large sums to pay for the interest due on
Egyptian debts by 1 December. He proposed to sell his 177,000 ordinary
shares in the Suez Canal company, which amounted to some 44 per cent
of the whole, the rest being held by French institutions. A French
syndicate proposed to buy up the khedive's holding but they reckoned
without Disraeli. Brushing aside the caution of Derby and other cabinet
colleagues, Disraeli rushed into the purchase of the shares by the British
Government. Not least of his problems was how to find £4 million in a
hurry when Parliament was not sitting. Disraeli's secretary, Monty Corry,
later told the tale that his chief, having got cabinet agreement, shouted
'Yes' to Corry, who promptly rushed off to Baron de Rothschild whom

he found at lunch. Corry requested '£4 million tomorrow'. Rothschild picked up a grape, ate it and spat out the pips. 'What is your security?' 'The British Government', came Corry's reply. 'You shall have it.' The deal went through and Britain became the largest holder of shares in the canal so essential to her trade. Europe was impressed and so was the Queen. Disraeli claimed 'the French government has been out-generaled'. In practice they had been very obliging, grateful for Britain's support in May. Despite this pardonable slip with the truth, Disraeli was right to be pleased with his achievement.

The centrepiece of Disraeli's foreign-policy excursions must be his handling of the so-called Eastern Crisis which began in 1875 and reached a climax in 1878. It raised many issues, some of limited concern, such as the reason for Britain's propping up the Turkish Empire in the 1870s, and others of abiding importance whenever foreign policy is considered. Should a nation pursue its own interests regardless of any higher moral concern? Seldom has the conduct of foreign policy so divided the country and so raised the political temperature.

5.2 The Balkans at the time of the 1878 Congress of Berlin

The Eastern Question related simply to the decline and possible collapse of the Turkish Empire, initially in Europe but, of equal concern to Britain, also in Asia. This empire comprised a vast assortment of territories which had come under Turkish rule in the fifteenth and sixteenth centuries and began to decay in the seventeenth. All decaying empires pose problems, not least what will fill the vacuum left behind. Britain had considerable economic interests at stake. The Ottoman Bank had a board of English directors and Britain supplied one-third of Turkey's imports. Perhaps more important Turkey was a barrier to Russian expansion. It was vital that Constantinople and the Straits should remain in Turkey's hands to keep the Russians out of the Mediterranean itself – the communication backbone of the British Empire. Turkey in Asia was likewise essential in keeping Russia from the Persian Gulf. As one British statesman said in the 1850s before the Crimean War, 'if we did not stop Russia on the Danube we should have to stop her on the Indus'. In Europe Turkey ruled a largely Slav, Greek Orthodox population who naturally looked to Russia as the greatest of the Slav powers. Russia herself saw the Turk as the national enemy. Russian tsars claimed to be the heirs of the East Roman Empire since Ivan III had married the daughter of the last Emperor at Constantinople. The liberation of that city was a Russian dream and the benefits of free access to the Mediterranean would be enormous. Such Russian ambitions worried not only Britain but also Austria who feared the destruction of the Turkish Empire as a preliminary to the break-up of her own, containing as it did many millions of subject Slavs. A Russian-dominated Balkans would at the very least reduce Austria to the level of a Russian satellite state.

The decay of the Turkish Empire was well underway by 1875. Greece had achieved independence in the 1820s and both Serbia and Romania effectively were independent in the 1850s. The Crimean War had temporarily extended the life of the Empire but the same ills of corrupt and inefficient government continued which Balkan nationalism found increasingly hard to bear. In 1875 Hercegovina and Bosnia rose in revolt. Austria feared their joining Serbia but appreciated that something had to be done, so Andrassy, the Austrian Foreign Minister, secured the support of all the European powers to issue a stiff warning to the Turks in December 1875, demanding reforms. Britain reluctantly agreed to this. Disraeli disliked the initiative coming from Vienna but saw the opportunity of fomenting divisions between Austria and Russia, and thereby breaking up the *Dreikaiserbund*. Nothing came of this 'Andrassy Note' and troubles continued in 1876. A Turkish mob murdered the French and German consuls in Salonika in Turkish Thrace (now Greece) in May. In April fresh anti-Turkish revolts had broken out in Bulgaria. Bismarck of Germany was primarily interested in preventing Austro-Russian conflict which could lead to the break-up of the *Dreikaiserbund*. On 13 May the *Dreikaiserbund* powers tried again with an even more forceful warning to the Turks to mend their ways. This Berlin Memorandum was rejected by Britain on 16 May. Disraeli even encouraged the Turks to reject it by sending the fleet to Besika Bay. Britain apparently stood alone against the *Dreikaiserbund*. In effect Disraeli called its bluff and heightened Britain's importance in Europe. As Disraeli wrote on 7 June:

> I look upon the tripartite confederacy to be at an end. It was an unnatural alliance, and never would have occurred had England maintained, of late years, her just position in public affairs.
>
> I think not only peace will be maintained, but that Her Majesty will be restored to her due and natural influence in the government of the world.
>
> (ibid., p. 128)

Britain's stand was applauded by the Marquis of Hartington, the new Liberal leader, and with a diplomatic triumph apparently safe in the bag Disraeli accepted an earldom from the Queen and went to the Lords. Already, however, as he accepted the title of Earl of Beaconsfield, problems were multiplying. News of appalling Turkish atrocities in Bulgaria set up more protests, particularly in the north of Britain. Disraeli initially sought to deny or play down Turkish inhumanity: I doubt 'that torture has been practised on a great scale.' Later in August he made the point that the upholding of British interests must remain supreme. 'What our duty is at this critical moment is to maintain the Empire of England.'

Gladstone, as we have seen, emerged from retirement in September to lead the campaign against Disraeli's stand. He was outraged at both the support given to inhuman butchers and also Britain's isolation from Christian Europe. Gladstone's Liberalism merged with the former Conservative tradition of espousing the 'Concert of Europe' to bring him to a pitch of moral indignation with Disraeli. As he wrote in a letter in August:

> Disraeli assumes his earldom amidst loud acclaims. I had better be mute about him and his influence generally, except as to a full acknowledgment of his genius and his good points of character. His government is supposed now to stand mainly upon its recent foreign policy: the most selfish and least worthy I have ever known. Whatever was open to any degree of exception in Palmerston, has this year received a tenfold development in Disraeli. Derby's influence, I think, has been for good; but too little of it.
>
> (Quoted in J. Morley, *Life of William Ewart Gladstone*, vol. III, London, Macmillan, 1903, p. 158)

The atrocity campaign resulted in paralysis in the government. The Cabinet was bitterly divided and public opinion made it impossible to support

Turkey. Derby's one initiative in the crisis was a conference at Constantinople. Reluctantly Disraeli agreed to Salisbury going as British representative. The conference met in December and Salisbury and the Russian representative, Ignatiev, made considerable progress towards agreement but to Disraeli's concern. As he complained to Derby: 'He [Salisbury] seems most prejudiced and not to be aware that his principal object in being sent to Constantinople is to keep the Russians out of Turkey, not to create an ideal existence for Turkish Christians.'

Disraeli need not have worried, the Turks refused all suggestions and the conference broke up having achieved nothing. Fresh demands were put to the Turks in what became known as the London Protocol, but without success. On 9 April Turkey rejected the demands, certain of secret British sympathy despite Britain's overt support for the reform package. This played straight into Russia's hands. As public opinion neutralized Britain and two deals with Austria in January and March in which she was promised Bosnia ensured her neutrality, Tsar Alexander II under the influence of Ignatiev and the Pan-slavists, declared war on Turkey. Russian troops advanced through the Balkans. Disraeli was dismayed yet helpless and the Queen was furious. 'It is not a question of upholding Turkey; it is a question of Russian or British supremacy in the world.'

The Cabinet would not hear of war. Not only the supine Derby but Salisbury too was opposed to war and support for the brutal Turks. In July 1877 Russian troops reached Plevna, just south of the Danube. Here they were heroically held by the Turkish garrison under Osman Pasha. It did not fall until 11 December 1877 and in these months British public opinion changed. By 1878 Turkish atrocities were forgotten and it was the Russian bully who was the object of popular hatred. On 20 January the Russians reached Adrianople and the Turkish capital seemed endangered. The Turks and the Russians signed an armistice in January and a peace in March. Salisbury became converted to the need to take firm action to deny Constantinople to the Russians. Derby opposed action, submitting his resignation first in January and having it accepted on a second submission in March. He was replaced by Salisbury who, in his own words, began 'to pick up the pieces of china'.

The Treaty of San Stefano that the Russians forced on the Turks was quite unacceptable to Britain. Although Constantinople remained in Turkish hands the large Russian garrison in the independent Bulgaria could seize it at any time. The 'new' Bulgaria also had a Mediterranean coast and as such gave the Russians access to that sea. Turkey in Europe was clearly at an end. The treaty was a victory for Ignatiev and the Russian 'hawks'. Gorchakov, the Russian Foreign Minister, saw the danger – Russia was isolated and bankrupt. Disraeli now gambled that Russia could be made to compromise without war. Warlike preparations were made. The British fleet had moved up to Constantinople in

February and in March the reserves were called up and Indian troops moved to Malta.

For two months it seemed war between Russia and Britain was possible but Salisbury, in a series of negotiations with Russia and Austria, secured a peaceful outcome. The 'doves' in Russia had gained the upper hand, in part simply because Russia could not afford a war. In May the outline of an agreement was reached and on 6 June agreement was made with Austria. The Turks finally accepted a settlement and reluctantly transferred Cyprus to Britain as an essential base for British support, particularly against Russia in Asia. For it was the Russian penetration of Asiatic Turkey which particularly worried Salisbury.

To ratify all the agreements a European Congress met in Berlin on 13 June 1878, and both Disraeli and Salisbury attended. It was the high point of Disraeli's career as he monopolized attention and seemed to have restored Britain to primacy in Europe. The 'new' Bulgaria was broken up and the southern section restored to Turkey, thus keeping Russian influence from the Mediterranean and pushing the threat to Constantinople further away. Russian troops were to be withdrawn and Austria was to gain control of Bosnia and Hercegovina. On the eastern side of the Black Sea Russian gains were limited, ensuring that the vital Trebizond–Tabriz caravan route was kept in Turkish hands. Disraeli returned in triumph to the offer of a dukedom and the order of the garter. He refused the first but accepted the latter on condition that Salisbury too received it, a fitting reward for the man who had done all the detailed work.

Whether the Turkish Empire really could be put together again Salisbury doubted. The best that could be hoped for was a period of calm in which Britain could strengthen her position in Asia. Turkey would be helped with money and advice and would in some respects resemble a British protectorate. Yet this position could crumble rapidly and indeed the whole settlement fell apart seven years later. Nevertheless, in 1878 the position was viewed as successful and had there been an election in the autumn of that year Disraeli would probably have returned with a comfortable majority. His description of 'Peace with honour' was widely accepted. Twelve months later his position had deteriorated, not only with the onset of economic recession (see chapter 3), but through two unlooked-for colonial disasters. Both Disraeli's supporters and detractors have fastened upon him the label 'imperialist'. To Gladstone it was a term of abuse indicating Disraeli's love of tawdry glory in the manner of the Bonapartist regime of Napoleon III. To Disraeli's Conservative successors he was the prophet of a new attitude and his premiership is sometimes seen as marking the break with the mid-Victorian dismissal of Empire as either an irrelevancy or, in Disraeli's own words of 1852, 'mill-stones around our neck'.

Even before Disraeli sounded the trumpet of imperial pride in his speech of 3 April 1872 at the Free Trade Hall, Manchester there were clear signs of a change in national mood with regard to the heterogeneous collection of territories that comprised the British Empire. Sir Charles Dilke had published his book *Problems of Greater Britain* in 1869. In it he pointed to the Empire as a possible life-boat of national grandeur in a forthcoming world of superpowers. John Ruskin, in his lectures at Oxford, extolled the virtues of Empire. Amongst his students was the young Cecil Rhodes. When Disraeli took up the theme of imperial splendour in Manchester and again in Crystal Palace he was acting as a good politician, trying to catch a changing tide. There is really little to suggest that in policy terms his government marks a break with the past. The rhetoric of 1872 was not followed up with substantial deeds. Fiji and Malaya were annexed in 1874 but these additions to the Empire arose from the activities of men on the spot and owed little to decisions taken in London. The Suez Canal was purchased in 1875 but Disraeli showed no desire to add Egypt to the Empire and happily settled for joint Franco-British management of Egyptian finances. The Queen was made Empress of India in 1876, a gesture that owed more to royal initiative than Disraelian imperialism. Cyprus was gained in 1878 but as one more strategic base to support Turkey rather than for the sake of acquiring territory. Disraeli showed no interest in Africa, the scene of so much imperial activity in the 1880s and 1890s, and the Colonial Office turned down the Protectorate of Zanzibar and East Africa made by the sultan of Zanzibar in 1879. Disraeli left the Empire to 'Twitters' – his derisory name for Lord Carnarvon, his Colonial Secretary. 'Twitters' was anxious to pursue traditional policies of economy and shedding responsibility. In South Africa he looked to the possibility of federating the four white states which would make possible security at decreased costs. British garrisons could be withdrawn and greater reliance placed on local forces to maintain law and order. In the light of this reasoning the independent Boer states of Transvaal and the Orange Free State were annexed to the crown in 1877 (see Map 5.4). Transvaal only had 17s 6d (87.5 pence) in the treasury and feared hostilities from the local Bantu, in particular the Zulus. This annexation was not the result of a new-found desire for territory but as a necessary first step to a semi-independent federated South Africa. The war against the Zulus which broke out in January 1879 was the work of the man on the spot, Sir Bartle Frere, High Commissioner in South Africa. When Michael Hicks Beach succeeded 'Twitters' as Colonial Secretary, he asserted in 1878, 'I really can't control him without a telegraph: I don't know that I could with one.' Hicks Beach issued a clear-cut order against attacking the Zulus but it arrived too late: two days after an ultimatum had been delivered to the Zulu king, Cetewayo. The result was a short and, for Britain, victorious war. However, before victory, disaster struck. At Isandhlwana an invading column of British soldiers was destroyed by

Zulu warriors. A shortage of screwdrivers prevented the opening of ammunition boxes fast enough to keep up a hail of fire. Later on the same day, 22 January 1879, honour was partly restored by the survival against overwhelming odds of a company of South Wales Borderers at Rorke's Drift – they had sufficient screwdrivers. The war itself was an embarrassment to the government despite its final outcome and, far from being an example of aggressive Disraelian imperialism, it was a perfect example of that dynamic which, once established, drove local officials ever on in the search for imperial security. In the same year a second war embarrassed the government; again, it was not of their making. In 1876 Disraeli had dispatched a new viceroy to India, Lord Lytton. Lytton was likely to adopt an aggressive posture and his selection for the job meant Disraeli had some responsibility for the events of 1879–80. In 1879 Lytton ordered the invasion of Afghanistan which, as in South Africa, involved costly disaster before ultimate victory. A British mission was murdered in Kabul and successful retribution by Sir Frederick Roberts came too late to help the government, now tainted with the charge of seeking expensive glory.

Gladstone denounced all aspects of the government's foreign policy in his Midlothian campaign of 1879–80: 'Remember the rights of the savage . . . remember that the happiness of his humble house, remember that the sanctity of life in the hill villages of Afghanistan, among the winter snows, is as inviolable in the eye of Almighty God as can be your own.' Income tax had risen to pay for Disraeli's military displays. Conscience and wallet joined forces. Beaconsfieldism was swept aside by such a potent alliance.

GLADSTONE'S SECOND MINISTRY 1880–5: 'RESTORING THE CONCERT OF EUROPE'!

Gladstone was heir to three differing traditions in the conduct of foreign policy. As already indicated, he looked via Aberdeen to Castlereagh and the Old Tory tradition of upholding the 'concert of Europe'. It was his so-called 'third principle' of foreign policy expressed in a famous speech given in November 1879:

> In my opinion the third sound principle is this – to strive to cultivate and maintain, ay, to the very uttermost, what is called the concert of Europe; to keep the Powers of Europe in union together. And why? Because by keeping all in union together you neutralize and fetter and bind up the selfish aims of each.
>
> (Quoted in Bourne, op. cit., p. 421)

He was also, as Liberal leader, heir to two rival traditions. One was that of Bright and Cobden which promoted peace, minimal expenditure and minimal engagement. His first principle in the speech referred to called for 'economy at home'. His second called for 'peace' and his fourth for an end to 'entangling engagements'. Yet Gladstone and even more his Whig colleagues like Hartington were heirs to Palmerston and his bombastic assertion of English power, particularly in the cause of Liberty. The bombast Gladstone left to Disraeli, but his sympathy with Liberalism abroad, especially the vision of Britain as the natural leader in the world struggle for freedom, could not be put aside so easily. In his sixth principle he embraced it: 'The foreign policy of England should always be inspired by the love of freedom.' In his and Earl Granville's attempt to reconcile these three traditions and at the same time grapple with the evils of Beaconsfieldism, the seeds of disaster lay. Each of the major countries in Europe in turn was alienated from Britain and it proved easier to condemn Disraeli's 'forward' imperial policy than to reverse it.

The Turkish entanglement was the most repellent to Gladstone and here a violent swing in British policy ensued. The 'one great anti-human specimen of humanity' defined Gladstone's feelings on the Turk. He was prevented by his cabinet colleagues from handing over Cyprus, with its majority of Greek-speaking inhabitants, to Greece, but he withdrew British advisers from Asiatic Turkey and in November 1880 and May 1881 used naval demonstrations not to bolster the Turkish Empire as 'Dizzy' had done but to coerce it, thus forcing their sultan, Abdul Hamid, nicknamed 'the Damned' to comply with the Berlin Treaty. In this way Gladstone saw Britain acting as the agent of 'the European concert for purposes of justice, peace and liberty'. The policy, whilst beneficial to Greece and the independent kingdom of Montenegro, to whom the Turks handed over territory, had disastrous repercussions for Britain. Turkey, not surprisingly, was infuriated at the loss of her former territory and moved out of the British sphere of influence. The first German military mission arrived in Constantinople in 1882 and completed the first stage in a process that was to make the Ottoman Empire a German ally in the First World War. Of more immediate consequence was the reforming of the *Dreikaiserbund* which Disraeli had so successfully disintegrated.

Austria, described by Gladstone in the election campaign of 1880, as 'that unflinching foe of freedom', was extremely concerned at the British volte-face in its approach to Turkey. The basis of Anglo-Austrian friendship was joint support for Turkey against Russia. Gladstone removed that base and Austria, already allied to Germany in 1879, succumbed to German pressure to reconstitute the *Dreikaiserbund* in June 1881. If Austria could not rely on British support against Russia to preserve Turkey then the next best thing was a deal with Russia. The new Russian tsar, Alexander III, was happy to turn from the Balkans and do a deal with the two conservative German states. By abandoning ambitions in the Balkans Russia could concentrate on Asian expansion and also use Austrian and German influence with Turkey to seal up the Straits to

British warships, thereby removing a deadly threat to Russia's south coast.

Gladstone had assumed that his approach to Turkey would improve relations with Russia. His actions ended on the brink of war with the Russian bear. One of the new Liberal Government's most clear successes on taking office was the satisfactory withdrawal from Afghanistan. Lytton and General Roberts, and even Salisbury, belonged to the 'forward' school which saw the defence of India best conducted on the Oxus river with Russia penned into central Asia. Gladstone and the new Liberal Viceroy, Lord Ripon, favoured the Indus. In 1880, therefore, British troops were withdrawn from Kabul and a satisfactory treaty made with the new ruler Amir Abdur Rahman. Britain would control his foreign policy in return for a payment of a subsidy and protection. But Russia's rulers were no more able to control their frontier generals and pro-consuls than was Britain and there was a steady advance south east from Khiva towards the Afghan frontier. In 1884 Russian forces conquered Merv and in 1885 Afghanistan itself seemed threatened when Afghan forces were defeated at Penjdeh (see Map 5.3). The vital issue was the control of the Zulficar Pass near to Penjdeh. Gladstone and Granville felt obliged to take a stand and troops were moved to India and railway construction towards the North-West Frontier was set in motion. Eleven million pounds of spending credit was voted by Parliament – clearly Britain intended to fight, with plans made to force the Straits and enter the Black Sea. The value of the *Dreikaiserbund* in preventing this move was demonstrated to the tsar. In June 1885, before resolution of the confrontation the Gladstone Government had fallen.

If any power should have been Britain's partner in reconstituting a liberal 'Concert of Europe', it should have been Republican France, yet even here relations deteriorated rapidly. The government was unhappy at the French seizure of Tunis in 1881 but it was the British occupation of Egypt in September 1882 that created a long-standing breach. The problem in Egypt arose from an upsurge of nationalist resentment at the Anglo-French joint financial control of 1879. Under the leadership of Colonel Ahmed Arabi, Egyptian opposition to Europeans became increasingly violent in 1882. Britain had two interests to protect: the financial stake of shareholders in the Egyptian debt and the Suez Canal. Riots in Alexandria in June led to the death of some fifty Europeans. The standard British response was a naval demonstration which took place in July but it got out of hand and produced the bombardment of Egyptian fortifications. Eventually faced with either abandonment of her Egyptian interests or invasion, Gladstone, under cabinet pressure, reluctantly sanctioned invasion. France was to share in this occupation, a demonstration yet again of Gladstonian commitment to the European ideal of co-operation. On 31 July the French government fell, a common enough occurrence during the Third Republic, and the new French ministry withdrew its

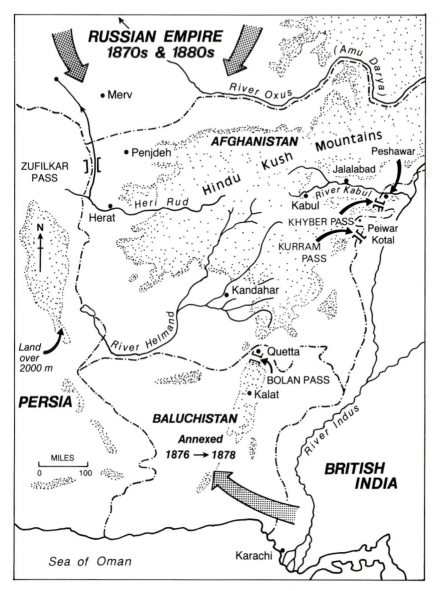

RUSSIAN EMPIRE
1870s & 1880s

(Amu Darya)

River Oxus

• Merv

• Penjdeh

AFGHANISTAN

Hindu Kush Mountains

Peshawar

Jalalabad

ZUFILKAR
PASS

Heri Rud

River Kabul

• Herat

Kabul

KHYBER PASS

Peiwar
Kotal

N

KURRAM
PASS

• Kandahar

Land
over
2000 m

River Helmand

Quetta

PERSIA

BOLAN PASS

• Kalat

BALUCHISTAN

MILES

Annexed
1876 → 1878

River Indus

0   100

BRITISH
INDIA

Sea of Oman

Karachi

5.3 Afghanistan about 1880

support for the occupation. With masterly efficiency Sir Garnet Wolseley occupied Egypt using 40,000 troops and 41,000 tons of supplies. It impressed the rest of Europe and Bismarck expected the declaration of a protectorate. Gladstone, embarrassed by Bright's resignation from the Cabinet, justified the occupation as a European act and denied the British intention of staying. Egyptian finances were put under the able management of Sir Evelyn Baring. Gladstone, however, unnecessarily compounded British difficulties by insisting that Egyptian finances should be partly under international control. The result was the setting up of the International Debt Commission for Egypt in March 1885. French and Russian votes tended to be automatically hostile forcing Britain to rely on the Germans for support. Here was Bismarck's 'bâton egyptienne' with which he could whack the British should they prove difficult elsewhere. Seldom has the pursuit of a moral ideal in foreign policy produced such embarrassing results. France was furious at the British occupation of what was generally held to be a French sphere of influence and spent the next twenty years trying to get Britain out.

The occupation of Egypt led to involvement with territory further afield, in this case, the Sudan. A massive religious rebellion against Egyptian rule had broken out under the inspired religious leadership of the Mahdi (which means simply 'the leader'). An attempt by the Egyptians to reconquer the Sudan in 1883 ended in disaster when 10,000 Egyptian soldiers under Colonel Hickes were annihilated at El Obeid. The British government of Gladstone refused to contemplate reconquest under the British flag and pressed the Egyptians to evacuate the remaining garrisons. To accomplish this task they were willing to supply a 'hero' in the eccentric form of General Charles Gordon. In practice he was a British version of the Mahdi – a religious fanatic possessed of courage and charisma. It was an appalling choice. Gordon arrived in Khartoum on 18 February 1884. His instructions were clear enough but Gordon was not given to obeying instructions except from God and the prophet Isaiah whom he consulted from time to time. Little wonder then that Sir Evelyn Baring in Cairo decided that Gordon was 'half-cracked'. There was no attempt to withdraw and instead he set about trying to control the country and expected reinforcements from Britain. The Queen and public opinion finally forced Gladstone, against his will, to send a relief expedition under another hero, Wolseley. Wolseley, the conquerer of Egypt, had been the agent of the 'concert of Europe' in Gladstone's eyes. Now, according to the Grand Old Man (GOM), he was waging war on a people struggling to be free. The difference between Egypt and the Sudan was not so obvious to men with less subtle intellects than the Prime Minister's, and when the expedition arrived at Khartoum three days too late to save Gordon from being hacked to death the 'GOM' became 'MOG' – Murderer of Gordon. The government found itself massively unpopular and Gladstone was hissed and booed in public. Only the confrontation with Russia in Afghanistan did something to distract public fury.

Events in the Sudan were the second imperial disaster to befall the government. In South Africa it rapidly became involved in what proved to be the First Boer War of 1880–1. The Boers of the Transvaal expected the new Liberal Government to reverse the annexation of 1877 as indicated in Gladstone's election speech. When this was not forthcoming they resorted to rebellion under their formidable President Kruger. The Cabinet and Colonial Office were advised by Frere and Wolseley to press on with a federated South Africa and there was not, therefore, the immediate independence that was demanded. Now that the Zulu menace had been removed and the bulk of the British soldiers too, the Boers decided to take what they had been refused. In December 1880 they inflicted a short sharp defeat on the Connaught Rangers and then in February 1881 a humiliating defeat at Majuba Hill when 280 British were killed or captured and wounded for the loss of one dead Boer and five wounded. There was the predictable demand for revenge and Hartington, in the Cabinet, argued for action. Gladstone felt that it was senseless to waste lives: 'Although we might have treated with you before these military miscarriages we cannot do so now until we offer up a certain number of victims in expiation of the blood that has been shed.' Gladstone pointed to the idiocy of such reasoning and eventually carried his Cabinet. Sir Evelyn Wood signed first an armistice and then the Convention of Pretoria with the Boers. This convention granted the Boers independence under the suzerainty of the British Crown. What 'suzerainty' meant no-one ever knew – which was its attraction. Attempts to define it later produced the second and greater Boer War of 1899–1902. Gladstone had also led the Boers to believe that the British would back down if confronted by force.

Southern Africa was also the scene of conflict with the greatest of European powers, Germany. Bismarck, Chancellor of the German Empire, detested Gladstone to whom he ascribed the title 'Professor' as a term of abuse. The British Prime Minister seemed to Bismarck to typify so many of the vices he saw in the German Progressives, his enemies in the Reichstag. He also saw danger in Gladstone's bid to resurrect a European 'concert' centred on a London–Paris–St Petersburg axis. Luckily for Bismarck such schemes were dead by 1882. He was delighted at the British occupation of Egypt which, as he rightly saw, would create a barrier to Anglo-French harmony. The German bid for empire in 1884 arose from a mixture of motives, and historians still have to guess at Bismarck's thinking. To some it was sheer frustration with Granville and the British Foreign Office. Germany had originally assumed that the area around the port of Walvis Bay was British and when German traders began to operate in the area they requested British protection be extended to them. Granville's evasion produced, eventually, a German announcement of a protectorate over the territory in April 1884. Possibly Bismarck was picking a harmless quarrel to serve him in the Reichstag elections, possibly he was bidding for an anti-British league with France, or, as his son Herbert said, he was trying to isolate the pro-British Crown Prince Frederick whose accession to the German throne Bismarck feared. His precise motivation remains a mystery. Britain in fact proved very accommodating, recognizing the German territory in June and refusing to quarrel with Germany at the Berlin Conference in November which met to consider the future of the Congo. Britain agreed happily to Belgian ownership of the lion's share. Fresh quarrels were then picked in January 1885 over the island of New Guinea, north of Australia, and then in May over East Africa. Here Bismarck appears to have been bidding for reconciliation with France through a common enmity with Britain. Luckily for Gladstone the French premier, Ferry, who was most inclined to co-operate with Germany, fell from power and French public opinion asserted the traditional hatred of the 'Hun'. Despite this happy chance Britain's world position seemed precarious in June 1885 when the Liberals fell from power. War with Russia still threatened over Afghanistan, the Straits were closed to British warships by the pressure of the *Dreikaiserbund*, and France was hostile over Egypt. Well might Salisbury claim that Gladstone had achieved his beloved 'concert of Europe' by uniting Europe against Britain.

THE ASCENDANCY OF LORD SALISBURY 1885–92

There can be little doubt that in or out of office, it was during these years that Britain's relations with the rest of the world were dominated by Robert Gascoigne Cecil. The Foreign Office had found a master of the stature of Palmerston or Castlereagh. For most of this period he served as both Prime Minister and Foreign Secretary. He took both offices in his short caretaker government of 1885 and although in June 1886 he sacrificed foreign affairs to Lord Northcote, when the Conservatives resumed office he replaced that unfortunate man in January 1887, and once again exercised almost sole control over policy decisions. Just as he left other ministers to manage their departments with a freedom that seems rare in the twentieth century, so he expected the same freedom from his cabinet colleagues. The influence of the permanent officials in the Foreign Office which became such a marked feature of the early twentieth century was kept firmly in check whilst Salisbury was in charge. They remained what they had been in Palmerston's day, glorified clerks. During the Gladstone governments of 1886 and 1892–4 there was to be no return to the pattern of party policies of the 1870s. Lord Rosebery took the Foreign Office on both occasions and if his freedom from cabinet interference was not as great as Salisbury's he was determined to preserve continuity. In 1890 he declared 'I will never be party to dropping the foreign policy of this country into the arena of party warfare.' This was a far cry from Midlothian. Salisbury returned in 1895 to take the Foreign Office and the premiership once again but although he continued to hold both offices until 1900 his grip was slipping from 1898 when serious illness led to a lengthy enforced absence from work. Chamberlain, Balfour and Lansdowne increasingly influenced the course of action from their positions in the Cabinet, as did officials like Francis Bertie, Assistant Under-Secretary from 1894 to 1903.

Salisbury's view of foreign policy was devoid of Gladstonian liberal baggage and Disraelian bombast. He saw his role as one of pursuing the interests of his country and these he recognized as threatened. As he wrote in 1887: 'Whatever happens will be for the worse and therefore it is in our interests that as little should happen as possible.' In the same year he put it even more dramatically to the Queen:

> If, in the present grouping of nations, which Prince Bismarck tells us is now taking place, England was left out in isolation, it might well happen that the adversaries, who are coming against each other on the Continent, might treat the English Empire as divisible booty, by which their differences might be adjusted; and, though England could defend herself, it would be at fearful risk, and cost.
>
> (Quoted in Bourne, op. cit., p. 426)

Yet he offered no preconceived solutions, merely an intelligent pragmatism. As he said in 1877: 'The commonest error in politics is sticking to the carcasses of dead policies.' But he recognized the force of public opinion in demanding certain lines of action which he, as a politician, was bound to admit into his calculations. He desired peace and was no jingoistic patriot but public opinion would not submit to national humiliation. He was not averse to working with any power and whilst recognizing France and Russia as the greatest threats in this period, he conveniently sought associations with both. Conversely he recognized Germany, Austria and Italy as the most likely partners but was anxious not to be locked permanently into an alliance system that would divide Europe and precipitate the European war he feared.

As indicated, he inherited a dismal position in 1885. The Queen, no friend of Gladstone, put it clearly: 'Mr Gladstone has alienated all other countries from us by his very changeable and unreliable policy – unintentionally no doubt.' After Salisbury's short government the Queen could happily write:

> Lord Beaconsfield raised up the position of Great Britain, from '74 to '80, in a marvellous manner. Mr Gladstone and Lord Granville pulled it down again during the five years of their mischievous and fatal misrule, but already in seven months Lord Salisbury raised our position again.
>
> (Quoted in C. Lowe, *The Reluctant Imperialists*, London, Routledge & Kegan Paul, 1967, p. 103)

Skill and luck played its part in Britain's escape from isolation. On 10 September the Russians decided to settle the Afghan question yielding the Zulficar Pass. A new Bulgarian crisis also broke out in September, drawing Britain and Austria once again together, and breaking up the reformed *Dreikaiserbund*. A rebellion broke out in Eastern Rumelia, a province of the Turkish Empire inhabited by Bulgarians, and led to a demand for union with Bulgaria. This was a direct challenge to the Berlin settlement and initially Salisbury opposed the changes as, of course, the Turks did. As it became clear that Russia too was opposed and that the new Bulgaria was no Russian satellite, Salisbury swung round to the idea of an enlarged Bulgaria as a better barrier to Russia than a decaying Turkish Empire, his support for which had always been less than Disraeli's. The solution finally accepted by the powers was Salisbury's – a personal union of the two principalities under Prince Alexander. On his return to office after the brief Gladstone Government of 1886, tensions over Bulgaria flared up anew. The Russians kidnapped Alexander and tried to rule the country under a Russian. Britain and Austria drew together with the cautious backing of Bismarck and eventually, in 1887, with Russia unwilling to risk a war, accepted Ferdinand of Coburg as king of the new Bulgaria. The *Dreikaiserbund* of 1881 was dead but Bismarck was anxious to preserve some links with St Petersburg and thus signed the Reinsurance Treaty with Russia in June 1887. His alliance with Austria still stood and so to avoid having to back Austria against Russia the wily German Chancellor was delighted to play godfather to an Anglo-Austrian deal which he hoped would relieve him of the need to confront the Russian bear.

Out of this Bulgarian crisis and fresh tension with France over Egypt came the Mediterranean agreements of 1887. Salisbury hoped to ease relations with the Republic by negotiating a satisfactory withdrawal from Egypt. Sir Henry Drummond Wolff engaged in a complex shuttle diplomacy between Constantinople (the Sultan was the titular ruler of Egypt), Cairo and London. The end result in May 1887 was an agreement for British withdrawal preserving rights of reoccupation and a privileged British position. This was too much for the French who, together with Russia, put pressure on the Sultan to reject the Agreement. Britain had already signed a vague accord with Italy in February and with Austria in March to preserve the status quo in the Mediterranean. This was widened in December 1887 when the second Mediterranean Agreement was signed which covered Bulgaria, the Straits and Asia Minor. Britain's conflict with Russia over Constantinople and with France over Egypt thus brought her associate membership of the Triple Alliance. Ironically, the more secure Britain was in Egypt the less inclined she was to fight for Constantinople and the more inclined she was to rely on Alexandria as a base from which to defend the route to India. By the end of the year Britain had decided to stay in Egypt and French attempts in 1889 to negotiate on the basis of the Drummond Wolff convention were rejected.

Even more than friendly agreement with Italy and Austria Salisbury trusted his faith in the power of the British fleet. France's hostility and her growing friendship with Russia forced Britain to begin a major programme of naval rearmament. By the Naval Defence Act of 1889 Salisbury signalled his preference for what he termed 'a free hand'. He did not wish to be too dependent on continental allies. By the Act the so-called 'Two Power Standard' was accepted by which Britain aimed to achieve a fleet bigger than the next two naval powers put together, in this case France and Russia. It was to prove expensive and the start of the arms race but Britain could afford it.

If relations with France remained chilly those with the German Empire flourished. In 1888 Salisbury could write to one British diplomat 'Our policy is identical with that of the Central Powers.' England and Germany and, to a large extent, Austria were satisfied powers. Bismarck, a year later, referred in the Reichstag to Britain as an 'old traditional ally'. Neither statesman wished friendship to become formal alliance for fear of the diplomatic repercussions. Yet Bismarck in 1889 did propose an alliance to Salisbury, although the chief purpose of this was probably to demonstrate to the young Kaiser Wilhelm II the unwillingness of Britain to sign such a deal and that in the light of this, good relations with Russia were essential. Salisbury obliged, if this was Bismarck's intention, letting the proposal in his own words 'lie upon the table'. In 1890 Salisbury was prepared to sign a far-reaching colonial deal with the German Empire which confirmed the friendly relations that existed. In return for Zanzibar and a strip of territory in East Africa, Germany was given the island of Heligoland off the North German coast. Salisbury described it as 'swapping a trouser button for a suit of clothes', and more importantly gaining vital German support against France over Egypt. Despite the cosiness of Anglo-German relations there were strict limits placed by Salisbury on this *entente*. He resisted the increasing pressure of the Kaiser and of Crispi, the Italian premier, for a formal alliance and by 1892 Germany was becoming irritated by British reluctance, particularly as her own good relations with Russia had deteriorated and a Franco-Russian alliance seemed imminent.

When the Conservative Government fell in 1892 the premier could feel well satisfied with his efforts. Compared with the friendless position of 1885 Britain was better placed. Firmly ensconced in Egypt with a more powerful fleet patrolling the seas she had the diplomatic backing of Austria, Italy and Germany. Many problems and threats remained but at least with Rosebery taking the Foreign Office in the new Liberal Government there would be continuity not the disastrous U-turns of 1880.

THE ROSEBERY INTERLUDE 1892–5

Because Gladstone needed Rosebery for the sake of his Irish policy he was forced to tolerate lines of action from his Foreign Secretary of which he strongly disapproved. Gladstone hated the Egyptian situation and when the khedive sought to assert his independence from Britain by sacking Lord Cromer in 1893, Gladstone declared that he would 'as soon set fire to Westminster Abbey' as send in more troops. The abbey did not go up in flames, Cromer was reinstated with extra British forces and Gladstone's impotence in the face of his aristocratic colleague was revealed. A similar clash over the annexation of Uganda in 1894 occurred. Rosebery insisted on British control of the headwaters of the Nile and the Prime Minister reluctantly acquiesced. Rosebery's relationship with his chief and his colleagues was indeed a strange one. He demanded not to be told the details of the Mediterranean Agreements so that he should not have to lie to his fellow ministers who appear to have remained in ignorance of this vital deal.

Rosebery was in many ways more hostile to France and Russia and more inclined to the Triple Alliance than Salisbury yet his relationship with Germany proved much more difficult. This arose in part from German suspicion of a Liberal Government but also from an arrogant assumption that the British tensions with France and Russia made the British Empire a dependant of Germany. Britain, it was felt, needed Germany more than Germany needed Britain and therefore Britannia would eventually be forced into the Triple Alliance on German terms. In the meantime the British should be made to realize this position and also be made to pay up in the form of colonial concessions. Rosebery himself contributed to these German presumptions by panic in July 1893 when a wrongly deciphered telegram made it appear that conflict was about to break out between France and Britain in South East Asia. Rosebery sent for the German ambassador and all but appealed for assistance. Germany became convinced that she could tweak the lion's tail with impunity and in 1894 made various difficulties for Britain in Africa and over the Pacific islands of Samoa. She torpedoed an agreement Britain had made with Belgium over the Congo and in Rosebery's words adopted a tone 'which she might properly use in addressing Monaco'.

In view of his growing irritation with Germany Rosebery, now Prime Minister, with the pliant Earl of Kimberley as Foreign Secretary, tried to improve relations with France and Russia. Progress was made over Siam (Thailand) and the outline of a deal on West Africa developed in October 1894. Any improvements in these areas however were more than undermined by the prospect of a coming clash on the Upper Nile. Sir Edward Grey, the Under-Secretary, made a public warning against the French making any attempt to penetrate the Sudan but the French attempt to cross from West Africa to the Nile, known as the Marchand expedition, went ahead with climactic consequences in September 1898. With Russia, as with the French, Rosebery succeeded in patching up relations in one area of the globe only to find fresh tension breaking out elsewhere. He deserves real credit for his persistence in achieving the Pamirs Agreement of 1895 which settled the issue of the North-West Frontier of the Indian Empire but Russian ambitions in northern China opened up a new area of conflict in Asia. Rosebery sought to co-operate with Russia to help the Armenians suffering appalling massacres under Turkish rule since the end of 1894. Britain hoped to enforce reform on the sultan with a scheme put to him in May 1895. Public pressure, partly whipped up by Gladstone's last political outing, demanded British action but the other European countries refused to join. Russia showed more interest in China, pressurizing the Japanese to hand back territory taken from the Chinese in the short war between the two nations in 1894–5. Germany and France co-operated with Russia in this venture rather than with Britain in the protection of Christian Armenians. In both the Far East and the Middle East Britain appeared impotent and in Europe her relations with the Triple Alliance were much weakened almost to the point of her old isolation. Rosebery's attempt to improve relations with France and Russia had failed and he left the country diplomatically much weaker than he had found it. Nevertheless, his bid for improved relations with France and Russia in response to German provocation was a fore-runner of what was to be achieved ten years later.

THE PASSING OF SALISBURY'S ASCENDANCY 1895–1902

Introduction

Salisbury returned to the premiership and the Foreign Office in June 1895. As ten years previously he inherited a sorry collection of problems worldwide. The Eastern Question, how to respond to the decaying Turk-ish Empire, seemed more unanswerable than ever. A fresh clash with France over the Nile looked likely and Russian ambitions in northern China excited concern. In Southern Africa tension with the Boer Repub-lics of the Transvaal and the Orange Free State was greater than usual and German backing for the troublesome Boers a distinct possibility. In July a completely unlooked-for clash with the USA started a war scare. The one bright spot on the gloomy canvas was the new naval building programme begun against Gladstone's wishes by the Liberal Govern-ment. The 'Two Power Standard' would be a reality by the late 1890s. Salisbury's hold on decision-making was less firm than in his previous government. He was older, more forgetful and more short-sighted than ever, described by Lord Esher as sitting in 'a crumpled heap like Grandpa Smallweed – evidently wearied out'. His cabinet colleagues were more assertive. George Goschen at the Admiralty was quite capable of influ-encing foreign policy and Joseph Chamberlain at the Colonial Office, brash and overflowing with masculine magnetism and energy, was going to be very troublesome. Salisbury complained in November 1895 that

'Chamberlain wants to go to war with every power in the world, and has no thoughts but Imperialism.'

The abandonment of Constantinople 1895–7

The Armenian massacres of 1894 and later in 1896 created a public outcry in which traditional support for the Turks and their sultan, Abdul Hamid, was well nigh impossible. Salisbury inherited from Rosebery an attempt to aid the unfortunate Armenians. He also tried to square this policy with the long-standing British aim of keeping Russia out of Constantinople. To accomplish both these tasks he wanted the fleet to move up through the Straits. Goschen and the Admiralty were convinced that Britain could not now force the Straits with their improved defences and the prospects of the Russian fleet ahead and the French fleet behind. The assumption of British naval power as an agent for British interests in the Straits which had gone unchallenged for fifty years was now ended. The other powers would not agree to put pressure on Turkey and the Armenians were left to suffer. As Salisbury bemoaned, Europeans from Archangel to Cadiz did not care 'whether the Armenians are exterminated or not'. In 1896 during a state visit by the tsar to Britain Salisbury hinted that Britain's commitment to the defence of Constantinople was not what it had been. Austria, fearing a falling-away of British enthusiasm for the status quo refused to renew the Mediterranean Agreements on the old informal basis but insisted on a tighter, more binding treaty. Salisbury would not agree and the Agreements lapsed in 1897 leaving Britain isolated. Salisbury's last real involvement with the Eastern Question related to the Greco-Turkish War of 1897. He could not prevent the conflict but he minimized the consequences to the Greeks of defeat and British naval power enabled him to insist on the virtual independence of Crete under a Greek governor. Turkey drifted from the British to the German orbit, symbolized by the Kaiser's visit to Constantinople in 1898. Austria, now lacking British support, signed a treaty with Russia on 5 May 1897. It was purely negative and put the Balkans 'on ice'. Both powers accepted the status quo. Russia could now afford to wait for the fruits to fall and in the meantime northern China appeared to be ripe for the picking. Britain, as Salisbury indicated in his letter to Sir Philip Currie, the British ambassador at Constantinople, simply dug in on the Nile, but Britain's isolation seemed complete.

The splendour of isolation – Fashoda

As described, it was British possession of Egypt which rankled with the French and they found it difficult to accept British ownership of the whole Nile valley – yet this was just what Britain was resolved on. Whilst the Sudan was under the Mahdi's followers it could be safely left but in

March 1896 Salisbury's Government took the decision to advance from Egypt into the Sudan. This was partly a response to an Italian appeal for help against Dervish attacks on some of their troops. A slow, methodical advance began up the Nile under a new hero, Herbert Kitchener, an engineering officer of ruthless efficiency. The French employed one of their heroes, Marchand, to reach the Nile from their Central African territories. In June 1896 Marchand was ordered to advance to the upper Nile and thereby improve France's bargaining position. Kitchener's triumph was one of logistics and organization whilst Marchand's was one of sheer intrepid courage. In January 1898 Salisbury gave Kitchener the order to make the final advance to Khartoum. On 2 September, across the river from Khartoum at Omdurman, the Dervish army was routed. Western technology versus primitive courage left little doubt about the outcome. The British Egyptian Army lost 48 men, the Dervishes possibly 11,000. The Kalifa, the Mahdi's successor, was hunted down. Gordon was revenged. Four days after Omdurman Kitchener learned of Marchand's presence further up the Nile at Fashoda. In the middle of the month confrontation occurred. France was ordered out. Russia would offer her no support and her forces on the spot were outnumbered and the ultimate arbiter would be the guns of the British fleet in the Mediterranean. Marchand withdrew, and after six months of prolonged argument during which popular passions flared in both countries, France conceded the Nile to Britain. In many ways it was the lancing of a boil, finally settling the Nile question and making ultimate reconciliation possible. In the meantime the French felt only the pain of the operation.

The weakness of isolation – the appeasement of the USA

In July 1895 the British government received a blunt demand from the American government that Britain should submit a boundary dispute between British Guiana and Venezuela to arbitration. The USA asserted the Monroe doctrine, which claimed USA supremacy in the affairs of the New World both North and South. In December President Cleveland publicly made more belligerent noises on the same subject. Salisbury took the matter calmly, insisting that it would fizzle out and that it was largely created for home consumption. The threat of crisis caused consternation. As one junior minister complained, 'we expect the French to hate us and are quite prepared to reciprocate; but the Americans No!' The Cabinet insisted that Britain agree to arbitration. The looming crisis promptly disappeared and in fact the final result in October 1899 favoured Britain but the incident clearly showed her unwillingness to confront her giant offspring across the Atlantic as she had under Palmerston in the 1840s. This same lesson of weakness was again illustrated by negotiations over the projected Panama Canal. In the 1850s it had been agreed that any such canal would be jointly controlled. In 1901 under the Hay–Pauncefote Treaty US control was accepted by Britain. Her acceptance two years previously of America's victory over Spain and US ownership of Puerto Rico and a base on Cuba added up to British realization of USA predominance in the New World. Britain would no longer challenge her claims and most British warships were now withdrawn from their station in the West Indies. The beat of the world's policeman was shrinking.

South Africa – a big colonial war: 1899–1902

Throughout Victoria's reign there had been a succession of little wars around the globe as Zulus, Afghans, Ashantis or Dervishes clashed with British imperial might. To most Britons the only difficulty about such conflicts was that they might entail an extra two pennies on the income tax. The reign finished, however, with a little war that got completely out of control, cost 30,000 lives and £300 million, and forced income tax through the shilling barrier.

The essential British interest at stake in South Africa was the naval base at the Cape. It was decided that the government of the mixed South African population, composed of several black tribes and two white tribes, should be conducted as cheaply as possible. In the 1870s the answer had seemed to lie in the federation of the four states: two British, Cape Province and Natal, and two Boer, the Transvaal and the Orange Free State (see Map 5.4). As we have seen, the attempt ended in disaster at Majuba Hill in 1881 and the settlements of 1882 and 1884 stored up trouble for the future by deliberately leaving Britain's relationship with the two Boer republics unclear. Two developments of the 1880s produced growing tension and made the Gladstonian settlement unacceptable to Britain. In 1886 gold was discovered at Witwatersrand and the great new mining town of Johannesburg sprang into existence overnight. The Transvaal ceased to be a sleepy backwater of Dutch farmers who seemed hardly to have changed since the seventeenth century. Into the Transvaal poured foreigners, the uitlanders, seeking to make their fortunes. The largest single group were Britons. The British government in London and at the Cape viewed this development with both hope and concern. On the one hand, a massively enriched Transvaal which could become the economic heart of Southern Africa while not firmly under British control, was worrying – particularly if it developed links to the outside world that avoided the Cape. On the other, the growing non-Dutch population might provide a peaceful solution if they took over the Transvaal from the inside and federated to the British Empire. Which of these two courses might happen was not clear in the 1890s. The other major development upsetting existing relationships was the arrival of the Germans as a local power. They acquired German South West Africa in 1884 and in the 1890s began to show interest in the Transvaal. President

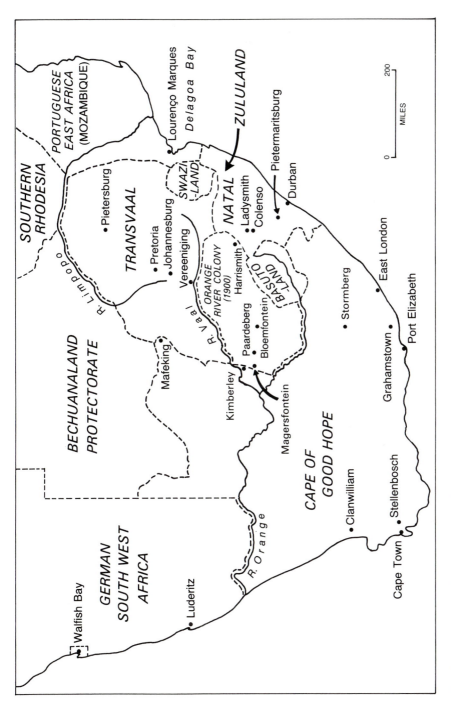

5.4 South Africa 1878–82, 1898–1902

Kruger shipped in German arms on a massive scale and looked to Germany for diplomatic support.

Salisbury certainly wished to avoid conflict in Southern Africa but after 1895 he left matters to his dynamic Colonial Secretary, Chamberlain. Initially, Chamberlain was happy to work through the Prime Minister of Cape Province, the multi-millionaire Cecil Rhodes. Rhodes was impatient to solve the Transvaal question. With Chamberlain's blessing he hatched a plot which would create a revolution in Johannesburg amongst the uitlanders to overthrow the South African republic. Rhodes was one of the leading mine-owners but his motives were a strange compound of financial interests, resentment at exploitive Boer taxes and fanatical patriotism. Rhodes believed in a vast British African Empire which would stretch from Cairo to Cape Town. The rebellion in Johannesburg would be supported by an armed invasion of his South Africa Company police under Dr L. S. Jameson. They would strike from Mafeking, a town on the railway which ran north from the Cape. The whole episode was a farce. The rebellion collapsed in 1896, Jameson was easily captured by the Boers and Rhodes forced to resign as Prime Minister of Cape Province. Chamberlain saved his own skin by denying any knowledge of the events. Kruger and the extreme Boer nationalists were strengthened and arms shipments were stepped up. The Kaiser chose his moment to intervene with his famous telegram to Kruger congratulating him and offering support. A German ship was sent to Delagoa Bay. Britain was furious and dispatched a battle squadron. The German cruiser withdrew.

Four years of manoeuvring for position followed. Britain sought to close off outside links to the Transvaal but it was not until 1899 that Portugal agreed to stop arms shipments. Britain was successful in buying off Germany by a treaty in August 1898 hastily signed whilst Salisbury was ill. Under its terms Britain promised Germany a share of the Portuguese Empire, should it break up. Salisbury likened the negotiations to two Jews in the bazaar at Constantinople haggling over property which did not belong to them. He found the whole business distasteful.

Chamberlain elected to solve the problem and defeat Kruger through the capabilities of Sir Alfred Milner who arrived in South Africa as High Commissioner and Lieutenant Governor of Cape Colony. Between the two men was a gulf of two centuries: Kruger, the tobacco-chewing frontiersman who believed in the literal truth of the Bible, and Milner, the brightest and best of Victorian Oxford. Negotiations turned on the question of uitlander rights. Milner insisted on a franchise that would destroy Kruger's hold on his country. Sixty thousand male uitlanders would outnumber the 30,000 Boer voters. The final crisis began in 1898 with the shooting of Tom Edgar, a boilermaker from Bootle. He was shot by a ZARP – a South African policeman – after a drunken brawl. It led to a mass petition being sent to the Queen asking for British intervention and protection. Milner himself sought to influence the Cabinet:

The case for intervention is overwhelming. . . . The spectacle of thousands of British subjects kept permanently in the position of helots . . . does steadily undermine the influence and reputation of Great Britain.
(Quoted in T. Pakenham, *The Boer War*, London, Weidenfeld & Nicolson, 1979, p. 59)

It worked and Chamberlain was able to demand concessions from the Boers' leaders. They agreed to meet Milner at the Bloemfontein Conference in May. In response to Milner's demand for franchise reform Kruger retorted 'It is our country you want.' Milner broke off negotiations and Chamberlain published Milner's dispatch. Public opinion in Britain was influenced and action demanded. Despite major concessions by the Boers in July, meeting most of the uitlander demands, Chamberlain persuaded the Cabinet on 8 September to send out 10,000 reinforcements. This decided the Boers to strike first and on 10 October they issued an ultimatum to the British Empire demanding the withdrawal of the reinforcements. War ensued.

In Britain 'jingoism' reached a pitch of excitement captured by Kipling in 'The Absent-minded Beggar', which begins:

When you've shouted 'Rule Britannia,' when you've sung
   'God save the Queen,'
  When you've finished killing Kruger with your mouth,
Will you kindly drop a shilling in my little tambourine
   For a gentleman in khaki ordered South? . . .

Like so many of Britain's wars this one began with a series of disasters in December. Sir Redvers Buller, the commander, divided his army corps into three and each section was shatteringly defeated in 'Black Week' by the accurate and deadly fire of the Boers. Britain's pride received a terrible blow yet the Queen rightly assessed the situation: 'We are not interested in the possibilities of defeat, they do not exist.' Reinforcements were rushed out and, to make sure, two heroes were appointed, the aged Lord Frederick Roberts and Kitchener of Khartoum. There were further defeats until the heroes arrived, notably at Spion Kop in January 1900, but superior numbers and resources told in the end. The Boers failed to make the most of their victories and settled down to indecisive sieges of Ladysmith, Kimberley and Mafeking, thus throwing away the advantages of mobility and accurate rifle fire. Each town was relieved in turn in the spring of 1900 with the news of a freed Mafeking setting off riotous rejoicing in London that has seldom been surpassed. On 5 June Roberts entered Pretoria and the war seemed over. Yet nearly two further years of hard and brutal fighting against Boer guerrillas was necessary to subdue the Dutch population. Only through Kitchener's 'methods of barbarism' could they be brought to sign the Peace of

Vereeniging in May 1902. Chamberlain had extended the Empire but it was a rather costly addition.

ISOLATION AND ITS PROBLEMS

Throughtout the Boer War Britain faced deep public hostility from all her European neighbours. Germany had been bought off with promises of the Portuguese Empire in 1898 and gains in Samoa in 1899. For the rest Britain relied on the rivalries of the European states and the size of her navy. Europe would not put aside her quarrels to league against Britain. Nevertheless the war exposed Britain's friendlessness and problems with Russia in northern China at the same time as the South African crisis led some members of the Cabinet, notably Chamberlain, to bid for a German alliance.

With regard to China, Britain's policy was 'open door'. She wished to avoid a partition of the decaying Manchu Empire which, after all, was a large market for British goods. British trade tended to be centred on Shanghai and the central and southern part of China. Salisbury was quite happy to placate Russia and give his blessing to the peaceful penetration of the north. Certainly he felt that singly Britain could not confront Russia on Chinese soil in view of her other conflicts around the globe. Tension arose with Russia in March 1898 when it seemed that the dismemberment of China was about to begin. The Russians worked their fleet to Port Arthur in northern China and then secured a lease on it and the neighbouring town of Talien Wan. Anti-Russian feeling flowed in Britain and whilst Salisbury was absent through illness talks were undertaken by Chamberlain for a German alliance. They came to nothing but they confirmed Germany's view that Britain needed her and that she could exact extensive compensation. As Salisbury put it, 'You ask too much for your friendship', and his return to political activity put an end to negotiations with Germany. He also peacefully defused the tension in northern China with an Anglo-Russian agreement to build a railway in the area. The outbreak of an anti-European uprising, the Boxer Rebellion (by the Society of the Righteous Harmonious Fists, hence the name 'Boxer'), in 1899 and the siege of western diplomats in the British Legation in Peking in 1900 raised once again the problem of the spoilation of China. Britain only reluctantly joined in the relief operation and was anxious to get a general agreement on Chinese territorial integrity and the 'open door'. There were extensive negotiations between Britain and Germany but in the end they came to very little. As Salisbury expressed the position Germany was in just before he retired from the Foreign Office in November 1900:

> She is in mortal terror on account of that long undefended frontier of hers on the Russian side. She will therefore never stand by us

against Russia; but is always rather inclined to curry favour with Russia by throwing us over. I have no wish to quarrel with her; but my faith in her in infinitesimal.

(Quoted in Bourne, op. cit., p. 168)

His successor, Lord Lansdowne, allied with Balfour and Chamberlain and felt like them that Britain could not go on muddling through her difficulties in an isolation that Chamberlain might declare 'splendid' in public but which privately he felt to be dangerous. Salisbury certainly did not see isolation as splendid, the vulgarity of the phrase appalled him, but isolation from European alliances was the lesser evil. Lansdowne undertook three initiatives to solve British difficulties. Until November of 1901 Germany and Britain, in the words of one historian, 'continued to grope for an understanding'. Salisbury offered powerful arguments against joining the Triple Alliance in a memorandum in May, and the growing influence of the Civil Service was notable in a memorandum from Francis Bertie, Assistant Under-Secretary, echoing Salisbury's position. Lansdowne accepted the strength of their arguments in November and the negotiations came to an end. His second line of attack was direct negotiation with Russia which eventually drew a blank. His third proved more successful and in very rapid negotiations a deal was struck with the adolescent power of Asia: Japan. In January 1902 a defensive pact was signed. Both powers undertook to aid the other if faced by more than one enemy. Britain would not have to face Russia and France alone in the Far East and this also ensured naval supremacy. Britain assumed that such a pact was motivated by the same defensive mentality on Japan's part. In fact, by insuring them against the kind of general European league that she faced in 1895, Japan could now contemplate war on Russia. To some observers this alliance was 'the end of isolation' and in strictly worded terms it was. Yet its purpose was to ensure continued isolation where it mattered, in Europe.

DIPLOMATIC REVOLUTION 1902–5

In 1898 a British army was confronting France on the Nile and a British naval squadron faced Russian ships in Port Arthur. In the same year, as we have seen, there was also talk of a British alliance with Germany. By 1905 there had been a dramatic about face in Britain's relations with the European powers. The British navy undertook its first study of war against Germany and a great new base at Scapa Flow in the Orkneys was begun to serve this new role. France had become a friend and the two armies began unofficial talks on co-operation.

A combination of circumstances produced this outcome. In October 1902, Lord Selborne, the First Lord of the Admiralty, presented the Cabinet with the following memorandum. Its content was worrying:

The more the composition of the new German fleet is examined the clearer it becomes that it is designed for a possible conflict with the British fleet. It cannot be designed for the purpose of playing a leading part in a future war between Germany and France and Russia. The issue of such a war can only be decided by armies and on land, and the great naval expenditure on which Germany has embarked involves a deliberate diminution of the military strength which Germany might otherwise have attained in relation to France and Russia.

(ibid., p. 478)

Within the Foreign Office there was an influential group of civil servants headed by Francis Bertie who were resentful of the years of German blackmail and anxious to free themselves of dependence on the Triple Alliance by reconciliation with France. In France too, now that the Nile was unobtainable, there was a desire to restore the *entente* with Britain and a desperate anxiety not to be dropped into conflict with the British Empire through a Russo-Japanese clash in the Far East. French ambitions had turned to Morocco and since Britain had the largest trading interests in that territory her goodwill to France was vital. After lengthy negotiations and a particularly successful goodwill visit to Paris by Edward VII in 1903, further progress eventually came about in 1904. It was the outbreak of the Russo-Japanese war in February that provided the final vital spur to agreement which was reached in April. Several long-standing niggling colonial disputes were settled, ranging from Siam to Madagascar and West Africa to Newfoundland, but the nub of the agreement was a French acceptance of British control of Egypt in return for British recognition of French predominance in Morocco.

There is a tendency to see this Anglo-French Entente purely through the lens of 1914, that is, as an alliance. It was not an anti-German alliance but a reinforcement of British isolation. Without Anglo-French tension Britain need not depend on German goodwill. She was freer than ever.

By 1905 Britain had coped well with decline and appeared far more secure than at any time in the past twenty years. Japan was in the process of removing the Russian threat in China, and in a new version of the alliance with Britain, extended her support to Britain's position in India. South Africa and Egypt had been secured and good relations established in the western hemisphere with the United States, although at the cost of accepting US supremacy in that part of the world. In the struggle for Empire Britain had emerged with the lion's share of Africa. Admittedly the French had a greater area but as Salisbury had pointed out much of it was 'very light soil' – the Sahara desert. The British navy was stronger than ever and under Balfour's leadership the Committee of Imperial Defence had been established in 1902 as the first real attempt at coordinated defence analysis and planning. Britain was still the only truly world power.

CONTROVERSY: BRITAIN IN AFRICA

Between 1870 and 1914 Great Britain, like most other western European powers, strode into Africa consolidating footholds on the coast and expanding into the interior of the continent. So much so, that by the outbreak of the First World War well over 90 per cent of African territory was in European hands and a very large percentage of this belonged to Britain (see Map 5.5). However, only a few years before this momentous process is supposed to have started, a Select Committee of the House of Commons on West African Settlements had strongly recommended 'an ultimate withdrawal from all [settlements] except probably Sierra Leone' (1865). Thus in a very short space of time Disraelian 'millstones' had become El Doradan dreams. As with many historical controversies it is not the events that are controversial but the motives of those involved and the subsequent explanations provided by later historians.

The earliest analyses of Victorian imperialism were straightforward enough if a little simplistic. Up to 1870 there had been a growing awareness of the burden of colonies that were more often than not troublesome and expensive, and invariably demanded independence from the mother country – notable examples being the American colonies, Canada and Australia. In this sense, then, little seemed to be gained by playing the colonial game and Britain appeared to enter a period of 'anti-imperialism'. However, in about 1870 there was a distinct change, with Britain feeling the chill wind of increasing competition from new industrial rivals and seeing the ever-increasing dominance of Bismarck's Germany in continental affairs. There was a retreat to colonies and empire as Britain was forced to look for new sources of raw materials and markets for her industry and trade. It was this stimulus that took Britons out to Africa. However, such historical interpretations as these, espoused by historians like H. E. Egerton in his *A Short History of British Colonial Policy* (1897), would soon be swept aside in the twentieth century as commentators tried to explain the phenomenon of imperialism and pinpoint the cause of Britain's imperial expansion, especially into Africa.

The first of these commentators was J. A. Hobson who wrote his seminal text *Imperialism: A Study* in 1902. It became the founder of a new dynasty of books that concentrated on the economic causes of imperialism and especially the role of investments or capitalist imperialism. Hobson's idea was simple:

> Over-production in the sense of an excessive manufacturing plant, and surplus capital which cannot find sound investments within the country

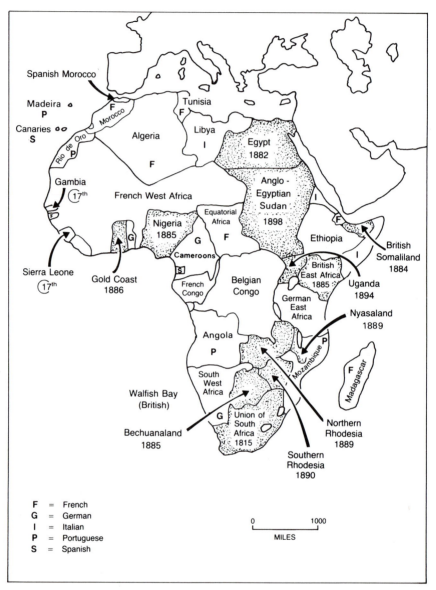

Spanish Morocco

Madeira **P**

Canaries **S**

Morocco

Rio de Oro **P**

Tunisia **F**

Algeria **F**

Libya **I**

Egypt 1882

Gambia 17th

French West Africa

Equatorial Africa

Nigeria 1885 **G**

G

F

Anglo - Egyptian Sudan 1898 **I**

Ethiopia **F**

British Somaliland 1884

Sierra Leone 17th

Gold Coast 1886

Cameroons **S**

French Congo

Belgian Congo

British East Africa 1885 **I**

Uganda 1894

German East Africa

Nyasaland 1889

Angola **P**

South West Africa

Mozambique **P**

Madagascar **F**

Walfish Bay (British)

G Union of South Africa 1815

Bechuanaland 1885

Southern Rhodesia 1890

Northern Rhodesia 1889

F	=	French
G	=	German
I	=	Italian
P	=	Portuguese
S	=	Spanish

0   1000

MILES

5.5 Africa – British imperial gains by 1914

force Great Britain, Germany, Holland, France, to place larger and larger portions of their economic resources outside the area of their political domain, and then stimulate a policy of political expansion so as to take in new areas.

In essence, he maintained that European countries invested in new areas and then found themselves having to annex these territories in order to

Table 5.1 British acquisitions of African territory [1871–1900]

Territory	Date of acquisition	Area in sq. miles	Population
Zanzibar/Pemba	1888	1,000,000	2,700,000
East African Prot.	1895		
Uganda Prot.	1894–1896	140,000	3,800,000
Somali Coast Prot.	1884–1885	68,000	?
Brit. Central Prot.	1889	42,217	688,049
Lagos	to 1889	21,000	3,000,000
Gambia	to 1888	3,550	215,000
Ashantee	1896–1901	70,000	2,000,000
Niger Prot.	1885–1898	500,000	40,000,000
Egypt	1882	400,000	9,734,405
Soudan (Egy)	1882	950,000	10,000,000
Griqualand West	1871–1880	15,197	83,373
Zululand	1879–1897	10,521	240,000
Brit. Bechuana.	1885–1886	51,424	72,736
Bechuana Prot.	1891	213,000	200,000
Transkei	1879–1885	2,535	153,582
Tembuland	1885	4,155	180,130
Pondoland	1894	4,040	188,000
Griqualand East	1879–1885	7,511	152,609
Brit. S. Afr. Caart.	1889	750,000	321,000
Transvaal	1900	119,139	870,000
Orange River Col.	1900	48,826	207,503
Total	–	4,421,115	74,806,387

Source: J. A. Hobson, *Imperialism: A Study*, 1902

Table 5.2 British foreign and colonial investments 1862–93

Year	In £ million	
	Amount	Annual increase (%)
1862	144	–
1872	600	45.6
1882	875	27.5
1893	1,698	74.8

Source: ibid.

protect their investments. However, much of Hobson's book is open to question, especially the statistical analysis of investments and annexations that simply does not match up as Tables 5.1 and 5.2 and the comment from the English historian A. J. P. Taylor suggests:

> The export of capital was certainly a striking feature of British economic life in the fifty years before 1914. But its greatest periods were before and after the time of ostensible imperialism. What is more

there is little correspondence between the areas of capitalist investment and political annexation. Hobson cheats on this.

(A. J. P. Taylor, *Englishmen and Others*, London,
Hamish Hamilton, 1956)

Despite the criticisms Hobson had opened up a new line of enquiry in the search for the explanation for Britain's activities in Africa. Soon after, another text appeared. This one, entitled *Imperialism: The Highest Stage of Capitalism* (1916), was by V. I. Lenin. In part it is an attempt to explain the absence of working-class revolution in the two most industrialized societies of western Europe – Germany and Great Britain. It also observes the connection between big business, investment abroad and colonial expansion. Lenin's contention was that capitalism had hybridized to produce a mutant which he termed monopoly capitalism. It was this higher stage of capitalism, which Marx could not have foreseen, which was creating empires and sustaining the capitalist system beyond its allotted term. Again, as with Hobson, the basic contention is persuasive but the evidence equally slight and error-ridden as Lenin read back into the nineteenth century the existence of huge national and international monopoly firms capable of exerting the influence that he assigns to them. Nevertheless the economic causes of imperialism have not stood by the influence of investment alone.

Obviously markets and raw materials had their place as did greed on the part of individual traders and governments. Other historians, among them D. C. M. Platt, have widened out the debate and suggested roles for the general European move towards protectionism in the late nineteenth century. This fits in neatly with the timescale and the more acquisitive actions of the powers in order to protect materials, markets and trade.

Persuasive as economic motives may be they cannot stand by themselves and the complexity of the problem can be seen in the variety of factors and influences that have been put forward as areas of explanation for imperialism. Prestige has been mentioned, especially for new nations like Germany and Italy, jostling to establish their positions in the pecking order amongst the older established nations. Diversion seems likely as imperial adventures helped to galvanize patriotic responses at home. Fear also played its part and not merely fear of being left out of the new great power game, but also fear of losing out to others and what this might mean for the future as the excerpts below suggest:

' . . . I am specially to point out,' Granville instructed Kirk, 'that at the present moment the attention of European Powers is directed to an unprecedented extent to the question of the formation of Settlements on the African coast, that action has been in recent cases prompt and secret, and that it is essential that a district situated like

that of Kilimanjaro . . . should not be placed under the protection of
another flag.'

(Quoted in R. Robinson and J. Gallagher, *Africa and the Victorians*,
London, Macmillan, 1961, p. 189)

Its annexation by France or Germany, and the seizure of a port would
be ruinous to British . . . influence on the East Coast. The proceedings
of the French in Madagascar make it all the more necessary to
guard . . . our sea route to India.

(ibid., p. 190)

There are those who have concentrated on the balance of power in
Europe and Bismarck's attempts to play off Britain and France against
each other in Africa in order to gain advantages for Germany in Europe.
The dynamics of empire itself may have created expansion and annexation, with neighbours keen to settle matters of cartography and get
borders drawn on maps as quickly as possible. The list seems endless
although C. C. Eldridge tries to draw it to a conclusion in his excellent
study, *Victorian Imperialism*:

The explanations put forward vary from a simple fit of absence of
mind, promoting 'Commerce, Christianity, and Civilisation', 'phil-
anthropy plus 5%' or 'The White Man's Burden', to the most sophisticated (and controversial) theories. These include imperialism as the
final stage of capitalism, the search for raw materials and markets,
outlets for surplus capital, over-production, under-consumption, trade
rivalries, tariff warfare, humanitarianism, missionary zeal, militarism,
nationalism, chauvinism, racism, social darwinism, new ruling elites,
the yellow press, fear, hysteria, social atavism, power politics, strategy,
national prestige, emigration, individual glory, contiguous development, insubordinate and ambitious men on the spot, scheming local
potentates, black nationalism, local power vacuums, the collapse of
indigenous societies and collaborating cliques, and the clash of cul-
tures. The list is overpowering to say the least and seems to touch
upon all of man's activities. All of these things, naturally, contributed
to the history of the period 1870–1914. It would seem that each
of the various, and apparently unconnected, chains of events which
constitute the New Imperialism had multiple causes which must be
given their due weight in any general historical explanation.

(C. C. Eldridge, *Victorian Imperialism*, London, Hodder &
Stoughton, 1978, pp. 144–5)

Amidst this welter of explanation there does stand one viewpoint that
seems to offer some direction. Often misinterpreted as purely a simplistic
theory is the work of Ronald Robinson and John Gallagher, notably in
the many editions of their book, *Africa and the Victorians*. The common
view is that Robinson and Gallagher rely on Egypt to explain the

scramble for territory in Africa – hence the tag 'Egyptocentric' theory of imperialism. Britain mistakenly stumbles into Egypt alone in 1882 through no fault of her own. The French who should have accompanied her but did not are besides themselves with anger and jealousy when Britain stays, and then in retribution the French enter on an orgy of annexation in West Africa that invites a similar response from Britain and other powers. Robinson and Gallagher's book contains a lot more than this and it is as much a way of looking at the British imperial phenomenon as it is a single cause explanation of it. They identify key themes and ideas and then tie these together into a structure that in itself allows for the analysis of imperialism. Continuity in imperialism is a main theme which leads them to reject utterly ideas of an age of 'anti-imperialism' before 1870, and they point to China and Africa itself to prove their point of the existence of 'informal' empire before 1870. They note that the informality is shouldered by various 'collaborative groups' such as explorers, merchants, traders and missionaries who promote and nurse the informal expansion of British interest up to 1870. Crisis areas and events are pinpointed that are African in nature and cause but international in their repercussions. In the north of the continent there is the problem of Egypt and the Sudan with financial worries, control of the Suez Canal and national revolt. In the South there is Cape Colony with its vital route to India and the rise of the increasingly economically independent Boer republics. In fact these Egyptian and Boer 'primitive' nationalisms create crisis in the north and south which the British government, ever mindful of French and German influence respectively, and the strategic importance of Suez and the Cape, must resolve. In order to do so the government, often with the help of men on the spot, move from 'informal' control to more direct control and eventually to 'formal' empire itself, even though annexation in one case involves a full-scale war. Finally, Robinson and Gallagher are keen to note the difference that lies between the terms 'causes' and 'motives'. For them the 'motives' of imperialism could be, on an individual level, greed or humanitarianism, or, on a government level, strategic protection or economic advantage. But, the 'causes' of imperialism were the crises in the north and south of Africa.

Of course, Robinson and Gallagher are as open to criticism as any historians who take on such a mammoth task. However, despite the work of Newbury who pre-dates French interest in annexing West Africa to well before Robinson and Gallagher's post-1882 date; Cooke, who believes that they have overplayed the importance of Egypt to French actions; and Stengers, who sees their concentration on Egypt to the exclusion of King Leopold of Belgium as unsustainable, Robinson and Gallagher's work remains the most important contribution to the debate of British motives for imperial expansion since its publication.

In all the long annals of imperialism, the partition of Africa is a remarkable freak. . . . It would be a gullible historiography which could see such gimcrack creations as necessary functions of the balance of power or as the highest stage of capitalism.

(Robinson and Gallagher, op. cit.)

BIBLIOGRAPHY

For an explanation of the grading system, see the preface p. xiii.

See the previous chapters for biographies of Gladstone, Disraeli, Salisbury, Rosebery, Chamberlain, etc.

General works

3 Bourne, K., *The Foreign Policy of Victorian England*, Oxford, 1970
4 Grenville, J. A. S., *Lord Salisbury and Foreign Policy*, London, Athlone Press, 1964
3 Hayes, P., *Modern British Foreign Policy – the Nineteenth Century 1814–1880*, London, A. & C. Black, 1975
3 Hayes, P., *Modern British Foreign Policy – the Twentieth Century 1880–1939*, London, A. & C. Black, 1978
2/3 Kennedy, P., *The Realities Behind Diplomacy*, London, Fontana, 1981
2/3 Kennedy, P., *Strategy and Diplomacy*, London, Fontana, 1981
3 Kennedy, P., *The Rise and Fall of the Great Powers*, London, Unwin Hyman, 1988
1 Lowe, J., *Rivalry and Accord*, London, Edward Arnold, 1988
4 Lowe, C. J., *The Reluctant Imperialists*, two volumes, London, Routledge & Kegan Paul, 1967
1 Morgan, M. C., *Foreign Affairs 1886–1914*, London, Collins, 1973
3 Porter, B., *Britain, Europe and the World 1850–1986*, London, Allen & Unwin, 1987
3/4 Taylor, A. J. P., *The Struggle for Mastery in Europe 1848–1918*, Oxford, Oxford University Press, 1954
2 Taylor, A. J. P., *The Troublemakers*, London, Hamish Hamilton, 1957 (This contains an excellent essay on Gladstonian foreign policy)

The Eastern Question

3 Anderson, H. S., *The Eastern Question 1774–1923*, London, Macmillan, 1966
2 Clayton, G. D., *Britain and the Eastern Question*, London, University Press, 1971
1 MacFie, A. L., *The Eastern Question*, London, Longman, 1989
4 Millman, R., *Britain and the Eastern Question*, Oxford, Oxford University Press, 1979
4 Shannon, R. T., *Gladstone and the Bulgarian Agitation 1876*, Brighton, Harvester, 1975

The Empire

3   Eldridge, C. C., *Victorian Imperialism*, London, Hodder & Stoughton, 1978

4   Fieldhouse, D. K., *Economics and Empire 1830–1914*, London, Weidenfeld & Nicolson, 1972

2/3   Judd, D., *The Victorian Empire*, London, Weidenfeld & Nicolson, 1970–1

2/3   Morris, J., *Heaven's Command*, New York, Harcourt Brace Jovanovich, 1973

2/3   Porter, B., *The Lion's Share*, London, Harlow, 1984

3/4   Robinson, R. and Gallagher, J., *Africa and the Victorians*, London, Macmillan, 1961

3   Thornton, A. P., *The Imperial Idea and its Enemies*, London, Macmillan, 1959

Military

3   Barnett, C., *Britain and Her Army*, London, Allen Lane, 1970

2   Forwell, B., *Queen Victoria's Little Wars*, London, Allen Lane, 1973

2   Forwell, B., *Eminent Victorian Soldiers*, London, Viking, 1986

4   Hamer, W. S., *The British Army: Civil–Military Relations 1885–1905*, Oxford, Oxford University Press, 1970

4   Kennedy, P., *The Rise and Fall of British Naval Mastery*, London, Allen & Unwin, 1976

2   Morris, D. R., *The Washing of the Spears: Zulu War 1878–79*, London, Cape, 1966

2   Padfield, P., *The Battleship Era*, London, Hart-Davies, 1972

3   Pakenham, T., *The Boer War*, London, Weidenfeld & Nicolson, 1979

Sources for coursework

There are many printed collections of documents relating to this period. Two small collections are contained in books referred to above; K. Bourne's has an interesting selection and C. J. Lowe's second volume is a collection of relevant original sources. There is much material in works like G. E. Buckle's *Letters of Queen Victoria*, London, John Murray, 1926–32 and Agatha Ramm's *The Political Correspondence of Mr. Gladstone 1868–1876*, Oxford, Oxford University Press, 1952 and *1876–1886*, 1962. Finally the more ambitious could go to the great classic compilations of documents like Temperley and Penser, *Foundations of British Foreign Policy from Pitt 1792–Salisbury 1902*, Cambridge, 1938.

6 The Liberal Party after Gladstone: recovery, triumph and death 1895–1935

INTRODUCTION: FORTY YEARS ON

By the early twentieth century Britain was already very different from what it had been when Gladstone and Disraeli had clashed over the 1867 Reform Bill. The toilet roll did now exist, at least in middle-class homes. The milk bottle appeared for the first time in 1907 and soap powder in the previous year. Britain had changed and was changing rapidly. The differences between 1904 and 1914 are marked. In 1904 there had been 2,500 horse buses in the capital but the last one was withdrawn from service on 4 August 1914, a date deserving of note for other reasons. Technological change was accelerating. Electric lights and trams were transforming the cities no less than the internal combustion engine. Type-writers and the telephone were creating a whole new world of work for young women, an alternative to the drudgery of domestic service. The servant problem produced grumbles in the houses of the wealthy but even here technology would come to the rescue with the new 'vacuum dust extractor'. Marconi's company was to erect wireless stations through-out the Empire in 1913, linking the king's dominions by means of the mysterious notion of communication through the air waves. Dirigible airships and the aeroplane ought to have been exciting the military mind but in England little such excitement was discernible. Perhaps more than any other gadget the humble bicycle should symbolize Edwardian Britain, freeing as it did villagers and town dwellers from their homes and the tyranny of the railway timetable.

There were considerably fewer villagers and more town-dwellers. By 1911 only one in four lived in the countryside. The population as a whole had passed 45 million by that date. Only in Ireland had the total declined, but even in mainland Britain the birth rate was falling and with it the annual rate of increase. By 1911 life-expectancy for men was 52 and for women 55. London retained its pre-eminence and was still a world phenomenon with its 7.25 million inhabitants. Manchester had passed the half-million mark and even little Glossop had reached 21,500 by 1911. An expanding economy had not only produced a bigger population and bigger cities but considerably greater wealth: gross domestic product per head had increased by 60 per cent between 1870 and 1913. The structure of the economy had clearly changed. The decline of agriculture has been referred to many times. It remained the country's biggest employer of men, if tenant farmers and labourers are included, and the ownership of land still conferred great prestige, but it had lost its primacy. By 1911 there were more coal-miners in mainland Britain than agricultural labourers. More than a million men dug coal.

The textile industry continued to grow up until 1914 but much more slowly than in the mid-nineteenth century. Over 600,000 drew their living from cotton. New areas of manufacture had also appeared. The electrical industry was now employing 118,000 workers. Vehicle manufacture grew from a mere 1,000 in 1881 to 93,000 by 1911. The service sector of the economy showed startling advances. The number of commercial travellers doubled in thirty years and those engaged in insurance topped 100,000 in 1911 compared to 17,346 in 1881. The expanding role of government showed in the growth of the civil service whose numbers more than tripled to reach 200,000. Local government officials also more than tripled in the same period. There were 190,000 elementary school teachers by 1900, 25 per cent of them women. The ranks of the middle class swelled from all these developments in the public and private sector.

The urban industrial society that stood triumphant everywhere but in Ireland had much to be proud of by the early twentieth century. The disorderly anarchy of the first flurry of industrialization seemed to have been replaced by a new urban civilization which surpassed that of ancient Rome. The police held the forces of crime and disorder in check, cities possessed new sewers and fresh water supplies. Cholera was a thing of the past. Parks, city art galleries and libraries provided for the recreational needs of the new urban man and woman. Well might E. Nesbit write in 1908 in *The House of Arden*:

> We live so safely now, we have nothing to be afraid of. When we have wars they are not in our own country. The police look after the burglars and even thunder is attended to by lightning rods.

This complacent summary of Edwardian England cannot stand unchallenged. The very success of British society highlighted its failures. Charles Booth's survey of the London poor, the first volume of which appeared in 1889, showed that 30 per cent of the population of the East End lay below his newly invented 'poverty line'. Ten years later Seebohm Rowntree carried out an even more precisely defined survey, in York, which confirmed Booth's findings. Nearly a third of Britons were paupers who lacked the basic necessities of life. There was a growing intolerance of slum housing in which so many of the new artisan class lived, and the poor physical condition of many Boer War recruits had caused extreme concern. In 1904 a special inquiry was set up into 'Physical Deterioration' which it was feared would undermine the strength of the Empire. There was an increased concern with class tensions and the dangers of the polarization of politics along class lines. As the Liberal intellectual J. A. Hobson said in an address to the National Liberal Club in 1912:

> The sentiment of severance between rich and poor, the spirit of class hostility has grown more conscious and acute. This is not a popular thing to say to a middle class audience but it is true.

This same concern shows up in literary form in John Galsworthy's play *Strife*. The Liberal MP Leo Chiozzo Money surveyed the new Britain of the twentieth century in a book entitled *Riches and Poverty*, published in 1905. He noted the increased wealth but clearly underlined its unfair distribution:

> Thus, to the conclusion that nearly one-half of the entire income of the nation is enjoyed by but one-ninth of its population, we must add another even more remarkable, viz.: that *more than one-third of the entire income of the United Kingdom is enjoyed by less than one-thirtieth of its people.*
>
> (Quoted in K. O. Morgan, *The Age of Lloyd George*, London, Allen & Unwin, 1978, p. 132)

What was the relevance of Liberalism to this changing and challenging world was a question that Liberals like Hobson and Chiozzo Money sought to answer. Could the Liberal Party hold onto the swollen ranks of the miners or win back the textile workers of Lancashire and the rapidly growing army of office workers in London?

'POLITICIANS IN SEARCH OF A CRY' 1895–1905

The Liberal Party which Sir Henry Campbell-Bannerman led in the first years of the twentieth century was not the same in composition as that which Mr Gladstone led to victory in 1868. The proportion of Liberal MPs who were landowners had fallen dramatically. In the 1860s it had been 49 per cent. By 1914 it was a mere 6 per cent. Those whose primary interest lay with finance and business rose from 30 to over 40 per cent. Lawyers, as always, continued to figure prominently, whether as solicitors like David Lloyd George or eminent barristers like H. H. Asquith and R. B. Haldane. Out of 272 Liberal MPs elected in December 1910 62 were lawyers. There was also a growing number of other professionals drawn from the ranks of teachers, journalists and social workers. Non-Conformists were much more in evidence at Westminster. Between 1895 and 1900 55 per cent of new Liberal MPs were Non-Conformists. This was a very much enlarged proportion from the 14 per cent of 1868. Even some working men now sat as Liberal MPs, particularly for mining districts, and in 1905 John Burns was the first working-class MP to enter the Cabinet. As he told the Prime Minister, Campbell-Bannerman, on news of the offer, 'Sir 'Enry you never did a more popular thing in your life.' The parliamentary Liberal Party was thus broader in social composition and reached further down the social scale than its Gladstonian predecessor. A recent survey concludes with the following:

> Despite such variations, it is still possible to identify a typical Liberal MP from 1895–1914. He was middle class and probably a businessman or a lawyer. He was likely to be a Nonconformist with a university or public school education who was over forty at the time of his election. His home or business probably was in the county, if not the constituency, for which he sat. He typically had gained governmental experience sitting on a town or county council, school board, or board of guardians, and he also probably was active in some local voluntary society. A Liberal MP was more likely to be of this type if he was first elected between 1895 and 1905, less likely if he was first elected after 1909.
>
> (Quoted in G. L. Bernstein, *Liberalism and Liberal Politics in Edwardian England*, London, Allen & Unwin, 1986, p. 17)

Wales and East Scotland were the rock-like foundations of nineteenth-century Liberalism (see the map of the Liberal heartland in chapter 2, p. 54). Other areas like the West Riding of Yorkshire and the North East coalfield also returned Liberal majorities. Middle-class constituencies were almost certain to be Conservative, working-class ones more likely to be Liberal, but their weaker party allegiance posed considerable problems. This shows very markedly in the large cities. Birmingham with Chamberlain's influence was no doubt a special case in its rejection of Liberalism but only Edinburgh and Leeds were consistently Liberal amongst the other major cities between 1885 and 1914. Large numbers of working-class voters were excluded from the franchise by being paupers or failed to qualify by moving house (tenants had to reside for more than one year in the same place to qualify). It has been estimated that four million adult males were without a vote in this way in 1900 and women were still, of course, completely excluded. Against this there were large numbers of middle- and upper-class voters who could vote more than once. In 1906 one estimate of plural voting has been put at 618,823 out of a total of 5,458,591 votes cast, indicating how much of an advantage the Unionists enjoyed under the electoral rules then prevailing.

Generalizations about what motivates voting habits are notoriously difficult to make, yet this does not prevent legions of pundits from making them. Why were the cotton operatives of Lancashire overwhelmingly Unionist in 1900, yet the woollen workers of Yorkshire overwhelmingly Liberal? Religious affiliations were clearly important. Non-Conformists and Roman Catholics were more likely to be Liberal and

Anglicans Unionist, but then large numbers of voters attended no church. Local Liberal Party activists tended to be middle-class businessmen as Table 6.1, based on three traditional Liberal areas, indicates.

Table 6.1 Occupations of local Liberals, 1899–1914

	Leicester Town Council	Executive, Leicester Liberal Association 1903–8	Leeds City Council	Executive, Leeds Liberal Federation 1899–1908	Norwich Town Council
Business					
Industry	13	14	19	10	7
Merchant	7	4	7	6	5
Other	2	4	5	3	6
Professional					
Law	2	2	9	4	8
Other*	10	19	14	8	3
Shopkeeper, Tradesman, Artisan, etc.*	12	8	18	6	12
Gentleman	5	1	2	0	1
Labour	8	4	3	1	2
Totals	59	56	77	38	44

*Examples of miscellaneous professionals include accountants, actuaries, teachers, ministers, journalists, salesmen and agents. Examples of non-industrial artisans are tailors, locksmiths, plumbers, a saddle-maker and a monumental mason.
Source: Bernstein, op. cit., p. 24.

The big problem for Liberalism in these areas and throughout the country as a whole was how could a party led by such a middle-class elite and inspired by Non-Conformists ever hope to excite the vital support of the working class? There was clearly a new challenge from the socialist parties and if the Independent Labour Party (ILP), founded in 1893, gained few seats itself it could deny seats to Liberals. The foundation of the Labour Representative Committee (LRC) in 1900 looked likely to heighten the threat.

How seriously threatened the Liberal Party was in these years is a difficult question to answer. Contemporaries were unsure as to whether it indicated a permanent decline or was merely the result of temporary adverse conditions. Historians have been divided ever since. Were the two election defeats of 1895 and 1900 a foretaste of decline and death in the inter-war years? Lord Rosebery, the leader in 1895, wondered if the party would now go the same way as the Belgian Liberal Party, towards extinction. There were clearly continuous deep-seated social trends that were weakening the party. The tendency to vote on class lines was unwelcome. The drift of the middle classes to the Conservatives had been a marked feature of British political life for three decades. The consequent reliance on the working-class vote was all the greater yet the new socialist parties might provide a focus for working-class loyalties. The hold on local Liberal parties by small middle-class cliques made it all the more hard to maintain working-class support. Non-Conformity which, as indicated, was a vital force to Liberalism, was losing much of its mid-Victorian vitality. Numbers continued to grow but much more slowly and they represented a smaller percentage of the adult population. Methodist membership had increased by a quarter of a million between 1871 and 1906 but the proportion had fallen from 4.1 per cent to 3.6 per cent as the population had increased at a faster rate. If these trends did spell doom then the victory of 1906 was a one-off aberration, a product of exceptionally favourable circumstances.

On the other side there was much to suggest that the party's troubles were themselves unusual and temporary, centred as they were on a leadership crisis and a not necessarily permanent fragmentation of the forces of the left. The great progressive coalition of 1868 had clearly split into some of its component parts. In the 1870s Isaac Butt and Charles Stewart Parnell had removed the Irish Liberals and renamed them Nationalists. Hartington and Chamberlain had walked out with an odd assortment of Whigs and radicals in 1886. Some working-class activists now preferred their own Labour organizations. All of these meant a diminution of the Liberal alliance. Gladstone's retirement in 1894 left no obvious replacement. As we saw in chapter 2, Rosebery's dalliance with the leadership was short-lived. His extensive stables had at least won the Derby twice during his time at Number 10 but this achievement did not commend him to his Non-Conformist followers. Relations with Sir William Harcourt, who was twenty years his senior and bitterly jealous, remained as bad as ever and when Gladstone, like some potent genie whom everyone thought to be safely stoppered up in a bottle, burst out again with his powerful speech in Liverpool in September 1895 against Turkish atrocities to Armenians, Rosebery decided to call it a day and resign the leadership. Harcourt continued as leader in the Commons and Lord Kimberley took over in the Lords. It looked like a re-run of the 1870s and some again called for the return of the Grand Old Man. At 87 this proved impossible even for him and Harcourt's difficulties multiplied. He made a poor showing in the debate on the invasion of the Transvaal headed by Dr Jameson (see chapter 5) and missed a golden opportunity to destroy Chamberlain. Rosebery remained as leader in waiting, active as a focus of loyalty for the many who hated Harcourt. On 14 December 1898 Harcourt suddenly announced his resignation and John Morley indicated that he was not available as successor. Of senior Liberals in the Commons only H. H. Asquith, a brilliant barrister and ex-Home Secretary, and Sir Henry Campbell-Bannerman, a far from brilliant ex-cabinet colleague, appeared as contenders. Asquith decided he could not afford the luxury of the position. He was dependent on his earnings at the bar, being a relatively poor man. Sir Henry was rich and at 62 was unanimously elected as leader on 6 February 1899. The Liberals had acquired a chief totally lacking in charisma, defective in debating talent and generally unknown. Ranged against him was the weighty prestige of Salisbury, the dynamic Chamberlain and the master of the parliamentary duel, Balfour. It was an uneven contest. Well might David Lloyd George, obscure backbencher from North Wales, bemoan the loss of Chamberlain to the Liberal Party.

There had always been tension amongst Liberals about Empire and foreign policy. The heirs of Cobden and Bright clashed with the heirs of Palmerston. Harcourt and Morley spoke for the former and Rosebery surrounded himself with a group of Liberal imperialists who spoke for the latter. The Boer War brought these tensions to a head. There had been signs before the war of a Liberal revival despite the leadership crisis. A string of by-elections had gone the Liberals' way and they could look forward to a massively improved position in a general election. The war divided the party more seriously than ever. 'Little Englanders', like the temperance reformer Sir Wilfred Lawson, were dubbed pro-Boers for their opposition. At the outbreak of war the leadership was left in the embarrassing position of abstaining whilst 186 Liberal MPs voted against the government for starting the war. Rosebery, with Asquith, Sir Edward Grey and Haldane in tow, supported the war and was anxious to promote a united patriotic front. The Liberal imperialists were bitterly at odds with the pro-Boers. The young Lloyd George emerged as a national figure when he threw his great oratorical gifts into the pro-Boer campaign. Sir Henry liked to take a middle line and keep the party together. In one vote in July 1900 forty-one Liberal imperialists supported the government, twenty-nine voted against and the rest abstained. It was a pathetic performance and small wonder the Liberals went down to a crushing defeat in the 'khaki election' of October 1900. They secured only 184 seats to the Conservatives' 402. Whilst the war continued so too did the divisions, in fact they intensified. A Liberal Imperialist Council was formed and there was a real possibility that Grey and Rosebery might leave the party. This prospect was viewed with some optimism by Campbell-Bannerman but that they might take Asquith with them was not. In June 1901 Sir Henry himself started up the argument with a speech at the National Reform Union. He condemned the use of concentration camps in the Transvaal for housing Boer civilians whilst the army pursued guerrillas in what was an expensive campaign. His speech ended with a famous phrase:

> What was this policy [of unconditional surrender]? . . . It was that now we had got the men we had been fighting against down, we

should punish them as severely as possible, devastate their country, burn their homes, break up their very instruments of agriculture and destroy the machinery by which food was produced. It was that we should sweep – as the Spaniards did in Cuba; and how we denounced the Spaniards – the women and children into camps in which they were destitute of all the decencies and comforts and many of the necessaries of life, and in some of which the death-rate rose so high as 430 in the 1,000 (shame). . . . A phrase often used was that 'war is war', but when one came to ask about it one was told that no war was going on, that it was not war. When was a war not a war? When it was carried on by methods of barbarism in South Africa.

> (Quoted in Morgan, op. cit., p. 118)

Rosebery condemned the argument in a speech at Chesterfield in December 1901 and widened the debate:

It is six years since the Liberals were in office. It is sixteen since they were in power. Meanwhile, the world has not stood still; but there is Toryism as great in Liberal circles, as great and deep, though it may be less conscious, as in the Carlton Club. There are men who sit still with the fly-blown phylacteries of obsolete policies bound round their foreheads, who do not remember that while they have been mumbling their incantations to themselves, the world has been marching and revolving, and that if they have any hope of leading it or guiding it they must march and move with it too. I hope, therefore, that when you have to write on your clean slate, you will write on it a policy adapted to 1901 or 1902, and not a policy adapted to 1892 or 1885. . . .

> (ibid., p. 119)

Here he seemed to be calling in particular for an end to a belief in Home Rule and for a revitalized party. Even pro-Boers like Lloyd George could agree with this. Rosebery was making public what many secretly felt. Liberalism had to make itself more relevant to the issues of the day. Temperance reform, Home Rule and disestablishment were not enough, 'old' Liberalism was played out. To Rosebery, as with Chamberlain, the future seemed to lie in a blend of imperialism and social reform. Many who were to be christened 'new' Liberals would take the social reform and leave the imperialism. In fact they saw a clash between the two, colourfully expressed by Lloyd George: 'There was not a lyddite shell which burst on the African hills that did not carry away an Old Age Pension.'

The new Liberalism with its more positive view of the state and constructive action goes back to the Oxford don T. H. Green in the early 1880s. Throughout the 1890s Green's theories had been taken up and developed by intellectuals like J. A. Hobson and future politicians like Herbert Samuel. They had formed a group nicknamed the 'Rainbow Circle' in 1893 to promote their ideas. The Boer War added a powerful spur to a more constructive view of the state. Conservatives like Balfour took up the notion of 'national efficiency', and Liberals like C. F. C. Masterman urged the adoption of state insurance schemes and labour bureaux such as had been tried in Germany. Perhaps one of the clearest expressions of this new Liberalism was to come later from Hobson in a book published in 1909 and entitled *The Crisis of Liberalism*. He urged more extensive social reform:

> Liberalism is now formally committed to a task which certainly involves a new conception of the State in its relation to the individual life and to private enterprise. That conception is not Socialism, in any accredited meaning of that term, though implying a considerable amount of increased public ownership and control of industry. From the standpoint which best presents its continuity with earlier Liberalism, it appears as a fuller appreciation and realization of individual liberty contained in the provision of equal opportunities for self-development.
>
> (Quoted in D. Read, *Edwardian England*, London, Harrap, 1972, p. 101)

Slowly the influence of men like Hobson and radical thinkers like Sidney and Beatrice Webb permeated Liberal thinking to provide the basis for action by a future Liberal Government. However, it was not a new positive Liberal programme that was to revive the party's fortunes and unite its warring factions but the mistakes of the Conservative Government.

The year 1902 was decisive in the change of fortune. Initially the divisions looked like deepening. Rosebery reappeared as president of a new Liberal League, a pressure group within the party, but with the threat of schism. Asquith, Grey and Sir Henry Fowler were its vice-presidents. Schism did not take place and the tide turned. In May the Boer War ended and the Conservative Government secured the passage of its celebrated Education Act. Here was an issue to unite Liberal factions. All rallied to the good old Non-Conformist cause. Robert Parks, Rosebery's chief adviser and treasurer of the League, was a leader of the Non-Conformist revolt against the Act. Lloyd George, after initial hesitation, put himself at the head of the Welsh revolt. Liberal politicians now had a cry. Hostility to rate-support for church schools and to the abolition of the Non-Conformist-dominated school boards was a perfect issue. By-elections swung against the Tories. The Liberals won Bury in May and Leeds North in July. The National Free Church Council had been set up in 1899 as a Non-Conformist pressure group and the Education Act and Unionist measures such as the 1904 Licensing Act and

'Chinese slavery' (see p. 102) led to a furious hatred of the government and an enthusiasm for the Liberals not seen since 1868.

This was only the start. In 1903 Chamberlain began his tariff reform campaign and presented the Liberals with a dream issue. Liberals could rally in defence of free trade and cheap food. The battles of the 1840s could be re-fought. The big Liberal loaf could be set against the small Tory loaf. Asquith emerged as the 'hammer' of protectionist arguments dogging Chamberlain's steps around the country. Liberals of all shades could feel outrage. Gladstonian purists could denounce a scheme which seemed to favour one section of the community, those gaining from tariffs, at the expense of the masses who would pay for them through dearer food. Social radicals could feel outrage at an attack on the poor. Here was a class issue which would not weaken the Liberals but cement their hold on the working-class vote. Protection, it was argued, was good for dukes but bad for the masses.

Several Conservative MPs crossed the floor of the House of Commons including the young Winston Churchill, MP for Oldham. By-election defeats became disastrous for the Unionists with five in 1903 and seven each in 1904 and 1905. It was in Lancashire particularly that the Liberals' defence of free trade produced the party's most spectacular revival. Lost to Liberalism in 1868 and only briefly recaptured in 1880, Lancashire swung dramatically to the free trade cause in 1906 and stayed there in 1910. As the *Manchester Guardian* reported in 1906:

> A candidate had only to be a Free Trader to get in, whether he was known or unknown, semi-Unionist or thorough Home Ruler. Protestant or Roman Catholic, entertaining or dull. He had only to be a Protectionist to lose all chance of getting in though he spoke with the tongues of men and angels, though he was a good employer to many electors, or had led the House of Commons or fought in the Crimea. (Quoted in A. K. Russell, *Liberal Landslide*, Newton Abbot, David & Charles, 1973, p. 173)

Throughout the county as a whole there was a swing of 13 per cent to the Liberals whose seats leapt from eleven to thirty-three.

Liberal Party organization responded to the opportunities provided by the Unionist 'home goals'. Herbert Gladstone, the Chief Whip, was the key figure. He worked at great personal cost to boost revenue and although his party could not equal the Unionists in resources Gladstone made the most of what they had. He sensibly decided to concentrate on London, and the seven or eight new agents appointed produced a revolution in the registration of Liberal voters. Their 1906 victory in places like Croydon was in no small part due to improved party organization. New support groups were encouraged. The National League of Young Liberals was set up in 1903 and had 300 branches by 1906. Gladstone's achievements as an organizer are shown in the fall in unopposed Unionist candidates. In 1900 the number had been a devastating 153, in 1906 it was 5. Associated with this is his eminently sensible deal with Ramsay MacDonald of the LRC. The splitting of the progressive vote had clearly rebounded to the Unionist advantage much as it was to do in the 1920s and the 1980s. An LRC victory at Barnard Castle in July 1903, with the official Liberal finishing a poor third, showed the advantages of an electoral pact. Clearly the LRC had not the resources for a full national campaign and both MacDonald and Gladstone could see advantages in giving progressive candidates a clear run at a Tory.

Negotiations had been opened in March and the Barnard Castle result was a powerful spur to final agreement which was settled in September. Labour would get a free run in some forty to fifty mainly Unionist seats in return for backing Liberals elsewhere. With some local friction the deal worked well in the 1906 election securing Labour a much increased representation and clearly helping many Liberals to reach Westminster. Gladstone himself was convinced the deal was rightly increasing working-class representation which had been denied in the 1890s. The LRC was not seen by him as a threat but part of a Liberal progressive federation. It was a healthy return to the grand alliance of 1868 which had seen his father triumphantly returned to Number 10.

The LRC and the Liberals could capitalize on an upswing of working-class consciousness directed at the Unionist government. Few governments seemed so narrowly plutocratic and aristocratic, an unholy merger of 'Hotel Cecil' and 'pushy' new money. Here was a government where Uncle Robert had handed over to nephew Arthur with yet another nephew, a son and a son-in-law in the same Cabinet. Had they not fought a war for the rich capitalists of the Rand? Had not Chamberlain's family, as Lloyd George had pointed out, made money out of war contracts? Had not the government shown itself contemptuous of Labour by importing Chinese 'slaves' into South Africa and refusing to reverse the Taff Vale judgment (see p. 102) of 1901? Finally, was not the whole tariff reform issue only the latest of the rich man's tricks to swindle the workers?

The timing of the election was determined in part by Lord Rosebery who looked like opening up old wounds when he spoke in Devon in November 1905 against Home Rule. Balfour resigned on 4 December hoping that Liberal divisions would quickly erupt and harm their chances in the election. There had, in fact, been a plot against Campbell-Bannerman by Grey, Haldane and Asquith to make him go to the Lords as a dummy Prime Minister whilst Asquith held the reins of power. This 'Relugas Compact', a reference from Grey's Scottish home, collapsed when Campbell-Bannerman made it perfectly clear to Asquith that he was staying in the Commons, but he offered him the Exchequer and the leadership of the Commons thereby declaring him 'crown prince'. Grey got the Foreign Office and Haldane the War Office. Rosebery got

g. The Liberal League's teeth were drawn and Rosebery was
ned to the race-course.

election in January 1906 was a Unionist nightmare. The Liberals
held on to their traditional areas of support but also made great gains
in Lancashire, London and the South East. In London Liberal seats
jumped from eight to thirty-nine with a swing of 15 per cent, rising to
21 per cent in parts of the suburbs. Only in Birmingham, Chamberlain's
citadel, was the Liberal tide held at bay. It was certainly a landslide in
terms of seats won and lost and the reversal of the previous result. Now
400 Liberals faced 157 Unionists. Yet the Liberals secured less than half
the poll. As always with the British 'first past the post' electoral system,
a modest change in the votes cast could produce a landslide in seats.

THE LAST LIBERAL GOVERNMENT 1905–15

Ploughing the sands 1905–8

Liberalism was apparently triumphant but what sort of Liberalism? It
had won largely on issues which had excited John Bright sixty years
before. Asquith in his approach to taxation and the role of the state
would not have offended Gladstone senior with the impeccable retrenchment principles explained in this speech in Cambridge in 1904:

> the most serious burden upon the industry of Great Britain . . . [was]
> the enormous and progressive increase in what the State took, and
> was taking, by taxation and by borrowing out of the pockets of the
> people of this country . . . if a Liberal Government came into power,
> the first duty they set before themselves would be a reduction in the
> country's expenditures . . . it would mean a great lightening of the
> burden lying upon every productive industry in this country.
>
> (Quoted in Bernstein, op. cit., p. 58)

There was clearly no overwhelming sense of mission to transform society,
still less a blueprint for action.

The new Liberalism was largely confined as yet to journals and the
Manchester Guardian. It had certainly not captured the Cabinet.
Campbell-Bannerman, the triumphant Prime Minister, was an old-
fashioned Gladstonian in his attitudes. Asquith, his deputy, was a prag-
matist from the right of the party who enjoyed the high society into
which his rich second wife had introduced him. Herbert Gladstone, the
architect of victory, became Home Secretary. He was well-meaning but
cautious. The Local Government Board which might be expected to
generate social reform was intensely conservative in its approach to
initiatives. Its new Liberal 'boss', John Burns, although once a socialist,
was not the man to shake it into life. The young David Lloyd George
became President of the Board of Trade and showed an energy and

administrative skill which made him a great minister, but as
political vision was still rooted in Welsh radicalism with little ?
the needs of urbanized England. In October 1906 in Cardiff, he
his audience only temperance, land reform, church disestablishment and
local Home Rule.

To English Liberals it was education which held pride of place. Non-
Conformist activists now expected the reward and the destruction of the
Balfourite monstrosity. The Liberal minister in charge, Augustine Birrell,
laboured manfully to produce a modest measure sailing between militant
Non-Conformity's demands for complete secular education and the
Roman Catholics who wanted protection for their schools. His efforts
were in vain. On 17 December 1906 the House of Lords killed the bill
which he had piloted through the Commons. Out of 602 noble Lords
only 85 nominally supported the government. A Plural Voting Bill was
also vetoed by the Lords as well as several minor measures. Here was
a direct challenge to democracy. An unelected upper house frustrating
a new huge Liberal majority in the Commons. To this challenge the
government had no answer. Lloyd George urged a dissolution but the
rest of the Cabinet urged caution. The following year brought fresh
humiliation. A Licensing Bill to please the anti-drink lobby of the party
was postponed until 1908 and then defeated in the Lords. An Irish
Councils Bill, to try and appease the Irish, was dropped when it was
quite clear that it did not go far enough for the Nationalists and anything
more would not pass the Lords. Another Education Bill in 1908 had to
be dropped. The programme of old Liberalism was receiving the old
treatment of 1892, and the result was likely to be another débâcle like
1895. By-elections began to run heavily against the government with the
loss of the solid Liberal seat of Mid-Devon in January 1908.

Yet although the first two years were deeply disappointing to activists
they were not devoid of legislative achievement. Perhaps the most
momentous of these was the Trades Disputes Act which formed the basis
of trade unions' legal position for the next sixty-five years. It was clear
that the new government would have to do something about the vulnerability of trade unions created by the Taff Vale case. Pressure from
Lib–Labs and the Labour Party made it a priority and they played a
vital role in shaping the final measure. Campbell-Bannerman and John
Burns were happy to agree to the Labour demand for full legal immunity
for trade unions but the lawyers in the Cabinet were outraged at this
notion of granting a uniquely privileged position to a section of the
community. The Cabinet, therefore, agreed to a modest Bill introduced
by the law officers on 28 March. A rival Labour Bill was introduced
offering complete freedom from damages. Without warning the Prime
Minister decided to support the Labour Bill and not his own government's: 'The great object then was, and still is, to place the two rival
powers of capital and labour on an equality so that the fight between

them, so far as fight is necessary, should be at least a fair one.' Despite the hostility of Asquith and the lawyers, Campbell-Bannerman got his way and it was the extensive bill that became law. From now on British trade unions enjoyed a most privileged legal position – a situation unique in the world. The House of Lords showed no inclination to interfere despite the sound legal arguments for amendment. Lord Lansdowne, the Tory leader in the Lords, saw nothing wrong with 'slaughtering' a Liberal Education Bill which did not command widespread working-class enthusiasm but a Trade Unions Act was another matter.

It was the Home Office under the diffident leadership of Herbert Gladstone that generated the greatest number of reforms in these first three years and his achievement is remarkable. A Workmen's Compensation Act in 1906 massively extended compensation for injury at work to a further six million workers. It brought in new categories of injury such as disease, and from the workers' point of view its most important provision was the shortening of time from two weeks to one before payment was made. Again Labour pressure lay behind the measure. Gladstone also decided to tackle the difficult question of miners' hours. More than any other issue it exposed class divisions inside the Liberal Party. The powerful miners' section demanded a straightforward limitation to eight hours. Many Liberal industrialists hated the whole idea of limiting adult male hours as a dangerous interference with market forces and profitability. In 1908 a measure was pushed through limiting miners' hours, in effect, to an eight-and-a-half-hour day, and thereby disappointing some miners. It was a political compromise but it did not prevent the secession of the Miners' Federation in 1909 to the Labour Party, potentially a serious blow to Liberalism.

The Home Office also introduced a mass of legislation reforming the penal system and securing children's rights. The system of probation as an alternative to prison was introduced in 1907. Together with a later act of 1914 allowing extra time for the payment of fines, it contributed to a considerable fall in prison population. The Borstal system for young offenders was set up in 1908 preventing the obvious dangers of thrusting youngsters in with hardened criminals in adult prisons. The Children's Act of 1908 prohibited the imprisonment of children under 14 and strictly limited it for those under 16.

If the major Liberal Education Bill failed, as indicated, important ordinances were made relating to schools. In 1907 the free place system at secondary schools was extended. In 1906, under Labour pressure and with much debate, the School Meals Act was passed enabling local authorities to provide free meals for needy children. By 1914 only half the education authorities were so doing but 31,000 children were receiving meals. The debate over this measure highlighted the vital issues of state versus individual responsibility and the passing of the Act marked a significant advance in the role of the state. Whether this ordinance was for good or ill is of course still debated. In 1907, with less controversy, an Act was passed which required medical inspections of children and permitted medical treatment. By 1914 75 per cent of all authorities were giving some treatment. Here again the government had not advanced with conviction or with a ready-made blueprint, but haltingly, and under backbench pressure. The results, however, were almost wholly beneficial.

Lloyd George at the Board of Trade proved himself more than a 'Welsh wind-bag'. He emerged as a skilful solver of administrative and political difficulties. Assisted by an able civil servant, Hubert Llewellyn-Smith, a large number of constructive measures were pushed through. A Merchant Shipping Act in 1906 massively improved conditions for seamen and forced foreign vessels using British ports to adopt the same standards. The first census of industrial production was made in 1907. This itself was indicative of the new extended role of the state. Without information, planning and government action were impossible. The establishment of the Port of London Authority in 1908 from a mass of competing interests showed Lloyd George's political skills at their best as did the settlement of a difficult railway dispute which threatened to escalate into a national strike. Lloyd George was clearly marked out for promotion.

All these measures were worthy and valuable but they made little popular impact at the time. Only one achieved really widespread appeal, the introduction of old age pensions by Asquith in his budget of 1908. Pensions had been on the political agenda in Britain for twenty years and ten other European countries had instituted them by 1906, the most notable being Germany in 1889. Pensions had figured prominently as election promises in the 1906 campaign. Despite the considerable pressure for pensions the government proceeded cautiously, anxious to avoid excessive increases in government expenditure. Asquith only promised action in 1907 and that for a year hence when he hoped a large surplus of revenue would ease the cost to the tax-payer. The scheme finally unveiled in 1908 was neither as universal as campaigners like Charles Booth had hoped, nor generous. It was only to be paid to the over 70s at the single rate of 5 shillings per week to those whose incomes were less than £26 per annum. Those who had habitually failed to work or had been in prison were excluded. Despite these concessions to Victorian thrift and morality it did break with the past. The state explicitly offered security without the stigma of the old poor law relief. It was received with universal acclaim.

Despite the popularity of this measure the prospects were not good for the Liberals when Campbell-Bannerman resigned as Prime Minister in April 1908 following a heart attack. Asquith succeeded him without any controversy. He had been heir apparent for some time but his tenure at Number 10 promised to be short-lived. In the course of 1908 seven seats were lost to the Conservatives in by-elections in all areas of the country. In 1907 there had also been three lost to Labour. This included a sensational result in Colne Valley where Victor Grayson carried a safe Liberal seat for the extreme left-wing position espoused by the ILP. A serious trade recession set in during 1908 and unemployment leapt ominously. In addition Asquith's Government faced a hostile House of Lords increasingly willing to block and emasculate Liberal legislation. Asquith's prospects did not look good.

Triumph and achievement 1909–11

The first three years of Asquith's premiership were a period of success almost unequalled by any other British government. Two general elections were fought and won in 1910. The dragon, in the shape of the House of Lords, was finally slain or at least had its teeth pulled, and perhaps the single most important piece of social legislation of the twentieth century was placed upon the statute books – the National Insurance Act of 1911.

Herbert Henry Asquith, the new Prime Minister, was 56 when he replaced Campbell-Bannerman. He was to prove an outstanding peacetime Prime Minister. He possessed a refined and disciplined mind which in Churchill's words, 'opened and closed like the well oiled breech of a gun'. As another cabinet colleague, Charles Hobhouse, recalled in his diary, Asquith had 'an extraordinary quickness in seizing the right point'. He dispatched government business with speed and efficiency leaving ample time for his numerous other pursuits amongst which literature, alcohol and young ladies figured prominently. He became somewhat notorious with regard to the last two categories. Asquith was a superb debater in the House of Commons until dinner time. On one evening after dinner in 1911 he was slumped on the front bench too drunk to speak. His other weakness also became more pronounced with age, as the suffragette Ethyl Smythe recalled in 1914: 'I think it disgraceful that millions of women shall be trampled underfoot because of the convictions of an old man who notoriously can't be left alone in a room with a young girl after dinner.' She was clearly biased but her complaint was rooted in fact. His failings apart Asquith was an outstanding political leader, holding together a strong team and uniquely avoiding any resignations for six years.

The team that he led must be accounted the strongest cabinet of the twentieth century in terms of talent and personality. Lloyd George was pre-eminent in both respects. Asquith promoted his Welsh colleague to the Exchequer. It is said that Lloyd George, or simply George as he then was, confessed himself a genius at the age of 13. As in most cases his perceptive intuition was correct. His was not the conventional mind of the English politician like Peel, Gladstone or Asquith schooled in classical scholarship. David George had left school at 16 to enter a small town solicitor's office. He was a local boy made good. He had a flair

Herbert Henry Asquith by Sir Leslie Ward

for popular oratory, a lightning and often cruel wit – of Balfour 'more a mannerism than a man' and of his fellow Liberal Herbert Samuel 'When they circumcised Samuel they threw away the wrong bit.' He also possessed charm in abundance, as Hobhouse put it, he had 'an unrivalled, indeed miraculous, power of picking other people's brains'. Lloyd George's disdain for conventional work habits at the Treasury drove some of his civil servants to distraction. Not for him the orderly submission of memos, he preferred an informal chat. He had an impish puck-like quality, fizzing with energy and ideas but lacking the high moral seriousness of a Gladstone or the gravitas of an Asquith. His cheerful irreverence is captured by his remark to Hobhouse in 1911, 'Good Heavens if one mayn't tell lies at election times, when may one tell them?' Perhaps there was a dangerous lack of morality for as John Burns said of him in 1911, 'Lloyd George's conscience is as good as new, for he has never used it.'

The energy and drive of the Cabinet was powerfully enhanced by the arrival in 1908 of Winston Spencer Churchill, in Lloyd George's former job of President of the Board of Trade. Grandson of a duke, son of the unfortunate Randolph Churchill, Winston was already a larger-than-life figure. Hobhouse described him in 1912: 'He is really a spoilt child with the brain of a genius.' Churchill seemed to have completely thrown off his Tory background and now embraced advanced Liberalism with enthusiasm. In an article in *The Nation* he urged 'a new constructive policy'. He espoused government action to tackle the evils of poverty and deprivation. The new Liberalism had found a spokesman of real weight in Cabinet. Lloyd George and Churchill between them gave a new dynamism to the government. Their importance is attested to by the Fabian Beatrice Webb who recorded in her diary during 1910:

> (*30 November 1910.*) . . . The big thing that has happened in the last two years is that Lloyd George and Winston Churchill have practically taken the *limelight*, not merely from their own colleagues, but from the Labour Party. They stand out as the most advanced politicians. And, if we get a Liberal majority and payment of members, we shall have any number of young Fabians rushing from Parliament, fully equipped for the fray – better than the Labour men – and enrolling themselves behind the two Radical leaders.
>
> (Quoted in Morgan, op. cit., p. 148)

If Churchill, Lloyd George and Asquith attracted the greatest attention there was plenty of other talent. Haldane at the War Office proved the most constructive army reformer since Cardwell. Junior ministers like John Simon, Charles Masterman and Herbert Samuel indicated that there was also depth of talent to call upon. However, it was the new Chancellor of the Exchequer who provided the instrument to revive Liberal fortunes with his bold budget of 1909. Nicknamed 'the People's Budget' it grew out of the need to provide extra cash for the old age pensions and dreadnought battleships but also the need to outwit the House of Lords and raise Liberal morale. Traditionally the Lords could not interfere with a money bill, therefore the budget was the obvious means to cock a snook at their lordships. Lloyd George appears to have deliberately exaggerated the deficit of £16 million, looking around for ideas for extra spending in order to justify the increase in taxes in key areas. It was a most unGladstonian approach. The victims of the budget were clearly the rich. An extra £7 million was raised by increasing higher rates of income tax on those earning over £3,000 per annum and introducing a super-tax on those earning more than £5,000 per annum. Estate duties were increased, as were stamp duties on shares. There were actually rebates for the lower income tax-payers with a new child allowance. Only 12,000 would be affected by the super-tax. By the standards of the twentieth century, especially later on, the tax burden on the rich was hardly oppressive but at the time it drew forth much criticism.

An extra £3.5 million was raised by taxes on beer, spirits and tobacco and if the Lords would not let through a Licensing Bill then revenge could be taken by these and increased licence fees for public houses. Temperance reformers were delighted. The rich were also hit by the new petrol duties and a road fund licence. The most bitter portion of the budget for the Lords was a series of land taxes. Lloyd George here was responding to a popular Liberal demand for land reform. The remarkable concentration of land ownership in Britain excited many critics and since the 1880s there had been a growing demand for attacks on these evil monopolies which were held to harm the community at large. Lloyd George's remedies were modest enough: a 20 per cent tax on the unearned value of land whenever it was sold without the owner contributing to its increased value; a half-penny in the pound duty on undeveloped land and minerals; and a 10 per cent reversion duty on the increased value of leased land every time a lease was ended. These taxes were only expected to bring in £500,000 per annum initially, but the Chancellor hoped that they would provide an expanding revenue in the future.

The importance of the budget lies not in the sums raised and projected, but in its political context. It worked on a firm commitment to constructive government – new roads under the Roads Board, £100,000 for a national system of labour exchanges, £200,000 for a Development Commission for developing rural life, etc. Conservatives might not object in principle to these but tariff reformers were furious that such constructive government and policies would be paid for by soaking the British rich not by taxing foreigners. The budget appeared to undermine the case for tariff reform and committed Britain to a national revenue system based on progressive direct taxation. The land taxes and the licensing duties were merely salt to rub in the Tory wounds.

The Cabinet did not anticipate the House of Lords' reaction. Fury robbed their lordships of their senses. It became increasingly likely that the Lords would reject the budget and precipitate a constitutional crisis. Churchill and Lloyd George could not believe their luck. Both raised the political temperature with fighting speeches deliberately stinging their opponents. At Newcastle in October Lloyd George delivered one of his most famous orations:

> Let them realize what they are doing. They are forcing a revolution, and they will get it. The Lords may decree a revolution, but the people will direct it. If they begin, issues will be raised that they little dream of. Questions will be asked which are now whispered in humble voices, and answers will be demanded then with authority. The question will be asked whether five hundred men, ordinary men chosen accidentally from among the unemployed, should override the

judgment – the deliberate judgment – of millions of people who are engaged in the industry which makes the wealth of the country.

That is one question. Another will be: Who ordained that a few should have the land of Britain as a perquisite? Who made ten thousand people owners of the soil, and the rest of us trespassers in the land of our birth? Who is it who is responsible for the scheme of things whereby one man is engaged through life in grinding labour to win a bare and precarious subsistence for himself, and when, at the end of his days, he claims at the hands of the community he served a poor pension of eightpence a day, he can only get it through a revolution, and another man who does not toil receives every hour of the day, every hour of the night, whilst he slumbers, more than his poor neighbour receives in a whole year of toil?

The budget was finally rejected on 30 November by 350 to 75. A general election would clearly be necessary. The Liberals would go to the country with the popular cry 'the peers against the people'. Rank-and-file Liberals could work enthusiastically in this cause, and party activists in both the Labour and Liberal parties who wished to break the pact of 1903 were forced to co-operate. January 1910 produced one of the highest turnouts of the century, 86.6 per cent. The Liberals did not do quite so well as they hoped but stifled any growing challenge from Labour. They finished with a clear working majority of 124:

Liberals	275
Unionists	273
Labour	40
Irish Nationalists	82

If the Unionists had recaptured much of the South and Midlands, the Liberals held on to the North and notably to Lancashire.

For over a month the government now dithered as to how to proceed. Pressure from activists forced it to undertake an assault on the House of Lords. The budget was quickly passed by 28 April and on the 14th Asquith had introduced a Parliament Bill which would cripple the Lords permanently. He and the Cabinet expected resistance which would force another election after which the King would agree to create enough peers to overwhelm opposition in the Lords and force the measures through. The crisis proved a long one partly because of the death of Edward VII on 6 May and partly because of the unexpected resistance from backbenchers in the Lords. The new inexperienced George V was pitched into the worst constitutional crisis of the century. To ease his burden Asquith agreed to try to solve the crisis by negotiation. Lloyd George showed himself to be distinctly enthusiastic for a deal, even talking of a national coalition. In the end negotiations failed on the issue of Home Rule. With the greatest reluctance the King promised his Prime

Minister that he could have the several hundred new peers he needed if the Liberals won a second general election.

The December election produced little change with a slightly lower turnout:

Liberals	272
Unionists	272
Labour	42
Irish Nationalists	84

The government retained a majority of 126 and the Parliament Bill could proceed. It passed the Commons with a huge majority and the tension centred on whether their lordships would submit to the inevitable and avoid the mass creation of peers or force the government into this step. A group of Tories wanted to fight to the last ditch. These last 'ditchers', led by the aged Lord Halsbury and Lord Willoughby de Broke, felt that Asquith was bluffing. Other Conservatives, including the official leadership, wanted to hedge. The 'ditchers' lost by seventeen votes in August 1911, and the Parliament Bill became law. The Lords could no longer interfere with any money bill and they were left in effect with only a two-year delay in all other measures including Home Rule. At the same time the length of a Parliament was reduced from seven years to five. Liberalism had at long last triumphed.

The year 1911 also produced another major legislative triumph – national insurance – and in so doing laid the foundations for a welfare state. The origins of the legislative landmark are diverse. Churchill at the Board of Trade wished to respond to the sharp rise in unemployment during the slump of 1908–9. With a young civil servant, William Beveridge, he prepared two schemes: one which he carried through and led to the setting up of labour exchanges throughout the country, the other, of unemployment insurance, was incomplete when Churchill was promoted to the Home Office in 1910. Lloyd George took over the Unemployment Insurance Bill in 1911. It was limited to select trades known to be susceptible to bouts of seasonal or cyclical unemployment such as construction, ship-building and engineering. Workers, employers and government would all contribute and weekly payments of 7 shillings for fifteen weeks would, it was hoped, tide the victims through the slumps. The scheme proved a huge success and by 1914 the government was preparing to extend it to other trades.

Health insurance was the other side of the measure. Although the unemployment insurance was unique in the world it was health insurance, already twenty-five years old in Germany, that proved a much more complex political problem. It grew from many roots, the widespread concern with national efficiency and the health of the nation, and the new concern with poverty. In 1909 a Royal Commission on the Poor Law reported on four years' research and made a mass of recommendations.

Lloyd George himself had visited Germany in 1908 and was fascinated by the German scheme. He eventually introduced one that was much more comprehensive and from which all workers earning less than £160 per annum would benefit. In return for 4 pennies from employees, 3 from employers and 2 from the state each week, the worker was entitled to a weekly benefit of 10 shillings whilst he was sick, and for the long term a 5 shillings a week disability payment was made. As well as this free medical treatment was available to the workers. A single payment of 50 shillings maternity benefit was introduced for workers' wives and benefits for widows and orphans were originally proposed but later dropped. Lloyd George's skill in piloting the measure on to the statute book was phenomenal, outwitting or compromising with different interest groups, trade unions, doctors, Friendly Societies and insurance companies. The Labour Party was not initially enthusiastic and was bought with the promise of payment for MPs which was carried through that same year. Widows and orphans were sacrificed to the insurance companies, and the doctors were outwitted by a well-timed appeal by Lloyd George over the heads of the British Medical Association leaders to the poorer rank and file of the medical profession. It was a massive achievement even though women and children only benefited indirectly. Initially it was not enormously popular, workers objected to the 4 pennies deduction from their wages and aristocratic ladies organized a protest by their servants at having to lick the stamps. The tide gradually turned and as the leading Unionist, Austen Chamberlain, complained, 'Confound Lloyd George he has strengthened the government again.'

Churchill's contribution to social reform in these years was not merely confined to the planning stages of national insurance. His Labour Exchanges Act of 1909 proved a major success. By 1913 there were 430 exchanges throughout the country. Churchill also grasped the nettle of the 'sweated trades' and pushed through the Trade Board Act in 1909 to raise wages in four occupations notorious for low wages and appalling conditions: tailoring, box making, lace and chain making. This move benefited 200,000 workers, 140,000 of them women, and six other trades were added in 1913. Here was another body blow to *laissez-faire*. The state was feeling its way forward to some notion of a minimum wage.

The troubled final years 1912–15

If 1911 was the year of the Liberal Party triumphant, 1912 showed just how fickle fate can be for politicians. Lloyd George was nearly ruined by the Marconi scandal. He and other leading Liberals had bought shares in the American Marconi Company just when a sister company, the British Marconi Company, had been awarded a valuable government contract. In strict terms there was no corruption but as one Liberal colleague pointed out their behaviour was 'certainly indiscreet and very nearly improper'. The whole affair was a passing embarrassment but far worse were a series of problems to which Asquith's Government appeared to have no ready answers.

The year 1912 was to be one of the worst of the century for strikes with 41 million working days lost. There were in excess of 11 million in 1913 and this general burst of union activity and militancy has prompted some historians to see an explosion of class conflict which threatened not only the Liberal Government but the whole fabric of Edwardian society. Union activity had many roots, the most important being the strengthened power of trade unions under the 1906 Act. The strikes were not, however, a precursor to revolution. The long period of deflation during the late nineteenth century had ended, and a modest inflation set in which forced workers to demand higher wages. This demand became more effective following recovery from the 1909 slump. There was now no great pool of unemployed to dampen militancy. The situation was exacerbated by the lack of any effective government machinery for solving disputes. During these years, therefore, the Board of Trade had to improvise conciliation and the government was driven piecemeal into legislation to allay grievances. It did not, however, have any cohesive strategy.

In 1911 a two-day rail strike was once again settled by Lloyd George and a Railway Traffic Act in 1913 allowed increased rates to pay for better wages and working conditions. In 1912 a lengthy national coal-strike forced the government further down the road to wage regulation with the setting up of District Boards to fix wages. The government explored the possibility of compulsory arbitration but trade union pressure led them to abandon the idea. By 1914 the worst seemed to be over but the Liberal Government had not found an answer to the problem of industrial relations which were to bedevil most governments well into the late twentieth century.

The issue of votes for women also posed a question for the government which it found difficult to answer. In principle Liberals were in favour of extending the franchise and in 1907 an Act had allowed women, for the first time, to serve on county and county borough councils, in which role they made, as is now being recognized, a significant contribution to the new Liberalism. The practicality, however, of enfranchising women for parliamentary elections was very complex. If women were to be given the vote on the same terms as men, that is as a householder franchise with the existing plural voting continuing, most Liberals feared that the result would be a substantial strengthening of the Unionist Party. Women's suffrage therefore would have to be part of a larger measure of franchise reform with all the complexities that that would entail. Since 1897 the suffragists of the National Union of Women's Suffrage Society had been campaigning. In 1903 a militant organization, the Women's Social and Political Union (WSPU), was formed by Mrs Emmeline

Pankhurst of Manchester. Beginning in 1905 it began to adopt militant tactics courting prison and public punishment. Too often they assailed their friends like Sir Edward Grey and Lloyd George and quite probably their activities, far from promoting their cause, actually turned moderate Liberals against them. A series of private members' bills were lost between 1907 and 1912, but in that year the government agreed to the insertion of women's franchise clauses into a general reform bill which would have ended plural voting and extended the male franchise. Unfortunately, the Speaker ruled that this changed the bill, and insisted that new bills would have to be introduced. The WSPU now resorted to extreme militancy. A house being built for Lloyd George was fired and a somewhat unbalanced suffragette threw herself under the King's horse during the 1913 Derby. From the safety of Paris, Emmeline Pankhurst's daughter Christabel orchestrated the campaign increasingly taking the WSPU down an anti-male highway which was completely counterproductive. The government reacted to the violence, which was that of only a tiny minority with the so-called 'Cat and Mouse' Act. Instead of the unpleasant forced feeding of offenders who were on hunger strike, such prisoners could be released until they had recovered their strength and then be re-arrested. In WSPU mythology this was one more example of the Liberal male oppression. In many respects the Act was a sensible and humane way of dealing with what the Liberal *Manchester Guardian* called 'diseased emotionalism'.

Ireland and Home Rule presented by far the greatest problem, to which the government searched in vain for a solution. The Parliament Act of 1911 had thrust Home Rule once again into the prominent position it had last held under Gladstone. Because of the deal struck with the Nationalists (see chapter 4) the Liberals were now completely dependent on the Irish Nationalists for their majority and could no longer use the excuse of the House of Lords' veto. The result was the Third Home Rule Bill introduced in April 1912. The Irish dimension of the ensuing crisis has been discussed in chapter 4. In mainland Britain it whipped up inter-party tension already inflamed by the Parliament Bill. The languid Balfour was replaced by the acerbic Andrew Bonar Law as Unionist leader and the volume of inter-party insult reached levels unheard for decades, as the Unionist minority in the Commons sought to preserve the Union itself. At times Conservative Party links with Unionist militancy in Northern Ireland hovered on the border of treason. The sympathies of the army with Unionist resistance became clear in the so-called Curragh Mutiny of March 1914. This was no mutiny but a badly handled sounding-out operation of army opinion, which produced a spate of resignations by army officers. The nub of the problem, then as now, lay in Northern Ireland and the Liberals recognized that some special treatment of Ulster with its Protestant majority would be necessary. Just how special was limited by pressure from the Irish Nationalists who could not agree to the total exclusion of Ulster from Home Rule. Asquith offered the Unionists a six-year exclusion which was discussed at a special conference at Buckingham Palace in the summer of 1914. No agreement was reached and the Third Home Rule Bill became law in September 1914. Its operation was suspended for the duration of the First World War. The problem had not been solved and the tensions had been exacerbated. The results of this were seen in 1916 and again in the violence of 1919–21. The events of these troubled years were seen by George Dangerfield in a wonderful book, *The Strange Death of Liberal England*, published in 1935, as the disintegration not only of a government but of a society. His work is a literary masterpiece if somewhat exaggerated in its conclusions.

By 1914 the worst of the strikes were over. The suffragette movement showed a capacity for theatricality but hardly threatened government or society. Ireland was indeed an unsolved problem but one that governments throughout the twentieth century have had to live with. Perhaps more serious for the Liberal Government was its hold on the working-class voters and the relationship of the Liberal Party with its Labour ally. Lloyd George once again made all the running, nailing the Liberal flag to the mast of land reform. There was an extensive rural land programme involving minimum wages for agricultural labourers, the building of 120,000 houses to let, thus doing away with tied cottages, and also the setting up of small holdings to let at reasonable prices. Farmers would get greater protection from the game rights of landlords and greater security of tenure. All the evidence suggests that this programme looked widely popular in rural constituencies. The urban land campaign was less successful. Its central theme was protection of leaseholders and the encouragement of housing and urban development. The latter was a tacit recognition of the failure of Burns's 1909 Housing Act. There is little to suggest that the campaign excited much enthusiasm in urban England and it was here that relations with the Labour Party were most ominous. Labour had made no dramatic parliamentary breakthrough in 1910 nor did it in subsequent by-elections but the growth of trade union membership from 2.6 million to 4.1 million between 1910 and 1914 provided the party with an expanding revenue. In 1912 the Miners' Federation of Great Britain had passed under the control of the Labour Party with serious implications for several Liberal seats in mining areas. At a local level there was a steady if unspectacular advance of Labour. If Labour had only 2 out of 64 seats in Sheffield it had 14 compared to only 12 Liberals in Leeds. In Liberal Leicester 10 Liberals faced 16 Conservatives and 14 Labour. By 1914 Labour was ready to contest 120 seats at the next general election. The Liberals would clearly have to renegotiate a new electoral pact and this would not be easy to enforce at a local level. The whole future of the Liberal Party is more fully discussed in a section at the end of this chapter. It belongs to the area of speculation and historical controversy.

The outbreak of war in August 1914 initially produced little change. Two members of the Cabinet resigned, John Morley and John Burns. Their departure produced no sensation. Lloyd George's decision to rally to the war effort was crucial. A united House of Commons accepted the government decision and the same government, in essence, continued for the next ten months. The major change was the arrival of Lord Kitchener at the War Office. He was left alone to run the army as Churchill, at the Admiralty, was left to run the navy. It was, in Churchill's famous phrase, 'business as usual'. The county cricket matches were played until the end of August. Voluntary recruitment, not conscription, would make up the army numbers. Income tax was raised by the Chancellor from one shilling and three pennies, to two shillings and sixpence, in his first war budget in November 1914. The railways were taken over by the Board of Trade but run by the same directors, and the 1913 dividend was guaranteed to share-holders. The Defence of the Realm Act, or DORA, as it was commonly know, was passed in 1914 and it gave the government wide powers which were steadily extended but overall this development of state power was only gradual. In March 1915 an agreement with the unions harnessed their influence to the war effort and showed the new respect and power they held in British society.

A general election was constitutionally due at the latest by January 1916. Asquith feared defeat. The Unionists had behaved as a 'patriotic' opposition but war setbacks would ensure the end of this honeymoon. Kitchener and the War Office failed to organize sufficient shell production leading to scandalous shortages at the battles of Neuve Chapelle, Ypres and Festubert. Lord Northcliffe, owner of the *Daily Mail* and *The Times*, was determined to take up the issue and drive the government from office. Setbacks over the Dardanelles campaign (see chapter 8) produced the resignation of Admiral Sir John Fisher, the First Sea Lord, and mounting criticism of his political boss Churchill. Asquith skilfully solved all these problems by a front-bench deal with Bonar Law. A coalition government was established and the last Liberal Government ended quietly. Asquith remained as Prime Minister and the Conservatives did rather badly in their share of the cabinet spoils. Nevertheless, Charles Hobhouse, one of the sacrificed Liberal ministers, recorded rather sourly in his diary:

> The disintegration of the Liberal Party is complete. We shall not return to power for some years, and only then because Labour is as broken as ourselves. Ll.G. and his Tory friends will soon get rid of Asquith, and the one or two genuine Liberals left of whom Grey and Crewe and W.R. are the most conscientious.
>
> (*Inside Asquith's Cabinet – From the Diaries of Charles Hobhouse*, London, John Murray, 1977, p. 247)

THE LIBERAL ACHIEVEMENT

One of the most constructive governments of the nineteenth and twentieth centuries had ended in May 1915. It had taken office in 1905 with no great blueprint of reform, yet the energy of ministers like Churchill and Lloyd George, and the growing influence and skills of civil servants such as Llewellyn-Smith and Beveridge, had produced an unparalleled spate of legislation. In part this was in response to political pressures and both Lloyd George and Churchill felt that the Labour Party had to be seen off by a large dose of social reform. Direct Labour pressure was responsible for some particular measures such as the Trades Disputes Act and the School Meals Act, both of 1906. The legislation was also a response to that most intangible phenomenon, the 'public mood'. The drive for national efficiency and the growing awareness of the unacceptable poverty created a climate where the new Liberalism could flourish. What had been acceptable in 1867 was not acceptable in 1907. There was a growing faith in the state's capacity to cure problems. No longer could it be left to local government which had shouldered most of the burden of social reform and improvement in Victorian England. The example of other European countries could also be a powerful stimulus. The dynamic new German Empire seemed to show that social reform and dramatic economic success could go hand in hand. Belgium showed the way in setting up infant welfare centres after 1903. Only after 1908 did the British Local Government Board really begin to encourage this development, largely due to the appointment of Dr Arthur Newsholme as Chief Medical Officer. No special legislation marks the most important of Edwardian achievements – the very real fall in infant mortality.

Many national disaster areas had been left untouched. The slums of the cities had to wait until the 1920s and the 1930s for a real assault and Burns's Housing Act of 1909 was more of a hindrance than a help to planning. State education, although modestly encouraged by the Liberals, remained markedly inferior to that of Germany. Only £250,000 went from the public purse to British universities in 1914 – a mere third of that spent by the state of Prussia alone – and the British working man remained the inferior of his German contemporary in secondary schooling. Despite these areas of neglect, social service spending had roughly doubled since 1906. Well might the old intone a blessing on that 'Lord George'.

THE WAR-TIME COALITION UNDER ASQUITH: MAY 1915 TO DECEMBER 1916

'Business as usual' proved impossible; Kitchener's mass army ensured this. By January 1915 two million men of the 17–45 age group were in the forces and in the course of 1915 a further 1.28 million joined them.

Eventually some 4.9 million industrial workers donned uniform. The implications of this were enormous. Women moved in to fill the gaps, with 800,000 going into engineering alone. Skirts and hair got shorter and 400,000 domestics abandoned service. The state's role steadily expanded, not according to any clear principles but as the need arose. Lloyd George found himself carried along by the dynamics of war to push for greater and greater control. In his new role as Minister of Munitions he pushed through extensive liquor control to aid production. Hours of drinking were cut and the afternoon rest period was not abandoned until the 1980s. Only in Carlisle, near a large munitions depot, was the brewery actually nationalized, again surviving until the 1980s as a state enterprise. Beer itself was weakened in the national cause. Two hundred factories and mines came under state control in the course of 1915–16. Prices and profits were regulated and a Rent Restriction Act was passed to help migrant munitions workers. County Agricultural Committees were devised in 1916 to impose production targets on farmers. The government came increasingly to control food prices, partly through the market mechanism of buying and releasing supplies. Taxation escalated. The new Chancellor of the Coalition Government, a Liberal, Reginald McKenna, a man often associated with pure *laissez-faire*, pushed up income tax to 25 pennies in the pound in 1916 and in the previous year an excess profits tax of 50 per cent had been introduced. More staggering the 'holy grail' of Liberalism had been sullied. In October 1915 McKenna abandoned free trade with 33 per cent duties imposed on luxury imports. The basic tenets of Victorian Liberalism were being eroded.

Asquith had marched the Edwardian progressive movement almost united into the alien landscape of total war. Born out of the iniquities of the Boer War and tariff reform the movement now found itself allied to the Tories and endorsing activities which would have shocked Campbell-Bannerman let alone Mr Gladstone. The acceptance of conscription perhaps more than any other issue ran counter to traditional Liberal tenets. By the middle of 1915 voluntary enlistment seemed to be inadequate to many as a means of filling the trenches in France. There was a growing demand for conscription from Unionist members of the coalition. Asquith resorted to his usual temporizing tactics. Lloyd George, the anti-war radical of 1900, identified with his Unionist colleagues not his radical supporters. In January 1916 Asquith gave in and the Military Service Act imposed compulsory enlistment on unmarried men aged 18 to 41. John Simon, the Liberal Home Secretary, resigned in protest. By April 1916 there was fresh pressure for general conscription. Lloyd George supported it but other Liberals threatened to resign if it was carried. Asquith dithered, distracted by the disaster in the Middle East and rebellion in Ireland, and the measure was finally accepted without resignations. Events in Ireland, however, forced Liberalism to accept fresh unpalatable actions. Rebellion was followed by illiberal, savage repression and despite Lloyd George's best efforts at compromise to appease Ireland, Unionist objections forced the dropping of immediate Home Rule as a cure for Ireland's ills. Free trade, personal liberty and now Home Rule had all been sacrificed on the altar of total war.

The coalition government itself was an unhappy amalgam. Asquith displayed political genius in playing off one personality against another, seemingly enhancing his own indispensability. Lloyd George exchanged the Exchequer for the new crisis centre of munitions. Asquith cleverly kept Bonar Law out of the Treasury (where he wanted to be) by the pretence that Lloyd George's departure was only temporary, and therefore McKenna, a Liberal, was drafted in to Number 11 to keep the place warm for the dynamic Welshman. Bonar Law contented himself with the Colonial Office. Only the easy-going Balfour, whom Asquith found congenial, secured an important post at the Admiralty in place of Churchill. Tensions and frustrations abounded. McKenna and Lloyd George hated one another. Bonar Law, like most Unionists, detested Lloyd George. All were increasingly frustrated by Kitchener, the one man whom the public had faith in and the man whom his colleagues increasingly saw as an obstacle to victory. He had become in Asquith's wife's phrase no more than 'a great poster'.

Lloyd George's energy and capacity for improvization rapidly solved the munitions crisis. Businessmen like Eric Geddes were drafted in by Lloyd George to control his expanding empire. The new ministry continually clashed with Kitchener. Geddes asked Kitchener on 26 July 1915 how many machine-guns per battalion were desirable. Kitchener replied that two was a minimum and four a maximum. Lloyd George's instructions to Geddes was indicative of his whole approach: 'Take Kitchener's maximum, square it multiply the result by two, and, when you are in sight of that, double it again for good measure.' Words were translated into deeds. Machine-gun production rose from 6,000 in 1915 to 33,000 in 1916. The monthly output of shells increased from 20,000 in May 1915 to one million by July 1916.

Lloyd George's energy contrasted with that of Asquith and blame for the muddle and defeats of 1915 and 1916 was laid at the Prime Minister's feet. Certainly there was no streamlining of the decision process. Decisions were taken in a leisurely fashion, some times first by a committee, like the one set up to supervise the Dardanelles campaign, and then again at other times by the whole Cabinet. It was a recipe for sloth and possibly defeat. The Dardanelles Committee was transformed into a smaller war council in November 1915. It rapidly degenerated into a larger inefficient body which met irregularly. As Sir Maurice Hankey, its secretary, complained in May 1916 there was 'Literally no one in this country who knows or has access to all the information naval, military and political on which future plans must be based'. Asquith's calm, a strength in peace, had become a liability in war. Churchill complained to his brother in 1916: 'Asquith reigns sodden, supine, supreme.' Less bitterly Lytton Strachey described the Prime Minister in a letter of 1916:

> I studied the Old Man with extreme vigour; and really he's a corker. He seemed much larger than he did when I last saw him (just two years ago) – a fleshy, sanguine, wine-bibbing medieval-Abbot of a personage – a gluttonous, lecherous, cynical old fellow – ough! . . . I've rarely seen anyone so obviously enjoying life; so obviously, I thought, *out* to enjoy it; almost, really, as if he'd deliberately decided that he *would*, and let all the rest go hang. Cynical, yes. It's hardly possible to doubt it; or perhaps one should say just 'case-hardened'. *Tiens!* One looks at him, and thinks of the war. . . . On the whole, one wants to stick a dagger in his ribs . . . and then, as well, one can't help liking him – I suppose because he *does* enjoy himself so much.
> (Quoted in S. E. Koss, *H. H. Asquith*, London, Allen Lane, 1976, p. 209)

In one sense it was not what Asquith did or did not do that mattered, it was how he was perceived. Image rather than reality was all important. The public demanded the appearance of dynamism, not languid calm. Lord Northcliffe, the powerful press baron, pursued Asquith with a vengeance. Defeats called for scapegoats. By the autumn of 1916 many Conservative members of Parliament and some members of the Cabinet felt that change was essential. Change did come, and quite unexpectedly. A mine assisted the war effort when it sank the cruiser carrying Kitchener on a visit to Russia. Lloyd George succeeded him as Minister of War and whilst he and Bonar Law remained loyal Asquith was safe as Prime Minister.

Asquith's downfall, however, came in December 1916 as a result of a series of complex political manoeuvrings. Bonar Law became convinced that his leadership of the Unionists was threatened by his loyalty to Asquith. He overcame his distrust of Lloyd George sufficiently to co-operate with him in demanding a streamlined War Cabinet. Lloyd George would chair it and Asquith would be excluded although remain as overall Prime Minister. Asquith refused and on 5 December resigned. Lloyd George was able to replace him with the support of the Conservatives and nearly half the Liberals, whose support had been canvassed by Dr Christopher Addison, a devotee of Lloyd George. The Labour Party, under Arthur Henderson, also threw in their lot with Lloyd George. Asquith was dumped. The result of this crisis was a disaster for the Liberal Party, half of whom remained loyal to 'Squiffy', who came to be viewed as the guardian of traditional Liberal values. The split was not healed until it was too late and the Liberal Party reduced to a third force condemned perpetually to the back benches.

THE WAR-TIME COALITION UNDER LLOYD GEORGE 1916–18

The new conductor was in many ways in a much weaker position than his predecessor in forcing the orchestra to follow his baton. The bulk of the parliamentary support was drawn from the Conservative benches and he was therefore dependent on the good will of Bonar Law. The need to avoid sparking off a Tory revolt handicapped the new Prime Minister in his handling of the army and navy chiefs. He eventually achieved victory over the latter but army commanders Haig and Robertson enjoyed an independence that the Prime Minister resented. The Conservatives now got a much stronger grasp on the levers of power. Bonar Law received the Exchequer and doubled it with the leadership of the House. Balfour replaced Grey as Foreign Secretary. In the new five-man War Cabinet Lloyd George was the sole Liberal. Bonar Law and Lord Curzon were Unionists, Henderson sat for Labour, and the imperial proconsul, Lord Milner, was drafted in, the symbol of national efficiency.

David Lloyd George by Walton Adams

Liberal talent was in short supply and Lloyd George had to make do with political second-raters until he got Churchill to join him in 1917. The galaxy of Liberal stars remained in the Asquithian camp. Partly to free himself of the Unionist stranglehold, partly in response to the quest for national efficiency, Lloyd George turned to non-political 'experts'. The historian H. A. L. Fisher took Education, Lord Devonport, the food-chain magnate, took the new Ministry of Food, and the press barons were drafted in to look after information and propaganda. Lloyd George himself evolved a new, almost presidential style with his Downing Street 'garden suburb' of attendants upon whom he relied to circumvent the normal processes of British ministerial government. The War Cabinet itself developed a proper secretariat which survives to this day as the Cabinet Office and for the first time minutes were kept of cabinet decisions.

The myth was carefully fostered of a 'national efficiency' government, exuding dynamic energy, taking decisions that the old 'wait and see' team would never have taken. More often than not the new government merely continued along those lines of development already well underway by December 1916. The pressure of war had its own logic. The Corn Production Act of 1917, which gave wide powers of control over farming built heavily on the already established County Agricultural Committees. Compulsory rationing came in only in 1918. The new men were as reluctant as the old to abandon market forces but like the old they strove for victory.

One of the most urgent problems was that posed by Germany's resort to unrestricted submarine warfare to starve Britain into defeat. It came close to success. In April 1917 545,000 tons of shipping were lost. The Admiralty was managing, by comparison, to sink one or two German U-boats per month. One of Lloyd George's experts, Sir Joseph Mackay, managed to boost production of ships and reduce turn-round time in the ports, but the sinkings continued. The Admiralty refused to work a convoy system which Lloyd George and his Cabinet Secretary, Sir Maurice Hankey, urged on them. The Unionist Sir Edward Carson had been appointed as political boss of the navy not because of any administrative talent, but because of his considerable abilities for making trouble on the back benches. As so often in British politics it was safer to have him in than out. Carson refused to coerce his admirals and threatened to resign. Lloyd George exercised great charm and pressure to get the navy to adopt the convoy system. In the end Carson was removed by promoting him to the War Cabinet and the expert businessman Eric Geddes took his place. The sinkings fell to 154,000 tons in November 1917. The country survived and Lloyd George had performed one of his most important services.

The other great crisis centred on the question of manpower. The army's insatiable demand for cannon fodder threatened industrial production. Sectors of industry competed with others for this vital scarce resource – labour. The army, it was decided, would only get 450,000 men in 1918 not the 1.2 million it demanded. This was to lead to a major political crisis and become entangled with the wider issue of civilian political control of the generals. The Somme offensive of 1916 with its 450,000 casualties for minimal gains had shaken Lloyd George's faith in both Field Marshal Douglas Haig, the commander in France, and the Cabinet's sole military adviser, Sir William Robertson, the Chief of the Imperial General Staff. The Prime Minister sought to avoid a repetition of the Somme and more directly to control military decisions. A popular but essentially weak Unionist, Lord Derby, was given the War Office in the hope that through him the War Cabinet would control the generals. Instead he became the tool of Robertson and Haig. Lloyd George who had almost a contempt for the abilities of his own military was possessed of a strange gullibility when it came to French generals. He attempted to subordinate Haig to the French commander in chief, Nivelle, in 1917 but failed. He also failed to stop a third battle of Ypres, better known as Passchendaele, with its 250,000 mud-covered casualties. Robertson was then skilfully, but at great risk to Lloyd George, outmanoeuvred. A general reserve of British and French divisions was set up in February 1918 under its own military experts. Robertson objected. He enjoyed much support stretching from Buckingham Palace, through Tory back-benchers to Asquith. Had Haig chosen to fully support his brother officer, Lloyd George would have been done for. Bonar Law and Milner remained loyal and Haig preferred to stay in France. Robertson read in the paper on the morning of 18 February that he had resigned. The Prime Minister had won a victory but five weeks later the German onslaught on Haig's weak Fifth Army threatened the whole allied cause with defeat. It was touch and go but by June the Germans had been held and an allied counter-offensive started which was to win the war by November. In May 1918 the army struck back accusing Lloyd George of being responsible for the spring defeats by withholding men. A senior figure at the War Office, General Maurice, in a letter to the press, accused the Prime Minister of lying to the House of Commons about the number of men in France. Lloyd George brazened it out and a tactical mistake by Asquith prevented the truth from emerging. Victory in France in the late summer and autumn made Lloyd George impreg-nable. He was the man who had won the war.

To his credit not only had the war been won but considerable strides had been made in domestic reforms too. Lloyd George was anxious to show that the old radical fires still burned and he turned to post-war reconstruction to illustrate this to his erstwhile radical backers. Dr Addison was appointed to a Ministry for Reconstruction and a host of social reformers were appointed to committees and commissions. Fisher produced a major Education Act in 1918 raising the school-leaving age to 14 and making provision for extended secondary and tertiary education. The most dramatic and extensive reform was a Franchise Act which Lloyd George skilfully got his Unionist colleagues to accept, promising them a reformed House of Lords (which they never got), and the retention of plural voting, a promise that was kept, to the concern of many Liberals. The Representation of the People's Act virtually tripled the electorate: 8.4 million women over the age of 30 could now vote, together with all men over 21. The electorate now numbered in excess of 21 million. Democracy had at last arrived in the United Kingdom.

How long the Kingdom would remain united was another question. Lloyd George's greatest failure was Ireland. An all-party Irish Convention which sat from May 1917 until the spring of 1918 broke up without agreement. Lloyd George could not afford to confront the Ulster Unionists. The problem was simply postponed. His other great failure lay in his handling of Arthur Henderson, the Labour leader, whom he had underestimated and in August 1917 unnecessarily antagonized over a proposed visit to Russia. Lloyd George accepted Henderson's resignation from the War Cabinet on 11 August. Henderson's devotion over the next twelve months to revamping a powerful independent Labour Party machine was to have unfortunate consequences for Lloyd George and the Liberals.

The fiction of Liberal unity had been maintained despite the Lloyd George–Asquith personality struggle. There had been in effect no real opposition to the government. The Maurice debate on 9 May 1918 ended this. Ninety-eight Liberals voted against the Prime Minister and with Asquith. Two separate organizations now emerged, first at Westminster, with their own Whips, and later in the constituencies. The Maurice debate had established battle lines. The election campaign in 1918 heightened the bitterness between 'Squiffites' and Lloyd George's 'Stage Army', as his Liberal MP supporters were nicknamed.

By now an election was long overdue and, with the new reform act, increasingly urgent. Lloyd George wished to remain at Number 10 and thus fight the election on coalition lines. Bonar Law feared his reputation as the man who had won the war, and wanted an anti-socialist alliance. The result was an electoral pact negotiated in July and the issuing of a letter of approval, jointly signed by Lloyd George and Bonar Law, to coalition-supporting MPs. This 'coupon', as it was satirically named, went to 159 Liberals and 373 Conservatives. Labour resolved to fight the election alone and withdrew from the coalition. The result was a complex election for a largely untried electorate. It clearly showed the extent of patriotic fervour that favoured the right.

It was not the men in uniform who had produced the result shown in Table 6.2, for only 900,000 voted. Lloyd George appeared to have triumphed but the victory in reality was the Conservatives'. The Labour

Table 6.2 The 1918 general election result

Coalition	Seats		Vote (%)	Opposition	Seats		Vote (%)
Con.	335	(374)*	32.6	Lab.	57†	(388)	22.2
Con. Uncouponed	48	(75)	6.1	Lib.	28‡	(258)	12.1
LG Lib.	133	(159)	13.5	S. Fein	73	(102)	4.5
Nat. Lab.	10	(18)	1.5	I. Nat.	7	(60)	2.2
	526			Others	16	(197)	5.3
					181		

* Figures in brackets denote number of candidates.
† Also Independent Labour at Anglesey and Aberdeen N., Co-operative at Kettering and National Socialist Party at West Ham (Silvertown) give the total of 61 sometimes quoted.
‡ 37 were elected as Liberals without the Coupon, but 9 of these took the government whip subsequently.
Source: M. Pugh, *The Making of Modern British Politics 1867–1939*, Oxford, Blackwell, 1982, p. 194.

Party despite its 57 MPs had done well. It was now no longer a minority party. There was little doubt that the losers were the Irish Nationalists and the 'Squiffites'. Asquith himself lost his seat.

THE PEACE-TIME COALITION 1918–22

The government of the last Liberal Prime Minister is still tainted with an unsavoury odour. The man who won the war became the man who was blamed for the 'Honours Scandal' – the sale of titles. The social reformer of 1911 became the man who allowed the Geddes axe to fall on government social expenditure and threw his Liberal reforming ministers to the Tory wolves. The hero of 1918 became the appeaser of 1922. The man of whom it was said that he could be prime minister for life was universally execrated four years later. Michael Foot, future leader of the Labour Party and son of a Liberal MP, records:

> I was brought up in a home where the name of David Lloyd George was, above all others, the most accursed. The charge was that he had broken the once so-powerful Liberal Party; that he had thrown open the gates to triumphant, gloating Toryism; that the deed had been done in pursuit of raw, personal ambition: a heavy indictment for sure and one not easily refuted or forgotten.
>
> (M. Foot, *Loyalists and Loners*, London, Collins, 1986, p. 142)

Stanley Baldwin, Conservative leader in the inter-war years, so detested the Welshman that he defaced his photograph in an album. Ramsay MacDonald always removed the photograph of Lloyd George at Chequers so that he would not have to look at it. To both left and right he became a demon of immoral political self-seeking. That there was in him an amorality cannot be denied. Keynes has provided one of the most famous literary portraits of this strange man:

How can I convey to the reader, who does not know him, any just impression of this extraordinary figure of our time, this siren, this goat-footed bard, this half-human visitor to our age from the hag-ridden magic and enchanted woods of Celtic antiquity? One catches in his company that flavour of final purposelessness, inner irresponsibility, existence outside or away from our Saxon good and evil, mixed with cunning, remorselessness, love of power, that lend fascination, enthralment and terror to the fair-seeming magician of North European folklore. . . . Lloyd George is rooted in nothing; he is void and without content; he lives and feeds on his immediate surroundings; he is an instrument and a player at the same time which plays on the company and is played on by them too; he is a prism, as I have heard him described, which collects light and distorts it and is most brilliant if the light comes from many quarters at once; a vampire and medium in one.

(G. Keynes (ed.), *Essays in Biography*, London, Mercury Books, 1961, p. 35)

In one sense his greatest offence was to challenge national preconceptions, including that most basic of English political virtues: team spirit. Lloyd George was a 'doer', fizzing with energy and ideas. The cosy confrontation of left and right eventually bored him, and the two political teams took their revenge by permanently excluding him from power.

For four years the Liberal radical led a government dependent on a Tory majority. He was loyally supported first by Bonar Law and then Austen Chamberlain, both of whom were natural seconds in command. Other Conservative cabinet ministers accepted him but with increasing resentment of his unpredictable gyrations. It is often said that he became more conservative with age and success, a normal process for most people. In the circumstances of his dependency on Conservative votes such a process would become doubly likely. Despite this, the coalition government was responsible for much that was progressive and liberal. Much of the Prime Minister's time was occupied by issues of foreign policy which are considered in chapter 8. In this area, his early position of revenge on Germany was rapidly reversed and he became the proponent of appeasement and reconciliation. Disengagement from the civil war in Russia was forced on his more anti-Bolshevik colleagues and Britain's speed of disarmament would even have satisfied the ghost of Gladstone. Only in his militant approach to Turkey did he appear belligerent and this again was in line with a great Liberal tradition of support for the Greeks against the ancient Turkish oppressor.

Extensive social reform marked the government, a clear continuation of the last pre-war Liberal Government. Old age pensions were raised from £26 5s per annum to £47 5s per annum. There was a massive extension of unemployment insurance, with an additional twelve million workers covered. Benefits were raised to 15s in 1920 and increased again in 1921 with additional payments for dependants. In view of the vast increase in the numbers of unemployed – to two million by December 1921 – the cost to the government was staggering. Fisher put into practice his Education Act with its extensive school-building programme. Teachers' salaries were doubled under the new arrangements proposed by the committee chaired by Lord Burnham in 1921.

Dr Christopher Addison proved to be the most controversial of Lloyd George's progressive ministers. He took over as president of the Local Government Board which was renamed the Ministry of Health in June 1919. Addison's Housing Act of the same year placed a duty on local authorities to build houses. The government offered help with substantial subsidies of £100 per house. A total of 70,000 homes were completed under the Act, short of what was hoped for, but far more than had previously been achieved. A Maternity and Child Welfare Act encouraged local authorities to extend the provision of clinics and push on with the good work of reducing infant mortality.

In dealing with two of the most insoluble of twentieth-century British problems Lloyd George's record was impressive. A wave of industrial militancy threatened to engulf the country. Trade unions, with their numbers spiralling, were in a self-confident mood. In the final year of the war 6 million working days had been lost, in 1919 it leapt to 35 million, falling to 26 million in 1920 then rising again to a climactic 85 million in 1921. The problem was initially left by Lloyd George as he concentrated on diplomacy and indeed was often absent from the country, but his negotiating skills had not deserted him. He ended a nine-day rail strike in 1919 with concessions over wages whilst still satisfying his right-wing cabinet colleagues that a tough line was being taken. Dockers secured great gains in 1920 with a national minimum wage, registration of dock labour and a forty-hour week. His handling of the mines in 1921 brought applause from Conservatives but bitter denunciation from the workers in the industry. A policy of prevarication delayed strike action and divided the miners from their allies in the transport unions who abandoned them to their defeat on what became known as Black Friday, 15 April 1921. Despite the numbers of working days lost Lloyd George's achievements had been considerable. His skill had avoided much of the brutality that marked similar class conflicts in Germany, France and Italy in the same years. Compromise, whatever the language used on each side, marked the disputes rather than bloody confrontation.

Bloody confrontation, however, marked the other great problem – Ireland. The Irish Nationalists had suffered disastrous defeats in the 1918 election, being replaced by Sinn Fein whose representatives refused to attend Westminster. Instead they established Dáil Eirean (the lower, i.e. elected, chamber of Parliament) in Dublin. This amounted to a declaration of independence. The British government responded with repression. The Dáil was declared illegal and war ensued between British troops and the IRA. The army and the Royal Irish Constabulary were reinforced with 'specials' drawn from ex-servicemen, nicknamed the 'Black and Tans' owing to the colours of their uniform. Atrocity and counter-atrocity marked this, as with all guerrilla wars. The methods of control used were clearly distasteful to the Liberals. Lloyd George showed his usual flexibility in finally producing a settlement. He supported firmness, wanting 'to seize murder by the throat', and then got the Sinn Fein leadership to accept an Irish Free State, retaining formal links with the Crown to placate the Conservatives, and the exclusion of Ulster to placate the Unionists. Ulster was given its own separate parliament and this division of Ireland came closest to solving the Irish Question which had defeated Peel and Gladstone. Perhaps it was his greatest political achievement but it brought him no friends. The Unionists felt betrayed by the settlement and Liberals felt outraged by the latest 'methods of barbarism'.

Whatever the radical reputation Lloyd George might have had and enhanced by the reforms of 1918–21 it was destroyed by his inability to control a Conservative back-bench revolt which demanded an end to waste. Middle-class impatience with continuing high taxation now that the war was over, produced the Anti-Waste League in January 1921. It promptly won a by-election in Dover and another in London in June. Addison was the chief victim of its campaign. His expenditure was curtailed and he himself removed from the Ministry of Health. Lloyd George totally failed to defend this most loyal of Liberal disciples, instead throwing him to the howling anti-waste wolves with a shabby speech of self-vindication. It was clearly a case of him laying down the life of his friend for his own. In response to further pressure the new Chancellor, Sir Robert Horne, set up the Geddes Committee to find areas of waste in government. Geddes wielded his axe with enthusiasm and proposed £76 million of economies. Most hit the armed forces but Fisher's education programme was also badly affected and 25 per cent of classes remained at the unacceptably high size of over sixty. All the schemes for continuation schools providing part-time education to the age of 16 were dropped. Fisher did manage to defend teachers' salaries after a bitter battle.

It was not, however, Lloyd George's waning radicalism which brought about his downfall. Conservatives were increasingly restless with what they felt was an alien master whose political assets were waning as the 1918 victory receded in the popular mind. There was particular distaste in many Conservative quarters for the reckless sale of honours to boost coalition Liberal funds. Knighthoods cost £10,000–£12,000, baronetcies as much as £35,000 and peerages somewhat more. Lloyd George left it to his secretary 'Bronco Bill' Sutherland and dubious agents like 'Maundy Gregory' to tout for custom. There was nothing new in this, merely the scale. Besides innumerable knighthoods, ninety peerages were created.

Even this volume of traffic might not have elicited the criticism it did, had it not been for the fact that the recipients were so unsavoury. Sir William Vesty, a war-time tax dodger, received a baronetcy, as did Joseph Robinson, previously convicted of fraud. Lloyd George was unrepentant. If people were fool enough to pay good money for something as worthless as a title, so what! It was far less corrupt than the practice in the USA where money paid to political parties bought legislation and special consideration for the donor. Conservative backbenchers did not see it this way. Something much valued was being debased.

Lloyd George and his closest associates, Churchill among them, had tried to carry through a fusion of the two parties in 1920. They had failed not so much on Conservative reluctance as the refusal of his own supporters to compromise on their Liberal name. Thereafter Lloyd George and the Liberals were a dwindling asset to the Conservatives as they lost by-election after by-election to Labour in industrial areas. Many Conservatives increasingly demanded an end to the coalition. The Conservative Party Chairman, Sir George Younger, denounced a scheme in January 1921 to hold a fresh election on a coalition ticket. Following a diplomatic crisis, which nearly produced war with Turkey in September 1922, the pressure for separation was irresistible. Lloyd George strove to regain control by going for a quick election. He carried most of the senior Conservatives in his Cabinet with him. He could not carry the Tory backbenchers who broke into revolt at a Carlton Club meeting on 19 October. An overwhelming majority rejected the coalition. Lloyd George resigned the same afternoon.

LINGERING DEATH 1922–35

The division between the 'Squiffites' and the Lloyd Georgites had hardened since December 1916. Policy disagreements in 1919 had added to the personality clash and the events of 1918 had hardened hearts. The election of that year had been crippling, as Herbert Gladstone was to recall later:

> The result of 1918 broke the party, not only in the House of Commons but in the country. Local associations perished or maintained a nominal existence. Masses of our best men passed away to Labour. Others gravitated to Conservatism or independence.
> (Quoted in C. Cook, *A Short History of the Liberal Party*, London, Macmillan, 1976, p. 81)

He was largely thinking of the 'Squiffites' or 'Wee Frees' as a small number of independent Liberals with whom he was associated were dubbed, but the comments on local associations applied equally, if not more so, to the coalition MPs where seats fell one by one in by-elections after 1918. Liberalism seemed to be withering at the grass roots.

It was not clear what the 'Squiffites' stood for, other than for 'Squiff' and against Lloyd George. Lloyd George and his coalitionists, once the emergency of the war had passed, seemed too much the prisoners of the Tories. Many radicals therefore turned to the Labour Party as did the working-class electorate in the big cities like Sheffield. Many of the middle class in the new atmosphere of Bolshevism and 'red scare' turned to the Conservatives, completing a process of drift begun in the 1860s. With debilitating drains of local support the warring antics of the two Liberal factions at Westminster completed the disaster. A completely separate Coalition Liberal organization did not come until 1920 when those Coalitionists who attended the NLF at Leamington Spa in May were howled down by the 'Squiffite' majority.

The ending of the coalition in 1922 and the subsequent general election was another landmark in the steepening decline of Liberal Party fortunes. In electoral terms it was a most complex event with four parties. Labour now overtook the combined total of Liberals as shown in Table 6.3. The Liberal Party was in the unenviable position of being the third party with all the disadvantages that this has under the British first-past-the-post electoral system. Many of the National or Coalition Liberals were only at Westminster by the grace of the Tories who had withdrawn opposition in certain constituencies. Some of these MPs were in fact to be inseparable from the Tory Party and now gave their support to Bonar Law. Lloyd George still hoped for the emergence of a centre party, a renewed coalition. The behaviour of many of the leading Conservatives like Austen Chamberlain and the Earl of Birkenhead, who refused to join Bonar Law's government, gave him grounds for hope.

Table 6.3 The 1922 general election result

	Total votes	% share	Candidates	MPs elected	Unopposed returns
Conservative	5,502,298	38.5	482	344	42
Liberal	2,668,143	18.9	333	60	6
National Liberal	1,412,772	9.4	144	53	4
Labour	4,237,349	29.7	414	142	4
Others	571,480	3.5	68	16	1
Total	14,392,330	100.0	1,441	615	57

Source: ibid., p. 86.

Baldwin, who succeeded the ailing Bonar Law in May 1923, put paid to any scheme of renewed coalition and skilfully divided Chamberlain and the other ex-ministers from their old chief by assuring them that protection and the introduction of tariffs were necessary. Since Bonar Law had promised in 1922 that the Conservatives would not do this without an election, Baldwin now 'honourably' called an election, only twelve months after winning a comfortable majority. Baldwin under-estimated the losses but was essentially correct in seeing that it would reunite the Tory Party in the old Chamberlainite cause. As a by-product it reunited the Liberals, but as the third force. Lloyd George had little alternative but to eat humble pie and effect reconciliation with Asquith who was accepted as leader of the party. The Liberals, thanks to Bald-win, now had an issue close to their hearts to fight, albeit one which was essentially negative and eighty years old: free trade. Lloyd George made a smaller than asked for contribution from his fund to the Liberals and this was to remain a bone of contention. In the event, a Liberal revival of promising proportions took place. They fielded more candi-dates than Labour but secured fewer MPs. The gains were mainly from Conservatives in rural or cathedral-city constituencies. The losses to Labour in crucial areas like Leicester, Derby and South Wales indicated a further weakening of the working-class base of Edwardian Liberalism. The 158 who triumphed were very precariously situated with small majorities. A swing to the Conservatives was likely to undo the progress. In other words the Liberals were already entering upon their future role as a party of Conservative protest voters – gaining when discontent with the Conservatives grew and fading as Conservatism became safe once more. This precarious position in the constituencies was matched by the difficulty of the situation at Westminster. Should the Liberals support Labour in an anti-Tory free trade alliance? This ran the risk of being tarnished with the Bolshevik brush and losing the very gains which had given them a boost. To deny Labour its chance would possibly speed up the working-class desertions. It was a cruel dilemma made worse by the unwillingness of MacDonald, leader of the Labour Party, to bargain and co-operate as Lloyd George would have wished. Asquith preferred to await the call for a Liberal ministry but essentially his position was his famous one of 'wait and see'. In the end the Liberals got the worst of all possible worlds. They were blamed for bringing in the first Labour Government but got no benefits. When Lloyd George realized that the best course lay in bringing down the government for its Russian policy, he was outmanoeuvred by both Baldwin and MacDonald who picked the ground for a showdown in the shape of the Campbell case. MacDonald could claim that the capitalist parties ganged up on him, and Baldwin could claim that only the Tory Party was an effective bastion against socialism. The Liberals faced their worst election disaster to date and in doing so ended the confused three-party system. MacDonald and Baldwin achieved their objective of squeezing the Liberal Party out.

On the surface the Conservatives were the greatest gainers with 412 seats. Labour shrank to 151 but the Liberals fell to 40. The latter were chronically short of money and fielded only 340 candidates, abandoning 136 seats they had fought in 1923. Not only was there a lack of money

Table 6.4 The 1923 general election result

	Votes	%	Candidates	Members	Unopposed
Conservative	5,514,541	38.0	536	258	35
Liberal	4,301,481	29.7	457	158	11
Labour	4,439,780	30.7	427	191	3
Communist	39,448	0.2	4	–	–
Nationalist	97,993	0.4	4	3	1
Others	154,452	1.0	18	5	–
Total	14,547,695	100.0	1,446	615	50

Source: ibid., p. 94.

but of will, at local level, to fight. Liberalism seemed to have little distinctive to say on the issues of the day. They were disappearing into the soft soggy central ground of British politics.

The years 1924–9 saw the last great attempt of the Liberals to be a major force in British politics before the heady, but temporary, revival of the 1980s. Asquith had lost his seat and was translated to the Lords. Lloyd George was elected chairman of the parliamentary party but he had to wait until 1926 for the party leadership and control of the machine. Between 1924 and 1926 unseemly wrangles continued over the Lloyd George party fund and finally over the General Strike to which Lloyd George was much more sympathetic than Asquith. However, Asquith suffered a stroke and in October 1926 he resigned. The party had no alternative but to turn to Lloyd George for leadership and cash. He gave them both and embarked on 'the last crusade' which culminated in the election of 1929. Money was poured from Lloyd George's fund into the party machine which was placed under Herbert Samuel. Constructive policies of far greater excitement and relevance than that of either Labour or the Conservative Party were researched and then offered to the public. The brightest and best, like J. M. Keynes, were recruited to assist in preparing this policy feast. The Green Book offered extensive reform and answers to the problem of a depressed agriculture. The Yellow Book on Britain's industrial failure in February 1928 had proposals for government planning far in advance of their time. In 1929 came the Orange Book on 'we can conquer unemployment'. It involved proposals for a massive public works programme of road building and housing schemes. In view of all this hype the performance in the election of 1929 was a grave disappointment. Lloyd George was certainly the most exciting of the political leaders. Baldwin's 'safety first' campaign was only marginally more boring than MacDonald's reassurance of 'no monkeying'. The great British public preferred the boring message. The pious platitudes of the two major parties were more reassuring than the Edwardian oratory of the ageing Welshman. The Liberals had massively increased their number of candidates and their share of the popular vote. The first-past-the-post system condemned them to 59 MPs in the new House of Commons. The last supreme effort had failed.

Fresh splits completed the ruin of a once great party. As in 1924, how far to support a Labour government caused much soul-searching amongst Liberals. Lloyd George pushed for a comprehensive deal involving electoral reform to remove the first-past-the-post system. Sir John Simon and a group of Conservative-minded Liberals declared war on the Labour Government and denounced Lloyd George's dialogue in November 1930. The 'Simonites' later became indistinguishable from Conservatives.

The crisis of August 1931 (see pp. 270–3) completed the fragmentation. Lloyd George was ill and Sir Herbert Samuel as acting leader of the party took the Liberals into a National Government that emerged. The party faced the election of 1931 split three ways: Simonite Liberal Nationals who gained 35 seats; Samuelite Liberals who gained 33; and Lloyd George Independent Liberals who gained 4. Both Simon and Samuel joined the coalition but Samuel withdrew in 1932 over the defence of free trade. Lloyd George had favoured a deal with Labour and detested his two enemies. MacDonald and Baldwin were now easily aligned in coalition, the spurious fighting of the 1920s forgotten. Lloyd George, sensing the hopeless mess, withdrew from active politics to write his memoirs.

The Liberal Party had ceased to count. They failed even to win by-elections; indeed they failed to fight in most of them. The general election of 1935 confirmed their virtual death. Only 159 candidates stood and only 21 MPs were elected. The Liberal Party had become one of the minority parties that decorate the British electoral scene, occasionally enlivening it, but essentially irrelevant.

CONCLUSION

The decay of the British Liberal Party was of course paralleled by the decay of other European Liberal parties in the twentieth century. In Germany the DVP and DDP both suffered a disastrous collapse in the 1920s from an already minority position. In France fragmented radicalism decayed more slowly but gave ground to the two parties of the left – the Socialists and the Communists. Perhaps the polarization of parties along class lines made the death of Liberal parties inevitable. Those great nineteenth-century issues of free trade and religious equality seemed irrelevant in the inter-war years. Protectionism seemed triumphant everywhere, and religion was in decline everywhere. Seebohm Rowntree's 1935 survey in York revealed that:

> the number of adults attending church has fallen from 17,060 in 1901 to 12,770 in 1935, notwithstanding the fact that during that period the

adult population of the city has increased from 48,000 to 72,248. . . . In 1901 adult attendances amounted to 35.5 per cent of the adult population; in 1935 it amounted to only 17.7 per cent.

(Quoted in A. Marwick, *The Deluge*, London, Macmillan, 1991, p. 298)

The old enemy, the landed elite, was not the formidable force it had been in the nineteenth century. Crowns and thrones had vanished, aristocracies had lost much of their power if not their glamour, and everywhere agriculture had suffered under the great surplus of food in the world. Perhaps when the British Liberal Party had slaughtered its own private foe, the House of Lords, it had completed its work. It was time to die.

Yet if the British Liberal Party had decayed and died as a major force in British politics, Liberalism had not. It had triumphed, its values taken over by the other two parties. To the Conservative Party was bequeathed the legacy of economic freedom and a faith in market forces; to the Labour Party the torch of social reform. Both espoused parliamentary democracy. Philip Kerr, Lord Lothian, accurately analysed the party's position in 1933:

From a party point of view Liberalism is in an almost hopeless position, so long as Baldwin is leader of the Conservative Party and Arthur Henderson the leading figure in the Labour Party. Both are democrats, liberally minded, supporters of disarmament and the League of Nations, and constitutionalists. . . . We have, therefore, no future by just talking [*sic*] what may be called the general principles of Liberalism and criticising certain aspects of the Government's policy. Apart from the stalwart remnant of the old guard the mass of voters will tend to vote for one or other of the two major parties, which at any rate have some hope of coming into power and are both, to-day, essentially liberal minded.

(Quoted in T. Wilson, *The Downfall of the Liberal Party*, London, Collins, 1966, p. 407)

This bequest to British party politics is symbolized at a personal level by Lloyd George's family. His son Gyllam became a member of a Conservative government and his daughter, Megan, a Labour MP.

CONTROVERSY

Much has been written on the decline of the Liberal Party, in seeking to understand its causes. Much has turned on the timing of decay and disaster. Was the Liberal Party alive and well in 1916 or already seriously stricken with a fatal disease? Was it the First World War and the subsequent splits in the leadership that killed it or was it already so weakened that it succumbed to these blows which it could otherwise have survived?

A magnificent introduction to this debate must be George Dangerfield's *The Strange Death of Liberal England*, published in 1935. Dangerfield's book is a literary masterpiece containing the central thesis that Liberal England tore itself apart in the years 1910–14. As a good read few history books surpass it, but not many historians would accept the Dangerfield thesis today. Doubts were shown in the 1960s when Professor Trevor Wilson, in the introduction to his book, *The Downfall of the Liberal Party*, took issue with Dangerfield:

> To make clear the view taken here about when the Liberal party 'reached the point of no return', it may be permissible to resort to allegory. The Liberal party can be compared to an individual who, after a period of robust health and great exertion, experienced symptoms of illness (Ireland, Labour unrest, the suffragettes). Before a thorough diagnosis could be made, he was involved in an encounter with a rampant omnibus (the First World War), which mounted the pavement and ran him over. After lingering painfully, he expired. A controversy has persisted ever since as to what killed him. One medical school argues that even without the bus he would soon have died; the intimations of illness were symptoms of a grave disease which would shortly have ended his life. Another school goes further, and says that the encounter with the bus would not have proved fatal had not the victim's health already been seriously impaired. Neither of these views is accepted here. The evidence for them is insufficient, because the ailments had not reached a stage where their ultimate effect could be known. How long, apart from the accident, the victim would have survived, what future (if any) he possessed, cannot be said. All that is known is that at one moment he was up and walking and at the next he was flat on his back, never to rise again; and in the interval he had been run over by a bus. If it is guess-work to say that the bus was responsible for his demise, it is the most warrantable guess that can be made.
>
> (T. Wilson, *The Downfall of the Liberal Party*, London, Collins, 1966, p. 20)

A year later, in *Socialists, Liberals and Labour – the struggle for London 1885–1914*, Paul Thompson argued the converse: that Liberalism was in serious trouble before 1914. His conclusions have, of course, been challenged. An important book by P. F. Clarke, *Lancashire and the New Liberalism*, published in 1971, took a much more hopeful view of the Liberal Party's ability to adapt to class politics. He argues at one stage:

> But, equally, the fragmentary evidence of the by-elections shows that

as late as November 1912 a Liberal candidate could hold his own in an industrial constituency, and that as late as February 1913 a Liberal candidate could actually gain ground. What this might have portended for a hypothetical General Election in 1915 is an open question.

(P. F. Clarke, *Lancashire and the New Liberalism*, Cambridge, Cambridge University Press, 1971, p. 359)

He concludes the book with the following:

Thus the first quarter of the twentieth century saw two sorts of change in British politics. The first sort centred upon the emergence of class politics in a stable form; the second sort upon the effective replacement of the Liberal party by the Labour party. But the first – with which this book is concerned – does not in any simple way explain the second. For one thing, the chronology is wrong. By 1910, the change to class politics was substantially complete. That from Liberalism to Labour had not really begun. Nor were there signs that it must begin. It was not a light thing to overturn one party and make another to put in its place. At the beginning of the second decade of the twentieth century it looked as though both Labour and Liberalism would be subsumed in progressivism.

(ibid.)

In other words, if Clarke was right, the Liberal Party was adapting to class politics and a bright future akin to the USA's Democratic Party awaited it, rather than the fate of the European parties.

The debate has continued throughout the 1970s and 1980s with a mountain of Ph.D. studies and articles, often dealing with regional analyses. The most important general works have been H. V. Emy's *Liberals, Radicals and Social Politics 1892–1914*, in 1973 and Ross McKibbin's *The Evolution of the Labour Party 1910–1924*, in 1974. The more recent, *Liberalism and Liberal Politics in Edwardian England*, by G. L. Bernstein in 1986 comes down on the side of the pessimists:

Thus, the best efforts of Liberal statesmanship to prepare the party to appeal more effectively to a working-class electorate in an era of class politics seemed to be failing. Neither the new liberalism nor Liberal policies of social reform represented a fundamental reorientation of the Liberal Party so that it could represent the interests of the working class rather than those of middle-class Nonconformists. The progressive alliance offered no solution to containing the challenge of Labour for the allegiance of the working-class voter. If class politics were coming, so was the decline of the Liberal Party – not imminently, perhaps but eventually and inevitably.

(Bernstein, op. cit., p. 201)

All students can do is look at as much evidence as possible, and come to their own conclusions. Like most academic historians they will doubt-less use information to support their own prejudices.

BIBLIOGRAPHY

For an explanation of the grading system, see the preface p. xiii.

Biographies

H. H. Asquith

3   Jenkins, R., London, Collins, 1964
2   Koss, S. E., London, Allen Lane, 1976

H. Campbell-Bannerman

3   Wilson, J., New York, St Martin's Press, 1973

W. S. Churchill

4   Churchill, R., *The Young Statesman*, London, Heinemann, 1967
2/3   Manchester, W., *The Last Lion: 1874–1932, Visions of Glory*, London, Michael Joseph, 1983
3   Pelling, H., London, Macmillan, 1974

Sir Edward Grey

3   Robbins, K., London, Cassell, 1971

D. Lloyd George

3   Grigg, J., *The Young Lloyd George*, London, Methuen, 1973
3   Grigg, J., *The People's Champion, 1902–1911*, London, Methuen, 1978
3   Grigg, J., *From Peace to War, 1912–1916*, London, Methuen, 1985
2   Pugh, M., Harlow, Longman, 1988

General works

4   Bernstein, G. L., *Liberalism and Liberal Politics in Edwardian England*, Boston, Allen & Unwin, 1986
4   Clarke, P. F., *Lancashire and the New Liberalism*, Cambridge, Cambridge University Press, 1971
4   Clarke, P. F., *Liberals and Social Democrats*, Cambridge, Cambridge University Press, 1978
2   Cook, C., *A Short History of the Liberal Party*, London, Macmillan, 1976
2/3   Douglas, R., *A History of the Liberal Party*, London, Sidgwick & Jackson, 1971
4   Emy, H. V., *Liberals, Radicals and Social Politics*, 1892–1914, Cambridge, Cambridge University Press, 1973

4   Freeden, M., *The New Liberalism*, Oxford, Oxford University Press, 1978
2   Hay, J. R., *Origins of the Liberal Welfare Reforms*, London, Macmillan, 1975
2   Jenkins, R., *Mr. Balfour's Poodle: Peers v. People*, London, Collins, 1952
2   Morgan, K. O., *The Age of Lloyd George*, London, Allen & Unwin, 1978
3   Morgan, K. O., *Consensus and Disunity: The Lloyd George Coalition*, Oxford, Oxford University Press, 1979
3   Pugh, M., *The Making of Modern British Politics 1867–1939*, Oxford, Blackwell, 1982
3   Read, D., *Edwardian England*, London, Harrop, 1972
1   Read, D., *Edwardian England*, London, History Association Pamphlet, 1980
4   Rowland, P., *The Last Liberal Government*, two vols, London, Barrie & Jenkins, 1968 and 1972
3   Russell, A. K., *Liberal Landslide: The General Election of 1906*, Newton Abbott, David & Charles, 1973
3   Wilson, T., *The Downfall of the Liberal Party*, London, Collins, 1966
1   *Women's Suffrage in Britain*, London, History Association Pamphlet, 1980

Sources for coursework

There is a mass of published primary material relating to this theme. Two introductory collections are K. O. Morgan's fine book, *The Age of Lloyd George* referred to above and, for much of the social background, E. Royston Pike's *Human Documents of the Lloyd George Era*, London, Allen & Unwin, 1972. Many of the principal actors have had their memoirs or diaries published. Asquith, for instance, can be looked at through his own reminiscences, *Fifty Years in Parliament* (London, Cassell, 1926), and *Memories and Reflections* (1928), and much more interestingly through the extensive correspondence with Venetia Stanley, with whom he was passionately in love whilst serving as Prime Minister, *Letters to Venetia Stanley*, Oxford, 1982. The diaries of one of his cabinet colleagues have also recently been published and provide fascinating insights, *Inside Asquith's Cabinet – From the Diaries of Charles Hobhouse*, London, John Murray, 1977. There is clearly ample opportunity to study this period at local level to attempt to map the decline of Liberal fortunes on local councils. For this and other lines of research local newspapers will be of great use.

7 The rise of Labour 1867–1940

INTRODUCTION

Not a single working-class MP emerged from the election in 1868 but by 1924 the first Labour Government, albeit a minority one, had taken office. In 1945 Britain returned its first Labour Government with an overall majority. In the seventy-seven years that separated 1868 and 1945 working men and working women had been given the vote, the Labour Party had been formed, the Liberal Party had declined and two world wars had fundamentally affected the political structures and attitudes in Britain. These eight decades were momentous ones because they saw the rise of Labour. However, the emergence of the working classes and the Labour Party into the political limelight was not a simple and natural progression as it has sometimes been portrayed in the past. If we are to seek out the steps by which Labour emerged then we embark on a long and complex path. Tony Crosland, Labour minister and writer, identified in *The Future of Socialism* (1956) twelve strands which contributed to the final product of a Labour Party capable of governing the country. Others would add more, but certainly there were key ideas, movements, organizations and individuals that moulded the Labour movement.

TRADE UNIONS

The nineteenth century had already seen many developments in the relationship between workers and their employers and the government. The Industrial Revolution and the changes it wrought in Britain had caused the very rapid growth of factory-based industry. With the factories came the concentrations of workers that seemed necessary for working-class movements and ideas to grow and spread. The distinguishing feature about such movements and ideas was, at least early on, their diversity of opinions, aims and approaches. It was not the simple development of trade unionism as we know it that characterized the early years of the nineteenth century but a proliferation of groups and goals. These ranged widely, from the simple desire to combine in trade and craft associations

to full-scale organization for radical reappraisals of politics and representation. In between these two extremes lay the multiple, individual
requirements of labouring men and women of Britain. This was a trait
that worked against the emergence of strongly organized national labour
movements. Trades were too diverse and working men and women were
separated not only by the different tasks they performed but also by
their geographic location in the country. Add to this their initial lack of
organization, funds, direction and aims, and the strengths shown by the
factory owners and employers, and then one can begin to appreciate the
difficulty involved.

No real progress could be made until amendments were made in 1825
to the Combination Laws (legislation of the eighteenth century which
had prevented workers joining together). Even then, the infant labouring
movements found the task of organization very difficult. Robert Owen's
Grand National Consolidated Trades Union of the early 1830s seemed
to accept in its very name the diversity of the labouring population.
Owen's failure to establish a truly national labouring movement hinted
both at the weakness of labour and the hostility of the property-owning
classes. It was in the 1830s and 1840s that the full range of interests of
the working classes could be seen. Some despaired of any improvement
and continued to work away at poorly paid tasks under appalling conditions with no hope of any improvement of their condition. Others tried
the road to self-improvement and self-help and this saw the emergence
of the co-operative movement, initially in Rochdale with the Pioneers,
but latterly throughout the country, and especially in the north. Yet
others preferred to attack their immediate problems and so joined a host
of organizations which, because of their numbers and diversity, in fact
helped to delay the formation of any potential national trades-based
movement. Campaigns for cheap bread, an eight-hour day, factory
reform, etc. proliferated in the mid-century, along with the rise of many
single-cause groups, such as the Anti-Poor Law League. They certainly
had a point and it was often easier to gain attention over a single evil
than to try and persuade the working man of the necessity to change
society itself. Some even challenged the wisdom of the strike as a weapon
in the working-class armoury.

Nevertheless there were efforts to change the status quo and the most
famous group must be the Chartists who on three separate occasions
between 1839 and 1848 put their famous six-point charter before Parliament only to have it rejected on each occasion. Led by middle-class
radicals and thinkers, the poor hapless crowds of working people who
made up the 'army' of Chartists often attended meetings and rallies
simply on the basis of their need for the food as well as out of curiosity
and interest. Such people would not form the baying crowds of rebellion
intent upon the overthrow of the existing order. Chartism was defeated
by its own image which sought to portray the working man as the

rebellious demander of 'rights' the correctness of which simply did not seem to make sense to property owners and politicians alike. Too often the Chartists seemed to confirm the worst fears of the guardians of social order.

Therefore, by the 1860s it is true to say that the concept of nationally organized labour as perceived by Owen in the 1830s was simply that – an idea of no substance. However, working-class organizations did exist and it was these that would provide the link into the great age of unionism in the 1890s and twentieth century.

The future of Labour lay in the hands of a few craft unions. These organizations had emerged to protect the interests of what Sidney and Beatrice Webb once termed the 'aristocracy of skilled workmen'. It was the skilled working men, especially engineers, who were in great demand as industry expanded and who commanded good wages and so could afford to put money and energy into their craft associations. These so-called 'new model unions' were very localized in origin and very narrow in membership. They had little to do with the great mass of the unskilled labouring people of the country and yet their efforts would in the long term provide the momentum for such people to emerge as a unionized force in their own right. The greatest service provided by these organizations was to portray the working man, albeit a skilled one, as a reasonable, peace-loving and valuable member of society. This was not an easy task in the 1860s with violence breaking out on the streets of England in the form of the Sheffield Outrages in 1866 which saw violent attacks on the persons and property of non-unioned workers. Moreover, the legal position of unions, which was far from assured, was also receiving attention in 1867 with the famous case of Hornby *v.* Close when the Boilermakers' Union lost a court case against a local branch secretary in Bradford who had absconded with the branch funds. This merely highlighted the weak and exposed position of unions.

It was in this less than promising atmosphere that the leaders of five of the main craft unions – Robert Applegarth of the Carpenters, William Allan of the Engineers, David Guile of the Ironfounders, Edwin Coulson of the Bricklayers, and George Odger of the Ladies' Shoemakers Society – joined together to form what became known as 'the Junta' or, more formally, the London Trades Council. They, along with many others in London and the provinces, believed that the time was right for another attempt at a nationally based trade union initiative. In part they had been persuaded by the good reception given to their efforts in the call for electoral reform, which had resulted in the 1867 second Reform Act. Although plagued by violence, not least in events such as the Hyde Park riots, these leaders of the respectable voice of the working man had impressed political leaders with their restraint and good sense. Although many showed some trepidation, the limited extension of the franchise in 1867 probably did the case of the craft unions more good than bad.

Certainly, the moderate voice of unionism was allowed to come through as the extract indicates:

> (*Question*) – Do you find that the possession of very large funds, and the fact that they belong to a very powerful organisation, such as your society is, lends generally to make the members of your society disposed to enter into such a dispute, or the contrary?

> (*Answer*) – I should say that the members generally are decidedly opposed to strikes, and that the fact of our having a large accumulated fund tends to encourage that feeling amongst them. They wish to conserve what they have got . . . and we believe all strikes are a complete waste of money, not only in relation to the workmen but also to the employers.

> (Evidence given by William Allan of the Engineers to the Royal Commission on Trade Unions 1867–9)

Whatever the cause, within the space of a year these specialized craft unions and their leaders were calling for their national organization. The proposal which was drawn up in Manchester on 21 February 1868 and circulated to all members of craft unions, calling for a Congress of Trades Councils, demonstrated the respectability of the movement and members. There were no clarion cries – instead clear and restrained proposals for discussion and action. The twelve points it listed were not revolutionary but legalistic and organizational with the association recognizing the 'rules of the game' and clearly intending to abide by them. Out of such an organization, as it stood, no nationally compelling movement to embrace the majority of the unskilled working people would emerge. A new approach would be needed but where would the impetus come from and what would arise out of it?

There was no doubt that the London bias built into the 'new model union' movement provided considerable stimulus for discontent. It was the 'provincial' pressure that saw the TUC emerge in Manchester. After all the labouring population was more associated with the Midlands and the north than the capital. In addition, the promise of Liberal reforms were for the most part unfulfilled. Though much had been attempted by both political parties the basic grievances of working people were valid ones. Simply the living and working conditions of the vast majority of people were appalling. Despite legislation, between one-third and one-half of town-dwellers were denied the bare necessities which would guarantee the maintenance of 'physical efficiency'. The employers' grip seemed to have tightened with sliding scale agreements that fixed wages to price movements, reduced rates, and the introduction of new labour-saving machinery.

The tactics pursued by the union leaders seemed to work against the working people. 'The Junta' wanted to control strikes and move along the path of industrial co-operation into what appeared to be a more Liberal Party, middle-class mould. They also wished to operate closed unions, those restricted to craft-based ones, and were very suspicious of calls for 'open' unions, or those for widespread non-craft-based membership. Feeding into this split was the arrival of more militant ideas through movements such as the International Workingmen's Association which was formed in London in 1864. Such militancy coincided with two key national events. The first was the trade depression in the late 1870s and early 1880s which made many unskilled workers determined to stop such suffering from happening again. Even the miners, who were relatively well off, suffered badly. In Northumberland in the 1870s a miner could earn just over 45 pence a day but by 1880 this had dropped to about 22 pence a day. The second event was the franchise reform of 1884 which meant that eventually the working people would hold the balance of political power. They might prefer to vote on the basis of the old divisions of Conservative and Liberal for the immediate future, but it became clear from the start that these parties would have to work harder in order to gain support from these new voters, and that at some time they would have to share the political stage with a new political party.

With these stimuli developed 'new unionism' which saw the emergence of large unions relying on bulk membership of unskilled workers and using the workers' weapon of the strike in order to gain the concessions and advantages their members deserved. The gap between the 'new model union' mentality and that of 'new unionism' is clear from this extract:

> To Trade Unionists I desire to make a special appeal. How long, *how long*, will you be content with the present half-hearted policy of your unions? I readily grant that good work has been done in the past by the unions, but, in Heaven's name, what good purpose are they serving now? All of them have large numbers out of employment even when their particular trade is busy. None of the important societies have any policy other than of endeavouring to keep wages from falling. The true Unionist policy of aggression seems entirely lost sight of; in fact the average Unionist of today is a man with a fossilized intellect, either hopelessly apathetic, or supporting a policy that plays directly into the hands of the capitalist exploiter.
>
> (Thomas Mann, *What a Compulsory Eight-Hour Working Day Means to the Worker*, 1886)

It was at the end of the 1880s that the strength and potential of 'new unionism' became clear, not only to employers and the government but also to working people themselves. In a short space of time strikes, around which legends would be woven, came upon the scene. Will Thorne's organization of the London gas-workers in the strike of 1888 which resulted in an eight-hour day for East Ham workers was the stimulus for further successful strikes in the capital and the provinces. More emotive than this in the same year was the strike that gave public awareness to the plight of match girls who suffered appalling industrial injury in their trade. The Bryant & May match girls' strike was remarkable in that the workers involved were women in low-profile, unskilled work. A less auspicious basis for a strike seemed hard to conceive but the revelations about conditions and especially 'phossy jaw' (phosphorus, used in the manufacture of matches, affected the bones of the face) ensured a lot of sympathy for their cause. They also benefited from the help of that tireless worker on behalf of female causes Annie Besant, who lent considerable weight and credibility to their campaign. It was becoming clear that workers, even if they were unskilled, could under certain circumstances present their grievances and have them rectified. The strike that was to prove this point more than any other was the dockers' strike of 1889.

The call for the 'docker's tanner' would be the rallying cry used by the dockers' leaders Tom Mann and Ben Tillett in this particularly symbolic piece of industrial action. The final achievement of a guaranteed 'tanner' (two and a half pence) per hour after five weeks of strike action was a success for the dockers and their leaders. However, it was the way in which the dispute had been handled which would alter the fundamental approach of strikers in the future. Tillett stood out as a brilliant organizer of the union. The dockers played on the appalling state that they and their families had fallen into as a result of poor rates of pay. In numerous marches and demonstrations, all of which were well orchestrated and organized in addition to being entirely peaceful, the basic message was put across. Tillett ensured that such activities received good press coverage. He also arranged for leading socialist figures and sympathizers to appear at dockers' rallies and meetings, such as the MP John Burns. The union went into the dispute well fortified for the fight with some £49,000 raised by subscription, much of it coming from the Australian dock-workers. Finally, the tactics pursued played to the strengths of the union and Tillett used the 'aristocracy' of dockers, the stevedores, to put maximum pressure on the owners. It was, all in all, a perfect example of how a union could orchestrate a dispute to its own benefit and ensure that the outcome was to its members' advantage. The strident calls made on the dockers' behalf by their leaders, which are clear from their General Manifesto, although successful in this instance did not mean that all owners and employers simply gave in to labour. 'New unionism's' lessons would be learned but over a period of time and the unions were as much hostage to change as were any other groups in society. The dockers' union's rocketing membership of 1890, a year that saw 40,000 men unionized, would diminish to 10,000 by 1910. The gas men, who could count 60,000 members in 1890 saw this number fall to 23,000 by 1892.

Adverse changes in the pattern of world trade and the rise of international competition saw many trades and industries under particular
pressure as the nineteenth century closed. The growth of technology also
played its part with improved equipment being capable of being worked
by unskilled labour. New working practices, such as piecework, meant
that workers tended to see themselves as individuals rather than part of
a group and thus the union feeling was weakened. More importantly,
the employers demonstrated the danger they felt by grouping together
to combat what they perceived as outrageous demands. The Federation
of Employers' Associations was formed in 1894 which gave employers a
national organization with political and financial clout. The allied
National Free Labour Association of 1893 meant a ready supply of non-
unionized workers capable of moving round the country at need. The
success of this approach was seen in the defeat of strikes in 1897 by the
Amalgamated Society of Engineers, textile workers and the miners. 'New
unionism' may well have been pointing the way forward for labour but
the path was not an easy one. Just how hard the task would become
was revealed in the opening years of the twentieth century. In 1900 a
union organizer of railwaymen on the Taff Vale railway line in South
Wales had found himself the victim of the owner's wrath after trying to
organize a pay increase. His colleagues leapt to his defence and went on
strike in August of that year. The union picketed to prevent the import
of black-leg labour and immediately invited legal proceedings on the part
of the owners. Although the dispute was settled inside eleven days the
litigation continued with disastrous consequences for the Taff Vale railwaymen and the trade union movement as a whole. The final judgment
held that the union was responsible for the actions of its members which
had cost the railway company £23,000 which the union now had to
reimburse the company, plus paying costs of some further £7,000.

> If trade unions are not above the law, how are these bodies to be
> sued? I have no doubt whatever that a trade union . . . could be sued
> in a representative action if the persons selected as defendants be
> persons who from their position may be taken fairly to represent the
> body. . . . The registered name is nothing more than a collective name
> for all the members. . . . I see nothing contrary to principle or contrary
> to the provisions of the Trade Union Acts in holding that a trade
> union may be sued by its registered name.
>
> (Judgment in favour of the Taff Vale Railway Company, 1901)

If anyone in the trade union movement believed that the fight was over,
this case and judgment quickly disabused them of that thought. With the
law standing as it was any dispute involving a strike and loss of income
for the owners would ultimately involve the union concerned in costs
and no union could afford such sums. The movement seemed to have
been emasculated just at a time when great progress was to be made. A

further consideration for all trade unionists was that co-operation with established political parties so far had brought them some way towards their goals but not far enough. Perhaps it was now time to consider another approach.

INTELLECTUALS AND OTHERS

The two great strands of intellectualism in the rise of labour were those associated with Marxist ideas and variants and those who could be labelled as 'reformists'. The Marxists came on the scene in 1881 with the formation of the Democratic Federation founded by H. M. Hyndman. Although aristocratic in background Hyndman was dedicated to the fall of capitalism and all its iniquities. He espoused his ideas in a number of texts and lectures, including *England for All: The Textbook of Democracy* (1881) and *Socialism Made Plain* (1883). In 1884 the Democratic Federation joined forces with Joseph Lane's Labour Emancipation League and became the Social Democratic Federation (SDF). The movement, and notably its leader, enjoyed social contacts and financial support but never seemed able to find its way politically. It remained an influential and much-vaunted group but one that never really exercised any power. Its membership was low, never getting above 12,000 even in its years of greatest popularity. As the historian G. D. H. Cole has put it Hyndman was 'cock of the walk in the SDF but he had not much of a dunghill to crow from'. Still, it was an organization of personalities and these ultimately played their part in the formation of an independent labour movement in Britain although their real legacy was preparing the way for the Communist Party of Great Britain.

The 'reformists' took their lead from Marx too but then diverged immediately. They believed that capitalist society was a way for the working classes progressively to increase their standard of living. Rather than promoting such ideas as class-war and revolution the reformists tended to see the future in terms of the eventual nurturing of a society dominated by the working classes who could exploit it for their own benefit. The organization associated most with reformist ideas is the Fabian Society, established in 1884, with an impressive list of intellectual members, including Sidney and Beatrice Webb, and George Bernard Shaw. The first real pronouncement from this group came in 1886 in the Fabian Programme:

The Fabian Society consists of Socialists.

It therefore aims at the reorganisation of Society by the emancipation of Land and Industrial Capital from individual and class ownership, and the vesting of them in the community for the general benefit. In this way only can the natural and acquired advantages of the country be equitably shared by the whole people.

The Society accordingly works for the extinction of private property in Land and of the consequent individual appropriation, in the form of Rent, of the price paid for permission to use the earth, as well as for the advantages of superior soils and sites.

The Society, further, works for the transfer to the community of the administration of such industrial Capital as can conveniently be managed socially. For, owing to the monopoly of the means of production in the past, industrial inventions and the transformation of surplus income into Capital have mainly enriched the proprietary class, the worker being now dependent on that class for leave to earn a living.

If these measures be carried out, without compensation (though not without such relief to expropriated individuals as may seem fit to the community), Rent and Interest will be added to the reward of labour, the idle class now living on the labour of others will necessarily disappear, and practical equality of opportunity will be maintained by the spontaneous action of economic forces with much less interference with personal liberty than the present system entails.

For the attainment of these ends the Fabian Society looks to the spread of Socialist opinions, and the social and political changes consequent thereon. It seeks to achieve these ends by the general dissemination of knowledge as to the relation between the individual and Society in its economic, ethical, and political aspects.

This was followed in 1889 by the *Fabian Essays*. This extract from Sidney Webb's 'The historic basis of Socialism' in *Fabian Essays* (1889), well illustrates the Fabian commitment to the 'inevitability of gradualness' – slow, peaceful democratic change leading to Socialism.

In the present Socialist movement these two streams are united: advocates of social reconstruction have learnt the lesson of Democracy, and know that it is through the slow and gradual turning of the popular mind to new principles that social reorganization bit by bit comes. All students of society who are abreast of their time, Socialists as well as Individualists, realize that important organic changes can only be (1) democratic, and thus acceptable to a majority of the people, and prepared for in the minds of all; (2) gradual, and thus causing no dislocation, however rapid may be the rate of progress; (3) not regarded as immoral by the mass of the people, and thus not subjectively demoralizing to them; and (4) in this country at any rate, constitutional and peaceful. Socialists may therefore be quite at one with Radicals in their political methods. Radicals, on the other hand, are perforce realizing that mere political levelling is insufficient to save a State from anarchy and despair. Both sections have been driven to recognize that the root of the difficulty is economic; and there is every day a wider consensus that the inevitable outcome of Democracy is the control by the people themselves, not only of their own political organization, but, through that, also of the main instruments of wealth production; the gradual substitution of organized co-operation for the anarchy of the competitive struggle; and the consequent recovery, in the only possible way, of what John Stuart Mill calls 'the enormous share which the possessors of the instruments of industry are able to take from the produce'. The economic side of the democratic ideal is, in fact, Socialism itself.

However at all stages the movement was one which seemed to enjoy the debate about socialist ideas rather than the practice of ensuring that these reached individual members of society. Academic debates about different theories of wages and rents were fine in their place but at least one commentator has suggested that Fabians like the Webbs 'almost believed that [revolution] could be accomplished through after-dinner conversations with Liberal ministers'. Nevertheless, as with the SDF, the Fabian Society provided a strand of socialist thinking that for good or ill played its part in the formation of the Labour movement as it prepared to enter the twentieth century.

Artistic movements played their part too, with John Ruskin and William Morris being outstanding in this aspect of Labour endeavour. Morris's theories were based on his view that:

> I can see no use in people having political freedom unless they use it as an instrument for leading reasonable and manlike lives; no good even in education if, when they are educated, people have only slavish work to do, and have to live lives too much beset with sordid anxiety for them to be able to think and feel with the more fortunate people who produced art and poetry and great thought. This release from slavery it is clear cannot come to people so long as they are subjected to the bare subsistence wages which are a necessity for competitive commerce.
>
> (William Morris to C. E. Maurice, 22 June 1883, 123, pp. 173–4)

Morris's and Ruskin's ideas were quaint with a call for a return to medieval guilds and craftsmanship through which each worker would become skilled in his or her own right and through such skill would discover the path to ultimate salvation both in a spiritual and political sense. Morris talked of 'working-class' art while Ruskin, like many Fabians, talked in terms of educating the working classes to save themselves. It was in recognition of Ruskin's influence that the study centre founded at Oxford in 1891 became known as Ruskin College.

A further strand was that of Christian socialism that can trace its development in the nineteenth century through the works of Charles Kingsley to the more obvious examples of the socialist ten commandments, which would be fixed to the wall of socialist Sunday Schools which emerged during the 1890s. The intertwining of the socialist and religious message was not reserved for Sunday Schools but became a major theme to be pursued by leading socialist proponents. Philip Snowden was one of these. In his lecture 'The Religion of Socialism' to the Keighley Labour Church on 17 February 1895 he certainly tried to storm the high moral ground on behalf of the movement and the working classes and belief in the 'righteousness' of the Labour cause was strong at this time. It was useful to be able to draw stark contrasts for supporters between 'good' and 'evil' in a biblical sense. The success of Non-Conformism, and especially Methodism, in the urban centres of the country since the early nineteenth century meant that such a message, and especially one couched in such a way, fell on eager ears, as is evidenced by the cries of approval that met Snowden's remarks in 1895:

> Mr. Philip Snowden on Socialism
> Modern Christianity and the Religion of Socialism
> Lectures on the Ethics of Socialism
>
> Mr. Snowden pointed out that Socialists were not bloody revolutionaries or dreamers, but a body of earnest men who were seeking to replace our present anarchical commercialism, our industrial struggle for existence, our system of profit-mongering and labour exploitation, by the collective ownership and co-operative management of all the means of production and distribution for the benefit of each and all alike. Yet Socialism aimed at something beyond a mere restricted demand for higher wages; its object was to realise those aspiring mutterings which had been faintly heard for ages, and to establish for the workers a true life – the development of the whole of man's capacities, the expanding of his affections, and the co-operating with the Divine order of the universe. Socialism did not claim to establish any new principle of morality or religion but it did claim to understand the moral law more clearly and perfectly than current philosophy or religion.
>
> . . . It was a religion that believed, with Ruskin, that whether there was one God, whether there were three gods, or 10,000 gods, little children should have their bellies filled and their bodies kept warm. It was a religion which judged men not by creeds, but by deeds (hear, hear). . . .
>
> (*Keighley News*, 9 February 1895 in Snowden Collection, Keighley
> Public Libraries)

However, it is very difficult to judge exactly what the impact of these intellectual forces was. Certainly an element of respectability was lent to the Labour movement by the calibre of the membership of such groups as the Fabians. Equally so these ideas were carried into print and circles which might not have so readily accepted them from lesser luminaries

LIBERTY

SOCIALIST
TEN COMMANDMENTS.

SOCIALISM THE HOPE OF THE WORLD

1.—Love your School Fellows, who will be your fellow workmen in life.

2.—Love learning, which is the food of the mind; be as grateful to your teachers as to your parents.

3.—Make every day holy by good and useful deeds and kindly actions.

4.—Honour good men, be courteous to all men, bow down to none.

5.—Do not hate or speak evil of anyone; do not be revengeful, but stand up for your rights and resist oppression.

6.—Do not be cowardly. Be a friend to the weak and love justice.

7. Remember that all the good things of the earth are produced by labour. Whoever enjoys them without working for them is stealing the bread of the workers.

8. Observe and think in order to discover the truth. Do not believe what is contrary to reason, and never deceive yourself or others.

9.—Do not think that he who loves his own country must hate and despise other nations, or wish for war, which is a remnant of barbarism.

10.—Look forward to the day when all men will be free citizens of one fatherland, and live together as brothers in peace and righteousness.

of the movement. Nevertheless, it is hard to escape from the feeling of 'armchair' socialism, given the heroic and self-sacrificing deeds of the ordinary trade union members who were the intellectuals' contemporaries. Certainly these groups demonstrate the diversity of the movement and the variety of impulses that gave rise to Labour. They enjoyed a privileged position in Labour history during this formative period but have been fortunate to retain their standing in the movement given later events and struggles in which they played no part.

THE POLITICAL ARENA

Until the 1890s the trade union movement had stayed aloof from politics preferring to become involved in individual disputes that furthered the material welfare of their respective members. Any political activity had so far been under the umbrella of the Liberal Party. The very first working-men MPs took their seats in Parliament in 1874 as Liberals, but men such as John Hardaker, a stone-mason, tended to represent that 'middle class' and artisan strand of trade unionism, that had emerged in the mid-nineteenth century, rather than the great mass of the labouring population that looked towards 'new unionism' or shied away from trade unionism altogether. However, the cosy idea of a new generation of 'working-class' Liberal voters who would continue to vote for the Liberal Party was not fulfilled. As one historian has noted:

> Even as late as 1890 the Labour movement was a weak vehicle for the political aspirations of the working class. Trade unionism was patchy and trades councils were only just beginning to emerge in many areas. In truth, the Liberal party had little to worry about and was confident in its estimation that at least two-thirds of the working-class voters would continue to vote Liberal in the future. It was the almost endemic weakness of organized Labour which deluded the Liberal party into thinking that it could stand still in the face of the 'little breezes' of discontent that occasionally emerged. What the national Liberal party, and its local organizations, failed to appreciate was the seething discontent which had erupted among trade unionists from the late 1880s onwards. This neglect combined with working-class anger and frustration to produce an independent Labour movement.
>
> (K. Laybourn, *The Rise of Labour. The British Labour Party 1890–1979*, London, Edward Arnold, 1988, p. 18)

The event more than any other that denoted this change in attitude seems to have been the Manningham Mills strike in Yorkshire in 1890–1. The mill-owner tried to force down the wages of the workers by as much as a third and several thousands went on strike, with the strength of feeling and support clearly visible in these verses:

Manningham strike verses

One day, when in a Bradford Street
A most wretched sight I saw.
A man with aching hand and feet,
For the day was cold and raw.

He stood an open street to tent
And a Manningham Strikes bill,
Of course I soon knew that it meant –
They were bent on winning still.

I threw some money in the street,
For by food they have to live,
Those strikers I shall always greet
And serve while I have to give.

But summer now is drawing near,
When the rose will bud and bloom,
And summer my glad tidings bear
For the strike hands now in gloom.

Their battle is one hard fought.
To keep the wolf from biting;
And workers say they have done right
In turning out and fighting.

(*Yorkshire Factory Times*, 10 April 1891)

Although unsuccessful in its immediate aims the strike symbolized the beginning of a process that was to take some years but which would eventually see the rise of an independent labour movement and political party. At one meeting before the dispute ended Charlie Glyde summed up the position: 'We have had two parties in the past, the can'ts and the won'ts and it is time that we had a party that will.' Speaking in April Glyde's words were prophetic enough but moves were already afoot to march along the path he was suggesting. John Lister, an independently wealthy landowner and disciple of Morris and Ruskin, was already setting up the structure for a Labour Union in Halifax that would become the forerunner of the Independent Labour Party (ILP). The extracts from his journal show what a momentous year 1891 was and also the importance played by visiting celebrities and especially those from the Fabian Society.

page 7   But 1891 saw a new spirit generating itself. In that year, a branch of the Fabian Society was established at Halifax of which Mr. C. N. Worsnop was, I believe, the main promoter. There was also trouble at this time about Clay Miners' Wages . . .

page 8   I was invited by Mr. C. N. Worsnop, of Halifax, to attend a meeting of the local Fabian Society, which was being called in order to arrange for a lecture by Mr. De Mattos, entitled 'What is Socialism' on Tuesday, the 29 May. That gentleman, who was afterwards Secretary of the ILP came to Halifax, delivered his lecture & stopped the night at Shibden Hall.

As a result of this lecture a Branch of the Fabian Society was established in Halifax, of which the Rev. Bryan Dale, M.A., was elected President. A course of lectures was also arranged. On the 18th of June my Diary informs me that I signed 'The Bases' of the Fabian Society and so became a full-fledged member.

page 10   'The Courier', in its issue of August 1st, under the headline of 'Labour Representation in Halifax' informed its readers that 'The Trades and Labour Council' are very likely to run two candidates in the Labour interest at the next (Municipal) Election in November.

page 11   We understand also that a few candidates will be run for the School Board Election. We expect & believe we shall see now, that the Fabians have joined with the Trades & Labour Council, that vacancies on Public Bodies will be filled up by Labour men – even to the extent of one of the *page 12*   sitting MPs being removed, & a working man put in his place.

Across West Yorkshire similar organizations and proponents of independent labour appeared soon to be joined by national figures and provincial trade unionists. Running ahead of itself the movement in embryo put the dockers' leader Ben Tillett forward as parliamentary candidate for West Bradford in 1892 but in spite of polling 2,749 votes the Tillett campaign was not sufficient to see him elected. Nevertheless, 1892 was a good year for James Keir Hardie in West Ham, John Burns in Battersea and Havelock Wilson in Middlesbrough, all of whom were elected.

Individual successes, gratifying as they may well be, would be no substitute for a concerted effort which could only come with national organization. Once again John Lister's careful records give us a detailed account:

page 53   A Labour Meeting was held towards the end of Septr. in Shibden Park, at which addresses were given by Keir Hardie, MP, Pete Curran; George Cowgill, of Bradford Trades & Labour Council; F. Roper, J. H. Beever & J. Lister.

Mr. Beever made a notable speech in moving a

Resolution in favour of the establishment of an I.L.P. party throughout the whole country. A similar Resolution also was moved, at a meeting in Halifax on the 18th Sept. by Keir Hardie in these words:–

That this mass meeting of the workers of Halifax & district is for opinion that the time has come when a National & Independent Labour Party must be formed & thereby pledges itself to support an Independent Labour policy.

page 66   The year 1893 was to see an event even more memorable in Labour Annals, viz;– the foundation of the National Independent Labour Party.

On Jany 13th & 14th of that year it was formed at a Conference held at the Labour Institute, Peckover St., Bradford. The delegates consisted of 121, of whom 94 were from Independent Labour organizations, 5 S.D.F. members, 12 Fabians, 4 from the Cumberland Workmen's Unions & 11 from 9 other organizations. At this conference Hardie was in the Chair.

Source: G. Firth, K. Laybourn and J. O'Connell (eds), *The Yorkshire Labour Movements*, Leeds University, 1980.

Keir Hardie exemplified the new mood of labour. A self-taught socialist thinker who was widely read, he had been a miner's union organizer in Scotland and had much experience of trade disputes. He also had a deep-seated suspicion of the older generation of trade unionists who appeared to have sold their labouring birthright for political advantage in a Liberal Party-dominated political world. Particularly galling to Hardie was the career of Henry Broadhurst who started as secretary of the TUC Parliamentary Committee and finished up as an Under-Secretary at the Home Office in Gladstone's Third Ministry. Working men as ministers of the Crown might be in the future – but as representatives of their own political party not as lackeys of Liberalism. Keir Hardie, along with others at Bradford was intent upon creating a Labour future through the medium of a Labour Party.

The ILP constitution is an interesting document. It was decided from the outset to avoid the use of the words 'socialist' or 'socialism' in the title of the new organization. However, although wary of the reaction such emotive words may cause amongst potential supporters and enemies, the party programme was certainly socialist. The emphasis on collective ownership and severe taxation policies for unearned income were mixed in with more acceptable calls for social and educational reforms and the broadening out of democracy. The first steps had been taken on the path to independence. The Labour movement now had a national persona, a programme and an organization but it was still small, under-financed and politically weak.

THE CONSTITUTION OF THE ILP ADOPTED AT BRADFORD, 13 and 14 JANUARY 1893

NAME		Independent Labour Party
OBJECT		The object of the Independent Labour Party shall be to secure the collective ownership of all the means of production, distribution and exchange.
MEMBERSHIP		No person opposed to the principle of the Independent Labour Party shall be eligible for membership.

PROGRAMME

SOCIAL	1	Abolition of overtime, piecework, and child labour under the age of fourteen years.
	2	The restriction by law of the working day to 8 hours.
	3	Provision for the sick, disabled, aged, widows, and orphans, the funds to be raised by a tax upon unearned increment.
	4	Collective ownership of the land, and of all means of production distribution and exchange.
	5	Free unsectarian education from school to university.
	6	Properly remunerated work for the unemployed.
POLITICAL		The Independent Labour Party is in favour of every proposal for extending electoral rights and democratising of Government.
FISCAL	1	Abolition of indirect taxation, and taxation, to extinction, of unearned incomes.
	2	A graduated income tax.

Source: Independent Labour Party, *Independent Labour Party, 1893–1943: Jubilee Souvenir*, 1943.

Keir Hardie, as a founding member of the ILP, was just one of many Labour politicians who sought entrance into Parliament as an independent politician. Up to this time working men such as John Hardaker in 1874 and Ben Pickard in 1885 had either sat as Liberals or Lib–Lab members. By 1886 nine such MPs existed and they were free to act as they wished over specifically labour issues but tended to follow a strict Liberal Party line over other issues. Hence their independence was severely curtailed albeit, most of the time, by choice and inclination. What was now needed was a succession of avowedly working-class candidates who would enter Parliament as such and be free to vote as they wished on whatever issue according to the dictates of their party programme and their consciences. The 1890s saw a spate of such candidatures and in the forefront was Keir Hardie whose election campaign of November 1896 in Bradford East is very revealing. Hardie's message was a simple and clear one: the iniquities of capitalism and privilege kept the working classes from reaching the new heights of social freedom. Instead they were consigned to harsh existences in towns and factories

Poster for the by-election at Bradford East in November 1896.

throughout the country. However, his message went unheard in the
general election of 1895 when twenty-five ILP members had failed to get
elected. It was perhaps for this reason that Hardie tried to broaden out
the appeal of the ILP message in the campaign of 1896. Listed among
the speakers due to address the audience at Hardie's meeting at St

George's Hall, Bradford, were people who could count themselves amongst the ranks of national personalities, such as Tom Mann. With them came the committed backbone of provincial labour organizations such as the West Riding Labour leaders. In addition there were personalities such as Margaret McMillan, the proponent of nursery education, and the Pankhursts as recognition of Hardie's support for the suffragist movement. Nevertheless the campaign of 1896 in East Bradford did not see Hardie elected. Once again it was time to move on to pastures new and Hardie would play a key role in the coming together of all like-minded socialist and labouring groups to produce a truly national political party that could honestly stand up in the country and parliament and claim that it spoke for labour. The election defeat of 1895 that had been so disastrous for the hopes of the ILP was equally catastrophic for the Liberal Party. The great Conservative majority held out no prospect of political co-operation from that quarter and labour's traditional political allies, the Liberals, were in disarray and reduced to a squabbling agglomeration of groups divided by what seemed to most workers as marginal issues of little importance other than to the 'Celtic' fringes. The only hope for Labour seemed to be with labour. The interest in the party could be found at the grassroots level where certain areas of the country enjoyed much labour influence in local government. By 1895 there were 600 borough council labour members in the country and in 1898 West Ham became the first local authority to go Labour. But the riddle was why the party of Labour, the ILP, established in 1893, could not show more for its few years' existence, when in theory it should have garnered the votes of the majority of the population – the working classes? It was the attempt to solve this riddle that eventually led to all politically minded groups, such as the ILP, meeting and allying with those associations that represented the working classes at work, the trades unions.

THE DRAWING TOGETHER OF THE STRANDS 1900–14

The TUC resolution of 1899 to devote its energies to increasing the number of labour members in the next Parliament was a key decision. Nothing would be achieved by this declaration if an organization was not established. Such an organization was needed to unite the efforts of the TUC, ILP, socialist societies and labour organizations. In February 1900 the Labour Representative Committee (LRC) came into existence. It was comprised of twelve members in the first instance with seven from the unions, two from the ILP, one Fabian and two from the SDF who left shortly after its formation. Despite the wave of optimism at its foundation its first year of operating was a disappointing one with only a dozen or so trade unions affiliating with a membership of 35,000 out of the unionized total of two million. Funds were low and the 1900 election had seen only two of the fifteen candidates fielded victorious –

Keir Hardie and Richard Bell. The greater number of candidates viewed their task in a far less optimistic fashion and upsets of mammoth proportions would be needed if the newly formed LRC was to enjoy immediate and lasting success.

With the disappointment of 1900 behind it the LRC looked more hopefully towards 1901 but in that year came the Taff Vale judgment which was a stab at the vitals of trade unionism in Britain. The trade unions realized that direct parliamentary action would be necessary to defend themselves. The LRC now took on a different persona, moving in from the fringes of political action to mainstream politics. The period 1902–3 saw a further 127 unions affiliate to the LRC, almost trebling the number that had affiliated in the LRC's first year of operation. With the greater numbers came increased funds and the possibility of fighting more by-elections and general elections. This period also saw the affiliation of key areas of the labouring population with traditionally moderate groups such as the textile workers joining, as well as the first of the powerful Miners' Federations. At last the labour movement seemed to be putting itself on a firm enough footing to be taken seriously by the population and the politicians. Certainly the Liberal Party saw the potential that the LRC wielded with its annual conferences, growing affiliations and membership, ever-increasing funds and use of its political levy to fund and discipline MPs. More worrying was the effect that such success could have on the Liberal Party's own future. This was brought home to party managers in the North-East Lanark by-election in 1901 when the miner Robert Smillie stood as a Labour Party candidate and split the vote with the Liberal candidate sufficiently to let the Conservative in. Herbert Gladstone, the Liberal Chief Whip, wrote to Campbell-Bannerman, his party leader: 'We must try to hit it off with the Labour people who are not really unreasonable . . . Lanark may be a pretty warning.' Gladstone's prophetic words seemed confirmed with further successes for the LRC in Clitheroe in 1903 and Woolwich and Barnard Castle, also in 1903. Ramsay MacDonald, a Scottish Home Ruler who had come to the ILP in 1894, via the Lib–Lab pact and the Marxist SDF, negotiated on behalf of Labour with Gladstone, the Liberal representative. The result of their negotiations was a secret agreement over electoral policies. The substance of the agreement, which was reached in August 1903, was that Labour would be given a free hand in thirty constituencies, thus providing them with the potential for a substantial group of MPs in Parliament. In return MacDonald promised help for some Liberal candidates and support for a future Liberal government. The agreement remained secret because of the likely reactions in each camp if the news were leaked too early. Certainly, many Liberals could foresee a future in which a larger Labour Party dominated by more militant trade unionism would threaten the Liberals themselves.

It was a timely move for the LRC and as we saw in chapter 6 the next general election, that of 1906, brought a sweeping Liberal victory with 400 seats but along with these came 29 LRC members to be joined by another later on. These 30 MPs were the ones who took the name of the Labour Party (there were 14 miner MPs and 12 Lib–Labs too). Most came from the heartlands of the early centres of labour support such as James Parker who triumphed in Halifax, the stamping-ground of John Lister. The message was very much the same, with the emphasis on social and economic legislation, and the attack on the Conservative Government and the identification of Labour with 'progress'. However, of prime importance for the LRC's many trade union supporters was the highlighting of the legislation affecting trade union rights and especially the need to reverse the decision of Taff Vale. The Liberals were not slow to assimilate the messages of 1906. Sitting on a massive majority they were in a position to enact legislative changes. One of the first was the Trades Disputes Act of 1906 which overturned the Taff Vale judgment. The introduction of a limited bill at first found itself under attack from the Labour MPs and the government decided to redraft it. The final measure was roundly criticized by owners. It gave union members the right to picket and completely protected trade union funds. It appeared to some to be a climbdown by the government and a charter to encourage the proliferation of strikes. To many, it was an example of the undue influence of the minority of Labour members on the government's policies and decisions. Further examples came with a new Workmen's Compensation Act, the School Meals Act and Medical Inspection Act. However, such a view belied the truth which was that Labour MPs, a few outstanding exceptions apart, were in H. M. Hyndman's phrase, 'dull and deferential'. They also suffered from the new Liberalism that pushed for a range of social reforms, many of them fundamentally affecting the working population. It was very difficult for Labour MPs to denounce the work of Liberals like Lloyd George who was promoting trade boards, labour exchanges and national insurance. But the post-1906 era of inactivity was not only determined by Liberal success. Another legal judgment, in 1909, was to knock back the Labour movement for some years. Trade unions had developed the practice of making a levy of their members for funds to finance Labour MPs (no MP, until 1911, received wages). In 1908 W. V. Osborne, a local branch secretary of the Railway Servants, refused to contribute on the grounds that he supported the Liberal Party. Taking his case to court Osborne was initially unsuccessful but on appeal he received the judgment he wanted from Lord Justice Farwell in December 1909, when it was ruled that unions should not make levies nor use funds to finance Labour MPs. It was a great blow to trade unions and the Labour Party alike. Although two years later MPs were paid, and in 1913 the Farwell decision was reversed in a new Trade Union Act, which provided for separate political funds, the Labour Party seemed considerably more exposed than it had done just a few years before in 1906. Worse was to follow with the apparent rise of militant and violent trade union disputes that seemed to consign the Labour Party to the rearguard of the Labour movement.

Union membership had continued to rise throughout the later nineteenth and early twentieth centuries. There was clearly an upward movement, seen in the way in which crucial events acted as stimuli to the swelling ranks of organized labour. The trend saw a massive spurt in the years just before the war with a 60 per cent increase in membership in the two years 1911–13. Certainly new-found strength acted as an encouragement to working-class politicians and union leaders. More importantly the move of the coal-miners from Liberal ranks to Labour ranks in 1909 heralded a key period of labour disputes because they carried their long-standing grievances with the mine owners with them. This was also a period of expansion in trade and industry and thus a period of increased trade union demands to allow their members to share in the new prosperity. At the same time the LRC seemed to be making little real headway against entrenched Liberal values in Parliament and so trade unions offered a more direct approach. This coincided with a growing militancy brought on by experimentation with ideas such as syndicalism which Tom Mann had brought back from his travels and propagated in areas of working-class Britain. In some of these areas his ideas took root, as with the Unofficial Reform Committee of the South Wales Miners' Federation which published in 1912 the pamphlet *The Miners' Next Step*. It took the idea of public ownership beyond that of simple nationalization. What these activists wanted was the workers' control of industry. Such militancy was portrayed as the workers taking independent action even over the heads of their union officials.

This was indeed the era of strike activity. Generally, in the opening years of the twentieth century, strikes cost between 1 and 3 million working days lost per annum. The years 1910–14 saw this average rise to 10 million and in 1912 41 million working days were lost as major unions joined forces and brought dispute after dispute. The key players were the dockers and seamen, who came together with other transport workers, but not the railwaymen, in 1910 in the National Transport Workers Federation. Such a grouping oddly enough was close to the syndicalist ideal of total stoppage by all unions or the workers' ultimate weapon – the general strike. Of course no such strike was achieved in these years and part of the trade union's weakness was that each of these three powerful bodies took turns in flexing its muscles and inevitably succumbed to government action in one form or another. Certainly, the public view of the strikes was one that did little good for the image of trade unionism and the newspapers were quick to point out the dangers of violence and extremism on the streets of England.

It was not until 1913 that the three unions managed to get together and put forward something resembling a joint plan of action. The extract from the *Labour Year Book* notes not only the combined strength of such an organization but also the costs involved of independent action:

At the Miners' Annual Conference in 1913, a resolution was passed, 'That the Executive Committee of the Miners' Federation approach the Executive Committees of other big Trade Unions with a view to co-operative action.'

The miners had a joint meeting with the representatives of the two industries most comparable to their own – railways and transport.

The three bodies have much in common. Their membership is considerable, the miners numbering 800,000, the railwaymen 270,000 and the transport workers 250,000. The miners have done much fighting; the railwaymen have come through struggles similar to our own; and the transport workers are famed for their fighting spirit and fighting qualities. But a great deal of suffering and privation has been caused. A strike on the railway system affects the miners and the transport workers. When the miners struck in 1912 the cost to the railwaymen alone was about £94,000.

The new body is not to be a rival to any other. Nor is it to be sectional in any sense. There is no suggestion that if one section of the miners determines to strike they will receive the assistance of the new alliance. Action is to be confined to joint national action. The predominant idea is that each of these great fighting organisations, before embarking upon any big movement, either defensive or aggressive, should formulate its programme, submit it to the others, and that upon joint proposals action should then be taken.

It will be wise, indeed essential, to have the working agreement ready for the days of peace after the war. It is then that we may expect an attack on Labour by the employers.

(Robert Smillie, *The Labour Year Book*, 1916)

Nevertheless such a new departure necessitated some lengthy and delicate negotiations which went on into 1914, by which time the course of international events changed the political picture as war broke out. An agreement was reached in December 1915 but it was by then purely academic.

On the surface the Labour movement seemed far from successful in 1914. It had emerged but still stood in the Liberal shadows in parliamentary terms and was bedevilled in trade union activity by division and public preconceptions. This is, however, too bleak a picture. Certainly the Labour movement had underachieved in the years up to 1914, especially in parliamentary elections, but it had made significant progress in other areas. It was very strong in local elections and enjoyed growing success in by-elections. The trade unions were expanding too. In 1914 membership stood at 4,145,000 and by 1920 this figure would double. Bleak as it might appear, the movement was about to enter on another period of significant development in the post-war years.

TEN MOMENTOUS YEARS 1914–24

Patriotism outweighed ideology in 1914. The call for all good socialists and workers to distance themselves from the barbarities of war was to be heard across the country as in this example from a provincial daily paper:

> Alone amongst the parties of Britain the Labour party is pledged against militarism. . . . We must take up the 'Fiery Cross' and carry it to the remotest hamlet in the country, call every man and woman to the colours. 'Down with militarism.' That is our cry – as it is also the cry of our comrades all over Europe. Blazen it on the banners. Write it on the pavement. Sing it in the streets.
>
> (*Bradford Pioneer*, 9 January 1914)

However, in reality these voices were few and increasingly muted as the popular enthusiasm for war grew, especially amongst the working classes, who saw the opportunity for adventure. Such romantic views did not last long and the war experience was important for many reasons in forming new attitudes and approaches adopted by Labour in the post-war era. First, the expectations of those who fought in the conflict were raised and their desire to see significant improvements in their working and living conditions contributed to the increase in trade union membership and a propensity to vote Labour. Whether a new, more homogeneous working class came out of the war experience, as some commentators have suggested, is debatable but it is easy to discern a greater urgency after 1918. Second, the needs of war forced on governments the necessity of adopting increasingly interventionist policies. In fact, war was an experiment in state intervention on a scale that had never been attempted before – after all this was total war. The Defence of the Realm Act (DORA) passed in 1914 saw powers given to government to regulate society on an unprecedented level. Both industry and agriculture came under close control as did working practices. The formation of specialized ministries saw the full force and weight of government direction. The Ministry of Munitions in 1915, for instance, overcame a crisis in this area of supply. The coalition governments saw both conscription and the mass employment of women. In the end it proved necessary, but also perfectly feasible, to bring in and operate food rationing in 1918. Third, the war provided the opportunity for Lloyd George and Asquith to air their differences more publicly. Initially Lloyd George was the victor forming a second coalition government in December 1916. This signalled the defection of many leading Liberals which considerably weakened the party in the post-war era. Fourth, the Labour Party's organization made some gains. The sensible and patriotic approach of the leaders and most of the workforce did much to enhance their standing. Moreover, organizations such as the War Emergency Committee, established in 1914, played their part in trying to restructure the party itself. Under Arthur Henderson's steady hand this and other organizations tried to prepare the Labour movement for the post-war era. Such moves were made all the more important considering the government's change to the electoral system in 1918. The Representation of the People Act 1918 trebled the electorate to 22 million, giving the vote to all men over 21 and all women over 30.

Peace brought a long-overdue election and in it Lloyd George, along with the Conservative leader Bonar Law, tried to keep the coalition together giving each candidate a jointly signed letter (contemptuously called a 'coupon' by Asquith) endorsing their candidature. The so-called 'coupon' election had the results Lloyd George wanted with the coalition getting 484 seats, 61 eventually going to Labour and a mere 26 to the Asquith-led group of Liberals. Labour feelings were mixed because in the last election 42 seats had been won but the total popular vote they received had increased from about half a million in 1910 to two million in 1918. They fielded 361 candidates in 1918 compared to a mere 78 in 1910 but their success rate was much less. Worse was to follow with their leaders – MacDonald, Snowden and Henderson – all losing their seats. The work of Henderson, both in organization and providing a new constitution for the party, had not had time to take effect before the election. He had set the party on its way with the beginnings of a local Labour Party branch organization and the creation of a 21-member party executive. Significantly the latter saw a dominance of trade union members and socialists giving 13 seats to them out of the final figure of 23. The Executive was to be elected annually at the party conference and the unions were to exercise a block vote. The new Labour Party programme was itemized in *Labour and the New Social Order* which saw the key priorities as: a national minimum wage, control of industry, financial reform and surplus wealth employed for the common good. The election of 1918 came too soon and the emotive effects of victory and patriotism muddied the waters of democracy, hence Labour's relatively poor showing. What is clear from 1918 is that despite having only 61 seats in all Labour was now a political and parliamentary force to be reckoned with.

Of course, what was not known in 1918 was the very rapid change in fortunes for both the Labour Party and the Liberals that the next few momentous years would hold. In the first place, the Labour Party organization continued to improve with four important sub-committees established to cover organization and elections, policy and programmes, literature, research and publicity, and finance and general purposes. Along with the active grassroots organizations dominated by the ILP branches and the acquisition of the *Daily Herald* the party's centralized structure began to take shape. In addition special attention was paid to the new political force of the female vote not only emancipated by the Act of 1918 but by the experience of war itself. This period also saw the first full-time paid agents of the party put to work in key areas. At the same time Britain's post-war economic difficulties made themselves known. Huge debts and loss of markets and trade were compounded by slow demobilization giving way to a much more rapid flooding of the labour market. The very short immediate post-war boom had given way by 1921 to economic collapse with a 50 per cent reduction in exports and unemployment reaching two million. The inevitable strikes followed, stimulated by the huge increase in trade union membership which grew from more than 2.5 million in 1910 to over 8.3 million in 1920. In addition, deregulation of industry had allowed certain groups such as the mine owners, in the face of economic downturn, to cut wage levels and thus bring about strikes. The extract shows the full effects of these across-the-board cuts which were hard for returning soldiers and heroes to take:

Flat Rate Changes
(applied nationally from the dates given below)

1917   *17 September*: 1s. 6d. per day to all colliery workers of 16 years of age and over, and 9d. per day to those under 16 years. To be paid for every day on which a worker works, and for every day on which a worker is ready and able to work, but is prevented owing to the work of the pit, seam or place being stopped by causes other than strikes, excluding recognised holidays, Sundays, stop-days, etc., but including days on which the work of the pit, seam or place is temporarily stopped through lack of trade (first 'War wage').

1918   *1st July*: The same (second 'War wage').

1919   *9th January*: 2s. per shift worked, or per day worked. 1s. in the case of workers under 16 years of age (Sankey wage).

1920   *12th March*: 20 per cent increase on gross wages, excluding War wage and Sankey wage, subject to a minimum increase of 2s. per day for adults, 1s. per day for persons of 16 years and under 18 years of age, and 9d. per day for those under 16 years of age.

        4th November: 2s. per day for workers over 18 years of age, 1s. for those of 16 years and under 18 years of age, and 9d. for workers under 16 years of age together with Bonus on Output resulting in:

1921   *3rd January*: An addition of 1s. 6d per day for adults, 9d. per day for youths and 6¾d. per day for boys.

1st February: A reduction of 2s. per day for adults, 1s. per day for youths and 9d. per day for boys.

1st March: A reduction of 1s. 6d. per day for adults, 9d. per day for youths, and 6¾d. per day for boys.

(R. Page Arnot, *The Miners' Years of Struggle. A History of the Miners' Federation of Great Britain from 1910 Onwards*, London, Allen & Unwin, 1953, p. 332)

The initial success in gaining some increases soon gave way to swingeing cuts. Strikes by the miners raised the prospect of a revival of the Triple Alliance but the miners found that promises made by other workers were not kept and that they stood alone against the owners. The desertion of the other unions on 15 April 1921, 'Black Friday' as it became known, led to the eventual capitulation of the miners in the summer of 1921 as the letter from their executive shows:

We, therefore, strongly urge you, with the knowledge of the seriousness of the situation, to accept this agreement, which we have provisionally agreed to today, and authorise your Committee to sign the terms by Friday next.

Yours, on behalf of the Executive Committee,

HERBERT SMITH, Acting President.
JAMES ROBSON, Treasurer.
FRANK HODGES, Secretary.

June 28th, 1921.

(ibid., p. 331)

Certainly this was a severe blow to the workers and the whole trade union movement but more importantly it also raised the question of how much the workers could rely on the government of the day to provide. them with their needs.

Meanwhile, the Liberal Party and especially Lloyd George's portion of it involved in the coalition with the Conservatives, found their position increasingly untenable. By 1922 troubles at home and abroad had decided the majority of Conservatives now under Austen Chamberlain's leadership to take action. In October of that year the Conservatives met at the Carlton Club and they resolved, far from unanimously, to readopt the ailing Bonar Law as leader and to distance the party from Lloyd George, his Liberals and the coalition. The ensuing election saw a big Conservative majority returned but more significantly 142 Labour members were elected, with the Liberals coming in third with about 120 seats. It was a triumph for Henderson's organization which was now bearing a heavy crop of electoral fruit and the election saw the Labour Party take over as the official opposition in Parliament: another milestone in the party's history.

Bonar Law's ill-health meant Baldwin took over the leadership of the Conservatives. Plagued by the economic condition of the country he decided to adopt a policy of protection to solve the crisis. The idea of protection raised the hackles of the Liberals and they joined with the Labour Party in opposing the government which forced Baldwin to seek a 'mandate' on the issue at a general election which was called for December 1923. The Conservatives were returned in large numbers, getting 258 seats but not the overall majority Baldwin wanted. Thus Labour's increase to 191 with the Liberals' 158 enabled James Ramsay MacDonald to take power as Britain's first Labour Prime Minister on 21 January 1924, albeit as a minority leader and only for ten months.

RED SCARES 1924–6

1924 was an inauspicious year: any hopes of a new labour order being formed had to be postponed because of the immediate objective of finding a solution to the economic problems. MacDonald made this clear with his appointment of Philip Snowden to the post of Chancellor of the Exchequer where his ministerial colleague concentrated on the national debts rather than any redistributive taxation policy. The government's only major achievement was the Wheatley Housing Act which gave generous subsidies to builders and stirred councils into action later in the 1920s. Much time was taken up by foreign affairs, MacDonald coping with this too, but as it turned out approaches to the Soviet government for a treaty tended to confirm the worst suspicions of Labour's opponents. Conservatives and Liberals combined to bring down the government, which was easily done given Labour's minority position. The election that took place that autumn became notorious for the so-called Zinoviev letter, part of which appears below:

EXECUTIVE COMMITTEE, THIRD COMMUNIST
INTERNATIONAL PRESIDIUM

MOSCOW
September 15 1924

To the Central Committee, British Communist Party
DEAR COMRADES, – The time is approaching for the Parliament of England to consider the Treaty concluded between the Governments of Great Britain and the S.S.S.R. for the purpose of ratification. The fierce campaign raised by the British bourgeoisie around the question shows that the majority of the same . . . are against the treaty. . . .

It is indispensable to stir up the masses of the British proletariat, to bring into movement the army of unemployed proletarians. . . . It is imperative that the group in the Labour Party sympathising with the treaty should bring increased pressure to bear upon the Government and Parliamentary circles in favour of ratification of the treaty. . . .

A settlement of relations between the two countries will assist in the revolutionising of the international and British proletariat not less than a successful rising in any of the working districts of England, as the establishment of closer relations between the British and Russian proletariat, the exchange of delegations and workers, etc., will make it possible for us to extend and develop the propaganda and ideals of Leninism in England and the Colonies. . . .

From your last report it is evident that agitation propaganda in the Army is weak, in the Navy a very little better . . . it would be desirable to have cells in all the units of the troops, particularly among those quartered in the large centres . . . and also among factories working on munitions and at military store depots. . . .

Desiring you all success, both in organisation and in your struggle.

With Communist greetings,

Zinoviev,
President of the Presidium of the I.K.K.I.

MacManus,
Member of the Presidium.

Kuusinen,
Secretary.

No matter how unlikely the drift of the text may seem it was a godsend for political opponents. The September date does tend to give credence to the idea that the letter was held back for an opportune moment when it could do most damage. Inevitably, as would have been the case without a Zinoviev letter, the Labour Party did not secure enough seats to return to government. In fact numbers fell from 191 to 151, although this tends to obscure the real gains that Labour made. First, the party increased its overall vote by one million. Second, the sweeping Conservative victory giving them 419 seats was won at the expense of the Liberal vote not the Labour vote. In fact, the overall losers in 1924 were the Liberals who were now reduced to a mere 40 seats and eclipsed as a political force from that time on.

The first Labour Government had made gains and losses. The intelligent, urbane MacDonald impressed as a leader especially with his presence and speeches, perhaps deserving Shinwell's epithet of 'a Prince among men'. His government had made no real mistakes on the domestic front and the sensible approach to problems and policies, despite the 'Red Scare', won some admiration for Labour. MacDonald was convinced of the good job they had done and was at pains to explain to the King:

> They have shown the country that they have the capacity to govern in an equal degree with the other Parties in the House . . . and, considering their lack of experience, . . . have acquitted themselves with credit in the House of Commons. [. . .] The Labour Government has also shown the country that patriotism is not a monopoly of any single class or party. Finally, they can justly claim that they have left the international situation in a more favourable position than that which they inherited. They have in fact demonstrated that they, no less than any other party, recognize their duties and responsibilities, and have done much to dispel the fantastic and extravagant belief which at one time found expression that they were nothing but a band of irresponsible revolutionaries intent on wreckage and destruction.
> (M. Cowling, *The Impact of Labour*, Cambridge, Cambridge University Press, 1971, p. 359)

On the other hand some of the mud smeared in 1924 stuck and Labour had to make very visible its distance from the more extreme political views. However, some sections of the Labour Party, and especially the ILP, were less than pleased with Labour's first experience of government. After all there had been no attempt to move towards nationalization – quite sensibly, given the economic situation and lack of a majority, but this was seen as a major betrayal of an article of faith enshrined in Clause Four of the Labour Party's programme. Similarly a Labour government invoking the Emergency Powers Act to stop industrial action stuck in many throats. The differences exposed would be tested to the full in the next years and while the parliamentary Labour Party languished in opposition the trade unions took up the challenge.

GENERAL STRIKE 1926

Although the miners had managed to get a pay increase in 1924 a sharp downturn in trade in the following year cruelly snatched this advantage away. It was tantamount to incitement to strike and the miners reacted predictably but this time they made sure of approaching the Unions' General Council and extracting an assurance of help. Perhaps conscious of their desertion in 1921 the Council responded positively and thus brought closer the possibility of a nationwide strike in support of the miners. The government wanted to avoid this and Baldwin gave subsidies to the mining industry to cover the lost wages while establishing the Samuel Commission whose brief it was to sort out a compromise and bring the owners and workers together in an agreement. Not trusting to luck Baldwin also began to make preparations and provision against a further escalation of the strike action, should Samuel fail. The concessions of 31 July 1925, called 'Red Friday' because of the unions' apparent victory, were short-lived because both the owners and the workers rejected Samuel's plans. The unions sent out secret notices for a national strike to begin on 4 May. Within a short space of time a remarkable number of the workforce was on strike with key groups joining in such as power workers, iron and steel workers, builders, printers, railwaymen, dockers and those involved in road transport. The message to all workers was a simple one but the government, well prepared with its own propaganda journal ready to come off the press, had other ideas. It was easy for it to point out the seeming iniquity and unfairness of the strike and also to raise serious questions about the constitutionality of the union's actions:

> The General Strike is in operation, expressing in no uncertain terms a direct challenge to ordered Government. It would be futile to attempt to minimise the seriousness of such a challenge, constituting as it does an effort to force upon some 42,000,000 British citizens the will of less than 4,000,000 others engaged in the vital services of the country. The strike is intended as a direct hold-up of the nation to ransom.
>
> (*The British Gazette*, 6 May 1926)

The unions could protest and put their own case both in inflammatory cartoons and more restrained print:

> The General Council does not challenge the Constitution. It is not seeking to substitute unconstitutional government. Nor is it desirous of undermining our Parliamentary institutions. The sole aim of the Council is to secure for the miners a decent standard of life. The Council is engaged in an Industrial Dispute. There is no Constitutional Crisis. . . .
>
> It is . . . fantastic for the Prime Minister to pretend that the Trade Unions are engaged in an attack upon the Constitution of the Country. Every instruction issued by the General Council is evidence of their determination to maintain the struggle strictly on the basis of an industrial dispute. They have ordered every member taking part to be exemplary in his conduct and not to give any cause for police interference. They are not attacking the Constitution. They are not fighting the community. They are defending the mine workers against the mine-owners.
>
> (*The British Worker*, 7 May 1926)

However, the truth was that they had neither the organization nor the inclination to hold the country to ransom. The government response of using troops, police, special constables, volunteers and undergraduates proved quite workable at least for a short time. Serious doubts were raised about the legality of the unions' actions and suggestions were made as to the level of moral and financial burden the general strike might foist upon the unions. Nevertheless, for the unions as well the first week appeared to go well and most importantly for all concerned peacefully:

On this same Monday morning (May 10th) there appeared in the *British Worker* under the heading 'ALL'S WELL' a 'General Council's message to Trade Union members':

We are entering upon the second week of the general stoppage in support of the mine-workers against the attack upon their standard of life by the coal-owners. Nothing could be more wonderful than the magnificent response of millions of workers to the call of their leaders. From every town and city in the country reports are pouring into the General Council headquarters stating that all ranks are solid, that the working men and women are resolute in their determination to resist the unjust attack upon the mining community.

The General Council desire to express their keen appreciation of the loyalty of the Trade Union members to whom the call was issued and by whom such a splendid response has been made. They are especially desirous of commending the workers on their strict obedience to the instruction to avoid all conflict and to conduct themselves in an orderly manner. Their behaviour during the first week of the stoppage is a great example to the whole world.

The General Council's message at the opening of the second week is: – 'Stand Firm. Be Loyal to Instructions and Trust your Leaders.'

(Page Arnot, op. cit., p. 444)

The progress of the action in the second week was followed closely by the country through newspapers as well as with the help of BBC radio which kept sending out up to date bulletins:

Tuesday, May 11th – afternoon bulletin:
Still no sign of relaxation of the strike situation as a whole.
Tuesday, May 11th – evening bulletin:
There is as yet little sign of a general collapse of the strike.
Wednesday, May 12th – 10 a.m. bulletin:
The position as a whole is still one of deadlock.

(ibid., p. 445)

However, on the Wednesday suddenly the deadlock was broken and the nine-day-old strike was called off:

Two short hours later came the noon bulletin on the B.B.C.: 'General Strike ceases today.'

Incredulous miners, workers, and general public clustered round the radio. Stunning confirmation reached them in the announcer's reading of a message from the King-Emperor in Buckingham Palace addressed 'to my people':

The nation has just passed through a period of extreme anxiety.

It was today announced that the General Strike had been brought to an end.

At such a moment it is supremely important to bring together all my people to confront the difficult situation which still remains.

This task requires the co-operation of all able and well-disposed men in the country.

(ibid.)

It was a victory for good sense: the government had been prepared to fight and the unions had not been prepared to escalate the action as they would have to do. The miners were left to struggle on which they did for a further six months, but finally they too succumbed and returned to work for less money. Obstinacy on both sides prevented a quicker solution and Lord Birkenhead claimed: 'It would be possible to say without exaggeration that the Miners' leaders were the stupidest men in England if we had not on frequent occasions to meet the owners.' Agreements, such as the one shown for Lambton pit in County Durham, were typical of the final outcome with wages reduced across the board for all mining activities:

LAMBTON. – D PIT. – Agreement 25 Apr. '27 (11852). – Maudlin Seam. *Hewing score prices.* Bargain Flat, whole reduced from 14s. 9d. to 11s. 9d., broken reduced from 11s. 1d. to 8s. 1d. West Flat, whole reduced from 14s. 9d. to 14s. 8d., broken reduced from 11s. 1d. to 11s. *Filling.* Bargain Flat reduced from 5s. 9d. to 4s. 2d. per score. *Bottom,* fillers 9d. per length of 4 feet, hewers 1s. 5d. per length of 4 feet. *Nightshift,* 6d. per score. *Consideration,* hewers and fillers, 9d. per hour. *Bordrooms* (22½ square feet) 6s. 6d.; own working, 8s. 2d. per yard. *Putters.* First rank reduced from 2s. 5d. to 1s. 10d., second rank reduced from 2s. 6d. to 1s. 11d., third rank reduced from 2s. 7d. to 2s., fourth rank reduced from 2s. 8d. to 2s. 1d., per score.

(Durham Coal Owners Association, *Abstract of Accounts and Agreements submitted to the District Commission from January 1, 1926 to March 2, 1928*, p. 46)

The final insult for the unions was the Trades Disputes Act of 1927 which declared sympathy strikes illegal as well as general ones. Moreover, it changed the character of the 1913 Act by making it the task of the individual member to declare in writing his intention of 'contracting in' to the political fund as opposed to 'contracting out' as it was before. The unions suffered as a result with a sharp decline in membership post 1926 and a consequent severe loss of funds.

Despite the emotive attacks in 1926 and a concentrated press campaign, notably in Conservative newspapers, the Labour Party emerged from the strike seemingly untainted. It had distanced itself from the unions' direct action, or so it certainly seemed to the unions and the more militant sections of the movement. With the strike being essentially peaceful, short and, apart from the miners, amicably settled Labour did not seem to suffer. In fact, 1927 distinctly strengthened its hand especially in a time of rising unemployment, the issue that would come to dominate British politics for at least the next ten years. Certainly Labour made the most of it. Individual candidates made much of unemployment in the election campaign of 1929 as did the party in its national publicity. The attack was successful and the Labour Party won for the first time a majority of the seats in Parliament, securing 288 in all. However, they were denied an absolute majority because the Conservatives mustered 260 seats and the Liberals 59. Nevertheless, with Baldwin's resignation on 4 June 1929, MacDonald became Labour Prime Minister for the second time.

THE LAST DECADE 1929–40

Macdonald's Cabinet saw Snowden return as Chancellor, Henderson become Foreign Secretary, J. H. Thomas as minister with responsibility for unemployment and Margaret Bondfield as the first woman cabinet minister at Housing. In foreign affairs there were close links with the League of Nations, support for disarmament conferences and negotiations for naval limitations, but at home little was achieved as far as the major Labour articles of faith were concerned. Casting a huge shadow over all of this was the growing problem of unemployment which was compounded, shortly after Labour took office, by the Wall Street Crash. The malign influence of the American stock market collapse spread throughout the world, hitting the European financial centres very badly. The economic slump and crisis that ensued was compounded by an already established post-war policy in Britain of trying to restore the pound to the gold standard and parity to the dollar. This had been achieved at some expense in 1925 and politicians were determined that it should remain in force. Labour's new Chancellor, Snowden, had very fixed ideas on how to cope with the new financial crisis, and thus retain confidence in a gold-backed pound. Snowden was something of a throw-back to the great traditions of Liberal radicalism and all the suggested policies to solve the current financial problems – coming off the gold standard, devaluation of the pound and protectionist policies – were anathema to him. Instead he adopted the ultimately disastrous policies of putting up taxes and reducing government expenditure. The latter of course helped to increase unemployment rather than decrease it and it climbed steadily to 23 per cent of the working population in 1931.

Nevertheless, Snowden's position in the government, the confidence with which he espoused his policies and his secrecy over treasury information gained him party support and confounded potential opponents. His budget of 1930 pursued the policies with vigour, with taxes rising across the board affecting the population as a whole. But, as always with indirect taxes the poorer sections suffered most. However, what money came in did so at the expense of reducing production and trade with the consequence of increasing unemployment, and as the dole queues grew in size so did the government's benefit burden. Balancing the budget became impossible. A commission of inquiry, the Gregory Commission, had already called for across-the-board cuts in benefit payments of up to 30 per cent in its report in June 1931. A further inquiry by the May Committee also reported the necessity of paring down the budget by £120 million of which £67 million could be gained from a 20 per cent cut in benefits. The government rejected Gregory's proposals out of hand but were forced to consider May's as the pressure for action became intense. Snowden realized that desperate situations called for desperate remedies and had already accepted the principle of sacrifice earlier in the year, as this speech of February 1931 shows. The problem would be convincing the majority of the party.

'I say with all the seriousness I can command that the national position is so grave that drastic and disagreeable measures will have to be taken', he said. 'Expenditure which may be easy and tolerable in prosperous times becomes intolerable in a state of grave industrial depression. . . . An increase in taxation in present conditions which fell on industry would be the last straw. Schemes involving heavy expenditure, however desirable they may be, will have to wait until prosperity returns.

This is necessary – I say this more particularly to my Honourable Friends behind – to uphold the present standard of living, and no class will ultimately benefit more by present economy than the wage-earners.

I have been in active political life for forty years, and my only object has been to improve the lot of the toiling millions. That is still my aim and object, and, if I ask for some temporary suspensions, some temporary sacrifice, it is because that is necessary to make future progress possible.'

(Colin Cross, *Philip Snowden*, London, Barrie & Rockliff, 1966, pp. 265–6)

Snowden, along with MacDonald, Henderson, Thomas and Graham formed the Cabinet Economic Committee in August 1931 but before it could formally meet its members had decided that £78 million of savings were necessary. Their problem was that full cabinet approval would be necessary and the Cabinet had already made it plain that its limit on savings was £56 million with none of it to come from cuts in benefits. At the same time Snowden was furiously negotiating with both American and French banks to get a loan of £80 million to bolster the pound –

but it was too late. The flight from the pound had begun and gold was flowing out of the country at an alarming rate as foreign investors feared a British banking collapse. It was on 24 August 1931 that MacDonald forced the issue in Cabinet with a vote of eleven for the cuts and nine against. Although victorious, MacDonald's faction carried far fewer cabinet heavyweights than the rebels and he felt his only action was to resign which he did on the morning of 24 August. Instead, however, of a call for a Baldwin Conservative administration, Labour members were amazed to hear the announcement at noon of a MacDonald-led national coalition government. Selfless as this action seemed to many with Mac-Donald putting party division to one side in the nation's time of greatest need, those less charitably inclined seriously questioned MacDonald's motives, intentions and morals. The vilification of MacDonald began:

> We'll hang Ramsay Mac on a sour apple tree,
> We'll hang Snowden and Thomas to keep him company;
> For that's the place where traitors ought to be.

Lynching was a capital offence but expulsion from the Party was severe enough and, in all, MacDonald and some dozen others found this their penalty.

The debate about MacDonald continued, and still does, but his priority was to lead the new government into the election of October 1931 to get a 'mandate' for their actions. His message seemed more attractive than that presented by Labour. The National Government was given its 'mandate' with a staggering return of 556, only 13 of them Labour, and took office for the next nine years. Labour could only muster 52 seats. Just as the great era of unemployment was about to turn the screw relentlessly on the working classes of Britain, the Labour Party, shorn of its leadership, was at its lowest ebb since 1910.

The National Government took the pound off the gold standard and what had been recently unthinkable became a reality. The value of the pound fell, but not catastrophically, and exports became cheaper for a short time. Protection was adopted with the Import Duties Act of 1932 establishing a 10 per cent general tariff but with some exclusions. This was reinforced in 1932 at the Imperial Economic Conference in Ottawa by the adoption of the principle of imperial preference on foods from the Dominions and goods from Britain. With low interest rates and a building boom after extensive slum clearance some signs of recovery were in the air. These were helped by subsidies to industry and agriculture, the latter gaining from the quota system that limited foreign food imports, and the establishing of marketing boards for foods like milk and bacon. However, this era was also the one described as the 'Hungry Thirties', and the economic activity and regeneration cited seems at variance with the image of hunger, deprivation and unemployment. The 'Hungry Thirties' were no myth and there is no doubt that some areas, notably the north with its heavy industry and regions dominated by single trades, suffered badly. The lower rates in London and Birmingham were of little help to the unemployed masses on Tyneside who were experiencing rates as high as 70 per cent in some communities. It is not surprising that workers from this region have a completely different view on the 1930s from workers in other areas. Their struggles became legendary as did their marches and demonstrations and none more so than the crusade that set off from Jarrow.

Where, however, did all this leave the Labour Party? The picture looked black in 1931 but the bleakness of the MacDonald desertion, high unemployment and trade union disarray did not paint a completely desolate landscape as the results of the election statistics testify. In 1931 and again in 1935 a National Government was returned but this time under Baldwin's Conservative leadership. The vagaries of the British first-past-the-post electoral system meant that even with a reduced national turnout in the 1935 election Labour secured 1.7 million more votes than was achieved in 1931, and this was sufficient to gain them a further 102 seats bringing their total to 154. In part this level of recovery would be explained by government policy, such as means testing – the most hated of regulations brought in by the government in September 1931 – continuing hardship in traditional working-class areas, especially in the north of the country, and also by Labour's own regathering of its strengths through organizational, resource and policy changes. This trend would continue in the mid- and later 1930s so that Labour could present itself after the war as a fully developed political force.

In 1932 Labour launched its 'A Million Members and Power' national publicity campaign and a year later tried to establish financial schemes to aid constituency organizations in putting forward candidates for election. However, it was in the area of policy that most energy was expended with Hugh Dalton and Herbert Morrison as key members of the Policy Sub-Committee which began to produce a range of documents, texts and statements about party policy. The year 1937 saw *Labour's Immediate Programme* but it also saw the birth of a new paper, the *Tribune*, which became an alternative source of ideas and debate for the left of the party. Many of the 'young Turks' who would be swept into Parliament in 1945 used this organ to make their early mark in the party's policy debates. Slow but steady progress was made towards recovery.

At the annual conference meetings, and especially the 1935 Brighton Conference, differences could be talked through – in this instance the Party's attitude to fascism as exampled by Mussolini's recent invasion of Abyssinia. Consequent upon this was Labour's attitude towards defence and especially the question of rearmament. The talks were fierce and the exchanges hard, and not for the first time did Labour resort to compromise in this area with one faction, led by Bevin and Dalton, favouring rearmament, especially after the start of the Spanish Civil War in 1936, and another faction, led by Sir Stafford Cripps, supporting 'united front' policies and a sanctions approach. The compromise was not resolved until there was a distinct shift to the right in the party which saw Bevin become chairman of the General Council of the TUC and Dalton become chairman of the NEC of the Party. In 1937 the parliamentary Labour Party supported the armed forces estimates and at the Bournemouth Conference in the same year the party adopted rearmament, albeit hedged about with many an 'if' and a 'maybe'. The struggle of the mid-1930s over defence was indicative of a wider political contest going on within the party itself. Most notable was a vociferous, and influential, group of left Labour MPs, especially Sir Stafford Cripps, who diverted much of Labour's attention in a succession of calls for a 'united front'. The latter was really the desire for a British version of the French Popular Front, a coming together of a whole range of leftist political groups, including the Communist Party, that would be necessary to defeat the National Government. Their assumption was that Labour could not do it alone and therefore a major grouping, along the lines described, would be essential for success. Cripps enjoyed some notoriety for his views and was still trying to bring about this end as late as January 1939 when he placed his 'Cripps Memorandum' before the Labour Party's NEC. This time he was willing to extend his invitation to Liberals as well. Although nothing came of this plan it did succeed in leading the Labour Party down some blind alleys in the late 1930s and certainly took much effort away from other, perhaps more demanding, issues. The left's actions in these years were distracting rather than destructive but they ensured that Labour's crusade stayed firmly on the ground.

However, as we have seen with other events in Labour history, gains were made even in this era. The level of debate in the party was intense and the 1930s allowed Labour some time to prepare for coming trials. A new generation of Labour supporters had appeared, ones used to the idea of Labour in power, and after the experience of the war it was these activists, well grounded in the party's ideas and image, who would become the 'Class of '45' and take their seats in a Parliament that had a majority Labour government for the very first time. The rise of Labour was almost complete.

CONTROVERSY: THE 1931 CRISIS

MacDonald's role in the 1931 crisis has created an ongoing historical debate as to his intentions at this time. The key questions are: how genuine was MacDonald's response in 1931? Did he simply see the National Government as the only path in a blinding flash as he resigned, or did his hopes lie in this direction well before the fateful 24 August?

Was MacDonald the scheming opportunist or simply converted on the road to Buckingham Palace?

MacDonald's career suggests something of an upwardly mobile young man with an eye for the main chance. The inauspicious beginnings in Lossiemouth were left behind as a bright and able mind saw him claw himself into the ranks of the lower middle class as a teacher, union official and journalist. His very useful marriage to Margaret in 1896 gave him no further financial worries and meant that he could give his full energies to a political career. He eagerly sought advancement and soon ditched his Liberal sympathies seizing on the opportunity presented by the Lib–Lab pact of 1903. His opportunism was renounced in 1914 when he withdrew from the party's leadership over the war. He regained it in 1922 and despite previous protestations about Labour never taking power as a minority government, he seized his chance in 1924. His career shows that, as K. O. Morgan in his *Labour People* (1987) suggests, MacDonald was too adept at becoming one of 'them' rather than staying one of 'us'. Certainly, MacNeil Weir, in his biography of 1938, sees MacDonald the schemer at work in 1931:

> The members of the Labour Cabinet naturally assumed on that Sunday night 23 August (1931) that Mr Baldwin would be asked to form a government. But it is significant that MacDonald had something quite different in view. Without a word of consultation with his Cabinet colleagues, without even informing them of his intentions to set up a National government with himself as Prime Minister, he proceeded to carry out his long-thought-out plan.
>
> The impression left on the minds of those who heard that speech [about the formation of the National government] . . . was that the whole thing had been arranged long before and that, while in Cabinet and Committee they had been making panic-stricken efforts to balance the Budget, the whole business had been humbug and make-believe.
>
> (L. MacNeil Weir, *The Tragedy of Ramsay MacDonald*, London, Secker & Warburg, 1938, pp. 383–4)

Yet others have cast the shadow of blame more widely and tended to portray MacDonald as making a major blunder and miscalculation, as Snowden did:

> When the Labour Cabinet as a whole declined to agree to a reduction of unemployment pay, Mr MacDonald assumed too hurriedly that this involved the resignation of his government. He neither showed nor expressed any grief at this regrettable development. On the contrary, he set about the formation of the National government with an enthusiasm which showed that the adventure was highly agreeable to him.
>
> (Quoted in Laybourn, op. cit., p. 68)

Rose is among those who suggest that others must carry the blame. His candidate would be George V:

> But the King decided to go one better. He induced MacDonald to lead the new ministry and so proclaim to the world that Britain spoke with a united and resolute voice in her determination to remain solvent.
>
> （K. Rose, *King George V*, London, Macmillan, 1983, p. 379）

More recently, David Marquand has portrayed MacDonald as a seizer of opportunities no matter how late they came his way. In fact Marquand is convinced that the fateful decision was taken as late as the night of the 23rd or even the morning of the 24th itself.

> My general impression is that J.R.M. feels himself to be *the* indispensable leader of a new political party which is bound to come into office within his life-time – a correct forecast, I think. He is no longer *intent* on social reform – any indignation he ever had at the present distribution of wealth he has lost; his real and intimate life is associating with non-political aristocratic society, surrounded with the beauty and dignity which wealth can buy and social experience can direct. Ramsay MacDonald is not distinguished either in intellect or character, and he has some very mean traits in his nature. But he has great gifts as a political leader, he has personal charm, he has vitality, he is assiduous, self-controlled and skilful.
>
> （From M. Cole (ed.), *Beatrice Webb Diaries*, London, Longman, 1952, p. 111）

This view was supported by some interpretations of MacDonald's actions before Marquand's book came on the scene with its great advantage of access to MacDonald's personal papers.

> On Sunday night, August 23, the drama came to its climax. The Cabinet prepared for all other economies, split on a ten per cent cut in unemployment benefit. It was long believed that there was a majority against the cut, but it has been established that there was a majority of either one or two for it. MacDonald decided that the minority was too great to permit him to carry on. He left his Cabinet colleagues to go to Buckingham Palace with the intention, as they understood it, of resigning. One of his colleagues described him as being jaunty. The King's Secretary, Sir Clive Wigram, speaks of him arriving at Buckingham Palace 'scared and unbalanced'. . . . MacDonald returned from the Palace to tell his colleagues that he had undertaken, supported by Baldwin and Samuel, to lead a National Government.
>
> （H. Boardman, *The Glory of Parliament*, London, Allen & Unwin 1960）

Whatever the timing, and even with access to MacDonald's papers it seems we shall never know definitely, the reaction to MacDonald's actions was predictable. Dalton gives one view, more charitable than some, of a man panicked into making a decision:

MacDonald sits alone on the other side of the long table . . . he has to tell us that the Government is at an end. He is very sorry. We shall curse him, and he is afraid that he has caused us great embarrassment. But the gravity of the crisis is not yet widely understood. . . .

He thinks the crisis could have been avoided if the Cabinet hadn't changed its mind at a critical point. A plan had been drawn up and agreed, which would have sufficed to secure the loan required. But then the Cabinet went back on it . . . this made necessary a Government of Persons, not Parties. He is going through with this . . . all members of the government will resign together, and then the new administration will be formed. . . .

And then we disperse. Going out, Willy Lunn and I speak vigorously against J.R.M. And I apparently am clearly audible. . . . There are a lot of pressmen outside. . . . To one pressman I say 'Just for a handful of panic he left us.'

(H. Dalton, *Call Back Yesterday: Memoirs 1886–1931*, 1953)

Others were less charitable and preferred to see the schemer at work with added attacks of an overinflated ego and lack of political principles and loyalty:

Here lies Ramsay Mac
A friend of all humanity,
Too many pats upon the back
Inflated Ramsay's vanity.
The Blarney stone he oft-times kissed,
But departed in his glory:
Having been born a socialist
He died a bloody Tory.
(R. C. Challinor, 'Letter from MacDonald to Clarke', *Bulletin of the Society for the Study of Labour History*, 27 (1973), pp. 34–5)

Selfless national leader or betrayer of his party – MacDonald's political career really ended in 1935 with Baldwin's assumption of the leadership of the second National Coalition Government. MacDonald could not win Seaham to secure a seat and was forced to end his political days a sad figure as member for the Scottish Universities.

BIBLIOGRAPHY

For an explanation of the grading system, see the preface p. xiii.

Biographies

Aneurin Bevan

3   Foot, M., *Aneurin Bevan 1887–1945*, vol. 1, London, MacGibbon & Kee, 1962
3   Campbell, J., *Nye Bevan and the Mirage of British Socialism*, London, Weidenfeld & Nicolson, 1987

Ernest Bevin

3   Bullock, A., *The Life and Times of Ernest Bevin*, vols 1 and 2, London, Heinemann, 1960 and 1967

Hugh Dalton

3   Pimlott, B., *Hugh Dalton*, London, J. Cape, 1985

Arthur Henderson

3   Wrigley, C., *Arthur Henderson*, GPC Books, 1990

James Ramsay MacDonald

3   Lord Elton, *The Life and Times of James Ramsay MacDonald 1866–1919*, London, Collins, 1939
3   MacNeil Weir, L., *The Tragedy of Ramsay MacDonald*, London, Secker & Warburg, 1938
4   Marquand, D., *Ramsay MacDonald*, London, J. Cape, 1977

Keir Hardie

3   Donaghue, B. and Jones, G. W., *Herbert Morrison*, London, Weidenfeld & Nicolson, 1973
3   Morgan, K. O., *Keir Hardie: Radical and Socialist*, London, Weidenfeld & Nicolson, 1975
3   Stewart, W., *J. Keir Hardie*, London, np, 1925

Philip Snowden

2/3   Laybourn, K., *Philip Snowden*, Aldershot, Gower Publications, 1988

Autobiographies

2/3 Mann, T., *Memoirs*, London, MacGibbon & Kee, 1967
3   Lord Morrison, *An Autobiography*, Odhams, np, 1960
2/3 Tillett, B., *Memories and Reflections*, John Long, np, 1931

General works

1   Adelman, P., *The Rise of the Labour Party 1880–1945*, London, Longman, 1972
2   Bagwell, P. S., *The Railwaymen*, London, Allen & Unwin, 1963
2   Belchem, J., *Class, Party and the Political System in Britain 1867–1914*, Oxford, Blackwell, 1990
3   Briggs, A. and Saville, J. (eds), *Essays in Labour History 1886–1923*, London, Macmillan, 1971
3   Brown, K. D. (ed.), *The First Labour Party 1906–1914*, Beckenham, Croom Helm, 1985
1   Browne, H., *The Rise of British Trade Unions 1825–1914*, London, Longman, 1979
3   Burgess, K., *The Challenge of Labour*, London, Croom Helm, 1980
3   Cole, G. D. H., *British Working-class Politics 1832–1914*, London, Routledge, 1941
3   Cole, G. D. H., *A History of the Labour Party Since 1914*, London, Allen & Unwin, 1948
3   Cole, G. D. H., *A Short History of the British Working-class Movement 1789–1947*, London, Allen & Unwin, 1948
1   Constantine, S., *Unemployment in Britain Between the Wars*, London, Longman, 1980
4   Cowling, M., *The Impact of Labour 1920–1924*, Cambridge, Cambridge University Press, 1971
3   Foote, G., *Labour Party Political Thought: A History*, London, Croom Helm, 1986
2   Gregory, R., *The Miners in British Politics*, Oxford, Oxford University Press, 1968
1   Hobley, L. F., *The Trade Union Story*, Glasgow, Blackie, 1969
3   Laybourn, K., *The Rise of Labour: The British Labour Party 1890–1979*, London, Arnold, 1988
2   Lovell, J., *Stevedores and Dockers*, London, Macmillan, 1969
3   McKibbin, R., *The Evolution of the Labour Party 1910–1924*, Oxford, Oxford University Press, 1974
3   Middlemas, K., *Politics in Industrial Society: The Experience of the British System Since 1911*, London, Deutsch, 1979
3   Miliband, R., *Parliamentary Socialism: A Study on the Politics of Labour*, London, Allen & Unwin, 1961
2   Morris, M., *The British General Strike*, London, Historical Association, 1973
2   Musson, A. E., *British Trade Unions 1800–1875*, London, Methuen, 1972
2/3 Pelling, H., *The British Communist Party: A Historical Profile*, Black, np, 1958
2/3 Pelling, H., *The Origins of the Labour Party 1880–1900*, Oxford, Oxford University Press, 1965
1/2 Pelling H., *A Short History of the Labour Party*, London, Macmillan, 1968

2   Pelling, H., *A History of British Trade Unionism*, Harmondsworth, Penguin, 1963

3   Pimlott, B., *Labour and the Left in the 1930s*, London, Cambridge University Press, 1977

3   Price, R., *Labour and British Society*, London, Croom Helm, 1986

2/3 Renshaw, P., *The General Strike*, London, Eyre Methuen, 1975

2/3 Skelley, J., *1926: The General Strike*, London, Lawrence & Wishart, 1976

3   Skildelsky, R., *Politics and the Slump. The Labour Government of 1929–1931*, London, Macmillan, 1967

2/3 Symons, J., *The General Strike: A Historical Portrait*, London, Cresset Library, 1987

3   Tanner, D., *Political Change and the Labour Party 1900–1919*, Cambridge, Cambridge University Press, 1990

3   Thompson, E. P., *The Making of the English Working-class*, Harmondsworth, Penguin, 1968

3   Thompson, P., *Socialists, Liberals and Labour: The Struggle for London 1885–1914*, London, Routledge, 1967

3   Webb, S. and B., *The History of British Trade Unionism*, London, Longman, 1920

3   Wrigley, C. (ed.), *A History of British Industrial Relations 1875–1914*, Brighton, Harvester, 1982

Sources for coursework

Few areas of history have gained more than the studies of local political movements and especially the role of trade unions and the Labour party in the various regional localities where they were particularly strong. M. Savage, *The Dynamics of Working-class Politics, the Labour Movement in Preston 1880–1940* (1988) is such a study. But its like can be found in many locations such as G. Firth, K. Laybourn and J. O'Connell (eds), *Yorkshire Labour Movements 1780–1926: A Guide to Historical Sources*, which was produced by the University of Leeds (nd). Equally so one will find much more material in the reference sections and local history sections of libraries and museums such as those in Wakefield, Halifax, Leeds, Durham, Manchester and Liverpool.

Along with the local historical sources there are, as usual, a number of important papers, letters and diaries in published form. *The Fabian Essays* (1889) Jubilee edition (London, Allen & Unwin, 1948), M. Cole (ed.), *Beatrice Webb Diaries 1912–1924* and *1924–1932* (London, Longman, 1952 and 1956), H. Dalton, *The Political Diary of Hugh Dalton 1918–1940* and *1945–1960* ed. B. Pimlott (London, Cape, 1987), H. Dalton, *The Second World War Diary of Hugh Dalton 1940–1945* (London, Cape, 1986), R. Barker (ed.), *Ramsay MacDonald: Political Writings* (London, Allen Lane, 1972).

Finally, there are outstanding collections of materials to be found at the Museum of Labour History in London along with its counterpart in Liverpool which has less on offer at present but will be expanding over the coming years.

8 British foreign policy 1905–45: the German Question

INTRODUCTION

The Eastern Question had deeply concerned the Foreign Office through-out the greater part of the nineteenth century. Essentially this related to the decline and disappearance of the Turkish Empire in Eastern Europe and the Middle East. For much of the first half of the twentieth century the problem was one in reverse, the appearance and growth of German power in Central Europe. This German Question had a far more devas-tating impact on Britain and her people. For ten of the forty years considered here she was engaged in a life-or-death struggle with this new force, and for a further fifteen years of the forty preparing for these struggles. Only briefly, in the 1920s, did the German menace seem to be absent and Britain could return to her old concerns of the Russian threat to India and Persia (Iran). Even in the 1920s, however, the most insoluble problem seemed to be how Europe should relate to the tempor-arily beaten Germany. The rows of neat white headstones in northern France provide a mournful testimony to the impact of this 'question' on ordinary Britons. Seven hundred and fifty thousand died between 1914 and 1918 (to which must be added at least 200,000 deaths from imperial forces), with perhaps a further two million being wounded. Two hundred and sixty-five thousand were killed in the Second World War in the armed forces, with a further 60,000 civilian deaths. The damage to British cities was on a scale unimaginable in the mid-nineteenth century, and the cost of the two wars was such as would have shocked Gladstone to the depth of his prudent being.

Germany in 1867 was a geographical expression. The word contained no terror for Britons, nor was it to do so for the next thirty years. The new German Empire had come into being in 1871 by dint of Prussia defeating France in a short aggressive war. This Second Reich posed no threat. The heir to the throne of the new Germany was married to Queen Victoria's daughter and was, in contrast to Herr Bismarck the Chancellor, an admirer of Mr Gladstone as the embodiment of Liberal virtues. Germany might possess the finest army in Europe but this

First World War headstone. Photograph: M. L. Pearce

seemed to contribute to the European balance of power rather than upset it. She would check France and Russia, hitherto perceived as the greatest threats to British interests. Bismarck, the real ruler of Germany until 1890, was certainly respected in Britain despite his dislike of Gladstone and his Liberal nostrums. His diplomatic manoeuvres might not always be approved of, but he was clearly a great European statesman.

A combination of circumstances in the 1890s began to worsen relations. At root lay the growth of the German economy which year by year raised Germany far above her continental neighbours and threatened to create that continental domination which Britain had always feared, whether it be from sixteenth-century Spain or Napoleonic France. Germans certainly recognized the coming struggle, as the great spokesman for German imperialism, Karl Peters, wrote in a national newspaper *Der Tag* in 1911:

> The City of London is the great devouring beast, through which foreign peoples are plundered; and Downing Street is in the service of Throgmorton Street. The rivalry of a healthy, hard-working nationality like the German does not suit such forces. Germany is for the normal John Bull what Spain was in the sixteenth century, France in the nineteenth, and Russia in the twentieth.
>
> (Quoted in P. Kennedy, *The Rise of Anglo-German Antagonism*, London, Allen & Unwin, 1980, p. 313)

In Britain the growth of German power was treated with some trepidation. Lord Esher, confidante of King Edward and a defence expert, recorded in 1907:

> there is no doubt that within measurable distance there looms a titanic struggle between Germany and Europe for mastery. The years 1793–1815 will be repeated, only Germany, not France, will be trying for European domination. She has 70,000,000 of people and is determined to have commercial pre-eminence. To do this *England* has got to be crippled and the Low Countries added to the German Empire.
>
> (ibid., p. 310)

But it was not just the rivalry of a new power with an old power. The USA had surpassed Britain in economic muscle in the 1880s without eliciting the same antagonism. Clearly in part it was the physical proximity of the new force to Britain, but it was also the style and behaviour of this force. There was a lack of restraint, a boisterous bullying and a rejoicing in power which frightened Germany's neighbours. The Kaiser, Wilhelm II, Queen Victoria's grandson, came to symbolize the new Germany with his restless energy, his unpredictability and his boastful bombast allied to a personal arrogance.

Germany's pursuit of empire in the 1890s was accepted by Britain and France, as was the decision to undertake the construction of a large fleet, reported in *The Times* in 1899: 'It would be ridiculous as well as futile to object though Great Britain can hardly be expected to welcome a policy which may make a considerable addition to our Naval estimates a reality.' In spite of these signs, Britain's conflicts with France and Russia in the last decade of the nineteenth century still inclined her friendship with the German Reich and her Triple Alliance partners, Austria-Hungary and Italy. Certain members of the British Cabinet, notably Chamberlain, urged open alliance with Germany which at various times between 1899 and 1901 was actively considered. Yet German behaviour irritated. From the Kaiser down, it was assumed in Berlin that Germany had a 'free hand'. British conflicts with France and Russia ensured that Britain needed Germany more than Germany needed

Britain. Rosebery's panic request for assistance in 1893, and Chamberlain's bid for alliance in 1898 seemed to confirm German assumptions (see chapter 5 p. 172). German behaviour bred anti-German prejudice amongst the diplomats of the Foreign Office. As one was later to put it: 'We were never so badly treated by Germany as in the years when we were always making concessions in order to gain their real friendship.' The consequence, as we have seen, was the Anglo-French Entente, an attempt to remove the German capacity to blackmail Britain. It was not at this stage an anti-German alliance. Over the next ten years it became one, as Germany changed from nuisance and potential enemy to *the* enemy.

Some historians, particularly Marxist ones, have seen this transformation as the inevitable product of economic and attendant colonial rivalry. Germany was Britain's closest competitor in world trade, as the figures in Table 8.1 showing the percentages of world trade indicate, and in particular markets, like South America and parts of the Middle East. German commercial interests were expanding, sometimes at the expense of British ones. There was also some resentment of the German penetration of the home market. Midlands iron, steel and engineering interests were particularly affected. However, hostility to this development was certainly not constant or dominating. The 'Made in Germany' phobia was at its greatest at such times as the 1902 trade recession when large numbers of goods were dumped in Britain at cheap prices. It declined thereafter with the great revival and expansion in the economy that occurred after 1903.

Table 8.1 Share of world trade (%)

	1880	1900	1913
Britain	23	20	17
Germany	10	13	13
France	11	9	8
USA	10	11	11
Others	46	47	51

Source: After Kennedy, op. cit., p. 92.

It is the interdependence of the British and German economies that is striking, not their rivalries. Britain was Germany's best customer and 20 per cent of all Germany's imports came from the British Empire. If Germany had a visible trade surplus with Britain, she had a deficit with India and Australia with whom Britain had a surplus. Britain's invisible earnings more than wiped out her overall trade deficit, and Germany contributed considerably to those invisibles. Most of her growing merchant marine was insured by Lloyd's of London. It seemed to most Britons by 1914 that their country was coping comfortably – indeed benefiting – with any German economic challenge. If the German merchant marine had increased from 1.9 million tons to 3.1 million tons, then Britain's had increased from 9.6 to 12.1. If German goods were reaching China, Britain was still exporting four times as much to that vast market in 1912. The world was big enough for the two of them.

The same was equally true of colonial interests. France had always been Britain's biggest colonial rival not Germany. Furthermore, almost all colonial disputes had been settled amicably by 1914. Britain did not wish to deny Germany a 'third world' empire, and even her penetration of the sensitive area of the Middle East through such schemes as the Berlin–Baghdad Railway could be dealt with peacefully. A sensible deal was struck in June 1914 in this case. When conflict did arise between the two countries over Morocco in 1905–6 and again in 1911 it was not essentially about Morocco but about France (see p. 285). Germany and Britain did not go to war over colonies nor directly over trade.

More than anything else it was the decision of the German government to build a first-class battle fleet that antagonized the United Kingdom. As early as 1897 Tirpitz, the new head of the German Admiralty, had written:

> For Germany the most dangerous enemy at the present time is England. It is also the enemy against which we most urgently require a certain measure of naval force as a political power factor . . . our fleet must be so constructed that it can unfold its greatest military potential between Heligoland and the Thames. . . . The military situation against England demands battleships in as great a number as possible.
> (Quoted in Kennedy, op. cit., p. 292)

The recognition of this threat by the British Admiralty had come in a memorandum of 1902 (quoted on pp. 175–6). Japan's destruction of the Russian fleet in 1905 heightened Germany's naval position. Tirpitz and the Kaiser were aiming, under the 1900 Navy Law, for a fleet of thirty-eight battleships. In 1899 Tirpitz had even talked of a fleet of forty-five battleships. These were clearly and solely directed against Great Britain. First Sea Lord Admiral Fisher put it succinctly to King Edward in 1906:

> Our only probable enemy is Germany. Germany keeps her whole fleet always concentrated within a few hours of England. We must therefore keep a fleet twice as powerful as that of Germany always concentrated within a few hours of Germany.
> (Quoted in P. Kennedy, *Strategy and Diplomacy*, London, Fontana, 1984, p. 142)

The Second Reich now posed the most serious threat to Britain since Napoleon had attempted his invasion in 1805. Should Germany gain command of the seas, her superior army would place Britain at her mercy. Britain responded to the challenge with a rapid expansion of her navy and a concentration in home waters. Under Admiral Fisher's direction she initiated a qualitative leap in ship construction in 1905 with the laying down of HMS *Dreadnought*. Using the high-pressure steam turbine to improve speed and concentrating her fire power into eight 12-inch guns she made all existing battleships almost obsolete. She was launched in 1906.

If HMS *Dreadnought* gave Britain a qualitative superiority it also weakened her quantitative lead built up over the years. Germany rapidly seized her chance and also built dreadnoughts as quickly as possible. What followed was a naval arms race which attracted public attention. The dreadnought battleship became the symbol of national vitality and a focus of patriotic pride. The leisurely building under the first two years of the Liberal Government gave the Germans the chance to catch up. Tirpitz accelerated the German building programme in 1908 with a target of some fifty-eight German dreadnoughts planned by the 1920s. The resulting naval scare in Britain early in 1909 created a cabinet crisis as to whether or not to build eight further ships. Radicals objected to 'bloated armaments', and the Unionist press trumpeted the German menace. Inside the Cabinet Sir Edward Grey and the Admiralty pressed for eight. Asquith's compromise of four now and four later, if needed, kept the government together and satisfied public opinion. Germany refused every attempt to end the race. The Kaiser told one British official he would not discuss any limitations with a foreign government. The effects of German naval expansion were quite clear to the German Foreign Office as one 1908 dispatch from Count Metternich, the German ambassador in London, to his Chancellor, Bulow, indicates: 'It is not Germany's economic development that is year by year injuring relations with England but the rapid growth of the German fleet.' The build-up was drawing Britain more and more into the French camp and all the original assumptions of Tirpitz's policy, predicated as it was on a 'free hand', were now seen to be untrue. Yet the Kaiser and Tirpitz would not halt the development. A further acceleration occurred on Germany's part in 1912, despite the obvious British counter-response.

The last serious attempt to secure naval agreement took place in 1912 when the British War Minister, R. B. Haldane, visited Berlin. The talks never got underway and in spite of mention of a 'naval holiday' in 1913 by Churchill, and the German army's needs forcing Tirpitz to cut back his naval programme, no formal agreement was ever reached. By 1914 Britain had a clear and growing lead in the naval race. Her new super dreadnoughts, like the *Queen Elizabeth*, were about to appear; oil-fired, faster and with their 15-inch guns, superior to anything in the German navy. Tirpitz, the underdog at this point, was anxious to avoid war in July 1914. Thus although naval rivalry did not precipitate conflict it was vital in preparing both nations psychologically for war. A spate of popular political thrillers centring on the German menace arose from the situation. Erskine Childers's *The Riddle of the Sands* (1903) and William LeQueux's *The Invasion of 1910* (1906) are perhaps the most famous. It is often fashionable today to dismiss the whole naval scare as a creation of the newspapers. Although the Northcliffe press, the *Daily Mail* and *Daily Mirror*, certainly played a part in heightening tension, the tension itself was not a press plot but the result of a very real and serious menace to the British homeland to which any government would have had to respond. The German government's decision to build up a large battle fleet stationed in the North Sea inevitably made Britain an enemy.

If the British response to the naval challenge cannot really be faulted, the general attitude of the Foreign Office to Germany has been subjected to much criticism. Many of the diplomats who were to staff the embassies and the London Office in the years before the First World War had developed massive prejudices against Germany and distrusted her every action. Much of this went back to the 1890s when Germany had felt itself in a position to blackmail Britain. Eyre Crowe, senior clerk in the Foreign Office 1905–12 and then Assistant Under-Secretary, was a potent anti-German influence. He was a genuine expert on the Second Reich, having a German mother and a German wife and having been brought up in Germany himself. In a forceful and influential memorandum produced in January 1907 he argued that Germany was either consciously aiming at the establishment of a German hegemony at first in Europe and eventually in the world, or that 'the great German design is in reality no more than the expression of a vague, confused and unpractical statesmanship not realising its own drift'. Crowe's views were shared by others. Grey's private secretary, Sir William Tyrell was to write in 1911:

> It is depressing to find that after six years experience of Germany the inclination here is to believe she can be placated by small concessions . . . what she wants is the hegemony of Europe.
> (Quoted in Z. Steiner, *Britain and the Origins of the First World War*, London, Macmillan, 1977, p. 42)

The two permanent chiefs of the Foreign Office, Charles Hardinge (1905–10) and Arthur Nicholson (1910–16) shared these sentiments. As Nicholson, with a fervour almost unequalled, put it: 'As long as he was Head of the Foreign Office Britain never, never should be friends with Germany.'

All these diplomats were almost obsessed with what they saw as the German bid for European domination and the fear that unless France and, later, Russia were supported firmly by Britain, both countries would pass under German influence. This would leave an isolated and vulnerable Britain. At times their sensitivity bordered on the ludicrous as when the Foreign Office prohibited in 1907 a friendly visit to Germany by the band of the Coldstream Guards for fear that the French might lose faith in their Entente partners. Under the influence of these professionals, and the crises between 1905 and 1911, the Entente with France came to resemble an alliance more than an understanding. The War Office increasingly lent its support to this process. In April 1905 the British General Staff played a war game involving a German invasion of Belgium and France. It reached the conclusion that a small British force could significantly aid French survival, and in 1906 the first secret staff talks began between the British and the French.

In 1907 Grey and the Foreign Office pulled off what they saw as their greatest achievement, a reconciliation with Russia. Many of the older sources of conflict had been either settled or resolved. Japan's triumph in 1905 removed the Russian threat to China and British support for Turkey had already been abandoned in the 1890s. A new era of conflict over Persia posed the thorniest problems, but on 31 August 1907 an Anglo-Russian Convention was signed settling disputes over Afghanistan, Tibet and Persia. Persia was divided into three spheres; one of Russian influence in the north, one of British influence in the south and around the Gulf, and a neutral zone in the middle. The British Foreign Office was delighted, as was the War Office, which had for long wrestled with the insoluble problem of how to reinforce India with enough troops to defend her from a Russian onslaught. Instead of the defence of India, British military planners now turned with enthusiasm to the preparation of a British Expeditionary Force (BEF) to serve in northern France against Germany. From the army's point of view the most dramatic reversal of roles had occurred. From 1908 onwards the attention of both the army and the navy was now firmly fixed on Germany.

Partly under pressure of the perceived general threat, and partly as a result of the inadequacies revealed during the Boer War, a series of major reforms was carried through by Haldane as Secretary for War 1905–12. He belatedly gave Britain's armed forces a General Staff as a planning authority, and new official manuals went out to the whole of the regular army. In 1907 came his Territorial and Reserve Forces Bill which went some way towards solving a long-standing problem of insufficient reserves. The Territorials came into existence in 1908 and by 1910 there were 276,618 of them. In 1909 officer training corps were established at many public and secondary schools to provide a supply of young officers. By the end of that year Haldane's achievements were remarkable. An expeditionary force of six infantry divisions and one cavalry division could be ready for dispatch to France within fifteen days of any hostilities beginning. Britain had gained a small but efficient military capability which was to prove its worth following the crisis of 1914.

A series of crises before the outbreak of war heightened the diplomatic tension and prepared Englishmen and women for the idea of war with Germany. They were also vitally instrumental in transforming the

Entente of 1904 into an alliance. The first of these crises began in March 1905 over Morocco. It was precipitated by Germany who decided to challenge the new Entente and expose the hollowness of British friend-ship to the French. France was vulnerable to diplomatic pressure in view of the weakness of her ally, Russia, and hamstrung successively by war and revolution. The French army was weakened in morale by the Dreyfus affair and a new premier, Rouvier, was inclined to deal with Germany. The crisis began with the dramatic visit of the Kaiser to Tangier on 31 March 1905. The idea was not his own but had been 'cooked up' by the German Foreign Office. In fact the poor man had a miserable day with a rough ride on a small boat and a well-nigh uncontrollable horse on dry land. Nevertheless, he did his duty in a speech casting down the gauntlet to France by proclaiming Morocco's independence and asserting German power. Germany demanded an international conference to settle the future of this North African state, hoping to rub France's nose in the dirt in the process, and at the same time expose the uselessness of British friendship to her Entente partner. The French Foreign Minister Delcassé wanted to refuse to attend the proposed conference and call Germany's bluff. His cabinet colleagues were not made of such stuff and gave in, forcing Delcassé to resign on 6 June. A conference eventually met at Algeçiras in Spain in January 1906. The new Liberal Foreign Secretary Grey found this his most pressing problem. He followed both his inclination and the advice of his civil servants and decided to give France full diplomatic support to prevent her capitulation to Germany. As Charles Hardinge, the Permanent Under-Secretary, pointed out, 'If France is left in the lurch, an agreement, or alliance, between France, Germany and Russia in the near future is certain.' Fortunately, the chief British delegate, Arthur Nicholson, successfully orchestrated an effective anti-German front at Algeçiras, lining up all the powers, bar Austria, against Germany. France gained control of the Moroccan police and banks, and Germany was humiliated. The outcome bred resentment of Britain in Berlin and a surprising faith in her on the part of France. The Entente had survived and even been strengthened. Furthermore it impressed the Russians who were more ready now, under French pres-sure, to do a deal with Britain (see p. 284).

The Anglo-Russian Entente was a development of some concern to the Germans, and the visit of Edward VII to Revel in June 1908 was greeted in many German papers as evidence of the encirclement of Germany. The Bosnian crisis of 1908–9 only indirectly involved Britain but during it Germany sought to fracture the Entente and force Russia into subservience. She secured a great triumph in diplomatic terms, causing Russia to back down and submit to the Austrian annexation of Bosnia, without compensation for Russia or her Balkan client Serbia. Britain could not offer Russia the help and support she had offered France in 1905–6. The Balkans were not an area of British interest and

8.1 The Balkans 1913

Grey was well aware that many of his cabinet colleagues and his Liberal backbenchers disliked the new friendship with tsarist, reactionary Russia. Nicholson and the diplomats need not have feared that the humiliation of Russia would drive her into dependency on Germany. It produced exactly the opposite result, a fierce determination to avoid humiliation again and the beginning of a vast rearmament programme which was to terrify Germany by 1914.

Despite the promptings of diplomats like Nicholson, Britain only hesitatingly moved closer to Russia and France and towards confrontation with Germany. Tensions over Persia remained with Russia and on several occasions it seemed that Russia had broken the Convention of 1907. Grey, unlike many of his colleagues, did not wish to commit Britain to a full alliance with France. Even had he so wished, Liberal MPs would have prevented it. Only the insensitive behaviour of Germany drove Britain closer to Russia and France. Had the German government used greater subtlety, the encirclement they so feared could have been easily avoided. Unfortunately, subtlety was not the obvious feature of German diplomacy and politicians in France, like Rouvier and Caillaux, who favoured *rapprochement*, had their task made more difficult as did pro-Germans in Britain like Haldane. The German naval challenge was at its greatest between 1909 and 1912 and, as indicated above, every British olive branch was rejected.

The second Moroccan crisis of 1911 brought Britain and Germany to a head-on confrontation, with France more or less trailing behind Britain in anti-German militancy. The crisis began when internal unrest in Morocco led the French to take military action and thus technically breach the agreement of 1906. The Germans decided to create a crisis out of which they hoped to make colonial gains. In the words of the German Foreign Secretary: 'It is necessary to thump the table. However, the only objective of this is to make the French negotiate.' Germany wanted the French Congo in return for accepting a French Morocco. To emphasize the point she dispatched, on 1 July, the gunboat *Panther* to the Moroccan port of Agadir, 'to protect German interests'. Since there were no German interests there it appeared to the British as a simple attempt to intimidate France. The Foreign Office was particularly worried because on the very same day Joseph Caillaux had become French premier and he favoured negotiation. Germany's thumping of the table made Caillaux's policy of concession all the harder to sell in France and was thus counter-productive, but it was the British reaction that caused the greatest shock in Berlin. On 21 July Lloyd George, making a speech at the Mansion House, inserted the words that Britain was not to be treated, 'as if she were of no account in the cabinet of nations . . . peace at that price would be a humiliation intolerable for a great country like ours to endure'. It was meant as a warning to both France and Germany but it was interpreted in Germany as another humiliating threat. Throughout August and September war seemed possible, Lloyd George and Churchill became militant anti-Germans and Grey had a difficult time walking a knife-edge between provoking Germany and seeming to let down France. Eventually the crisis ended with an agreement signed in November 1911, giving France a protectorate over Morocco and Germany a small portion of the French Congo.

The Moroccan crisis had profound results. It brought to power a much more anti-German government in France with Poincaré and strengthened the Entente with Britain, leading to the Anglo-French Naval Agreement of 1912. In both London and Berlin the men in charge were frightened by the public passions unleashed and both Grey and Bethmann-Hollweg, the German Chancellor, sought improved relations. In a sense they struggled against forces beyond their control. In Germany there was an upsurge of anti-British feeling and a demand for no more humiliations. With the help of this mood, Tirpitz got his enlarged navy in 1912. If radical Liberal backbenchers supported Grey's search for *détente* with

Germany, Churchill and Lloyd George had moved the balance in the Cabinet to a stronger anti-German line and the press supported this.

The crisis also set off a train of events which crookedly ran like a fizzing gunpowder trail to August 1914. On 29 September 1911 Italy declared war on Turkey in a bid to claim Tripoli in compensation for the French control over Morocco. Turkey, weakened by this war, found itself faced in 1912 by a Balkan League organized by Hartwig, the Russian ambassador in Belgrade. Russia was to have her revenge for the Bosnian crisis. In the course of October 1912 the Turkish Empire in Europe was finally destroyed and Serbia, Greece and Bulgaria were victorious. It was a disaster not only for Turkey but for Austria who was now faced by a much stronger Serbia to the south already bitterly resentful of the Austrian annexation of Bosnia in 1908. Peace amongst the great powers was kept. Grey worked happily with Germany to restrain both Austria and Russia and the resulting Treaty of London in May 1913 seemed a triumph for the 'Concert of Europe'. Austria gained a concession that Serbia should not have an Adriatic port and an independent Albania was thus set up. Russia accepted this on her client's behalf, happy that her interests had been advanced in the Balkans by the destruction of Turkey. A brief second Balkan war followed in June 1913 when Serbia and Bulgaria fell out. It resulted in an even larger Serbia, much to Austria's alarm, but again Germany restrained her. There had been co-operation over the Balkans and some of the heat of the naval rivalry was disappearing as the German army budget took precedence over Tirpitz's navy. Agreements over Portuguese colonies in South Africa in June 1913 and the Berlin–Baghdad Railway in June 1914 seemed to confirm this trend.

It was not the prospect of European war that occupied the British government in 1914 but the crisis over Ireland. Europe seemed calmer than it had been for a long time. Even the fierce Germanophobe, Nicholson, was writing in May 1914 'Since I have been at the Foreign Office I have not seen such calm waters.' The next month four British battleships visited Kiel on a goodwill mission, but in that same June events in a faraway Sarajevo completed the gunpowder trail set fizzing in 1911. Bosnian nationalists assassinated the heir to the Austrian throne, Arch-Duke Franz Ferdinand, on the 28th. They had been partly armed and encouraged by the Serbian Secret Service. Austria, with German support, decided to seek a showdown with Serbia even, it seems, at the risk of precipitating a general European war. Both powers hoped that the conflict could be localized but, if not, then at least Britain might stay out. On 23 July Austria sent a tough and unacceptable ultimatum to Serbia and five days later declared war on her. Grey was later criticized for not taking a more positive line either to deter Germany by clear threats or to restrain France and Russia. In reality he could do little other than pursue the cautious line he did. He wished to restrain France and Russia

and could not make a forthright statement to Germany of his sup_
for France in the event of an attack because in a meeting on 24 July the
Cabinet would not agree to such a declaration. All his proposals for a
conference to settle the dispute and localize it were rejected by both
Germany and Austria.

On 31 July Russia ordered general mobilization to threaten Austria.
Germany responded on 1 August with a declaration of war on Russia.
Germany only had one war plan, the so-called Schlieffen Plan, for dealing
with the Franco-Russian alliance of 1894, which she now applied and
declared war on France on 3 August, with troops entering Belgium to
get to her on 4 August. To the last Britain's position was unclear. In a
letter of 31 July Grey wrote: 'All I could say was that our attitude would
be determined largely by public opinion here and that the neutrality of
Belgium would appeal strongly to public opinion.' Grey wished to support France even apart from the violation of Belgian territory, but he
recognized that his cabinet colleagues were less sure. On 2 August the
Cabinet agreed to protect France's northern coasts in accordance with
the Naval Agreement of 1912. On 3 August an appeal was received from
Belgium for assistance. Crowds in the streets cheered for intervention
and when Grey made a balanced unemotional statement to the Commons
of the need to support France it was clear that House and nation were for
war. An ultimatum was dispatched to Germany on 4 August requesting
withdrawal from Belgium. Nothing was heard from Berlin and at 11.00
p.m. Churchill at the Admiralty dispatched action telegrams to the fleet.
The First World War had begun. Grey was later to explain and justify
Britain's declaration of war in his memoirs:

> We felt that to stand aside would mean the domination of Germany;
> the subordination of France and Russia; the isolation of Britain, the
> hatred of her by both those who had feared and those who had wished
> for her intervention in the war; and ultimately that Germany would
> wield the whole power of the Continent. How would she use it as
> regards Britain? Could anyone feel comfortable about that question?
> Could anyone give to it truthfully in his heart any but a sinister and
> foreboding answer?
>
> (E. Grey, *Twenty-Five Years*, London, Cassell, 1925, p. 19)

THE FIRST WORLD WAR 1914–18

On 6 August the Cabinet authorized the dispatch of the British
Expeditionary Force (BEF) to France. Initially, only four, not six, infantry divisions were sent, plus a cavalry division, numbering 100,000 men
in all. On 23 August the BEF saw its first action with the Germans at
Mons. The movement of this highly effective regular force was a model
of efficiency and a credit to Haldane and the General Staff. Sir John

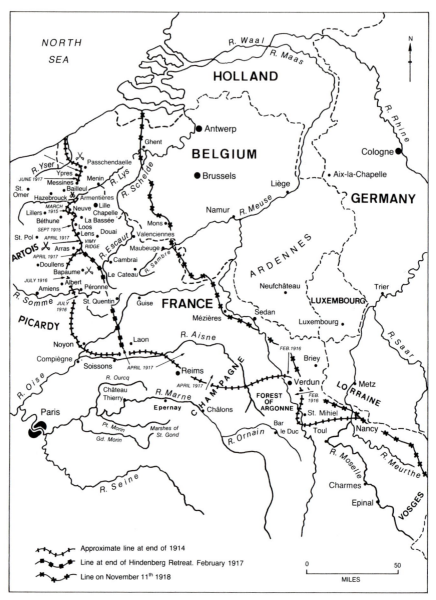

8.2 The Western Front

French, its commander, was ordered to take up a position on the left of
the French Fifth Army. The BEF and the Fifth found themselves massively outnumbered by the huge German right wing swinging through
Belgium in accordance with the Schlieffen Plan. Lanrezac, commander
of the Fifth, began to retreat on the 23rd forcing the BEF to do the
same. Over the next two weeks the army trudged south with the French.

On the river Marne east of Paris they halted and took part, hesitatingly it must be admitted, in the great counter-attack which with hindsight was to be the turning point of the war. On 10 September the Germans began to retreat to the river Aisne. The Schlieffen Plan had failed. France had not been knocked out by a single sledge-hammer blow and a long war of attrition would follow. The German Kaiser dismissed the Chief of the German General Staff, Von Moltke. It was a confession of failure.

Slowly the BEF and the French pursued the retreating Germans, but failed to force them from their new line on the Chemin des Dames above the valley of the Aisne. The Germans now produced the war's secret weapon, the spade, and trenches were dug. Siege warfare replaced a war of movement. The French sought to outflank the Germans to the north, and the Germans sought to outflank the French to the north and the trenches snaked their way up to the Channel. French and British forces joined with the remnants of the Belgian army holding a corner of that small country. Within that tiny corner lay the beautiful old Flemish town of Ypres to which the BEF was transported by rail and bus at the beginning of October (see Map 8.2). It arrived only to be virtually destroyed in the lengthy series of pushes and counter-pushes, between 12 October and 11 November, known as the First Battle of Ypres. The town was held at terrible costs. Commonsense dictated a straightening of the line behind the town but success in 1914 dictated holding on to this bulge, or salient, and the result was a bloody killing field which would soak up the blood from one million casualties, let alone the dead, over the next four years. The BEF had played a part in stopping the German bid for victory in 1914 but at the price of destroying the old regular army. As the Second Highland Light Infantry marched out of the front line on 16 November to rest only 30 men remained out of a battalion of 30 officers and 977 other ranks which had left Aldershot three months before. The army as a whole had suffered 89,000 casualties. A new army would have to be created.

Already this creation was underway. The new Minister of War, Lord Kitchener, decided the war would be long and the British Empire would have to become a major land power with seventy divisions. By the end of 1914 voluntary recruiting had brought in nearly 1.2 million men. The following year produced just over this figure and 1916 again just under 1.2 million. It would take time to transform these raw recruits into an effective fighting force. In the meantime the French would bear the brunt of the fighting, as they had in 1914. The British would have to rely on the Territorials, a total of 250,000 men, to hold their sector of the Western Front until Kitchener's new armies arrived. The Empire also began to make its significant contribution. The Indian Army Corps arrived at Marseilles at the end of September 1914 and was near Ypres by the end of the year. The first Canadian division was in France by

February 1915. One year after the BEF had landed it had swollen to twenty-eight divisions of infantry.

Throughout 1915 the French sought to drive the Germans out of their country with a series of costly offensives. The Germans concentrated on driving the Russians back from their borders. The Germans succeeded but the French did not. Britain's role in France was a very junior one. The expanding BEF took over more of the front but her contribution to the assaults was subsidiary and marred by serious shortages of guns and ammunition. The BEF lost blood and gained experience at Neuve Chapelle, the Second Battle of Ypres and Loos. In the second of these battles it was the Germans who attacked in April using gas for the first time. The chlorine used was terrible in its effects and with the element of surprise assisted a local breakthrough, stopped heroically by the newly arrived Canadians. Ypres was again saved but at great cost. Failure at Loos in September cost Sir John French his job as Commander in Chief and he was replaced by Sir Douglas Haig.

Other fronts had also opened in 1915 to widen the war. Turkey's entry on the German side led to conflict in Mesopotamia, where Britain strove to safeguard her Middle East oil supplies, and on the Egyptian border with Turkish Palestine. But it was on neither of these fronts that the British government focused its attention, concentrating instead upon a dramatic stroke to drive Turkey from the war altogether by seizing the Straits and Constantinople itself. It was a hastily improvised affair to relieve pressure on the Russians and to begin with only the navy was to bombard the defending forts. After initial success mines sank a third of the bombarding force. It became a complex combined operation. More and more troops were fed into what proved to be a fresh killing ground just as deadly as the Western Front. 'Gallipoli' as it became known used up 410,000 imperial troops, of which the ANZAC corps from Australia and New Zealand became the most famous. There were 213,000 casualties, the majority from disease as in all previous wars. Evacuation eventually occurred in January 1916, the exercise itself having achieved nothing. Henceforth the major British efforts against the Turkish Empire would be on the Suez and Persian Gulf fronts.

By January 1916 the BEF had topped the one million mark, comprising thirty-eight infantry divisions and five cavalry divisions. By July the total was fifty-seven divisions, the largest army Britain had ever possessed, and with it Haig proposed to win the war with 'the big push'. The push would take place in the valley of the Somme where the British and French sections met. It could thus be a joint Anglo-French venture. The German attack on the French further east at Verdun reduced the French contribution but made a major British effort all the more necessary. Kitchener's new armies were going to win the war, on the Somme, in the summer of 1916. An eight-day preliminary bombardment of 1,732,873 shells must surely annihilate the enemy. It did not. On 1 July 1916 57,470

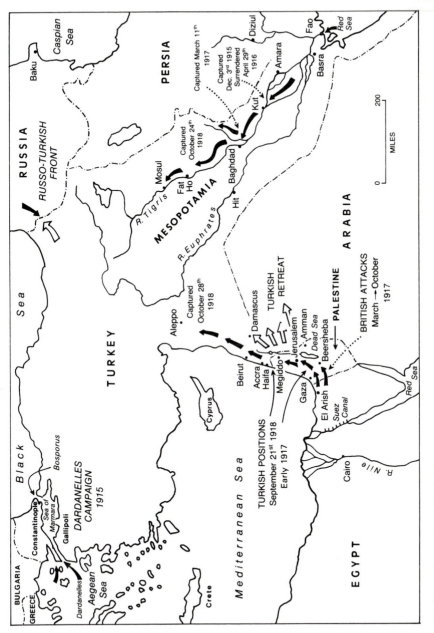

BULGARIA
GREECE
Dardanelles
Aegean Sea
Crete
Constantinople
Sea of Marmara
Gallipoli
Bosporus
DARDANELLES CAMPAIGN 1915

Black Sea

Baku
Caspian Sea

RUSSIA
RUSSO-TURKISH FRONT

PERSIA

Diziul
Fao
Red Sea
Basra

Captured March 11th 1917
Captured Dec. 3rd 1915
Surrendered April 29th 1916
Amara
Kut

Mosul
Captured October 24th 1918
Fat Ho
R. Tigris
Hit
Baghdad
MESOPOTAMIA
R. Euphrates

TURKEY

Cyprus

Mediterranean Sea

Aleppo
Captured October 28th 1918
Damascus
TURKISH RETREAT
Amman
Jerusalem
Dead Sea
Beersheba
PALESTINE
Beirut
Accra
Haifa
Megiddo
Gaza
El Arish
Suez Canal
Red Sea

TURKISH POSITIONS
September 21st 1918
Early 1917

BRITISH ATTACKS
March → October 1917

ARABIA

EGYPT

Cairo
R. Nile

0   200
MILES

8.3 The Middle East 1914–18

of the new armies' personnel became casualties. Nearly 20,000 were dead. It was the worst day in the British army's history. All along the fourteen-mile front men left their trenches at 7.30 a.m. on a beautiful summer's morning. Most of the deaths had occurred by 8.00 a.m. German machine guns had not been knocked out and repeatedly a single gun would cut a swathe through the partially trained young enthusiasts. Haig persevered with the battle until November. Slowly they edged forward, a cruel slogging match, finally resulting in over 400,000 imperial casualties. The Germans lost about the same. The Battle of the Somme was the graveyard of the old peace-time German army. In the words of the new mastermind of the German army, Ludendorff, 'The army had been fought to a standstill and was utterly worn out.' The Somme has gone down in British mythology as a prime example of military blundering. In reality it was an example of what continental warfare means, especially when an army is new, half-trained and inadequately supplied with the necessary heavy guns and shells. It is impossible to improvise a mass army without suffering the consequences. It is also impossible to fight on a continental scale without casualties particularly when the enemy is as well trained as the imperial German army. It has become a common fallacy to compare the idiocies of the First World War generals with supposedly superior leadership in the Second World War. The difference in casualties between the two is marked, but then so was the amount of fighting that the British army did in both wars. In 1916 it took on nearly 95 different divisions of the German army during the course of battle, out of the 125 on the Western Front. In the Second World War such scale of fighting was left to the Red Army which was to bleed even more profusely than the British on the Somme.

The achievement of raising, supplying and servicing such vast forces that existed by 1916 was in itself staggering. There were fifty-eight hospitals in the British sector by 1916 and 70,000 beds. It was the first war in which more men died encountering the enemy rather than from disease or neglect. The men were fed on a sometimes monotonous but healthy diet. By 1918 the Army Service Corps was issuing monthly 67.5 million pounds of meat and 90 million pounds of bread. The technology of the internal combustion engine was readily applied and by 1918 56,000 trucks and 34,000 motorcycles were in use with the BEF. The tank was adopted with enthusiasm, making its first appearance on the Somme in 1916. Air power expanded dramatically and in April 1918 the Royal Air Force was created as an independent service. When the war ended plans were well advanced for a strategic bombing attack on Germany.

In 1917 Britain began to assume the more important role in offensives on the Western Front. France, although retaining the biggest army to the end, was increasingly exhausted, and, as the mutinies of 1917 demonstrated, increasingly disinclined to fight. Haig launched a large supporting attack at Arras in April 1917 to assist the Nivelle offensive of that year.

The Canadian capture of Vimy Ridge was the only notable triumph of this costly subsidiary operation. There were 159,000 casualties spread over thirty-nine days. In July Haig was able to launch his own campaign in Flanders, the Third Battle of Ypres. The advancing line finally reached the village of Passchendaele in November with a loss of 250,000 casualties. No breakthrough had been achieved but heavy pressure and equal losses had been inflicted on the Germans. The battle in the mud came to symbolize the hell of the First World War. Haig summarized the fighting, not too inaccurately, in his official dispatch:

> Notwithstanding the many difficulties, much has been achieved. Our captures in Flanders since the commencement of operations at the end of July amount to 24,065 prisoners, 74 guns, 941 machine guns and 138 trench mortars. It is certain that the enemy's losses considerably exceeded ours. Most important of all, our new and hastily trained Armies have shown once again that they are capable of meeting and beating the enemy's best troops, even under conditions which favoured his defence to a degree which it required the greatest endurance, determination and heroism to overcome.
>
> (Sir Douglas Haig, *Despatches*, London, Dent, 1919,
> 1979 edn, p. 133)

The poet Siegfried Sassoon also summarized the fighting of 1917 in 'Attack':

> At dawn the ridge emerges massed and dun
> In the wild purple of the glow'ring sun,
> Smouldering through spouts of drifting smoke that shroud
> The menacing scarred slope; and, one by one,
> Tanks creep and topple forward to the wire.
> The barrage roars and lifts. Then, clumsily bowed
> With bombs and guns and shovels and battle-gear,
> Men jostle and climb to meet the bristling fire.
> Lines of grey, muttering faces, masked with fear,
> They leave their trenches, going over the top,
> While time ticks blank and busy on their wrists,
> And hope, with furtive eyes and grappling fists,
> Flounders in mud. O Jesus, make it stop!

The year ended with another abortive battle which at first promised much. At Cambrai, on 20 November, a mass force of tanks broke into the German trenches in dramatic fashion. The reserves, however, were kept too far back, and a successful German counter-attack regained the lost ground.

The defeat of Russia and her departure from the war was ultimately more than made up for by the entry of the United States in April 1917. In the long run Germany could no longer win. In the short term, however, the closing down of the Eastern Front made possible the transfer of more German troops to the west and the last chance of a knock-out blow to win the war before the Americans arrived in vast numbers. On 21 March 1918 a great German offensive began against the weakened British Fifth Army holding a front on the Somme. Despite terrible casualties, and a considerable retreat, the front held. Two more major German onslaughts followed. The allies were not beaten although once again the Germans reached the Marne – only 37 miles from Paris. In June and July the allies passed rapidly from defence to attack and to their surprise the Germans crumbled. One of the greatest allied victories was the battle of Amiens in August 1918. The German front collapsed after a vast bombardment of four million shells. It was the 'black day' of the German army, as Ludendorff christened this defeat, inflicted by the BEF under Haig's leadership. This time instead of continuing with an attack as the defence hardened the offensive was shifted to a fresh part of the line. The crumbling of the powerful German war machine became obvious as it began a slow but steady retreat. What is not obvious is the leading role of the British Army which played the greatest part in this final victory.

The formidable German defence known as the Hindenburg Line was broken. Tanks played a part but it was primarily a triumph of artillery. On 28 and 29 September 943,947 rounds were fired by the British army. By 1918 such men were gratified for the way their own artillery facilitated victory. The Germans requested an armistice and on 11 November the guns at last fell silent. The British army had won the greatest victory in its history. Its men just wanted to go home.

On other fronts, Britain had played a major part in defeating Germany by depriving her of her allies, a vital factor leading up to the German decision to ask for an armistice. In the Middle East, the Turkish Empire was assaulted by over one million imperial troops, many from India. Both Baghdad and Jerusalem had been captured by the end of 1917. Damascus fell in October 1918 as did Mosul in northern Iraq. Turkey surrendered at the end of October. British forces, for so long trapped around the Greek port of Salonika, took part with the French in finally effecting a break-out and driving Bulgaria from the war at the end of September. The threat of an advance north into the Danube valley contributed to the Austrian decision to seek peace early in November.

In addition to these subsidiary fronts Britain's greatest contribution to victory lay with the navy which from the beginning had imposed a blockade on Germany. This slowly strangled her economy. Death by malnutrition came to hundreds of thousands of German nationals, particularly children. Much of the food shortages were due to mistakes made by the German High Command after 1916. Fertilizer production was neglected as the mighty German chemicals industry concentrated on the production of explosives. The German merchant marine ceased to exist and surface raiders were quickly hunted down. Only once did the German high seas fleet seek to justify the expense of its creation and assault the blockading British fleet. The short confused action known as the Battle of Jutland resulted in 1916. Six thousand British sailors and 2,551 Germans died in eight minutes of fighting. The Germans claimed a victory but in the famous words of one American journalist: 'The German fleet has assaulted its jailor but is still in jail.' The only answer to the British blockade seemed to be the use of submarines to impose a counter-blockade on Britain. This had been tried in 1915 with some success but had to be called off because of American protests. The new military team who took over the management of Germany's war effort in 1918, Hindenberg and Ludendorff, decided to reactivate unrestricted submarine warfare. It was a gamble based on the contention that Britain could be brought to her knees before USA involvement proved decisive. In the early part of 1917 one ship in four that left Britain did not return and the Admiralty admitted that such losses could bring defeat by November. As described in chapter 6 the gamble failed and the convoy system, along with other defensive and offensive measures, enabled two million US soldiers to be transported to France by the summer of 1918.

Victory came finally to the strongest side. As Table 8.2 indicates Germany faced superior resources, particularly after the USA entered the war in 1917. That it took so long to defeat her was a result of the superb quality of the German army, the advantages of interior lines of communications and the power of the defensive. It also took many years to bring resources to bear. It was only in 1918 that Haig had sufficient guns *and* ammunition to pound his way to victory. The leading role of the British army in the campaigns of 1918 has already been pointed to. Her financial contribution to victory is even more impressive, as summarized in Table 8.3.

Table 8.2 Comparative balance of resources 1914–18 (%)

	Germany/Austria-Hungary	France/Russia & Britain (1914)	Britain/USA/France (1918)
Percentages of world manufacturing production (1913)	19.2	27.9	51.7
Energy consumption (1913), metric million tons of coal equivalent	236.4	311.8	798.8
Steel production (1913), in million tons	20.2	17.1	44.1
Total industrial potential (UK in 1900 = 100)	178.4	261.1	472.6

	Expenditure at 1913 prices ($ billions)	Total mobilized forces (millions)
Allies:		
British Empire	23.0	9.5
France	9.3	8.2
Russia	5.4	13.0
Italy	3.2	5.6
United States	17.1	3.8
Other Allies*	–0.3	2.6
Total	57.7	42.7
Central Powers:		
Germany	19.9	13.25
Austria-Hungary	4.7	9.00
Bulgaria, Turkey	0.1	2.85
Total	24.7	25.10

*Belgium, Romania, Portugal, Greece, Serbia.

ARMISTICE AND PEACE

The end of the war made the British think seriously about what they had been fighting for. In vague terms they had fought to stop the German domination of Europe which simply meant stopping Germany from being the victor. In a speech on 5 January 1918, Lloyd George had tried to explain what the war was about and what the consequences of victory would be. Among them he listed the restoration of Belgium and Serbia to their 1914 positions and also the return of Alsace and Lorraine to France. Perhaps more difficulty would follow from his fourth proposed change, the re-creation of an independent Poland, last seen in the 1790s. He concluded:

> If, then, we are asked what we are fighting for, we reply, as we have often replied – we are fighting for a just and lasting peace – and we believe that, before permanent peace can be hoped for, three conditions must be fulfilled. First, the sanctity of treaties must be re-established; secondly, a territorial settlement must be securely based on the right of self-determination or the consent of the governed; and, lastly, we must seek by the creation of some international organization to limit the burden of armaments and diminish the probability of war.

This all sounded very idealistic and laudable. Lloyd George was being a Liberal in the best Gladstonian tradition. What he was also trying to do was to counter the charge emerging from the new Bolshevik Russia that the war was a war of imperial aggrandizement. The Bolsheviks sought to embarrass the allies by publishing details of the secret agreement between the allies for gains – particularly at Turkey's expense. Britain certainly sought to gain territory from Turkey, as the secret Sykes–Picot pact with France in May 1916 indicated. Australia, South Africa, Japan and Britain all intended to keep the parcels of German Empire they had conquered, but these gains did not amount to an explanation of motives. They were consequences of fighting not causes for fighting. Britain's fundamental aim was sensible and age-old: the security of the British Isles. Given the period, such objectives were garnished, as Lloyd George's speech indicates, with Liberal ideological decoration.

The conditions of the armistice itself fulfilled much that Britain desired. The German army withdrew from Belgium and its fleet surrendered at Scapa Flow in the Orkneys. There, its officers decided to scuttle their ships rather than hand them over. The pride of both Tirpitz and the Kaiser sank one by one on 21 June 1919 as they lay at anchor in the waters of Scapa Flow. In private the British were rather pleased, as it avoided the embarrassing issue of dividing the ships amongst the victors.

The Peace Conference opened in Paris on 18 January 1919. President Wilson had arrived the previous month on the battleship *George Washington* and been feted as the liberal hero who had saved Europe. Lloyd George arrived in Paris with a large retinue in the new year. The two hundred-strong British delegation took over the Hotel Majestic but Lloyd George had a fashionable apartment with his mistress, Frances Stevenson, in attendance. The Foreign Secretary, Balfour, took the flat above the Prime Minister. For over six months Lloyd George spent more time in Paris than in London. The conference revealed both his diplomatic skills and an inner moral weakness. As always he was the master of fast footwork, sliding over difficulties to elicit compromises but there was no principle to guide him as, in their different ways, both the French premier Georges Clemenceau and President Woodrow Wilson possessed. Lloyd George was in many respects the prisoner of his own election campaign fought in December 1918. He himself had little sympathy with a punitive peace but under pressure from the *Daily Mail* with such headlines as 'The Huns Must Pay', Lloyd George abandoned his own feelings and in the heat of the election endorsed extreme opinions in which he clearly did not believe. To allay suspicions that he was 'soft' on Germany he deliberately appointed a known hard-line representative on the Reparations Commission, Billy Hughes, the Australian premier. The Commission's high demands were later to cause him embarrassment.

Initially Lloyd George co-operated with Clemenceau to force the Americans to moderate their idealistic stance and accept extensive reparations from Germany and the disposal of the German colonies to the victors. In taking this line Lloyd George was very conscious of the *Daily Mail* and his fire-breathing backbenchers who had dispatched a threatening telegram to him in April reminding him of his election pledges. Under this sort of pressure Lloyd George got the principle of unlimited liability for the Germans accepted by the Americans, and the War Guilt Clause (231) written into the Treaty; both were to be a source of endless argument later. The exact sum was to be fixed later but by getting disability payments and allowances for dependants of the dead he doubled Britain's share of any resulting payments. With this he was able to return to Westminster for a dramatic victory over his critics on 16 April.

On his return to Paris, Lloyd George swung the British delegation firmly against what seemed to be excessive French demands on Germany. He forced the French to abandon their claim to the Rhineland, which he feared would be an Alsace and Lorraine in reverse. Only with great reluctance and under the promise of an Anglo-American guarantee would the French agree to accept the Rhineland as German but disarmed and occupied by allied troops for fifteen years. On Germany's eastern frontier Lloyd George again sought to minimize her losses to the new state of Poland. He forced the French to agree to a plebiscite in Upper Silesia and refused to allow the Poles to incorporate the German city of Danzig. They should enjoy its port facilities but it would become a free city under the League of Nations. Germany's resentment of the whole eastern settlement filled Lloyd George and the Foreign Office with dismay. Clearly Germany would seek to change it and she remained the most powerful economy in Europe despite her losses and the disarmament clauses. The latter limited Germany's army to 100,000 men with no tanks, her navy to 15,000 with no submarines and only six battleships of humble size, and she was allowed no airforce.

THE AUDIT OF WAR

On the surface, the signing of the Versailles Settlement by Germany at the end of June 1919 gave Britain all she could wish for. The German navy was rusting in the waters of Scapa Flow and no other European power could challenge the huge British naval forces of 58 battleships and battlecruisers, 12 aircraft carriers, 103 cruisers and even 122 submarines. Her airforce, with 20,000 aircraft, was the biggest in the world as well. Her Empire reached its largest extent and gains had been made in Africa with the acquisition of German East Africa. More importantly a vast new empire in the Middle East had been taken from Turkey. Palestine kept the French away from Egypt and the Suez Canal. Possession of Iraq and effective control of a nominally independent Persia gave Britain control over vast oil supplies. Diplomatically she appeared stronger than ever. Japan had behaved as a faithful ally in the Far East while Russia, the old rival in Asia, seemed to have disappeared as a great power under the triple catastrophes of war, revolution and civil war. Her territorial

Legend:
- |||||| Sudetenland
- Lost by Germany 1919
- ■ Saar: League of Nations control 1919–35
- Demilitarised Rhineland 1919–36
- Austria–Hungary until 1918
- ⊠ Plebiscite areas
- ⫽ Former territory of Imperial Russia

0 — 200
MILES

NORWAY
SWEDEN
FINLAND
Oslo
Helsinki
Leningrad
Baltic Sea
Stockholm
ESTONIA
North Sea
LATVIA
Riga
U.S.S.R.
DENMARK
LITHUANIA
Danzig free city
Memel
Minsk
Copenhagen
Vilna
EAST PRUSSIA
Kiel
HOLLAND
Berlin
Poznan
Warsaw
BELGIUM
Bonn
GERMANY
Weimar
Saxony
POLAND
Saar
LUX.
Cracow
Lvov
Prague
Alsace-Lorraine
Bavaria
CZECHOSLOVAKIA
FRANCE
Munich
Vienna
Bessarabia
SWITZERLAND
AUSTRIA
Graz
Budapest
Transylvania
Süd Tirol
HUNGARY
Cluj
Trent
Slovenia
Trieste
RUMANIA
Croatia
YUGOSLAVIA
Bucharest
Sarajevo
Belgrade
Serbia
Mediterranean Sea
ITALY
Adriatic Sea
Bosnia
BULGARIA
Monte-negro
Sofia
ALBANIA
Maced-onia
GREECE
TURKEY

8.4 European frontiers 1919–37

losses at Versailles had been worse than those of Germany, her European frontiers pushed back to those of the mid-seventeenth century. True, France had made gains and this caused some concern to the alarmists, but economically and morally she was shattered, with her losses of men twice that of Britain. Italy was treated as a joke, her contribution to victory not well appreciated, as the British ambassador had written in November 1917, 'As for the Italians what can you expect from a nation, the majority of which, would be better employed selling ice cream.' The navy could be relied upon to deter Italy from any undesirable action, as in January 1919 when she wished to intervene in Montenegro and restore its king. Britain felt that the Montenegran inalienable right to murder each other, as and when they considered it necessary, should be upheld and the navy forced the Italians to agree. Only the United States and its strange, woolly-minded President gave cause for concern but even here the problem was to solve itself when Wilson fell ill and Congress simply withdrew from Europe and from most world affairs.

The widespread feeling that Britain was now safe can be readily understood. It was not until 1932 that a committee was even set up to study the lessons of the First World War. The army could return to being a colonial police force, most of the navy could hibernate and the RAF could be scrapped. British interests were clear as a Foreign Office memorandum of 1926 put it:

> We . . . have no territorial ambitions nor desire for aggrandisement. We have got all that we want – perhaps more. Our sole object is to keep what we want and live in peace. . . . The fact is that war and rumours of war, quarrels and friction, in any corner of the world spell loss and harm to British commercial and financial interests . . . so manifold and ubiquitous are British trade and British finance that, whatever else may be the outcome of a disturbance of the peace, we shall be the losers.
>
> (*Documents on British Foreign Policy 1919–1939*, vol. I, p. 846)

Like some lady of advanced middle age who had over-exerted herself, Britain now wanted a cup of tea and a snooze.

Yet the more perceptive of Britain's citizens were well aware that the world situation in 1919 was pregnant with future problems and difficulties. Britain's relative economic decline had been accelerated (this is looked at more fully in chapter 9). What was clear in 1919 was the increased power of the dollar and the shift in the world's financial centre of gravity from London to New York. Overall Britain was owed as much as she owed, but she was not likely to recover debts from Russia or even France unless France could extract money from defeated Germany. The national debt had multiplied eleven-fold and interest payments alone would consume 40 per cent of government spending, not the 12 per cent of 1913. There would clearly be great pressure for economies. In the meantime the USA insisted that Britain should honour her borrowings. The USA, as well as being Britain's creditor, now appeared as a formidable naval rival, intent on building the world's biggest fleet. Her resources would ensure that she could achieve her goal. Two centuries of British naval mastery was about to end. The other world giant, Russia, might appear temporarily removed from the list of great powers, but she would recover and a Bolshevik Russia with its message of world revolution threatened to be more menacing than tsarist Russia. Under prodding from Churchill, Lloyd George agreed reluctantly to intervention in 1919, but by the end of the year British troops were withdrawn having achieved nothing. A hostile Bolshevik regime might well seek to subvert His Majesty's Dominions in India as well as posing a renewed threat to the Middle East. It was in the Middle East that the first breaches in the Peace Settlement were made and the British public's unwillingness to enforce its terms was clearly displayed. A Turkish national uprising under Mustapha Kemal rejected the terms of the Treaty of Sèvres. After a victorious war against the Greeks there was a confrontation with the small British garrison holding the Straits in 1922. Lloyd George found there was no support for his bellicose stance and after complex negotiations, the Treaty of Lausanne was signed in July 1923. Turkey had stood up to the victors of 1918 and made great gains.

In the Far East Japanese power had been consolidated. As one British diplomat put it, 'While the Japanese gave us negligible help, they helped themselves to our trade and a fair amount of booty.' Their dominance in northern China threatened to usurp Britain's preponderance in the south and this threat was backed up by Japan's modern, concentrated fleet.

The perceptive were also conscious of future problems in Europe. Germany had temporarily been removed from the list of great powers, but it was only temporarily. The Peace Treaty appeared harsh to most Germans but in practice it hardly affected her fundamental strength. She had been irritated and outraged but not weakened. It was a recipe for disaster. Lloyd George, like most of the British delegation in Paris, felt that the settlement of Eastern Europe was unrealistic and likely to produce fresh conflict. The British Prime Minister showed great perspicacity in his so-called Fontainebleau Memorandum of March 1919:

> I cannot imagine any greater cause for future war than that the German people, who have proved themselves one of the most powerful and vigorous races of the world, should be surrounded by a number of small States, many of them consisting of peoples who have never previously set up a stable government for themselves, but each containing large masses of Germans clamouring for reunion with their native land.
>
> (Quoted in P. Kennedy, *The Realities Behind Diplomacy*, op. cit., p. 217)

From an early stage Britain clearly was prepared to accept revision of the Treaty. As with reparations, Lloyd George quickly came to regret the extent and harshness of the burden imposed on Germany. Like many Englishmen he regarded a healthy German economy as vital for British economic revival. The man who played along with populist anti-German sentiment in the election of 1918 became the father of appeasement.

Relations with France rapidly deteriorated. As Lord Curzon, Foreign Secretary from 1919 to 1922, was to put it:

> the Foreign Office is only too painfully aware that in almost every quarter of the globe, whether it be Silesia or Bavaria or Hungary or the Balkans – Morocco or Egypt or Turkey or Mesopotamia – the representatives of France are actively pursuing a policy which is either unfriendly to British interests or, if not that, is consecrated to the promotion of a French interest which is inconsistent with ours.
>
> (Quoted in S. Marks, *The Illusion of Peace: International Relations in Europe 1918–33*, London, Macmillan, 1976, p. 34)

Throughout the 1920s there was a growing distaste for France and her obsession with security against Germany. Relations deteriorated to the point where some of the service chiefs began to consider the French airforce as the biggest threat to the United Kingdom.

Away from the Continent there were further distractions. The Empire might have reached its greatest extent in 1919 but it was not as united as it had been in 1900 or 1914. Canada, Australia and South Africa were all anxious to emphasize their individuality and independence. Even in India, which had made a massive contribution to the imperial war effort, there was a growing impatience with colonial white control. As the Amritsar massacre of April 1919 showed, Britain would be increasingly faced with ruling by the gun or surrendering control. Gone were the days when 4,000 Britons could awe, or con, the native population into subservience. Rule by the gun was hardly a viable alternative for a 'Liberal' power. The concept of independence was hardly more acceptable.

Finally, at home there was a growing unwillingness to shoulder the burden of greatness. The cost in blood and treasure of being the world's policeman was too great. There was initially a public idolization of Wilson's League of Nations. Could not this preserve the world, as it was, more cheaply? Could not Britain remain rich and great but somehow find someone else to do the work? The service chiefs and the Foreign Office were aware of the discrepancies between needs and resources. In December 1918, Balfour, the then Foreign Secretary expressed this concern in an official minute:

> We talk of huge protectorates all over the place. I am really frightened at the responsibilities which we are taking upon ourselves, because

who has to bear the responsibilities? Two offices in the main – the Treasury and the War Office. . . . Where are they going to find the men and the money for these things?

(Quoted in M. Howard, *The Continental Commitment*, London, Temple Smith, 1972, p. 71)

In July 1920 the General Staff gave a depressing summary of needs against resources. British troops were on call everywhere – fighting insurrection in Ireland, India and Egypt; separating Jews and Arabs in Palestine; and trying to guard the Straits and Persian oil supplies – 'In sum our liabilities are so vast and at the same time so indeterminate that to assess them must be largely a matter of conjecture.' The future to those in the know was far from rosy, but to the men and women in the street the storm had passed. The League of Nations could look after the world. Britain could take a well-deserved rest.

NO WAR FOR TEN YEARS 1919–32

In 1919 Lloyd George told the service chiefs that they need not anticipate a major war for another ten years. This policy became the gospel of British foreign and defence planning in the 1920s and defence spending slid remorselessly. Britain signed only armaments-limitation agreements on the navy but she disarmed none the less, reaching her lowest point of military weakness in 1931–2. All parties were responsible for this development. Churchill, as Chancellor of the Exchequer under Baldwin in the era 1924–9, was as enthusiastic a disarmer as any member of MacDonald's two Labour governments of 1924 and 1929–31. It was the army that suffered the most from these economies. A voluntary army starved of new equipment, and used to operating in small units as a colonial police force replaced the vast conscript army of 1918. Armoured warfare, a British concept, was also abandoned.

In the RAF the story was much the same with large numbers of its machines being scrapped, and fresh ones not being ordered. In a sense this was not too disastrous as the rapid obsolescence of planes ensured that Britain, unlike Italy and France, entered the 1930s with no great weight of antique bi-planes which she would be reluctant to replace. The navy was the subject of international agreement. Under pressure from the USA, and the threat of a bigger and more expensive arms race (of which only HMS *Hood*, the new giant British battlecruiser, was the surviving monument), Britain agreed to an international naval conference which met in Washington in November 1921. It ended Britain's naval mastery. She agreed to parity with the USA: 525,000 tons of capital ships each, while Japan was to have 315,000 and Italy and France 175,000. It ended the threat of an arms race but produced a British navy relatively weaker than at any time since the 1670s. It also ended the

Anglo-Japanese Alliance. These two developments were to have very serious repercussions for Britain's position in Asia where a concentrated Japanese fleet now faced an ageing portion of the British navy. In 1927 a conference in Geneva sought to extend limitations to cruisers and other craft, but it broke up with much Anglo-American animosity. It required Ramsay MacDonald and the second Labour Government to achieve agreement in this area at the London Naval Conference of 1930.

Underlying this general trend to disarmament lay the serious deterioration in the British economy in the 1920s. Britain's share of world trade continued to decline and the export-dependent economy performed far less well than that of the USA, France or Germany. By 1929 many of those features that would make Britain the 'sick lady' of Europe in the 1970s were visible. In view of the decline, particularly of exports, there was a growing anxiety to revive pre-war markets. Germany had absorbed 8.3 per cent of British exports in 1913. By 1921 it was 2.4 per cent. Russia was also seen as a potential market to be opened up after the Bolshevik seizure of power. Economic interests welcomed appeasement of both these powers as well as the USA.

Russia after the Bolshevik success posed special problems. She was the pariah of Europe, uninvited to the Peace Conference, and she had lost heavily. All promises by her former Entente partners were regarded as negated by the revolution and Russia's withdrawal from the war. The west's intervention on behalf of anti-Bolshevik forces in the Civil War left a legacy of suspicion and hate. Her revenge was the repudiation of all war debts and nationalization without compensation of all western interests in Russia. In addition her new leaders Lenin and Trotsky were committed to the concept of world revolution. Communism could be exported to Britain and her Empire. The Communist Party of Great Britain was founded in April 1920 and in the same year the Communist International (Comintern), on Lenin's instructions, turned it and all western communist parties into 'the intellectual slaves of Moscow'. In the troubled early years of the 1920s, when class conflict and industrial strife seemed to many to promise revolution, both the Foreign Office and the secret intelligence community took the Russian threat of subversion very seriously. It was the relationship with Russia that, more than anything else, distinguished the foreign policies of the Labour and Conservative governments in the inter-war years.

The first Labour Government in 1924 decided to recognize the USSR but the attempt to settle the debt question via a complex commercial treaty and a loan contributed to its fall on the charge of being 'soft' on Bolshevism. The Zinoviev Letter (see chapter 7) fuelled the 'red scare' paranoia and the replacement Conservative Government found a convenient bogy in Bolshevik Russia. Austen Chamberlain, the Foreign Secretary, was the least inclined to push hostility to breaking point but even he wrote to Baldwin in 1925 that:

A great mass of information has accumulated in this office proving the continuous hostile activities of Soviet Agencies against the British Empire, more particularly in the East. Nearly all this information is of the most highly secret character, which I do not circulate to Ministers lest any carelessness in the handling of the papers should endanger our sources of information.

(Quoted in C. Andrew, *Secret Service*, London, Sceptre, 1986, p. 450)

The ideological threat of subversion at home, powerfully encouraged by the General Strike of 1926, received reinforcement by a refurbished threat to India. This was the old tsarist threat with additional red relish. The completion of a new branch of the trans-Caspian railway in 1925 revived all the earlier fears of an invasion of Afghanistan (see chapter 5, p. 144). To this good old strategic threat was added that of communist subversion of India.

The General Staff at the same time was frightening itself with assessments of eighty divisions poised for a descent on the Indian sub-continent. This, together with a genuine conviction of Russian subversion in Britain, led to the breaking of diplomatic ties in May 1927. The hawks, led by Churchill and Sir William Joynson Hicks, the Home Secretary, were all to get the better of Chamberlain. After a Secret Service raid on the Russian trade mission, Arcos in London (which, incidentally, failed to turn up the evidence of subversion thought to exist), the Russian ambassador was expelled. By 1928 realism was asserting itself and the General Staff no longer believed in eighty divisions poised for a descent. Instead there was a reassessment that the Soviet Union's munitions production could not support a major war. The second Labour Government restored diplomatic relations in October 1929. It required the growing menace of Hitler to thaw relations still further and see the USSR accepted as a member of the League of Nations in 1934.

For all the obsessions of the Secret Service and Tory die-hards with the communist threat it was the problem of Germany that dominated Foreign Office thinking. How was a beaten but fundamentally unweakened Germany to be integrated into the European family of nations? British statesmen felt that they needed the German economy as a partner for ailing British industry; they also shared the German assessment of the impermanence of the boundary settlement of eastern Europe. Appeasement has come to be associated with Neville Chamberlain and with the two or three years immediately prior to the outbreak of war in 1939. In practice it began with Lloyd George in 1919 as soon as the ink was dry on the Treaty of Versailles. It continued throughout the 1920s under MacDonald, as Labour premier and Foreign Secretary in 1924, and under Austen Chamberlain, as Foreign Secretary from 1924 to 1929. Labour was possibly more enthusiastic than Chamberlain, who was less anti-French than MacDonald, but both parties pushed ahead with

unscrambling the Versailles Settlement and trying to win German acceptance of something less than domination of the Continent.

Reparations presented the most immediate problem and were the
subject of endless conferences between 1919 and 1922. Germany was
presented with a bill in 1921 for 50 billion gold marks. The French were
determined to extract compensation; the British rapidly lost interest in
the face of determined German resistance. Relations between France
and Britain deteriorated. Britain refused to ratify her original Versailles
guarantee of French frontiers on the grounds that the USA had withdrawn, and Britain disagreed with French encouragement for the Poles
in their claims with Russia, while France disagreed with Britain's backing
of the Greeks in their claims with the Turks. By the end of 1922 Britain's
and France's attitudes to reparations and Germany seemed miles apart.
Britain was for a moratorium to allow the German economy time to
recover, and France for full and punctual payments. On 9 January 1923
the Reparations Commission, against British advice, decided to occupy
the Ruhr to force Germany to pay. In the short term it was a French
victory. The new German government of Gustave Stresemann agreed to
come to the negotiating table. The result was the Dawes Plan of 1924,
named after the American banker, Charles G. Dawes, who chaired a
committee of inquiry, but British diplomats and the Labour Prime Minister, Ramsay MacDonald, also played a key role in the London Conference of July 1924 which obtained Franco-German acceptance of the
Plan. The French agreed to leave the Ruhr and the Germans to resume
payments, but allied controls were weakened and future sanctions against
default virtually impossible. A large American loan to Germany eased
the whole process. It seemed a triumph for MacDonald.

Less successful was MacDonald's tackling of the other real cause of
Franco-German tension, the question of French security and disarmament. The League of Nations seemed the obvious agency for promoting
this and in 1923 a scheme known as the Draft Treaty of Mutual Assistance had been put before the League's Assembly. It obligated all League
members to come to the aid of the victim of aggression. France was
delighted, and approved. Britain, aware of her wide imperial commitments and under pressure from dominions like Canada, rejected the
scheme. MacDonald then promoted an alternative which, taking its name
from the League's headquarters, became known as the Geneva Protocol.
It involved a careful system of compulsory arbitration and disarmament.
It was disliked by the new Conservative Government which took office
at the end of the year. Austen Chamberlain, the Foreign Secretary,
preferred direct great power negotiation and treaties. The Geneva Protocol was dropped but Chamberlain sought to give the French security at
minimal British cost. Stresemann sought to speed up the evacuation of
German territory, not due until 1935, and wished to avoid a full-scale
Anglo-French alliance. The result of all these considerations was the

Locarno Treaty of 1925 which Chamberlain considered his greatest achievement. France and Germany promised peace and the inviolability of their common frontiers. No longer would France threaten the Ruhr, nor Germany Alsace. Britain and Italy agreed to stand as guarantors of the settlement. In tribute to Chamberlain the signing ceremonies were held on his sixty-second birthday on 16 October. He had made Britain the arbiter of Europe, but unfortunately the armed forces had neither the means nor any plan for enforcement. The real victor was Stresemann. He emphasized that this was a valid treaty in contrast to the *diktat* of Versailles. The Poles and the Czechs noted anxiously that the Germans did not promise to respect their eastern frontiers, only to seek change peacefully. As one historian has put it, 'Locarno was widely interpreted as a green light for Germany in the east.' Stresemann had also secured the evacuation of Cologne and reduced the level of occupation in the remaining zones. Moreover, he had headed off an Anglo-French Entente of real meaning.

In 1926 Germany gained entry to the League of Nations and took one of the permanent seats on the League's Council. She was now fully recognized as a great power and Stresemann availed himself of every opportunity to press for more and more concessions, no sooner having gained one than bringing pressure to bear for a new one in return for ratification of the first. In January 1927 the Inter-Allied Military Control Commission (IMCC) was withdrawn altogether from Germany, making verification of German disarmament impossible. In 1929 Stresemann secured two further great concessions: one, the Young Plan (approved at the Hague Conference in August of that year) on reparations which reduced the overall burden on Germany to a third of the original total and removed all the effective controls on Germany. The other, also agreed at the Hague Conference, was to withdraw all troops from Germany by June 1930. Stresemann was aided in the extracting of these concessions by the return of a Labour Government in May. MacDonald was far less sympathetic to French security fears than Chamberlain. Ten weeks after the last French troops left German soil the unknown Nazi Party suddenly leapt to prominence in Germany with 107 seats in the September 1930 Reichstag elections. Perhaps democracy was not safe in Germany and feeding tit-bits to a tiger not the way to keep it quiet.

The onset of world recession in 1929 and the gathering gloom of 1930 and 1931 as the jobless totals mounted in Britain and Germany, produced opposite results in the two countries. In Britain the demand for economies and disarmament intensified. In Germany a shrill and frightening nationalism drowned all other cries. MacDonald and his Foreign Secretary Arthur Henderson worked hard to produce a world Disarmament Conference at Geneva. It finally met in February 1932, after MacDonald's Labour Cabinet had fallen in August 1931. Henderson, in tribute to his preparatory work, was appointed its chairman. The conference achieved no agreement. German demands met French flat refusals. Ironically one month after the Disarmament Conference opened Britain formally abandoned the ten-year rule and invited the Chiefs of Staff to prepare to remedy the worst difficulties and neglect. In practice this meant little. The Chancellor of the Exchequer promptly introduced the lowest military estimates of the inter-war years. The Empire was almost defenceless without a disarmament conference. Britain had unilaterally disarmed and public opinion was overwhelmingly behind Henderson. In February 1933 the Oxford Union passed its famous resolution: that, 'This House will not fight for King or country.' No British government, despite its unease and a deteriorating world situation, dared to rearm before 1935.

No agreement was reached on disarmament but a conference chaired by MacDonald, now Prime Minister of a coalition government, finally ended reparations at Lausanne in June 1932. The world economic blizzard made collection of further reparations impossible. Germany had secured another victory, but it came too late to prevent Hitler's accession to power in January 1933. From this time on the German question would begin to acquire a new ominous urgency.

DEALING WITH HITLER 1933–9

No war is inevitable until it breaks out, as A. J. P. Taylor frequently stressed, and war with Germany in 1933 did not seem inevitable. Hitler inherited a strong moral position prepared by Stresemann. There was a widespread feeling in Britain that Germany had been harshly treated in 1919. There was often more sympathy for her position than that of France as the *Punch* cartoon of 1933 indicates. Although Hitler walked out of the Disarmament Conference, many Britons felt that it was French intransigence that had wrecked the conference not Hitler's intemperance. Britain resisted any ideas of guaranteeing the eastern European settlement as the French Foreign Minister, Louis Barthou, wanted. There was going to be no eastern Locarno if the British Foreign Office could help it. A Foreign Office memorandum of November 1935 clearly expressed the general nature of British policy to Germany:

> The fundamental idea is of course that the ex-Allied Powers should come to terms with Germany in order to remove grievances by friendly arrangement and by the process of give and take, before Germany once again takes the law into her own hands. This is the only constructive policy open to Europe – the alternatives of drift and encirclement are avowedly policies of negation and despair. There will in this memorandum be no suggestion that this policy should be abandoned.

Here is a rejection of Grey and Eyre Crowe. There was to be no restraint by encirclement, and no alliance such as Barthou and Pierre Laval

THE MYSTERIOUS CIVILIAN.

French Gendarme. "SEE THAT FELLOW? I SUSPECT HIM OF CARRYING CONCEALED ARMS. I OUGHT TO SEARCH HIM."

P.C. John Bull. "VERY LIKELY, MATE. AND I MUST SAY YOU SEEM TO HAVE RIGGED YOURSELF OUT FOR THE JOB PRETTY THOROUGHLY."

wanted. This sprang partly from a feeling that Grey's *entente* policy had been counter-productive, forcing Germany to lash out in 1914, and partly from a distaste for communist Russia. Many in Britain preferred Hitler to Stalin. Certainly it was widely accepted, particularly in the Conservative Party, that any conflict with Germany would only benefit Russia. The 'Red Bear' needed treating with extreme caution. The French might welcome Russia to the League of Nations in 1934 and even sign a tentative alliance in 1935, but Britain remained sceptical.

The USA was wedded to isolation more than ever and the Dominions, vital components of the war effort of 1914, seemed reluctant to involve themselves as General Hertzog of South Africa put it in 1937:

> if a European war did come because England continued to associate with France in a policy in respect of central and eastern Europe calculated to threaten Germany's existence through unwillingness to set right the injustices flowing from the Treaty of Versailles, South Africa cannot be expected to take part in the war.

The attitude of the USA and the Dominions powerfully reinforced appeasement. The Labour Party was later to make capital out of the failure of the National Government's appeasement policy yet the Labour Party was even more opposed to rearmament than the Tory Party. C. R. Attlee, the new leader of the Labour Party in 1935, said in May:

> As a Party we do not stand for unilateral disarmament. . . . We stand for Collective Security through the League of Nations. We reject the use of force as an instrument of policy. We stand for the reduction of armaments and pooled security. . . . We have stated that this country must be prepared to make its contribution to collective security. Our policy is not one of seeking security through rearmament, but through disarmament. Our aim is the reduction of armaments, and then the complete abolition of all national armaments and the creation of an International Police Force under the League.

The parliamentary party opposed rearmament until 1937 and the Party Conference, even in 1938, did the same – despite their dislike for fascist Germany. There was a certain hypocrisy in their demand for action without a willingness to support the call.

Fear and a sense of weakness also added weight to the arguments for finding a *modus vivendi*. The slump slashed government revenues. Defence spending was now pared to the bone. Although economic recovery had set in by 1934, the Treasury felt that peace was essential to nurse the patient back to full health. There was also a general horror of war. Gone was the 'jingo' patriotism of 1914. The war poets, with their haunting evocation of the trenches and belief in the futility of war, coloured much public perception by the 1930s. A growing awareness of what modern warfare meant added to this sense of horror. As Stanley

Baldwin famously put it, 'The bomber will always get through.' Civilians would now die in their thousands and maybe millions from explosions and poisonous gas. As Germany began to develop her airforce this fear seemed to be rooted in a terrible reality. All these considerations explain why Britain sought to find a way to live with Nazi Germany.

On Germany's side too there seemed little to make conflict inevitable. Hitler appeared personally well-disposed to Britain. As he wrote in *Mein Kampf*:

> Cool and cautious consideration shows that it is these two States, Great Britain and Italy, whose own most natural interests are least in opposition to the conditions essential to the existence of the German nation, and are, in fact, to a certain extent, identical with them.

At least until 1938 he appears to have striven to achieve an understanding with the offshore island. Although the world economic crisis produced a decline in Anglo-German trade, mutual economic ties remained an important link for both countries. An Anglo-German Payments Agreement was signed in 1934, and renegotiated, after Germany's absorption of Austria, in 1938 with concessions favourable to Britain. The depressed British coal and textile industries found a market in Germany and there was a real reluctance until 1939 to do anything to weaken the German economy.

In 1933 it was not Germany but Japan that seemed to pose the greatest threat to imperial security. In September of 1931 the Japanese army in Korea had invaded the north Chinese province of Manchuria, apparently without instruction from Tokyo. Within a year Manchuria was conquered and a Japanese puppet state of Manchukuo established. As yet this was no vital threat either to the Empire or British Chinese interests which were further south but it was a flagrant affront to the League of Nations and the principle of collective security. Britain, absorbed in her domestic economic crisis, was unwilling to take action and the League merely dispatched a commission of inquiry under Lord Lytton. The end result was the most ineffective sanctions possible, such as non-recognition of Manchukuo passports. Even so they drove Japan to leave the League of Nations in March 1933, and a further attack on China took place in May. A truce was arranged but it seemed to the Foreign Office that there was no restraining force on Japan and the extent of her ambitions remained a mystery. The USA had refused to co-operate and the USSR was viewed as potentially even more menacing than Japan. In 1932 the Chiefs of Staff reported: 'The whole of our territory in the Far East, as well as the coastline of India, the Dominions and our vast trade and shipping lies open to attack.'

Work was re-started on fortifying Singapore as the cornerstone of imperial defence in the Far East, but the prospects were deeply worrying. Could the reduced British army defend the Empire? Australia was probably not very reassured by the Chiefs of Staff's analysis of 1932. 'Provided that the British Fleet arrives in time and finds a properly equipped base at Singapore, Australia has nothing to fear beyond sporadic attacks.' Japanese unpredictability grew and she abandoned the Naval Limitation Treaty in 1934 and the Admiralty and the Foreign Office groped for a solution. This menace in the Far East was to play a vital part in encouraging appeasement of Germany. In 1936 the Chiefs of Staff warned: 'The greater our commitments to Europe, the less will be our ability to secure our Empire and its communications.'

In 1937 Japan resumed her attack on China this time unrestrained in the region. Britain could do nothing without the USA, who would not budge from her self-obsessed isolation. In the last analysis China was less of a vital interest than those which Nazi Germany could threaten, so reluctant acceptance of Japanese aggression was all that was possible. The logical policy that was favoured by many in the Foreign Office was a deal with Japan but fear of upsetting the USA was paramount. A selfish and morally smug America played a major part in precipitating the Second World War by its very inaction in the 1930s.

If Britain dithered between resistance and conciliation with Japan, the same dilemma existed in Europe with both Germany and Italy, and the same policy of dither repeated itself for the same reasons. Over the four years after his coming to power Hitler pursued essentially the same revisionist policies as his predecessors but with the gambler's capacity for taking risks. The result was that the Foreign Office was repeatedly pre-empted. Some concessions that had been prepared to ensnare Germany into the fold of respectability were taken without negotiation or reciprocal concession. Britain had decided that some form of German rearmament was inevitable after the failure of the Geneva Conference. She hoped for some deal involving an air pact. Early in 1935 Hitler announced the existence of an airforce, and then on 16 March the reintroduction of conscription. Sir John Simon, the British Foreign Secretary, visited Berlin just after this, but since Hitler had already taken the proposed British rearmament concession there was little to discuss.

Britain reluctantly began to rearm herself as a White Paper of March 1935 outlined. The conduct of the Labour opposition was marked by a head-burying exercise that outdid the average ostrich in skill. Attlee wanted the weight of 'the whole world's opinion' to restrain potential aggressors and condemned rearmament. It was Neville Chamberlain, the Chancellor of the Exchequer, who recognized the need for armament expansion albeit in a moderate way. There was, however, desperate anxiety to avoid an arms race. Likewise there was a flirtation with diplomatic grouping to restrain Hitler. Anthony Eden, number two at the Foreign Office, visited Moscow in the spring but there was no thought of an alliance. Italy was considered a more suitable and acceptable partner as it was felt that it was Italy under Mussolini that had restrained

Germany in 1934 from seizing Austria. In April the Prime Minister, MacDonald, with Sir John Simon attended a conference at Stresa in northern Italy. Britain, France and Italy then issued a declaration on 11 April condemning German unilateral rearmament and reaffirming their commitment to Locarno. Any possibility that Hitler might be confronted with a solid block of opposition was shortlived and it was Britain who took the first step to fragmenting the Stresa Front. On 18 June 1935 she signed the Anglo-German Naval Agreement sanctioning Germany's building of a fleet that was 35 per cent the size of Britain's. The new Foreign Secretary, Sir Samuel Hoare, was bounced into the Agreement by the German ambassador, Von Ribbentrop. It was a selfish act by which Britain seemed to bless German rearmament as long as her own particular naval needs were met. It was signed with one eye on the Japanese menace and the desire to avoid simultaneous confrontation with a naval power in Europe and in Asia. It was, of course, what Britain had sought prior to 1914 and singularly failed to get. Hitler appears to have been genuine in his desire to avoid confrontation with Britain and avoid the mistakes of the Kaiser, but in any case he was giving away very little as the Agreement in effect allowed Germany to build as fast as she could.

France was furious with Britain, but Britain was already suspicious of France's flirtation with the USSR. Both of these powers had negotiated a limited pact during May 1935. It was, however, the Italian invasion of Abyssinia in October 1935 that finally sealed the fate of any united front against Hitler.

Throughout 1935 Mussolini had been drawing closer to France with the two powers signing a military convention for the protection of Austria in June. France was quite happy for Italy to seize the backward state of Abyssinia in East Africa, as was the British Foreign Office. No vital British interests were involved and a secret committee under Sir John Maffey made this point in a memorandum in June. Unfortunately Abyssinia was a member of the League of Nations and public opinion being obsessed with the League made any brutal sacrifice of poor Abyssinia impossible. *Realpolitik* was in conflict with the public's morality. Nevertheless, the Foreign Secretary, Hoare, urged on by his senior civil servant, Sir Robert Vansittart, who was anti-German in the best Eyre Crowe tradition, proceeded to negotiate a deal with the French Prime Minister, Laval. The resulting Hoare–Laval pact proposed to give Mussolini three-fifths of Abyssinia. Unfortunately for Hoare the pact was leaked to the press and a wave of righteous pro-League indignation swept him from office. Baldwin, the Prime Minister, abandoned him as a scapegoat and appointed the young Sir Anthony Eden as his successor. Eden had a reputation for being a friend of the League.

The half-hearted sanctions imposed on Italy in November 1935 were continued but oil, the one vital material whose denial would have stopped

Italy, was not included. Mussolini knew of the Maffey report and Britain's unwillingness to fight. In fact the Italian Secret Service were reading much classified British information. Security was lamentable at the British embassy where Italian employees seemed to have easy access to material. In the British Legation in the Vatican the premises were shared with the Italian army and were not occupied at night. Classified information was left lying around. The whole episode was a disaster. Italy was infuriated by the sanctions yet still conquered Abyssinia. France and Britain's mutual suspicions were heightened and Hitler was encouraged.

Taking advantage of the Stresa partners' differences Hitler decided on his biggest gamble. On 7 March 1936 he ordered his troops into the demilitarized Rhineland. By doing this he not only breached Versailles but also Locarno. With encouragement from Britain, France would probably have acted and could have defeated the still small German army. London gave no such encouragement. Germany, in the words of the leading Liberal Lord Lothian, 'had walked into her own back garden'. The Labour Party agreed with the inactivity favoured by Baldwin and Eden and Hitler encouraged the inaction by promising pacts left, right and centre. As one of the few opponents of appeasement, General Sir Edward Spears pointed out in 1936:

> having invaded the Rhineland this year and having offered a treaty of 25 years' duration, next year they will take Austria and offer a treaty of 50 years; that after that it will be the turn of Memel and the Corridor, when they will offer a treaty of 75 years, and we can look forward to eternal peace once France and England have disappeared.

Spears was not listened to, the 'back garden' argument meshed nicely with public desire to prolong 'the long week-end'.

In many ways 1936 marked a key turning point in Britain's relations with Germany. The balance of power shifted dramatically to the latter. Until 1936 appeasement was motivated by inertia and a desire to be fair to a maltreated power. After 1936 fear and a sense of inadequacy were heavily influencing British official thinking. There was no choice left but appeasement. Italy swung rapidly towards *détente*, and then *entente*, with Germany. Mussolini was irritated by British policy over Abyssinia and unimpressed by his Locarno partners' response to the occupation of the Rhineland. The outbreak of the Spanish Civil War in July 1936 drew the two dictators together as backers of General Franco. By November 1936 Mussolini was talking of a Rome–Berlin axis around which the affairs of Europe would revolve. French nerves, in some ways, snapped with the occupation of the Rhineland. France's position *vis-à-vis* Germany now deteriorated rapidly. Worsening relations with Italy meant another seventeen or eighteen divisions would be needed in the defence of North Africa. Belgium declared her neutrality in 1936, cruelly undermining all French military strategy to date. France would now have to extend the defence of her eastern frontier, the so-called Maginot Line, westwards to the sea. It would be hideously expensive and a very slow business. France, unlike Britain or Germany, was much slower to recover from the economic slump and bitter political tensions between right and left weakened her capacity for decisive action. The outbreak of the Spanish Civil War added to these tensions. This meant that from 1936 any resistance to Hitler must come from Britain and it was Britain who now clearly took the lead in dealing with the German leader. Yet Britain herself at the end of that year was made sadly aware of her vulnerability. In a famous debate on air power on 20 July 1934 Churchill had warned the government of the growing German air menace:

> We are a rich and easy prey. No country is so vulnerable, and no country would better repay pillage than our own. . . . *With our enormous metropolis here, the greatest target in the world, a kind of tremendous, fat, valuable cow tied up to attract the beast of prey*, we are in a position in which we have never been before, and in which no other country is at the present time.
>
> *Let us remember this: our weakness does not only involve ourselves; our weakness involves also the stability of Europe.*
>
> (W. S. Churchill, *The Second World War*, vol. I, London, Odhams, 1948, p. 92)

Baldwin, for the government, claimed that the Germans as yet posed no threat and that an expanding British airforce offered security. Such complacency disappeared in the autumn of 1936 and British Intelligence performed a volte-face suddenly convincing itself that the *Luftwaffe* was outstripping Britain which had little hope of catching up. Apocalyptic prophecies of mass destruction were accepted. Group Captain Arthur Harris was the RAF representative on the Joint Planning Committee of the Chiefs of Staff and, possibly under his influence, the committee argued that Germany would be able to deliver a series of knock-out attacks on London by 1939. We now know that such reports were wildly inaccurate, as Germany did not possess such a capacity in 1938 or 1939. The British response to these predictions was one of extreme caution in confronting Germany and a rapid expansion of air defences which was to pay off in 1940.

Whilst rearmament began to get seriously underway from 1936 with the appointment of Sir Thomas Inskip as Minister for the Co-ordination of Defence, it was the RAF and the navy that were given priority. There was an abhorrence of fighting another continental war on the lines of 1914–18. The army was neglected. It was assumed that France could and should deal with the German army with minimal British assistance – 'limited liability' as it was described was less popular in Paris than in London. British defence priorities can be clearly seen from Table 8.4.

Table 8.4 Actual expenditure by departments, 1932–9 (£ million)

Financial year	Admiralty	Air Ministry	War Office	Civil Defence	Total
1932	50.2	17.0	36.0	–	103.2
1933	53.4	16.7	37.5	–	107.6
1934	56.6	17.7	39.6	–	113.9
1935	64.9	27.5	44.5	–	136.9
1936	81.0	50.0	54.5	0.7	186.2
1937	102.0	81.8	78.1	3.4	265.3
1938	127.3	133.8	121.4	17.8	400.3
1939	149.3	248.6	243.6	59.0	700.5

Note: figures rounded up or down to the nearest thousand.
Source: After *Parliamentary Papers*, 1933–7, Air, Army and Navy Appropriation Accounts; T.161/999/S.46095: 'Defence expenditure before and during the present war.'

Following the occupation of the Rhineland what Churchill christened the 'loaded pause' ensued. For many Britons attention was shifted from Hitler to events in Spain and Italy. It was a diversion from the real menace. Italy gave extensive aid to Franco and by 1937 there were 60,000 Italian volunteers in Spain. Germany gave less help but her Condor Legion of aircraft could test themselves at the Spanish people's expense. To much of the British left it became a crusade to aid the Republic against what was perceived as a general fascist threat. It confirmed the trend already begun over Abyssinia, to concentrate hatred on Mussolini who was no threat to Britain but to oppose rearmament against Hitler who was. Speeches against fascism abounded, plaudits of the League and collective security brought applause from Labour Party Conferences. Rearmament remained a dirty word. The British government proposed a policy of strict non-intervention in Spain and a farcical Non-Intervention Committee was set up with Germany, Italy and Russia taking part while at the same time feeding the conflict in Spain. After a brief inclination to intervention in 1936 the French government gave way to British pressure and observed a strict neutrality. Britain's attitude was governed by a fear of a communist Spain and a desire to regain Mussolini as a counter-weight to Hitler. The National Government and the Foreign Office refused as yet to lump the two dictators into the same camp and accept the division of Europe on ideological grounds, as the left did. Italy was treated with kidgloves. In June 1936 sanctions over Abyssinia had been withdrawn and Italy's flagrant intervention in Spain ignored. Even sinkings of British ships in the Mediterranean, trading with Republican Spain, were put down to 'unknown' submarines. They were clearly Italian and in September 1937, following a conference in Nyons in France, joint British and French destroyer patrols put an end to the submarines. It was a rare show of force but throughout 1938 conciliation of Mussolini dominated government policy. The proposal to recognize

Italian Abyssinia drove Eden from the Cabinet in February 1938, a gesture on his part towards his League supporters. The closer Mussolini came to Hitler the more the Foreign Office sought to win his good offices to influence the greater menace.

In May 1937 Neville Chamberlain had become Prime Minister. As has already been made clear he did not invent appeasement. It already had a long history. In fact he had been the father of the rearmament programme, and in many ways Chamberlain was the supreme realist. He hated war every bit as much as Attlee and the Labour Party, but he had an ill-concealed contempt for their windy rhetoric. If peace could be preserved Chamberlain would seek to preserve it. At least peace could be preserved long enough for the British rearmament programme to give the Empire a chance of survival. His arrival at Number 10 gave a new clarity and direction to foreign policy which it had lacked under Baldwin and MacDonald. Chamberlain ruled his Cabinet with a rod of iron. He was not loved by his backbenchers but he was respected. The Labour Party returned his contempt with hatred. Chamberlain quickly asserted control over policy, with Vansittart, the Permanent Under-Secretary, being promoted to the meaningless post of Chief Diplomatic Adviser early in 1938, and Eden being replaced by the more malleable Viscount Halifax in February of that year. Like most dominant prime ministers of the twentieth century, Chamberlain often relied on his own personal advisers. Sir Horace Wilson, the government's chief industrial adviser, was the most important of these.

Chamberlain hoped to head off some sudden 'mad-cap' scheme by Hitler which would precipitate war. His hand was not strong enough and he knew it. He has often been criticized for not trying harder to entice the USA from her isolation, but most historians today would probably agree with Chamberlain's assessment that such an exercise was futile. He has also often been criticized for being too suspicious of Russia. Chamberlain, like most Conservatives, felt an intuitive dislike for the Bolshevik regime and saw no more virtue in Stalin than Hitler. He also saw the Soviet Union as enfeebled in view of its murderous purges of its own army in 1937 and 1938. The only hope seemed to lie in an energetic pursuit of that policy begun by Lloyd George: the satisfaction of Germany's legitimate grievances – appeasement. In November 1937 Halifax, not yet Foreign Secretary, visited Berlin and indicated that Britain would have no objection to Germany's peaceful settlement of her disputes with Poland and Czechoslovakia. Hitler's sudden improvised march into Austria in March 1938 was accepted. There was no French government on that day, thanks to one of the interminable ministerial crises of the French Republic. Italy had signed Austria away and Britain could do nothing. Austria was German-speaking and would have joined Germany in 1919 had she been allowed. Commonsense and morality dictated inaction.

The crisis over Czechoslovakia was less easily resolved. Within the new state were 3.2 million Germans living in the border region of the Sudetenland. To transfer these areas over to Germany in accordance with the principle of self-determination would end Czechoslovakia's viability as an independent state. Hitler intended to destroy this 'French aircraft carrier in the middle of Europe'. The timing, like so many of Hitler's moves, was fortuitous. The leader of the Germans in Sudetenland, Conrad Henlein, visited Hitler in March, and in April made a series of demands on the Czech government which added up to autonomy for the region. In May a misunderstanding led to the Czechs mobilizing, thinking that a German attack was imminent. No such attack was planned but Hitler was forced to admit this and thereby made to appear to suffer a defeat. He resolved on war and ordered his generals to prepare to smash the Czech state by the end of September. The resulting crisis led Chamberlain to seize the initiative and try to defuse the situation. France had a clear treaty with Czechoslovakia as did Russia. Hitler made a warlike speech on 12 September and there was rioting in the Sudeten German towns. Chamberlain courageously flew to meet Hitler at Berchtesgarden, taking the dictator completely by surprise. It was a diplomatic coup. Chamberlain agreed in principle to the transfer of the majority of the German-speaking area to the Reich, although he told the Führer that the French and his own Cabinet would have to agree. The Cabinet agreed on the 18th and the French a day later. The Czechs, after bitter arguments, had no alternative but to yield to Franco-British pressure and they also agreed on 21 September. The next day Chamberlain returned to Germany and met Hitler at Bad Godesberg to inform him of the success of his missions. Much to Chamberlain's fury Hitler upped his demands. He now wanted concessions to Hungary and Poland and immediate German occupation. On his return to London Chamberlain found more opposition in the Cabinet and from the French. War was possible. The fleet was mobilized on the 28th and the Czechs and the French began to call up reservists. In Germany Hitler's nerve nearly broke. The German people were sullenly hostile to war and unknown to the Führer some generals were actually planning a coup to remove their chief. Chamberlain, irritated by Hitler, was still unconvinced of either the value of fighting or the possibility of winning. Hitler reluctantly agreed to a suggestion from Mussolini for a conference in Munich to settle the question and avoid war. The Prime Minister gladly agreed to attend and announced his third visit to Germany to a cheering House of Commons. The result was a diplomatic victory for Hitler. Chamberlain and Daladier, the French premier, agreed to all the Bad Godesberg demands in return for a four power guarantee of the remaining state of Czechoslovakia. Daladier felt it was a necessary defeat, Chamberlain felt it was a victory. The cheering crowds that greeted his return marked the depth of horror felt by the British people at the prospect of war. The famous joint Anglo-German declaration of peaceful intent signed by Hitler and Chamberlain was a last-minute improvisation. It meant little to Hitler who strangely enough was much irritated by being robbed of his war and felt outmanoeuvred by Chamberlain. The British Prime Minister was a national hero. He carried his Cabinet with only one resignation and secured a massive endorsement from the House of Commons. Churchill's splendid speech of criticism had made little impact on the vote:

> We really must not waste time after all this long debate upon the difference between the positions reached at Berchtesgarden, at Godesberg, and at Munich. They can be very simply epitomised, if the House will permit me to vary the metaphor. £1 was demanded at the pistol's point. When it was given, £2 were demanded at the pistol's point. Finally, the Dictator consented to take £1 17s. 6d. and the rest in promises of good will for the future.
>
> All is over. Silent, mournful, abandoned, broken, Czechoslovakia recedes into the darkness. She has suffered in every respect by her associations with France, under whose guidance and policy she has been actuated for so long.
>
> (Churchill, op. cit., p. 256)

The great British public was grateful for a war averted. Not for them the purple passages of Churchill or the sarcasm of Vansittart's 'If at first you can't concede, then fly, fly and fly again.' For many the problem of Czechoslovakia was nothing to do with them.

Twelve months after the Munich meeting Britain and Germany were at war. It was a war over Poland in which traditionally Britain had little interest, and whose safety she had consistently refused to guarantee. A revolution had taken place in British foreign policy. There had been less of a change in German policy, although Hitler appears to have reached the conclusion that Britain must be counted amongst Germany's enemies. In January 1939 he ordered the implementation of the Z Plan – the creation of a large navy which would be able to challenge Britain by 1943. The navy was now to have priority over the army. Despite this, there was to be no seeking of confrontation with Britain in 1939. Instead Germany sought to tidy up the remnants of Czechoslovakia and to solve the Polish question by tying Poland to Germany's side as an anti-Bolshevik satellite.

A variety of circumstances and pressures transformed Chamberlain's policy. There seemed to be hope of greater support from the USA. President Roosevelt attacked the US Neutrality Act in a speech in January 1939. Private messages of support were sent out to Chamberlain from October 1938 onwards, as Roosevelt sought to stiffen British resistance to Hitler. How serious such support would be would depend on Congress but it was heartening, none the less. There was also a new self-confidence over British defences by early 1939. The Industrial Intelligence Committee run by Desmond Morton predicted in February 1939 that British aircraft production would overtake that of Germany later in the year. The new British monoplanes would be equal or superior to those of Germany, and radar, just coming into service, might prevent the bomber from getting through. Much intelligence information also indicated that the German economy was in serious trouble with the extensive German rearmament programme and that it could not sustain a long war. The decision was also taken in February massively to extend Britain's defence spending and to abandon limited liability. The Cabinet had reached the conclusion that France, now deprived of the thirty-five divisions of the Czech army, would need what Britain had so long refused to contemplate: an 'effort of blood' on Britain's part. It was resolved to create a continental army of thirty-two divisions, doubling the territorial army. As the defence expenditure shown in Table 8.5 indicates this required a huge rise in spending on the army. Britain in effect had decided to rearm, regardless of the cost and the strain it put on her economy. In part these changes were a product of a flood of intelligence information from Germany of plans for a dramatic, sudden blow at Holland or France. In response to this the British government at long last made a clear-cut military commitment to France and began serious Chief of Staff talks. It was also resolved to fight in the event of any German moves against Holland, Belgium or Switzerland.

There was thus already a new spirit abroad in London before the events of 15 March when Hitler broke the Munich Agreement by marching into Prague. Czechoslovakia was the first non-German state to be seized. Bohemia was declared a German Protectorate. The next day Chamberlain in a speech in Birmingham delivered his strongest warning yet to Germany:

> The events which have taken place this week in complete disregard of the principles laid down by the German government itself seem to fall into a different category, and they must cause us all to be asking ourselves: 'Is this the end of an old adventure, or is it the beginning of a new? Is this the last attack upon a small State, or is it to be followed by others? Is this, in fact, a step in the direction of an attempt to dominate the world by force? . . . No greater mistake could be made than to suppose that, because it believes war to be a senseless and cruel thing, this nation has so lost its fibre that it will not take part to the utmost of its power in resisting such a challenge if it ever were made.
>
> (Quoted in P. Bell, *The Origins of the Second World War*, London, Longman, 1978, p. 252)

The Cabinet, and in particular the Foreign Secretary Lord Halifax, felt that it was a vital signal to Germany that she must go no further.

However, more than speeches would be required to convince Hitler, and a complete reversal of policy ensued in a bid to signal effectively to the Third Reich. It was this sudden reversal of policy that produced war in September 1939. The signalling to Hitler failed. His reaction was that of a high-stake poker player to what he believed was a bluff. Possibly it was a bluff on Chamberlain's part as he was still clinging desperately to a belief in the necessity of peace, but public opinion swung increasingly to demand a firm line with Hitler. Newspapers which had distanced themselves from European events in 1938 now expressed outrage. As in January and May 1938 rumours of German aggression now influenced events. It came to be widely believed in London that a German move to seize Romania was contemplated for October. This belatedly led the British Cabinet to take up the 1934 Barthou scheme of an Eastern Locarno. Britain would now guarantee the eastern European settlement, something it had refused to do since 1919.

As yet Hitler appears to have had no fixed plans. Negotiations were begun with the Poles on 21 March for the resolution of the Germans' claims. Hitler appears to have hoped for the peaceful return of Danzig which was essentially a German city. Once again rumour translated these into German plans for smashing Poland. In reality anti-Nazi forces in Germany were feeding British intelligence with warnings in the hope of stiffening resistance to Hitler. Britain reacted quickly to this fresh threat and on 31 March Chamberlain made a public declaration of support for Poland. Britain would fight if Poland was attacked. In many senses this was disastrous because, for one, Britain could not aid Poland. By her guarantee she encouraged the Poles to be more inflexible with Hitler and so induced Hitler to call Britain's bluff. On 1 April Hitler ordered plans to be prepared for an attack on Poland by 1 September.

Italy now added to the tension by landing troops in Albania. The results were Anglo-French guarantees to Greece and Romania, on 13 April, followed ten days later by the announcement of conscription in Britain. The one action which could have deterred Hitler was a clear military alliance with Russia, a belated return to the Triple Entente of 1914. For years Russia had been angling for this. The pro-western Russian Foreign Minister, Litvinov, had been repeatedly snubbed and Russia had been pointedly ignored at Munich. The British government was suspicious of Bolshevik Russia and regarded it with an even greater moral repugnance than it did Nazi Germany. It is worth recalling that by 1939 the blood spilt by Hitler was a puddle compared to the oceans that were Stalin's responsibility. The British Chiefs of Staff were also dubious about Russia's military capability after the purges in the Red Army. Reluctantly Britain began to explore the possibility of a deal with the Soviet ogre. It was already dangerously late. On 3 May Litvinov was replaced by the anti-western Molotov. It was not until the end of July that Britain agreed to military talks and in a leisurely and unconvincing fashion a low-level delegation reached Russia in August. The French were desperate for agreement; not so Britain. Admiral Reginald Aylmer Ranfurly Plunket Ernle-Erle-Drax travelled by ship rather than plane and had no proper accreditation on arrival. Negotiations with Marshal Vorashilov became a farce, finally breaking down over the Polish refusal to allow Russian troops to enter Poland before a German attack. On 23 August the diplomatic bombshell of the Nazi–Soviet pact burst upon Europe. Russia and Germany had signed a non-aggression pact and secretly decided to partition Poland. Hitler's demands for Danzig and transit rights across the Polish Corridor had been refused by Poland. Hitler was now determined to have war and take much more than his original demands. On 1 September German tanks and aircraft struck. Hitler had called Britain's bluff. Even now Chamberlain delayed in sending an ultimatum to Germany. His speech to the House of Commons on 2 September seemed indecisive and left the way open for the climb-down that Hitler expected. The House was impatient and as Arthur Greenwood rose with the words 'Speaking for the Labour Party', the famous shout was heard 'Speak for England.' Commons and Cabinet demanded action. That night the Cabinet resolved to present an ulti-matum to Germany the next morning demanding withdrawal from Poland. As Chamberlain concluded with the words 'this means war', a clap of thunder echoed around Downing Street and lightning lit up the Cabinet Room. War came the next day, 3 September 1939 at 11 o'clock, a Sunday, the very hour the last terrible conflict had ended.

THE SECOND WORLD WAR 1939–45

Britain's position in 1939 *vis-à-vis* Germany was almost in every way weaker than it had been in 1914. The new British Expeditionary Force that had crossed to France in 1939 was the inferior to its predecessor. It was initially smaller and arrived later. It was also less effective as a fighting unit. Two years of muddled planning and a sudden decision for breakneck expansion was not a recipe for success. The British had first developed the tank and the early theorists of its use, General Fuller and Basil Liddell-Hart, were also British. By 1939 however the initiative in tank warfare had passed to the *Wehrmacht* that already had six panzer divisions in existence. Britain trailed badly in armoured warfare and was never to match the Germans throughout the six years of combat. The decision to turn cavalry regiments into tank units gave British armoured formations dash but also many of the weaknesses of these ancient darlings of the British army. The British navy was certainly superior in size to that of Germany but most of the battleships were old and, ship for ship, inferior. Britain had developed aircraft carriers ahead of anyone else but by 1939 she was seriously inferior to the Japanese in this key branch of naval warfare. British carriers still relied on the Fairey Swordfish torpedo bomber. If the navy was going to have to fight Germany, Japan and Italy it would be in serious trouble. Only the airforce appeared to give ground for confidence in 1939. By 1940 British aircraft production would surpass that of Germany's, and the new monoplane fighters and new generation of bombers provided for by the expansion programme of 1938–9 would be the equal or superior of anything possessed by Britain's enemies. In the meantime Germany still enjoyed a considerable superiority in aircraft and her use of dive bombers to provide the *Wehrmacht* with fast-moving artillery was unrivalled by anything Britain possessed. Nor could much comfort be drawn from support abroad. Russia, a British ally in 1914, was now friendly with Germany and, if not her ally, she was a willing supplier of materials. There would be no eastern front to relieve pressure on the west. France was not the fighting force she had been. Her army was large but antiquated in equipment and training but most seriously of all obsessed by defence and the so-called 'Maginot spirit'. Frenchmen were not going to die as they had done in 1914. France would wait for the British. There was little prospect in 1939 of US participation. Furthermore the Neutrality Acts remained in force. Unlike in the First World War the USA could not be a source of munitions on tick.

Perhaps more important than any of these military and diplomatic weaknesses was a fundamental economic weakness. Despite the economic recovery of the 1930s the British economy's relative decline had continued. In 1914 Britain had possessed 13.6 per cent of the world's manufacturing capacity but by 1938 it had fallen to between 9 and 10 per cent. Of even deeper concern was the financial weakness of the country. Throughout the inter-war years the collapse of exports had created a balance of payments crisis. How was Britain to pay for the war? Her gold and international currency reserves were at a relatively much lower level than they had been in 1914. In March of 1939 the Treasury pointed out the danger of the enlarged armaments programme. War itself presented the country with the prospect of bankruptcy by 1941. Perhaps Chamberlain had been right to resist conflict on an economic basis alone.

In reality there was little conflict for the first ten months of the war. There was to be no Mons or Le Cateau and no retreat to the Marne. The BEF took up its station in France and slowly expanded to ten divisions by May 1940. No shots were fired, no bombs were dropped. Hitler's forces quickly conquered Poland without British or French interference. Leaflets were dropped over Germany proclaiming their wickedness but nothing more terrible. In the words of one American correspondent it was the 'Phoney War'. A naval blockade was imposed but with access (thanks to her August pact) to Russian raw materials Germany was less seriously affected than she had been in 1914–18. Only at sea were there occasional flurries of drama. A U-boat penetrated the defences of Scapa Flow and sank the battleship *Royal Oak* in October

1939. In December the German pocket-battleship, the *Admiral Graf Spee*, was caught by a force of three smaller British ships and scuttled off the River Plate estuary in South America. It was a heartening Christmas present for the British people but of no great consequence.

On 30 November 1939 Russia suddenly declared war on Finland. The previous month not only had Poland been occupied but the three Baltic states of Latvia, Lithuania and Estonia had been forced to accept Soviet garrisons. Stalin had, in effect, restored the frontiers of tsarist Russia. Russia sought to safeguard Leningrad with an exchange of territory with Finland. The Finns refused and in the ensuing conflict gave the Red Army a very bloody nose. Anti-Bolshevik feeling in Britain and France heightened and the Allies proposed in January 1940 to send an expeditionary force to help the Finns. This decision to take on the Russians as well as Germany now appears as military lunacy. Finnish resistance collapsed before the Allies could move and Stalin offered a modest peace which the Finns accepted. The effects of the Baltic war were to draw the Allies' and German eyes northwards to Scandinavia. The iron ore of Sweden was vital to the German war effort and the Allies had hoped to cut the supply as a by-product of a Finnish campaign. They now planned to mine the Norwegian coastal route to Germany to achieve the same end. Hitler struck first and so ended the 'Phoney War'.

On 9 April Denmark was occupied and in a lightning campaign of great boldness Norway was seized by the German army from under the nose of the British navy. The campaign revealed the superiority of the *Wehrmacht*, the appalling incompetence of many British units and, most worrying of all, the fact that air power could negate naval supremacy. Churchill, who was invited by Chamberlain to become First Lord of the Admiralty at the outbreak of war, seems to have totally failed to appreciate the impact of air power. The only allied gain from the whole campaign was the massive damage done to the German navy particularly at Narvik Fiord where the heroic feats of the Royal Navy saw the destruction of ten destroyers. The consequences of these losses were to be felt two months later when Germany began to contemplate the invasion of Britain.

The Norwegian campaign had one other consequence of importance for British survival. On 10 May Churchill replaced Chamberlain as Prime Minister. The muddles of the campaign produced one of the great parliamentary occasions in British history, a two-day debate beginning on 7 May 1940. It was one of those rare political crises when the Commons asserted itself. Much of the most serious damage was not done by Labour opposition but by Conservative rebels. Leo Amery made a celebrated speech ending with the famous words Cromwell had used in 1653: 'You have sat here too long for any good you have been doing. Depart I say and let us have done with you. In the name of God, go.' Lloyd George made his last really effective performance in the House on 8 May:

Sir Winston Churchill, 1941. Photograph: Walter Stoneman

> He [Chamberlain] has appealed for sacrifice. The nation is prepared for every sacrifice provided it has leadership. . . . I say solemnly that the Prime Minister should give an example of sacrifice, because there is nothing which can contribute to victory in this war than that he should sacrifice the seals of office.

On the vote of confidence the usual government majority of over 200 fell to 81. Thirty-three Conservatives voted with the opposition and large numbers abstained. Labour refused to serve under Chamberlain who now resolved to resign. The alternatives were Halifax and Churchill. Halifax was the favourite with the King and the senior figures of both parties but he was a peer. Churchill refused to say whether he would serve under Halifax. Chamberlain advised the King to settle for Churchill who became Prime Minister aged 64 on 10 May.

On the same day one of the most brilliant and breath-taking of military campaigns opened when the German armies swept into Holland and

Belgium. It seemed to the Allies like a re-run of 1914 and the Schlieffen Plan and in response the BEF and the best part of the French army moved north into Belgium to meet the Germans and ensure that this time the line of trenches was not on French soil. In fact the key German attack came through the Ardennes which the French General Staff thought impenetrable. Seven of the ten German armoured divisions pushed their way slowly to the River Meuse on the French border. On meeting some of the weakest French formations they crossed at Sedan and then broke out and overran the plains of northern France behind the main French armies and the BEF. This crossing of the Meuse on 13 May was a disaster for the Allies. The German aircraft roamed the skies and the Stuka dive-bombers provided artillery for the fast-moving panzer divisions. Here was the perfect example of *blitzkrieg* – the warfare theorized by British writers two decades earlier. By 20 May the Channel was reached and the BEF and thirty French divisions were trapped. Lord Gort, the commander of the British Forces, decided to try and escape with his men via the port of Dunkirk rather than fight his way out to the south. His decision saved the BEF but abandoned France. The heroic fighting of the French First Army around Lille enabled the BEF to escape between 26 May and 4 June. In all, 224,000 British and 95,000 French troops escaped to Britain to fight another day. It was a terrible defeat yet it was an unlooked-for deliverance. The rest of France was rapidly overrun. On 14 June the Germans entered Paris and Italy had declared her entry into the war three days earlier. On 22 June France agreed to surrender. Standing up to Hitler appeared to be a dreadful error. The battle of France was lost.

The new British government resolved to fight on. There was little hope of victory and it must appear as one of the strangest decisions. Hitler had an unbeatable army, a powerful and menacing airforce and now the resources of the Continent to call on. Churchill had the navy, Spitfires backed by radar, and rhetoric. It looked and was an unequal contest. Yet the rhetoric is some of the finest in the English language, its impact today sadly weakened by over-repetition. Churchill's words still deserve attention. As the German tanks crossed the Meuse on 13 May he announced his programme to the House of Commons:

> You ask, What is our policy? I will say: it is to wage war, by sea, land and air, with all our might and with all the strength that God can give us: to wage war against a monstrous tyranny, never surpassed in the dark, lamentable catalogue of human crime. That is our policy. You ask, what is our aim? I can answer in one word: Victory – victory at all costs, victory in spite of all terror, victory, however long and hard the road may be; for without victory there is no survival.

A month later in the deep gloom of defeat he made the speech that echoes down the years:

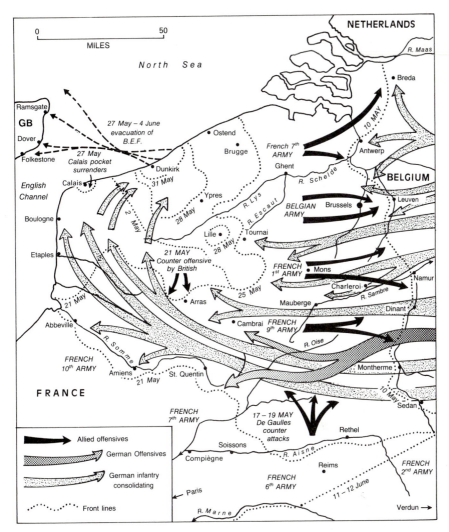

8.5 The fall of France 1940

What General Weygand called the Battle of France is over. I expect that the Battle of Britain is about to begin. . . . Let us therefore brace ourselves to our duties, and so bear ourselves that, if the British Empire and its Commonwealth last for a thousand years, men will still say: 'This was their finest hour.'

Like the Battle of Waterloo the Battle of Britain was a 'close run thing'. Just over 700 Me 109s with a further 227 Me 110s faced 650 Hurricanes and Spitfires in a duel for the command of the air. Without air supremacy no invasion of Britain was possible; with it, it might not be necessary. As well as excellent fighters, the technological equal of

Germany's, Britain possessed radar and ultra. Both gave invaluable intelligence information. Radar warned of an approach and ultra, a guarded secret until 1974, increasingly enabled Britain to read secret German signals and know their detailed plans. Despite these advantages the Germans nearly won. By the end of August severe damage had been done by German bombers to British fighter bases in the south-east of England and this continued into the first week in September. Barges were being assembled at Boulogne for invasion and on the 7th an invasion alert was ordered. That very day the Germans made a vital mistake. Huge waves of bombers appeared but instead of making for the battered airfields they headed for London, and began the task of flattening the capital. The *Luftwaffe* was unprepared for such a task and its bombs and bombers were simply too small. The RAF was given a respite. On 15 September a massive raid was broken up with the loss of sixty German aircraft. Two days later Hitler postponed plans for the invasion until further notice. In October it was put off until 1941 and in January 1941 put off indefinitely. Britain had won its battle and survived.

In November, Field Marshal Goering, head of the *Luftwaffe*, ordered concentrated night-time bombing of Britain's ports and industrial centres. On 14 November Coventry was particularly badly hit and from then until May 1941 the drone of aircraft spelled a frightening sleepless night for the inhabitants of Britain's cities. It ended in May 1941 when the bulk of the German airforce was moved east to assault Russia. This 'Blitz' had caused the death of 30,000 civilians but it was irrelevant to the outcome of the war. Morale was not broken and wartime aircraft production continued to rise. The Blitz also excited the sympathy and support of the USA which now became increasingly vital to Britain's continued war effort. In November 1939 Roosevelt had persuaded Congress to amend the Neutrality Acts to allow arms sales to Britain and France on a cash-and-carry basis. Until his re-election for a third term in November 1940 Roosevelt had to move cautiously in the face of isolationist critics. His ambassador to Britain, Joseph Kennedy, was not optimistic about Britain's chances in the summer and autumn of 1940. Yet the clear resolution to carry on the war was shown in the determined way in which Britain crippled the French fleet at Oran in July 1940 to prevent it falling into German hands. Roosevelt believed that every aid possible should be given in the fight against Hitler's Germany. In September came the exchange of fifty old US destroyers for bases in the West Indies and, following his successful election, Lend-Lease. Congress finally approved this in March 1941 and Britain could now shop on credit. It averted bankruptcy and gave the United Kingdom $750 million worth of arms in 1941 alone. The worrying long-term implications of becoming simply the sword of the United States whilst British exports and the domestic economy crumbled were disregarded. Churchill was pursuing victory 'whatever the cost'. As chapter 11 indicates Britain in many ways became far more committed to total war than Germany and her citizens had greater burdens of taxation and cuts in consumer goods. By 1944 Germany was still producing consumer goods at 85 per cent of the rate of 1939. In Britain it was 54 per cent.

Despite the sacrifices, the increasing US help and the rising arms production there was little that Britain could do to defeat Germany directly. Survival remained a first priority and if direct attack on the homeland and the threat of invasion receded after the spring of 1941 there was still the menace of the U-boat. Food and raw materials were essential for national survival and without control of the Atlantic the 'Arsenal of Democracy', as Roosevelt christened the USA, could not help Britain. The battle for control of the sea lanes to Britain was more deadly than any of the attrition conflicts of the First World War. Out of 145,000 merchant seamen 32,000 died. All were civilian volunteers yet they suffered a casualty rate higher than that of the services. A third of British merchant shipping was sunk and at various points between 1940 and 1943 starvation and defeat seemed possible. But the German U-boat crews suffered an even worse attrition rate with 785 out of 1,162 German submarines lost. The German naval command reckoned that they needed to sink 700,000 tons a month to blockade Britain. Nearly 4 million tons were sunk in 1940 and over 4 million in 1941. In 1942 it reached 7 million tons and by the end of the year 200 U-boats were operational compared to only 46 in the spring of 1940. In March 1943 sinkings almost reached the 700,000 tons target. It was the worst month of the war.

Convoys and depth charges were not enough in this war to deal with the submarine menace. There was a shortage of escort vessels, although this was partly remedied by increasing US assistance in 1941. Aircraft were found to be particularly valuable in spotting U-boats and attacking them but here again there was a shortage, leaving a vital gap in the mid-Atlantic until April 1943 when long-range Liberators closed it and escort carriers became more frequent. British science and technology also made a vital contribution. The development of the centimetric radar enabled allied planes to detect and attack U-boats without their prior knowledge. Its widespread application inflicted heavy German casualties. Ultra and the breaking of the German codes proved particularly vital. The capture of U110 on 8 May 1941 with its enigma machine and codes intact enabled Britain to crack the German naval code which, unlike those of the other two German services, had eluded British cryptographers. This produced an immediate drop in sinkings and the destruction of German supply ships which could keep U-boats and surface raiders at sea. The Germans changed their code in February 1942 but again it was cracked in December and, following another change in March, rapidly cracked once more. In May 1943 Doenitz, the U-boat commander-in-chief, confessed failure as the number of U-boat losses rose massively. The battle of the Atlantic had also been won.

Wars, however, are not won merely by surviving attacks and since Britain could not seriously think of invading Europe, her only way of striking at Germany was through the expanding British bomber force. Unlike the *Luftwaffe*, the RAF had long been committed to the plan of a strategic air offensive but until 1942–3 the necessary heavy bombers, in the form of Halifaxes and Lancasters, were not there. Britain had attempted, as Germany had done in 1940, to inflict destruction with medium bombers. Although strategic targets were selected the bombing became indiscriminate terror bombing. An enquiry of 1941 revealed that only 30 per cent came within five miles of their target and this fell to only 10 per cent in the heavily industrialized Ruhr. As the new heavy bombers, laid down in the 1939–40 rearmament programme, became ready in 1942–3, a massive intensification of the strategic air offensive in Germany could take place. The mastermind, appointed in 1942, behind the British bombing offensive was Air Chief Marshal Sir Arthur Harris. Since accurate day-time bombing was too dangerous and accurate night-time bombing impossible, even with improved navigational aids, the inevitable option was mass area terror bombing. The first 1,000-strong bomber raid on Cologne in May 1942 was largely carried out by the old medium bombers but it was a foretaste of what was to come. The Ruhr was hit repeatedly in 1943, and then Hamburg and increasingly Berlin. In Hamburg alone 50,000 people were killed. The US 8th Airforce with its Flying Fortresses struck by day, convinced that accurate day-time bombing was possible if the bombers were armed heavily enough. On 14 October 1943 the Americans attacked the crucial ball-bearing factory at Schwenfurt and did great damage, but the losses suffered were prohibitive with 60 out of 291 planes lost. In the same year the famous 617 Squadron of Wing-Commander Guy Gibson showed that accurate bombing was possible when he destroyed the Moehne and Eder dams on the Ruhr. But again the losses were staggering with 8 out of 19 Lancasters lost. Even night-time area bombing became more and more costly and by March 1944 the *Luftwaffe* was winning the battle for the control of German airspace. Between November 1943 and March 1944 over a thousand British bombers were lost. Long-range escort fighters were the answer and the Americans produced one in the P51B Mustang, the ultimate fighter of the war. After an intermission in spring and summer 1944 to assist the Normandy landings, both Bomber Command and the US 8th Airforce renewed their assault. This time the devastation was beyond question, and also beyond question was its effects in destroying the German war-machine. By January 1945 production of aviation fuel in Germany had dropped to 11,000 tons. In May 1944 it had been 156,000 tons.

Controversy still surrounds the strategic bombing offensive. Could it be morally justified and was it worth it? It clearly fell short of the claims of its original backers that it would break German morale, and up to

Table 8.5 Bomber production and bomb tonnages delivered 1940–5

| | Germany | | Britain and America† | |
	Bombers	*Bomb tonnage* on UK*	*Bombers*	*Bomb tonnage on Europe*
1940	2,852	36,844	3,529	14,631
1941	3,373	21,858	4,668	35,509
1942	4,502	3,260	18,880	53,755
1943	4,789	2,298	37,083	226,513
1944	1,982	9,151	42,906	1,188,577
1945	–	761	23,554	477,051
	17,498	74,172	130,620	1,996,036

* including V-weapons
† American figures included only for 1942–5
Source: R. Overy, *The Air War*, London, Europa Publications, 1980, p. 120.

1944 it did not prevent the growth of German military production. Yet it did produce a massive switch of German resources to deal with it. By 1944 two million people in the Third Reich were engaged in anti-aircraft defence and 30 per cent of gun output and 20 per cent of heavy ammunition was devoted to the same end. The conclusion of Overy, one of Britain's leading historians on the subject is:

> But bombing was much more effective than the Allies believed. The important consequence of the bombing was not that it failed to stem the increase in arms production, but that it prevented the increase from being very considerably greater than it was. Bombing placed a ceiling on German war production which was well below what Germany, with skilful and more urgent management of its resources, was capable of producing after 1943.
>
> (ibid., p. 123)

In many ways strategic bombing was the Second World War's version of the war of attrition. If British generals and politicians congratulated themselves on avoiding a repetition of the Somme such avoidance was not obvious to the young men of Bomber Command, 55,573 of whom died.

From when the BEF left France in June 1940 to that memorable day exactly four years later when they re-entered western Europe, the British army engaged only in side-shows against the *Wehrmacht*. Italy's entry into the war opened up the sort of diversionary front much beloved by Churchill. The war in the Mediterranean absorbed most of Britain's attention and resources from 1940 to 1944. It certainly did not absorb the attention and resources of Germany. In the bleak autumn days of 1940 victories over the Italians did much to hearten the British public. Half of the Italian fleet was knocked out for the loss of two Swordfish torpedo bombers in a daring raid on Taranto in November 1940. The Japanese took note of the battle. A lumbering Italian army began to advance from Libya into Egypt. A daring British counter-attack with massively inferior forces was launched under General O'Connor. By February 1941 125,000 Italian prisoners had been taken and the whole of North Africa was within Britain's grasp. Unfortunately that month two events ensured that this would not happen for another two years. Hitler dispatched Erwin Rommel with a small armoured force to North Africa to prop up the Italians and Britain diverted 50,000 men to Greece to help stem the German invasion of the Balkans. The scenes witnessed at Dunkirk and in Norway were repeated yet again with the navy rescuing the army in April 1941. In North Africa Rommel did not wait either for reinforcements or orders but launched an attack which threw the British back to the Egyptian border. Only the conquest of the Italian East African Empire of Eritrea and Ethiopia by May 1941 offered any compensation.

Ultimate British defeat must have been inevitable had Hitler not made two decisions in 1941. The first was to attack Russia in June and had even a fraction of the 200 German divisions used there been sent to the Mediterranean, Rommel would have chased the British from the Middle East. The other, almost incomprehensible decision by the Führer, was to declare war on the United States in December 1941, following the Japanese attack on Pearl Harbor. This enabled Roosevelt to direct US efforts to defeating what he and the US Chiefs of Staff regarded as the more dangerous enemy: Germany. Churchill's assessment of the situation was surely correct: 'Hitler's fate was sealed. Mussolini's fate was sealed. As for the Japanese they would be ground to powder. All the rest was merely the proper application of overwhelming force.' It would take time for this 'overwhelming force' to be applied and 1942 contained more than a smattering of disasters. In North Africa, despite reinforcements of tanks and planes, the British 8th Army was out-fought and out-generalled by Rommel's Afrika Korps. In June the British garrison at Tobruk capitulated and 35,000 marched into captivity. In the Far East, even more humiliating defeats afflicted the British Empire as the Japanese launched a tide of conquests which threatened to sweep British power away. Hong Kong was indefensible and fell on Christmas Day 1941 after heroic resistance. This could not be said of Singapore which in theory was the linchpin of Britain's position in the Far East. The British army in Malaya was out-fought in humiliating fashion losing 25,000, mainly as prisoners, for the loss of 4,600 Japanese troops. Singapore's fall on 15 February was a military disaster and disgrace unparalleled in British history. General Percival with 85,000 men surrendered to the inferior forces of General Yamashita. The Japanese then successfully bundled the British out of Burma and reached the Indian frontier, the limit of their advance. It had been a brilliant offensive carried out

Table 8.6 Comparative balance of resources 1938

	Population (millions)	Total labour force (millions)	% of world manufacturing*
Allied powers			
USA	141.9	52.8 (1940)	32.2
USSR	170.4	70.0	18.5
UK	47.6	22.9 (1939)	9.2
Total	359.9	145.7	59.9
Axis powers			
Germany	79.2†	36.2 (1939)	10.7
Italy	43.4	21.0 (1936)	2.7
Japan	72.8	34.1 (1940)	3.5
Total	195.4	91.3	16.9

Production	Steel (m. tons)	Coal (m. tons)	Electricity (mrd. kWh)	Motor vehicles
Allied powers				
USA	28.8	354.5	116.6	2,489,085
USSR	18.0	132.9	39.4	200,000
UK	10.5	230.7	25.7	447,561
Total	57.3	718.1	181.7	3,136,646
Axis powers				
Germany†	23.3	186.2	58.3	340,719
Italy	2.3	1.9	15.5	70,777
Japan	5.8‡	53.0‡	35 (1939)	32,744
Total	31.4	241.1	108.8	444,240

* 1936–8 average
† Including Austria
‡ Figure for steel is 1937; that for coal is an estimate for 1938

with limited forces. The oil-rich Dutch East Indies (Indonesia), the object of the attack, was now in Japanese possession. It would take the British and Americans three years to push Japan back.

Despite the reverses of 1941 and 1942, Churchill's hold on power and his control of the generals was much firmer than Lloyd George's had been in the First World War. He did not make Lloyd George's mistake of trying to be Prime Minister without the Party leadership and when Chamberlain died late in 1940 he had himself elected as leader of the Conservative Party. Attlee served him loyally as deputy Prime Minister and the powerful figure of Ernest Bevin guaranteed the loyalty of the trade unions. General Sir Alan Brooke became Chief of the Imperial General Staff in December 1941 and worked with great skill to execute Churchill's better ideas and head off his more lunatic ones, of which there

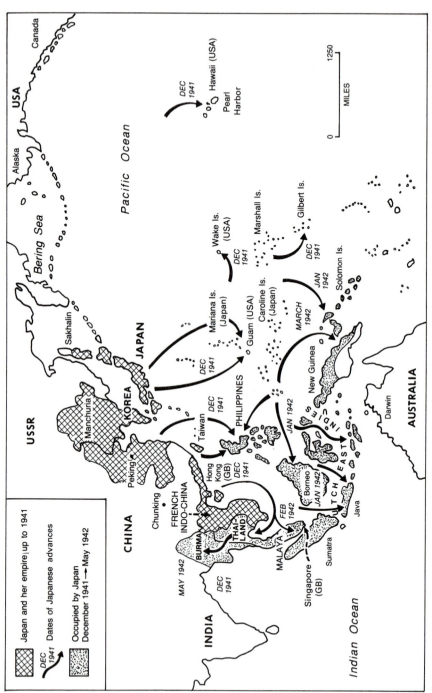

8.6 The war in the Pacific

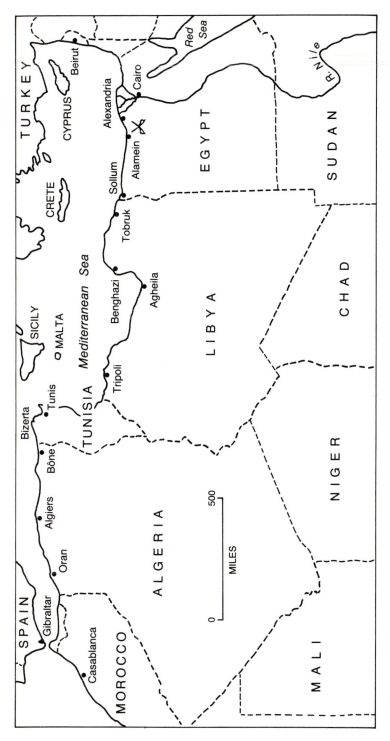

8.7 The war in North Africa

were many. In 1942 there was something of an upsurge of discontent with his leadership but minor Cabinet reshuffles saw off the mutterings and a vote of no confidence in July was defeated 475 to 25.

In the course of 1942 the tide turned and the proper application of overwhelming force slowly began to have its effect. With successive victories Churchill's position became impregnable. Churchill's new team in North Africa, Generals Alexander and Montgomery, won a decisive victory over the Afrika Korps at the end of October and early November 1942. Faced with six times as many tanks and overpowering superiority in the air, Rommel retreated from El Alamein, defeated after a hard struggle. Four German divisions were involved, compared to the 200 divisions fighting the Russians. Four days after Rommel began his long retreat, Anglo-American forces landed in Algiers to complete the conquest of North Africa. The Germans retreated to Tunisia where after a futile and mistaken reinforcement they surrendered in June 1943.

There was strong pressure from the hard-pressed Russians and many US generals for a direct invasion of France in 1943. A second front might end the war quickly. Churchill and his advisers met Roosevelt at Casablanca in January 1943 to decide future strategies. British nervousness triumphed and it was decided to put off until 1944 the opening of the second front. In the meantime the British Mediterranean strategy would be followed. Following the surrender of the German and Italian forces in Tunis came the successful invasion of Sicily in July. The same month saw Mussolini overthrown and in September the new Italian government asked for an armistice and tried to join the Allies. The Germans moved quickly and occupied most of Italy. Naples was captured by the Allies in October, but the Germans established a firm defensive line south of Rome which prevented further advance. Rome did not fall until June 1944 by which time the long-awaited second front had opened.

Throughout 1943 and early 1944 there was a vast build-up of resources in Britain. She was an unsinkable aircraft carrier anchored off the coast of Europe, from which the overwhelming force of the USA could be applied to storm Hitler's fortress Europe. Britain was increasingly the junior partner in the alliance as indicated by the selection of the American General Eisenhower to command the landings. The final assault on Normandy, codenamed Operation Overlord, was a triumph of meticulous planning and economic muscle. Total control of the sea enabled 5,000 ships to cross the Channel unhindered. The *Luftwaffe* was driven from the skies as more than 12,000 allied planes faced 500 German ones. Elaborate deception plans kept a vital part of the *Wehrmacht* in the Pas de Calais in the north of France, awaiting what Hitler was convinced was the real invasion. In two days 185,000 men and 19,000 vehicles were landed. By the end of the Battle for Normandy 1.2 million Americans and 850,000 British and Canadian troops had been put ashore. The British engaged the bulk of the German forces around Caen in a long slogging battle of attrition. The Americans broke out near Avranches at the end of July and in a vast sweep trapped much of the German army in the Falaise Pocket. France was then rapidly liberated. The German forces in the west collapsed and occupied Paris fell on 25 August. In September the Allies had a 25:1 superiority in aircraft and a 20:1 superiority in tanks. The application of overwhelming force had triumphed. To many it seemed that the war could end in 1944. The American General Patten raced east to Alsace until shortages of petrol brought him to a halt. The British advanced north into Belgium, liberating Brussels on 3 September. The supply facilities at Antwerp were vital and delay in opening up the port and the River Scheldt postponed further advance. The German forces in the west had time to re-group and the opportunity for victory that autumn evaporated. On 16 September General Montgomery established a small bridgehead over the Rhine at Arnhem using airborne troops. It turned into a military disaster as ground forces could not reach them before they were overwhelmed by a panzer division brought up unexpectedly to rest.

Much to the surprise of the Allies the Germans chose to use their scant resources in an aggressive stroke through the Ardennes, a repetition, in very different circumstances, of the attack in 1940. It met with initial success against the Americans in that area but the *Wehrmacht* lost a further 120,000 men. Final defeat was to come rapidly in the spring of 1945 but the British people were now thoroughly weary too, and the previous year had produced an unpleasant shock for the inhabitants of London and the south-east. The launching of Hitler's new terror weapon the V1, and later V2, rockets had produced an impact out of all proportions to casualties. It was lucky these rockets had come so late and their launch sites could be overrun by the advancing allied armies.

On the frontiers of the Third Reich enormous Soviet armies covered eastern Europe like some vast glacier and pushed the *Wehrmacht* back to its heartland. Churchill and Roosevelt had met Stalin at Teheran in December 1943 when the prospect of dismembering and deindustrializing Germany had been considered. In October 1944 Churchill had flown to Moscow and discussed the future of eastern Europe. Bulgaria and Romania would be Russian and Greece British. In February 1945, at Yalta in the Crimea, the three leaders met for a second time to settle the future. Roosevelt was dying but insisted on getting Russian membership of the new United Nations organization, and also a Russian declaration of war on Japan. He secured promises on both counts but Poland was abandoned to the Russian glacier. It was not to melt for another forty-five years. Germany was to be divided into American, Russian and British zones of occupation. If the western Allies chose to give the French a share of theirs that was their affair. All three of the allied powers would occupy a part of Berlin even though the city would lie behind the western halt-line and therefore be in the Russian zone. The future of Europe was set in Soviet ice.

The terms of Yalta were rapidly executed in the spring of 1945. The German armies in the west collapsed. The Americans seized an unblown bridge at Remegan and pushed rapidly into south Germany. The British moved north and on Lüneberg Heath Montgomery had the distinction of taking the surrender of the German forces on 4 May, although the war officially ended four days later. In the Far East the end came more quickly than expected largely as a result of US activity. The British army managed to recover some of its lost pride in a final victorious offensive in Burma under General Sir William Slim. But, before Singapore could be re-taken the Japanese surrendered. Fearful conventional saturation bombing by the US brought no submission and finally two atomic bombs made even the most heroic of Japanese accept the inevitability of defeat. On 2 September 1945 the Second World War ended.

ASSESSMENT

The division and occupation of Germany in 1945 appeared to have solved the German question. If not quite the extreme solution proposed at Teheran it looked like giving security to eastern and western Europe for many years. The price for the Continent, apart from the immediate devastation, was the occupation of eastern Europe by the Red Army. Poland had been saved from the SS but handed over to the KGB. Democracy had triumphed in western Europe where it had always been strongest but a despotism, no less antiquated for being decorated with a red star, now entrenched itself in the east. The horrific scenes that greeted allied troops as they liberated German concentration camps, no less than the cheering crowds in Belgium and France, all seemed to point to the war as a crusade of liberty against evil. And so it was in the west. In the east, however, one monstrous tyranny had replaced another as the one eastern European democracy, Czechoslovakia, came to realize.

Perhaps Britain had much to be proud of. Her physical suffering had been less than most combatants yet she sacrificed a great deal. She had fought for six years not because she was attacked like the Americans and Russians but in defence of international law and her honour. Perhaps also she fought for freedom. She was no longer *the* world power. Congress in Washington, not the Commons at Westminster, was now the most vital forum of political debate. The British fleet ceased to be the largest in the world in 1944. The Far Eastern Empire could not survive the shock of the Japanese victories. The troops of the Mikado had defeated those of the king emperor. Yellow men had beaten white men. The collapse from world power to European off-shore island would be very rapid. Britain's exports in 1945 stood at only 30 per cent of their 1938 total and without continued American assistance her people would have faced unbelievable hardship. The war for Danzig, set in motion by Hitler, ended with Danzig in Russian hands and Britain a client state of the USA. Perhaps Chamberlain had been right to seek to solve the German question by means other than war.

CONTROVERSY

Munich and Chamberlain became synonymous with weakness. The young at the time who were to fight the Second World War, and their children, grew up to regard the Munich Pact as a page of shame in the national story. The best that might be claimed about it was that it gained time. Even this last qualification was challenged by Churchill in Volume I of *The Second World War*, published in 1948. Churchill sees Munich, in the first instance, as morally reprehensible:

> For the French Government to leave her faithful ally Czechoslovakia to her fate was a melancholy lapse from which flowed terrible consequences. Not only wise and fair policy, but chivalry, honour, and sympathy for a small threatened people made an overwhelming concentration. Great Britain, who would certainly have fought if bound by treaty obligations, was nevertheless now deeply involved, and it must be recorded with regret that the British Government not only acquiesced but encouraged the French Government in a fatal course.

Second, it was both militarily disastrous and shortsighted:

> The subjugation of Czechoslovakia robbed the Allies of the Czech Army of twenty-one regular divisions, fifteen or sixteen second-line divisions already mobilised, and also their mountain fortress line which, in the days of Munich, had required the deployment of thirty German divisions, or the main strength of the mobile and fully-trained German Army. According to Generals Halder and Jodl there were but thirteen German divisions, of which only five were composed of first-line troops, left in the West at the time of the Munich arrangement. We certainly suffered a loss through the fall of Czechoslovakia equivalent to some thirty-five divisions. Besides this the Skoda works, the second most important arsenal in central Europe, the production of which between August, 1938, and September, 1939, was in itself nearly equal to the actual output of British arms factories in that period, was made to change sides adversely.

Others at the same time, and since, have argued that it was a necessary consequence of weakness and Chamberlain did what had to be done in the circumstances. R. A. Butler, a junior minister at the Foreign Office in 1938, takes this line and incidently quotes from one of the classic works of the 1938 crisis, *Munich: Prologue to Tragedy* (1948), by Sir John Wheeler-Bennett:

> Throughout the fateful weeks of September I was off-stage in Geneva where, however, I conducted two important interviews with the Foreign Ministers of the Soviet Union and of France. The former convinced me that Russia had no intention of coming to the help of the Czechs, even if the Czechs had wanted this, which they didn't; the latter gave me the measure of France's political unreliability. These two factors were interrelated, since a French declaration of war was stipulated by the Russians to be a condition of their own intervention. I am thus convinced that Sir John Wheeler-Bennett's conclusion about the inevitability of the Munich agreement was correct and, in view of his own vehement and sustained reaction to appeasement, all the more creditable to his historical mastery. 'Let us say of the Munich Settlement', he wrote, 'that it was inescapable; that, faced with the lack of preparedness in Britain's armaments and defences, with the lack of unity at home and in the Commonwealth, with the collapse of French morale, and with the uncertainty of Russia to fight, Mr. Chamberlain had no alternative to do other than he did; let us pay tribute to his persistence in carrying out a policy which he honestly believed to be right. Let us accept and admit all these things, but in so doing let us not omit the shame and humiliation that were ours; let us not forget that, in order to save our own skins – that because we were too weak to protect ourselves – we were forced to sacrifice a small Power to slavery.'
>
> (R. A. Butler, *The Art of the Possible*, London, Hamish Hamilton, 1971, pp. 66–7)

Ten years before Butler's book, A. J. P. Taylor, the doyen of British diplomatic historians, had produced his famous, or infamous, *Origins of the Second World War*. It contained the following assertions on the morality of Munich:

> The settlement at Munich was a triumph for British policy, which had worked precisely to this end; not a triumph for Hitler, who had started with no such clear intention. Nor was it merely a triumph for selfish or cynical British statesmen, indifferent to the fate of far-off peoples or calculating that Hitler might be launched into war against Soviet Russia. It was a triumph for all that was best and most enlightened in British life; a triumph for those who had preached equal justice between peoples; a triumph for those who had courageously denounced the harshness and short-sightedness of Versailles. Brailsford, the leading Socialist authority on foreign affairs, wrote in 1920 of the peace settlement: 'The worst offence was the subjection of over three million Germans to Czech rule.' This was the offence redressed

at Munich. Idealists could claim that British policy had been tardy and hesitant. In 1938 it atoned for these failings. With skill and persistence, Chamberlain brought first the French, and then the Czechs, to follow the moral line.

(pp. 234–5)

Since then historians have continued to chip away at the Churchillian explanation. In 1989 D. C. Watt's magnificent volume *How War Came* appeared. Essentially a study of 1939 it points out at the beginning of chapter 3:

> The world celebrated the Munich Agreement as Hitler's greatest victory. In the British Parliament, Churchill, Anthony Eden and Duff Cooper (the First Lord of the Admiralty, who resigned his office rather than lend his agreement to so dishonourable an action) attacked it bitterly. . . .
>
> Yet Hitler regarded Munich as a defeat. 'That senile old rascal', Neville Chamberlain, with his governess's manner and his bourgeois indecisiveness, had defeated him. When Hitler had stood on the balcony of the Reichs Chancellery three days earlier to inspect the troops about to launch the assault on Czechoslovakia, the Berlin crowds had greeted him glumly, silently. When Chamberlain drove through the streets of Munich the crowds shouted for joy and relief, threw flowers, and even shouted '*Heil* Chamberlain'.
>
> (D. C. Watt, *How War Came*, London, Heinemann, 1989, p. 00)

John Charmley, in another 1989 study of the war's origins, *Chamberlain and the Lost Peace*, makes a clear defence of Chamberlain's actions:

> Unlike Churchill, Chamberlain had knowledge both of what passed for the French war-plan and of the latest report of the British Chiefs of Staff. After a 'squib offensive (to bring us in)', the French plan was to wait behind the Maginot Line until the British had expanded their army and the economic blockade began to bite; this was not a strategy which promised speedy relief to the Czechs (as the Poles were to discover a year later). There were plans to march into Libya – but these presupposed that Italy would enter the war and, as the British Chiefs of Staff report emphasised, such a development would be exceedingly unfavourable to the Allies. The Chiefs were adamant that there was nothing that either Power could do to 'prevent Germany from overruning Bohemia and inflicting a decisive defeat on Czechoslovakia'. Britain was still a year away from the time when her rearmament programme would be substantially complete; the omens for war were not good.
>
> (J. C. Charmley, *Chamberlain and the Lost Peace*, London, Hodder
> & Stoughton, 1989, p. 134)

Finally, 1989 brought an incidental restatement of the Churchillian view in the memoirs of Denis Healey, admittedly writing as an informed observer rather than as a professional historian:

> Controversy continues about the Munich Agreement. I am still convinced that Chamberlain's policy was politically and strategically disastrous, as well as morally contemptible. He really believed that he had brought us 'Peace in our time', and continued to trust Hitler until the occupation of the rest of Czechoslovakia the following Easter. As a result of this the Allies lost thirty Czech divisions, as well as fortifications which the German generals admitted at Nuremburg they would have found it very difficult to overcome. Above all, Hitler made far better use of the time he gained to build up his military power than did Chamberlain and Daladier. On the other hand, it is incontestable that the British Parliament and people were not psychologically ready for war in 1938. The most difficult question is whether Hitler would have backed down if Chamberlain had stood firm. No one will ever know the answer.
>
> (D. Healey, *The Time of My Life*, London, Michael Joseph, 1989, pp. 37–8)

The above paragraph ends with the following truth:

> The judgement of historians is no more reliable than that of politicians in such matters.

Wise words the student of history would do well to remember.

BIBLIOGRAPHY

For an explanation of the grading system, see the preface p. xiii.

General works

3/4   Andrew C., *Secret Service*, London, Heinemann, 1985
3   Barnett, C., *Britain and her Army*, London, Allen Lane, 1970
3   Dilks, D. (ed.), *Retreat from Power*, Vol. 1, London, Macmillan, 1981
3   Hayes, P., *Modern British Foreign Policy 1880–1939*, London, A. & C. Black, 1978
2/3   Kennedy, P., *The Realities behind Diplomacy*, London, Fontana, 1981
2/3   Kennedy, P., *Strategy and Diplomacy*, London, Allen & Unwin, 1983
3   Kennedy, P., *The Rise and Fall of Great Powers*, London, Unwin Hyman, 1988
3   Porter, B., *Britain, Europe and the World 1850–1986*, London, Allen & Unwin, 1987
3   Taylor, A. J. P., *English History 1914–1945*, Oxford, 1965

Causes of the First World War

3   Joll, J., *The Origins of the First World War*, London, Longman, 1984
4   Kennedy, P., *The Rise of Anglo-German Antagonism*, London, Allen & Unwin, 1980
2   Langhorne, R., *The Collapse of the Concert of Europe*, London, Macmillan, 1981
1   Lowe, J., *Rivalry and Accord*, London, Arnold, 1988
1   Martel, G., *The Origins of the First World War*, London, Longman, 1988
2   Padfield, P., *The Great Naval Race*, London, Hart Davis, 1974
3   Robbins, K., *Sir Edward Grey*, London, Cassell, 1971
4   Steiner, Z., *The Foreign Office and Foreign Policy 1898–1914*, Cambridge, Cambridge University Press, 1969
3   Steiner, Z., *Britain and the Origins of the First World War*, London, Macmillan, 1977
3/4 Taylor, A. J. P., *The Struggle for the Mastery of Europe 1848–1918*, Oxford, 1954
2/3 Turner, L. C. F., *Origins of the First World War*, London, Arnold, 1970

First World War

3   Fussell, P., *The Great War and Modern Memory*, Oxford, Oxford University Press, 1975
2/3 Keegan, J., *The Face of Battle*, London, Cape, 1976 (contains an excellent section on the Somme)
3   Liddell Hart, B., *History of the First World War*, two vols, London, Cassell, 1930
2   MacDonald, L., *The Roses of No-Man's Land*, London, Michael Joseph, 1980
2   MacDonald, L., *The Somme*, London, Papermac edition, 1989
2   Middlebrook, M., *The First Day of the Somme*, London, Allen Lane, 1971
1/2 Taylor, A. J. P., *The First World War*, London, Hamish Hamilton, 1963 (illustrated)
2   Terraine, J., *The Great War*, London, Hutchinson, 1965
3   Terraine, J., *Douglas Haig*, London, Hutchinson, 1963
2/3 Terraine, J., *To Win a War*, London, Sidgwick & Jackson, 1978
2   Winter, D., *Death's Men*, London, Allen Lane, 1978

Inter-war

3   Bell, P. M. H., *Origins of the Second World War*, London, Longman, 1978
4   Bond, B., *British Military Policy between the Two World Wars*, Oxford, Clarendon Press, 1980
3   Carlton, D., *A. Eden*, London, Allen Lane, 1981
3   Charmley, J. C., *Chamberlain and the Lost Peace*, London, Hodder & Stoughton, 1989
2   Gilbert, M., *The Roots of Appeasement*, London, Weidenfeld & Nicolson, 1966
2   Howard, M., *The Continental Commitment*, London, Temple Smith, 1972
2/3 Manchester, W., *Churchill: The Caged Lion 1932–1940*, London, Michael Joseph, 1988
2   Marks, S., *The Illusion of Peace*, London, Macmillan, 1976
3   Robbins, K., *Munich 1938*, London, Cassell, 1968

2/3	Rock, W. R., *British Appeasement in the 1930s*, London, Arnold, 1977
3	Taylor, A. J. P., *Origins of the Second World War*, London, Hamish Hamilton, 1961
2/3	Thorne, C., *The Approach of War*, London, Macmillan, 1967
4	Wark, W., *The Ultimate Enemy: British Intelligence and Nazi Germany*, Oxford, Oxford University Press, 1985
3/4	Watt, D. C., *How War Came*, London, Heinemann, 1989

Second World War

3	Gilbert, M., *The Second World War*, London, Weidenfeld & Nicolson, 1989
2/3	Grigg, J., *1943: The Victory that Never Was*, London, Methuen, 1980
2/3	Keegan, J., *Six Armies in Normandy*, Harmondsworth, 1983
3	Keegan, J., *The Second World War*, London, Hutchinson, 1989
2	Kitchen, M., *A World in Flames*, London, Longman, 1990
2/3	Lewin, R., *Ultra Goes to War*, London, Hutchinson, 1978
3	Liddell Hart, B., *History of the Second World War*, London, Cassell, 1970
3	Lukacs, J., *The Last European War 1939–December 1941*, London, Routledge & Kegan Paul, 1977
3	Overy, R., *The Air War*, London, Europa Publications, 1980
1	Shackleton, R., *The Second World War*, London, Historical Association, 1991
1	Wood, A., *War in Europe 1939–1945*, London, Longman, 1987

Sources for coursework

Official collections of documents and the official histories of the wars are a vast mine of possible material: for example, *British Documents on the Origins of War 1898–1914*, eleven volumes (1926–38). These volumes were just in time for completion as the Second World War began and publication of the later conflict began in 1946, *Documents on British Foreign Policy 1919–1939*. In addition there is a welter of memoirs and published diaries which can be used. Pride of literary place amongst these must go to Churchill's works on both the First and Second World Wars: W. S. Churchill, *The World Crisis* (1923) and *The Second World War*, six volumes (London, Odhams, 1948 onwards). Grey published his memoirs, *Twenty-Five Years*, London, Cassell, in 1925 and Eden published his *Facing the Dictators* in 1962. One of the most fascinating developments in the 1970s was the revelations about Ultra, the code-breaking operation so vital to success in the Second World War – see F. W. Winterbottom, *The Ultra Secret* (London, Weidenfeld & Nicolson, 1974). The whole area of military intelligence has slowly been opened up and become a fascinating one to explore.

At a more mundane level, in one sense, there has been a recent outpouring of reminiscences of the First World War by ordinary participants, military and civilian, who are fast themselves becoming things of the past. Lyn MacDonald and Martin Middlebrook have shown in a series of books since the 1970s what skilled writers can do in weaving together individual tales into a forceful narrative. Many students could seek to emulate their turning oral history into literary history. Possibly the most important resource centre for this topic will be the Imperial War Museum which holds a mass of material, and many millions of photographs, and has an excellent education section.

9   Britain between the wars

INTRODUCTION

The dole queue has become the symbol of the inter-war years, and photographs of the Jarrow protest marchers of 1936 almost a clichéd comment on the two decades of unemployment and economic decay which stand out in the popular mind as a key feature of the twenty years which separate the first war against Germany from the replay in 1939. Older Britons, who have enjoyed the affluence of the late 1950s onwards look back to childhoods of apparent deprivation. Slums in London still survived, ugly mementoes of the nineteenth century. Yet Londoners who visited Glasgow were appalled that even their London hell-holes did not match the squalor of parts of Clydeside. In many rural areas the water-closet, let alone the toilet roll, had not arrived. Often water was still drawn from wells and the only source of power lay in oil lamps and wood-burning fires. The great burst of welfare legislation brought about by the post-war Labour Government led its supporters to blacken the pre-war decades. On the one side lay the sunny uplands of Britain with a National Health Service and universal benefits; on the other a world downtrodden and deprived, untouched by the light of regenerative Social-ism. The presence of so many living memories today far from aiding the assessment of this period often distorts it. Comparisons are nearly always made, unfavourably with the present and unfavourably with the years before 1914. The 1920s and 1930s were in fact years of considerable social and economic progress. Side by side with the picture of the dole queue and urban squalor must be placed a myriad images of the new consumer society symbolized by chain stores like Woolworth's and Marks & Spencer. It is an age therefore of marked contradictions and any analysis must initially face the question of the impact of the First World War. Many contemporaries saw in this cataclysm an explanation of all that was wrong with their world.

IE EFFECTS OF THE FIRST WORLD WAR

In 1914 London was the financial capital of the world, the pound approximating to a world currency. The old staple industries of coal, cotton, ship-building and iron were still booming. The first two in particular relied heavily on exports for their prosperity. Exports as a whole amounted to 23.2 per cent of net national income in 1913. The British merchant marine was 42 per cent of the world's total, which explained the vast ship-building industry. Taxation was minimal with the standard rate of income tax one shilling and two pennies in the pound (6 pence), and this was only applicable to the relatively wealthy with incomes over £160 per annum. Government expenditure might have risen under the Liberal governments of 1905–15 but central and local government expenditure remained a mere 13 per cent of GNP. Britain remained the model of a Liberal economic state and her greatness appeared to rest on the continued working of free trade and a freely convertible currency. The market mechanism had served the country well, it seemed, with more than a century of uninterrupted economic growth and rising living standards. If there had been slumps, like those of 1879 or 1908–9, they had been short lived and sharp. Unemployment would rise but then prices and wages would fall and the growth cycle would start again and unemployment would quickly disappear. God worked through the market 'his wonders to perform' and millions gave weekly thanks in their churches and chapels for his goodness.

The post-war world was different. Unemployment after the short boom of 1919–20 remained obstinately above one million for the whole of the inter-war years reaching crisis proportions in the slumps of 1920–1 and 1931–3. Even in a relatively good year like 1924 it never fell below 9 per cent. The old staple industries never again attained the old levels of prosperity and world dominance. Coal, cotton and ship-building entered a period of long slow decline. Exports declined and London lost its primacy to New York, and the pound lost out to the dollar. The world's money market entered a period of turbulence which led bankers to look back on the pre-war world as some blissful golden age before the fall. 'Paradise lost' was their interpretation of the new world of the 1920s. The state's role had vastly increased. By 1918 total central and local government expenditure stood at over 50 per cent of GNP. Income tax had risen dramatically to a standard rate of six shillings (30 pence) by 1919, and it applied to all those on incomes over £130 per annum – a much lower threshold in actual and real terms. For the first time income tax touched the better off among the working class. Despite cuts in expenditure in the early 1920s the state's role never returned to the levels of the pre-war world, never falling below 24 per cent of GNP. Likewise income tax never returned to the light burden of 1913.

A simple 'before and after' scenario led many commentators to seek to explain these dramatic changes as a consequence of the war. Clearly it did have an impact on the British economy and society, but whether it permanently twisted Britain out of a track of development that she would otherwise have taken is less clear. The most devastating result of the war must have been the deaths, mainly of young men. Out of 6,146,574 serving soldiers, sailors and airmen, 722,785 were killed – 11.8 per cent. To these must be added the merchant seamen who lost their lives and a few hundred civilian victims of bombing raids. The result of this was an inevitable increase in the proportion of women in the population and, of course, widows. Arthur Marwick puts it thus:

> The balance of females over the age of fourteen, therefore (discounting any other minor factors involved), rose from 595 per thousand in 1911 to 638 per thousand in 1921, and the proportion of widows per thousand of the population rose from 38 to 43. There is no exact measure of the quantity of personal agony concealed behind these figures, but society, in later years, exhibited all the signs of having suffered a deep mental wound.
>
> (A. Marwick, *The Deluge – British Society and the First World War*, London, Macmillan, 1965, p. 290)

There was much talk later of a lost generation. In reality 11.8 per cent does not add up to a lost generation but, as Marwick points out, to a vast amount of human suffering. It is more excusable to talk of a lost generation higher up the social scale. Subalterns suffered proportionately more than lower ranks. A curious analysis of the ducal peerage, a peculiarly narrow sample it must be admitted, reveals that 48 per cent of male members born between 1880 and 1939 died violent deaths, a higher rate than even the murderous Wars of the Roses produced in the fifteenth century.

Despite the death rate there is, however, little to show that the basic demographic trends of British society were altered. Of far more long-term significance was the fall in infant mortality and the increase in life expectancy. The losses in the 1860s of infants was on a scale to dwarf even the horror of the Western Front. Changes in emigration patterns which declined markedly in the inter-war years, as much from improvements at home as American attempts to exclude migrants, made a significant contribution. So too did the trend to smaller families, the average size of which fell from 4.35 in 1919 to 3.59 in 1939. None of these developments was interrupted by the First World War and together they did more to shape the demographic structure of twentieth-century Britain than all the blood-letting in France. Nor can the loss of so many young men be held responsible for the mediocre performance of the British economy in the 1920s. France and Germany both suffered proportionately higher losses, in France's case double that of Britain, yet these neighbouring economies each showed much greater dynamism than did Britain.

Other direct losses were the sinking of millions of tons of shipping. This again can hardly be held to have contributed directly to the problems of the 1920s, when it was the surplus of ships, not the dearth, which brought misery to British ship-building centres. As indicated in chapter 8 the capital expenditure on the war by Britain and her Empire exceeded that of any other belligerent, but simply to write this off as loss can be misleading. Wars are not necessarily economic disasters. Britain emerged from the lengthy Napoleonic Wars of the early nineteenth century a far bigger economy, as did the USA in the two World Wars of the twentieth century. In Britain there was a steep drop in economic activity in 1914 followed by a rapid rise. National income per head of population increased in the period 1915–18. Much reference is made to the build-up of foreign debt and the sale of overseas assets to pay for increased imports from the USA. In reality neither of these was of vast significance. Britain lent her allies £1,419 million and owed, mainly the USA, £1,285 million. The problem lay in Russia's reneging on her debts and the USA's insistence on payment in full. Eventually all debts were effectively cancelled although the US Treasury keeps a theoretical record of debt and interest owing. In all, £250 million of investments were either sold off or deposited as securities for US loans and then unredeemed. This was a small fraction of Britain's investment and Professor Milward, in his study of the economic effects of the two world wars, concluded in 1984 that the overall post-war earning capacity of British foreign investment was not seriously weakened. Depreciation of such assets in the 1930s and the general disruption to the international money markets were more harmful than direct losses.

It was the loss of overseas export markets during the war that probably did the most serious economic damage to Britain. The great cotton textile industry of Lancashire was the chief victim. The loss of the Indian market was the most serious. This came partly from the development of Indian industry encouraged by raising the tariffs in 1917 from 3.5 per cent to 7.5 per cent. Japanese competition also bit into the market. In 1913 Britain had supplied 97 per cent of Indian piece good imports and Japan 0.3 per cent. By 1936 it was 43 per cent and 55 per cent respectively. In China also, the second major market for textiles, native production and Japanese competition combined to squeeze out the British. Textiles and other products lost out to the Americans in South America. The Argentinian market showed the biggest losses. Elsewhere in the world British coal exports never recovered their pre-war levels. In many ways the First World War proved to be the occasion rather than the cause of these losses. It speeded up a process which was probably inevitable and the decline continued after the war years. The explanation lay in world-wide changes and the basic inefficiencies of the old established British staple industries in the face of newer competition. Had it not been for the First World War it is possible that the British would have found it easier to adjust but this is by no means certain.

It cannot thus be argued that the First World War was an economic disaster for Britain. It posed problems but it also provided opportunities leading to a much higher pitch of industrial activity, as indicated by the rise in national income. A vast new aircraft industry was created. By 1919 52,027 aircraft had been produced. There was an increase in the use of sophisticated machinery in engineering such as universal milling machines. Machine tools in general received a massive stimulus, many having to be imported from the USA. The overall effect on the efficiency of British industry was probably positive.

The permanent social consequences of the First World War are equally difficult to assess. Specific quaint national customs such as British Summer Time and afternoon closing of public houses were due solely to the war. Cigarette smoking became much more popular. Munitions workers as well as the troops had taken them up in preference to pipes and the cigar, bearing more tax, became an upper-class luxury. Rationing encouraged queueing and the average beer remained permanently weaker than its Edwardian predecessor. The price of a pint went up from 3 pennies to 5 pennies (2 pence). In 1918 alcohol sales were only 50 per cent of those of 1900. The famous slogan 'Homes fit for Heroes', pointed up a serious decline in houses produced by the war. Fewer were built despite increasing needs. This deterioration in living conditions was probably responsible for the increase in deaths from respiratory diseases during the war. Despite these particular setbacks, in general, all the evidence points to considerable social progress during the war. Life expectancy at birth rose, between 1911 and 1921, from 49 for men to 56 and from 53 to 60 for women. The war period showed the steepest drop in infant mortality rates in the first thirty years of the century and there is ample evidence to suggest that the whole civilian population was markedly healthier at the end of the war than at the beginning. The war appears to have accelerated developments already underway, such as better maternity care. More work and better pay for the bulk of the population seems to have been the case. Industrial canteens and subsidized meals for workers became more common. State benefits of all kinds were extended. The provision of school meals for children was extended. In Scotland the sums spent feeding children rose from £7 million in 1912–13 to £29 million in 1917–18. Health insurance set up by the 1911 Act was given automatically to the armed forces and their wives now received maternity benefits. Winter, in his study of the effects of the war on the British people, concludes:

But we should not underestimate the significance of these wartime developments, either for the social history of Britain or for the history of the war itself. In this context it is possible only to suggest that if German workers in 1917–18 had commanded the real incomes of their British counterparts, and if their families had been able to maintain the nutritional levels we have described above, the outcome of the war may well have been reversed. Clearly a full-scale comparison with German conditions would be necessary to establish this claim, but the available literature seems to show that it was precisely on the level of defending civilian living standards that the German war economy failed. The consequences were clear: better health among British civilians; much greater deprivation, stress, and despair as well as deteriorating standards of health among a German population which paid the price British civilians never had to pay for their country's war effort.

(J. M. Winter, *The Great War and the British People*, London, Macmillan, 1986, p. 245)

Not only was the population healthier, there is much to suggest that the war prompted greater social equality. Wage rates improved and the average working week was reduced from 55 to 48 hours. It was the poorest group in society, the unskilled, who came out best and the gap between skilled and unskilled narrowed, as the figures in Table 9.1 indicate. The very rich lost out due to much heavier taxation and their share of national income decreased. The number of servants fell dramatically as women found more profitable work elsewhere. The rigid class

Table 9.1 Real wages of some manual workers 1886–1926 (1913 = 100)

	1886	*1913*	*1920*	*1926*
Skilled grades				
Bricklayers	80	100	94	104
Coalgetters	63	100	110	97
Cotton spinners	79	100	118	106
Engineering turners	77	100	118	106
Railway engine drivers	93	100	91	117
Semi-skilled grades				
Painters	83	100	105	117
Coalmining putters and fillers	72	100	123	96
Cotton grinders	72	100	118	96
Engineering machinemen	73	100	109	98
Railway guards	89	100	104	123
Unskilled grades				
Building labourers	75	100	124	121
Coalmining labourers	72	100	123	99
Cotton weavers (women)	82	100	125	112
Engineering labourers	82	100	120	125
Railway goods porters	91	100	125	127

Source: After J. W. F. Rowe, *Wages in Practice and Theory*, 1928, p. 18.

divisions, particularly between middle- and working-class families began to erode. The possession of a servant and the paying of income tax had been the hallmark of middle-class respectability before 1914. By 1918 fewer had servants and many more paid income tax. Britain was a healthier and more socially equal society as a result of her struggle with Germany.

THE PROBLEM OF UNEMPLOYMENT

Unemployment became the political issue in the inter-war years in a way it had never been before, nor was to be again until the late 1970s. Between 1921 and 1939 it remained stubbornly at what in the nineteenth century would have been regarded as crisis level with troughs of misery in 1922 and 1932. A book published in 1922 entitled *The Third Winter of Unemployment* registered that something horribly new and unexpected had happened. In the 1930s a spate of literary and political works publicized the misery of the distressed areas. George Orwell's *The Road to Wigan Pier*, published in 1937, is perhaps the best known today. The worst was over by that year but the flood of books demonstrates that it gripped the popular imagination and dominated much political thinking after the Second World War.

The causes of this double decade of heightened job losses are not difficult to understand. There had always been seasonal and cyclical unemployment. The trade cycle of boom and slump had accustomed Victorians and Edwardians to periodic unemployment due to over-production and a downturn in demand as a result – usually of flooding some foreign market. Unemployment would rise, as in 1908–9, and then, as the demand rose again and balanced supply, there would be a recovery. The bulk of lay-offs tended to be borne by the unskilled and the least well-off in society, and the whole question was usually discussed, if it was discussed at all, as part of the general issue of poverty.

There were three such cyclical slumps in the inter-war years – 1921–2, 1929–33 and 1937, the second of these being particularly severe and long-lasting. In addition to these three general recessions persistent 'structural' unemployment afflicted most industries and all parts of the country to varying degrees, but none more so than the old staple export industries of Britain: coal, textiles, iron and steel and ship-building. In other words these industries were now entering terminal decline from which there was no permanent recovery. Agriculture, as indicated in chapter 1, had faced such a decline since the 1870s with steady job losses and a consequent drift of labourers to the towns and abroad. The war-time revival proved short-lived, and agricultural decline continued after the First World War. By 1938 there were only 593,000 labourers in agriculture, as compared with one million before 1914, and the overall proportion of the workforce fell from 6.2 per cent to 4.2 per cent.

Table 9.2 Britain's official unemployment statistics 1900–84 (%)

Year	Official series	Year	Official series	Year	Official series
1900	2.5	1929	10.4	1958	2.2
1901	3.3	1930	16.0	1959	2.3
1902	4.0	1931	21.3	1960	1.7
1903	4.7	1932	22.1	1961	1.6
1904	6.0	1933	19.9	1962	2.1
1905	5.0	1934	16.7	1963	2.6
1906	3.6	1935	15.5	1964	1.7
1907	3.7	1936	13.1	1965	1.5
1908	7.8	1937	10.8	1966	1.6
1909	7.7	1938	13.5	1967	2.5
1910	4.7	1939	11.6	1968	2.5
1911	3.0	1940	9.7	1969	2.5
1912	3.2	1941	6.6	1970	2.6
1913	2.1	1942	2.4	1971	3.5
1914	3.3	1943	0.8	1972	3.8
1915	1.1	1944	0.7	1973	2.7
1916	0.4	1945	1.2	1974	2.6
1917	0.6	1946	2.5	1975	4.2
1918	0.8	1947	3.1	1976	5.7
1919	2.1	1948	1.8	1977	6.2
1920	2.0	1949	1.6	1978	6.1
1921	12.9	1950	1.5	1979	5.7
1922	14.3	1951	1.2	1980	7.4
1923	11.7	1952	2.1	1981	11.4
1924	10.3	1953	1.8	1982	12.1
1925	11.3	1954	1.5	1983	12.9
1926	12.5	1955	1.2	1984	13.1
1927	9.7	1956	1.3		
1928	10.8	1957	1.6		

Source: Figures taken from a variety of sources.

If agriculture had been declining for sixty years by 1938, the decline of the staple industries of Victorian Britain was new. Coal production never again reached the levels of 1913 when 287 million tons were produced, by one million miners. In 1933 only 207 million tons were produced, by half a million men. This was a reversal of two hundred years of steady expansion. There was a world glut of coal as more countries, like Poland, began to exploit their resources, and new sources of power, such as hydroelectric power in Italy reduced the demand for exports from Britain. Three-quarters of the decline in coal production can be blamed on loss of export demand but other factors, for example coal-burning ships being replaced by oil-fired vessels, played their part. In 1914 97 per cent of ships used coal but by 1937 the figure was only 49 per cent. After 1927 there was a steady closure of pits, but supply always seemed too great for demand until rearmament got underway in the late 1930s. British pits were often small and inefficient. Closures produced gains in productivity and new technology (mechanical cutting, for instance) was adopted. In 1936 55 per cent of British coal was cut mechanically compared to only 8 per cent in 1913. Investment was, however, always too little. Coal-mining areas were amongst the worst affected by structural unemployment but the decline of British ship-building produced the most concentrated pockets of misery. Clydeside, Northern Ireland, Barrow and the north-east were all devastated by the collapse in demand. A world surplus of ships and new innovative competitors like Germany and Sweden spelled doom. In 1913 the United Kingdom supplied 80 per cent of the foreign market. By 1936–8 it was 20 per cent. The decline in government orders for warships added to the problem. Management was often unadventurous and a highly unionized labour force was difficult to manage, insisting as it did on a rigid demarcation of job responsibility. This tendency was intensified by decline as every group of workers tried to preserve their jobs. A ship-building town like Jarrow suffered appallingly from the death of its leading industry. In 1934 67.8 per cent of that town's workforce was unemployed.

The effects of the First World War on textiles have already been mentioned. As indicated, it was foreign competition, particularly from Japan and India, that produced decline. Tiny Glossop was particularly badly hit by Asian competition in the coarser cloths in which it specialized. Its inflexible weaving methods could not adapt and the vast mills faced closure. Unemployment reached 14 per cent by 1929 and with the onset of world recession it reached 55.6 per cent by 1931. Various parts of Lancashire were nearly as bad, although the smaller, more specialized enterprises survived better. As with coal and ship-building the future was bleak. The iron and steel industry was also very depressed throughout the 1920s and suffered along with other staple industries proportionately more during the early 1930s than did the newer industries. Steel production fell from 9.6 million tons in 1929 to 5.2 million tons in 1932. Unlike coal, textiles and ship-building, iron and steel was not a dying industry, but like them it suffered from too many inefficient units which lacked modern technology and management. Once again more efficient foreign competition meant the misery of redundancy for hundreds of British firms. South Wales, already suffering the effect of the decline in coal mining, was badly affected with 73 per cent unemployed in Dowlais when the steel works closed. Although iron and steel did eventually revive strongly with rearmament it was a leaner and fitter industry employing fewer men.

All of these factors point to the regional nature of unemployment. Glossop, Jarrow and Dowlais endured catastrophe but Oxford and Coventry had only 5 per cent unemployment in 1934. The country was undergoing major change; some regions were dying, others were growing. It was those regions most dependent on exports that were the hardest hit. The explanation for this lay largely in changes abroad. As Disraeli had pointed out in the 1830s the world would not suffer Britain to be its workshop for ever. The British doubtless contributed to their failure. Management was often conservative and blind to new product requirements. Unions were resistant to change and Britain had the most unionized workforce in the world. The Conservative Government of 1924–9 added to the problems by returning to the gold standard in 1925 with a pound overvalued by at least 10 per cent. A dollar value of 4.86 to the pound was good for the City of London's reputation as a financial centre but it was bad news for exporters. Yet political moves like this were not the cause of structural unemployment. It was a natural and inevitable consequence of irresistible change.

The great slump of 1929–33 intensified the misery of persistent structural unemployment and those areas already depressed suffered even more. That there was a slump in 1929 is not surprising after the galloping expansion in production in the USA and Germany in the 1920s. The newer industries in Britain had shared in this in a modest way. Supply outstripped demand as it had done so often in the past but this time other features of the world economy intensified the resulting slump. It was not the Wall Street Crash which ushered in disaster in Britain. The primary producers of the Third World were already badly depressed in late 1928 and these absorbed 40 per cent of British exports. The collapse in the USA clearly intensified the worldwide slump as US money was withdrawn and primary producers in particular faced catastrophic balance of payments problems. Governments everywhere sought to solve their problems by raising tariff barriers and this made a recovery of world trade all the harder to achieve. The whole world's exchange mechanism was badly damaged with consequent long-term effect. The economies most dependent on exports were bound to suffer more severely although the slump in domestic-oriented industries was less pronounced in Britain than in Germany or the USA. In these sections of the British economy, housing and construction for example, the modest expansion of the 1920s produced only a modest slump.

Just as the depression in agriculture in the late nineteenth century induced population shifts so now did the slump in the old staple industries. Emigration continued from the country in the 1920s but this was becoming more difficult, particularly for those bound for the USA with its new policy of exclusion and quota acts. Most of the change was from one region to another as Table 9.3 indicates. Glossop lost 16 per cent of its population between 1929 and 1939, mostly from amongst the young. Welshmen and women moved to London stirring up the resentment that existing communities often feel for the newly arrived. For those who stayed, poverty was the most obvious result of unemployment. All the social investigations of the period agreed on this. In the East End of London Llewellyn Smith's *New Survey of London* (1934) found unemployment to be the biggest single cause. Even in York, one of the

Table 9.3 Regional gains (+) or losses (−) through migration in Britain 1923–36

Region	1923–31	1933–6
London and Home Counties	+62,205	+71,623
South-east	+8,733	+18,334
South-west	+10,582	+11,445
Midlands	−4,964	+5,521
North-west	−19,275	−6,942
North-east	−30,516	−24,180
Scotland	−37,559	+1,299
Wales	−31,350	−22,092
Net inward (+) or outward (−) balance of overseas migration	−42,144	+55,008

Source: M. P. Fogarty, *Prospects of the Industrial Areas of Great Britain*

northern cities not extensively damaged by the slump, Rowntree found in 1936 that unemployment explained 28.6 per cent of the poverty in that city. Since the institution of national insurance in 1911 and its later extension most workers were entitled to dole money. In 1931 a married man with three children received 29s 3d (£1.46) per week. A single adult male received 17 shillings per week (85 pence) and an insured unemployed woman 15 shillings per week (75 pence). This entailed, for most workers, a serious reduction in living standards. An average textile worker's wage was 48 shillings for men (£2.40) and a miner 45 shillings (£2.22½). Many members of unemployed households recall feeling hungry and George Orwell in *The Road to Wigan Pier* touchingly describes the scene in Wigan of scrambles for coal from the spoil heaps and dirt trains:

> Everyone knows that the unemployed have got to get fuel somehow. So every afternoon several hundred men risk their necks and several hundred women scrabble in the mud for hours – and all for half a hundredweight of inferior fuel, value ninepence.
>
> That scene stays in my mind as one of my pictures of Lancashire: the dumpy, shawled women, with their sacking aprons and their heavy black clogs, kneeling in the cindery mud and the bitter wind, searching eagerly for tiny chips of coal. They are glad enough to do it. In winter they are desperate for fuel; it is more important almost than food. Meanwhile all round, as far as the eye can see, are the slag-heaps and hoisting gear of collieries, and not one of those collieries can sell all the coal it is capable of producing.

The imposition of the means test in 1931 for all those unemployed for more than six months was particularly resented. The means test was carried out by a local Public Assistance Committee, often the old poor law guardians. All family income, savings and even possessions could be taken into account and a recommended reduction in benefit be made:

> A Lancashire miner, with wife and six children, had, before his unemployment, managed to save £15, which was banked in the Co-op. Under the means test this man received a ruling: 'Not a case for help so long as this sum is on deposit.'
>
> A Tyneside man with an invalid wife, seven children of school age, and one girl of sixteen years, wages 8s. One boy fourteen years not working, and one son in the army sending home 5s. 3d. per week. His benefit is reduced from 37s 9d. to 21s. 9d. because of the wages of the daughter and the money from the son in the army. Therefore two adults, two adolescents, and seven children have to live on 35s. a week, out of which rent also has to be paid.
>
> A Llanelly part-time worker earning on an average £1 3s. a week, with wife to maintain and 10s. rent to pay. He is refused benefit entirely, although no other source of income is available.
>
> (W. Hannington, *The Problem of the Distressed Areas*, London, Gollancz, 1937, p. 47)

By January 1932 there were nearly one million people subject to the means test in order to be able to receive the transitional benefit that resulted.

Poverty often led to ill-health. It became a hotly debated issue as to whether unemployment did produce a deterioration in health. One study suggested that 3,000 deaths in childbirth could be put down to poverty. In fact mortality rates remained higher in the depressed areas of the north than in the more prosperous areas of the south, but this had always been the case. In 1935 the Minister of Health, Sir Kingsley Wood, made the claim that 'there is at present no available medical evidence of any increase in physical impairment as a result of the economic depression or unemployment'. Certainly conclusive evidence was hard to find and the overall trend towards a healthier, longer-lived society continued throughout the 1930s, although the progress in the depressed areas was slower than elsewhere.

There is little to show that adult crime increased as a result of unemployment, other than the technical offence of suicide. There was apparently a 60 per cent increase in suicides of the under-25s in the years 1921–31 but it is difficult to correlate the rise directly with unemployment. Post-war trauma might also be advanced as an explanation. Juvenile crime increased markedly between 1929 and 1936 but then again it increased even more in the unemployment-free world of the 1950s and 1960s. It is thus difficult to show that the slump produced social breakdown in Britain. Clearly it created pockets of heightened misery but long-standing social trends like increased life expectancy, declining family size, lower alcohol consumption, more consumer goods and less religious observance continued.

Politically unemployment produced no revolution. There was a brief and minor upsurge in support for Communists and Fascists but nothing to equal the support such groups enjoyed in France, a country with much lower rates of unemployment. There was a series of hunger marches and demonstrations, mostly organized by Wal Hannington's National Unemployed Workers' Movement (NUWM). The organization began in London in late 1920 and became a national movement in 1921. Most of its leaders, including Hannington, were Communists but it enjoyed a wider degree of support. By 1932 it had some 50,000 paying members organized into 386 branches. Even so the movement never acquired the active support of even a minority of the unemployed. It campaigned for better benefits and against the means test. Apart from help with individual cases it is difficult to see what it achieved in general terms. The TUC and the Labour Party kept it at arm's length and its leaders were harassed by the government.

The hunger march organized in 1922 proved to be the first of many. Unemployed Welsh miners marched to London in 1927 against TUC advice. In 1931 over thirty towns and cities experienced minor battles between police and the unemployed. Not surprisingly 1931 was the worst year for violent demonstrations with the first fatalities occurring in Belfast. Troops had to be called in, as they were in Rochdale in January. Merseyside witnessed violent clashes in September. The police and not the army contained the situation. A great march to, and a demonstration in, London against the means test was the culmination of the NUWM activities in 1932. It brought almost unanimous criticism from the press and little support from Labour MPs, frightened of being associated with a Communist-organized event. A further march to the capital in 1934 was proposed. Rumours that the government planned to stop it led to the formation of the National Council for Civil Liberties. In the end the march was allowed to take place and it passed off peacefully.

The most famous of the marches was, of course, that from Jarrow in 1936. It was specific in its objective: work for Jarrow, and was organized not by the NUWM but by the local council and Ellen Wilkinson, the newly elected Labour MP. It was a model of good organization and good behaviour and a propaganda triumph. It also failed to gain help for the town and the marchers had their unemployment pay stopped for the duration on the grounds that they would not be available for work whilst on the march.

The chief success of the NUWM, the Jarrow marchers and all the other protesters against the misery of the depression lay in the future. In their own decade they achieved little of concrete value. They did, however, shape the post-war perceptions of the 1930s and ensured the attachment of the word 'Hungry' to the 1930s in the popular mind. Most of the victims of the slump, whether in Glossop, Jarrow, Dowlais or Clydeside, had two real options, leave and go south or stay in a state of resigned poverty. Most did the latter.

INTER-WAR GOVERNMENT POLICIES

The responses of the different governments in the inter-war period were muddled. They, no more than anyone else, could not offer practical solutions to the problem. Liberals, Conservatives and Labour politicians all fudged and fumbled in a situation essentially new to them. Their responses may possibly be analysed under two headings: 'relief' and 'cure', although these two are certainly not mutually exclusive. The key element in relief was the operation of welfare payments to the unemployed – the dole. The 1911 Insurance Act had been massively extended under the 1920 Act to most workers other than those in agriculture or domestic service, who still gained relief under the old poor law. The amount paid was increased in 1920 and again in 1921 when allowances for dependants were added. The original scheme had been devised to deal with the temporary cyclical unemployment of Victorian and Edwardian Britain. It was assumed to be self-financing. The high numbers of long-term unemployed in the 1920s exhausted the fund which was £25 million in debt by 1928 and was being supplemented by payments from the Treasury. Those who had exhausted their claims under the national insurance scheme were receiving 'transitional' benefits from the Treasury. Thus, before the onset of the great slump, the relief system was in a state of some administrative confusion. The Local Government Act of 1929 abolished the poor law guardians and transferred their duties to the local authorities who operated Public Assistance Committees partially funded from the rates. The massive leap in the numbers of the unemployed produced a crisis for the MacDonald Labour Government of 1929–31. It was responsible for an Unemployment Act in 1930 which extended payments and made claims easier. By 1931 benefit was costing the government £125 million per annum compared to £51 million in 1929, and it was the arguments over whether to cut this total that brought about the fall of the MacDonald Government in August of that year (see chapter 7).

In view of falling prices the real value of benefit had risen considerably by comparison with the early 1920s. The new National Government was determined to show its commitment to economy by tightening the controls on unemployment payments. Benefits were cut by 10 per cent and payments to 134,000 married women stopped. It was the introduction of the means test, referred to above, on those claiming 'transitional' benefit which excited the most protest. The Public Assistance Committees, or PACs, were to carry out this test and their enthusiasm varied from area to area. Some Labour-controlled PACs refused to operate the system and in Rotherham and Durham they were superseded by commissioners from London. As the worst of the slump passed the National Government decided to act on a report and nationalize the whole system, which went ahead as the Unemployment Act of 1934. This set up the Unemployment Assistance Board which took the responsibility out of the hands of the PACs and local authorities. The cuts of 1931 were reversed and following effective Labour protests the new proposed 'transitional' benefits were made more generous. The Act in one sense finally settled the question of relief payments and removed it from the party political agenda. In 1936 agricultural workers were brought under the scheme. By the end of the 1930s Britain had one of the most advanced unemployment welfare systems in the world which, if not generous, took the revolutionary edge off a potentially dangerous situation.

Relief was easier to organize than a 'cure'. The whole notion of 'economic policy' was alien to those governing Britain. Economic literacy was not considered to be a requirement for those seeking political office. It had hardly changed from 1851 when Disraeli had protested his unsuitability for the Exchequer on the grounds of ignorance only to be informed by Lord Derby that 'it did not matter, they give you the figures'. Winston Churchill, Chancellor of the Exchequer from 1924 to 1929, freely admitted his inability to argue with the financial experts of the City who urged him to return to the gold standard. There was a general consensus amongst politicians and 'experts' at the Treasury that the solution lay in a return to the pre-war world. A sound currency and a balanced budget would restore 'business confidence' and the free market would do the rest. The Labour Chancellor in 1924 and again in 1929–31, Philip Snowden, was as rigidly orthodox as Gladstone. MacDonald, the Labour leader, was happier working in the realms of moral generalities. In Churchill's brutal words he managed to 'cram the minimum amount of thought into the maximum amount of words'. There was no coherent socialist answer, merely socialist words and goodwill. Baldwin in the Conservative Party offered the same recipe minus the socialist words.

There was in the 1920s a retreat from the interventionism of the First World War. The Corn Production Acts of 1917 and 1920 were repealed and agriculture returned to languish in its pre-war state. The railways and mines were handed back to private ownership as the governments of 1921 to 1923 viewed their priority to be the cutting of government spending to restore confidence. To please the City Churchill accepted the return to the gold standard at the pre-war level of $4.86. It is generally now regarded as a mistake but it hardly caused the depression in the staple industries which were already badly afflicted. As unemployment persisted in the north, Wales, Scotland and Northern Ireland so there was slow acceptance of the need for further government action but without any real clear strategy. In 1926 Baldwin's Government was responsible for the Mining Industry Act to encourage voluntary amalgamation. In 1928 the Ministry of Labour inaugurated a scheme of industrial transfer to help removal of miners from the depressed areas to the prosperous ones. The 1929 election showed that neither Labour nor the Conservatives had any real answer to the depressed areas. The Liberals at least had policies but the electorate was not inclined to trust Lloyd George, and whether the schemes would have worked is much questioned by economists today. The Labour Government of 1929–31 therefore had no clearer idea than Baldwin's Government of how to deal with the problem. Certainly relief was easier than cure but since the Labour Chancellor still believed essentially that cure depended on cutting expenditure, and relief depended on extending it, the result was an impasse.

The National Government of 1931 nominally under MacDonald was dominated by the Conservatives and, from November, by Neville Chamberlain, as Chancellor of the Exchequer. Chamberlain believed that a balanced budget and a tight hold on government spending were essential to restore business confidence. Like most economics experts at the time he rejected the kind of Keynesian ideas promoted by outsiders like Oswald Mosley and Lloyd George. The only departures from orthodoxy which helped the situation were the abandonment of the gold standard in October 1931 and the introduction of protective tariffs in 1932. The first was forced on the government and the resulting fall in the pound helped exports. Chamberlain, a true son of Joseph, embraced tariffs. Their effects were to cut imports. What part they played in overall recovery is difficult to assess. Chamberlain's cheap money policy did play a part. The bank rate was cut in June 1932 to 2 per cent and it remained at this level until 1939. Movements of capital were controlled by means of the Exchange Equalization Account and sterling stabilized. The result of this cheap money policy was the stimulation of domestic investment particularly in the great building boom of the 1930s which powered the economy out of recession.

Despite the denunciation of Socialism by the National Government there was a growing acceptance of intervention by the state to tackle specific problems. Agricultural Marketing Acts of 1931 and 1933 set up boards for potatoes, milk, pigs and many more in order to rationalize the marketing of these products. A Wheat Act of 1932 gave a guaranteed standard price. The state intervened more forcefully in both the textile and iron and steel industries to encourage reconstruction, modernization and loss of surplus inefficient producers. The Cotton Spinning Act of 1936 avoided direct intervention but was an enabling measure and offered financial guarantees. To aid ship-building the North Atlantic Shipping Act was passed which allowed work to start again on the *Queen Mary* and in 1935 a subsidy was introduced for tramp or coastal shipping to encourage the 'scrap and build' scheme. The sums were small but amounted to an abandonment of the principle of leaving the industry to its fate. *Laissez-faire* was a fading doctrine. The Special Areas Act of 1934 set up two commissioners with five sub-commissioners to try to help the distressed industrial regions. Their powers, like their financial resources, were strictly limited. By 1938 they had set up 121 new firms and created 14,900 jobs – hardly a massive contribution to solving the problems of the distressed areas. Direct government help was thus very limited, but the overall recovery of the British economy in the 1930s was an achievement of which Chamberlain and his cabinet colleagues could be proud. Economic growth after 1932 was very impressive when compared with other countries and with Britain's past performance as Table 9.4 indicates. Only Nazi Germany could boast a better record in reducing unemployment and the political and social costs of that example were unacceptable to most decent-minded Britons. The National Government did not solve the problem of the distressed areas but it eased their plight and made the painful process of economic adjustment bearable whilst preserving the decencies of a democratic and tolerant society.

Table 9.4 Comparison of industrial production and output per man-hour (% per annum)

	Rate of growth of industrial production				Rate of growth of output per man-hour			
	1901–13	1913–37	1913–29	1929–37	1870–1913	1913–38	1913–29	1929–38
UK	2.3	2.0	1.3	3.4	1.5	2.1	2.1	2.1
Germany	4.7	1.2	0.9	3.0	2.1*	1.2	0.8	2.1
France	4.2	0.8	2.0	−2.8	1.8	2.3	2.8	1.6
USA	4.9	2.9	4.2	0.4	2.4*	3.0	2.8	3.3

Note: *Refers to 1871–1913.
Source: After N. K. Buxton and D. H. Aldcroft, *British Industry between the Wars*, London, Scolar Press, 1979, p. 14.

PROSPERITY AND GROWTH

If nearly one-quarter of the labour force was unemployed in 1932 it must be borne in mind that three-quarters were employed and for most of the inter-war period, with the possible exception of 1921–2, 90 per cent were in work. These not only had jobs but were enjoying rising living standards. By 1938 the average Briton was 30 per cent better off than in 1913. This advance had been erratic and was unevenly distributed. The unemployed certainly did not share in the prosperity and those in the new industries and service sector of the south-east and the Midlands benefited far more than those in the traditional industries of the north. The numbers in vehicle manufacture more than doubled to over half a million, overtaking textiles and iron and steel as a mass employer in the process. Morris in Cowley and Austin in Longbridge adopted mass production techniques.

The numbers in electrical engineering doubled to over 300,000. The chemical industry enjoyed substantial growth and the electrical supply industry mushroomed. Those in white-collar jobs formed an expanding segment of the workforce as government bureaucracy and the service sector called for more and more clerical officers. There was less and less need for unskilled workers, and women as much as men benefited from this change. They enjoyed increasing opportunities for employment outside domestic service. The more prosperous professionals might still run to employing a maid but increasingly they had to make do with the vacuum cleaner.

The consumer society of the post-Second World War era has its roots firmly in the rising affluence of the inter-war decades. Not only were real wages increasing but smaller families meant higher living standards. The average family size fell from 4.2 in 1929 to 3.59 by 1939 as couples consciously chose greater affluence in preference to more children. A working-class family in 1914 spent 40 per cent of its income on food and 16 per cent on rent. By 1938 these figures were 35 per cent and 9 per cent. The difference did not go into traditional expenditure on liquid refreshment because alcohol consumption continued to fall. Some of the spare cash went on luxury foods and consumer goods but most went into housing and building societies. By 1939 three million cars were on the road. The price of vehicles had fallen with mass production: an Austin Seven in 1931 sold for £118. Admittedly, this put it outside the reach of most working-class families whose income was likely to be in the region of £150 per annum. The motorbike and sidecar proved a cheaper substitute and still opened up the 'wide blue yonder' for a small family. Electrical goods of all sorts multiplied. Vacuum cleaner sales reached 400,000 in 1938. Radios entered most homes. There were nine million radio licences issued by 1939. Off the peg clothing, gambling on the pools, seaside holidays and visits to the cinema all absorbed more and more spare cash generated by expanding wealth. Woolworth's with its boast of 'nothing more than sixpence' and Marks & Spencer began to decorate the high streets.

Perhaps more than anything else the achievement of inter-war Britain was to rehouse so many of its citizens and make enormous strides in destroying the slums of Victorian Britain. There were 4.3 million homes built, 2.5 million of them in the 1930s. The home amounted to a huge investment which most people seemed to value. A property-owning democracy was born. House prices fell through these years, and the ownership of a house became possible for the better-off working class. Millions moved to the suburbs from the squalid town centres and the national craze for gardening flourished in Harrow, Edgware, Sudbury, around the capital, as on the leafy edges of most great cities. In 1914 only 10 per cent owned their own home, by 1939 the figure was 31 per cent. Clearly the overwhelming majority of these were middle class, yet the lot of the working class also improved markedly with the creation of council estates made possible by a series of acts beginning with the Addison Act of 1919. Over a million council houses were built for rent with a government subsidy of £208 million. Most were of high quality and contained the latest amenities such as baths and electricity.

As might be expected from this heightened affluence, and from the improvement in diet and housing in particular, the health of the nation showed a remarkable progress. Infant mortality rates continued to fall although, as noted earlier, the fall was more notable in the south than in the north and Scotland. In York Rowntree found a dramatic improvement between 1900 and 1936. At the beginning of the century out of every thousand live births 160 infants had died before the age of one. By 1936 the rate was down to 54.6. The old killers of the nineteenth century like tuberculosis were disappearing and the new killers of the old and middle aged – heart disease and cancers – were increasing. Rowntree found in York a generally much healthier population in 1936 compared to 1900. Children were on average two inches taller and five pounds heavier. Another valuable survey, besides that of Rowntree, was carried out in the 1930s. This was by Sir John Boyd Orr of the Rowett Institute in Aberdeen. It was published in 1936 entitled *Food, Health and Income* and it showed a considerable improvement in diet with a 64 per cent increase in consumption of fresh vegetables and 88 per cent increase in fruits since 1900. Orr, like Rowntree, did however show that the general improvement was more marked in the richer segments of society and the better-off working class.

Despite the continued gross imbalance in the distribution of affluence nearly all were better off and the advantage of increased wealth and shorter hours of work showed itself in the spread of leisure activities. Prime amongst these must be listening to the radio and visiting the cinema. Cinemas were 'palaces' of the people; the twentieth-century monuments to the common man. They spread throughout the 1920s to almost every community in the country. Even depressed Glossop boasted its 'Empire'. It lacked the grandeur of the great city cinemas but like thousands of others up and down the country it was filled nightly. Even the unemployed escaped into the magic world of Hollywood. When the 'talkies' began in 1929 there were already 3,300 cinemas. By 1938 there were 4,967 and 1,000 million tickets were sold in that year. The cinema attracted rich and poor alike and since most of the films were American they helped to break down the traditional British class barriers.

Radio broadcasts by the BBC began in 1922 and a new culture was created. By 1930 there were 3.5 million radio licences and by 1938 some 9 million. Over three-quarters of the homes in Britain had access to a wider world. News and music predominated and the serious high-

High Street, Glossop, *c.* 1934

mindedness of Sir John Reith, the first Director-General, stamped itself on this new medium. Only in July 1939 did ITMA, with Tommy Handley, begin a new development in light comedy entertainment which was to keep the nation laughing through the war.

Reading also increased in these years. Just over 50 million books had been borrowed from libraries before the First World War. In 1939 247 million books were issued. Book sales also multiplied, largely to middle-class consumers, but the birth of the sixpenny (2½ pence) Penguin paper-back in 1935 made book purchases a possibility for the less well-off. The press also expanded its circulation and readership. In 1910 daily sales had been approximately 4 million, led by the *Daily Mail*, and the *News Chronicle*. By 1939 the *Daily Express* alone had a circulation of 2.5 million and the total daily newspaper sales exceeded 10 million. The *News of the World*, with nearly 4 million copies, led the field of Sunday papers of which over 5 million copies were produced each week. Cinema, radio, books and newspapers all made vital contributions to the integration and shape of modern British society, breaking down centuries-old barriers of class and region.

Affluence meant the British obsession with sport could be given increased indulgence. The 'sport of kings' flourished as never before at Ascot and Newmarket, but in 1926 the first dog track was opened at Belle Vue, Manchester, to be followed in 1927 by one at White City in London. Football drew vast well-behaved crowds. Tennis attracted a growing middle-class following of participants and spectators. 'Nice' girls could meet 'nice' boys at the local tennis club, and Wimbledon provided idols for polite society. Cricket transcended all barriers. Hobbs, Sutcliffe and the young Hutton could elicit hero worship from people of all walks of life, and a test match against Australia raised or dashed national morale according to the result. The radio and cinema newsreel high-lighted the existing interest in sport and fed off the enthusiasm too.

CONCLUSION: SEVENTY YEARS ON

Much remained of the Britain of the 1860s. There had been no cataclysm like the Russian revolution to shake society to its foundations. Rural Britain had slowly continued to give way to urban, or more accurately *sub*urban, Britain. Agricultural labourers remained amongst the poorest paid workers on just over 30 shillings (£1.50) a week. The gentry and the aristocracy who employed them still owned vast swathes of the country and their stately homes still housed gatherings of the mighty at weekends. It was a world turned into fantastic farce in the stories of P. G. Wodehouse and wittily, yet nostalgically, savaged by Evelyn Waugh. The popular thrillers of writers like Agatha Christie were often set in this exalted environment of country houses replete with dark passages, pantries and threatening butlers. Yet it was a dying world in more than the sense that Agatha Christie intended. There was a spate of land sales. The ownership of England changed more rapidly than at any time since the Reformation. In 1919 over a million acres were sold and in 1920 even more. Death duties, raised in 1919 to 40 per cent on estates over £2 million, often forced sales but there was also the desire to cash in on increased wartime land values when rents had not risen. Agricultural depression returned in the 1920s and power and prosperity slid remorse-lessly into the hands of the new entrepreneurs of the consumer society, like the owners of the new football pools. No Prime Minister from 1908 to 1940 was drawn from the old ruling elite. Baldwin had been to Harrow but his wealth was not landed. Asquith, Lloyd George, Bonar Law and MacDonald were all self-made men.

The industrial antithesis of rural England, in the shape of the dark satanic mills, was also fading. Cotton no more than corn was king. In Glossop old money in the form of Lord Howard, lord of the manor, sold up in 1925 but the great industrial families who had controlled the town before the war also departed as mills closed or were saved only by integration into bigger combines. Power passed to less elevated social groups. The council was no longer dominated by the Liberal Partingtons who had owned the local paper mill, nor the Tory Hill-Woods, with their cotton kingdom. A petit-bourgeois mix of shop-keepers, school-masters and artisans inherited the management of this distressed com-munity.

The new England epitomized by the sprawling London suburbs, the prosperous car workers of Cowley or even the new neat council estates, was a less class-conscious society. Vast inequalities of wealth remained in Britain but overall it was less unequal than in Edwardian England. At the top 1.1 per cent of the population took 30 per cent of the national income in 1910. In 1929 1.5 per cent took 23 per cent. The numbers of those who could be classified as middle class rose with the expansion of service industries and state employment like civil servants and teachers. The decline in keeping servants ended the rigid divisions between working and middle classes. Within the working classes the erosion of differentials encouraged by the First World War has already been pointed out. The aristocracy of labour was losing its privileges just as the landed aristocracy was. The headmaster of the new grammar school in Glossop could still instruct pupils in the 1920s not to speak to their parents if the parents were in mill clothes, but the instruction to his pupils already seemed to be hideously eccentric.

Education remained one of the neglected areas of the inter-war years despite the high hopes of Fisher in Lloyd George's coalition (see chapter 6, p. 221). It reflected and perpetuated the class structure. In the early 1930s 14 per cent of 11-year-olds went to secondary school. The vast majority stayed on in their elementary schools until they left at 14. Of those attending secondary school within the state system more than half were fee-payers, largely drawn from the middle and lower middle classes. The financial crisis of 1931–2 led governments to cut free places so that non-fee-paying pupils actually fell, from 49 per cent in 1932 to 44 per cent by 1934. The situation in higher education was worse. Less than 3 per cent of the age-group enjoyed any sort of higher education and the proportion did not improve between 1924 and 1938. Only three new university colleges were created between the First and Second World Wars. By the outbreak of the Second World War Britain still had fewer students at university than Germany had before 1914.

Despite the slow pace of educational change the overall trend towards social equality remains clear and it was matched by the trend towards greater sexual equality. The granting of votes to women, first in 1918, and then in 1928 on the same terms as men, was perhaps the most symbolic aspect of this change. It meant 14.5 million women electors could outvote 12.25 million males. Perhaps more important in the lives of most women were other legal changes, for example the 1919 Sex Disqualification Removal Act, and the Matrimonial Causes Act in 1923, which gave women equal rights in divorce. Women's pay in almost all areas remained lower than men's and the entry of women into the higher professions was slow. By 1931 it was only 7.5 per cent, but the expanding opportunities in nursing, teaching and above all clerical work at least freed girls from the old tyranny of domestic service, although the process was not fully complete until after the Second World War. The growing acceptance of family planning and the trend towards smaller families was probably the most liberating development for females. In 1926 the prohibition on giving information on birth control at welfare centres was lifted (against the wishes of the government who suffered defeat in the House of Lords on this issue). Changes in fashion and manners also freed girls. Women could smoke in public and began to enter that bastion of male privilege: the public house.

The changes in British society in these years amounted to no giddy revolution. Ecstasy and agony were left to be experienced by Soviet Russia and Nazi Germany but in each case there was more of the latter than the former. Liberal America and France enjoyed huge changes in the 1920s followed by a painful hangover in the 1930s. Neither experience was felt as intently in Britain. An old world declined and a new one gently emerged. As indicated at the end of chapter 6, liberal values appeared triumphant despite the demise of the Liberal Party. The *Punch* portrayal of Abyssinia in 1935 might well be compared with that of 1867 shown in chapter 1 (see p. 10).

Britain was a less formally religious society, as church attendance figures indicate. The silver screen was now the opium of the people. Yet there was a heightened concern to alleviate suffering despite the increased materialism. Petty snobberies remained. Jews might still be excluded from golf clubs or abused in the East End, but there was a conscious rejection of the brutalities of Nazism. Only in Northern Ireland did the primitive tribalism of Catholic–Protestant antagonism survive. In Glasgow and Liverpool it slowly subsided into mere football rivalry. The British thought of themselves as decent and on the whole behaved decently. There were no genocidal lunacies as had disfigured Russia and Germany nor anything equivalent to isolated atrocities such as those perpetrated by the Klu Klux Klan and Cagoulards in America and France respectively. The extreme right and the extreme left remained harmless minorities. Most of the population, regardless of their party political loyalty, were attached to their society and its customs. The monarchy successfully came to express this stability. To Mussolini and Hitler Britain was decadent but its willingness to stand up for decency, decadent or not, ensured their defeat and the emergence of a 'decent' Europe in the post-war era.

CONTROVERSY

Various detailed academic debates concerning our interpretation of the inter-war years exist. How far unemployment affected health produced controversy in the 1930s and more recently there has been debate concerning the extent of recovery of the British economy. B. W. E. Alford, in *Depression and Recovery? British Economic Growth 1918–1939* (1972), is critical of the more extravagant claims. Yet it is not these debates that form the central controversy. It is the perception of the whole inter-war years as either a period of misery, the 'Hungry Thirties', or as a period

THE BLACK MAN'S BURDEN.

ABYSSINIA. "I SOMETIMES WONDER WHETHER IT WAS WORTH MY WHILE JOINING THIS EUROPEAN LEAGUE."

of social and economic progress. Noreen Branson and Margot Heine-mann, in their conclusion to their *Britain in the Nineteen Thirties* (1971), wrote:

> It is easily forgotten how much of the social legislation which we now take for granted as part of the fabric of British life was as recently as the thirties either non-existent or embryonic. There were no family allowances, no universally available free medical treatment, no free secondary education except for a handful of children, no free milk in schools except for a tiny minority. There were still relatively few council houses. Old age pensions were a pittance, which many people were not entitled to anyway. (p. 323)

By comparison Stephen Constantine in his *Social Conditions in Britain 1918–1939* (1983), concludes:

> Research shows that more attention ought to be paid than has been customary to the signs of substantial improvement in social conditions between the wars. Those subordinate images of affluence are not deceitful. For the majority of the British people, life in Britain before the Second World War was a good deal better in material terms than it had been just before the First World War. (p. 42)

Perhaps the final word ought to go to the investigative pioneer See-bohm Rowntree whose two surveys of York, conducted in 1899 and 1936, gave him a unique ability to assess his age:

> The economic condition of the workers is better by 30 per cent than in 1899, though working hours are shorter. Housing is immeasurably better, health is better, education is better. Cheap means of transport, the provision of public libraries and cheap books, the wireless, the cinema and other places of entertainment, have placed within the reach of everyone forms of recreation unknown, and some of them unthought of, forty years ago. It is gratifying that so much progress has been achieved, but if instead of looking backward we look for-ward, then we see how far the standard of living of many workers falls short of any standard which could be regarded, even for the time being, as satisfactory. Great though the progress made during the last forty years has been, there is no cause for satisfaction in the fact that in a country so rich as England, over 30 per cent of the workers in a typical provincial city should have incomes so small that it is beyond their means to live even at the stringently economical level adopted as a minimum in this survey, nor in the fact that almost half the children of working-class parents spend the first five years of their lives in poverty and that almost a third of them live below the poverty line for ten years or more.
>
> (S. Rowntree, *Poverty and Progress*, London, Longman, 1941)

BIBLIOGRAPHY

For an explanation of the grading system, see the preface p. xiii.

2   Aldcroft, D. H., *The British Economy between the Wars*, London, P. Allan, 1983 (a good short introduction)

4   Aldcroft, D. H., *The Inter-War Economy*, London, Batsford, 1970

3   Branson, N., *Britain in the Nineteen Twenties*, London, Weidenfeld & Nicolson, 1975

3   Branson, N., and Heinemann, M., *Britain in the Nineteen Thirties*, London, Weidenfeld & Nicolson, 1971

3   Buxton, N. K. and Aldcroft, D. H., *British Industry between the Wars*, London, Scolar Press, 1979

3/4   Cannadine, D., *The Decline and Fall of the British Aristocracy*, New Haven and London, Yale, 1990

1   Constantine, S., *Unemployment in Britain between the Wars*, London, Longman, 1980

1   Constantine, S., *Social Conditions in Britain 1918–1939*, London, Methuen, 1983

4   Halsey, A. H. (ed.), *British Social Trends since 1900*, London, Macmillan, 1988

3   Hannington, W., *The Problem of the Distressed Areas*, London, Gollancz, 1937

1   Howego, J., *London in the 1920s and 1930s from Old Photographs*, London, Batsford, 1978

4   Llewellyn Smith, H. (ed.), *The New Survey of London Life and Labour*, London, London School of Economics, 1934

3   Marwick, A., *The Deluge – British Society and the First World War*, London, Macmillan, 1984

3   Mowat, C. L., *Britain between the Wars 1918–1940*, London, Methuen, 1955

2   Muggeridge, M., *The Thirties*, London, Collins, 2nd edn, 1971

3   Perkin, H., *The Rise of Professional Society*, London, Routledge, 1989

3   Priestley, J. B., *English Journey*, London, Gollancz, 1934, repr. Penguin, 1977

2   Orwell, G., *The Road to Wigan Pier*, London, Gollancz, 1937, repr. Penguin, 1962

4   Rowntree, B. S., *Poverty and Progress*, London, Longman, 1941

3   Stevenson, J., *Social Conditions in Britain between the Wars*, London, Penguin, 1977

3   Stevenson, J., *British Society 1914–45*, London, Penguin, 1984

3   Stevenson, J. and Cook, C., *The Slump – Society and Problems during the Depression*, London, Cape, 1977

2/3   Taylor, A. J. P., *English History 1914–1945*, Oxford, Oxford University Press, 1966

4   Winter, J. M., *The Great War and the British People*, London, Macmillan, 1986

Sources for coursework

Many of the above works contain excellent bibliographies with guidance for further reading. Of those published in the 1930s, like Llewellyn Smith's survey or Priestley's *English Journey*, many provide excellent starting points for any study. Local newspapers, family archives, including old photographs, interviews with survivors and specialized local collections in reference libraries all offer opportunities for personal research. In addition, major national collections also exist, like the Museum of Labour History in Liverpool and other predominantly industrial towns.

10 The Conservative Party of the Chamberlains 1906–40

INTRODUCTION

The suggestion in 1885 that the leading family in the Tory Party in the next century would be the Chamberlains would have brought the speaker a certificate of lunacy. Yet the party of the landed gentry was to pass from the aristocratic custody of the Cecils into the hands of a Birmingham dynasty of screw manufacturers. Joseph, the radical hope of 1885, was never to gain the leadership of the Tory Party but his two sons, Austen and Neville, were each to hold this position. This is both testimony to the glorious unpredictability of British politics, and also symbolic of the major changes which overtook the Conservatives and British society in the late nineteenth and early twentieth centuries.

The Conservatives of the inter-war years were clearly different from what they had been in 1867 – the voice of the squirearchy. Even as late as 1900 nearly 40 per cent of Conservative MPs were still from the landed classes and only 30 per cent from industry and commerce. In the first decade of the twentieth century 30 per cent could still claim some connection with the aristocracy. Balfour had written to his uncle Lord Salisbury, the Prime Minister, in August 1891, advising the appointment of a northern manufacturer as Postmaster General. He claimed that his nominee, a certain W. L. Jackson: 'has great tact and judgement – middle class tact and judgement I admit, but good of their kind . . . he is that *rara avis*, a successful manufacturer who is fit for something besides manufacturing.' In fact the party was already changing despite the traditional background of Balfour and uncle Robert. Of new MPs who entered Parliament on the Tory side in 1900 42 per cent were from industry and commerce and only 29 per cent from the traditional landed elite. After 1918 two-thirds of the parliamentary party were either businessmen or professionals. Only 15 per cent were landed. The middle classes, whose drift to the Conservatives had been marked by the late 1870s, had now captured the parliamentary party. The Tories had become the party of suburbia rather than the party of broad acres.

Tories were also to appeal successfully to a large segment of the working classes. In both Liverpool and Birmingham there was strong working-class Conservatism in the 1890s. Only in the Scotland division of Liverpool, where there was an Irish immigrant majority, did the Unionist candidate lose regularly between 1885 and 1945. It was the presence of this Irish community that was probably responsible for the strength of working-class Conservatism elsewhere in the city. A similar swing to the Tories developed in Glasgow and western Scotland where again there was large-scale Irish immigration. In Birmingham Joseph Chamberlain's defection to the Tory Party consolidated an already strong Conservative working-class base. Patriotism and anti-immigrant feeling were both vital components of the appeal of Unionism in the Midlands. The tripling of the electorate in 1918, far from spelling disaster, ushered in an era of election victories. Democracy did not spell doom for the Tories. Unlike so many of the European Conservative parties of the nineteenth century, tied to declining aristocratic power and agriculture, that of Britain adapted and adjusted to the new industrial urban society. The Cecils giving way to the Chamberlains was part of this process.

What Conservatism was in the early twentieth century is perhaps harder to define than it was even in 1867. Lord Hugh Cecil, son of Lord Salisbury, produced a book in 1912 entitled *Conservatism*. He admitted a preference for what existed and had been tried over the 'unknown' – a vague, but possibly sufficient, definition of 'Conservatism'. As in the nineteenth century the party tended to define itself in terms of what it was against. Cecil admitted that 'Conservatives have no difficulty in welcoming the social activity of the state', but he went on to denounce the injustice of redistributing wealth from the rich to the poor. It was this opposition to 'excessive socialistic redistribution' which had appeal to the middle-class voters and MPs. Stanley Baldwin, a new Tory MP in 1908 and no die-hard reactionary (he was one of the twelve rebels to support the Liberals' Old Age Pension in 1908), neatly expressed this common Conservative view of redistribution: 'It is one thing to do good to your soul by renouncing your own earthly goods, but it is quite another to do good to another man's soul by taking away his goods.'

The Russian Revolution of 1917 tainted socialism with anarchy and destruction. Throughout the 1920s Bolshevism could be used to magnify the redistributive threat of Britain's own home-grown Labour Party whose very growth strengthened the Conservatives as the defenders of property against a despoiling state. As in the nineteenth century, when British Conservatism was in reaction to the French Revolution and its tame British 'liberal' heirs, so in the twentieth century the Russian Revolution served the Tory Party well and 'red scares' proved an electoral asset.

Many Conservatives also saw themselves as the defenders of morality in an increasingly immoral world. They were no longer simply the party of the Anglican Church (although for tradition's sake it would defend the Church of Wales against Liberal disestablishment in 1914). Baldwin was to see his role in the 1920s as a moral one in terms of both healing class divisions and cleansing the state from the immorality and political corruption of Lloyd George. Baldwin's cousin, the poet Rudyard Kipling, had felt a violent distaste in 1912 for the whiff of corruption generated by the Marconi scandal. His poem 'Gehasi' was a denunciation of Rufus Isaacs, the Liberal lawyer at the centre of it. Kipling, like many, saw the Tories as the natural guardians of political morality. Sir William Joynson Hicks, Baldwin's Home Secretary from 1924 to 1929, made it almost a crusade to purify the land of personal immorality. Night-clubs were raided for after-hours drinking, proceedings against literary and artistic 'obscenities' encouraged, and the police ordered to stamp out unseemly acts in the parks.

Conservatives also saw themselves as the defenders of the nation. They were the party of patriotism. It was Disraeli's most valuable bequest. Even patriotism, however, was usually seen in negative terms as the defence of the realm against threats: the threat of the German navy before 1914, the threat of foreign economic competition. Tariff reform was a patriotic Conservative answer. The Liberal policy of Home Rule threatened to split the Empire's heart. Conservative Unionists were the defenders of the 'United Kingdom'. The bitterness generated by this defence in the years before the First World War was probably unparalleled in British party politics. Property, morality and Britain itself all seemed threatened and Conservatives saw themselves as the most suitable and effective guardians.

Political parties also have a momentum of their own, regardless of any fundamental philosophy. They are a team or a business corporation whose object, above all else, is to win and succeed at the expense of their rivals. Once in existence with a powerful machinery of agents, local committees and regional and national staff they generate support and political activity without the need for any bedrock beliefs. Balfour, Baldwin and Neville Chamberlain were all from Conservative families and attached themselves to the familial political machine without having to think about whether they were Conservatives or what 'Conservatism' was. To both Balfour and Neville Chamberlain the Conservative Party was primarily an instrument for efficient government. Party was the rather unfortunate concomitant of democracy. Neville Chamberlain clearly expressed this early in his political career:

> It has been found, however, that public interest cannot be stimulated in local concerns unless it is worked up by an efficient organisation. Such organisations are only maintained by the political parties and it is for that reason that in my judgment the Party system is on the whole the best for local elections in spite of its obvious drawbacks and even inconsistencies.

(Quoted in D. Dilks, *Neville Chamberlain*, Cambridge, Cambridge University Press, 1984, p. 127)

He was the true son of his father Joe. Politics was about getting things done and solving problems and the Conservative and Unionist Party, particularly in the inter-war years, seemed to be the party of sound and sensible government where abstract ideas were kept to a minimum. In this sense 'Conservatism' was almost an anti-political belief and the Conservative Party the no-nonsense approach of the businessman erected into a political system.

The party's machine remained formidable throughout these years. Like anything else it had its ups and downs and the period after the party agent R. W. E. Middleton's retirement in 1903 was a trough. Following the defeats of 1910, Balfour initiated reforms which led to the creation of a new office of Chairman of the Party organization. The Chief Whip's role was now confined to parliamentary matters. The Liberal Unionist organization was amalgamated with the Conservatives at the same time. Further extensive reform followed in the 1920s under J. C. C. Davidson as Party Chairman from 1926. Change was necessary to cope with the new mass electorate. Registration of voters was now no longer the vital matter it had been in the nineteenth century but postal voting was established in 1918 and the Conservatives came to terms with the organizational demands of this quicker than their rivals. A political education centre was set up at Ashridge in Kent and a Research Department to brief speakers with the necessary facts and analyses. Neville Chamberlain took over as its director in 1930 and the department set about preparing future blueprints for action when the Tories returned to office. First-rate assistants were appointed to Central Office, amongst these the mysterious Joseph Ball formerly of MI5. He set out successfully to penetrate Labour Party headquarters through an agent at the Labour Party's printers in order to get advance warning of Labour propaganda. Despite such quaint initiatives the real strength of the Tory Party machine lay in its army of agents, of which there were 352, together with 99 women organizers, all of whom received training between 1924 and 1937. This was far more than the decrepit Liberal Party organization of these years could manage, or the Labour Party, which depended on trade union organizers doubling up as its agents. Women played a vital part in the local organization, raising funds and serving as volunteers at elections. In this sense the Conservatives gave women a greater political role than their rivals. Their generosity did not extend to promoting women in Parliament. There were only twelve women out of 534 Conservative candidates in 1924 and never more than three sitting as MPs throughout the 1920s.

OUT OF OFFICE 1905–15

Joseph Chamberlain, as we have seen in chapters 2 and 3, was taken prisoner by Lord Salisbury and apparently tamed. He remained a dynamic force and as Baldwin said of Lloyd George, a dynamic force is a very terrible thing. Chamberlain placed himself at the head of the protectionist movement inside the Conservative Party with his speech calling for tariffs in 1903. The party became bitterly divided on the issue and lost the general election of 1906. It was a calamity: the worst defeat suffered in the party's history. Only 157 seats were held. Nowhere except in the West Midlands did they retain a majority of the popular votes cast. Lancashire and London, the twin bases of the revival under Disraeli and Salisbury, were lost. In most constituencies the number of Conservative voters remained little changed from 1900 while the number of Liberal and Labour voters increased by over 25 per cent. Many had voted for the first time to reject tariff reform. Yet if the country had rejected it the Conservative Party appeared to have endorsed it more than ever. In the new House of Commons 109 Chamberlainite tariff reformers faced 16 free traders and 32 supporters of Balfour's compromise position. Hence the *Punch* cartoon shown here is at pains to point out Chamberlain's control of the party's direction.

The Cecil clan had done badly, Arthur Balfour himself lost in East Manchester, as did his brother Gerald in Leeds. Lord Hugh Cecil, Balfour's cousin and a leading free trade Tory, lost at Greenwich. Joseph Chamberlain and his son Austen retained their seats. Balfour was found a safe constituency in the City of London where the victorious Conservative was persuaded to resign. He immediately faced a tussle with the Chamberlainites for control of the party. Both declared their loyalty to Balfour but in an exchange of letters known from their date as the 'Valentine Letters', Balfour endorsed tariff reform as the first, constructive work of the Unionist Party. He was saved from further trouble and temporarily, at least, guaranteed his position by Joseph Chamberlain's paralysing stroke in July 1906.

Stopping rather than forwarding 'constructive legislation' became the forte of Balfour's party after 1906. Rather ominously the Tory leader had said at Nottingham on 15 January: 'the great Unionist party should still control whether in power or whether in opposition the destinies of this great Empire.' The House of Lords was the instrument of control and between 1906 and 1908 its Unionist majority was able to challenge and mutilate various Liberal measures making Balfour's boast a reality. In April 1906 he expounded his strategy clearly in a letter to Lord Lansdowne, the Unionist leader in the Lords:

I do not think the House of Lords will be able to escape the duty of making serious modifications in important Government measures, but, if this is done with caution and tact, I do not believe that they will do themselves any harm. On the contrary, as the rejection of the Home Rule Bill undoubtedly strengthened their position, I think it is quite possible that your House may come out of the ordeal

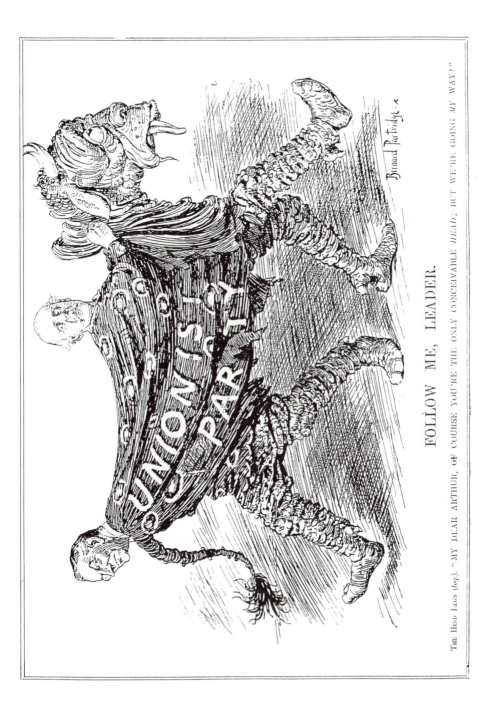

Bernard Partridge

FOLLOW ME, LEADER.

The Hind Legs (log). "MY DEAR ARTHUR, OF COURSE YOU'RE THE ONLY CONCEIVABLE *HEAD*; BUT WE'RE GOING *MY* WAY!"

strengthened rather than weakened by the inevitable difficulties of the next few years.

(Quoted in R. Jenkins, *Mr Balfour's Poodle: Peers v. People*, Glasgow and London, Collins, 1952, p. 40)

The consequences of this great aristocratic challenge to democracy have already been examined in chapter 6. The caution and tact referred to above by Balfour was clearly lacking in 1909 when he and Lansdowne decided to use the Lords to reject Lloyd George's budget. Their motive appears to have been one of a desire to uphold party unity at all costs. The budget would replace the divisive issue of tariff reform. In fact, the tariff reformers were ardent opponents of the budget. Lloyd George proposed progressive direct taxes and taxes on luxury consumption as the fiscal solution to increased state spending on defence and social reform. It was a central plank in tariff reform theory that only tariffs could pay for these desirable objectives. Lord Hugh Cecil and Austen Chamberlain could join forces against the socialism of Lloyd George and hang the consequences.

The results of the January 1910 election were a disappointment to both the Conservatives and the Liberals. The progressive alliance of Liberal, Labour and Irish Nationalists still kept the Conservatives as a clear minority. They gained 47 per cent of the popular vote and 273 seats. They overtook the Liberals in popular votes but were still inferior in seats. The Conservative majority that seemed likely in 1908 had evaporated. Tariff reform had little appeal as the economy revived and Lloyd George's budget strategy and the behaviour of the House of Lords had provided an effective progressive rallying cry. The Unionists gained 116 seats, particularly in the south. A majority of London seats returned to the Conservative fold but Lancashire was not attracted by tariff reform. Southern England gave a two to one Conservative majority in terms of seats won. In the north it was the reverse. Overall Asquith retained a working majority of 124.

The Unionist House of Lords now faced a direct assault, hardly a promising battleground for the party. The conflict has already been surveyed in chapter 6. Balfour and some other leading Conservatives were attracted by Lloyd George's quaint idea of a cross-party programme of action but in the end compromise proved impossible. Party feelings were running high. Behind the issue of the Lords lay that of Home Rule which stirred many Tory patriots to the depths of their political being. The Lords' rejection of the Parliament Bill produced the second election of 1910 in December. Before it Balfour was trapped by Asquith into promising a referendum on tariff reform if the Conservatives 'were returned to power'. He hoped to secure a similar pledge from the Liberals on Home Rule. He failed but alienated the fanatic tariff reformers in his party. Further division ensued following the election which produced virtually no change in the overall composition of the Commons. Balfour and Lansdowne now favoured surrender to the Liberals and the passing of the Parliament Bill. Failure to do this would entail the mass creation of peers, making a mockery of the Lords and destroying what was still an important political Tory weapon, given their large majority in the Upper House. Two-year delaying powers could still be used effectively to frustrate a Liberal–radical programme. The Unionists now divided afresh into 'Ditchers', like the aged Lord Halsbury, backed by Austen Chamberlain, Sir Edward Carson and F. E. Smith. They, it was said, would die in the last ditch to frustrate the Bill. The 'Hedgers' followed Balfour's cool appraisal of the party needs and recognized that the passage of the Bill was essential to avoid the enormity of mass creation of peers. The Bill just passed but the wounds left in the Unionist Party were deep.

No-one questioned Balfour's intellectual primacy but three election defeats, his climbdown on tariff reform, and now the Parliament Bill, heightened criticism of his leadership. Leo Maxse of the right-wing *National Review*, for long a critic of Balfour, coined the abbreviation BMG in his September 1911 issue – Balfour Must Go. Before the débâcle of 1910–11 there had been many Unionists who pointed out Balfour's deficiencies as a popular leader. As one Conservative had forcefully put it to Balfour's Private Secretary in 1907:

> But he is not understood (and therefore looked on suspiciously) in the country. His intellect is far greater than that of his party and even than that of the bulk of his colleagues – and his thoughts and language are sometimes not understood by them. He is often over the heads of his audience – outside the H. of C. – and for this reason . . . they honestly don't know what his quality is – and therefore sincerely think he is vacillating. If he could consider that the major portion of his party were . . . stupid and uneducated and get himself down to their level he would be better understood and appreciated.
>
> (Quoted in M. Egremont, *Balfour*, London, Collins, 1980, p. 213)

In office such eccentricities were often considered endearing, in opposition they were irritating and demonstrated, it seemed to many, Balfour's self-imposed exile from the real world. He appears by the action of 1911 to have had enough of division and criticism and when in October the 'Halsbury Club' of die-hard 'Ditchers' was formed, Balfour decided to resign.

The ensuing struggle for the leadership threw up a very contrasting figure. The two front-runners were Austen Chamberlain, the heir to his father's tariff reform kingdom, and Walter Long. In many ways they symbolized the uneasy alliance which was the Unionist Party in Edwardian England. Walter Long was a peppery country squire not noted for his intellect. He had little enthusiasm for tariff reform and had been a 'Hedger' during the Parliament Crisis. He did, however, command considerable support from traditional elements in the party. Austen was simply the banner bearer of his formidable father. He had been schooled for political success by Joseph and had accepted his role. He would fulfil his father's dreams of tariff reform and the premiership. Yet there was a lack of steel. His very appearance was modelled on his father. Underneath the surface was a thoroughly decent intelligent upper-middle-class Englishman who enjoyed his family life more than power. It was for his father's sake that he would be leader rather than his own, but unlike his father he would not brutally seize his chance. In Churchill's famous phrase, 'he always played the game and he always lost it'. To get around a damaging split in the party Austen decided to withdraw and persuaded Long to do the same. The beneficiary of this generosity was a teetotalling, dour Scot of Ulster and Canadian extraction. Andrew Bonar Law was a 53-year-old businessman who had only entered Parliament in 1900. He was a respected member of the Unionist front bench on account of his clear exposition of tariff reform issues. As one admirer said, 'Bonar Law's style was like the hammering of a skilled riveter, every blow hitting the nail on the head.' His simple directness appealed to a frustrated party fed up with Balfour's dialectical niceties. Here was a leader who would lead them into battle, without philosophic doubt. He was elected unanimously with no contest. His manager had been the Canadian newspaper tycoon Max Aitken who was Unionist MP for Ashton-under-Lyne. Aitken told how he said to Bonar Law as they left the Carlton Club, 'You are a great man now.' Bonar Law's simple directness showed in his reply, 'If I am a great man then a good many great men must have been frauds.'

Bonar Law made it quite clear to Asquith, the Liberal Prime Minister, that he would have to adopt a different style to Balfour. 'I am afraid I shall have to show myself very vicious this session', he said once as they walked together at the opening of the parliamentary session. Bonar Law appreciated the expectations of his troops. His Scottish accent, his disdain for polite society and strong liquor, his simple love of milk pudding and chess could all be forgotten and forgiven in return for his violent denunciation of Home Rule. He espoused Ulster's cause with an enthusiasm Balfour could never have conjured up. Bonar Law was clearly uniting his party on this issue but genuine political fervour lay behind this political calculation. At times his support for Ulster's resistance to Home Rule bordered on the criminal. In a great Unionist rally at Blenheim Palace in July 1912 he declared that 'there are things stronger than parliamentary majorities'. He himself seemed to be supporting armed resistance to a lawful government:

> Before I occupied the position which I now fill in the Party I said
> that, in my belief, if an attempt were made to deprive these men of

their birth-right – as part of a corrupt Parliamentary bargain – they would be justified in resisting such an attempt by all means in their power, including force. I said it then, and I repeat now with a full sense of the responsibility which attaches to my position, that, in my opinion, if such an attempt is made, I can imagine no length of resistance to which Ulster can go in which I should not be prepared to support them, and in which, in my belief, they would not be supported by the overwhelming majority of the British people.

(Quoted in R. Blake, *Bonar Law – The Unknown Prime Minister*, London, Eyre & Spottiswoode, 1955, p. 130)

At no other time in the twentieth century have British party passions become so embittered to the point that many talked of the breakdown of constitutional government. Bonar Law wanted a political settlement, the exclusion of Ulster from Home Rule Ireland, but he was prepared to go to extraordinary lengths to extract this concession. In February and March 1914 as the Home Rule Bill slowly approached its final passage, despite the Lords' two-year veto, Bonar Law seriously considered using the Lords to reject the annual Mutiny Bill upon which discipline in the army rested.

The use of the 'orange card', as Lord Randolph Churchill had christened it back in 1886, was a dangerous policy which threatened to extend to the whole of the United Kingdom the tribal passions of Ulster. In many ways it appeared to be electorally unpromising in England by 1914. The breakdown of the Liberal–Labour Pact in various by-elections in 1912–13 had benefited the Conservatives. But the defence of constitutional government against Unionist extremism could re-cement the progressive alliance and damn the Conservatives to another five years of opposition. There were various ominous signs that the coming election of 1915 would not be favourable. What was to become a common pattern of twentieth-century British politics seemed to be operating. There had been a mid-term swing of 4.4 per cent against the government but by 1914 it was recovering its popularity. The passage of the Plural Voting Bill, which would be on the statute book before the next general election despite the House of Lords, was generally calculated to cost the Conservatives thirty seats. Only the bitter fragmentation of the forces of the left could give the Conservatives hope of success yet their very emphasis on Ulster and opposition to Home Rule, in order to preserve Unionist harmony, enabled Asquith to keep his coalition together. Ramsay MacDonald of the Labour Party and Redmond of the Irish Nationalists would cleave to the Liberals because of this one issue. Bonar Law resisted appeals to embrace more positive social reform. There was still considerable resistance to tariff reform within the party and Bonar Law had to abandon his plans to repudiate Balfour's pledge of November 1910 on a referendum. The Unionists were trapped in the policy blackhole of Ulster fanaticism.

Initially the war added to their dilemma. Two days before its outbreak Bonar Law and Lansdowne had written to offer their 'unhesitating support' to the government. As the patriotic party they could do little else. The only alternative was to abandon Westminster for the trenches of France and ninety-eight Conservatives did just this by January 1915. The party truce meant a suspension of by-election contests, but there was considerable and growing frustration on the back benches as Conservatives felt themselves to be the natural leaders of the country at war. Bonar Law feared open party warfare which might divide the country disastrously at a time of great peril. He worked to avoid a replay of 1900 when the Boer War had been managed by the Conservatives but denounced by most of the left and had indeed been instrumental in forging the Edwardian progressive alliance.

THE CONSERVATIVES IN COALITION 1915–22

The May Crisis of 1915 which ended the last purely Liberal Government appears initially as a Liberal triumph (see chapter 6, pp. 209–10). Bonar Law and the Tory front bench did rather badly in sharing the spoils of office. Bonar Law himself only got the Colonial Office with seven other Unionists in the Cabinet compared to twelve Liberals. Only Balfour gained one of the six vital offices – the Admiralty. Many of the Conservative leaders were not displeased to see Bonar Law so humiliated and looked forward to his replacement. It was on the advice of Curzon, a leading Tory grandee, that Asquith chose to omit Bonar Law from the key Cabinet Committee in August 1915. Bonar Law's anger is clear from this letter:

'Dear Mr. Asquith,

'I am greatly surprised to learn that you have not included my name in the Committee which was decided upon in yesterday's cabinet. It is the most important Committee which has been set up since the present Government was formed and as the leader of our Party in the House of Commons it is difficult for me to understand on what principle you left me out of it without previously consulting me.

'Yours very truly,
A. Bonar Law.'

Asquith enjoyed playing on the tensions between new Conservative colleagues. He had had plenty of experience doing it with Liberals and he saw no reason why his talents of dividing and ruling should not extend his premiership in the future.

Yet the war, as we saw in chapter 6, proved disastrous for the Liberals fragmenting the progressive alliance and ultimately ushering in a quarter of a century of Conservative dominance. Home Rule, although on the statute books, was shelved. Redmond, of the Irish Nationalists, refused to join Asquith's Cabinet but the Ulster Unionists' leader Edward Carson was brought in as Attorney General. It was the Conservatives who seemed increasingly more at home in the situation of directing total war. They could more readily accept conscription than the Liberals. The harsh suppression of the Easter Rising in Dublin in 1916 could be expected from a Tory Government but not one led by a Liberal. The final crisis which brought about Asquith's fall was as much a product of Conservative in-fighting as Liberal rivalries. Carson appeared to be intriguing with Lloyd George and even the rigidly honourable Austen Chamberlain was to write in a letter: 'We have little confidence in Bonar Law's judgement, and none in his strength of character.'

As Bonar Law's loyalty to Asquith seemed to be undermining his position in his own party he decided reluctantly to throw in his hand with Lloyd George in forcing a government reconstruction, and in the process strengthen his own position against the plots and intrigues of men like Carson and Lord Curzon. In offering their resignations to Asquith on 5 December it may be that some of the Tory leaders, notably Curzon, hoped to ditch Bonar Law and Lloyd George in a reshuffle. Whatever the intention the result was Lloyd George's accession to the premiership and Bonar Law in a much enhanced position as Chancellor of the Exchequer. The Unionists were now in a stronger position. Lloyd George might be a Liberal and acknowledged as a virtual dictator of the war effort, but he was increasingly dependent on Tory votes in the Commons. The progressive alliance disintegrated. The Liberals were split between the followers of Lloyd George and Asquith. Labour withdrew from the coalition in November 1918 and resolved to fight the next election against allcomers. The Irish Nationalists faced a surge of electoral support for Sinn Fein.

Despite this favourable split many Conservatives were deeply worried by the implications of the new electorate conjured up by the Parliament Act of 1918. There would now be 22 million voters not 8 million. The working class would dominate as never before. They had secured various concessions to sugar the democratic pill. Plural voting was retained and there was an extension of university seats. Postal voting was introduced to enable the men in the forces to vote and conscientious objectors were excluded for five years. To make doubly sure that the appeal of the Labour Party should not triumph Bonar Law and the leader of the Unionists wanted to fight the election under Lloyd George's continued leadership. The Welshman might still lead nominally but the election underlined his dependence on the Tories. Bonar Law stated as much to a meeting of Conservative MPs on 12 November:

By our own action we have made Mr. Lloyd George the flag bearer of the very principles upon which we should appeal to the country. It is not his Liberal friends, it is the Unionist Party which has made him Prime Minister, and made it possible for him to do the great work that has been done by this Government.

(Quoted in Blake, op. cit., p. 387)

He also explained the element of fear behind the decision to continue the coalition:

Remember this, that at this moment Mr. Lloyd George commands an amount of influence in every constituency as great as has ever been exercised by any Prime Minister in our political history.

(ibid., p. 388)

But this said, it was not just mere party calculation but a genuine belief that the country could best be served by coalition government. Those who won the war should also win the peace. Many of the Conservative leaders found coalition cosy. Balfour, Austen Chamberlain, Curzon and F. E. Smith (now elevated to the Lord Chancellorship as Lord Birkenhead), all enjoyed the freedom from the game of party warfare. As 'superior' persons they could rule the country in its best interests. The little Welshman had enough popular appeal to keep them in power and keep Labour at bay. Many assumed that they had discovered a new Joseph Chamberlain and that, like Chamberlain, Lloyd George would slowly transmute from Radical to Unionist.

The decision to fight the election as a coalition proved a triumph for the Conservatives. Coalition Conservatives, that is those in receipt of the 'coupon' (see p. 218), gained 335 seats with only 32.6 per cent of the popular vote. In addition there were another 48 uncouponed Conservatives. Thus the Conservatives alone had a majority in the new Parliament, a majority of overwhelming proportions as the Sinn Feiners did not take their 73 seats and the other opposition parties were too fragmented. Democracy had come to Britain. The demon that so many Conservatives had feared in the mid-nineteenth century now endorsed their party above all others.

The achievements and failures of the coalition have already been discussed in chapter 6. In 1906 Protection had been the Conservatives' chief rallying cry; in 1910 and the few years afterwards it was Ulster. And it was these issues more than any others which moved Bonar Law. All the rest he admitted was merely playing games. Anti-German fervour had drowned all other issues in 1918 and with this, and through this, Conservatism could easily accommodate itself to democracy. After 1918, Conservatives were increasingly associated with the old Gladstonian principle of retrenchment. The bloated role of the state produced by the war and the crushing taxation excited the anti-waste campaign. Lloyd George's boundless energy and the reforming zeal of such Liberal ministers as Addison and Fisher looked likely to perpetuate a much enhanced role for the state. Conservatives increasingly found this unsupportable. As the new party of retrenchment it could also hope to attract ex-Liberal voters and make itself the sole barrier to the Labour Party's triumph. Conservative power within the coalition gradually asserted itself. Addison was dumped and his housing programme severely modified. The Ministry of Food was abolished in March 1921 and back-bench pressure forced the Cabinet to drop a plan produced by Sir Eric Geddes to nationalize the railways. Coal was de-controlled in 1921 and the Sankey Commission recommendations ignored. The Ministry of Transport was abolished in 1922. Austen Chamberlain, as Chancellor of the Exchequer from 1919 to 1921, fully endorsed this trend and his successor, Sir Robert Horne, was if anything even more enthusiastic. The Conservative Party was increasingly becoming the party of 'economy', Its appeal to income-tax payers was obvious.

In March 1921 Bonar Law resigned as Lord Privy Seal and leader of the Conservative Party. Dangerously high blood pressure necessitated a complete rest. There was no doubt about his successor. Austen could now complete his dead father's ambition and become leader of the Unionist Party being unanimously elected at a meeting at the Carlton Club. Bonar Law's retirement was a disaster for Lloyd George. Austen was no less loyal – if anything more so – but he lacked Bonar Law's hold on his party and failed to register its emotions. He seemed a distant figure to most of his followers. As one cabinet colleague wrote in 1921, 'I respect Austen very much but he is aloof and reserved. I seldom see him and never seem to get to know him any better.' Even Bonar Law would have found it difficult to control the growing resentment on the Tory benches towards the little Welshman. There had always been some back-bench hostility to Lloyd George and these die-hards, as they were called, gained influence and power within the party as Lloyd George upset or ignored vital Unionist sentiments. The Liberal Viceroy of India, Edwin Montagu, upset many with his apparent moves towards Indian self-government. The Irish settlement of 1921, despite the safeguarding of Ulster, seemed to many a great betrayal of the Union. What was not done also caused upset. The pledges given in 1917 to reform the House of Lords, re-creating an effective second chamber, were not carried out. Tariff reform was ignored, to the disgust of enthusiasts like Leo Amery, biographer of the great Joseph Chamberlain. Agriculture was neglected to the irritation of the squirearchy. In addition, there was a distaste for the style and 'corruption' of the Welshman. There was also frustration at being kept out of office. Only half the cabinet members were Conservatives, despite their strength in the Commons, and many ambitious junior ministers felt a deep frustration with a coalition system which blocked their way to a cabinet position. By the early part of 1922 hostility to the continuation of the coalition was becoming dangerously inflamed.

Talk of a second coalition election was firmly knocked on the head by Sir George Younger, the chairman of the party organization. An influential Conservative backbencher and future Party Chairman, J. C. C. Davidson was to write in January:

> I was talking to S. B. [Stanley Baldwin] the other day (he is against an election) and he is inclined to share the opinion that our own people fervently desire to know where they stand and what they stand for.
>   The re-establishment of a great Conservative Party with
>   Honest Government
>   Drastic Economy
>   National Security
>   and
>   No Adventures abroad or at home
> would carry great weight in the country.
>
> (ibid., p. 437)

It is in such comments that we see much of the programme of the inter-war Conservative Party.

Three leading Conservatives determined the timing of the breakup of the coalition. Austen Chamberlain, by his stiff-necked loyalty to Lloyd George and his determination to push ahead with a plan for a coalition election in 1922 against the advice of the Party Chairman, national agent and Chief Whip, ensured the humiliating rebuff he received at the Carlton Club meeting of 19 October. Chamberlain lectured the party on the need to continue the coalition. He was followed by Stanley Baldwin, President of the Board of Trade in the Coalition Government. He denounced the coalition and its Prime Minister:

> [The Prime Minister] is a dynamic force, and it is from that very fact that our troubles, in our opinion, arise. A dynamic force is a very terrible thing; it may crush you but it is not necessarily right. It is owing to that dynamic force, and that remarkable personality, that the Liberal Party, to which he formerly belonged, has been smashed to pieces; and it is my firm conviction that, in time, the same thing will happen to our party. I do not propose to elaborate, in an assembly like this, the dangers and the perils of that happening. . . . I think that if the present association is continued, and if this meeting agrees that it should be continued, you will see some more breaking up, and I believe the process must go on inevitably until the old Conservative Party is smashed to atoms and lost in ruins.
>
> (Quoted in Jenkins, op. cit., pp. 52–3)

The reappearance of Bonar Law delivered the *coup de grâce* to Chamberlain. In him, now apparently recovered, the party had an alternative leader. His vote for an end to the coalition brought Lloyd George and

Chamberlain down and dissolved the coalition partnership. It also brought Bonar Law to Number 10.

THE CONSERVATIVES IN POWER OCTOBER 1922 TO JANUARY 1924: 'THE SECOND ELEVEN'

The government that Bonar Law formed, after having had himself formally re-elected as party leader, was not distinguished by anything other than the quantity of blue blood. Only four of the sixteen cabinet members could be correctly addressed as 'Mr'. There were seven peers. It would not have looked out of place, as it was remarked, in the eighteenth century. Only Bonar Law and Curzon had senior cabinet experience. It was an alliance of die-hard reactionaries, like the Marquis of Salisbury, and discontented junior ministers from the coalition, like Leo Amery. Stanley Baldwin, a minister of minimal cabinet experience, but at least some, was rocketed to the Exchequer, a sign of Bonar Law's desperation. All the Lloyd George coalitionists were mortified and refused to co-operate – except Curzon who neatly, as in 1916, did a quick jump from the sinking ship to land safely on the one now afloat. It became one of Bonar Law's priorities to win back much of the talent of the party. He was gratified when Neville Chamberlain, Austen's younger brother, accepted an appointment outside the Cabinet.

The general election that followed the breakup of the coalition must rank as one of the most confused and confusing in recent British history. The Conservatives confronted two Liberal parties and the Labour Party. The issues at stake were not very clear. Bonar Law took tranquillity as his theme:

> The crying need of the nation at this moment, a need which in my judgement far exceeds any, is that we should have tranquillity and stability at home and abroad, so that free scope should be given to the initiative and enterprise of our citizens.
>
> (Quoted in Blake, op. cit., p. 467)

Not since the days of Lord Salisbury at his most somnolent had the nation been promised such repose. The two Liberal parties could offer very little. Lloyd George was too surprised by the speed of it all, and Asquith had had no ideas since 1916. Labour had an idea, the capital levy, a tax on war profits, but decided that like all other ideas at this time it was potentially a vote loser and dropped it half-way through the campaign. The Conservatives nominally supported tariff reform but, like Labour with their central plank, dropped it. Bonar Law had promised that tariff reform would not be introduced without a second general election.

The general public decided that they could snore more safely under the Conservatives and the result fully justified the likes of Baldwin and

Younger in breaking up the coalition. With 344 seats the Conservatives had a majority of 77 over all other parties. The press had helped considerably. Lord Rothermere's *Daily Mail* and *Daily Mirror* supported the Conservatives as did Beaverbrook's *Daily Express*. Beaverbrook carried his enthusiasm even further and convinced unofficial Conservative supporters to stand against Lloyd George Liberals where there was no official Unionist candidate. Lloyd George's dog was an unwilling ally of Bonar Law on the occasion of a visit to Lloyd George's house at Churt by Lord Riddell, owner of the *News of the World*; the dog, a large chow, pinned the influential aristocrat in an empty room for nearly an hour while Lloyd George was out. The *News of the World* abandoned its usual stance and supported the Conservatives in November 1922, whether due to the chow or other circumstances is not clear.

Bonar Law's brief government on the whole lived *down* to its promises to do little. The one notable success was in foreign policy where Lord Curzon successfully extricated the country from confrontation with Turkey and produced the satisfactory Lausanne Settlement (see chapter 8). Baldwin as Chancellor of the Exchequer set off for Washington to settle the question of war debts. His inexperience showed in every way. He settled quickly for harsh terms, much harsher than the terms gained later by France and Italy, and he totally failed to link payments to America to the condition that Britain receive from others what was owed to her. Britain appeared as the honourable 'muggins'. Bonar Law clearly felt so and was for rejecting the terms when Baldwin returned. Unfortunately, Baldwin had already made a public statement broadcasting the terms at his landing at Southampton. The rest of the Cabinet reluctantly felt that Baldwin would have to be supported and Bonar Law gave in, writing by way of retaliation an anonymous letter to *The Times* denouncing the terms which his own government had accepted.

The only notable achievement at home was a Housing Act in 1923, put through by Neville Chamberlain who had been rapidly promoted to the Ministry of Health in March of that year. It provided a subsidy to encourage the building of small houses. It was more limited than Addison's Act and was designed to ensure that local authorities exercised thrift and caution but it did at least do something to promote more houses even if the chief beneficiaries were the lower middle class. Bonar Law duly reduced the scale of prime ministerial government as it had existed under Lloyd George – the 'garden suburb of Number 10', as it had become known, was dismantled and the great swollen body of secretarial and personal advisers was slimmed down. Sir Maurice Hankey (Cabinet Secretary), however, and the Cabinet Office were retained. Bonar Law himself was increasingly ill and it eventually became clear that he was suffering from an incurable throat cancer and in May 1923 he resigned. The succession was unclear. Bonar Law himself refused to make any recommendations to the king. Of the existing Cabinet, Curzon, the

George Curzon, Marquess of Kedleston
by Harry Furness

Foreign Secretary, and Baldwin as Chancellor were the leading contestants. Neither was ideal: Curzon was an eccentric if talented peer. (It was said that he had attempted to hail a bus and ordered it to take him to the Carlton House Terrace. He was surprised to find that 'the fellow flatly refused'.) Baldwin was still something of a political dwarf – 'little Baldwin' as Lloyd George had once described him. His rise to eminence was due solely to his speech at the Carlton Club and the lead he had given in breaking the coalition. His performance so far as Chancellor of the Exchequer hardly inspired great faith in his abilities. The king did eventually send for Baldwin. Balfour was consulted by George V and advised against Curzon. One of Baldwin's friends, J. C. C. Davidson, serving in Bonar Law's private office, seems to have drafted a memorandum for the king which strongly recommended Baldwin. It was passed off as Bonar Law's opinion. In fact, Baldwin was probably the favoured choice of most Conservative MPs in the circumstances. His arrival at

Number 10 in May 1923 was one of the strangest and unlooked-for political advances in British history. Curzon was mortified and it is reported that he wept like a child, sobbing that Baldwin was 'not even a public figure, a man of no experience and of the utmost insignificance, of the utmost insignificance'.

The new Prime Minister was 55 and so far had spent fifteen years as an MP. He was the wealthy son of a West Midlands ironmaster and had taken over the parliamentary seat of Bewdley in his native county of Worcestershire on the death of his father. He had finished at Cambridge with a third class degree and this had followed an undistinguished career at Harrow. He was not stupid but inclined to relax too readily and this was to give rise to the widely held belief that he was simply lazy. Clearly he had some talents that had raised him up. He had a gift for words and a real feel for the cadences and music of his native tongue which he used to extol the virtues of a vanishing rural England. He was also approachable and likeable. He was the first Prime Minister to address his colleagues by their christian names and BBC technicians recalled his relaxed and easy-going banter after a broadcast. It was his mastery of this latter technique which made him a formidable politician in the inter-war years. He learned faster than any of his rivals that the microphone took the politician into the voter's parlour, and the homely chat was more appropriate than the grandiloquence of a MacDonald or a Lloyd George. He was a complete contrast to the dour, hard-working Bonar Law who had first taken Baldwin into government in 1916. Not for Baldwin the methodical paperwork, the ploughing through civil service filled in-trays and boxes. He liked to talk and spent far more hours than most Prime Ministers in the Commons talking to both his own supporters and opponents. It was very hard to dislike him.

The driving passion of his political life was an intense disapproval of Lloyd George, and a desire to see the nation much as his family firm had been in his youth:

> It was a place where nobody ever got the sack and where . . . a number of old gentlemen used to spend their days sitting on the handles of wheelbarrows smoking their pipes. Oddly enough, it was not an inefficient community.
>
> (Quoted in Jenkins, op. cit., p. 94)

He was determined to exclude Lloyd George from power and if possible see the Liberals replaced by Labour. English politics could then proceed on a calm course. Not for Baldwin the passionate commitments of Bonar Law to Ulster nor Churchill's new-found detestation of Bolshevism. He saw himself as a healer, a man to minimize class tensions and sectarian hatreds by means of an appeal to decency and the vision of a gentle, kindly England. In 1925 he spoke against a die-hard Conservative backbencher measure to substitute 'contracting-in' for 'contracting-out' of the political levy which trade unions used to finance the Labour Party:

> Although I know that there are those who work for different ends from most of us in this House, yet there are many in all ranks and all parties who will re-echo my prayer 'Give peace in our time, O Lord.'
>
> (Quoted in R. A. Butler (ed.), *The Conservatives*, London, Allen & Unwin, 1977, p. 297)

Baldwin correctly felt that the British political system functioned best when two parties which shared more than they disagreed about could engage in ritualistic and gentlemanly conflict. He wished to avoid the dangerous party rivalry of 1911–14 when passions threatened the whole British parliamentary system. On the other hand, clearcut two-party rivalry would keep down faction and minimize the opportunities for unprincipled rogues like Lloyd George.

In his conduct of cabinet government he wished to undo the evil of Lloyd George. As one of his colleagues described: 'He wasn't – nor did he ever attempt to be – a Winston or a Lloyd George but the chairman of a competent board of managers.' There was none of the constant interference or over-ruling that had marked Lloyd George's premiership. Each minister was left to rule his department. Baldwin thought and talked about the middle- and long-distance issues, not the immediate, day-to-day problems. His lack of concentration on detail could be infuriating to ministers of a different persuasion. Chamberlain was irritated in a vital cabinet sub-committee meeting to find Baldwin passing a note to Churchill as Chancellor of the Exchequer bearing the following weighty information:

MATCHES

LENT AT 10.30 A.M.

RETURNED?

Baldwin's major decision as Prime Minister in 1923 was on the surface extraordinary. With a large majority already, which could run for another five years, he decided to hold another election on the issue of tariff reform in line with the pledge given in 1922. The election result was a surprising setback for the Conservatives. Although their share of the popular vote only fell from 38.2 per cent in 1922 to 38.1 per cent in 1923 they lost 87 seats as a result of the healing of the split between Asquith and Lloyd George. The result was the first Labour Government under MacDonald (see chapter 7). Baldwin, however, had succeeded in reuniting his party. Austen Chamberlain, Birkenhead and the other members of the 'first eleven' now returned to the Tory fold. Austen Chamberlain had no high opinion of Baldwin. When Balfour had presciently remarked that he found it difficult to gauge S.B.'s intelligence Austen, less presciently, remarked that it was impossible to gauge what did not exist. Nevertheless, Baldwin's charm, and the hard work of Neville Chamberlain brought Austen back to the opposition front bench. All that Baldwin had to do now was to wait for the inevitable downfall of the minority Labour Government. The Liberals had the opprobrium of putting Labour in and many middle-class Conservatives who had voted Liberal in 1923 would now vote Conservative to defend the social order. The Liberals also had the oppobrium of putting Labour out and many Radicals could vote Labour for the betrayal. The result was completely satisfactory to MacDonald and Baldwin. Lloyd George and the Liberals were well and truly dished. The general election of 1924 restored the two-party system that Baldwin had hoped to see. The Conservatives led by a moderate and progressive man could be the guardians of the social order. Labour, led by an almost equally moderate and progressive man, could talk about what threatened the social order. Lloyd George could be consigned to the political refuse heap.

BALDWIN'S SECOND MINISTRY 1924–9

The Conservatives had secured 48 per cent of the popular vote and 419 seats, a massive majority of over 200. Baldwin now had ample talent available, a board of directors who could be left each to their own departments to run things. Austen Chamberlain took the Foreign Office, and his brother Neville refused the Treasury, preferring to go back to the Ministry of Health where he proved the most constructive of inter-war politicians. The aged Balfour and the drunken Birkenhead were found places and most extraordinary of all, the wayward Liberal, Church-ill, was not only found a place but to his own astonishment was offered the Exchequer. Churchill had moved to the Conservative Party in the last two years, increasingly obsessed by the Bolshevik menace and his loss of a parliamentary seat in 1922. He was offered the safe Conservative seat of Epping and re-entered Parliament now under the colours he had first worn at Oldham in 1900. His hatred of Bolshevism endeared him to many die-hards in the Tory party:

> Judged by every standard which history has applied to Governments, the Soviet Government of Russia is one of the worst tyrannies that has ever existed in the world. It accords no political rights. It rules by terror. It punishes political opinions. It suppresses free speech. It tolerates no newspapers but its own. It persecutes Christianity with a zeal and a cunning never equalled since the times of the Roman Emperors. It is engaged at this moment in trampling down the peoples of Georgia and executing their leaders by hundreds.
> (Quoted in M. Gilbert, *W. S. Churchill*, vol. V, London, Heinemann, 1976, p. 48)

Baldwin decided that Churchill was probably much less trouble in than out of government and furthermore it was one more nail in Lloyd George's political coffin if this ex-Liberal colleague could be won over.

As Chancellor Churchill threw all his rumbustious energy into the new role. His debating skills strengthened the front bench. Neville Chamberlain in a letter to Baldwin expressed his admiration for the new Chancellor, and also some reservations:

> What a brilliant creature he is! But there is somehow a great gulf fixed between him and me which I don't think I shall ever cross. I like him. I like his humour and his vitality. I like his courage. I liked the way he took that – to me – very unexpected line over the coal crisis in Cabinet. But not for all the joys of Paradise would I be a member of his staff! Mercurial! A much abused word, but it is the literal description of his temperament.
>
> (Quoted in Dilks, op. cit., p. 441)

Churchill's stewardship of the nation's finances tends always to be seen in the light of the return to the gold standard in 1925 at too high a parity for the pound. The dominance of Keynesian economic thinking after 1945 has led to an almost unanimous condemnation of Churchill's decision and acclaim for Keynes's prescience in his criticism of Churchill. His *Economic Consequences of Mr. Churchill* gained great influence in the light of future events and even in the 1980s a television programme on the Great Depression could still accord prime causation to the return to the gold standard. This is clearly a gross exaggeration, as indicated in chapter 9. The root causes of the decline of Britain's staple industries were far deeper than a misjudgement in 1925. Churchill himself had misgivings as one of his draft papers at the time shows:

> The whole question of a return to the Gold Standard must not be dealt with only upon its financial and currency aspects. The merchant, the manufacturer, the workman and the consumer have interests which, though largely common, do not by any means exactly coincide either with each other or with the financial and currency interests.
>
> (Quoted in H. Pelling, *W. S. Churchill*, London, Macmillan, 1974, p. 301)

Given that he received almost unanimous advice to return to the pre-war parity he had little option but to do so. The result possibly intensified the problems of the old export industries but it was not a decisive cause of these problems. The return to gold has overshadowed much of Churchill's work as a progressive and constructive reformer. In 1925 he not only did the expected Conservative thing and reduced income tax to the benefit of the middle classes, he also took over a scheme of Neville Chamberlain's and introduced a contributory scheme of pensions for widows and orphans, and reduced the age for pensions to 65 instead of

70. In his later budgets he tended to have to wrestle with the consequences of the coal dispute and the General Strike. He longed for the opportunity to put through some grand plan of reform and in 1928 succeeded in forcing through the derating of agriculture and the reduction of rates to 25 per cent for industry. This cut right across much of Neville Chamberlain's work and at one time almost produced the latter's resignation but a compromise was finally agreed upon. As Chancellor, as with every office he held, Churchill's enthusiasm knew few restraints. The ex-First Lord of the Admiralty, the proponent of more and bigger battleships in 1912, now became, in the words of the First Sea Lord, 'economy mad', and fought a lengthy battle to slash the navy's cruiser building programme. Baldwin had to intervene to defend the Admiralty from the energy of his Chancellor.

The handling of the coal dispute and the General Strike was of course the major domestic problem facing the government and the one issue in which Baldwin himself played a central role. This flare-up of class tension was just the sort of development Baldwin wished to avoid. His role, however, was vital in limiting its potential for political and social disruption. Bonar Law had displayed a cold if rational detachment from the ills of unemployment. He had refused to see a deputation of the unemployed pointing out truthfully, but tactlessly, that it was a waste of their shoe-leather. Baldwin could never behave like this. His language and gestures were those of the healer. He was the pourer of oil on troubled waters. His gestures, like the torpedoing of his own party's bill to amend the payment of the political levy mentioned above, had built up a fund of goodwill on the Labour benches and amongst the trade union movement. To many of the die-hards in his own party he was seen as a semi-socialist. The dispute in the declining mining industry tested all of Baldwin's goodwill and skills of political manoeuvre. The demand of the mine-owners for wage cuts and the refusal of the miners to agree to this produced a dangerous impasse in what was still the nation's largest industry. After initially refusing to solve the problem by a government subsidy, at the last minute Baldwin climbed down to TUC pressure and on 30 July 1925 granted a nine-month subsidy to avert conflict. Churchill fully supported the deal. A commission of inquiry under Herbert Samuel was set up to recommend a suitable solution. Baldwin came in for fierce criticism for his conciliatory line. It is often said that this was merely a device by the government to gain time and make preparations to face a full-blown confrontation. In reality Baldwin was as usual anxious to explore every possible avenue to avoid conflict. The conflict eventually came when the subsidy ran out in 1926. Baldwin and the TUC leaders were still anxious for a solution but many of his cabinet colleagues felt that the government should show no weakness and both the miners, under the Marxist A. J. Cook and the mine-owners were bent on confrontation. The Samuel Commission reported on 11 March and its recommendations of wage cuts were unacceptable to the miners, as was reorganization to the employers. Negotiations with Baldwin and Birkenhead in the forefront continued until 2 May. On 1 May the owners had locked the miners out for their refusal to accept wage cuts. Negotiations still continued with Baldwin and such TUC leaders as J. H. Thomas still desperate for a settlement when news came that the printers at the *Daily Mail* had closed the paper. Baldwin yielded to his more militant cabinet colleagues and broke off negotiations on the evening of Sunday 2 May. Leo Amery recalled the event in his diary

> . . . at 9.30 we assembled in Winston's room and passed the evening as best we could until about 11. Then Stanley came in very tired and threw himself into an armchair leaving it to F. E. to read out as far as they had got with the discussions. . . .
>
> While we were discussing the news arrived that the Daily Mail had been suppressed altogether by the printers because they did not like its leading article. We had already had information that in the Sunday Express and other papers articles had been considerably censored or dropped out. This turned the scale.
>
> (Quoted in Gilbert, op. cit., p. 150)

It has been suggested that Baldwin used the printers' unofficial action as an excuse to escape from commitments made to Thomas that he could not deliver in view of the hostility of his colleagues. Whatever the truth he was exhausted and now accepted a General Strike as inevitable. It began on 4 May but efficient preparations had already been made by a civil servant, Sir John Anderson, and there was every prospect of defeating it. Baldwin still aimed to keep the temperature down and play on the unwillingness of the TUC leaders to push things to extremes. He himself reined in extremists, like Churchill, and limited the activities of the armed forces to avoid provocation. Baldwin claimed to distinguish between the coal dispute, which was a legitimate industrial dispute, and the General Strike which was a political issue. He broadcast to the nation on Saturday 8 May:

> I am a man of peace. I am longing, and looking and praying for peace. But I will not surrender the safety and the security of the British Constitution. It placed me in power eighteen months ago by the largest majority accorded to any party for many, many years. Have I done anything to forfeit that confidence? Cannot you trust me to ensure a square deal and to ensure even justice between man and man?
>
> (Quoted in Jenkins, op. cit., p. 103)

His prayers were answered and the TUC called it off on 12 May using the figleaf of official proposals from Herbert Samuel as a cover for the nakedness of their defeat. Baldwin continued to apply lashings of oil to the troubled waters, saying to Ernest Bevin on that day:

> You know my record. You know the object of my policy, and I think you can trust me to consider what has been said. . . . You will want my co-operation, and I shall want yours to make good the damage done to the trade, and try to make this country a little better and a happier place than it has been in recent years. That will be my steady endeavour.
>
> (Quoted in D. Southgate (ed.), *The Conservative Leadership*, London, Macmillan, 1974, p. 213)

Miners and mine-owners still refused to compromise and after a final spasm of attempted conciliation Baldwin lapsed into exhausted inertia. The miners were eventually starved into submission. The dispute had finally lanced the boil of industrial relations. It had exposed the hollowness of revolutionary rhetoric from the left and ushered in a period of greater harmony in industrial relations. The syndicalist dream floating in the minds of many socialists since before the First World War vanished. The miners suffered defeat and the union membership fell but there was no general witch-hunt. Baldwin's handling of the dispute was successful and probably in the best interests of the country. Thereafter, he rather lost his touch. He was suffering from nervous exhaustion. The government put through a Trade Disputes Act in May 1927. It declared sympathetic and general strikes illegal. It did little to reduce trade union power in reality. Chamberlain wished to turn it into a general constructive measure with a compulsory 'cooling-off' period in any dispute. Baldwin shied away from this. He agreed, against Chamberlain's advice, to include that which he had vigorously opposed in 1925, namely a change in the rules governing the political levy. Although it might be argued that this was perfectly fair and legal it appeared vindictive as the matter had nothing to do with the strike itself.

It was not only Baldwin's rhetoric which set the tone for progressive Conservatism in this government. Neville Chamberlain at the Ministry of Health proved to be a constructive politician in the best tradition of his radical father. Chamberlain's own experience in local government gave him an enormous advantage and he was often more knowledgeable than his civil servants on the intricacies and possibilities of particular projects. Over the next four years he put through twenty-one acts, many of great complexity. They dealt with housing, public health, the provision of parks and leisure facilities and, most important, the wholesale reform of local government in 1928–9. With Chamberlain's encouragement just under a million new houses had been built by the time of the government's defeat. The health of the nation had improved, with infant mortality falling to 45 per 1,000 in 1928. Chamberlain's own mother had died in childbirth and the provision of maternity and child welfare clinics was a concern particularly dear to him. His greatest work was the vast reform of local government, begun in 1928. The old Poor Law was swept away and its functions transferred to the counties and county boroughs. Its health functions were now separated from poor relief. These local authorities also took over the maintenance of roads. The system of central government support was changed from percentage grants to block grants. It was the most complex measure proposed in the inter-war years with 115 clauses and 12 schedules. Chamberlain's speech of introduction on 26 November 1928 of two-and-a-half hours was universally greeted as a masterpiece of succinct exposition. It was bold of the government to push through such a complex measure so late in its life, and the new increased rating assessments were received by many households just before polling day in May 1929. It was courageous but electorally harmful.

Other measures by the government added to this programme of reform. An Equal Franchise Act in April 1928 equalized the franchise for men and women at 21 and added five million new women voters – the 'flapper' vote as it was nicknamed.

Balfour, as Lord President, was largely responsible for a redefinition of Britain's relations with the Dominions following the Imperial Conference of 1926. It was Balfour, the subtle wordsmith, who found the phraseology to express the new commonwealth partnership:

> [A]utonomous communities within the British Empire, equal in status, in no way subordinate one to another in any respect of their domestic or internal affairs though united by a common allegiance to the Crown and freely associated as members of the British Commonwealth of nations.

In contrast to the horror expressed by the Conservative Party in the 1980s to nationalization it is worth remembering that Baldwin's government developed the legal framework of public corporations later much extended by the post-war Labour Government. In 1926 the British Broadcasting Corporation was created by royal charter financed from licence fees. A Conservative Government opted for a state monopoly rather than the free market model of broadcasting adopted in the USA. In many ways the BBC embodied the high-minded values of upper-middle-class British reformers who had shaped the development of the modern British state since the 1830s. Lord Reith, first Director-General of the BBC, accepted the job of cultural dictator to the nation. He had the missionary zeal of many Scots Calvinists and worked to bring to every fireside 'all that was best in every department of human knowledge, endeavour and achievement'. In the same year as the BBC was established the Central Electricity Board was also set up to provide a nation-wide power grid. It was fed by private generating companies but the state's role had been extended once again to fulfil the needs of an increasingly complex society.

The great failure of the government lay with the issue of unemployment. It never fell below the one million mark, not even in the period of economic boom, and from 1928 the situation was worsening. The government had no real answer, other than the extension of relief (see chapter 9). Only Lloyd George and the Liberals actually offered a policy and whether this would have worked is open to question (see chapter 6). Lloyd George's campaign certainly hurt the Conservatives and in the 1929 election 33 out of the 35 Liberal gains were at the Conservatives' expense. Unemployment, the new increased rates, a more dynamic Liberal Party and the moderate yet imposing figure of MacDonald all worked to destroy the Conservative majority. The result was a disappointment to Baldwin who had hoped to cling on with a small majority, but at least his successor would be MacDonald who hated Lloyd George nearly as much as Baldwin himself. Despite electoral defeat Baldwin's achievements had been considerable. He had reunited his party, destroyed Lloyd George and helped to launch a moderate, 'safe', Labour Party as an alternative government. He had also softened and blunted the edges of class conflict and reduced the whole temperature of British political life. The acerbic exchanges of party warfare in the years before the First World War faded into distant memory. Parliamentary democracy and decent English values had been saved in part by 'Stanley Boy'. It no longer seemed appropriate to talk of forming regiments of stockbrokers as Bonar Law had (to suppress the revolution), or to train a battleship's guns on Liverpool as had happened in the era of industrial militancy just after the First World War. Baldwin had done much to create that consensus that so strongly showed itself in the Second World War. His very role as leader also meant that his government, like those consensus governments after the Second World War, failed to tackle the very real problem of relative economic decline. Britain and Baldwin opted for a quiet smoke on the wheelbarrow. It was not, however, possible, despite Baldwin's reminiscences quoted earlier to combine it with efficiency.

Table 10.1 The May 1929 general election result

	Millions of votes cast	*Number of seats won*
Conservative	8.7	260
Liberal	5.3	59
Labour	8.4	288

Source: After D. Butler, *British Political Fact*, London, Macmillan, 1986.

OUT OF OFFICE AND IN AGAIN 1929–31

Defeat brought faction, plots and disarray to the Conservatives. J. C. C. Davidson, Baldwin's loyal Party Chairman had to go. The author of the defeated 'safety first' campaign, he was the obvious scapegoat. He clung on until the end of May 1930 by which time Baldwin could no longer save him and he was replaced by Neville Chamberlain whose own loyalty to Baldwin was now in doubt. He wrote a month later:

> I have come to the conclusion that if S. B. would go the whole party would heave a sigh of relief. Everywhere I hear that there is no confidence in his leadership or belief in his determination to carry any policy through.
>
> (Quoted in R. R. James, *The British Revolution*, London, Hamish Hamilton, 1977, p. 226)

Baldwin would never be an effective leader of the opposition. He lacked the devotion to partisan party warfare. He was too conciliatory to please his backbenchers. There could be none of the devastating verbal assaults on the Treasury bench that Churchill could make like this one, made in January 1931:

> What is the Prime Minister going to do? I spoke the other day, after he had been defeated in an important division about his wonderful skill in falling without hurting himself. He falls, but up he comes again, smiling, a little dishevelled but still smiling. But this is a juncture, a situation, which will try to the fullest the peculiar arts in which he excels. I remember when I was a child, being taken to the celebrated Barnum's Circus which contained an exhibition of freaks and monstrosities, but the exhibit on the programme which I most desired to see was the one described as 'The Boneless Wonder'. My parents judged that that spectacle would be too revolting and demoralizing for my youthful eyes, and I have waited fifty years to see the boneless wonder sitting on the Treasury Bench.
>
> (Quoted in Gilbert, op. cit., p. 389)

Churchill himself parted company from Baldwin and threw himself in with the extreme right-wing of the Tory Party in opposition to moves towards dominion status for India. Baldwin's last government had appointed Edward Wood, Lord Irwin, as Viceroy. Faced with the growing agitation of Gandhi and the Congress Party for independence Irwin, whilst upholding order, sought to negotiate and in October 1929 announced that dominion status – self-government – was an acceptable objective. Churchill and Birkenhead, along with many others, were outraged. Churchill denounced Gandhi as 'a seditious Middle Temple lawyer now posing as a fakir of a type well known in the East, striding half-naked up the steps of the Viceregal Palace'. Baldwin sympathized with the halting steps of MacDonald's Labour Government towards providing self-government for India, and he clashed openly with Churchill in the Commons in 1931. The conflict was to run for another four years and to do Churchill, in the end, much more harm than Baldwin.

A more serious challenge to Baldwin's leadership was to come from the two great newspaper tycoons: Lord Rothermere of the *Daily Mail* and Lord Beaverbrook of the *Daily Express*. Beaverbrook decided to launch a crusade for Empire free trade – a new version of tariff reform. Rothermere threw in the support of his newspaper empire and early in 1930 the United Empire Party was born. Candidates were put up at by-elections and the criticism of Baldwin became more and more strident. Baldwin had to call a special meeting of MPs and candidates to carry a vote of confidence. He delivered a stinging attack on the newspaper barons. Rothermere had mistakenly demanded of Baldwin to know the names of his next Cabinet – Baldwin rejected such a request:

> We are told that unless we make peace with these noblemen, candidates are to be run all over the country. The Lloyd George candidates at the last election smelt; these will stink. The challenge has been issued. . . . I accept, as I accepted the challenge of the T.U.C.
>
> (Quoted in Jenkins, op. cit., p. 115)

Baldwin got a vote of confidence but only by 150 to 80. A second vote was taken at a meeting in October which was won by 462 to 116, but the need for two votes in such a short space of time was indicative of the insecurity of his position. In February 1931 an empire crusader beat the official Conservative candidate into third place. The Conservative chief agent demanded Baldwin's resignation. If he was no great fighter in the Commons against the Labour Party Baldwin chose to stand his ground and fight now. A fresh by-election was due in the safe Conservative seat of St George's, Westminster. All the signs were that Beaverbrook and Rothermere would triumph here. The official Conservative withdrew and in desperation Baldwin thought to resign his own seat and stake all on a last-ditch personal contest. 'Think of the effect on your successor', Chamberlain plaintively objected. 'I don't give a damn about my successor, Neville', was the reply. In fact a Baldwin defender was found to stand – Duff Cooper. Baldwin contributed to his victory with a famous denunciation of the two press lords:

> What the proprietorship of these papers is aiming at is power, and power without responsibility – the prerogative of the harlot throughout the ages . . . this contest is not a contest as to who is to lead the party, but as to who is to appoint the leader of the party.
>
> (ibid., p. 120)

His leadership was safe. Luckily the Churchill campaign and the Empire free-trade campaign never coalesced, but a party so noted for maintaining a dignified face of unity in public could hardly have looked less united in the two years of MacDonald's Government.

As MacDonald's difficulties mounted Baldwin accepted the notion of a fresh election and a possible return to power. As he told an audience in Lancashire in April 1931 the government was cracked and crumbling, held up only by Lloyd George, and 'I would as soon have a building in which I was interested underpinned by a stick of dynamite.' He had lost none of his animosity for the 'Welsh goat'. He at least allowed himself to get his annual French holiday in, and made it quite clear to everyone that he was opposed to any coalition, before disaster struck. He was half-way to Aix when the August Crisis forced him to be recalled on the 13th. He was still very reluctant to contemplate coalition and, after extensive discussion, left the 'whole matter in Chamberlain's hands', and returned to Aix. The worsening banking crisis and the splits in the Labour Cabinet (see pp. 267–8) again forced Baldwin's return. He was still deeply reluctant to take part in a coalition and was not moved by Chamberlain's arguments of the advantage of splitting the Labour Party. Chamberlain and Baldwin were called to Downing Street on 23 August. Chamberlain urged MacDonald to carry on as leader of a coalition but MacDonald seemed reluctant and Baldwin came away assuming, as he told his wife in a letter, that he would have to form a government. The next day MacDonald changed his mind and at a conference at Buckingham Palace, involving Baldwin and Samuel for the Liberals, MacDonald agreed to a coalition. Samuel drafted the summary of the agreement:

1. National Government to be formed to deal with the present financial emergency.
2. It will not be a Coalition in the ordinary sense of the term, but co-operation of individuals.
3. When the emergency is dealt with, the Government's work will have finished and the Parties will return to their ordinary position.
4. The economies and imports shall be equitable and shall generally follow the lines of the suggestions attached, designed to enable a loan to be raised in New York and Paris.
5. The elections which may follow the end of the Government will not be fought by the Government but by the Parties.
6. If there is any legislation which is necessary to pass for special departmental or other reasons and it is generally accepted by the different Parties, it may be undertaken.
7. The Cabinet shall be reduced to a minimum.

(Quoted in K. Middlemas and J. Barnes, *Baldwin*, London, Weidenfeld & Nicolson, 1969, p. 629)

It appears that the original intention was a short-lived emergency government, not a long-lived coalition. Events in September, however, were to transform the situation.

THE NATIONAL GOVERNMENT 1931–40

The original Cabinet formed in August contained only ten members: four Conservatives, with Baldwin as Lord President and Neville Chamberlain back as Health Minister; four Labour members; and two Liberals. Baldwin was happy to serve under MacDonald whom he respected and liked. Lloyd George was, of course, not included. The Almighty, or so it seemed to the two other party leaders, had shown his support for their view of the old Liberal by ensuring that he was in hospital undergoing a serious operation during the political crisis. The formation of the National Government did not end the crisis which actually intensified during September. Fresh loans were arranged to prop up the pound and keep it in its 1925 parity. Snowden, continuing as Chancellor, introduced an emergency budget raising taxes and making cuts of £70 million. All public employees were to take cuts of 10 per cent in their salaries except the police who got away with 5 per cent and teachers who were sentenced to 15 per cent. The bulk of the Labour Party broke into furious opposition and Parliament has seldom been so acrimonious. On 15 September the fleet at Invergordon mutinied and the run on the pound accelerated. On 21 September there was nothing else to do but go off the gold standard and devalue the pound. It fell from $4.86 to $3.80 and eventually to $3.40. It ended the crisis. The government formed to save the pound had failed but it did not seem to matter.

The bitter Labour opposition and vitriolic attacks on Snowden and MacDonald convinced them of the virtue of having an election under coalition colours. The Conservatives came to the conclusion that an election would be beneficial on two accounts: enabling tariffs to be introduced and allowing them to cash in on a favourable situation. A group of Liberals, twenty-nine strong, aligned themselves behind Sir John Simon as the Liberal National Party and accepted the idea of an emergency tariff. As the cartoon indicates, they were the essential base of the so-called National Government. MacDonald and Baldwin decided on an election and by agreeing that the three parties could issue their own manifestos even kept the free-trade Samuelites in the coalition. The government would appeal for a doctor's mandate, an appeal for power to put things right. The result was a triumph for the National Government and for the Conservatives in particular. The Conservatives alone had seized 55 per cent of the popular vote and 473 seats (see Table 10.2). Many of the Conservative gains were brought about by the withdrawal of the Liberal candidate and the rise in the Conservative vote by 3 million was approximately the same as the fall in the Liberal vote since 1929. The Simonite fusion of Liberal Nationals with the Conservatives was mirrored in many local anti-socialist pacts which eventually produced fusion. At Plymouth in 1932 such a deal was struck, and in 1934 in

TEAM WORK.

WITH MR. PUNCH'S RENEWED COMPLIMENTS TO MAC AND SIMON IN THEIR REFINED
EQUESTRIAN ACT.

Doncaster and Ipswich similar co-operation was evident. Liberalism was withering at the grass roots as never before, but its demise strengthened the Baldwin version of Conservatism. His Liberal Toryism, and his personal standing in Parliament, was much enhanced by this development. Possibly 100 new Conservative MPs owed their success to the withdrawal of Liberal candidates in 1931. Political survival for these, and perhaps a further 50, depended on the progressive tint that Baldwin gave to the Conservative Party.

Table 10.2 The October 1931 general election result

	Millions of votes cast	Number of seats won		Millions of votes cast	Number of seats won
Conservative	12.0	473	Independent Liberal	0.1	4
National Labour	0.3	13	Labour	6.6	52
Liberal National	0.8	35	Communist	0.07	–
Liberal	1.4	33	New Party	0.04	–
			Others	0.2	5

Source: After Butler, op. cit.

The election triumph and the added strength of the Conservatives made a Cabinet reshuffle inevitable but MacDonald, despite his sense of being a Conservative prisoner, kept Number 10, and only Number 11 out of twenty cabinet offices went to the Conservatives. Snowden had not contested his seat and now had to hand over the Exchequer to Neville Chamberlain – the most important gain that the Conservatives made. Snowden remained in the Cabinet as Lord Privy Seal and three Samuelites and two Simonites helped to maintain the image of a coalition. The Samuelites managed to swallow the introduction of a tariff in February 1932 but the agreement at the Ottawa Conference in August 1932, to introduce imperial preference (see chapter 3), was too much for these free-trade purists and Samuel and Snowden withdrew to be replaced by Conservatives. Despite the increasing Conservative domination, MacDonald's presence at Number 10 until June 1935, and the prominence of ex-Liberal Sir John Simon as Foreign Secretary, still ensured the National character of the government. Churchill and other Tory die-hards were excluded. Progressive Conservatives like Samuel Hoare and Lord Irwin predominated. Baldwin's position was ideal from his point of view, as a civil servant from the Cabinet Office, Tom Jones, noted: 'This being second not first suits him perfectly, and frees him from final decisions and therefore from worry.'

Neville Chamberlain was the undisputed number three in the government and was in many ways its workhorse. As Chancellor he nursed the economy back to health and its revival by 1935 made possible the election victory of that year. He was no great financial radical but by comparison with Snowden's Gladstonian orthodoxy he was certainly innovative. The introduction of a general 10 per cent tariff in February 1932 marked a break with Britain's Victorian free-trade heritage. It was also a display of filial duty to the memory of his father the great Joseph Chamberlain. It was Chamberlain who bore the brunt of the negotiations at the Ottawa Conference in July and August that at long last brought in a moderate system of imperial preference. He also took a leading role at the Lausanne Conference which finally ended the unhappy saga of reparations. In April 1932 he introduced the first of his six budgets. Further cuts in spending were announced and tea duties raised. A new Exchequer Equalization Fund was established with which to defend sterling in the future. In June he carried through a major achievement by a conversion of the national debt reducing interest payments from 5 per cent to 3.5 per cent, thereby saving the Treasury £23 million per annum. Low interest rates helped to stimulate the great home-building boom which both powered the economy out of recession and conferred great social benefits. In 1934 income tax was lowered as the economy recovered and unemployment benefits were restored to their 1930 level which, in view of the extensive deflation, was a considerable improvement in real terms. The reductions in public sector pay were partially relaxed and Chamberlain announced that 'the first chapter of Great Expectations had succeeded Bleak House'. In 1935 public salaries were completely restored to their pre-crisis levels. The worst of the slump seemed to be over although as chapter 9 indicates the regional persistencies of depression meant that recovery was patchy. But recovery was still sufficiently strong to enable the government to win a convincing electoral victory.

Throughout Europe the economic crisis of the early 1930s threatened Liberal democracies and in Germany swept one away. The threat came both from the extreme left and the extreme right. The NUWM and the Communist Party were seen as the more dangerous initially and the government took a tough line with both organizations, discouraging marches and using police to break up demonstrations. By December 1932 there had been 1,300 arrests and 421 convictions. The police had used over a hundred baton charges. The hard core of the activists was much weakened by imprisonments. Wal Hannington, the NUWM founder, was given three months in November 1932 and its chairman, Sid Elias, was gaoled for two years for sedition. The government strengthened its hand in 1934 with the Incitement to Disaffection Act – better known as the Sedition Bill. It was designed to tighten the law against incitement of 'His Majesty's forces', and gave magistrates the power to order searches for seditious materials. This was later modified after extensive protests. In fact, the Act was little used and by 1934 the most dramatic phase of the left-wing challenge was over.

The British Union of Fascists (BUF) was increasingly seen as the more dangerous group. It was formed in October 1932 by Sir Oswald Mosley, ex-Conservative MP and ex-Labour minister. Mosley had already founded one party called simply 'The New Party'. Money had been supplied by William Morris, later Lord Nuffield. It contested twenty-four seats in 1931 and formed its own newspaper: *Action*. The New Party was not a success with a total vote of 36,377 in the October general election. Mosley was not deterred and inspired by a visit to Italy in January 1932 he decided that only fascism could save the country from the drift and muddle which threatened to see communism emerge triumphant. He wrote in 1932 in *The Greater Britain*:

> In such a situation, new ideas will not come peacefully; they will come violently, as they have come elsewhere. In the final economic crisis to which neglect may lead, argument, reason, persuasion vanish and organised force alone prevails. In such a situation, the eternal protagonists in the history of all modern crises must struggle for the mastery of the State. Either Fascism or Communism emerges victorious; if it be the latter, the story of Britain is told.
>
> (Quoted in C. Cook and J. Stevenson, *The Slump – Society and Politics during the Depression*, London, Cape, 1977, p. 200)

The BUF's blackshirt uniform was modelled on Mussolini's followers. The movement grew throughout 1933. Mosley addressed an audience of 10,000 at the Albert Hall in London and in January 1934 gained the backing of Lord Rothermere's newspaper empire. *The Daily Mail* carried an article entitled 'Hurrah for the Blackshirts'. A meeting at Olympia in June 1934 did the movement great damage when the brutality of its stewards towards hecklers was widely reported and brought extreme criticism not only from its natural left-wing critics but also from Conservative MPs. Rothermere withdrew his support as a consequence of Olympia. The BUF grew more extreme, increasingly playing up anti-semitism. Its membership probably peaked in 1934 but violent incidents provoked by demonstrations continued into 1935 and 1936. There were deliberately provocative marches through Jewish areas – particularly in the East End of London. A major riot occurred in Cable Street, Stepney, with 88 arrests and 70 injuries. Later Mosley addressed 12,000 in Victoria Park, Bethnal Green, in October 1936. It was in the East End that Mosley was able to build up his biggest following although there was also substantial support in Lancashire and Yorkshire. Most commentators agree on the relative youth of the BUF's membership. Two-thirds of the 103 leaders in 1935 were under 40, and there was a strong ex-military element in the leadership too. Outside the East End, where there appears to have been a genuine working-class following, members were mainly lower middle class, the same social group that predominated in the NSDAP, the Nazi equivalent in Germany. The full extent of the support is difficult to gauge. In its most favoured areas it gained between 15 and 25 per cent of the vote in local county council elections held in 1937. It never secured parliamentary representation since Britain did not have the system of proportional representation that enabled Hitler to make a parliamentary breakthrough in Germany.

In 1936 the government dealt fascism a body blow when it put through the Public Order Act. There had been complaints about the partiality of the police and their failure to defend Jews and their property. Certainly the Special Branch appears to have been much more concerned with the threat from the NUWM and the Communist Party, both of which it infiltrated, rather than the BUF, which it did not. Sir John Simon, the Home Secretary, clearly stated the government's position in July 1936:

> I should like to feel assured that not only the senior officials at Scotland Yard and the higher ranks in the police divisions, but each individual police officer who may be called to deal with anti-Jewish incidents is made fully aware that grossly abusive language of the Jews, either individually or as a race, is a serious offence and that there can be no question in this matter of good-humoured toleration of language which in other circumstances might not call for intervention on the part of the police.
>
> (ibid., p. 237)

The Public Order Act came into force in January 1937 and prohibited the wearing of uniforms for political purposes and sought to limit paramilitary forces. It also gave chief constables the right to ban processions which could lead to serious disorder. Thereafter the BUF withered away, clearly identified in the public mind with an alien culture which was increasingly seen as a menace. Both fascism and communism fed on one another in a symbiotic relationship: the BUF needed a communist menace to attract the middle classes to its standard and the communists sought to play up the fascist threat to heighten its importance in broad left popular fronts. In reality both enjoyed the support of tiny minorities and these minorities were firmly, yet sensibly, dealt with by a humane and liberal government. The presence of the National Government and the economic revival after 1933 ensured that the middle and lower middle classes did not desert parliamentary democracy. In Germany the middle classes deserted the liberal DDP and DVP to vote fascist. In Britain all that occurred is that Liberals voted for Baldwin and MacDonald, a nominal Conservative and a nominal Socialist. In reality the liberal voters perceived that they were still voting for liberals.

The National Government's policy with regard to India emphasizes the point. The second Labour Government, following on the work of Irwin and the Simon Report, committed Britain to a wide measure of provincial self-government. It was Baldwin's support of this that led Churchill to withdraw from the Shadow Cabinet in January 1931. In March Churchill publicly complained:

The Conservative leaders have decided that we are to work with the Socialists, and that we must make our action conform with theirs. We therefore have against us at the present time the official machinery of all the three great parties in the State. We meet under a ban. Every Member of Parliament or Peer who comes here must face the displeasure of the party Whips. Mr Baldwin has declared that the three-party collusion must continue, and in support of that decision he has appealed to all those sentiments of personal loyalty and partisan feeling which a leader can command.

(Quoted in Gilbert, op. cit., p. 398)

The new National Government fulfilled Churchill's fears. The left-wing Conservative Sir Samuel Hoare was appointed Secretary for India and proceeded with reform. Two more conferences were held before a government White Paper was produced in 1933. A lengthy Select Committee sat taking evidence and Churchill behaved with extraordinary intemperance, accusing Hoare of tampering with evidence to the Committee. At 60 he appeared increasingly as a marginalized 'has-been'. The India Bill with an elephantine gestation period finally became law in August 1935. Baldwin defended it stoutly in and out of Parliament:

There is a wind of nationalism and freedom blowing round the world, and blowing as strongly in Asia as anywhere in the world. And are we less true Conservatives because we say: 'the time has now come'? Are those who say 'the time may come – some day', are they the truer Conservatives?

(Quoted in Dilks, op. cit., p. 361)

He, with Hoare, deserves much of the credit for this half-way house on the road to Indian independence.

Both gained promotion that year. MacDonald decided to step down as Prime Minister. There was much discontent with his leadership on the back benches; he was a physical and mental shadow of his former self, and this once very articulate man was now prone to ghastly meanderings. In answer to Lloyd George in February 1933 he confused the House with the following: 'He thinks he is the only impatient man in this House to get things done. I will beat him 50 per cent any day he likes. . . . No doubt he has a hawk-like desire for action, without bridle and saddle, across the Atlantic.' Baldwin later recalled his colleague's plight:

Poor old Ramsay was a doughty fighter in his early days: it was tragic to see him in his closing days as PM, losing the thread of his speech and turning to ask a colleague why people were laughing – detested by his old friends, despised by the Conservatives.

(Quoted in Middlemas and Barnes, op. cit., p. 803)

In June 1935 MacDonald swopped places with Baldwin, mistakenly deciding to prolong his own political obituary. Baldwin certainly lacked vigour but he was an improvement on MacDonald. Hoare was moved to the Foreign Office as reward for his struggle with Churchill over India. An election was due by 1936. Labour had made a considerable recovery in popularity since 1933. In both municipal and by-elections it was doing very well and in 1934 by-election results continued the trend with Labour wins in North Hammersmith and West Ham, followed by further wins in the autumn. Labour then captured the London County Council in November 1934 for the first time. This steady advance was worrying for the government. Chamberlain and Baldwin were increasingly convinced that rearmament was necessary as a response to Germany. A white paper on defence had been published in March 1935 to be vigorously attacked by Clement Attlee for Labour, and Sir Archibald Sinclair for the Liberals. The apparent strength in the country of semi-pacifist sentiments was a cause of deep concern. At Fulham in 1933 the Conservatives had been defeated in a by-election largely on the armaments issue and Labour gave every sign that it intended to denounce the government as warmongers. Chamberlain expressed the government's dilemma clearly:

> The Labour Party obviously intends to fasten upon our backs the accusation of being 'warmongers' and they are suggesting that we have 'hush hush' plans for rearmament which we are concealing from the people. As a matter of fact we are working on plans for rearmament at an early date for the situation in Europe is most alarming. . . . We are not sufficiently advanced to reveal our ideas to the public, but of course we cannot deny the general charge of rearmament and no doubt if we try to keep our ideas secret till after the election, we should either fail, or if we succeeded, lay ourselves open to the far more damaging accusation that we had deliberately deceived the people. . . . I have therefore suggested that we should take the bold course of actually appealing to the country on a defence programme, thus turning the Labour party's dishonest weapon into a boomerang.
> (Quoted in M. Cowling, *The Impact of Hitler*, Cambridge, Cambridge University Press, 1975, p. 92)

Churchill, from the Tory back benches, urged the government into rapid rearmament despite public opinion and the Labour Party. Baldwin was more circumspect. He entirely agreed that action was necessary and had already made vital contributions to future defence requirements. He was largely responsible for the setting up of the shadow-factory network (industries which could switch to war work as necessary) and technical research groups in 1934 which later bore much fruit in an enlarged and efficient RAF. He was also fearful of a divided country or a Labour victory, which would mean no armaments. The looming Abyssinian crisis in the autumn of 1935 made the situation increasingly critical. A clear-cut rearmament programme was necessary to be carried out by a government with a solid future. There were some favourable signs for the government. The Royal Jubilee had seen a celebration of national solidarity and the ending of the slump in most areas. Baldwin decided that he could appeal to the electorate on the basis of a modest rearmament programme and win. It was vital to hold the Liberal vote and not seem to be bending to Churchill and the wild men of the right. He handled the situation brilliantly, reassuring the moderates with 'there will be no great armaments', and expressing loyalty and support for the League of Nations and collective security. At the end of October in his own deeply personal way he sounded a note of quiet patriotism and a call to be on guard.

> We live under the shadow of the last War and its memories still sicken us. We remember what modern warfare is, with no glory in it but the heroism of man. Have you thought what it has meant to the world to have had that swath of death cut through the loveliest and best of our contemporaries, how public life has suffered because those who would have been ready to take over from our tired and disillusioned generation are not there?
>
> Perhaps we avert our thoughts from these terrors, and send them roaming over this 'dear, dear land' of ours. . . . We think, perhaps of the level evening sun over an English meadow, with the rooks tumbling noisily home into the elms, of the ploughman 'with his team on the world's rim, creeping like the hands of a clock', one of those garnered memories of the long peace of the countryside that a wise man takes about with him as a viaticum. To what risks do we expose our treasures – irreplaceable treasures, for you cannot build up beauty like that in a few years of mass-production? Make no mistake; every piece of all the life that we and our fathers have made in this land, every thing we have and hold and cherish, is in jeopardy in this great issue.
>
> (Quoted in Middlemas and Barnes, op. cit., p. 867)

By comparison the Labour manifesto seemed shrill:

> This Government is a danger to the peace of the world, to the security of this country. . . . Whilst paying lip service to the League, it is planning a vast and expensive rearmament programme which will only stimulate similar programmes elsewhere . . . the best defence is not huge competitive national armaments, but the organisation of collective security against any aggressor and the agreed reduction of national armaments elsewhere. Labour will propose to other nations the complete abolition of all the national air forces, the effective international control of civil aviation, and the creation of an international air police; large reductions by international agreement in the naval and military

forces, and the abolition of the private manufacture of, and trade in arms.

(ibid., p. 866)

Herbert Morrison who made much of the running for Labour made wild and unconvincing attacks on this patently peace-loving government. Baldwin's final speech rebutted the charges but promised security:

The defence forces of the country must be brought up to such a state of efficiency that we may be able to make our proper contribution in the cause of collective security. This means just what it says . . . it is a lie to say that the Government had already made its plans to introduce conscription. A lie, the biggest yet. . . . In this my last appeal to the country before polling day, I pledge the National Government to work faithfully for security at home and peace throughout the world, spending not a penny more on our defence forces than is necessary for the safety of our people, and striving always to bring the nations into agreement for the all-round reduction of armaments in a world where collective security has been made the sure protection against aggression.

(ibid., p. 868)

It was a masterful performance and he had done his country a great service. The results were a deep disappointment for the Labour Party, as the figures in Table 10.3 reveal.

Table 10.3 The November 1935 general election result

	Millions of votes cast	Number of seats won
Conservative	11.8	432
Liberal	1.4	20
Labour	8.3	154
Independent Labour Party	0.1	4
Communist	0.03	1
Others	0.3	4

Source: After Butler, op. cit.

Churchill in his memoirs was later to damn Baldwin and his skilful footwork:

Thus an administration more disastrous than any in our history saw all its errors and shortcomings acclaimed by the nation. There was however a bill to be paid, and it took the new House of Commons nearly ten years to pay it.

(W. S. Churchill, *The Second World War*, vol. I, London, Cassell, 1948, p. 141)

At the time he wrote to Baldwin on 7 October: 'Things are in such a state that it is a blessing to have at the head of affairs a man whom people will rally round.' That, of course, was before it became clear that Baldwin was not going to find a place for Churchill in his Cabinet after the election. The one great government casualty was Ramsay MacDonald, decisively defeated in a vicious contest at Seaham. To save him, a safe university seat was found. It was a sad end for a socialist leader. Baldwin himself was clearly past his prime. Victory was quickly followed by the humiliation which arose from the outcry over the Hoare–Laval Pact (see p. 315). Hoare was ditched and made a scapegoat for government policy and the young Anthony Eden was appointed in his place as a sop to the League of Nations lobby. The government's handling of the Italy–Abyssinia conflict caused problems. Chamberlain forced the government's hand in June with a speech to the 1900 Club urging the ending of sanctions against Italy. It was an ominous intrusion by the Chancellor into the realm of foreign affairs, and a direct challenge to Eden, the new Foreign Minister. It exposed Baldwin as the supine figurehead of a drifting vessel. He was subjected to devastating criticism from his old enemy Lloyd George:

> I have been in this House very nearly half a century. . . . I have never before heard a British Minister . . . come down to the House of Commons and say that Britain was beaten, Britain and her Empire beaten and that we must abandon an enterprise we had taken in hand.
> (Quoted in Middlemas and Barnes, op. cit., p. 940)

He appears already to have been on the point of a nervous breakdown, and was desperately tired and ordered to take a three-month rest. Neville Chamberlain was more than ever the driving force and linchpin of the government. On Baldwin's return he faced an onslaught from Churchill during the debate on the address following the opening of Parliament in December:

> The Government cannot make up their minds, or they cannot get the Prime Minister to make up his mind. So they go on, in strange paradox, decided only to be undecided, resolved to be irresolute, adamant for drift, solid for fluidity, all-powerful to be impotent. So we go on, preparing more months and years – precious – perhaps vital – to the greatness of Britain – for the locusts to eat.
> (ibid., pp. 969–70)

Baldwin's response was to do his reputation irreparable damage in the post-war world:

> That was the feeling in the country in 1933. My position as a leader of a great party was not altogether a comfortable one. I asked myself what chance was there – when that feeling that was given expression

to in Fulham was common throughout the country – what chance was there within the next year or two of that feeling being so changed that the country would give a mandate for rearmament? Supposing I had gone to the country and said that Germany was rearming and we must rearm, does anybody think that this pacific democracy would have rallied to that cry at that moment! I cannot think of anything that would have made the loss of the election from my point of view more certain.

(ibid., p. 970)

Churchill, and others, chose to misrepresent it as putting party before country. In practice Baldwin was merely stating the obvious – that in a democracy governments can only basically do what public opinion will tolerate. The public, so anxious for peace in the early 1930s, made Baldwin its scapegoat for its own unwillingness to face reality.

Baldwin's last great trial and opportunity for redemption came from an unexpected direction – Buckingham Palace. The old king, George V, died in January 1936. A gruff and direct sailor he had earned real national affection. He was succeeded by his eldest son, Edward, a youthful 42-year-old. The Prince had a certain outward popular charm but he was impatient of many of the more tiresome aspects of the kingly profession. He also had a taste for married women. One long affair had lasted sixteen years, much to his parents' concern. In 1934 he met and fell in love with Mrs Wallis Simpson and promptly ended his long-standing affair with Mrs Dudley Ward. The new object of his affections posed greater problems. Mrs Simpson saw no real objections to a twice-divorced American becoming Queen of England. Nor, it seems did Edward. The British press preserved a discreet silence but the French papers had a field day. The new king was also causing problems in other directions. He was strongly pro-German and careless with official information. The Foreign Office therefore carefully limited his access to delicate issues. The crisis over Mrs Simpson developed in the latter part of 1936 when she secured a divorce from Mr Simpson, and was thus available to marry. On 16 November Baldwin answered the king's question as to whether the marriage would be approved by informing him firmly that it would not. The king then told his Prime Minister that he would abdicate. The story of the affair only broke in the British press on 3 December and to the king's surprise its tone was critical. The king agreed to abdicate. Churchill and Beaverbrook tried to rally a king's Party but when Churchill rose to speak in the House of Commons, urging delay, he was howled down. Baldwin, by comparison, made one of the best speeches of his career on 10 December explaining the whole sorry business in simple yet moving terms. He restored his reputation for tact and commonsense management of difficult circumstances. On such a high, he chose to retire and went in May 1937, immediately after the coronation of George VI. He had led the Conservative Party for fourteen years and held office for over eleven. Such an unlikely leader and Prime Minister had outwitted a remarkable number of formidable political opponents.

His successor was beyond dispute. Neville Chamberlain was crown prince and slipped unchallenged into Number 10 and the leadership of the Conservative Party. At long last the Chamberlain dynasty was officially in control of the party it had influenced and directed for forty years. Neville was a complete contrast to Baldwin in style of leadership and personality, if not in policy. A year before his accession *The Spectator* carried out an illuminating portrayal of the future Prime Minister:

> He is not in any sense a platform man. In public he seems cold and unsympathetic, more like the chairman of a municipal committee anxious to keep down the rates than a leader of the nation. Even in the House of Commons he appears aloof and slightly magisterial. Apart from Mr Baldwin he has few friends even among his colleagues, and the back-benchers hardly know him at all, for he is not easily approachable in the Lobby and seldom, if ever, visits the smoking-room. He jokes with difficulty. I recall a dreadful occasion when in his Budget statement in 1932 he referred to the longevity of men with great fortunes that would one day fall into the maw of the Treasury by means of Death Duties, and addressed them in the rather brutal words of the Duke of Wellington to his troops: 'Come on, you rascals, you cannot live for ever.' His humour on the rare occasion that he employs it is self-conscious and studied and rather tasteless, like that of a man striving to be the life and soul of a funeral party.
>
> Yet with all these drawbacks he is the one man on the Government Front Bench today who could take charge in a crisis. He has a real relish for the cut-and-thrust of debate. I have watched him through a stormy all-night sitting calm, unruffled, a slightly contemptuous smile on his face, while the steady stream of insult and invective flowed upon him from the Socialist benches, and then rising to speak equipped with the succinct and smashing answer. He is quite fearless. No Parliamentary attack can daunt him, and I am certain that the international situation, however much it may worsen, will never unnerve him. He will never bend to pressure or play for cheap applause.
>
> (*The Spectator*, 24 April 1936)

Chamberlain gripped his cabinet colleagues and the government machine with a firmness totally lacking under Baldwin and MacDonald. He also gave his parliamentary troops fresh heart with his relish for the business of debate. His own diary records one such triumph in April 1938:

> It was so long since our people had heard a real fighting speech that they went delirious with joy and I don't remember ever hearing the

Neville Chamberlain, 1940. By Andrew MacLaren

cheering so prolonged as it was when I sat down. The Chief Whip says he has never known such enthusiasm over the lead the party is getting and of course that is not surprising when you remember that for 14 years they have had only S. B. or Ramsay.

(Quoted in Butler, op. cit., p. 385)

The Labour Party tended to hate him, not for his policy so much as his personality. Baldwin had tried to soften his approach as Chamberlain recalled in 1927:

Stanley begged me to remember that I was addressing a meeting of gentlemen. I always gave him the impression, he said, when I spoke in the H. of C. that I looked on the Labour Party as dirt. The fact is that intellectually, with a few exceptions, they *are* dirt.

(ibid., p. 312)

Time did not soften him and his successful years as Chancellor of the Exchequer gave him fresh confidence in himself. The antics of the Labour Party in the 1930s only reinforced his contempt.

His premiership was to be genuinely tragic. Like Asquith and the Younger Pitt he was a great master of domestic affairs forced by circumstances to wrestle with the problems of war. Unlike Pitt and Asquith he did not have time to establish his reputation as a great peace-time Prime

Minister. From the first the problems of dealing with Hitler absorbed his energy. He could not complete his work of building a comfortable environment for the British people. Rearmament absorbed a bigger and bigger share of the nation's resources and a man who was through and through a lover of peace was forced to take his country into war. This story is told elsewhere, as is the dramatic saga of his downfall in May 1940 (see chapter 8). Churchill the outcast of the 1930s was accepted that month as the nation's saviour by the very Parliament that had howled him down four years earlier.

ASSESSMENT

In the seven inter-war elections held under the new democratic franchise of 1918, the Conservatives secured majorities in five of them and in both of the others, 1923 and 1929, had the largest share of the popular vote. Even in 1929 when Labour secured more seats, 288 to 260, the Conservatives had more votes, 38.2 per cent to 37.1 per cent. They held office for 18 of the 21 inter-war years. It was a remarkable achievement for the party, which, under Lord Salisbury, had faced the onset of democracy with such trepidation. Much clearly favoured its success. In the 1920s the great progressive alliance of Edwardian England which had kept the Conservatives out of office for ten years fragmented. The Irish Nationalists who had been the consistent opponents of the Tories since 1886 disappeared. The Northern Irish contingent that remained after the setting up of the Free State was overwhelmingly Unionist. In other words, the Ireland which since 1868 had been a constant debit of around sixty-five seats at Westminster became an asset of around eight seats. The breakdown of the pact between Labour and the Liberals benefited the Conservatives in the 1920s. In 1922 the Liberal and Labour parties managed to gain 58.6 per cent of the vote but secured only 258 seats between them. In 1906, with the pact in operation, 54.9 per cent of the popular vote gave them 430 seats. The Liberals' collapse in 1924 was brought about by the increase in Labour candidates from 422 to 512. This produced the loss of many Liberal seats won in 1923, not to Labour, but to the Conservatives. As in the 1980s a divided left opposition was a blessing to the Tory Party. In the special circumstances of 1931, with a partial carrying over to 1935, division in both the Labour and Liberal parties rebounded even more powerfully to the Conservatives who, despite bitter arguments within their own ranks, never, except at the odd by-election, actually carried their quarrels onto the hustings.

The strength of the Conservative organization and its resources has already been mentioned. The new electorate lacked traditional party loyalties and in this situation efficient organization was all the more vital. The press was another Conservative asset. In the 1920s and the early

1930s it was overwhelmingly Conservative even if proprietors, like Beaverbrook of the *Express* and Rothermere of the *Daily Mail*, were unpredictable friends of the Tory Party. By 1939 the situation had changed considerably. In 1938 the *Daily Mirror* changed sides to support Labour, and the *Daily Herald*, funded by the TUC as a Labour paper, had grown in circulation to rival the *Express*. The disappearance of the Liberals as a force meant the reunification of the progressive alliance under the Labour banner by 1939 and together with more press support the Labour victory of 1945 becomes really understandable.

The actual nature of the inter-war Conservative Party and its leaders must in part explain its success. It was notably moderate and even progressive. It securely occupied the centre ground of British politics. Baldwin was denounced by his own chief agent as a semi-socialist. Chamberlain might rally the party faithful with the rhetoric of party warfare but he was a notable progressive reformer, deeply committed to improving the condition of the people. The first halting steps in nationalization were taken in the 1920s and in the course of the 1930s faith in state intervention to soften the impact of industrial decline in the depressed regions became more marked (see chapter 9). Even in other areas of the economy public control grew. The London Passenger Transport Board was established in 1933 and the British Overseas Airways Corporation in 1939. Baldwin did indeed practise centrist consensus politics. The Liberals fragmented and, tainted with the odour of political corruption emanating from Lloyd George, were increasingly marginalized and the Labour Party could often be relied upon to shoot itself in the foot with bitter internecine disputes. The Labour stand on international affairs was almost contemptible in the 1930s engulfing themselves in 'windy rhetoric' about the League of Nations and international morality but persistently refusing to endorse rearmament which would give meaning to their speeches. Only slowly could the likes of Bevin and Dalton make headway against the party's love of fantasy. In the meantime Baldwin and Chamberlain gathered in the votes and when comparison is made with the management of other countries in the difficult circumstances of the 1930s they emerge with much credit. Life was massively better for the vast bulk of Englishmen and women by 1939. Democratic decencies were preserved and a cohesive, orderly society reluctantly embarked on the salvation of Europe.

CONTROVERSY

The central historical debate in these years of British politics must turn on whether the leading figures MacDonald, Baldwin and Chamberlain are seen through polemical works like *The Guilty Men*, a pamphlet published in 1940, or in the light of revisionist biographies written since

1970. Both left and right in the post-war world turned upon the leaders of Britain during the 'Devil's Decade'. *The Guilty Men* was simply a party political pamphlet to rubbish the fallen Tory leaders but its prime author, the future Labour leader Michael Foot, had not changed his mind thirty years later:

> Were the Guilty Men truly guilty? The term, it may be recalled, first gained notoriety as the title of a popular pamphlet published in 1940. It soon entered general political parlance as a convenient way of identifying those who played the leading roles in guiding the nation towards the disaster of Dunkirk, the most dangerous moment in British history since 1066.
>
> It won respectability, even at the loss of some precision, as what may be called the Churchillian view of modern times: the notion that the British people saved themselves in their finest hour from the shame and stupidity of the previous decade. And often the guilty men have seemed to offer evidence against themselves. None of the memoirs and apologies hitherto written on their behalf has done much to parry the indictment, and one of them, the 'official' biography of Guilty Man Number Two, Stanley Baldwin, (pride of place as Guilty Man Number One must surely always be allotted to Neville Chamberlain) sounded like another witness for the prosecution.
>
> (M. Foot, *Loyalists and Loners*, London, Collins, 1986, p. 180)

What came close to creating a national consensus that the guilty men were guilty was Churchill's massive *War Memoirs*, published in 1948. Churchill himself had said, 'poor Neville, he will come very badly out of history. I know, I shall write it.' This is exactly what he did. Churchill's animosity to Baldwin in particular colours the first volume. Twelve years later his resentment was undimmed as he wrote of his exclusion from the new position of defence co-ordinator in 1936:

> Mr. Baldwin certainly had good reason to use the last flickers of his power against one who had exposed his mistakes so severely and so often. Moreover as a profoundly astute Party manager, thinking in majorities and aiming at a quiet life between elections, he did not wish to have my disturbing aid. He thought no doubt that he had dealt me a politically fatal stroke, and I felt he might well be right. How little can we foresee the consequences either of wise or unwise action, of virtue or of malice!
>
> (ibid., p. 157)

The post-war historical orthodoxy created by both right and left against the National Government has only gradually been eroded. Three massive scholarly biographies of the three Prime Ministers of the decade have sought to defend their subjects. David Marquand's *MacDonald*, published in 1977, attempts to give the first Labour premier a fairer hearing. Middlemas and Barnes's *Baldwin*, published in 1969, presents the reader with a challenging 1,000 pages – on none of which is there a hint that the subject is 'guilty man number two'. 'Guilty man number one', in Michael Foot's phrase, still awaits complete redemption, but it is well in hand as David Dilks has produced one volume on Neville Chamberlain which takes his life up to 1929 and the presentation is of an exceptionally able and progressive politician. Volume two covering the vital years at Number 10 is still in preparation but the shift in public perceptions of Neville Chamberlain is well marked by the BBC programme of 1988, 'Three Cheers for Mr Chamberlain', a sympathetic interpretation of his handling of the Munich Crisis. Perhaps the students of the 1990s and beyond can achieve more of that dispassionate objectivity that historians claim to seek but usually fail to find.

BIBLIOGRAPHY

For an explanation of the grading system, see the preface p. xiii.

Biographies

Baldwin

2   Jenkins, R., London, Collins, 1987
4   Middlemas, K. and Barnes, J., London, Weidenfeld & Nicolson, 1969
2   Young, K., London, Weidenfeld & Nicolson, 1976

Bonar Law

3   Blake, R., London, Eyre & Spottiswoode, 1955

The Chamberlains

4   Dilks, D., *Neville Chamberlain*, Cambridge, Cambridge University Press, 1984 (up to 1929)
3   Dutton, D., *Austen Chamberlain: Gentleman in Politics*, Bolton, Ross Anderson Publications, 1985
3   Elletson, D. H., London, John Murray, 1966
4   Feiling, K., *Neville Chamberlain*, London, Macmillan, 1970
2   Montgomery Hyde, H., *Neville Chamberlain*, London, Weidenfeld & Nicolson, 1976
2   Thorpe, D., chapter in *The Uncrowned Prime Ministers*, London, Dark Horse Publishing, 1980

Winston Churchill

4   Gilbert M., *W. S. Churchill*, Vol. 5, 1922–1939, London, Heinemann, 1976

3   James, R. R., *Churchill – A Study in Failure*, London, Weidenfeld & Nicolson, 1970
3   Pelling, H., *W. S. Churchill*, London, Macmillan, 1974

George V

3   Rose, K., London, Macmillan, 1983

Edward VII

3   Donaldson, F., London, Weidenfeld & Nicolson, 1970

Oswald Mosley

3   Skidelsky, R., London, Macmillan, 1975

General works

2   Blake, R., *The Conservative Party: Peel to Churchill*, London, Eyre & Spottiswoode, 1970
2   Blake, R., *The Decline of Power*, London, Granada, 1985
3   Butler, R. A. (ed.), *The Conservatives*, London, Allen & Unwin, 1977
3   Cook, C. and Stevenson, J., *The Slump – Society and Politics During the Depression*, London, Cape, 1977
4   Cowling, M., *The Impact of Hitler*, Cambridge, Cambridge University Press, 1975
4   Cowling, M., *The Impact of Labour 1920–1924*, Cambridge, Cambridge University Press, 1971
3   Mowat, C. L., *Britain Between the Wars, 1918–1940*, London, Methuen, 1955
3   Pugh, M., *The Making of British Politics 1867–1939*, Oxford, Blackwell, 1982
4   Ramsden, J., *The Age of Balfour and Baldwin 1902–1940*, London, Longman, 1978
3   Southgate, D. (ed.), *The Conservative Leadership*, London, Macmillan, 1974
3   Taylor, A. J. P., *England 1914–1945*, Oxford, Oxford University Press, 1966

Sources for coursework

Many of the above works contain extensive bibliographies. There is a wealth of printed primary material, and full biographies like Gilbert's *Churchill* and Barnes and Middlemas's *Baldwin* contain much primary information to be quarried. Most politicians have published memoirs of varying degrees of reliability. One of great value must be *Memoirs of a Conservative*, edited by R. R. James (London, Weidenfeld & Nicolson, 1969). These are the memoirs of J. C. C. Davidson for 1910–37. Also of outstanding value are the *Whitehall Diaries* of T. Jones, deputy secretary to the Cabinet in the 1920s (London, Oxford University Press, 1969). Ian Colvin used the published cabinet papers to tell the story of

The Chamberlain Cabinet (London, Gollancz, 1971). A. J. P. Taylor's book referred to above contains one of the most readable and amusing bibliographies ever written and provides a detailed guide to much that is available.

11 Socialist Britain 1940–51: the home front

INTRODUCTION

By 1939 Labour's story had only partly unfolded. The taking of power in 1924 and 1929 demonstrated that a new political force had arrived but after the debilitating and humiliating defeat of 1931, which left a rump of 50 MPs in the Commons, it appeared that Labour was back to square one. This was, however, a false impression, but certainly the party would need some time to recover and the dissension that broke out between rival groups and factions over the problems of the economy, foreign affairs and social reform ensured that the 1930s were years of unfulfilled promise for the Labour Party. This impression was, if anything, heightened by Labour's leader Clement Attlee. The son of a very successful solicitor, and a product of Oxford, he enjoyed private means and did not have to practise his chosen profession of law. In 1907 he joined the Fabians, and the ILP in 1908 – the same year that he started as a social worker in the East End of London. He worked there, with only a brief respite for war service, until 1922. By this time he had been mayor of Stepney, a London alderman and in 1922 he became Labour MP for Limehouse. Junior posts followed in the 1924 and 1929–31 Labour Governments. A small undistinguished man, not known for his conversation, he seemed to have taken on the leadership of Labour by default in 1935. Even as leader he still seemed to play a backseat role and many could not understand how such a humble little man had risen above so many Labour lions. It seemed to be the latter, men like Hugh Dalton, who steered the party away from pacifism and appeasement and it was no surprise when his leadership was challenged on the eve of war itself.

This is a very superficial picture of Attlee and Labour but one which seems to suggest that Labour could only take power either as a minority or in coalition with other parties. This position of apparent weakness was an anomaly in British politics and one that later coalition and national governments did much to prolong. But, the substance of Labour success lay dormant while the greater battles across Europe, Africa and the Far East raged. But even in this period of apparent loss for Labour their position was being strengthened. Their radical policies for social and economic reforms enshrined in the Party Programme of 1918, and including the famous Clause Four, calling for public ownership by nationalization, could not only be attacked by opponents on political and philosophical grounds, but also on the grounds of the impracticalities of such grand schemes and social experimentation. The first two of these criticisms could be countered by an overwhelming vote of support in a general election and that came in 1945. The final criticism presented Labour with something of a riddle. The practicalities of their plans could only be shown when they were in power but office might elude them until they could demonstrate the feasibility of what they planned. The circle of the argument was broken for them by the experience of war. It was the marshalling of the resources of the nation on a grand scale, one not really attempted before, that demonstrated the practicality of the widespread and wholesale influence of the state for the public good, which in the case of 1939–45 meant for victory over the enemy. The war also gave Labour an added impetus in that the experience of the war years changed British society in ways that political debate and party policy discussions could never do. The physical, mental and psychological experience of war, allied to its vast emotional impact, drew the realities of Britain's condition and future very clearly for the vast majority of the population. If they could not see where Britain ought to be going from a national standpoint they knew full well what their individual desires were. In the end it was the Labour Party's programme and widespread appeal that ushered in the 1945–51 government whose achievements in the spheres of social and economic welfare reforms must stand proudly against those of any other government in the modern era, if not of all time. War had shown what a united and untiring nation could achieve in military terms.

The election of 1945 would hold out the hope of what might be achieved by the same people working untiringly and unselfishly for themselves. Moreover, the framework for putting policy into action was not, in 1945, in question. The state had been galvanized and had used the resources of the British population to create victory over Germany. It was not too much to hope that the same power, and enterprise, of the state, could also be galvanized in order to create the Britain of the postwar era where the same brave population would usher in a new dawn of social and economic justice. Many who lived through the era of war and the Labour Government speak fondly of the years of deprivation and sacrifice they faced. Many claim that these were some of the happiest years they can remember despite the savagery of conflict and the self-denial during the era of austerity. Historians have taken very opposing views of the war years and the Labour Government's achievements. In the 1980s it became fashionable to be critical of the 1945–51 Labour administration and to claim that the welfare state and nationalization were experiments that Britain could ill afford in economic terms. Correlli Barnett, in what has been an influential text, *The Audit of War* (1986), has stressed the costs of this socialist experiment and directly related to it Britain's decline in economic terms in the 1950s and 1960s and beyond. The controversial arguments surrounding Barnett's argument and his critics' responses, which are equally vociferous, will be dealt with at the end of this chapter. What cannot be doubted by any historian is the enormity of the change in the state's role and involvement in the day-to-day life of the British public from 1940 onwards.

THE PEOPLE AS SERVANTS OF THE STATE

In September 1939 all pretence of a negotiated diplomatic restraint of Germany's aggressive moves was abandoned. With Chamberlain's harrowing words 'This country is now at war with Germany', the government swung immediately into action in a realistic, some might claim pessimistic, way. The reassuring concern of the government ready for anything that saw the sand-bagging of public buildings, the issuing of gas-masks, civil defence warnings and advice and preparations for the evacuation of children from centres of population hid the reality of special orders for one million coffins to cope with the slaughter from the skies that was expected at any moment. The period known as the 'Phoney War' gave the government a little respite but this was put to good use as the country's political and military leaders presided over the biggest extension of state power and control that had ever been seen in Britain. The speed of government reaction can be judged by the wide-ranging reports listed in the contents of the *Daily Telegraph* for 4 September 1939, the day after war was declared.

The military preparations for mobilization of all forces, the calling up of reserves and the taking in of volunteers and conscriptees went on naturally enough. It was, though, the civilian effort orchestrated by the government that would reveal the feasibility of extensive and successful state action. Civil defence, especially from air and gas attack (although the latter never came); the mobilization and direction of the labour force for the war effort, including that most valuable of labour reserves, women; evacuation on a massive scale of the nation's children; rationing of virtually all goods and particularly food; the taking into production of millions of acres of spare, wasted and under-used land; and the amassing of aluminium pots and pans, iron railings and all manner of ordinary household articles for war materials. All of this required the wholesale organization, control and direction of the British population.

It is easy, though, in the light of eventual victory and the tendency to see the war experience as 'Britain's finest hour', to overplay the preparedness of the British government and people. Most simply did not know what to expect and those who believed they did and thought in terms

News Summary: Other Pages

HOME

Prime Minister's broadcast announcement that Britain was at war with Germany. (P. 9.)

Official declaration of war in "London Gazette" (P. 11.)

Socialists and Liberals refused to be represented in War Cabinet; will give aid from outside. (P. 10.)

Anglo-French declaration that civilian populations will be spared in conduct of hostilities. (P. 11.)

Recruiting offices besieged. (P. 10.)

London crowds' calmness when air-raid warning sounded. (P. 9.)

Theatres and cinemas closed. (P. 6.)

Scheme for rationing certain foods may be introduced within next fortnight. (P. 10.)

Gold coin or bullion or foreign exchange to be offered for sale to Treasury. (P. 4.)

Board of Trade to insure cargoes and commodities against war risks from this morning. (P. 4.)

Government plans for growing more food at home. (P. 11.)

Consumption of coal, gas and electricity to be reduced 25 per cent. to conserve fuel supplies. (P. 6.)

Doctors and nurses in emergency hospital services called out for immediate duty. (P. 11.)

Traders warned of penalties for doing business with the enemy. (P. 4.)

Provisions of National Service (Armed Forces) Act. (P. 6.)

PARLIAMENT

Two days' debates in both Houses of Parliament. (Pp. 5 and 6.)

EMPIRE

Manifestations of loyalty to Britain by Dominions and Colonies. (P. 10.)

FOREIGN

M. Daladier's broadcast: "We are fighting for liberty." (P. 10.)

French envoy's last words with von Ribbentrop. (P. 9.)

Proclamation invoking Neutrality Act to be made in U.S.; Roosevelt calls Cabinet. (P. 10.)

Franco broadcasts appeal to Governments and nations to localise the war. (P. 7.)

Text of German reply to British ultimatum. (P. 7.)

Unrest among Germans. (P. 9.)

FINANCE

Problems of financing in war. (P. 3.)

Many advances in heavy dealing on Wall Street. (P. 3.)

SPORT

Doncaster Race Committee abandons four-day meeting. (P. 13.)

Sports gatherings prohibited. (P. 6.)

From *The Daily Telegraph*, 4 September, 1939

of a more modern version of 1914–18 were to be sadly disabused in a very short space of time, especially the ordinary non-combatant citizen who had mostly escaped, family losses apart, relatively unscathed in the last great conflict. The Emergency Powers Act of 22 May 1940, which was passed in its entirety in a single day, gave the British government unlimited authority over British citizens and their property. This of course was additional to those powers granted to Parliament, and not rescinded since the last war. It is interesting to note that although there was no necessity for Parliament to do so most of the key policy issues of the war years were in fact raised and debated in Parliament: a visible example of the spirit of democracy that Britain was seeking to defend.

Although some plans had been well laid others proved more difficult to implement and problematic in their results. Lord Chatfield, Minister Co-Ordinator for Home Defence, relied on people like S. P. Vivian in the first instance, who had worked in a similar capacity in the First World War. Vivian's scheme for national registration, suggested but not adopted in 1917, was accepted on 30 September 1939. A less than dynamic Leslie Burgin, a Liberal Nationalist, was appointed Minister of Supply but did not start at his office until August 1939. Food distribution would be his main task as many expected a war of attrition and the British effort could be considerably aided by 'tightening the belt', or simply reducing consumption. The move by the Ministry to raise food prices by seven points on the retail price index in November 1939 was not going to be enough by itself to control demand and thus restrict supply. A system of rationing would be necessary but unfortunately the system adopted, one that tied consumers to specific retailers, made the work of keeping track of individuals and families in a time of great population movement unnecessarily time-consuming and labour intensive. Bacon, butter and sugar were the first to be rationed but average calorific intake, even in these times, was supposed to be 3,000 a day. Consumption of meat decreased by 27 per cent, the amount of eggs (rationed to one per person per week in 1943) consumed fell by 56 per cent, sugar by 35 per cent and fruit by 56 per cent. There were some increases, such as potatoes by 54 per cent, as arable land under cultivation increased by half. Moreover, the very sensible ideas that were suggested to extract the greatest use from food materials, such as feeding cereals directly to the human population rather than indirectly via beasts to be slaughtered, were not recognized until the second year of the war. Most people were prepared to knuckle under even though a small minority operated on an extensive, lucrative and expanding black market which did give access to luxuries, both food and consumer goods, to those who could, and were willing to, pay – whatever the cost. For the majority, deprived of free choice, burdened by bureaucracy and queues and despairing of seeing once common products ever again, the British population had the comfort of knowing that at least their meagre diet was a healthy one. More importantly the diet was guaranteed to the majority of the population and for many it would be the first time that they would eat a healthy and nutritious diet over a long period. Certainly the lessons of rationing were not ignored and the system would be honed and developed. It existed in Britain up to 1955 for many goods and was a testimony to the patience of the British people and just how far down the resources barrel the country had stretched its arm in gaining final victory by 1945.

As with rationing, ARP also made its way into the everyday vocabulary of British people at war. Air Raid Protection was believed to be essential especially with destruction from the deadly *Luftwaffe* expected at any moment. The destruction did come but later in the war than anticipated and in more specifically concentrated areas. An efficient system of protection was essential not only from bombs but also, it was believed – erroneously as it turned out – from gas attack. The government and other organizations produced a mass of advice on what to do in the event of an air attack. The first efforts at preparing for warning the population of attack were a little amateurish but the precautions they advised worked, as those caught in the much reported false alarm of 4 September found out. The 'Phoney War' made such precautions seem an over-reaction but government orders to provide black-out curtains, taped over windows in homes and all public buildings proved essential to safety later on. Companies like Reckitt & Sons soon alerted consumers to the usefulness of their products, like Dettol, in the event of injuries. Others simply tried to avoid injury altogether with the outsized steel cages, or Morrison shelters, in which people slept inside their houses, and the Anderson shelters for use outside.

The threat of invasion was so real in 1940 it was decided that German invasion tactics including the dropping of parachutists, as in Holland and Belgium, could best be countered by a Local Defence Volunteer reserve force. Anthony Eden, the newly appointed Secretary of State for War, announced plans for such a force on the BBC on Tuesday 14 May 1940. The call went out for all men aged between 17 and 65 who for whatever reason were excused military service to enrol. A quarter of a million had responded in the first twenty-four hours and by the end of June this had risen to 1.5 million volunteers, not very far short of the British army's wartime strength. Age, at least early on, proved no barrier, and even later restrictions were waived by the War Office, and a number of men in their eighties and veterans of wars fought in the previous century found themselves serving their country. Thus a vast assortment of all classes of people were thrown together in the levelling experience of military duty. The local gentry rubbed shoulders with professional classes, tradesmen and the working classes. Their motto of 'Kill the Bosche' owed more to intention than reality, but their service was undoubtedly immensely helpful in the war effort. They released troops from necessary but sometimes secondary duties such as observation and surveillance. They trained hard and worked tirelessly in case the threat of invasion became a reality. Their antics amused local inhabitants and their enthusiasm often proved too great for their own good but they found an affectionate niche, if partly deprecatory, in the hearts of many ordinary folk. They were certainly the butt of many jokes. The Home Guard, as the Local Defence Volunteer reserve force became in July 1940, might be known as 'Dad's Army' and be criticized for taking a position in local society higher than their rank deserved, but any additional organization of willing labour, whether trained to fight effectively or not, proved invaluable for the home front. Any aid offered to fire-fighters, air-raid wardens and rescue personnel helped the war effort, as did constant vigilance in whatever form.

Certainly a paranoia developed around any suggestion of slackness at home. It might be shirking of duty or simply 'careless talk' but the implied help to Britain's enemies was a clear message. The Ministry of Information spent a large proportion of its budget on a rolling campaign to warn citizens of the dangers of loose talk. The enemy within was felt to be at least as dangerous as the enemy without battering on the doors of the British Isles, although most would claim that it was fear of the dropping bomb rather than the slipping tongue that kept most people watchful. For the first time, apart from some very localized and limited damages and casualties in the 1914–18 conflict, the British people lay open to attack. The effectiveness of attack from the skies had been ably demonstrated by the experiences of the Spanish Civil War. The damages and losses were severe enough in the end but nothing near the scale feared. Nevertheless large areas of many cities, and especially London, were devastated and the severe housing shortages after the war were due in some measure to the success of the *Luftwaffe* attacks in the early part of the war. But, just as in Germany later on with bombing and even saturation bombing, the blitz appeared not to break the morale of the people under the bombs, if anything it appeared to improve it.

Perhaps the greatest effort during the earliest part of the war went into getting people, and especially children, out of the target cities and industrial areas. The fear of the destruction by bombing was immense and incidents of that fear winning over British bravery were kept well concealed from the public. On one occasion a quarter of the population of Plymouth fled to the surrounding hills to escape an infernal attack of incendiary bombs that destroyed 30,000 homes. The government refused to allow film shot of the exodus to be shown and the authorized newsreels merely showed Churchill visiting the city later on. Such control was useful in keeping the war effort running smoothly and the government made very free use of Regulation 2D, which allowed for censorship of the news in papers. Part of the fear was what would happen to city dwellers simply caught in such a raid. Concern centred on children. In one such evacuation, from Liverpool, government instructions received just before noon on 31 August 1939 were immediately circulated to all schools. Between Friday 1 September and Wednesday 6 September 226 special trains filled with evacuees left the city. It was a testing time for parents, teachers, the receiving families and of course the children. For most children, especially those from the great industrial cities, it would be their first experience of travel outside the confines of their brick environment. Equally so it would be many people's first experience of what city life must be like for millions of families and the young guests often had a shock or two in store for their hosts:

> Less measurable, but if anything even more inflammatory, were the social habits of many evacuees. Foster-parents were horrified to find many of Liverpool's little girls had never worn knickers and a large percentage had never possessed pyjamas. But in the conditions of poverty many children came from, underwear and sleep attire were hardly priorities. As another evacuated schoolteacher remembered: ' . . . the foster-parents expected them to have nighties on, but of course they didn't, they just took off the top layer and got into

bed!' Bed-wetting was a major problem, although not perhaps to be unexpected given the emotional upheaval.

> (P. Ayers, *Women at War*, Birkenhead, Liver Press, 1988, p. 4)

These revelations begin to give some idea of the scale of personal experiences that every Briton underwent in the years 1939 to 1945. It is true that with the 'Phoney War' many evacuees came back to their homes and survived the bombing of the cities along with their parents but the shared experience of evacuation was a valuable one. As one historian has put it, writing about the war experience in total, 'It was a levelling experience – levelling in the risks of war, in food, in shelter, in clothing, in amusement.' It is worth bearing in mind that over a million people were evacuated, and for many it was the first time they had mixed with other classes of British society.

This was overwhelmingly a time of sheer exhausting effort on the part of the British people with men and women working very long hours for guaranteed but modest pay. As one diarist of the time, working herself as a part-time nurse in hospital put it:

> several [patients] were munitions workers suffering from over fatigue. I do hope the long hours will be knocked off. The people cannot do it.
>
> (Vere Hodgson, *A Few Eggs and No Oranges: A Diary*, London, Dennis Dobson, 1976, p. 42)

For others their jobs allowed them the time to take a second job, with vicars, for example, doubling up as postmen. For most, though, all their waking hours were devoted to their contribution to the war effort.

More than ever before the vital role of women, already having been instrumental to success in 1914–18, was recognized. In December 1941 Churchill announced:

> The part-time employment of women in industry has already been developed but nothing like on the scale which must be reached in the months which lie before us . . . an immense variety of arrangements are possible to enable women to divide up domestic tasks and then be free to work, close at hand, in the factory or field. The treatment of the problem must be flexible.

However, very quickly towards the end of December 1941 the National Service No. 2 Act provided for all single women aged 20 and 21 to be taken into service and by 1942 the age limit had been dropped to 19. All were to choose:

> auxiliary services or important jobs in industry. Those who opted for the former would not be posted to combatant duties unless they volunteered for them. With this formula, the Act gained general

acceptance. The Wartime Social Survey found 97 per cent of women agreed emphatically that women should undertake war work.

(A. Calder, *The People's War: Britain 1939–1945*, Cambridge, Cambridge University Press, 1971, pp. 268–9)

Their vital industrial work, especially in the munitions factories, revealed the importance of women in the war effort. However, underpinning this was the administrative framework and state-led interventionism that made such a marshalling of labour resources a possibility, and finally a reality. Britain had come a long way along the road of bureaucracy with registration, labour direction and the classification of work into essential and non-essential categories. The more astute recognized the irony of the situation as remarked by Mollie Panter-Downes, another diarist, who in her *London War Notes* said of the Ministry of Labour directives, 'It is the stiffest dose of totalitarian principles that a democracy has ever had to swallow in order to save the democratic ideal from totalitarian destruction.' The end result could not be argued with but the means employed were not entirely to escape criticism. It did not need the likes of young journalists like Michael Foot, editor of the *Evening Standard*, to call the government's over-use of Regulation 2D powers into question – as he did in 1942. The ordinary citizen was well aware that not all was being revealed. The year before, a *Mass Observation Report* found:

> Universal criticism and dissatisfaction with post blitz administration stronger in Liverpool than any other town. . . . A situation of doubt and rumour – almost complete absence of information and explanation. . . . A loudspeaker van toured but only to give information about transport services.
>
> (Report No. 706, 22 May 1941)

Mollie Panter-Downes, just one of many who questioned what was going on, refers in her diary to this 'curious hush-hush war to keep things as impersonal as an official communiqué'. She constantly criticized the 'Ministry of Information which does not inform', but in common with most others accepted the necessity to withhold information on the grounds of national security. Like Vere Hodgson she resigned herself to sacrifice and the cheering possibility of making it home, 'in time for the Brains Trust', one of the most popular radio programmes of the era. The BBC became the lifeline of all Britons and its services increased massively during the war. In September 1939 it had 24 transmitters operating but by May 1945 this had risen to 121. The BBC became in many ways the 'official voice of Britain', although the Ministry of Information, working from Senate House at London University, censored all material at source before it was then made available to the BBC, newspapers and the newsreel companies. At least as important as its role as information-giver was the BBC's role as morale booster with figures like Tommy

Handley, and his hit show ITMA, and Rob Wilton raising spirits and indulging in the traditional British pastime of ridiculing pompous authority and organizational incompetence, with the Home Guard as prime target on both counts. The radio was also the way that Churchill communicated best with his people. He was a master of radio presentation and Vere Hodgson noted in her diary on Wednesday 1 July 1942, after hearing a broadcast by Churchill, 'Mr Churchill's speech did not offer much comfort. He dominated as he always does and we surrender to his over-powering will.'

The comforts of the war, even for those sat around the radio, were few and the hardships were legion. British people, and especially women workers, put in double and triple shifts, more than their German counterparts did. However, the role of British women did not end with factory labour and back-breaking work on the land. Most of the female workers were also wives and mothers and their work was simply added to by volunteer and conscripted duties. The armed forces also found that women were eager to take a leading role in the war effort. The Auxiliary Territorial Service, formed in 1938, belatedly joined the Women's Royal Naval Service and the Women's Royal Air Force both of which were already in existence. By 1939 all three female branches of the services could muster some 20,000 personnel. By the end of the war this had leapt to just under 500,000. Women, in addition to the traditional clerical duties, took on specialized tasks such as fighter controllers and plotters, radar operators, as well as work with signals, transport and anti-aircraft gun batteries. Some of the most effective intelligence officers were women, and their skill as code-breakers was especially useful. In April 1941 the ATS was sent to the Middle East and the WRNS to Singapore, both enjoying full military status. Despite the very active service engaged in by women in the armed forces the old prejudices seemed still to be at work because technically they were non-combatants so they could not win a VC, whatever the level of their endeavour and bravery.

On the civilian side the Civil Defence Corps and the Women's Volunteer Service (WVS) proved invaluable. The Defence Corps with its fire-fighting duties allied to rescue and demolition work again highlighted the plight of women. Compensation was at a rate two-thirds of that for men doing the same dangerous tasks. The WVS' duties were varied. In Liverpool they organized a Housewives' Service for women who could not leave home but might be valuable in emergencies with some tuition in basic first aid and air-raid precautions. Otherwise it was a continual round of offering help to the shell-shocked and wounded, serving refreshments, taking in a bit of washing for those bombed out or going through remains to help identify injured and dead.

If time, blood, energy, pain, exhaustion and belt-tightening were not enough, the British government also demanded money from its people. On an income of £1,000 per annum, far more than most Britons enjoyed, the income tax levied was 38 per cent. On unearned incomes of £1,000 the tax rate was 94 per cent, and luxuries had a tax levied of 100 per cent their full value. In addition to taxation the government asked for, and received, massive war bond contributions that amassed £8.467 billion. This represented a saving of £177 per person, and all this at a time of severe austerity and want. Of course even this massive sum was nowhere near enough to cover the costs of the war, but it was another selfless action and a testimony to the British people's desire to help the government win the war.

Inevitably, with the coming of Lend-Lease (see chapter 14) and eventually American military aid, plus the increasingly diffuse tactics of Hitler multiplying fronts and commitments, the war did take on a different character. The days of worrying about invasion and the countryside being laid waste disappeared as 1941 gave way to 1942. It was the latter year that saw allied victories, the first since the Battle of Britain. By 1943 victories were becoming the norm. Lord Woolton, the Minister of Food, had promised the British people the 'fruits' of victory in Africa and Mollie Panter-Downes noted in her diary on 24 October 1943 that he was true to his word. Oranges appeared, albeit for consumption by children. On 6 September 1944 blackout restrictions were relaxed and in January of that year the government had doubled the level of permitted spending on essential repairs to houses from £100 to £200. Soon, for the first time in years, it would become legal to purchase a large-scale map, sound a factory hooter, have a car radio, sleep in an uncamouflaged tent and release a racing-pigeon without police permission. However, strict controls were still in force for virtually all commodities, and would remain so for some years to come. But the successes on the field of battle had made the meagre fare of life more palatable to the British people. By 1945 victory was expected and it was duly delivered. The surrender from Germany came and 8 May 1945 became Victory in Europe (VE) day. The celebrations were joyous and ecstatic but, as Churchill warned, the respite the British people could allow themselves could only number a few days. The tasks ahead would be as testing as the trial by war that had occupied the waking and sleeping hours of every man, woman and child in the country for the past six years.

Exactly how far-reaching the war experience was is difficult to quantify. Certainly, a glance at any street in London or other large city would have revealed a great deal: men – and women – in uniform, civilians struggling to look fashionable in utility clothes (designed to use the minimum of materials) and the ever-present gas mask cases, with everyone having half an ear open for the air-raid siren and half an eye on the nearest shelter. If a raid came it would mean another uncomfortable night in the Underground, or at home, until the all-clear was sounded. Under such circumstances it is hardly surprising that changes in British social attitudes came about in a very short space of time. Certainly there was camaraderie and a leavening of the social mix in factories, army units and the Home Guard. Many would endorse the words of J. B. Priestley that 'British people were never as good as they were in the Second World War.' There is always a danger of looking back and seeing only the good things while ignoring personal tragedies, the pain of separation, the immorality of the black market, the exploitation of many and the suffering of others that lasted well beyond the all too brief days of victory. Nevertheless, the overwhelming impression seemed to be a positive one and the contrast between the return of the soldier in 1945 and that of his counterpart in 1918 seemed stark. For in the intervening years not only had the country changed, and the people with it, but their expectations reflected the changes they had experienced. A 'land fit for heroes' could no longer be a pipe-dream; it had to become a reality this time, and throughout the years of conflict there were clear signs that momentous changes were possible and would become reality when victory had been gained.

A 'STEP TOWARDS UTOPIA'

In 1939 there had been 20,000 women in the three branches of the armed forces; for men the figure was around 500,000. By 1945 there were nearly 500,000 women and 4.5 million men in uniform. In all 15 million men and 7 million women, in one capacity or another, had been called into service by the state in the years of its greatest need. Twenty-two million people represented, in rough terms, around half the population of the country, thrown together, rubbing shoulders and moving up and down the length of the country. Before the war over half of Britain's population had never spent a night away from their own home but by 1945 60 million changes of address had been registered in the six years of war, and two million homes had been devastated, gutted, damaged and destroyed by bombing. It is little wonder that the word reconstruction went far beyond simple rebuilding programmes; it was the encouragement of what Ben Morris termed the desire to take a 'step towards Utopia'. J. B. Priestley's prophetic words, taken from one of his many radio broadcasts, that 'Britain was being bombed into democracy', were about to be put to the test. Not this time a democracy in an electoral form, but a fuller type of democracy as graphically described by *The Times* on 1 July 1940:

> If we speak of democracy, we do not mean a democracy which maintains the right to vote but forgets the right to work and the right to live. If we speak of freedom, we do not mean a rugged individualism which excludes social organization and economic planning. If we speak of equality, we do not mean a political equality nullified by social and economic privilege.

It must have been encouraging for the Labour Party to read such comments in the Tory press, and certainly the war years opened well enough for the party, for it did very well out of the ministerial appointments made by Churchill in May 1940. Attlee was appointed Lord Privy Seal, becoming deputy Prime Minister in 1942. Other leading Labour politicians also received the call. Men like Cripps, Greenwood, Morrison and Dalton, and Bevin from the trade unions, all served in senior positions. The war offered the opportunity for the Labour Party to show off its array of talent and ability at ministerial level. Churchill was quick to recognize the riches at his disposal and many of these men found their way into his inner War Cabinet that took direction of the country's efforts. Attlee's role was central and only he, of all Churchill's colleagues in these years, was a continuous member of the War Cabinet for the duration. He was also the only politician who was in the War Cabinet, on the Defence Committee and the Lord President's Committee. The first two he served as deputy and the last as Chairman. He was the most powerful and effective figure of the politicians charged with the control, direction and responsibility for the Home Front. The important role played not only by Attlee but by Labour as a whole is demonstrated by the work of Arthur Greenwood, Labour MP for Wakefield, who was made Minister with Responsibility for Reconstruction in 1941. As such he set to work teams of researchers, planners and specialists to come up with ideas and recommendations. He established the Inter-Departmental Committee on Social Insurance and Allied Services. This was more or less a continuation of the Labour Party's interest in and proposals on these topics that had been much in evidence before the war started. It was Labour's Hugh Dalton, now serving at the Board of Trade, who had outlined plans for schemes of social welfare and the creation of full employment in *Labour's Immediate Programme* of 1937. These suggestions appeared again in *Labour's War Aims* in 1939, and in *Labour, the War and Peace* and *Labour's Home Policy* in 1940. They reached fruition in *Let's Face the Future* in 1945 when the references to National Health Service, national insurance and house-building programmes reappeared. By this date, such an extensive, albeit vague, programme proposed by a Labour ministry was no longer a pipe-dream but an entirely feasible step forward. Attlee and Bevin in particular had taken a leading role, along with others, in what might be termed the 'domestic' ministries. Those concerns that were less than dashing in war-time, but had been the bread and butter of victory, suddenly became the chief focus of attention after 1945: housing, health and employment.

By 1945 the Labour Party and its politicians were prepared. Changes during the war had, in general, been piecemeal and responsive to needs. For example, R. A. Butler's decision to provide school meals was reported in the *Liverpool Daily Post* of 4 November 1941:

If children can be kept warm in school and have a good meal, it will be much better than having to walk home several miles. Nowadays, when so many women are engaged on war work, children may be neglected at midday.

Such moves paved the way in 1945 for wholesale, government-led changes of even greater social significance. What war had done was, first, to show what was possible, such as the creation of a national fire service, by the Labour politician Herbert Morrison, or the government control of gas and electricity along with the railways. Second, it had shown what was necessary with an under-nourished, vermin ridden inner-city under-class of families which became graphic exports to a more complacent rural and middle-class populace which simply, for the most part, did not know that such deprivations and conditions existed. Third, it had helped to create the means, desire and spirit to bring such great social changes and reforms about. As Michael Foot claimed of the war, 'It was the nearest thing I have seen in my lifetime to the operation of a democratic socialist state.' Certainly the challenge facing Britain was recognized in official and semi-official circles with the Ministry of Information releasing films such as 'Land of Promise', and suggesting the use of war-time planning expertise to wage 'another war for freedom' and 'a full planned economy'. Part of the success was the almost saturation coverage that such ideas received. Priestley's *Out of the People* (1941); Macmillan's series of pamphlets like R. H. Tawney's *Why Britain Fights*, on sale at 3 pennies; the *Picture Post* series with its circulation of 8 million in 1941, outlining Britain's future with titles such as 'Health for All'; and the sixpenny Penguin books such as Eleanor Rathbone's, *A Case for Family Allowances*, were all best-sellers in their own right. The ideas themselves were freely discussed, especially in the army, under the auspices of its Bureau of Current Affairs which ensured that all soldiers received one hour a week set aside for discussion of all aspects of current concern. Those who talked were, after all, the children of those who had fought in 1914–18, and, as one old soldier put it, 'much of war is about waiting around, thinking and talking'. Most found plenty of opportunity for this in the six years of combat.

The desire for a new future did not stop at reading and talking. The idea of a political movement based on the common weal, much voiced by Priestley, was made a reality by Sir Richard Acland, the Liberal MP for Barnstaple, in 1942. The Commonwealth 'party' opposed what it called reaction and stood for common ownership of land and productive resources to serve as a foundation for a more morally correct basis to society. Its electoral success was brief with by-election victories at Eddisbury in 1943 and Skipton in 1944. It did take Chelmsford in the 1945 general election but no more. As an organization its impact in the war years was important because it became yet another stimulus to reform and change, providing extra impetus to the government to make plans, present discussion documents and even prepare White Papers. In this its influence was out of all proportion to its numbers and political role inside Parliament.

A long hard look at industry was also needed. Ernest Bevin, that most charismatic of trade-union officials, who had been imaginatively called into the government by Churchill, proved a cornerstone of victory. He could lead the trade-union movement in a direction that traditional politicians would find hard going. Who better to get the unions to accept directives such as Order 1305 forbidding strike activity? But even Bevin could not make men work more than 24 hours a day, as many miners and factory workers were trying to do with their own work being supplemented by voluntary duties. The men at Betteshanger pit in Kent revealed that they could take no more in 1942 when they went on strike. It was not treason, nor even avarice, that prompted their action but plain simple exhaustion. Bevin's plans for 1943 resulted in the extension of the call-up to all boys aged over seventeen and a half. These had their names entered in a numbered ballot and all those whose numbers ended in '0' or '09' were taken away to work in the pits and became known as 'Bevin Boys'. The plan did not stop strikes nor did it revive the more worrying flagging levels of coal production, but it was an example of the imaginative and charismatic part played by one leader of labour. Moreover, the strikes, which spread to the Yorkshire pits, demonstrated graphically what might be in store for the next peace-time government of the country unless serious consideration was given to social issues.

One factor more than any other that symbolizes both the political will and the popular desire to make a break and attack the greatest weaknesses of British society – 'want, disease, idleness, ignorance and squalor' – was the Beveridge Report. Sir Wiliam Beveridge had been made Chairman of a Ministry of Health social insurance committee in June 1941. By 1 December 1942 the report, carrying Beveridge's name, was on the table of the House of Commons. Its message was clear. It envisaged a future of state and citizen co-operation, with a unified social insurance system, a national minimum income, a national medical service and benefits for birth, marriage and death. The report proposed a legislative bombshell which frightened many Tories and excited many Labour supporters. The press was in no doubt about the momentous nature of the proposals being made:

[The report] has transformed this aspiration [freedom from want] into a plainly realizable project of national endeavour. . . . The central proposals must surely be accepted as the basis of Government action. . . . The Government has been presented with an opportunity for marking this decisive epoch with a great social measure which will

go far towards restoring the faith of ordinary men and women throughout the world in the power of democracy.

(The Times, 2 December 1942)

one of the most remarkable state documents ever drafted. . . . The
true test of the Beveridge Plan is whether or not it will inspire,
regardless of vested interests, a nation-wide determination to set right
what is so plainly wrong and a series of prompt decisions by the
Government to ensure that whatever else this war may bring, social
security and economic progress shall march together.

(The Economist, 5 December 1942)

The general public was simply excited and there are few government
reports that have become best-sellers, but inside a year Beveridge's had
sold 265,000 complete copies, 369,000 shortened versions and 40,000 to
the American market. Mollie Panter-Downes in her diary for 13
December 1942 noted how Londoners had queued for hours for the
privilege of buying a 'two shilling slab of involved economics'. A Gallup
poll of about this time reported that nineteen out of every twenty people
questioned had heard of the report, and many may well have thought it
a cure-all.

Popularity does not mean instant political success and Churchill was
very worried that such issues, as raised by Beveridge, would distract
from the war effort in 1942 and 1943, which would be key years for the
country. In a sense he was right, for Beveridge and his report caused
both the Labour Party and the government its greatest difficulties in the
Commons during the course of the war. A Labour resolution that the
government should support and implement the Beveridge Report was
defeated by 335 to 119. Ninety-seven Labour MPs had voted against the
government and of the twenty-three who voted with the government,
twenty-two were ministers. Obviously, the latter, as representatives of
the government, had victory as their top priority. In fact, Attlee was a
Beveridge Report enthusiast although many Labour supporters were not.
This was especially true of Beveridge's later reports and the production
of a White Paper entitled *Full Employment in a Free Society*. Many saw
this as a crutch for capitalism draped in a socialist cloak and refused to
lend their support to anything less than full-blown socialism, like Aneurin
Bevan. Even those Labour politicians who could see the good points of
Beveridge's reports were wary of the man and his intentions, like Hugh
Dalton who, when talking to Labour Party delegates from Bishop Auck-
land, put it in these terms:

I knew Beveridge better than most people having served both under
and over him; that he is not 'one of us' and has no first-hand knowledge of industrial conditions; that there are a number of things in his
Report to which we could not subscribe, e.g. the penalizing of miners

and railway workers because their jobs are inherently more risky than a carpenter's, and the proposal to take twenty years to reach the appropriate rate of old-age pension.

(*The Second World War Diary of Hugh Dalton 1940–45*, ed. B. Pimlott, London, Cape, 1986, p. 564)

In spite of dissenting voices the Beveridge Report, closely followed by others like Mr Justice Uthwatt's *Compensation and Benefit* in September 1942, had drawn the lines very clearly for politicians and people. What had been the stuff of dreams and imagination had, through the magnifying glass of war, become the just deserts and rights of all Britons. It was time for the state to consider its new role as servant of the people.

'LABOUR IS THE PARTY OF THE FUTURE'

Attlee's optimistic view of his own party's role in the post-war world did not fit in with Churchill's proposal on 18 May 1945 that the Coalition Government should continue in office until the defeat of Japan. The Labour Party rejected the idea at the Blackpool Conference that year, and Churchill formed a caretaker government until he asked for a dissolution on 15 June so that elections could take place on 5 July. Uniquely in British electoral history the balloting was extended, and votes not counted, until 26 July, to allow for the vast numbers of armed services voters to cast their votes. Arrangements were also made for parliamentary candidates in the services to be transported home to stand in elections. James Callaghan, later Labour Prime Minister, was in the Indian Ocean when the election was announced but managed to get home in time to win a Cardiff constituency for Labour. The great question of British politics was decided in some exotic locations that year and the Egyptian one is particularly symbolic. It was in Cairo, as an extension of the current affairs interests engendered in soldiers, that permission was granted for a 'mock' parliament. This Labour-dominated assembly met and talked and gave its seal of approval to radical programmes like land nationalization, nationalization of banks, transport and mines, and freedom for India. The army closed the Cairo parliament before it got out of hand and the government denied the forces copies of Beveridge's *Full Employment in a Free Society* but the general mood of feeling was clear to see. What most could not believe, nor even contemplate, was that this mood would manifest in terms of votes when the time came. Churchill expected victory as did the pundits who favoured the war leader and the Tories. Churchill played it safe in campaigning, and made radio speeches stressing the leadership qualities of the Conservative Party. Critical remarks about Attlee and the Labour Party and their unfitness to govern no longer seemed applicable, and a new Tory strategy of attack had yet to emerge. Their enemies had been hardened by five

years of ministerial experience and grave crisis from which they had
emerged as triumphantly as Churchill and the Tories. Indeed Labour's
campaign had a much more modern look to it and suggested a much
wider appeal to the community as a whole. From the simple black and
white of the party manifesto *Let Us Face the Future* as much as on the
billboards and hoardings it is clear to see what the Labour programme
was:

> What will the Labour Party do?
>
> First, the whole of the national resources, in land, material and
> labour must be fully employed. Production must be raised to the
> highest level and related to purchasing power. Over-production is not
> the cause of depression and unemployment; it is under-consumption
> that is responsible. It is doubtful whether we have ever, except in
> war, used the whole of our productive capacity. This must be corrected
> because, upon our ability to produce and organise a fair and generous
> distribution of the product, the standard of living of our people
> depends.
>
> Secondly, a high and constant purchasing power can be maintained
> through good wages, social services and insurance, and taxation which
> bears less heavily on the lower-income groups . . .
>
> Thirdly, planned investment in essential industries and on houses,
> schools, hospitals and civic centres will occupy a large field of capital
> expenditure . . .
>
> Fourthly, the Bank of England with its financial powers must be
> brought under public ownership, and the operations of the other banks
> harmonised with industrial needs.
>
> By these and other means full employment can be achieved.

Besides appeal, logic and the moral high-ground, the Labour Party's
policies also appealed to the outrage felt by many people that what
should have been done after the last war was still waiting to be started.

Labour had a double-figure lead in the polls, although this had been
the case since 1942, and in fact their lead soon fell back when serious
campaigning started. Although 1945 cannot boast the largest of turnouts
with 73.3 per cent it was an election with a big swing of votes: 12 per
cent over the 1935 results which increased Labour members from 154 to
393. With 48 per cent of the vote, against the Tories' 39.6 per cent,
Labour had an overall majority, of 146 seats, for the first time in its
history. Churchill resigned immediately and at 7.30 on the evening of 26
July 1945 Clement Attlee accepted the King's commission as Prime Minister of Great Britain. The experiment in socialism could now begin. The
'Pathenews' report of 30 July 1945 that claimed 'Let's face it whoever
imagined such a result' was soon forgotten as Attlee named his new
government. The names of the men occupying the senior posts were all
familiar: Morrison as Lord President, Greenwood as Lord Privy Seal,

Dalton as Chancellor of the Exchequer, Bevin as Foreign Secretary, Cripps as President of the Board of Trade and Bevan as Minister of Health. The only surprises were Morrison's attempt to delay forming a government until the Parliamentary Labour Party (PLP) met, hoping for victory himself, and the appointment of Dalton and Bevin each of whom was expected to get the other's post. Some uncertainty surrounds this first major decision of the new Labour Prime Minister because he appears to have suggested Dalton might get the post of Foreign Secretary early on. He may have been influenced personally by Churchill, the king and the cabinet secretary. Two considerations appear to have been exercising people's minds. The first was that Bevin, a political maverick, simply did not get on with Morrison and to have the two of them at loggerheads over domestic issues would be disastrous, hence Bevin became favourite for the Foreign Office, out of harm's way. Second, Dalton had favoured, before the war, an alliance with Russia, and thus, in the new post-war era of growing suspicion, was a less than safe choice for Foreign Secretary when diplomacy would be dominated by the questions of Russia and eastern Europe. Bevin as a trade unionist, but not pro-Russian, seemed the better choice to many as Foreign Secretary, thus leaving the complex economic negotiations of post-war loans to the more economically well-versed and adept Dalton. The only remaining controversy appears to be exactly how many times Attlee changed his mind in a given 24-hour period. These senior seasoned campaigners who could provide wise, experienced and skilled leadership found themselves injected with the enthusiasm of youth. In excess of 250 of the 393 Labour MPs who entered Parliament in 1945 were entirely new to the experience. Each group was just as excited as the other. James Callaghan, a new member, later recorded in his biography, 'to me it was a new world and I was enthralled'. Hugh Dalton, an old hand, resorted in his memoirs to a line from Edward Carpenter's Socialist Hymn:

England is risen and the day is here.

THE STATE AS SERVANT OF THE PEOPLE

The momentous years of the first Labour Government 1945–50 have given rise to much discussion. The ushering in of the welfare state and the policies of nationalization have been variously assessed as the final victory of socialist principles and the natural progression of the political consensus of the war years. Some of the arguments centre on the very tenuous links between the Labour Party pronouncements of the 1930s and before, and the quite radical reforms that found their way on to the statute books. Even more debatable, especially for the left, is how closely the achievements of the Labour Government approximated to socialism. Were they, after all, only carrying out what naturally followed from the war effort, or was there a genuine feeling of a socialist new dawn to be created by widespread mould-breaking legislative action? In truth politics is not as simple as having convictions and then doing something about them once in power. The post-war world found politics to be in a much more complex state than this. Britain had come out of the war with the spirit to do something to change her society, and maybe also had a range of blueprints, but it would be made perfectly plain in a short space of time that desire and intent also needed wherewithal. Britain came out of the war an economic cripple and one whose only crutch of support would be the USA. Much of Labour policy would not be dictated directly by the USA, but by the range of economic props the USA was willing to provide. This was made plain by the US decision to end Lend-Lease on 21 August 1945 which necessitated lengthy negotiations by Lord Keynes in the USA in order to secure a loan. This was an inauspicious start for the new government. Dalton's first budget was an optimistic one that reflected a desire to expand with its reductions of income tax and purchase tax. In reality this was something of a side-show while the real economic decision-making took place across the Atlantic. The USA agreed to give Britain a loan of $4.4 billion. This was less than asked for, and included $650 million already written off to USA debts. It also came with conditions. First, after 1951 interest would be charged at 2 per cent and, more contentiously, by 1947 Britain would be obliged to make sterling a fully convertible currency. The terms were stiff but agreed to, and with a Canadian loan of $1.25 billion, the Labour Government now had the economic and financial flexibility, or so it believed, to carry forward its legislative programme.

In a sense the programme had already started. As the Labour historian Laybourn has claimed, 'the Labour government welfare programme was a rich mosaic of wartime collectivism, Labour policies and practical necessity'. He might also have added 'inheritance'. One example of the wartime inheritance was the 1944 Education Act. Here was a reform, sibling to later ones, that would provide for part of the post-war welfare state. It had created a new Ministry of Education, 146 local education authorities, raised the school-leaving age to 15, and tackled the vexed question of religious instruction by making non-denominational worship compulsory along with religious education, but both were covered by a 'conscience' clause that permitted exclusion. The Act was the creation of a Conservative, R. A. Butler, thus testifying to the cross-party concern on welfare issues in this era. *The Times* noted, at the White Paper stage in July 1943, that it was 'the greatest and grandest educational advance since 1870'. It was after the Act became law that further social reforms were mentioned in an address from the throne in November 1944. It was these reforms, lauded at the time by Churchill and Eden as well as Labour politicians, that the government now intended to put into force. With the benefit of pledges made so recently by their political opponents, and with a large majority, there was little opposition to many of the proposals now brought forward. The Trades Disputes Act was repealed in May 1946. This fulfilled Labour's old promise to the unions by returning to them their legal position of 1926 before the General Strike necessitated changes. In addition it restored the political levy which was used by the party to cover expenses. Trade unionists could however contract out of the arrangement. James Griffiths's National Insurance Act was passed in the same year. This provided for immediate increases to 26 shillings a week in both sickness and unemployment benefits, while extending the period over which such payments were made. Family allowances, maternity benefits and widows' benefits were also introduced in this year.

The pace of reform was relentless in these early years, but one piece of legislation stands out for its benefits to society and the acrimony of debate, and that was the National Health Service Act of 1946. Whereas national insurance had taken its guidelines directly from Beveridge the Health measure would be a different affair completely. The historian Peter Calvocoressi has claimed that the NHS Act was 'perhaps the most beneficial reform ever enacted in England'. This may well be the case, but it came up against some intense pressure from vested interests, and finally appeared in a slightly truncated form. The need for a national health service had been recognized by the British Medical Association (BMA) as early as 1918. This need was restated in a report entitled *General Medical Services for the Nation*, published in 1930. During the war the nation's health became a defence concern; it also became a major area for discussion by the planners on the reconstruction committees. The issues were left to successive Ministers of Health, Ernest Brown and then Henry Willink, to suggest reforms. Willink came up with a proposal of revamping the organization and contracting general practitioners to the service. The proposals were debated in March 1944 with some dissenting voices but Willink was over-run by the tide of political events. In the new Labour Government Aneurin Bevan was Minister of Health. The charismatic Welsh orator, who was MP for Ebbw Vale and the son of a miner, wanted more than the Willink proposals. His imaginative and far-reaching plans for the health services are a warning to those who seek too readily for simplistic and concrete links between war-time and Labour legislation. Bevan wanted all hospitals including voluntary ones involved in the service, GPs to be put on a basic salary, and controls brought in over the sale of practices. After a first reading in March 1946 the Bill had its second reading on 11 May and Conservatives placed an amendment that was defeated by 359 to 172. Bevan was labelled by his opponents as a 'man in a hurry'. Despite continued Conservative opposition the Bill received its third reading in July, and Royal Assent in December 1946. The BMA took the offensive, prompted, it must be said, by the financial implications as well as those for patient care. A ballot ensued in November 1946 and gave a 55 per cent vote in favour of non-cooperation under the terms of the new Act. Bevan and the government were faced by a doctors' revolt which lasted through 1947. The medical profession's feelings were reaffirmed at the BMA council on 17 March 1948. Bevan succumbed to pressure in April of that year omitting the idea of full-time contracts that prevented doctors from giving some of their time to private patients and consultancy. Parts of the Act had been successfully cut away with the BMA acting as surgeon. Many later sympathized with Bevan's description of the Tories as 'lower than vermin', a remark made in Manchester in July 1948. The National Health Service was inaugurated on 5 July 1948 and it was none the less one of if not the finest achievement in social legislation in the history of Britain. It would last unchanged until 1989.

Housing was another priority area. So many people had nowhere to live or lodged with relatives or friends, a prerequisite for being placed on the housing list. With so many houses destroyed in the war and resources being channelled into what seemed more important areas the housing stock available for habitation dropped rapidly. In the 1930s houses were being built at a rate of up to 350,000 a year but in 1945 only 3,000 houses were built. At the same time the demobilization of nearly 5 million service personnel put an inordinate strain on scant resources and the meagre amount of accommodation available. For most people it was the unpleasant feeling of having nowhere of their own to live or even having no roof over their head at all. The housing problem in post-war Britain was graphically revealed by protesting squatters in London and other cities who demanded, besides water and bedding, simple accommodation. For many, simple hostel accommodation was what they received. Nevertheless, simple was far preferable to spartan and unpleasant – as many of the alternatives were. Hostels were far from ideal especially for families and the use of locations such as aerodromes, which had accommodation formerly used by airmen, as with the serried ranks of Nissen huts at Stoneycross in the New Forest which was still in use as late as 1951, was *in extremis*. The government tried hard to increase house-building programmes but many of the splendid target figures achieved between 1948–51 (200,000 houses per annum) included large numbers of what were intended to be temporary dwellings. Pre-fabricated houses, or pre-fabs, were designed to make up for the shortage of bricks and mortar. Initially they were aluminium framed dwellings but later concrete pre-fabs appeared. It is a sobering thought that many people throughout the country still live in these houses erected by the post-war Labour Government.

While the structure of the welfare state was taking shape the Labour Government had a second goal in mind. This was the keeping of faith with the founders of the party's constitution in 1918. 'Clause Four', which called for public ownership, was the other leg that would support the

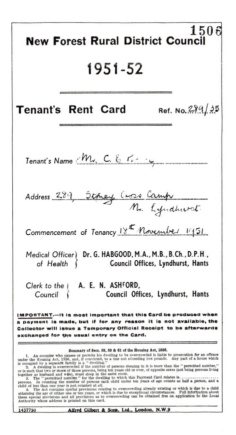

body of the new Britain. The Party Conference in 1944, under the promptings of Ian Mikardo, had once again pledged itself to nationalization. The war demonstrated the effects of government control of utilities and transport, as well as the feasibility. Public ownership seemed only a short step from government control. However, the commitment was to an article of faith rather than a planned policy, and Labour has been criticized since for the piecemeal and diffuse approach to nationalization. In 1946 it nationalized the Bank of England, Civil Aviation, Cable and Wireless and coal. The following year saw railways, electricity and road haulage added, while gas went in 1948. Indicative of the mood of enthusiasm, but lack of thought, was the thinking out of details on the hoof. As one historian has noted, 'it was only by trial and error that the organisational structures, finances, compensation, pricing policies and relations with workers were worked out'. No plan or strategy seemed to exist and each utility and interest was taken on its own merits with the very process of nationalization seen as some kind of magic wand. There was also opposition to many of the proposals. Some of these came from Tories, like their objections to road transport, and the desire to exclude some users. At other times it was Labour's own supporters, as with complaints about the levels of compensation for pit-owners. The government's proposals for iron and steel really raised opposition hackles and a fierce rearguard action was fought all the way from the initial proposals in 1948 to the final act of 1950. As one might suspect the government found it more difficult to operate freely as its term of office came to a close. An example would be the 800 opposition amendments to the gas proposals in 1948. What is certain is that there was no attempt to try to push the idea of nationalization into the public sector beyond the great industries and utilities. It is for this reason that the Labour Government has been taken to task by its socialist critics who also might see its other activities in this field as ones that strengthened the capitalist state rather than helping to engineer its demise.

Often forgotten amongst the social reforms and nationalization programmes are the significant parliamentary reforms carried out by this government. In part it was the House of Lords' opposition to the steel Bill that created a desire to extend the powers of the 1911 Parliament Act. In 1949 a Parliament Act cut the delaying powers of the Lords to one year. A year earlier the government had also passed a Parliamentary Reform Act. This was designed to redraw the constituency boundaries so that they were more in line with modern population trends and concentrations. In the following election the number of MPs dropped from 640 to 625 and the Labour Party suffered worse than its opponents as a result of this reform. The noble gesture in this matter was countered by the gains to be made by outlawing plural voting, or the tradition that some graduates and businessmen in London exercised two votes in elections. This was considered unfair and its abolition was another blow against unwarranted privilege.

The American money that had allowed such an extensive programme of welfare reform and nationalization to come into being had strings attached. It was these strings that would strangle the Labour Government's further attempts to build the 'New Jerusalem' in the years after 1947. The decision to honour the loan conditions, although noble, was disastrous. Putting the pound on full convertibility with the dollar on 15 July 1947 saw a run on sterling. The fuel crisis caused by the incompetence of the minister in charge, Manny Shinwell, along with a coal shortage and a very severe winter intensified the economic difficulties. Higher American prices ensured a balance of payments crisis and foreign gold and currency reserves were hastily withdrawn from the country, so much so that the government had to suspend convertibility on 20 August. Dalton, injudicious enough to leak budget details, resigned and was replaced at the Exchequer by Sir Stafford Cripps whose name became linked for all time with the term 'austerity'. Cripps's policy was to raise the level of exports while reducing the level of imports for which he employed a licensing system and continued rationing. This was introduced at the same time as a complete control on prices and incomes

BUYING PERMIT

This permit contains _____ 40 _____ *Utility Furniture Units*
and the following *Priority Dockets*

_____ / _____ Curtain material
_____ / _____ Floor covering
_____ / _____ Mattresses
_____ _____ Blankets
_____ 3 _____ Sheets

| To be quoted in any correspondence |
| Reference Number 6299785 |

The person to whom this permit is issued **MUST**
complete these particulars **BEFORE** using it

1. Name   Mr. W. L. Pearce

2. Address

3. National Registration (Identity Card) Number
or Service Number and Rank

AREA OF VALIDITY

For the purpose of obtaining Utility Furniture, this permit may be used only at a shop
within a radius of 15 miles of the address to which the furniture is to be delivered

or anywhere in _____ 24 NOV 1947 _____
Date of issue _____ , 194 _____

Please see Notes inside the front and back covers

51—2710

EC 615287
D

priority docket

for 20 square yards of

Linoleum or Felt Base

Series 2

Priority dockets are NOT equivalent to When they

EC 615287
D

Important—

UN/F 573411

priority docket

for

UTILITY MATTRESS

First Series

Priority dockets are
NOT equivalent to
coupons. When they
relate to rationed
goods and do not have
coupon - equivalent
documents attached,
the appropriate num-
ber of coupons must
also be surrendered.

overleaf.

CONSUMER RATIONING ORDER
GENERAL LICENCE S.R. & O. 1944. No. 809

certificate

(Series 1)

*permitting the supply without the surrender of coupons to
the person by whom it is endorsed overleaf of*

DS, **C** 352277

SHEETS

in respect of which the appropriate number of coupons
does not exceed

SIX COUPONS

issued on behalf of the
BOARD OF TRADE by
This document is valid only when it is
(a) stamped or signed by the issuing office
and (b) endorsed overleaf with the name and address of the
person to be supplied
A trader who has supplied sheets against this document may
deposit it in his coupon account for **SIX** coupons

UTILITY FURNITURE OFFICE
SOUTHPORT, LANCS

6

see overleaf

involving a wages freeze. It was harsh medicine for a population already expert at extreme self-denial. 'Marshall aid' (see chapter 14, p. 554) was extended but huge loans were soon swallowed up by the implementation of the previous year's reforms which were proving costly. Cripps relied on safe budgetary measures raising taxes and duties in April 1948. Some respite came with the 1949 budget with reductions in excise duties but increases in other taxes. However, tinkering with beer duty and introducing a pools betting tax was again not enough and devaluation came in 1949. Some claimed that this was not only too strong a medicine but not even necessary. Younger members of the party, like Hugh Gaitskell, doubted the need for the remedy and pointed to Britain's economic recovery with indices such as industrial production well above 1938 levels, but Cripps prevailed. The pound sank from $4.03 to $2.80. It was the economic crises of convertibility and devaluation that put the brakes on the government's legislative activity. It is significant that shortly after devaluation, which was on 18 September 1949, Attlee announced cuts of £140 million in capital expenditure and £120 million in current expenditure plus bank loan restrictions. Even the National Health Service appeared to be a possible target for cuts until Bevan pre-empted the Cabinet by announcing on 25 September 1949 that 'the health service is sacrosanct'. With Morrison talking of health charges the seeds were sown here for future debate and acrimony in the party.

For ordinary Britons little seemed to have changed, rationing was still in force and would remain so until July 1955. As the historian Paul

Addison has remarked, the home front 'ran on without a war to sustain it', and was all the more difficult to comprehend. The returning soldiers found all goods in short supply and for many with the resumption of married life came the baby boom of 1947 which brought its own problems. The government tried to help and newly-weds, and new parents, were entitled to priority dockets and supplementary rations as the illustrations show. Utility clothes and furniture were the only goods available to the vast majority of the population. Relaxations were made when possible but financial stringencies made them more belated than the government hoped for. The end of clothes rationing was ordered by Harold Wilson on 14 March 1949. But while clothes became 'coupon free', food remained rationed well into the next decade. Economics had triumphed over politics and the Labour Government's intense activity was slowing down as the change to a new decade approached.

'THE RETREAT FROM JERUSALEM'

Kenneth Morgan's description of the last months of the Labour administrations of 1950 and 1951 succinctly encapsulates the slackening of the pace and desire for reform, both on the nationalization and welfare fronts. It was simply impossible to continue with the economic stringency of the years biting deeply into the vitals of the body of Britain. The underlying indicators of import, export and production figures may have been promising, but the greater forces of international currency markets and USA dominance of world finance and trade had conspired to push Britain into the economic second division along with so many others. The retreat was none the less very unpalatable to many Labour supporters. It seemed to be a fundamental betrayal of principles and a waste of all the hard work to talk in terms of slowing down the pace of change. Anything less than full-blown socialism, for some, was anathema to the very existence of the party itself. Two personalities exemplified the growing split in the party. On one side there was Herbert Morrison, from a poor London background and a Labour stalwart since before the First World War, who had become the linchpin of Labour's domestic policies. While the government was forced to change the tenor of its policy Morrison, rightly or wrongly, was associated with the so-called retreat. Cripps and Gaitskell also stood by him. On the other side there was Aneurin Bevan, all fiery Welsh mining socialism of the old school, who brooked no compromise. The field of conflict was the National Health Service and the need for all areas of government activity to sustain spending cuts in the age of austerity. The National Health Service was popular but the costs escalated, nearly tripling from the 1946 estimates and by 1951 they had reached £365 million. The debate apparently centred on health charges for prescriptions and eye tests, but in reality, for Bevan at least, it was a matter of principle with the service 'sacrosanct'. The National

Health was a service for all Britons and the government ought to keep faith with promises made in 1946 and again in 1948. The debate was terminated for a while by the election of 1950. Despite the troubles that had welled up, especially towards the end of the government's term, it had survived intact with not one loss at by-elections. Unusually the announcement was made on 11 January for an election day on 23 February, the first early year election since 1910. Labour, despite leading at the polls expected losses because the boundary changes, enacted in the 1948 Representation of the People Act, would become operative. However, the contest, thanks to a reinvigorated Conservative Party and its organization, and the fact that 475 Liberals muddied the electoral waters, proved a close one. Labour polled 46.1 per cent of the votes and gained 315 seats, a loss of 76; the Conservatives polled 43.5 per cent which gave them an increased 299 seats. Overall the Labour majority was a mere five seats on an 84 per cent turnout.

Morrison's idea of 'consolidation', his electoral slogan, looked less than possible especially with a revival of the NHS debate which proved very damaging to the party. Cripps's attempt to impose charges in the spring of 1950 were opposed by Bevan, still Minister of Health. Bevan's success was shortlived, though, because Cripps dropped charges in favour of a ceiling on NHS spending. Bevan had been got another way, and in any case was moved from Health to the Ministry of Labour in January 1951, and thus was no longer able to protect his beloved NHS. Cripps gave way to Gaitskell at the Exchequer who launched a fresh attack on the NHS in the spring of 1951 which did bring in charges. Bevan had no choice, politically or morally, but to resign which he did on 22 April, taking Harold Wilson with him. In exile Bevan became the focus for dissent from the left of the party and viewed the PLP as fair game.

The political commentator Peter Hennessey has claimed that 'From February 1950 to the government's fall in October 1951 it was consolidation at best and damage limitation and crisis management at worse.' As is usual in politics when difficulties come they abound and intensify. The additional financial burden of fighting in Korea was an unwelcome extra in 1950, and, as we shall see in chapter 14, foreign policy in general was a bone of contention. The trade unions' patience, once very thin was now non-existent. Self-imposed wage restraint was rapidly becoming a thing of the past as the TUC discovered when they tried to extend it, unsuccessfully, in 1950. The years of deprivation in the war and austerity after were taking their toll on the working people. There were docks strikes in 1948 and again in 1949, with the latter necessitating the use of troops in order to move food. But strikes were on the increase and the government was forced to employ residual war-time powers like those under Order 1305 which allowed for strike-breaking and the arrest and imprisonment of strikers. These powers were used extensively, another nail in the coffin of the government as far as the left was concerned.

Bevan took great pleasure, as Minister of Labour, in repealing these orders, so offensive to the left. However, it was in a situation of increasing political crisis and economic difficulty, allied to loss of key personnel, that Attlee decided to call another election in October 1951. A spirited campaign ensued with Labour making up lost ground in the opinion polls and Churchill suing the *Daily Mirror*, successfully, for a front-page 'slur' suggesting that the Conservative leader was a gun-toting warmonger with an itchy finger on the trigger. The turnout was 82.5 per cent, split fairly evenly, with Labour getting 48.8 per cent and Conservatives 48 per cent of the votes cast. This was also the first British election to have televised party political broadcasts, except that the number of voters with a television receiver was very small indeed. Although they polled nearly 14 million votes, the largest number ever cast for a single party in Britain, the Labour Government fell. The Conservatives with 321 seats, against Labour's 295, had an overall Commons majority of 17. The great socialist experiment had come to a close.

AFTERTHOUGHT

Clement Attlee moved into opposition in 1951 and stayed there as leader until he accepted a peerage in 1955. His demeanour, a small apparently nondescript and taciturn man, belied an acute political expertise. Once said never to waste a word when a syllable would do, Attlee was known for his tight-lipped silences even in conversations. It is possible that the Dalton mix-up over the Foreign Secretaryship could have come with the king's misinterpretation of an Attlee grunt when discussing the possible make-up of the Cabinet in 1945. The king, not known for his wit, was moved to comment on his first meeting that 'Clem' might better be called 'Clam'. In fact the two men enjoyed a closer relationship in the end than many monarchs and Prime Ministers. Attlee was not an overly modest man, despite appearances, although he did record in his diary on that triumphant 26 July 1945 that, for him and his party, it had been 'Quite an exciting day.' Certainly he was nobody's fool. Politically adept he had a command over the structures of government, especially at the highest level, that was unrivalled. Some claim that he overcomplicated government and certainly by 1951 he had presided over a proliferation of cabinet committees, 148 in all, and 313 *ad hoc* committees. However, his mastery of day-to-day government was supreme and rivals found him a tough old stager, failing despite many attempts to remove him from the leadership. Certainly, the longer the gap between 1945–51 and the present day, the more Attlee emerges as a wholly remarkable figure in political terms. His work on social welfare and nationalization is that which many Labour leaders hark back to and hold up as the epitome of the caring and egalitarian socialist government at the service of the people. Equally so Attlee's government has been criticized, even vilified, by successive generations of Conservatives who would now claim that it was the start and cause of Britain's long and painful delusion that ushered her to the brink of disaster in the 1960s and for most of the 1970s. Political consensus became a dirty word in Mrs Thatcher's Britain. The arguments surrounding these two standpoints will be analysed in later chapters. What is worth dwelling on is Attlee's success in exciting such diverse passions and being indirectly responsible for momentous political changes thirty, and maybe even forty, years after he left office. This is what puts Attlee, and the Labour achievements of 1945–51, in perspective. It is difficult to agree with Peter Hennessey's view that 'from 1945 to 1951 Britain was run by a real life Captain Mainwaring'. Attlee, like most astute and successful men had a fair measure of himself, and the limerick below gives a hint of the inner man, even though it was penned by Attlee in old age:

> Few thought he was even a starter,
> There were many who thought themselves smarter,
> But he ended PM,
> CH and OM,
> An earl and a Knight of the Garter.

Attacked by the extreme left for betrayal, the Labour Government's achievements were worthy of great praise. It was no simple task. Many of their reforms were some of the most momentous to pass through Parliament, but the achievement was made all the greater because they came after six unrelenting years of effort in winning the war. To follow straight on into one of the most energetic series of parliamentary sessions on record, and all at a time of intense economic crises, was a triumph indeed.

CONTROVERSY

The latest historical controversy of this era takes a holistic view of these years and questions the very basis of what might be called the Labour Government's experiment with state control of welfare and the economy. On the one side there are those who are proponents of Attlee and the Labour Government, seeing the post-war experience as truly the first steps in the creation of the 'New Jerusalem'. This viewpoint has been forcefully promoted by writers such as Kenneth Morgan in his *Labour in Power* (1984), which includes the following passage:

> The Attlee government was . . . unique in its structural cohesiveness and in its legislative vitality. Its legacy lived on in a broad influence over the Labour and progressive left, over political and economic thought and, indeed, over much of cultural life for a full quarter of

a century after 1951. It was without doubt the most effective of all
Labour governments, perhaps amongst the most effective of any Brit-
ish government since the passage of the 1832 Reform Act.
(K. O. Morgan, *Labour in Power 1945–51*, Oxford, Oxford University
Press, 1984, p. 402)

This is high praise indeed, but equally passionate statements have been
made in recent years about the disastrous nature of the Labour experiment. In fact, Attlee's contemporaries were far from certain about the
wisdom of the path he chose to tread after 1945. Even before Labour
won its sweeping victory in 1945, Professor Friedrich Hayek, of the
London School of Economics, was clearly shouting warnings to all who
would hear him. In his seminal work, *The Road to Serfdom* (1944), he
seriously challenged the woolly thinking that suggested there were merits
in state-controlled economies. He suggested that such economies could
only operate if they also had the parallel state apparatus of a tyrannical
regime. Even though those who tried to practise such tyranny – such as
Albert Speer in Germany – claimed that this was not the case, Hayek's
book became a bible for those who wished to question the usefulness,
worth and possibility of an overweaning state. It is interesting to note
that in the later 1970s Conservatives harked back to Hayek's works and
the professor has become something of a prophet for the intellectual
gurus of the Tory Party, such as Sir Keith Joseph. An article in *The
Economist* in 1982 succinctly summed up the path on which Hayek's
thinking had set the new Conservative Party:

Mrs Margaret Thatcher sees her task as replacing the Attleean consensus which left Britain with low industrial productivity, resource-hungry
State concerns and a welfare system that discourages thrift and breeds
bureaucracy. She says that it will take two parliaments to break that
mould and is privately uncertain whether even she can pull it off.
(*The Economist*, 4 September 1982, p. 26)

It was in 1986 that the new contribution to the Attlee Labour Government debate appeared in the form of Correlli Barnett's *The Audit of
War*. Barnett saw 1945 as a watershed in British history, but one that
marked its decline rather than its greatness. Simply the British electorate
had made a mistake in 1945 and would rue its poor choice for the best
part of forty years, if not longer. They would see Britain's precipitant
fall from a seemingly great height as she spiralled ever downward with
cataclysmic results for the country both at home and abroad:

As that descent took its course the illusions and the dreams of 1945
would fade one by one – the imperial and Commonwealth role, the
world-power role, British industrial genius, and, at the last, New
Jerusalem itself, a dream turned to a dank reality of a segregated,

subliterate, unskilled, unhealthy and institutionalised proletariat hanging on the nipple of state maternalism.
(C. Barnett, *The Audit of War: The Illusion and Reality of Great Britain as a Great Nation*, London, Macmillan, 1986, p. 304)

Barnett's work has prospered given the political circumstances of Britain in the late 1970s and 1980s, and it has become a very influential text. It enjoys the whiff of orthodoxy and therefore is readily received, both as a book and wisdom, in government circles where familiarity with its contents seems obligatory. However, such mute acceptance of a single idea would seriously undermine historical research. Certainly, many have voiced different opinions, such as Sidney Pollard who explains Britain's position in 1950 in an entirely different light even allowing for the Attlee Government of 1945–51:

At the end of the war . . . [Britain] was still among the richest nations of the world, ahead by far of the war-shattered economies of Europe. On the Continent, only the neutrals, Sweden and Switzerland, were better off than Britain, and elsewhere only the United States and Canada. Britain was among the technical leaders, especially in the promising high-technology industries of the future: aircraft, electronics, vehicles. The problem that exercised the statesmen of the day was whether the rest of Europe, even its industrialised parts, would ever be able to come within reach of, let alone catch up with, Britain. Nor was that lead a temporary fluke, a result of the more destructive effects of the war on the Continent. On the contrary, the British lead in 1950 was fully in line with that of 1938: and even more so with that of earlier decades, when the British position had been firmly in the van of Europe.
(S. Pollard, *The Wasting of the British Economy*, London, Croom Helm, 1982, p. 2)

As always a simple and generalized set of answers does not aid the historian in his or her assessment of historical events and personalities. What is certainly true is the impact, for good or ill, that the Attlee Labour Government had on British history. As Peter Hennessey has claimed, 'It is a glowing tribute to the Attlee administration that after forty years their light should shine sufficiently brightly to illuminate contemporary debate.'

BIBLIOGRAPHY

For an explanation of the grading system, see the preface p. xiii.

Biographies

Clement Attlee

3   Burridge, T., *Clement Attlee: A Political Biography*, London, Cape, 1985
3   Harris, K., *Attlee*, London, Weidenfeld & Nicolson, 1982

Aneurin Bevan

3   Campbell, J., *Nye Bevan and the Mirage of British Socialism*, London, Weidenfeld & Nicolson, 1987
3   Foot, M., *Aneurin Bevan, Vol. II 1945–60* London, Davis Poynter, 1973

Ernest Bevin

3   Bullock, A., *The Life and Times of Ernest Bevin*, Vols 1 and 2, London, Heinemann, 1960 and 1967

R. A. Butler

3   Howard, A., *RAB: The Life of R. A. Butler*, London, Cape, 1987

Winston Churchill

3   Seldon, A., *Churchill's Indian Summer: The Conservative Government 1951–55*, London, Hodder & Stoughton, 1981

Anthony Eden

3   Eden, A., *Full Circle*, London, Cassell, 1960
2/3 James, R. R., *Anthony Eden*, London, Weidenfeld & Nicolson, 1986
– and see bibliographies to other chapters in this book.

Although the biographies of the great provide a lot of material for the student it should be apparent from this chapter that the events of 1939–45 at least were the years of the common people. Moreover, many political memoirs concentrate on the events of the war itself and the political and military decision-making processes many of which simply did not directly affect the ordinary person's everyday working life. Thus the list of biographies above ought to be leavened by the personal memoirs of people such as Vere Hodgson, *A Few Eggs and No Oranges: A Dairy* (London, Dennis Dobson, 1976) and Mollie Panter-Downes, *London War Notes* (London, Longman, 1972). However, such reminiscences tend to be from one end of the social spectrum and there is an obvious need to match this with the lives of working-class people too. Books such as Pat Ayres's *Women at War* (Rock Ferry, Birkenhead, Liver Press, 1988) give a broader coverage of the social spectrum and also add a regional flavour to the experience of war.

Of the general texts that exist there is a clear dividing line between the popular and leisure books and those for the academic market. The following are in the first category, and all contain personal reminiscences and a mass of photographic material:

2/3   Addison, P., *Now the War is Over*, London, Cape, 1985
2   Briggs, S., *Keep Smiling Through: The Home Front 1939–1945*, Cambridge, Cambridge University Press, 1986
2/3   Calder, A., *The People's War in Britain 1939–1945*, Cambridge, Cambridge University Press, 1971
2   Jenkins, A., *The Forties*, London, Methuen, 1977
2   Landels, W., *The Time of Our Lives: A Pictorial History of Great Britain since 1945*, London, Elm Tree/Hamish Hamilton, 1981
2/3   Minns, R., *Bombers and Mash: The Domestic Front 1939–1945*, London, Virago, 1980

There is a range of books at a more academic level, including:

3   Barnett, C., *The Audit of War: The Illusion and Reality of Britain as a Great Nation*, London, Macmillan, 1986
3   Cairncross, A., *Years of Recovery: British Economic Policy 1945–51*, London, Methuen, 1985
3   Campbell, J., *Nye Bevan and the Mirage of British Socialism*, London, Weidenfeld & Nicolson, 1987
3/4   Dalton, H., *The Second World War: Diary of Hugh Dalton 1939–1945*, ed. B. Pimlott, London, Cape, 1983
3/4   Hennessey, P., and Seldon, A., *Ruling Performance: British Governments from Attlee to Thatcher*, Oxford, Blackwell, 1989
3   Morgan, K. O., *Labour in Power*, Oxford, Oxford University Press, 1984
3/4   Pollard, S., *The Wasting of the British Economy*, London, Croom Helm, 1982

Sources for coursework

There is a problem with using the obvious sources for coursework – newspapers – and that is that the government used a strict system of censorship in the press and elsewhere. This simply means that these sources have to be handled more carefully and any judgements made in the light of this knowledge need to be tempered. There is much printed material available and the obvious place to look is in the very informative *Mass-Observation Reports* carried out by central and local government and their agencies. There are growing numbers of local collections of war-time materials and local reference libraries and history groups should prove a fruitful source of such materials. Newsreels provide another interesting, although censored source, and these are becoming available in the commercial market with video cassettes now on sale in the high street. Obviously these are heavily edited collections but the material may still prove helpful. Robert Kee's collection of photographs provides more visual evidence (*We'll Meet Again: Photographs of Daily Life in Britain During World War II*, London, Dent, 1984).

Personal diaries and memoirs like those listed above will be useful as will personal reminiscences of family and friends who may well be able to give an interesting oral account of their lives at this period. However, the historian should be aware of the difficulties of working with oral evidence, as failing memory and different viewpoints will distort accounts.

12 Consensus Britain 1951–79

INTRODUCTION

The years of consensus are marked at their beginning by the wartime coalition governments and at their end by the Thatcher Conservative Governments. In between lay nearly forty years of so-called political consensus which was characterized by two themes. First, there was broad agreement by both parties on the style of government in Britain which became, after 1951, increasingly one of governmental consultation with key groups in society and especially the trade unions – the move towards corporatism. Second, there was equally broad agreement about the range of policies to be pursued by either party when in government. The latter were easily identifiable and owed their paternity to two great personalities who had shaped both economic and social policy in the recent past. On the one hand there was John Maynard Keynes whose name was synonymous with the government's use of fiscal techniques to control the economy, especially on the demand side, and thus ensure full employment. On the other hand there was William Beveridge whose influence gave rise to a commitment to the provision of social welfare to the country's citizens as well as control of essential sectors of the economy. Both ideas were certainly well within the remit of any Labour government. After the 'Hungry Thirties' the promise, or commitment to, full employment was the least that a Labour government could take to the electorate. Similarly, government control of welfare, and some goods and services, also fitted neatly into the party's ideas of nationalization and a controlled economy, and the principles of social justice. For the Conservatives the acceptance of consensus was less easy but none the less necessary. The experience of the war years had shown the population's growing awareness of their plight, not against Germany as such, but against the injustices that had marred so many lives in the years up to 1939. The spirit of the war years was clearly carried into the post-war years and the population's expectations had risen. Most of the electorate did expect a land fit for heroes and waited in anticipation for jobs, housing, health services, better education for their children, and a growing need for

Full employment and production

Labour 1951

Full employment through six years of peace is the greatest of all Labour's achievements. It has never happened before. It has meant a revolution in the lives of our people. Today, there are half a million unfilled vacancies at the employment exchanges. Under Labour – more jobs than workers. Under the Tories – more workers than jobs.

Largely due to full employment, with everyone contributing to the national product, production in Britain since 1945 has risen twice as fast each year as under the Tories. Our industrial and agricultural output is now 50 per cent above pre-war, but we must do better still to improve our living standards, to fulfil our obligations in collective defence and to play our part in assisting under-developed regions. Almost 20 per cent of the national income is now devoted to new capital equipment for the nation. This is higher than ever in British history.

World shortage of raw materials has steeply raised the prices of our imports and reopened the dollar gap. The difficulties are great. But we can conquer them.

Full employment

Conservative 1955

Under Conservative administration a working population of record peace-time size has been kept fully employed, without Socialist controls and without continual inflation. Our record speaks for itself. In the intensely competitive times ahead, continued full employment must mean, not only everyone in a job, but everyone doing their job to the full. Only with a high output-high earnings economy can we maintain and improve our trading position.

The Government has sought, with an encouraging measure of success, to create the right climate of confidence and to foster the idea of a common interest and task. Team-work is an essential driving force of a dynamic economy. There is really only one side in modern industry, and all of us are on it. As Conservatives we have always believed this.

Labour 1959

We do not say that the task of combining an expanding economy with full employment and steady prices is an easy one. Indeed it will remain impossible until we have a Government which is prepared to use all measures, including the Budget, in order to expand production and simultaneously to ensure that welfare is developed and prosperity fairly shared. Labour's five-year programme of action has been carefully worked out to achieve these aims.

Employment and economic change

Conservative 1959

So long as Conservative policies of sound currency and expanding trade are continued, and unity at home maintained, full employment is safe. But patches of *local* unemployment can be created by swift changes in markets, methods and machines.

Labour 1964

The aims are simple enough: we want full employment; a faster rate of industrial expansion; a sensible distribution of industry throughout the country; an end to the present chaos in traffic and transport; a brake on rising prices and a solution to our balance of payments problems.

Growth without inflation

Conservative 1964

In thirteen years of Conservative government the living standards of the British people have improved more than in the whole of the previous half-century.

The working population is up by two million and over 98 per cent are in jobs. Rising incomes and lower taxes have made possible a spectacular increase in spending on the essentials, the comforts and what were once regarded as the luxuries of life. At the same time, personal savings have grown from £100m in 1951 to nearly £2,000m, last year – providing funds for the modernisation of Britain, security for the individual, and substance to the Conservative concept of a property-owning democracy.

greater equality and justice. If the Conservative Party needed persuading that this was the new path for British politics then the massive Labour victory in the 1945 election was sufficient. A Labour majority of 146 seats and a clear lead of 9 per cent in the popular vote over the Conservatives was the most graphic way of demonstrating that the nature of British politics was about to change. With it the parties would also have to adapt to new ideas and policies and if the Conservatives wished to remain a force in British politics then they too would have to change as they had done in the twentieth century.

The terrain which the two parties shared was littered with landmarks which successive governments would toil towards and thus tread familiar paths. The great areas of mutual concern were clear for all to see. First, Keynesian full employment was a necessary goal as the two parties' election manifestos from 1951 to 1964 show. The high rates of unemployment of the 1930s, albeit with sharp regional variations, were politically unacceptable in the post-war world. By managing demand governments could hope to control these levels and for some years both parties were successful with unemployment not exceeding an average of 3 per cent in any twelve months between 1948 and 1970. Second, there was a visible commitment to the mixed economy. The idea of a government taking a hand in the managing of the economy in order to achieve certain goals was clearly a possibility, as had been demonstrated in the years 1939–45. It was a short step to believing that such control could be used to achieve social and economic objectives just as it had been used to achieve a military one. Labour was evidently committed to the public ownership of basic utilities and to taking an active role in managing the economy. The Conservatives were not far behind, once again mindful of the political costs of taking a contrary standpoint, and also willing to embrace the new ideas of post-war Britain. Third, the first two points seemed to assume a greater role for trade unions. After all, these organizations, not yet in the era of declining membership, were equally committed to full employment and most had nationalization as a principle written into their own charters. Governments would at least have to deal with the trade unions and Labour established an early precedent of full consultation with them in the years up to 1951. This privilege, and the strength given to the unions by full employment, meant that they became a key element in the consensus years. When the economy was performing adequately then the unions were useful allies but when economic needs meant that governments tried to curtail union activity and demands then industrial relations problems arose. Fourth, the expectations of the population and the commitment of Labour to social justice gave the country the welfare state in all its manifestations. Certainly the advantages of such a system were clear to many but the costs involved were huge. Spending on the welfare state continued to rise and this expenditure meant a growing reliance on high levels of taxation in order to pay for the services provided. Fifth, there was a consensus that spread from domestic politics into foreign policy. As we shall see in chapter 14 there was a shared opinion on the major issues of foreign policy in the post-war world such as the retreat from Empire, Britain's commitment to the Atlantic Alliance and her role as a nuclear power.

Underpinning the concept of consensus, certainly as far as domestic affairs are concerned, is the idea of interventionist governments or governments as 'problem-solvers'. However, governments only become solvers when they have solutions to offer and it became abundantly clear when Britain's relative economic decline became fully manifest that no government up to 1979 had any clear idea of how to tackle such a problem let alone solve it. By the time of the end of consensus many of the foundations of the ideal were already crumbling. Full employment rapidly disappeared over the horizon, persuading governments to opt for growth as a panacea for all the nation's economic ills. The continuous enlargement of the state's role created financial embarrassment and bureaucratic muddle. As the state's role grew so, in the words of Richard Rose, the 'government's reach exceeded its grasp'. And, as a final ignominy, it appeared that governments created more problems than they actually solved.

Although some commentators would reject the idea of consensus ever having existed, such as Ben Pimlott, the doubts raised are more concerned with self-perception of politicians of the day and the rhetoric of inter-party debate. A close analysis of the issues and the policies adopted and the decisions made indicate that a broad consensus did exist. It did not prevent discord, party political debate nor parties presenting themselves as alternatives to each other at election times. But the broad agreement to walk the same terrain using the same compass and map remained. More damning as a criticism of consensus are the words of the one person who can justly claim to have brought it to an end, even if it was dying on its feet at the time, Margaret Thatcher. Mrs Thatcher claimed in 1981 that consensus was, 'the process of abandoning all beliefs, principles, values and policies . . . avoiding the very issues that have got to be solved merely to get people to come to an agreement on the way ahead'.

From the great wave of national hope in 1945 to the despairing decade of the 1970s the era of political consensus left its mark on Britain. The broader aspects of the ways in which this period of modern British history has been analysed will be dealt with later. However, before judgement can be made the cases for the defence and the prosecution should be heard.

CONSERVATIVE GOVERNMENTS WITH LABOUR POLICIES 1951–64

The effect of the 1945 election defeat cannot be underestimated as far as the Conservative Party was concerned. The loss was a body blow to party and leader alike. In part it was the people voicing their desire for a different future and in part an uncertainty about Churchill and the party he led. Certainly it was too easy to see Churchill as the political adventurer who liked war and was opposed to the post-war reconstruction. Although not inaccurate in all ways this assessment belied Churchill's eventual willingness to take the broad consensual view of British politics. However, the victory of the 1951 election had to be worked for, although, as with most, luck also played its part. The Labour Party's difficulties with post-war Europe, the Russian threat, communist subversion and events like the Berlin blockade suggested that experienced and, in the popular imagination, sterner leaders would not be a bad thing in the circumstances. Thus, the old war horse, Churchill, found the disadvantages of 1945 turned into the advantages of 1951. It was, however, inside the party that the real battles were fought and the election eventually won. The party certainly promoted its leadership assets as statesmen rather than warmongers, and both Churchill and Eden were portrayed thus. R. A. Butler, as Chairman of the Conservative Research Department, oversaw many of the policy formulations and set up special groups such as the Industrial Policy Committee. In 1947 Reginald Maudling, with his *Industrial Charter*, announced at the Party Conference the Conservatives' commitment to the idea of a mixed economy and the principle of co-partnership in industry. By 1949 these ideas were being honed for inclusion in the party's manifesto. Organizationally too the party was regrouping. Maxwell-Fyfe, later Lord Kilmuir, masterminded a modernization of the internal structure of the party with rule changes that gave it a more democratic appearance. In addition Lord Woolton's reorganization of the Central Office and growing recruitment campaign especially amongst the young announced the party's readiness to return to the fight and present itself to the British people as an alternative government in both 1950 and 1951.

Oddly enough the British people had also shown themselves ready for a change. A decade of austerity, first in war and latterly in peace, saw a reaction against rationing and the continued housing shortage. Freedom became an important concept and one which the Conservative Party picked up on earlier than their Labour counterparts. A passing reference in the 1949 party policy document became the election cry of 1951 with 'Set the People Free'. When it came to polling day the Conservatives found themselves with a palatable message and the right language to put it across. They polled about the same percentage as the Labour Party but their 321 seats, as opposed to their opponents' 295, gave them an overall majority of 17 in the new Parliament. It remained to be seen whether the Labour cries of fear that the Conservatives once in power would begin to dismantle the welfare state and nationalized industries were well-founded, or whether consensus would prevail.

The Conservative manifesto of 1951

The Conservative aim is to increase our national output. Here is the surest way to keep our people fully employed, to halt the rising cost of living, and to preserve our social services. Hard work, good management, thrift – all must receive their due incentive and reward.

All industries remaining nationalised will come within the purview of the Monopolies' Commission and there will also be strict Parliamentary review of their activities.

We seek to create an industrial system that is not only efficient but human. The Conservative Workers' Charter for Industry will be brought into being as early as possible, and extended to agriculture wherever practicable. The scheme will be worked out with trade unions and employers, and then laid before Parliament.

Housing is the first of the social services. It is also one of the keys to increased productivity. Work, family life, health and education are all undermined by overcrowded homes. Therefore a Conservative and Unionist Government will give housing a priority second only to national defence. Our target remains 300,000 houses a year. There should be no reduction in the number of houses and flats built to let but more freedom must be given to the private builder. In a property-owning democracy, the more people who own their homes the better.

CHURCHILL'S GOVERNMENT 1951–5

For many Labour supporters Churchill's election victory in 1951 threatened to spell the dismantling of the New Jerusalem. They were seriously adrift in their assessment of the grand old man. In that very election year Churchill had claimed that Britain needed 'several administrations, if only to allow for Socialist legislation to reach its full fruition'. With only 20 per cent of industry and commerce in state hands in 1951 Churchill seemed correct in his assumption that there was a long way to go before socialism claimed victory in Britain. Certainly the new Tory administration had its reservations about nationalization and it was in this sphere that the new government did move to reverse the previous government's policy, if only in a token fashion. The Conservatives denationalized iron and steel and road haulage (although not until May 1953) but retained the other publicly owned utilities and services. The rest of the administration's policies could just as easily have come from a Labour government as a Tory one.

Churchill put together a broadly based team of ministers chosen from the centre and left of the party. Eden was appointed Foreign Minister; Butler, a Tory radical, Chancellor of the Exchequer; Walter Monckton, known for his conciliatory approach, to the Ministry of Labour; Harold Macmillan to Housing; and Peter Thorneycroft to the Board of Trade. Less successful were the appointments of Lord Alexander of Tunis to Defence and Florence Horsbrugh to Education. Also criticized was Churchill's desire to appoint overlords to collections of ministries thus reviving comments about the War Cabinet of 1940–5. Churchill's first request of his cabinet colleagues was for them to take a 20 per cent pay cut with himself taking a 30 per cent reduction thus creating a precedent for Mrs Thatcher forty years later. The Conservatives had inherited the shaky economic situation facing Labour in their last months in power. On the surface it looked bad with spiralling deficits on the country's balance of payments racing to £700 million. Many were alarmed and predicted a crisis as great as that of 1931 but they were mistaken. Churchill took appropriate steps and imposed credit restrictions, reduced imports, cut government food subsidies and drastically reduced travel allowances. However, the Robot Plan for sterling convertibility was repeated in February 1952 and Butler played his part too by raising interest rates from 2 to 4 per cent in an attempt to restrict demand. In fact it is not certain that the policies helped greatly. The ending of the Korean War and general optimism returning did at least as much to turn around the apparently dire situation. By the end of 1952 the country was back in the black, to the tune of £300 million as far as its balance of payments was concerned. Churchill may well have been very lucky and but for the want of waiting a few months Attlee could have bequeathed his successors the same long run that Churchill gave the Tories.

The year of 1952 opened in sadness with the death of the popular George VI on 6 February. His daughter, Elizabeth, was crowned Queen of England in the summer of the following year. The new Elizabethan age seemed to herald a new prosperity but the government was painfully aware that it needed to be seen to be doing things. The population at large expected more than austerity. As *The Times* had pointed out even before the Tories returned to power, 'There is real and mounting distaste for restrictions, whether needed or not, and a resentment of bureaucratic meddling.' The government was keen to de-control, with identity cards abolished in February 1952, and the ending of rationing on all goods in 1954. Again the Conservatives were fortunate because Labour, or at least Wilson, had talked of 'bonfires of controls' in the dying months of the Labour administration. There were token economies in government, as with the ministers' salaries, and official cars were cut from 722 to 444. The civil service also saw cuts to its staff of 25,640 but this amounted to tampering rather than fundamental change. However, the need to economize was reduced as the administration moved into its second full year and gained the benefit of renewed economic confidence. The schemes used by Labour to give aid to depressed areas were retained by the Conservatives as were the financial supports for farmers. However, most memorable of the policies pursued by the government were those relating to housing. It was Harold Macmillan's great achievement to provide the organization and wherewithal to keep the promise made at the Party Conference of 300,000 houses. In 1953 327,000 houses were built and in 1954 354,000. But it was not simply in construction numbers that the Conservatives were seen to be successful. In 1952 Macmillan increased the housing subsidy from £22 to £35 per home. Local authorities were granted powers to license private contractors to build in their localities on a one to one basis. The following year saw such licenses extended to all sizes of houses and Macmillan pursued an active policy of encouraging the provision of mortgages. The planned New Towns were completed and at least part of the demands of the electorate were being met. Macmillan's achievements were impressive and perhaps he took Churchill's words to heart when the younger man was informed that this could 'make or break his political career'. In retrospect the achievement has tarnished a little with criticisms of Macmillan trying to do too much too quickly and compromising on standards. Nevertheless, the Tories kept faith with one of the basic principles of post-war policy, the provision of adequate housing for the population.

Education saw little positive action until the appointment of David Eccles to the Ministry late on in the government's life, in 1954. The proposed plans for improving technical schools were immediately implemented and by 1955 twice as many children were staying on in schools and colleges until the age of 17 than had been in 1951. Across the board the country enjoyed rising social benefits and the government progressively increased these throughout its term of office. By 1955 social benefits were marginally more in real terms than they had been in 1951 – yet another indication that the Conservatives were far from overturning the Labour welfare state.

Despite this activity the overwhelming character of this government was the number of issues that it ignored, left alone, shelved or decided to take no action on at all. Herein might lay some of its popularity. The period 1951–5 may well have been Churchill's 'Indian Summer' but it was a lazy one in terms of legislative enactments. Churchill summed it up himself a little later when he outlined his priorities as 'Houses, meat and not being scuppered'. This left plenty of scope for inactivity. Education was certainly one area in which more could have been done especially in the realms of technical education which, for many educationalists, were lagging behind alarmingly. Trade unions were also considered but the rhetoric of the *Industrial Charter* and the strong position of many trades made action seem somewhat foolhardy especially when little appeared to be gained by it. The issue was discussed in Cabinet but proposals for trade union legislation were talked down and eventually put on ice. A similar tale surrounds another issue with its roots in the post-war years: immigration. By the later 1950s something like 26,000 migrants a year from the West Indies were coming into Britain and their presence made the achievement of full employment more difficult. Again the Cabinet discussed this issue but took no action as far as immigration controls were concerned and thus, perhaps, stored up problems for later governments especially as racial prejudice took its position in the front line of the arguments being espoused by many of the electorate. The Health Service was left intact although some changes were made, such as increasing prescription charges to 2/- (10 pence). However, the Labour Party's fears about the dismantling of the service or at least radical changes were once again unfounded. When issues could not be avoided the government acted quickly to stop acrimony. They gave in to the farmers' lobby in March 1955 despite Butler's view that more favourable treatment for this powerful group would be inflationary. As for union disputes, they also were quickly settled, especially as the government's term approached its end. As Hugh Massingham, a former editor of *The Nation* and an old-style radical, claimed of Monckton, 'In Union circles it is often said that he is the best Minister of Labour for years, but it is not what the employers think.'

By a mixture of inactivity, good fortune and keeping confrontation to the minimum the Conservatives arrived in 1954 at the head of an increasingly prosperous country. The successive Butler budgets had done their job. It is an interesting comment on the close similarity of the policies pursued by both parties that on 13 February 1954 *The Economist* called this economic policy pursued by successive Chancellors 'Butskellism'.

> Mr Butskell is already a well-known figure in dinner-table conversations in both Westminster and Whitehall. The time has come to introduce him to a wider audience. He is a composite of the present Chancellor and the previous one. Whenever there is a tendency to excess conservatism within the Conservative Party, such as a clamour for too much imperial preference, for a wild dash to convertibility, or even for a little more unemployment to teach the workers a lesson, Mr Butskell speaks up for the cause of moderation from the Government side of the House. When there is a clamour for even graver irresponsibilities from the Labour benches, Mr Butskell has hitherto spoken up from the other.

'Butskellism' referred to the hardly discernible differences between the two leading economic proponents of each of the main political parties – Butler for the Conservatives and Gaitskell for Labour. Certainly as far as contemporaries were concerned consensus was alive and well in the 1950s. Butler's use of interest rates in his budgets to control demand appeared to work although it developed the pattern of higher and rapidly changing rates of interest that have become more familiar in the modern era. Whatever the methods the policy achieved the desired results. As *The Times* reported in December 1954:

> With production and consumption in this country at the highest levels of all time, the population fully employed and the external balance of payments still to all outward appearances satisfactory, the present state of the national economy gives little grounds for complaint.

Although Butler pushed up the bank rate to 4.5 per cent in February 1955 the 'miser' turned 'spendthrift' in the April budget of that year. *The Observer* may well have been right that 'Britain is very prosperous, the prosperity is widely diffused with full employment and higher wages than ever before.' Even so Butler's 'election bribe' of a sixpenny (2½ pence) reduction in income tax and higher personal allowances did not go amiss when it came to polling time.

Despite the outward signs of prosperity and contentment in the country the Conservatives themselves were entering a worrying time. Their majority was small and they had already suffered the problem of over-influential backbenchers, most notably in the introduction of competitive television to break the BBC monopoly, against the wishes of the party leaders in July 1954. Of more concern still was the likely outcome of the next election. A secret Conservative Central Office poll in 1954 indicated wholesale changes would be necessary if the Conservatives were to stay in power. A new leader was essential but Churchill's standing and obstinacy – reportedly he once told Cabinet 'I know that you are trying to get rid of me . . . but I won't go' – created severe problems. The old man was suffering from ill-health although reports of his total incapacity in the last years of this government's term seem exaggerated. The party was saved from further problems when Churchill decided to retire in April 1955, only four months after the outburst in Cabinet, thus leaving the way open for Anthony Eden who crowned a long and distinguished career as Foreign Minister in war-time and peace-time governments by becoming caretaker Prime Minister in Churchill's stead. His first priority, however, was to organize the party for the coming election and to decide on its date. After some hesitation he chose 26 May.

The Conservatives entered the fray with an uncontroversial track record, a popular leader and recognized statesman, and a united party. The electorate that had grown prosperous with the Tories would find it difficult not to vote for them again but in part, victory would be decided by the opposition that could be mustered by Labour. If the odds were not already stacked in Eden's favour then Labour ensured that the new Conservative leader would be returned handsomely.

It was a great pity that Attlee's last years as Labour leader were some of his most unhappiest as the party, recently victorious, united and triumphant, was about to break apart and in doing so allow a Conservative dominance of British politics to emerge. The political disaster area that the Labour Party became had its roots in many events. Within party circles there was the continuing split with the left and the Bevanites who numbered some thirty-two MPs in 1951, and possibly rose to fifty-seven later on in the decade. Wilson, Driberg, Castle, Foot, Mikardo, Crossman and Bevan's wife Jennie Lee were all identified with the party's inability to unite. Proposals and counter proposals flew at Labour Conferences, especially over further nationalization. This issue became something of an albatross. Gaitskell and the right of the party wanted to revise the ideas on Clause Four and adapt Labour Party policy to new perceived needs. These 'revisionists' placed their faith in the ideas of men like Tony Crosland who wanted an expanding welfare state fuelled by growth and driven on by managerial efficiency. Although the right received support from the larger unions and the TUC as a whole there was the great stumbling block of Clause Four that was as much a part of union belief as it was the party's constitution. Although key union figures like Deakin of the Transport Workers, Williamson of the Municipal Workers and Lawther of the Miners supported the party over the left it would not compromise over Clause Four.

Between them Bevanites, trade unions and the 'revisionists' were creating enough problems and conflicts to keep the party entirely occupied. The rifts deepened in 1952 with fifty-seven MPs refusing to follow the Party Whip and facing strong calls for expulsion. Bevan pushed too hard in 1954 in challenging Gaitskell for the party treasuryship in April and defying instructions to support proposals in the Commons for hydrogen bomb manufacture.

Defence, and especially the issue of the hydrogen bomb, had become a key debate within the Labour Party. The party itself had started Britain on the nuclear weapons age and it felt, given the present state of international tension and suspicion, that a continuation of this policy was a correct course of action. Hence the decision to support the construction of such a bomb in the Commons. Unfortunately for party unity a small but vociferous section did not see it in this way. The party's dilemma is well illustrated by its manifesto for the 1955 election:

Labour manifesto 1955

[Forward With Labour:
Labour's Policy for the Consideration of the Nation]

As we in Britain prepare to go to the poll, the Hydrogen Bomb looms over all mankind. What can we do to meet that menace? The existence of this terrible weapon on both sides of the Iron Curtain maintains an uneasy balance under the threat of mutual destruction. But deterrents can at best only give us a breathing space. We are faced with the choice between world co-operation and world annihilation. The time is short.

The dangers of the bomb were well known but the party's commitment to its existence remained especially amongst the leadership. Elsewhere Labour MPs were taking a different view of the issues with many leading lights joining the H-Bomb National Committee, the forerunner of the Campaign for Nuclear Disarmament (CND). Such apparent division within the party made its task so much more difficult in the general election. It is no wonder that the Conservative Party found the contest in May much to its liking.

Labour presented easy targets to their opponents and the Tories made the most of the divisive nature of their main rivals. It was too easy to portray the ageing Attlee as the puppet of the Bevanites and the more radical elements of the party whose policies might well be a threat to consensus itself. The claims that the Conservatives of 1951 would preside over the wrecking of the Labour achievements of 1945–51 had been proved false. Moreover, Labour's manifesto sounded dull apart from re-establishing a free National Health Service and a promise to abolish the national examination at 11 which determined entry into the different grades of schooling available. This was the first sign of Labour's long cold period in opposition explained by Cronin in these terms:

> By the 1950s Labour ceased to offer a compelling reformist vision or even a clear alternative to the Tories. Its middle-class supporters soon began to swing back and forth between Labour and the Conservatives depending on the fickle perceptions of the moment, and its working-class base to alternate between abstention and reluctant support.
>
> (J. E. Cronin, *Labour and Society in Britain 1918–1979*, London, Batsford, 1984, p. 13)

On the other hand the electorate could look to Conservative success and feel safe that the best policies of the post-war consensus were safe in Tory hands, as their manifesto suggested (see p. 471).

There was nothing here to worry the voter of whatever class. The state's role would be maintained, within certain limits, prosperity was assured, standards of living would rise and world peace would become a reality. The Conservatives certainly judged the mood correctly and got the message right. They even got the message across. Although this was the last election not to be fully covered by the broadcasters, television and radio did play their part. The Conservatives were certainly up to the public relations exercise and appeared on television, aware of the fact that there were now three times as many television sets as there had been in 1951. There was a 76.8 per cent turnout and the Conservatives raised their number of seats from 322 to 345 while Labour fell back from 294 to 277. The Conservatives had the lion's share of the popular vote and a majority of 54 seats. It was the first time in ninety years that the party in power had improved on its position in the previous election. The scene was set for a second Conservative Government to carry on the work of the first. However, Eden's premiership was to be brief and ill-fated bearing the label of the Suez disaster and his own increasing ill-health.

Programme for prosperity

The economic policy of the Conservative Party is to help create the conditions in which the British people can steadily improve their standard of living. As long as we conduct our affairs wisely and get on with the job of raising the national product year by year, the country can be twice as well off in twenty-five years time as it is now.

So we say: Let us strive to double our standard of living within this period. Let everyone have a firmer stake in the fortunes of his country. Let everyone have a fuller chance to earn more and to own more, to get on and to have more enjoyment as well. Given the boon of world peace, all this can be ours, if we will work for it and save for it and so deserve to have it.

An expanding economy

If Britain is to seize the opportunities which our trade policy can open up, economic arrangements at home have got to be as modern and go-ahead as we can possibly make them.

Conservatives neither minimise nor exaggerate the part that Governments can play in bringing these conditions about. It is for the State to give a lead, to provide incentive, support and advice, to protect the public interest and to restrain abuse. But it is certainly no proper function of the State in normal times to go into trade itself, to interfere in the day-to-day running of business, or to tell housewives how to do their shopping. Within broad but well-defined limits of basic public concern, we insist on freedom of action for producers and freedom of choice for consumers.

EDEN'S BRIEF INTERLUDE 1955–7

The Conservative Party had won the prizes at the election in 1955 but they soon reaped the economic whirlwind of Butler's too-lax last budget of the 1951–5 administration. Almost immediately Butler was forced to take emergency counter-inflationary measures. Not only was he under pressure at home to do so but the British Chancellor also had to take the opportunity at an International Monetary Fund Conference to quash rumours of an imminent devaluation of the pound. The October budget in the autumn of 1955 rapidly wiped out the April bonanza with increases in purchase tax, profits tax, and reductions in housing subsidies. Rapidly, however, the Middle East would take centre stage and dominate the events of the rest of Eden's term. The home front did not escape, though, and the economy could have done without the threat to vital oil supplies and the disruption of trade. Eden's end came quickly and with it was finally nailed the fallacy of Britain's pretensions to greatness and a global role. These events are covered in chapter 14 and such was their all-consuming importance most other political business of the day was forced into the background.

ASLEF came out on strike in May 1955 to add to the government's problems and the succession of problems persuaded Eden that a team change was necessary at the end of the year and so he shuffled his Cabinet. Butler's standing as Chancellor had fallen rapidly and he was moved to become Leader of the House. Macmillan took his place and Selwyn Lloyd became Foreign Secretary. Macmillan furthered his claims to the party's leadership, albeit still as an outsider, with a determined performance at the Exchequer. The base lending rate was raised to 5.5 per cent – the highest it had been for over thirty years and in February Macmillan cut subsidies on food, reduced public investment and restricted hire purchase. The latter had had obvious inflationary tendencies and those who wanted to join in the country's prosperity could always purchase on 'the never-never'. Macmillan saw the danger here and stepped in on this occasion to restrict schemes to delay payment for purchases. In his first budget he balanced giving with one hand, through income tax relief, by taking away with the other hand, via increased profits tax and tobacco duty. He did, however, introduce the Premium Bond Scheme which proved an effective way to take money out of circulation and thus reduce demand. Both Eden and Macmillan were at least in one mind over this. The ever-present concern over consumer-fuelled inflationary tendencies was in the forefront of the government's thinking. The publication of the White Paper in March 1956, on the economic implications of full employment stressed the need for government to get the position between itself, industry and unions correct so that constructive and agreed limitations on wages and prices could be reached. However, the government rejected totally, much to the annoyance of the younger blood in the party, any thoughts of interference and restraint imposed by itself. It was made clear that there would be no wage freeze nor any formal incomes policy. In fact so keen was the government not to antagonize the unions that it missed a perfect opportunity to edge the unions towards more modern working practices by excluding them from its Monopolies and Restrictive Practices Act which became law in 1956. Some saw this as a golden opportunity squandered, believing that outmoded working practices enshrined in union and shop-floor lore would have to be swept aside if British industry was to overcome its lack of productivity.

Not that the economic ills of the slump of 1955–6 could be laid at the door of the unions alone. It was weakness of several causes which was making Britain ill not a simple single disease. The problems were structural ones but the solutions were cosmetic. While tinkering with demand could give the appearance of economic strength, in reality it only created a façade of prosperity. However, the latter sowed the seeds for economic self-destruction as the comments from Conservative MP Robert Boothby suggest:

> What are the four main causes of our present trouble?
>
> The greatest has been excessive public expenditure ever since the war. I am oppressed by the expenditure on defence. This has been an expenditure . . . of hundreds of millions of pounds, absolutely wasted.
>
> On my second point I may not carry all Hon. Members with me. A system of progressive taxation on earned income is the greatest hamper to our economic advance. No man can save out of earnings, even if he is at the top of his profession. He can only save out of speculation or property deals. That is all wrong.
>
> Thirdly, the actions of employers and workers who are responsible for determining the rate of wages and the prices which inevitably follow, by bidding up for higher wages, in conditions of full employment. Employers have tried to bribe labour away from one industry to another, and the trade unions have been tempted – I do not altogether blame them – to take advantage of full employment to force up wages to heights which the economy cannot stand.
>
> I now come to excessive imports . . . all of which we should be producing ourselves in far greater quantities. Sooner or later we shall have to cut our dollar imports to the level of our dollar earnings.
>
> (Lord Boothby, *My Yesterday, Your Tomorrow*, London, Hutchinson, 1962, pp. 158–9)

Away from the economic problems, social and moral questions were also exercising the government. A main issue of the day was that of capital punishment. On 13 July 1955 Ruth Ellis had been hanged for murder. This raised the debate about the merits of capital punishment in a civilized society. Leading the proponents of abolition was the Labour MP Sydney Silverman who introduced a bill to that effect into Parliament in 1956. The Commons was given a free vote but the Lords rejected the proposal on 10 July. Although not of immense political importance the issue was one of many that would come to the forefront of the political stage in the 1950s and 1960s and exercise the political parties' moral majorities on more than one occasion. Another was the vexed question of West Indian immigration. Eden added to his reputation for indecisiveness, perhaps unfairly being touted in the press because of his refusal to reshuffle his ministers, delay in naming the election day, and vacillation over the early recall of Parliament to deal with the economic crisis, and now because of his reference to Cabinet of the West Indian issue. Some ministers, like Duncan Sandys, foretold of the risks of violence particularly in areas like Lambeth in London or parts of Birmingham. Other cabinet colleagues were divided between a ban on immigration or free entry. In the end the cabinet committee report suggested taking no action which probably proved the easiest thing to do anyway.

'YOU'VE NEVER HAD IT SO GOOD'

Macmillan assumed control of the country amidst some grave doubts. Suez was a body-blow, Eden's loss expected but untimely, and the economy far from healthy both internally and externally. Macmillan's first task was to name his team. He found a place for Butler, his unsuccessful rival in the leadership race, but as Home Secretary not Foreign Secretary. The latter went to Selwyn Lloyd, amidst much astonishment. Lloyd was an obvious scapegoat for the Suez débâcle but as Macmillan remarked 'one head on a charger should be enough', and anyway Lloyd's retention would give Macmillan plenty of opportunity to impose his own ideas. Peter Thorneycroft became Chancellor of the Exchequer and was to prove a troublesome colleague for Macmillan before his resignation in 1958. Duncan Sandys was Minister of Defence and Quintin Hogg Minister of Education with David Eccles President of the Board of Trade. A number of younger men also appeared such as Julian Amery, Iain Macleod and Reginald Maudling. This new Cabinet was faced with a number of problems. Many were related to British foreign policy which is the subject of chapter 14. On the domestic front economic worries persisted. Butler's last bout of 'stop' measures designed to bring the country's finances under control lasted longer than expected. Thorneycroft was keen to keep a tight monetary control and was in favour of fairly drastic measures to do so. The need for this was obvious to the Chancellor. At the end of May he reported to Macmillan that the country's liabilities amounted to £4 billion and its assets to a mere £850 million. The Prime Minister was acutely aware of the discrepancy and that is why he gave his now-famous speech at the Bedford football ground on 20 July 1957. Macmillan will forever be associated with the words: 'Let's be frank about it; most of our people have never had it so good'; what is always forgotten is the warning that followed on from this assertion:

> What is beginning to worry some of us is 'Is it too good to be true?' or perhaps I should say 'Is it too good to last?' For amidst all this prosperity, there is one problem that has troubled us – in one way or another – ever since the war. It's the problem of rising prices. Our constant concern today is – can prices be steadied while at the same time we maintain full employment in an expanding economy? Can we control inflation? This is the problem of our time.
>
> (D. Kavanagh and P. Morris, *Consensus Politics from Attlee to Thatcher*, Oxford, Blackwell, 1989, p. 40)

By the end of 1957 economic policy and the way forward had become an open argument between Prime Minister and Chancellor. Thorneycroft believed that public expenditure needed to be kept under strict control and he was, as Macmillan himself reported, 'very worried about the civil estimates which show a great rise for 1958–1959'. Macmillan put down such rises to 'inescapable causes' and the natural consequences of running a mixed economy and a welfare state. Certainly, he was personally opposed to any stringent economic measures fearing a return to the division-ridden days of the 1930s that were so firmly etched on his mind. In the end the break came over Thorneycroft's proposals for cuts of £163 million, a paltry sum on its own, and nearly matched by the cuts acceptable to the rest of the Cabinet. In reality, it was a much more major decision than this. Thorneycroft resigned on 6 January 1958 and took his Treasury team with him. One of them, Enoch Powell, has since said that the whole issue was about the future of the country's economic policy:

> The year 1957 marked the end of seven years of decline in government expenditure as a proportion of national income. Through the subsequent six years of Conservative and six years of Socialist administration it rose steadily and rapidly.

Thorneycroft's high bank rate of 7 per cent in September 1957 was rapidly brought down in stages by the new Chancellor Derek Heathcote-Amory to 4.5 per cent in the August of 1959. The pathway for economic policy was clearly marked out for the foreseeable future.

A similar safe track was sought on the union front. The hand-in-glove relationship between unions and government was to be maintained. The policy of giving union officials recognition and appointments to major committees continued. It has been claimed that by 1958 employees achieved parity of representation on 850 committees, including such influential ones as the economic planning boards. So close were the relationships that Crosland in opposition could write in 1956, 'the atmosphere in Whitehall is almost deferential, the desire not to offend positively ostentatious'. Certainly, Macmillan was keen to avoid industrial strife, and at times it appeared that he was keen to do so at any cost. His diary is very pessimistic in the spring of 1957:

> 15 March – Engineering, railways, coalmines, power stations – this is the dreary sequence over the next few days, threatening a General strike.
>
> (A. Horne, *Harold Macmillan*, vol. II, London, Macmillan, 1988–90, p. 66)

Macmillan arranged for the railwaymen to be bought off by Sir Brian Robertson and they settled for 5 per cent increases rather than the 3 per cent proposed by the independent report set to investigate the claim. The total cost was £42 million, all to come from the British public. The other disputes were also quickly settled but the long honeymoon of government and union co-operation which had lasted since the beginning of the war was about to come to an end.

The year 1957 saw 8.5 million days lost because of industrial disputes – the highest figure since the general strike year of 1926. In addition the co-operation of leadership exemplified by the days of Bevin and Deakin was over and there was no clearer sign of this than in their own union the TGWU. Frank Cousins took over as TUC leader in 1956 and shifted the unions, and especially the TGWU, significantly to the left. He removed the ban on communists becoming office holders and shifted power from the leadership to the shop-floor, and especially to the more militant shop-stewards. This shift was seen most clearly in pay bargaining where demands were translated up to union representatives rather than the leaders imposing wage settlements from above. Such moves would be a blow to a government used to co-operation and dealing with union leaders rather than the rank-and-file membership. Industrial relations would also become a thorn in the side of successive governments.

Britain was fortunate to have in Rab (as he was known) Butler, as Home Secretary, what many people believed to be 'the best prime minister the country never had'. Certainly, he was well up to the task of his department and took the opportunity to set in motion many plans and schemes which are familiar parts of life today. One of the big issues was capital punishment. Overall it was not a party issue and opinions varied but there were persistent calls for reassessment since Ruth Ellis was hanged in 1955. In 1957 the issue was raised again and this time a Homicide Bill was the result which proposed to reserve capital punishment for five special cases of murder. It was an interesting compromise, the plan being to monitor the effect of reduced deterrent and accustom the public to abolition by stages. Allied to this was Butler's White Paper on *Penal Practices in a Changing Society*, published in February 1959, the recommendations of which would be implemented by the Home Office in the following years.

On defence the government committed itself to providing Britain with a continued nuclear deterrent in the shape of the hydrogen bomb with the airforce taking delivery of its first weapons in 1958. This decision was not entirely a defence one. The spiralling costs of conventional defence were biting deeply into public expenditure, already at levels high enough to worry the government. Military orders were monopolizing much productive capacity with defence contracts taking up 24 per cent of shipping and 14 per cent of engineering thus depriving the export market. A nuclear deterrent would place Britain firmly on the world stage again and help to reduce defence spending. What was not realized at the time was that nuclear weaponry would easily outstrip the costs of conventional weaponry when research costs, delivery systems and the like were taken into account. With a current defence budget in 1952 greater, per capita, than that of the USA, savings were the order of the day and attempts to pare away at defence budgets had proved unsuccessful at least on the scale desired. The decision had its repercussions elsewhere and in 1957 the Campaign for Nuclear Disarmament (CND) came into being, organizing the first of its Aldermaston marches in 1958. It was a campaign that was to grow and take particular root in the Labour Party with consequences for both major political parties.

The government also carried out some extensive legislative proposals concerning local government reorganization, compensation for compulsorily purchased property, New Towns and loans to the farming community. Principal amongst these was the 1957 Rent Act. There was particular concern about the state of much rented property and the Act was designed to relax some controls to allow landlords to charge higher rents. The government believed that this would give landlords the money to improve property. Labour saw it differently and claimed it was a 'Landlords' Charter' that would simply put extra rent into their pockets. The Act took 810,000 properties out of rent control and allowed for increases in the remaining 4.3 million controlled properties.

Equally contentious was the call for reform of the House of Lords. Criticisms of such a privileged second chamber, relying as it did on hereditary succession, were growing and the demand for change was quite strident especially from the opposition benches. However, the government would not abandon the second chamber and so it settled for compromise in its Life Peers Bill of 1957. Hereditary peerages were safeguarded but the composition of the House would be changed, albeit slowly, by the creation of nominated life peers with both parties being given rights to nominate men and women. Quite remarkable though was the name of Robert Boothby which appeared on the first list of ten men and four women to be so elevated. Boothby had been Macmillan's wife's lover and had caused the Prime Minister years of sorrow and anguish while the affair lasted.

In education the Conservatives had increased the number of technical schools, established colleges of advanced technology and university institutes of technology. The policy and promise of de-control continued and a White Paper of 1957 recommended that conscription, in the form of national service, should cease. In the event it was not abolished until 1960. The persistent problem of immigration ran on and was worsened by disturbances in both Nottingham and Notting Hill in London in August 1958, but the government was quick to decide in September of that year that there would be no controls on Commonwealth immigration into Britain despite the obvious intensity of feeling. Although the government's opinions were to change in succeeding years the issue seemed to recede with immigration figures showing falls in both 1958 and 1959.

Macmillan picked 1959 to become the election year, choosing to go to the nation after the Tories had enjoyed four and a half years in office. The time seemed opportune with a 7 per cent lead in the opinion polls. The four-week campaign proved hard going but the Conservative message was a powerful one – prosperity and experience of government at home and abroad:

The Conservative record

Eight years ago was a turning point in British history. The Labour Government had failed in grappling with the problems of the post-war world. Under Conservative leadership this country set out upon a new path. It is leading to prosperity and opportunity for all.

The British economy is sounder today than at any time since the first world war. Sterling has been re-established as a strong and respected currency. Under Conservative government we have earned abroad £1,600 million more than we have spent. Our exports have reached the highest peak ever. Overseas, mostly in the Commonwealth, we are investing nearly double what we could manage eight years ago. Capital investment at home, to build for the future, is over half as large again. To match this, and make it possible, people are saving more than ever before.

The paraphernalia of controls have been swept away. The call-up is being abolished. We have cut taxes in seven Budgets, whilst continuing to develop the social services. We have provided over two million new homes and almost two million new school places, a better health service and a modern pensions plan. We have now stabilised the cost of living while maintaining full employment. We have shown that Conservative freedom works. Life *is* better with the Conservatives.

In the international field, thanks to the initiative of the Conservative Government, the diplomatic deadlock between East and West has now been broken. The Prime Minister's visit to Russia in February began a sequence of events which has led to the present easing of tension. The proposed exchange of visits between President Eisenhower and Mr. Khrushchev is the most recent proof of this. It is our determination to see that this process continues and to make a success of the important negotiations which we trust will follow.

The main issues at this election are therefore simple: (1) Do you want to go ahead on the lines which have brought prosperity at home? (2) Do you want your present leaders to represent you abroad?

On the other hand the Labour campaign seemed to lack genuine alternatives (see p. 479). The party leader Hugh Gaitskell did the Labour cause considerable harm with continual promises about significantly raised levels of benefits whilst admitting that there would be no increases in income tax. For a while the ruse worked and the middle of the month-long campaign belonged to Labour but the bluff was called before election day and the Tories finished strongly rejecting the 'have your cake and eat it' policy of Gaitskell summed up in Macmillan's own words: 'if this is an auction, I am not in it'.

Labour was also suffering publicly from the split in the party between harder-line Bevanites and the 'Keep Left' group and Gaitskell's own revisionists. Clause Four was a major bone of contention, as was defence policy and especially nuclear weapons. A patching-up of sorts occurred

Labour manifesto 1959

[Britain Belongs to You:
The Labour Party's Policy for Consideration by the British People]

We welcome this Election; it gives us, at last, the chance to end eight years of Tory rule. In a television chat with President Eisenhower, Mr. Macmillan told us that the old division of Britain into the two nations, the Haves and the Have Nots, has disappeared. Tory prosperity, he suggested, is shared by all. In fact, the contrast between the extremes of wealth and poverty is sharper today than eight years ago. The business man with a tax-free expense account, the speculator with tax-free capital gains, and the retiring company director with a tax-free redundancy payment due to a take-over bid – these people have indeed 'never had it so good'.

It is not so good for the widowed mother with children, the chronic sick, the 400,000 unemployed, and the millions of old age pensioners who have no adequate superannuation. While many of those at work have been able to maintain and even improve their standard of living by collective bargaining, the sick, the disabled and the old have continually seen the value of state benefits and small savings whittled away by rising prices. Instead of recognising this problem as the greatest social challenge of our time, the Prime Minister blandly denies it exists.

before the election and Bevan even worked loyally for Gaitskell taking on the nuclear disarmers with the memorable reference to British foreign ministers going 'naked into the Conference Chamber' but it was all to no avail. The divisions were real ones and had been publicly aired over many years and Labour, not for the first or the last time, seemed to be its own worst enemy.

Macmillan fought a hard campaign, travelling 2,500 miles and speaking at seventy-four meetings and it was during this tour that the famous words 'You've never had it so good' were supposedly spoken to one worker Macmillan met. The sentiment was right and the electorate realized that the Tories had provided them with a more comfortable standard of living, and the party had of course given them a timely reminder in the pre-election budget which cut income tax, purchase tax and reduced duty on beer. No wonder Macmillan considered the consumer durable revolution his greatest electoral asset. With a turnout of 78 per cent the Conservatives increased their number of seats from 342 to 365 while Labour fell back from 281 to 258. The Conservatives entered a third term with yet another increased majority, this time of 100 seats. While the 'good times rolled' the electorate was content but although the Tories' third consecutive term started promisingly enough in a short time the problems would amass and carry them away.

THE CONSERVATIVES IN POWER 1959–64

On the surface the position of the Conservative Party in 1959 appeared its strongest for many years and the events of the first two years in power did nothing to undermine that strength. The economy appeared to be responsive to 'stop–go' tactics even though some economists had severe doubts about the policy – not least because it did appear to rest its case on a single element of Keynesian economics. If the economy had a tendency to 'overheat' then it needed 'cooling down' with strict controls which although bringing temporary unemployment would soon redress any imbalance in the balance of payments. After a sufficient dose of economic medicine then reinflation could proceed. This tended to ignore some deeper seated problems such as the continuing tendency for wages to rise on a yearly basis regardless, and the rapidly rising costs of many staple imports including food. Heathcote-Amory had wanted to return to a bit of stern medicine after the election but Macmillan vetoed this on the basis that it would be unseemly after the pre-election budget and talk of prosperity. Non-budgets followed which allowed a balance of payments deficit to increase and in 1960, amidst popular criticism, Heathcote-Amory resigned to be replaced by Selwyn Lloyd. By this time the deficit was a worrying £258 million and within a short time speculation had risen about another sterling crisis. An emergency budget was given in July 1961 with bank rate once again hitting 7 per cent and import controls imposing increases of 10 per cent. Most controversial of all, though, was the so-called 'pay-pause' imposed on all government employees, in the faint hope that the private sector would feel morally bound to come into line. With thirty-five outstanding pay claims, and wages tending to rise 50 per cent faster than output, the concern can be appreciated. The budget established the National Economic Development Council, or 'Neddy' as it was known, but the trade unions who were supposed to play a part only reluctantly took up their seat on it. The unions also boycotted other initiatives such as the National Incomes Commission and the government's attempts to impose a 2.5 per cent pay guideline. In August the government had to ask the IMF for help and received a credit of £714 million. With unemployment rapidly rising, and due to hit 800,000 in the following year, the 'good times' were definitely over.

Further problems mounted. The rapidly rising rate of immigration to Britain, especially from the West Indies, was giving cause for yet more concern. From the relatively low entry figures of around 20,000 in 1959, 1960 saw an increase to 56,100 and 1961 a further rise to 115,150. There was strong evidence to suggest the rush was partly in anticipation of controls but the impression given was the first signs of a huge deluge of migrants. Although many previous migrants had found jobs and provided many essential services there were rising fears about ghettos, strain on social services, rising unemployment and racial conflict. The government's Commonwealth Immigration Act of July 1962 was implemented initially for a five-year trial period. The Conservatives, in political terms, were on a hiding to nothing. Prospective migrants had to fulfil one of three criteria: a job offer in Britain, possession of educational qualifications or skills that were in demand, or be part of the general quota. The opposition were quick to seize on the anomalies of unskilled Irish labour entering with no restrictions and how the conditions would not really affect white colonials. Gaitskell labelled the measure 'Cruel and brutal anti-colour legislation' but his own party would be forced to firm up controls in the very near future.

A further worry to Macmillan was the rising tide of political opposition to the Tory administration. This was seen most graphically in a series of very damaging by-elections which in 1961–2 not only spelled lack of popularity for the government but also gave the whiff of Liberal Party resurrection. The key loss came at Orpington in Kent in March 1962 when a Conservative majority of 14,760 was turned into a Liberal one of 7,855. The early successes of the administration in terms of new motorway building, the Robbins Report on Higher Education which heralded the opening of the University of Sussex in 1961 and the inauguration of others at York, East Anglia, Kent, Lancaster and Warwick were soon forgotten. Even the apparent triumph of purchasing Polaris missiles for the quite reasonable sum of £350 million faded into the background as the more immediate uncertainties took hold. There was also increasing clamour for someone's head and the phrase 'Macmillan must go' seemed to strike the premier's panic button. In July 1962 he oversaw a fundamental Cabinet reshuffle with seven full Cabinet Ministers, including his Chancellor Selwyn Lloyd, being ousted. The others included Lords Kilmuir and Mills, Watkinson and Eccles; in addition, nine junior ministers not in the Cabinet also departed. The mayhem earned the epithet 'The Night of the Long Knives' and some critical comment from other politicians, many of whom shared Jeremy Thorpe's stinging appraisal of Macmillan's action as 'Greater love hath no man than to lay down his friends for his life.' Whether Macmillan feared a plot against him or genuinely wanted to bring in new young talent to replace an increasingly ageing and unimaginative team is not entirely clear, but the political ramifications of these actions were. Macmillan succeeded in creating intense bitterness in the party which eventually played no little part in his departure from the political scene in a short space of time.

The normal function of government rapidly deteriorated in this second Macmillan administration. Few legislative enactments graced the last years of this administration as foreign affairs continued to dominate. One interesting one, ironically to play a part in the leadership succession after Macmillan's departure, was the Peerages Renunciation Act of 1963. Its passage owed much to Lord Stansgate, Anthony Wedgwood-Benn, who desired to continue political life even though he was heir to a title that would take him to the Lords and thus debar him. His long fight resulted in the Act which he used immediately, and others like Lord Hailsham latterly. The Act protected hereditary claims as renunciation could only be made on one's own behalf not that of children who could take the title in normal succession. Thus Tony Benn's political career continued.

Transport had been one area of some success with the new motorway building programme which had notched up 300 miles by 1964. Railways were a different matter, though, and the White Paper entitled *The Reshaping of Britain's Railways* had some unwelcomed news for unions and commuters alike. Dr Richard Beeching, the new head of British Railways, had plans which called for the closing down of one-third of the existing routes in an attempt to rationalize the service and make it cost effective. The move was not popular and people talked in terms of the 'Beeching Axe' slicing through one of the great symbols of the country's prosperity. It was, however, only the first of several unpleasant shocks that the British public would face as the reality of Britain's decaying industrial heritage came to the surface in the 1960s and 1970s.

By this time, however, Dr Beeching was seeing, along with all other Britons, the demise of the Macmillan Government. It was to be a very messy end. The first inklings of trouble came with the unfortunate William Vassall 'spy' case. Vassall, a government employee, was given eighteen years imprisonment in October 1962 for spying on behalf of the Russian government. He had been blackmailed – something, given the morals of the days, his homosexuality made easy – and an unsavoury whiff began to emanate from government circles. Hardly had the tabloids had time to catch their breath than the ex-Head of the Soviet Department of MI6, Kim Philby, defected in January 1963. Worse was to follow with a much more damaging scandal.

The Minister of Defence, John Profumo, had been having an affair with Christine Keeler, a model and call-girl, since 1961. Although, Lord Hailsham was to point out, a little indelicately, marital infidelity was not the preserve of the Tory Party, there were extreme circumstances in this case. Keeler, whose immoral earnings were keeping a certain Stephen Ward, who would commit suicide over the case, was also sleeping with Captain Ivanov of the Russian embassy. Cross-pillow talk was feared and Profumo's position was desperate. Believing nothing to have been leaked via his affair and Keeler's other lovers, Profumo decided to brazen it out with dreadful consequences. He stood up in the House of Commons on 22 March and simply lied to the House claiming that his liaison with Christine Keeler had ended in 1961 and that recent love letters were now simply tokens of an affair long over. His explanation was accepted until further revelations made it impossible for him to continue the pretence and he was forced to admit his lies and tender his resignation to Macmillan. Worse was to follow with Harold Wilson baiting the luckless Macmillan in the Commons and forcing Macmillan to talk publicly about matters that were personally distasteful to him. The Labour Party had a field day and the government's standing sank lower and lower as each day passed. Calls for security enquiries and attacks on Macmillan's failure to act early and decisively over the affair mounted as the weeks passed.

Further ammunition was given to the opposition by the revelations about landlord exploitation of tenants especially in areas of London where one such landlord, Peter Rachman, gave his name to this growing national scandal of 'Rachmanism'. As the carriers of the 1957 Rent Act the Conservatives seemed to be the perfect target for attacks. It is understandable then that Macmillan was already making plans for his own departure but these were set awry by his own illness which necessitated an operation and his earlier retirement. The key question was – 'Who was to be his successor?' As with all successions the pundits had their favourites but the field seemed larger than usual with Hailsham, Maudling, Macleod, Heath, Butler and one or two others being named. Hailsham and Butler were the favourites but Macmillan had other ideas. In his diary for 4 October 1963 there lies the following comment about the leadership, even before his illness manifested itself: 'Butler would be fatal. Maudling uninspiring. Hailsham, with Maudling and the others in loyal support might still win.' It was from his hospital bed on 9 October that Macmillan informed Alec Douglas-Home, Lord Home, that he favoured him as the next leader of the party. With the announcement about Macmillan's resignation made at the Blackpool Conference, held on 10–12 October, all hell broke loose and hats came flying into the ring from every quarter. However, Home's announcement that he intended to renounce his title and stand persuaded Hailsham to do the same and the contest began. It was Home who came out on top much to the annoyance of some of the young contenders who, like Iain Macleod, suspected that the Tory party 'magic circle' had waved its wand over Home. Certainly, Macmillan had instructed Home to go to Blackpool and deal with 'those whose business it was to do so, to take soundings about the future leadership'. Macmillan had won but in many ways the party had lost and Home proved to be an easy target for the newly envigorated Labour Party when it came to a general election.

The quick demise of the Conservatives after the early false dawn seemed to mirror the exact opposite for Labour. Early disasters gave way to a rising tide of confidence and certainty. 1959 was a nadir for the party. It even raised questions like *Can Labour Win?* and few answers were forthcoming that pleased all elements of the party. Gaitskell was sure Labour could but on a number of conditions. One was the need to move with the times and distance the party from the old Clause Four mentality which had proved to be an electoral stumbling block. However, he was not successful in pushing this through and met stern resistance from the left of the party and the trade unions who still viewed Clause Four as an article of socialist faith. Gaitskell's thoughts were made plain at the 1959 party conference but to no avail:

> We may not be far from the frontier of this kind of giant State monopoly [but] . . . I cannot agree that we have reached the frontier of public ownership as a whole.
>
> At the same time I disagree equally with the other extreme view that public ownership is the be all and end all, the ultimate first principle and aim of socialism.
>
> (*The Diary of Hugh Gaitskell*, ed. P. M. Williams, London, Cape,
> 1983, p. 324)

However, the dissension caused was yet another weakness in an opposition that was finding it increasingly difficult to find, let alone justify, its role. A similar story of faction arose with the continuing debate over unilateral disarmament which Gaitskell thought an untenable position for a party seeking government, given the recent past and present international situation. Gaitskell went to the 1960 Scarborough Conference determined to sway the party to the leadership's side but found himself on the end of an embarrassing defeat. He went down fighting on this occasion and promised a re-match in the following year – which he won. As Kenneth Morgan has claimed Gaitskell 'won victory, but too much blood was spilt on the way'. At this stage the Conservatives were contentedly watching Labour bite itself and their problems had yet to surface. However, it was a cruel blow, in the shape of Gaitskell's untimely death after a viral infection, which brought a new leader to the forefront, Harold Wilson. After a brilliant university career both as student and academic Wilson entered government service through the experts' backdoor during war-time and made himself an enviable reputation. He had served at ministerial level, albeit junior, and had resigned with Bevan over the National Health Service prescription charges. He was a member of the Keep Left Group and co-authored *One Way Only* (1951) thus helping to establish a reputation as a left-winger which was reinforced as leader of the Tribune Group. However, Wilson was never herald of later militancy and his position in the party sits more easily in the centre. He rapidly rose in the party to become Shadow Chancellor and Foreign Secretary. He was an acknowledged political tactician of some skill and his provincial Yorkshire upbringing allied to wit and charm gave him a homely, approachable and trusting exterior. Not everyone would vouch for this impression now and certainly Wilson had his darker side, even if it be only jumping at shadows. Nevertheless, in 1963 he gave Labour a distinct advantage in the popularity stakes especially with Douglas-Home taking over the reins of power on behalf of the Conservatives.

The date for the election was set for 15 October 1964, and the campaigning proved to be gruelling. Labour were predicted the victors and certainly the comparison between the two parties' views of the country's future was stark. The Conservative rallying cry for *Prosperity with a Purpose* was no match for Labour's *New Britain*. The manifesto war was won hands down by Labour and even today the energy, enthusiasm and sense of purpose of the Labour document comes through despite the intervening years of disappointment:

Planning the new Britain

We offer no easy solution to our national problems. Time and effort will be required before they can be mastered. But Labour has a philosophy and a practical programme which is relevant to our contemporary needs. The starting point is our belief that the community must equip itself to take charge of its own destiny and no longer be ruled by market forces beyond its control. Labour does not accept that democracy is a five yearly visit to the polling booth that changes little but the men at the top. We are working for an active democracy, in which men and women as responsible citizens consciously assist in shaping the surroundings in which they live, and take part in deciding how the community's wealth is to be shared among all its members.

Two giant tasks now await the nation: first we must energise and modernise our industries – including their methods of promotion and training – to achieve the sustained economic expansion we need; second, we must ensure that a sufficient part of the new wealth created goes to meet urgent and now neglected human needs.

Labour needed an enormous swing to turn around the Conservative majority and turnout was lower than usual with 77.1 per cent. However, Labour won the popular vote and a swing, which was the largest since the war. Unfortunately, it was only sufficient to give them a five-seat majority which rapidly fell to four. It was victory but bitterly slight and Harold Wilson formed the first Labour administration in thirteen years full of the knowledge that it might be a very short stay in Number 10.

'THE WHITE HEAT OF THE TECHNOLOGICAL REVOLUTION' 1964–70

Wilson's campaigning phrase certainly hit a responsive chord being full of hope, modernity and regeneration. The character of this crusading ardour can be noted in Wilson's desire to make an impact with his 'first hundred days'. His Cabinet was, of necessity, an inexperienced one in terms of ministerial expertise. James Callaghan took the Chancellorship with George Brown, effectively Wilson's number two, becoming head of a new Department of Economic Affairs whose job it would be to oversee the National Plan; Patrick Gordon Walker took the Foreign Office and Lord Longford became Lord Privy Seal. A number of the left took

ministerial positions too, including Barbara Castle and Richard Crossman, and Jennie Lee became Minister of the Arts. The scale of the
problems facing this new team was soon revealed. The last Conservative
Chancellor, Reginald Maudling, had pinned his hopes on 'a dash for
growth', but growth without similar increases in productivity and exports
had created a widening balance of payments gap. The new administration
was horrified to learn that they had inherited an £800 million trade deficit
which would severely curtail their desire to spend on social services and
boost education and technology in order to honour their election pledges.
The great new dawn was beginning to resemble a gathering storm, and
one which would break around the Labour leadership. The government's
first budget would be crucial. It saw the bank rate rise to 7 per cent, a
15 per cent import surcharge and a loan from the USA of £2 billion. It
seemed to many as if little had changed. However, this would be an
unfair assessment as the same budget also increased pensions and abolished prescription charges. Working within the very tight political con-
straints of a slender majority the Labour Government succeeded in passing important pieces of legislation in the two years between 1964 and
the next general election of 1966.

The feeling of a new broom was best seen in the proliferation of new
departments in addition to that for Economic Affairs already mentioned.
There were ministries of Overseas Development, Land and Natural
Resources, and Technology, where the luckless Frank Cousins was mis-
placed. A Welsh department was also created. Acts were passed
empowering local authorities to grant pensioners concessionary fares on
transport in 1964; and a Trades Disputes Act, a Science and Technology
Act, a Race Relations Act and a Murder Act outlawing capital punishment, all came into force in 1965, as did the Monopolies and Mergers
Act. These years also saw important proposals for metrification, decimalization and the government's circular on comprehensive education, as
well as the Donovan Commission on the reform of the trade unions.
It proved impossible, given Labour's majority, to do more and many
administrations might have done less. Much time was also taken by
devising Labour's so-called National Plan. Wilson had to play the political
game very carefully because in August 1965 the Tory Party narrowly
elected a new leader, the first time Tory MPs had done so, and the new
adversary, Edward Heath, was more prepossessing than Alec Douglas-
Home. More symbolic still of the changing nature of British politics was
the death earlier in the year of Winston Churchill who was accorded the
honour of a state funeral. The old Tory Party appeared to have passed
away with Churchill, Macmillan and Home. Heath now took up the
mantle laid down and his prospects appeared to be good with Labour's
majority falling to three seats and government becoming almost impossible. It was not a question of would Wilson go to the country but when?
In the event it was after a successful by-election victory in Hull and

Wilson judged it was the right time to go to the polls. He set the date for the election as 31 March. The turnout was lower than 1964 at 75.8 per cent and Labour was having to weather continued economic struggles with severe balance of payments difficulties and the pound once again under pressure. However, wage increases were easing the political burden, and Heath's warnings of 'vote now pay later' fell on deaf ears. Wilson stood by the 1964 manifesto and campaigned effectively gaining an increase in Labour's seats from 316 to 363 while the Tories slipped from 304 to 253. The government's majority was 96 – more than sufficient for an effective administration to implement Labour's proposals.

LABOUR IN POWER 1966–70

The return to power was marred by the growing awareness of the economic crisis Britain faced and the very damaging seamen's strike in the summer of 1966 which necessitated the declaration of a state of emergency. The dispute hit the country's finances badly and added to balance of payments difficulties and pressure on sterling. It is this scenario that rapidly worsened and provided the backdrop for the Labour Government in these years. Once again the economic difficulties limited legislative action and the government was forced back on to other areas of executive action rather than fundamental structural changes. It is symbolic that the great National Plan was the first to fall by the wayside whilst very worthy but 'civilizing', rather than regenerating, pieces of legislation were entered on to the pages of the statute book. The latter were tantamount to a charter for greater equality, freedom and caring. Amongst the acts passed in 1967 were: the Criminal Justice Act which brought in suspended sentences; the Sexual Offences Act which permitted homosexual acts between consenting adults over the age of 21; the Abortion Act (the work of the Liberal David Steel but strongly supported by the government) which permitted abortion in certain circumstances; the Family Planning Act; and the Leasehold Reform Act. In 1968, despite the Race Relations Act, Gaitskell's famous earlier condemnation of the Tories turned bitter in the party's mouth as it passed the Commonwealth Immigrants Act which excluded Kenyan Asians. In 1969 the Representation of the People Act gave votes to 18-year-olds. The same year saw the Divorce Act and the Children and Young Persons Act. In the final year of the administration important precedents were set for women with the Equal Pay Act and the Matrimonial Property Act. In addition the Disabled Persons Act was also passed.

Labour also showed its historical roots with two pieces of legislation that suggested public ownership was still a guiding light in the movement, albeit a dim one for the leadership: the renationalization of iron and steel in 1967 and the 1968 Transport Act, which created national bus and freight companies. There was also a Shipbuilding Industry Act in

1967 and an Industrial Expansion Act in 1968. On the educational front the government announced plans to create thirty polytechnics in 1967, the charting of the Open University in 1969 and the comprehensive system of schooling which saw the grammar schools under attack with half of those in existence seeing their demise in these years. Similar fundamental changes were designed for local government and the civil service with extensive commissions of inquiry into both. That same year also saw the appointment of the Parliamentary Commissioner for Administration or the Ombudsman. The promises of the manifesto and election campaigns were being fulfilled but the unmistakable impression of fiddling while Rome, or in this case Britain, burned is apparent. Form rather than content was the order of the day, ideas without structure the weakness of the administration. There can be few arguments about the desire to change and alleviate problems and inequalities but the fundamental difficulties were those that needed the government's full attention. Worthy enactments are just that and their significance palls, despite their merits, in the face of economic crisis and one that had been brewing for many years.

There was a growing belief that Britain was living beyond her means and the steady increase in public expenditure was clearly evident, although it would get much worse as the 1970s unfolded. Between 1959 and 1964 spending remained much the same at about 33 per cent of GDP. By 1970, under Labour, this had risen to 38 per cent. Rising domestic inflation and industrial troubles put pressure on sterling and the government responded with strict controls. Ironically the run on sterling began the day the seamen's strike ended, on 1 July 1967. At this stage the Cabinet was opposed to drastic action which included the thought of devaluation. The latter was politically damaging; after all, the last devaluation had occurred in 1949 with Labour in government, but economically it made sense to many. Other issues also played their part and the French had made it clear that Britain's entry into the EEC would be made that much easier if she were economically sound. In Cabinet devaluation was rejected by seventeen votes to six on 19 July with the majority favouring a tight budget including hire-purchase controls, a 10 per cent increase in duties, defence cuts and 10 per cent surcharges. These were to be brought in with a prices and incomes policy that would impose a standstill for six months. The policy held although there were notable opponents, such as Frank Cousins and Clive Jenkins. Speculation continued into the new year despite relatively good indicators. Deficits continued although they were small ones but rumour played on rumour and the key question was: could Britain avoid this long drawn-out game of balance of payments deficits for a continuous period? The financial markets appeared to think that the answer was 'No'. Callaghan, the Chancellor, tried his best in his budget speech, fittingly for a native of Portsmouth and an ex-mariner, relying on seafaring metaphors: 'I sum up the prospects for 1967 in three short sentences. We are back on course. The ship is picking up speed. The economy is moving ahead. Every seaman knows the command at such a moment – "Steady as she goes".' Two months later the Arab–Israeli war closed the Suez Canal and restricted oil supplies. In sterling's fragile state it was a body-blow and by the autumn further docks strikes in Hull, Liverpool and London presented the world with a picture of industrial torpor.

Devaluation followed almost inevitably on 18 November. A cut in sterling's value of 14.3 per cent brought it down from \$2.80 to \$2.40. The move was accompanied by a further package of restrictions and controls including bank rate rising to 8 per cent. Callaghan resigned from the Exchequer, moving to the Home Office, and was replaced by Roy Jenkins who carried through further stringent controls in the budget of 1968 which saw the severest tax increases since the war and brought in £923 million of savings.

Underlying many of the ills of the economy and certainly a spark in the devaluation crisis was the role of the trade unions. The Donovan Commission's report on trade-union reform was published in 1968. It made no concrete recommendations, mainly because of the Commission's political composition, but the message was clear: the trade-union movement was too parochial, informal and unstructured to become the partner in government that many believed was necessary for Labour to succeed. The bland report necessitated a further display of intent by the government to address the problem and this turned out to be Barbara Castle's *In Place of Strife*, published in 1969. Hard negotiations took place and many points raised heated debate. Amongst the proposals made were compulsory 'cooling-off' periods in disputes, ballots in strikes that would harm the country's economic position, statutory rights to belong to trade unions, a Commission for Industrial Relations, rights against unfair dismissal, and strengthened collective pay bargaining. The proposals, enshrined in an Industrial Relations Bill in 1970, were not destined to become law, however. Unfortunately for the Labour Party the defeat of these proposals tended to confirm some suspicions that the party was tied too strongly to the union movement and this prevented it from being the effective government that the country needed in times of economic turmoil. Certainly, the Conservative Party homed in on this particular aspect of policy and Heath had already set up policy groups to look into the vexed question of trade union law and practices. It was obvious that the Conservative leader expected this to be a major arena of government action should he enter Number 10.

Heath's optimism in 1968 and 1969, despite the internal wranglings over Enoch Powell's infamous and misquoted 'rivers of blood' speech about continued immigration, soon disappeared. By late 1969 the Labour Government appeared to have turned a corner. The balance of payments at long last took a turn for the better and by 1970 there would be £1 billion surplus; the party seemed to become more attractive and moved into a poll lead; and Wilson seized the chance of a June election. Labour campaigned well and was given the lead in most polls and everyone expected a Wilson government to be returned. It was only in the last couple of days that the tide turned with poor trade figures for May and some sharp price rises. Imponderables like England failing in the World Cup and Powell's supporters voting with the Tories instead of against them may also have played a part. The result was a surprise with Heath's Conservatives picking up a comfortable victory on a low turnout of 72 per cent. The overall majority of thirty was certainly workable and Heath could begin to plan for a new Conservative administration.

THE CONSERVATIVES IN POWER 1970–4

Edward Heath's influence on the Tory Party since becoming its leader was considerable. The patrician air of landed and ducal public-school educated men had weakened a little to reveal the music-loving, sailing bachelor with a grammar-school background, even if the Oxford connection was maintained. Personality did not seem to affect policy and the old Tory ideas espoused best by Sir William Anstruther Grey, Chairman of the 1922 Committee, who claimed Tory policy amounted to 'a sound pound, prosperous agriculture and strong defence' still remained. Many in the party would have agreed with him but not necessarily Edward Heath. He felt a fresh image was needed and was aware in 1965, given Labour's position then, that government might come the Tories way sooner rather than later. He instituted thirty separate policy committees, calling on MPs and outside experts. As Edward Du Cann, Party Chairman from 1965–7 recalled, 'we decided that we must try to turn the Tory party into a ferment of ideas . . . a great deal was done in the twin fields of research and publications especially by the Conservative Political Centre'. In January 1970 the Shadow Cabinet fleshed out its new ideas during lengthy discussions at the Selsdon Park Hotel in Croydon. Heath emerged from this, at least to some sections of the disparaging press, as the new 'Selsdon Man'. The main thrust of the policy initiatives announced by Heath were to the right with reductions in direct taxation, increases in the size of the police force and an Industrial Relations Bill. Heath believed he had some clear ideas in mind when he made his grand design speech on 19 June, stating: 'This government is to be at the service of all the people, the whole of the time. Our purpose is not to divide but to unite and where there are differences to bring reconciliation to create one nation.'

The thrust of this revived 'One nation Toryism' was to be on three fronts. First, a reorganization of central and local government. Second, a major assault on the British economy and its all too obvious ills. Third, a consideration of the real problem of industrial relations. From such promising beginnings came Heath's humiliation and eventual defeat in 1974. His government has been criticized for its intransigence and desire to go too far too quickly when events conspired against them but it was those events on the domestic and international scenes which really brought about the Tories' failure in the Heath government of 1970–4.

The portent of things to come occurred in the very first weeks of the ministry. The electricity workers started a work to rule and created widespread blackouts reminiscent of war days. Heath's most senior, and able, colleague, Macleod, his new Chancellor of the Exchequer, died suddenly. He was replaced by the less experienced Anthony Barber whose abilities lay more in party management than financial affairs. Heath had fallen back on Home for the Foreign Office, Lord Carrington for Defence and Reginald Maudling at the Home Office. Barber's first budget in 1971, following the official start of decimalization, was designed to reinflate the economy but his tax cuts and much discussed abolition of free school milk and increases in the price of school meals along with increased prescription charges and dental fees, although offset by a new family income supplement for the poorest, did not do the trick. Further cuts of £550 million did not help either and in 1972 in his March budget he went for gargantuan tax cuts amounting to £1,380 million and promised pension increases for the autumn. It was unfortunate that such measures coincided with increasing balance of payments difficulties, high rates of inflation, high wage demands and massive increases in commodity prices on international markets. A large deficit on Britain's trade balance was recorded in 1975 of £700 million and a sterling crisis ensued. The government's response was to float the pound within limits in August 1971 and freely by June 1972. It was a far from auspicious start and the government, owing to severe financial difficulties, was unable to fulfil many of their promises of the election campaign.

However, 1971 had contained some good moments for the government, especially the Commons vote in favour of Britain's entry to the EEC. Heath felt that EEC membership would help to stimulate economic recovery but such plans and hopes would be swamped all too soon. An Immigration Bill also went on to the statute book in this year which unified the system of entry for all prospective migrants whether from the Commonwealth or not. Ironically for a government which was to experience such financial difficulties this was also the year in which the first North Sea oil concessions were auctioned. Bad news however came with financial difficulties for Rolls-Royce and Upper Clyde Shipbuilders with the government eventually mounting rescue operations for both companies which would take them into public ownership. This was certainly not a plank of the Conservative platform and presaged the later complete U-turn but it did show a genuine desire to curtail unemployment which was showing a worrying tendency to rise and would hit one million by January 1972. The real parliamentary work in 1971, though, had been done in the mammoth task, requiring sixty days and 450 hours of parliamentary time, to pass, on 5 August, the Industrial Relations Bill. This made collective industrial bargaining enforceable by law and established a National Industrial Relations Court.

The Heath Government's administrative reforms went ahead relatively smoothly. By the end of Heath's term central government had seen many significant changes. There was a reorganization of ministries to take into account the changing priorities and importances of various policy areas with some ministries splitting and others merging. A Central Policy Review Staff came into existence in the Cabinet Office clearing, indicating the changing nature of government. In local government the measures passed became operative in the 1974 local government reorganization of the 1972 Act which created forty-five counties with six metropolitan areas and a new tier of metropolitan districts. However, it was to be the two interrelated objectives of economic recovery and industrial relations which were to be the bane of Heath's administration. More so because traditional economic policies had been shown to be out of step with the events of the 1970s. The supposedly impossible, in Keynesian terms, appearance of inflation and stagnation at the same time, the so-called 'stagflation', which had appeared in the 1960s gave all economic pundits plenty to think about. Brendon Sewill, Director of the Conservative Research Department, has commented:

> There was a curious blank spot because everybody thought that inflation was the great problem but no one was actually prepared to say that Keynesian principle of full employment was a paramount aim that should be abandoned. Everyone said the trade unions were too powerful but nobody was prepared to say the only way to reduce their power was to increase unemployment. Nobody was prepared to take the mental leap away from total Keynesian tradition in which everyone had grown up during the 1940's, 1950's and 1960's.
>
> (*Contemporary Record*, vol. 3, no. 3 (February 1990), p. 38)

Certainly, the Heath Government identified part of the problem, as had previous governments, as being the trade unions. The woeful productivity figures and the ever-increasing demands for wage increases, not linked to improved output, were undermining any attempts to rectify the country's economic plight. It was obvious that Heath hoped to do something about this and equally obvious that the trade unions felt strong enough to take on a government that had made its intentions already patently obvious with the passing of the Industrial Relations Act. Particularly galling for the unions was the provision for the imposition of fines on unions not adhering to the National Industrial Relations Court's findings. The upshot was that 1972 opened with all 280,000 miners out on strike on 9 January in a very damaging six-week confrontation that lasted through until mid-February. The miners had rejected the government's offer, within its guidelines, of £2 maximum increase, and forced a rethink on the part of the Heath Government. Their dispute went to inquiry and the Wilberforce Commission came out in favour of giving the miners three times what the Coal Board was offering. The unions had won their first battle.

The second wave came with British Railways' work to rule which started in April and lasted until June. Heath realized that an offensive was opening up and declared in a speech at Perth in Scotland in May that 'we cannot, if we hope to prosper, allow our politics to be dictated by one section of the community'. The unions' reply was the dockers' strike of the summer which lasted until mid-August and involved 30,000 men. Such industrial disputes, now coming thick and fast, did Britain's international standing no good at all and inevitably put the strain on the pound necessitating it to float freely. Completely beyond Heath's control was the massive rise in international market prices for many staple imports which experienced increases of between 100 per cent and 300 per cent. The autumn saw worsening relations and the TUC intent upon suspending any union which registered under the Industrial Relations Act. Heath felt that a little simple rational thought was needed – after all the Conservatives' original policy for the unions had been *A Fair Deal at Work* – but co-operation and reconciliation certainly was not on the minds of many union leaders as the recent past events had suggested. It was therefore left for the government to impose a statutory prices and incomes policy which Heath wanted to do in three stages. Stage one began on 6 November 1972 and imposed a ninety-day wages and prices standstill. The policy was much criticized but in its first two stages (the second stage became operative in April 1973), it did appear to be working. The second stage had been announced with the budget, which was notable for the introduction of Value Added Tax, and established a Price Commission and a Pay Board. Pay increases were to be pegged at 4 per cent plus £1 per week up to a maximum of £250 per annum. More interestingly it also became an offence to strike. This was more than a little antagonistic and unfortunate in that later figures indicate that the economy was seeing some benefit of the changes brought by Heath with, for example, unemployment falling by 1974.

The years of stage one and stage two, 1972 and 1973, showed some improvements in economic performance but the fate of Heath is clearly spelled out in 1974 when stage three, implemented in October 1973, became fully operative. Despite the ban on strikes there were disputes with the gas workers, the civil service, for the first time going on strike, a miners' overtime ban and an ASLEF work to rule. Stage three instituted price controls, placed a wage-increase maximum of £350 per annum or 7 per cent or £2.35 per week whichever was the more acceptable, but exceptions were made for unsocial hours and the like.

Stage three had been announced just two days after the Arab–Israeli War of 1973 broke out. There was an immediate oil crisis and fears about energy crises which would throw the country into an even worse condition than it already was. With renewed industrial conflict through November and December, even though the war had ended, Heath's position began to look increasingly precarious. Such was the severity of the energy crisis and industrial disruption that the government was forced to implement a 'three-day week' in order to save energy. It was brought in on 13 December, in the depths of dark winter, with speed restrictions on motorways of 50 miles per hour, television ending at 10.30 p.m., energy-saving bans on use of floodlights and publicity displays and a raising of the minimum lending rate (successor to the bank rate) to 13 per cent. There soon followed notification of huge cuts in public expenditure amounting to £1,200 million. Heath's policies of expansion and spending were shot to pieces, his Industrial Relations Act was torn apart and the country had been reduced to some part-time twilight existence. The announcement of a miners' strike on 5 February 1974 was the last straw and Heath went to the country two days later announcing an election for 28 February.

Heath's administration, of all recent governments, is one that has been coloured most by the events it endured. Entry to the EEC, an achievement denied his two predecessors, was a major change in British history. The implications, economic and political, have yet to be fully felt by the country. Government reorganization was also a significant achievement as was an extensive taxation reform, and the Housing Finance Act of 1972. The government pursued a policy of selective eligibility for welfare benefits, marking a move away from previous attitudes to the state's role while still maintaining its central function. However, all of this has been swept aside by the industrial strife. Heath's was the first real attempt to tackle the problem of the trade unions and for a time his policy worked. The added burden of the oil crisis and rapidly rising commodity prices proved too much in the end as the unions entered a particularly militant period of their history. Heath will be forever linked to the complete turn-around in policy that was forced on him by necessity. His will always be the government of the U-turn.

It is not surprising that Heath went to the polls with the message of the Conservative campaign being 'Who governs?', and it was generally expected he would win, but the Conservatives suffered badly at the hands of minority groups and especially the reinvigorated Liberals who ended up with 20 per cent in the opinion polls by election day. The campaign of the Liberal leader, Jeremy Thorpe, with its call for moderation, proved a key one in the final result. The Liberals drew away key numbers of Conservative supporters and thus opened the door for the Labour Party. In fact Labour with only 37.1 per cent of the popular vote managed to amass 301 seats with the Conservatives on 37.9 per cent only managing 297 seats. Labour was the biggest party but 34 seats short of an overall majority. The government of Britain was up for grabs and Heath tried for four days to get enough support, on the right terms, to allow him to continue before conceding failure. Harold Wilson thus returned to Number 10 but as a minority Prime Minister and therefore only for a while. However, he made most of the opportunity, knowing that another election would be needed, or forced, in a very short space of time. The miners' dispute was brought to an end with the miners coming out of the whole episode financial gainers. Wilson felt safe in repealing the Industrial Relations Act and dismantling the Heath Government's pay policies. He also put in motion a renegotiation of Britain's entry to the EEC but in doing so created as many problems for his own party, which was deeply divided over the issue, as it did advantages. Although this issue was to raise itself once more in the near future Wilson's priorities were the economy and the unions. Both prices and wages continued to rise, by 8 per cent and 16 per cent respectively in the government's first six months. Worse was the position on the Stock Exchange which saw a sharp fall in share values from March to September, in fact a bigger fall than had been registered in the Great Crash of 1929. Wilson responded with two budgets and the creation of his so-called Social Contract. The latter was designed to win over the unions and cajole them into co-operation in the government's work. The March budget was fierce with tax increases amounting to £1,500 million and very large increases in the costs of coal, steel, electricity and postage all designed to take the strain from the government's finances by reducing subsidies. So severe were its effects that a further, mildly inflationary budget, was needed in July. In the meantime the government tried to work the Social Contract but found themselves faced with railwaymen's and hospital workers' disputes in May and July of 1974.

Despite the economic problems the government announced its intentions of attacking the last vestiges of private medicine in the NHS by abolishing the 'pay-bed' system and also roused Tory anger with a declaration to make the school system fully comprehensive. The opposition did not have to wait long to vent its anger in public. Wilson's 184-day administration was brought to a close in the autumn, with Labour 8 per cent in front in the opinion polls. For a second time in 1974 the public was asked to vote in a general election on 10 October. It was assumed that Labour would win. Wilson had caught the Tories in some disarray and they were, unusually, fighting amongst themselves in public, but the predicted landslide did not materialize for Wilson. The results, when declared, were bitterly disappointing for him. Labour was in government but with a paltry majority of three with 319 MPs ranged against the Conservatives 277 and 39 others.

LABOUR IN POWER 1974–9: WILSON AND CALLAGHAN

Wilson stayed with his Cabinet team for the most part with Healey at the Exchequer, Callaghan at the Foreign Office and Jenkins as Home Secretary. The two female ministers, Barbara Castle and Shirley Williams, were retained as were Michael Foot and Tony Wedgwood Benn. The economy dominated politics with inflation, which was to hit a 27 per cent high in 1975, low productivity, high labour costs, rising unemployment, strain on sterling and further problems with the balance of payments. It is quite right to shy away from those who wish to discuss *the* economic crisis of 1975–6 because in reality there were several. Overlying them all was a crisis of economic faith – were the days of Keynesian-inspired government economic policies over? Certainly as the crises worsened simple reference to Keynesian demand-side policies seemed increasingly unrealistic.

The new government continued to govern with its Industrial Bill, which became law in November 1975, and created National Enterprise Boards which facilitated state intervention in a whole range of businesses. Amongst those involved were Ferranti, Rolls-Royce, British Leyland and Harland & Wolf. The opposition cried out against nationalization 'through the back door' but had to face further threats of state extension in the form of the proposed Aircraft and Shipbuilding Bills. The government also established the British National Oil Corporation and retained a 51 per cent stake in it. In addition the long-awaited Sexual Equality Bill found its way on to the statute book in 1975. The promise to re-evaluate the entry to the EEC was also kept but the end result was more trouble than it was worth and brought out once again the divisions which existed in the Labour Party. These divisions were not only between the party and its main source of support, the trade unions, but also amongst leading proponents of the party itself. The eventual referendum that was granted resulted in a clear majority of the country in favour of staying in – 67.7 per cent against 32.3 per cent on a good turnout. Wilson was forced however to make it a question of conscience in Cabinet, which was split sixteen for and seven against, when ministers were not speaking on government policy from the dispatch box. If it was not an embarrassment then it was a difficult decision time. In April 1975 Denis Healey announced his 'rough and tough' budget. A further 2 pence went on income tax, taking it to 35 pence, a luxury category of VAT was announced at 25 per cent and all duties were raised by substantial amounts, but the government really needed trade-union help. Labour got it in July 1975 with an agreement to a compulsory limit on wage increases of £6 per week for those earning less than £8,500 and nothing for those earning above this figure. It was none too soon as wage increases had been allowed to rocket to 28 per cent above that of the previous year. There was some belief that the government was finally getting the situation under control and the voluntary pay limitation was clearly a good sign if it could be continued. It was felt that 1976 might prove to be a year of recovery despite the continuing jitters in many of the financial markets and institutions. What was not known was that according to his own accounts Harold Wilson had informed the Queen of his intention to leave office in December 1975. The impact of such a move, which eventually came in March 1976, would do little to inspire confidence.

Wilson gave the following reasons for retiring: he had spent thirty years on government and shadow front benches, eleven years in Cabinet, eight years as premier; and the party needed an opportunity for younger blood to be promoted, and a successor given time to impose authority before the next general election. Entirely reasonable as these may be Wilson has, sometimes a little uncharitably, been accused of cutting and running with major political and economic crises looming on the horizon. His last action as Prime Minister, his resignation honours, created furore in the political world and not least amongst his own backbenchers who were outraged by Wilson's use of the list to pay off old debts to all manner of celebrities and business people, many of whose public service activities throughout their lives were not too easy to discern. Given the immediate events following on his resignation, his far from popular press, periodically stoked up by tales of paranoia real or imagined in government, has stayed with him. Certainly he left no easy task for his successor but first of all that person would have to emerge from a party that had increasingly shown its divisions as the years of the 1970s unfolded.

Neither the party nor the country could really afford the diversion of a leadership election but one was necessary. On the first ballot six candidates presented themselves with Michael Foot representing the left of the party coming out ahead of Callaghan by 90 to 86 votes. In the second ballot there were only three survivors with Callaghan beating Foot 141 to 133 and Healey being omitted at a mere 38. In the third and deciding ballot Callaghan amassed 176 to Foot's 137. James Callaghan had become leader of the Labour Party and Prime Minister in one vote. His stout qualities, having had no formal education beyond school, his union background and long experience of both the party and Parliament stood him in good stead. Party intellectuals might sneer a little but his record was impressive. He had pioneered tax reforms while Chancellor in the 1960s and had come back from the dead after devaluation in 1967, serving a very useful rehabilitation period at the Home Office in the meantime and latterly re-emerging as a politician of substance as Foreign Secretary. Callaghan became the only Prime Minister in the twentieth century so far to have held all four of the great offices of state. It was simply unfortunate that his only government would have such an appalling start to its administration and one that heralded even worse to come.

While successive governments had struggled with the seeming irrecon-
cilables of the British economy, failing to arrest decline, and suffering
increases in all the undesirable indicators, the rest of the world had been
looking on. The previous decades' performances of fumble and bumble,
not helped by events beyond the governments' control, it must be admitted, began to concern international markets, investors, institutions and
financiers. The obvious victim of this doubt and uncertainty was going
to be the pound sterling. The government, perhaps bargaining on more
time than it had, decided on three strategies all of which needed trade-
union co-operation. Wage restraint was essential, public spending cuts
necessary, and acceptance of some rise in unemployment simply a fact
of life. These were, however, three unpalatable messages to take to the
trade-union movement but Callaghan and Healey did just this in 1976.
Healey imaginatively even tried to sugar the pill a little in his budget
proposals promising tax cuts if the unions would keep down their
demands. Leaders like the miners' Joe Gormley found the task difficult
and many unions simply rejected the targets the government had in mind.
However, in June a special TUC meeting agreed to 4.5 per cent average
wage increases. It seemed promising but all hopes of restraint and time
for manoeuvre disappeared as the pound came increasingly under pressure on the international markets, ironically started in the first instance
by a Bank of England strategy to sell pounds secretly. Very quickly the
Bank was stepping in to buy back huge amounts of currency to prop up
the pound. However, it was not in England that the solution could be
sought any longer and sterling's fate was in the hands of the currency
dealers. From a level of \$2.024 on 1 January 1976 it fell, and then
plummeted to \$1.637 on 28 September. Confidence in sterling had gone
and with it confidence in Britain and the British government. It would
be necessary to restore that confidence before the government could
even think of tackling the longer term ailments of the British economy.
The crisis in sterling reverberated around the world and also around the
country. With unemployment rising to over 1.5 million and inflation set
to reach 17 per cent before the end of the year the Cabinet was faced
with a difficult decision. It took six weeks and twenty-six cabinet meetings, while rival policies and options were argued through, but in the
end the government agreed to call in the IMF and put together a package.
The final deal involved loans of £3,900 million and was made on the
basis of strict conditions which saw a further £3,000 million expenditure
cuts by the government. With the package the worst of the storm was
over but the government's other worries were more than enough to keep
it on its toes.

The year 1976 was a startling one for political personalities. Wilson
departed political life but so too did Jeremy Thorpe, the Liberal leader,
under a cloud of financial and homosexual innuendoes. David Steel
succeeded Thorpe just as Margaret Thatcher had done the previous year

with Edward Heath. Roy Jenkins resigned as Home Secretary to become President of the EEC, and in February 1977 Foreign Secretary Anthony Crosland died to be succeeded by the 39-year-old Dr David Owen. On a less exalted level 1976 saw two Labour MPs defect to set up a Scottish Labour Party, and by-election losses were suffered at Workington and Walsall North. One economic crisis might have just been weathered but a political crisis was already looming. By January 1977 Labour, with the exclusion of the Speaker and deputies, could count on a majority of one. In a move of some imagination Callaghan set up a Liberal–Labour (Lib–Lab) Pact on 23 March to save the government and its legislation. Neither party wanted a general election. The Pact was straightforward enough with the Liberals getting the right to veto legislation before it reached the House of Commons. Promises were made by the Liberals to support Labour on Europe and devolution, and by Labour to aid Liberal measures on housing and local authorities. It was to last for a session and be reviewed. In fact it was renewed in July 1977. With the Pact in operation, until its end in the summer of 1978, the government could concentrate on other areas of legislation. Even the unions, for the time being at least, appeared to be operating inside the government's pay guidelines.

As with other governments lost in the morass of the economic débâcle of the 1970s, their legislative efforts are often ignored. Callaghan's government did bring in a number of significant bills and see them on to the statute book. The Police Act, setting up the Police Complaints Board, was one. The proposals over 'pay-beds' embodied in the National Health Service Act was another. The Education Act increased the pace of local authority adoption of comprehensive schooling by abolishing selective education. The Race Relations Act, which established the Race Relations Commission, was also passed. Other bills fared less well. The Dock Works Regulation Bill and the Aircraft and Shipbuilding Bill were both mauled in the Commons and the Lords. However, it was in their proposals for devolution that the government met its greatest defeat outside that of the unions and the economy. Devolution, or the decentralization of government so that groups within Britain, notably the Scots and the Welsh, could have some measure of self-government, has a long history in British politics. The renewed interest in the idea in the 1960s and the 1970s was mostly to do with national revival in the areas mentioned and the simple political fact of life that a series of close elections made each MP worth his weight in gold, a fact that had not been lost on the Labour Government in the recent necessity to ally with the Liberals. There was an equally potent counter-argument for keeping the kingdom intact from the point of view of economic and political efficiency, let alone any arguments concerning the potentially damaging effect that devolution might have on the constitution and Parliament's sovereignty. So the issue of devolution was bound to raise the political temperature. A Royal Commission in 1973 had recommended a Scottish Assembly and the 1974 election had seen 30 per cent of the vote in Scotland go to Scottish Nationalist members. From the dalliance of the 1960s, and the breakthroughs in Hamilton in 1967 and Carmarthen in 1966, both the Scottish National Party and Plaid Cymru had apparently become political forces of some weight. Labour's desire to pass a combined devolution bill was abandoned because of the stricture of parliamentary time and opposition to the measure. Separate bills were introduced for Scotland and Wales but with a back-bench proviso that when it came to national referenda a minimum of 40 per cent of those qualified to vote would be necessary for the bills to go forward. When the time came in 1979 Scotland voted 51.6 per cent in favour but the turnout only gave a positive figure of 32 per cent of those entitled to vote. In Wales the story was even worse with a rejection by four to one in the referendum itself. The results were disastrous for the government after spending so much time and energy on the legislation. However, by 1979 the devolution débâcle seemed to count for very little because the government was in the throes of one of the worst industrial disputes since 1926.

The government's policy on incomes had reached its fourth phase and Denis Healey announced in 1978 a 5 per cent limit on pay increases. However, union leaders, notably Jack Jones, soon to retire as leader of the TGWU, had already warned both Healey and Callaghan of the rising mood of militancy amongst their unions' members. Further blows were to come with the Ford workers striking against the government's 5 per cent pay limit and the Labour Conference itself rejecting the limit on 2 October. At the same time the brooding union feeling of being put upon for too long found its voice, and most notably in the shape of Alan Fisher of NUPE and Moss Evans of the TGWU, whose leadership at this time has been criticized by Morgan as both 'unpolitical and unthinking'. The new year opened up with a lorry drivers' claim for a 25 per cent increase soon supported by a separate tanker drivers' claim which was settled at 14 per cent. On 22 January 1.5 million public service workers, including those responsible for water, sewerage and refuse, put in additional claims after a day of action which was followed by six weeks of strikes. Most worrying for the government was the emergence of secondary picketing which Callaghan denounced as 'free collective vandalism' on account of the violence it caused. The public service workers eventually settled for 9 per cent plus £1 per week and by March the government's pay restraint was blown apart. Callaghan had already been the victim of misrepresentation when the newspapers turned his remark of 10 January that 'I do not think other people in the world would share the view that there is mounting chaos', into the more damaging 'Crisis, what Crisis?' There is no doubt that it was the last straw of union lack of restraint that brought the government down. Morgan claims:

Amidst overflowing rubbish bins, closed schools and undug graves the unions destroyed wantonly a government which could hardly have been gentler towards them, and which had steadfastly ruled out statutory restraints on pay or on the internal conduct of union affairs.

(K. O. Morgan, *Labour People. Leaders and Lieutenants: Hardie to Kinnock*, Oxford, Oxford University Press, 1987, p. 273)

The attack was nevertheless sufficient and it brought about a vote of no confidence in the government on 28 March 1979. The vote, amidst scenes rarely seen in the House of Commons, gave the dramatic result of 311 against the government, 310 for. Keeping to the convention Callaghan immediately announced a general election. Callaghan has been blamed repeatedly for rejecting the option of an early election in the autumn of 1978 and thus exposing the party and the country to the 'winter of discontent' which gave the opposition so much ammunition in the coming campaign that would see polling on 3 May. The Tories had a substantial lead, not unexpectedly, and their campaign was a safe one with no errors being made. The middle ground, especially for the nationalist parties, shrank and on a turnout of 76 per cent Margaret Thatcher became the first female Prime Minister when Callaghan conceded defeat early on 4 May. The Conservative overall majority would be forty-three and the tasks facing them severe with many outstanding problems to be settled before reconstruction could even hope to begin. What sort of reconstruction is still very much in the realm of the present and how far the Thatcher era has taken Britain and in what direction remains to be seen.

IRELAND 1922–90

In 1922 Ireland became a dominion but this still meant she retained links with Britain and the Empire. The aftermath of the Great War, let alone the Irish 'civil war', necessitated a continued relationship between the two countries. Economic difficulties tended to place political differences in perspective and for most of the rest of the 1920s and the 1930s Anglo-Irish relations never reached the same peak of public interest and concern as they had done in the years immediately before and after the First World War.

Part of the problem was that the Irish electorate had been wooed by the so-called 'Soldiers of Destiny' or Fianna Fail. The latter had settled its differences over the oath of loyalty and had taken its seats in the Dail, the Irish Parliament, in 1927. Fianna Fail was hardly pro-British, but there were political groups within southern Ireland that were and it was to these that British politicians turned for a maintenance of Anglo-Irish relations. When the more placatory government of W. T. Cosgrave was replaced by Eamon de Valera's Fianna Fail party in 1932 the chances of the symbolic constitutional bond between England and Ireland surviving very much longer seemed slim. De Valera was keen to make the distinction that although southern Ireland was in the Commonwealth she was definitely not 'of it'. A period of economic 'war' then followed with de Valera refusing to pay annuities due to England under the old land purchase acts, England retaliating with 20 per cent duties on Irish goods and de Valera responding with his own protectionist programme. With the return of de Valera's government in 1933 he put in motion constitutional revisions which would supplant the existing arrangements. The task was a lengthy one and took until 1937. Britain found no great support for her position, and some sympathy for Ireland, amongst the Commonwealth and Empire.

With the constitutional crisis of Edward VIII's abdication fresh in the memory and European affairs paramount Britain was keen to settle the Irish issue quickly. The Anglo-Irish talks of January to April 1938 were designed to find a final settlement. Three areas were tackled: the return of naval bases to the Irish government, an ending to the economic war between the two countries and trade agreements which favoured Irish goods over English ones. De Valera had effectively ended the 1921 Treaty between the two countries but although he had secured the greater sovereignty of the southern state the position of the northern one, and that of Ireland as a whole, was not much clearer. It had been hoped that the 1938 agreement would provide the springboard for negotiations between the south and the north but neither seemed inclined to use it.

De Valera's success, to a certain extent, sparked the more nationalist and extremist groups in the south once again. The IRA reactivated its campaigns of violence and in 1939–40 there was a series of bombings in England with five killed in Coventry. Two IRA men were hanged in 1940 under the Prevention of Violence (Special Provisions) Act of 1939. De Valera was not too pleased either and during the war the south interned 400 IRA men. This was mainly because the Irish government feared that their actions, if left unpunished, would compromise Ireland's neutrality. However, with the end of the war in 1945 and, more importantly, the granting of independence to India in 1947, the Irish government also decided to leave the Commonwealth declaring its own independence in 1948. The British government replied with the 1949 Ireland Act which stated that Northern Ireland remained part of the United Kingdom and would only cease to do so with the consent of the Province's Parliament. These events simply made even more rigid the divide which existed between north and south. Moreover, they prompted nationalist groups to renew their efforts to bring Ireland together in a single nation.

IRELAND IN THE YEARS OF CONSENSUS

In the 1950s and after it was the position of Northern Ireland and the maintenance of the union, effectively preventing a united Ireland, that predominated in Anglo-Irish relations. The euphoria of independence for the south was not enough for many nationalists. They still looked to the Catholic minorities in the north from the safe haven of an incomplete but free Ireland in the south. What they saw struck them as being far from comforting and distinctly unfair. The Catholic minorities were in an unenviable position. They were prejudiced against in housing and jobs and also suffered the iniquities of 'gerrymandering' which manipulated Catholic votes in local elections to ensure that they enjoyed only minority representation on councils even where Catholics predominated. In addition these groups also suffered, on occasions, the heavy-handed attention of the RUC and the B-Specials. It is not surprising then that the IRA and its political wing, Sinn Fein, turned its attention towards the north. In 1955 Sinn Fein secured a meagre 155,000 votes in the elections and had already declared its intention of not taking up its seats – 'abstentionism'. Even so these results were interpreted as sufficient support for the launching of a new campaign of violence that ran from 1956 to 1962. Relying on the old-fashioned 'flying squad' tactics of the 1920s and attacks on customs posts the IRA campaign was notable for its lack of success. In the north it was met with some indifference and in the south it prompted the government to reinstate internment. The IRA seemed to have run out of ideas and support. However, just when it was likely that the movement would disappear two events came rushing to the rescue. The first was inside the IRA itself. In 1962 a new leadership built around Cathal Goulding and Roy Johnstone emerged, and it was these two men who tried to re-fashion the IRA with an appeal to all working-class groups in the Province and an end to abstentionism. The movement took a distinctly left-wing turn and began to adopt socialist and Marxist ideas and rhetoric. The latter was more than many old hands, such as Joe Cahill and Sean MacStiophain, could take. Thus began the feud which would see the IRA split, in 1969, into the official wing and the Provisional Council or 'Provos'. The second event was the great outburst of civil rights campaigning that had started in the United States and was soon, in the 1960s, to spread to the whole of Europe including Northern Ireland.

It was reportedly Lord Brookborough, Prime Minister of the Province from 1943–63, who claimed that he would never employ a Catholic 'in whatever capacity'. The disabilities suffered by the Catholic minority were well known and it was Paul Rose, in 1965, who organized the Campaign for Democracy in Ulster and affiliated it in the same year to the National Council for Civil Liberties. It was out of this movement that the Northern Ireland Civil Rights Association (NICRA) grew which called for British standards of social justice in the Province. In fact, the Province's Prime Minister, Terence O'Neill (1963–9), had been trying to gain a greater voice for the Catholic minority but with little success. His efforts were to be overwhelmed by the reaction to the events of the

Derry Civil Rights march of October 1968. This was dispersed by the RUC in the presence of a number of Labour MPs. It was at this stage that Harold Wilson stepped in and instructed O'Neill to find a solution which he failed to do. In the spring and summer of 1969 violence erupted in Derry and Belfast and convinced the Labour leader that if Stormont could not keep the peace then Westminster would have to do so for it. On 14 August there was more massive destruction and the loss of six lives and two days later British troops were ordered into the Province. These events also saw the completion of the break in the IRA between the 'official' and 'provisional' wings of the movement.

Wilson's decision has been criticized. First, he suggested by it that a solution could be found by Westminster which was far from the truth. Second, he humiliated the Province's politicians by implying that they could not cope. Third, he gave a massive boost to the IRA who could portray the move as another English affront to Irish nationalism.

The 1970s started off with the formation of a new political party representing the views of Catholic minority interests – the SDLP – the Social Democratic Labour Party. There were attempts in the Province to use this new group as a political safety valve. Brian Faulkner, who replaced O'Neill as Prime Minister, tried to create a voice for it by offering it four cabinet committees. However, these moves were overrun by the fast changing and violent scene on the streets. The IRA killed its first British soldier of the Troubles in February 1971 and a further 175 people were destined to be killed that year with a further 400 losing their lives in 1972. While the IRA fought its corner for the nationalists the Loyalists could rely on the Ulster Defence Force (UDF) which had been murdering Catholics since 1966, before the Troubles of this era began. Just as the IRA was to be joined later by the even more extreme Irish National Liberation Army (INLA) so the UDF would spawn the Ulster Freedom Fighters (UFF). The level of sectarian violence forced the SDLP out of Stormont and by this time Wilson's Government had been replaced by that of Heath.

Reginald Maudling, Conservative Home Secretary, set part of the tone for the years 1970–2. It was after all he who voiced the concept of 'acceptable levels of violence' and exclaimed on leaving Belfast after a visit, 'What a bloody awful place'. Violence became second nature with the McGurk's Bar bomb in December 1971 which killed 15 Catholics. This was followed by a Civil Rights March on 30 January, in defiance of a ban, which became known as 'Bloody Sunday' and some have termed it 'Ireland's Sharpville'. Thirteen people were killed by troops and the IRA took reprisals with the bombing of the Parachute Regiment's barracks in Aldershot in the same year. It was these events which persuaded Ted Heath to take stronger actions, and in 1972 Parliament passed the Northern Ireland (Temporary Provisions) Act which suspended Stormont for a year in the first instance. However, what it effectively did was bring to an end the Stormont era and usher in the phase of 'direct rule' with William Whitelaw in control in the Province. It was never intended for 'direct rule' to become the norm but for this to be a means to an end, the end being a solution to the Troubles. Intense negotiations followed with meetings at Darlington, County Durham in July 1972 and at Sunningdale in 1973. A plebiscite had already shown that 57.4 per cent of the total electorate in the Province was in favour of continuing the Union. While talks and plans proliferated the violence was never very far away. 1972 had already seen the creation of special category prisoners but the IRA's hold was firm and July 1973 saw 'Bloody Friday' that involved the detonation of 20 bombs in Belfast which killed 11 and injured 120. Ten days later, on 31 July, 'Operation Motorman' was launched by the security forces which saw troops occupying the so-called 'no-go' areas. In this tense atmosphere the Sunningdale Agreement of December 1973 emerged and it would become the basis of the ill-fated plans of January 1974. The agreement suggested that Ulster be left to govern itself, that Britain retain its security role and that Dublin be brought into play as a member of a Council for Ireland. On 1 January 1974 'direct rule' theoretically ended but this was more a triumph of hope than reality. The Executive thus established lasted just a year. Fears of betrayal in unionists' minds, as Britain countenanced co-operation with the south, resulted in damaging and disruptive strikes throughout the Province.

1974 did not see any improvement at all and the change of government in that year mattered little to Ireland. Merlyn Rees, the new Labour spokesman on Ireland, pursued the power-sharing line as an extension of the Conservative idea and the response was much the same with the Ulster Workers' Council continuing to organize damaging strikes. Worse was to follow with the IRA taking the campaign to the mainland and this year saw the Birmingham Pub Bombings and the outraged government's response of the Prevention of Terrorism Act. Attempts to provide a forum for discussion with an Irish Convention were soured by the government's recognition of the IRA and the move into an uneasy and violent period of 'truce'. This move, although motivated by good intentions, undermined the role of the far less militant SDLP and struck the Unionists as the clearest of signs that the government was not to be trusted. Little progress was made inside or outside the Convention discussions which collapsed in 1976 without success and once again other problems piled on top of the Labour Government in the late 1970s. Uneasy though the situation was it seemed politic to let well enough alone for the most part. However, in 1979 the Callaghan Government did commit itself to increasing Ulster representation at Westminster but thoughts of a government deal with the Ulster Unionists was too much for one MP, Gerry Fitt. It was Fitt who was to absent himself in the crucial vote of no confidence that the government would lose by one, thus causing the general election that brought Margaret Thatcher into Number 10. Not for the first time Irish politics had a profound effect on the British people.

IRELAND IN THE THATCHER YEARS

The Conservative Prime Minister in 1979 inherited a legacy of IRA success in the 1970s. The IRA had succeeded on a number of levels. After the in-fighting of the late 1960s the apparently disparate and weakened groups that emerged should have presented little threat to the authorities. However, the emergence of the 'Provos' as a terrorist force of great commitment and sacrifice ensured that the cause of a united Ireland would not die. British governments, both in 1972 and 1975, had conspired to give the organization some 'legitimacy' by negotiating with it. The so-called 'truces' which emerged from the negotiations were short-lived but appeared to 'recognize' the organization as an entity. The IRA's activities both in Northern Ireland and mainland Britain brought reactions from the British governments that were tailor-made for publicity purposes.

The creation of 'special category' prisoners in 1972 enabled the imprisoned IRA to claim a certain notoriety. Merlyn Rees's removal of this status led IRA members to launch a variety of campaigns. 'Going to the blanket', or a refusal to wear prison uniform, was supplanted later in the 1970s by 'the dirty campaign' where inmates and cells were smeared with excrement. The mainland bombing campaign against both military and so-called 'soft' civilian targets had been supplemented by individual political assassination including that of Mrs Thatcher's close political confidante Airey Neave in March 1979. This was followed in August by the even more shocking Lord Mountbatten murder. These activities had brought a dual response with successive governments in the 1970s trying to establish the 'power-sharing' concept in the Province. At least this line appeared to have the possibility of some mileage in it as opposed to the other options of withdrawal, independence or Civil War all which were untenable, unthinkable or simply impossible. While politicians negotiated, the increasingly murky world of the security forces and clandestine operations saw 'acceptable levels of violence' escalate.

Mrs Thatcher's dual approach consisted of a strong line on the IRA and the pursuit of a political solution. In fact much the same tactics as previous Prime Ministers. The 1981 Hunger Strikers of the Maze prison, led by Bobby Sands, once again placed Northern Ireland and the IRA's cause on the front pages of the world's press. From March to August, Sands' life ebbed away and he was joined in a martyr's death by 10 other members of the IRA. Sternly resolute with 'the men of violence' Mrs Thatcher pursued negotiations with Garret FitzGerald the Republic's Prime Minister. The Anglo-Irish Inter-Governmental Council was established after their third summit meeting in November 1981 in London. It was left to James Prior, who had responsibility for the Province in the Cabinet, to put the plans for a new Northern Ireland Assembly into operation in 1982. At the same time Mrs Thatcher was also talking with the Irish leader Charles Haughey but any hopes of a helping hand from this direction in the development of policy were spiked by the aftermath of the hunger strikes, increasing economic difficulties in the north and south both in part related to Mrs Thatcher's own unbending approach to economic problems, and the south's refusal to toe the European line and apply economic sanctions on Argentina. The elections for the new Assembly in the north were a great disappointment for the British. One third of Catholics voted for Sinn Fein with their 'gun and ballot' slogan and the Reverend Ian Paisley's unofficial Democratic Unionists polled better than the Official Unionist Party as the north rapidly gravitated to the political extremes once again. Moreover, the SDLP and Sinn Fein both refused to take up their seats in the new Assembly and the expectations of 1981 gave way to the disappointments of 1982. Violence entered a new phase at this stage with ever more audacious attacks in the Province and on the mainland. It was not just the launching of new waves of widespread bombing, as with the London campaign in 1982 with the Hyde Park atrocity, but the almost disastrously successful Brighton Tory Party Conference bombing in October 1984. The government response was to step up counter-insurgency measures and build on the Prevention of Terrorism Act of 1974 which allowed the security forces to detain any suspected terrorist. Soon to follow would be the attempts to gag the IRA and Sinn Fein with bans on press and television coverage. On a more controversial note there were also accusations against the security forces in the 1980s of the operation of a 'shoot to kill' policy. Although denied the accusations have survived, effectively unanswered claim its proponents, despite the many reports and inquiries. In fact the whole question itself gave rise to yet other embarrassments and scandals for the Thatcher Government with the Stalker inquiry which eventually led to John Stalker himself being ignominiously removed from his investigations before his findings could be confirmed and published.

In this inauspicious climate of hate, suspicion and violence another initiative was launched with the 1983–5 New Irish Forum. Another Inter-Governmental summit was called but no real progress was made although it was now clear that 'power sharing' in the Province between Protestant and Catholic would have to be supplemented, if not replaced, by some form of joint control. The Brighton bombing was a reminder of the fact that not every group approved of such fraternization. A third summit followed at Hillsborough Castle, Belfast but the substance of the talks, which ranged over issues such as Ireland being given a consultative role in Northern Irish affairs, the retention of majority rule in the Province and the extent of British government financial assistance were such that it was unlikely to reach any firm conclusions. If anything the talks tended to confirm Unionists' fears and add to their feelings of being betrayed by the Conservative Government as their union was, so they felt, being negotiated away from under them by the very people who ought to be protecting it. Since 1985 little has changed and the government has retained its convictions over power sharing and consultative roles but its policies have been viewed with much scepticism by many groups. More worrying, in the increasingly complex world of Northern Ireland, was a new development in 1986 that saw loyalist groups murdering members of the RUC. Its Catholic counterpart was the internal power struggles within the INLA which have seen many murders and a break-off IPLA (Irish People's Liberation Army) in 1987. As the Thatcher era closed yet another initiative was under way with Peter Brooke, Secretary of State for Northern Ireland, involved in the 'talks about talks' in 1990. These too, like all other attempts to get a solution faltered and finally collapsed. In the meantime the violence has continued. There have been further instances of political assassinations with Ian Gow, the Conservative MP, falling victim to the IRA in the summer of 1990. Yet another 'near miss' audacious attack on the very centre of British political power took place in February 1991 when the new Prime Minister John Major, along with his Cabinet colleagues, found himself the target of an IRA rocket-launcher attack. Although Number 10 remained intact, as did the political leaders, the missiles got as far as the garden beyond the Prime Minister's residence. By this time the government was also facing the scandal of 'un-sound' convictions of a number of suspected IRA members who were imprisoned for their part in the bombing campaigns of the 1970s. 1991 saw the release from custody of the so-called Birmingham Six and Guildford Four. Both events were extremely embarrassing for the government in its Anglo-Irish policies.

The terror campaigns are far from over and the talking, although halted, has been interrupted rather than drawn to a conclusion. However, the parties involved seem as far away from reaching a solution as ever. Any further initiatives in the 1990s and beyond will have to buck the course of several centuries of bloody history if a solution to Ireland's affairs and problems is to be found.

CONSENSUS AND CONTROVERSY

Although this chapter commenced with an outline of what consensus politics was, the issues and events identified were meant to be a convenient rule of thumb for appraisal of an era in British political history. Consensus itself is controversial and few commentators mention it without justification, qualification or refutation. Kavanagh and Morris have noted a basic dilemma:

There is a problem about using the term consensus as a synonym for cross-party agreement. After all, disagreement about ends and means is the life blood of politics. Political disagreement arises inevitably from human diversity and the clash of individual and group interests. Politics is the activity of reconciling, in a fashion, these differences and establishing a common policy for society. An obvious problem follows: the idea of consensus is at odds with political activity. Was nothing at stake in general elections, were different party programmes false labels, was the party clash little more than a cover for rival personal ambitions?
(Kavanagh and Morris, op. cit., p. 10)

Increasingly presidential though British politics was to become in this era it was not merely about personal ambitions. The point about consensus is that it was underpinned in the political parties by a general agreement about their political goals even if their policies did not appear to show this. Kavanagh and Morris give a perfect example of this:

In the area of secondary education, the wartime Education Act (1944) inaugurated a tripartite system – grammar, secondary modern and technical schools. The 1945 Labour Government did not abolish private education or press ahead with comprehensive schools, as left-wingers wanted. The tripartite system dominated until 1964, when the Labour Government switched to support of comprehensives. Labour introduced an order in 1965 making comprehensive schooling mandatory, by insisting that all local authorities submit plans for reorganization. The new Conservative Government withdrew the order in 1970, leaving the decision about reorganization with the local authorities. Labour reimposed the order on its return to office in 1974, and the new Conservative Government in 1979 withdrew it again. On the surface, policy has clearly been discontinuous, according to which party is in office. Yet by 1979 more than 90 per cent of secondary schools were comprehensive and over a period of more than 20 years the largest number of such schools was actually created under a Conservative minister of education, Margaret Thatcher (1970–4).
(ibid., pp. 11–12)

Marxists have tended to agree with Ralph Miliband who claims that:

One of the most important aspects of the political life of advanced capitalism is precisely that the disagreements *between those political leaders who have genuinely been able to gain high office* have very seldom been the fundamental kind these leaders and other people so often suggest. What is really striking . . . is not their many differences but the extent of their agreement on truly fundamental issues. (Miliband's emphasis)
(R. Miliband, *The State in Capitalist Society*, London, Weidenfeld & Nicolson, 1969, p. 69)

However, this is not to say that the case is closed on consensus because there are those whose opinions differ. One such is Tony Benn who will admit consensus's existence but prefers to think in terms of periods of consensus with his third stage, which runs from 1945 to 1976, being that of 'welfare capitalist consensus'. Others, such as David Marquand, prefer to see consensus not as some era in its own right but simply part of a more general twentieth-century trend that can be linked back to the Liberal Yellow Book of 1928 (see chapter 6), and even before that.

Those who try to distance themselves from the idea of consensus ever having existed follow in Ben Pimlott's footsteps. He emphasizes the high level of party identification in the 1950s and 1960s with its clear grounding in class-based voting as examples of party differences as opposed to agreements. Furthermore, he stresses that politicians of the time thought they were divided on fundamental issues, which is a point shared with Michael Fraser:

> In a fundamental sense, there must always be a good deal of common ground between the main parties alternating in government in a free society. When in power, after all, they are governing the same country, with the same history, people, problems and elbow-room, or lack of it, within the same world. Because the two main parties coming out of the coalition government in 1945 had already hammered out, not without some hard bargaining and horse-trading, the broad policies for dealing after the war with those social problems that had been identified and prepared for during the war on the basis of the Beveridge Report, the Employment Policy White Paper and the Butler Education Act of 1944, there was for a time an unusual degree of apparent unity of aim. To say, however, that the situation after 1945 amounted to a 'consensus' is a myth of more recent origin. No one thought that at the time. The real position was like that of two trains, starting off from parallel platforms at some great London terminus and running for a time on broadly parallel lines but always heading for very different destinations.
>
> (In P. Hennessey and A. Seldon (eds), *Ruling Performance, British Governments from Attlee to Thatcher*, Oxford, Blackwell, 1989, p. 310)

Part of the problem surely lies in the fact that although the bases of post-war consensus, or at least the parties travelling together on parallel tracks, have been debunked, their influence and heritage continues to exist. Hence, all attempts to define this era are coloured by the era itself. If agreement between parties did not exist then similarities did. These may have been deemed hidden, or implicit, consensus by one set of analysts and clear and overt consensus by others. There seems, however, little doubt that there were some shared similarities, if only from the point of view of goals; that both parties also shared styles of government;

and, though rarely mentioned, that both had to work with a civil service brought up in the same era that produced consensus – the national effort to win the war. There were certainly more dynamic forces pushing British politics towards consensus than there were driving it apart in the years 1945–79. If that is sufficient to justify the term then consensus existed. Thus, many might endorse Vernon Bogdanor's assessment below:

> Compared with any previous thirty-year period – say 1915–1945, or 1885–1915 – the three decades following the Second World War are remarkable for their continuity. It seemed as if the world was standing still. Not only were the issues broadly the same at every general election – the management of the economy and the development of the welfare state – but it was agreed that these aims were to be secured through a social democratic consensus which provided for a mixed economy and for the provision of universal social benefits. Keynes and Beveridge, the underwriters of this settlement, had helped to create a type of politics in which incremental management was the key to success, and ideology – whether Bevanite or Powellite – the road to ruin. Thus, while the political struggle appeared to be between a socialist and a capitalist party, in reality the central issue from 1945 to 1974 was who could manage the mixed economy-cum-welfare state most effectively. The ideological underpinning was rhetorical, not real.
>
> (*The Contemporary Record*, vol. 1, no. 2 (Summer 1987))

BIBLIOGRAPHY

For an explanation of the grading system, see the preface p. xiii.

Biographies

Clement Attlee

3   Burridge, T., *Clement Attlee: A Political Biography*, London, Cape, 1985
3   Harris, K., *Attlee*, London, Weidenfeld & Nicolson, 1982

Aneurin Bevan

3   Campbell, J., *Nye Bevan and the Mirage of British Socialism*, London, Weidenfeld & Nicolson, 1987
3   Foot, M., *Aneurin Bevan, Vol. II 1945–1960*, London, Davis Poynter, 1973

R. A. Butler

3   Howard, A., *RAB: The Life of R. A. Butler*, London, Cape, 1987

Jim Callaghan

2   Kellner, P. and Hitchens, C., *Callaghan: The Road to Number 10*, London, Cassell, 1976

Winston Churchill

3/4   Seldon, A., *Churchill's Indian Summer: The Conservative Government 1951–55*, London, Hodder & Stoughton, 1981

Alec Douglas-Home

Home, Lord, *The Way the Wind Blows*, London, Collins, 1976

Anthony Eden

3   Carlton, S., *Anthony Eden*, London, Allen Lane, 1981
3   Eden, A., *Full Circle*, London, Cassell, 1960
2/3   James, R. R., *Anthony Eden*, London, Weidenfeld & Nicolson, 1986

Michael Foot

3   Foot M., *Debts of Honour*, London, Pan, 1981
2/3   Hoggart, S. and Leigh, D., *Michael Foot: A Portrait*, London, Hodder & Stoughton, 1981

Hugh Gaitskell

2/3   Haseler, S., *The Gaitskellers: Revisionism in the British Labour Party 1951–1964*, London, Macmillan, 1969
2/3   Rodgers, W. T. (ed.), *Hugh Gaitskell 1906–1963*, London, Thames & Hudson, 1964

Joe Gormley

2   Gormley, J., *Battered Cherub*, London, Hamish Hamilton, 1982

Denis Healey

3   Healey, D., *The Time of My Life*, London, Michael Joseph, 1989

Edward Heath

3   Laing, M., *Edward Heath: Prime Minister*, London, Sidgwick & Jackson, 1972

Jack Jones

2   Jones, J., *Union Man: The Autobiography of Jack Jones*, London, Collins, 1986

Harold Macmillan

2/3   Fisher, N., *Harold Macmillan: A Biography*, London, Weidenfeld & Nicolson, 1982
3/4   Horne, A., *Harold Macmillan 1894–1956 and 1956–*, London, Macmillan, 1988–90
2/3   Macmillan, H., *At the End of the Day*, London, Weidenfeld & Nicolson, 1986

Reginald Maudling

> Maudling, R., *Memoirs*, London, Sidgwick & Jackson, 1978

Harold Wilson

3   Wilson, H., *Memoirs 1916–1964: The Making of a Prime Minister*, London, Weidenfeld & Nicolson, 1986

3   Wilson, H., *The Labour Government 1964–1970: A Personal Memoir*, London, Weidenfeld & Nicolson, 1986

3   Wilson, H., *Final Term: The Labour Government of 1974–1976*, London, Weidenfeld & Nicolson, 1979

General texts

There has always been a lot of material on this period of British political history simply as a consequence of the vast amount of information that is stored away on modern policy decision-making, especially since the war. This has given rise to a large number of interesting and useful texts on the period. The Macmillan series on modern British elections is a fund of information and analysis. These texts run from 1955 to the present day compiled by a variety of authors, with Butler, Rose and Kavanagh being the most prominent. Besides this, Vernon Bogdanor and Robert Skidelsky's *The Age of Affluence 1951–1964* (London, Macmillan, 1974) is a good general text covering most of the era in question. Other useful studies include: R. Blake, *The Conservative Party from Peel to Thatcher* (London, Methuen, 1985); D. Boyce, *The Irish Question and British Politics 1968–1986* (London, Macmillan, 1988); D. Butler, *General Elections Since 1945* (Oxford, Blackwell, 1989); J. Harris, *Politics of Power* (London, Cape, 1977); M. Harrison, *Trade Unions and the Labour Party Since 1945* (London, Allen & Unwin, 1960); P. Hennessey and A. Seldon, *Ruling Performance* (Oxford, Blackwell, 1989); D. Kavanagh and P. Morris, *Consensus Politics from Attlee to Thatcher* (Oxford, Blackwell, 1989); B. Lapping, *The Labour Government 1964–1970* (Harmondsworth, Penguin, 1970); K. Laybourn, *The Rise of Labour: The British Labour Party 1890–1979* (London, Arnold, 1988).

Sources for coursework

There is a mass of material for the student who wishes to delve into modern British political history. There are several political memoirs including the ministerial diaries of Richard Crossman, Tony Benn and Barbara Castle which cover the latter period up to the 1970s. These complement such memoirs as Harold Evans's *Downing Street Diary: The Macmillan Years 1957–1963* (London, Hodder & Stoughton, 1981). Prime ministerial memoirs are also useful although not always reliable. Macmillan's, in the form of Horne's biography, is monumental but selective. Wilson's should be treated with some caution as should James Callaghan's *Time and Chance* (London, Collins, 1987), but Denis Healey's autobiography gives some balance to the Labour governments.

F. W. S. Craig's *British General Election Manifestos 1900–1975* (London, Macmillan, 1975) is a fund of contemporary party political thinking, prejudice and interest. In addition, most national newspapers of the day are available at reference libraries and local newspapers help reveal how parochial Britain viewed world events.

13 Thatcher's Britain – one hundred and twenty years on: 1979–90

INTRODUCTION

Of the 322 million people of the EC 56.5 million lived in the United Kingdom in the late 1980s. It was the third most populous country after Germany and Italy. Whereas the population of Britain had quadrupled in the nineteenth century the increase in the twentieth century to date has been less than 50 per cent. Life expectancy within the British Isles differed not very dramatically from the rest of Western Europe: at 77.2 years for females (1985) it was slightly better than Germany and slightly worse than France. Males, whilst having only 71.4 years to look forward to, had at least the consolation of knowing that they were slightly better off than French and German males. The rise in life expectation is probably the most significant change of the twentieth century. As pointed out in chapter 5 it was a mere 48 years for men in 1901 – almost identical to life expectation in Tanzania in 1985. In consequence of this change the age structure of the 1990s is very different. Over 20 per cent of the population is now over sixty compared to a mere 8 per cent in 1901. Those over eighty are now significantly increasing with considerable implications for health expenditure.

Another change in the population structure worth commenting on lies in the increase in those of new commonwealth origin. In 1950 they amounted to only 0.5 per cent of the population. By 1987 they were 5 per cent. Of this 5 per cent the largest group was from the Indian sub-continent. The second largest group was from the West Indies. The first black MPs for fifty years were elected in 1987, amongst them the first black female, and the presence of players of West Indian extraction in major international teams representing England is a marked development over the recent past.

The population shift from the old industrial areas of the north during the inter-war years has already been emphasized in chapter 9. By 1985 almost one in three lived in the south-east. With Britain's entry to the EEC the already well-developed shift in economic emphasis southwards was strengthened, but also a pull to the east has been clearly noticeable.

East Anglia has had the fastest growing population whereas ports like Liverpool have entered what appears to be terminal decline. Felixstowe has become a boom town with a vast container traffic. North Sea oil and gas and the boom in cereal production have added to the prosperity of the east. In all regions inner cities have decayed and suburban villages expanded. The vast increase in road facilities has been quickly saturated with the even more sensational expansion of car ownership. The motorway network completed since 1959 has cemented the country together even more firmly than the rail network of the nineteenth century.

In general those industries in decline in the inter-war years have continued to shrink often to minuscule proportions. The mighty ship-building industries of Edwardian Britain seem to have all but expired. Even in 1940 Britain was still the world's leading producer with 38 per cent of the global total. By 1977 it was 4 per cent and by 1980 output had halved again. Coal employing one million in 1914 was much depleted by the late 1980s despite the start of new high technology mines like Selby. In 1980 the National Coal Board had 232,000 employees. By 1987 it was 108,000 and shrinking. Textiles remained a substantial employer but woollens and man-made fibres predominated over cottons. Iron and steel producers have had very mixed fortunes. In the immediate post-war world they enjoyed the benefits of little foreign competition and in 1950 Britain produced 10 per cent of world output. By 1980 it was down to 1.6 per cent and British steel producers seemed the most inefficient outside the Soviet Union. Since then there has been a major shake out and productivity has increased. The new industries of the inter-war years have, like iron and steel, enjoyed mixed fortunes. Chemicals and even electrical manufacture have survived and grown but the car industry, the spearhead of the post-war economy, has suffered serious shrinkage with crises developing in the 1970s. British productivity lagged seriously behind her competitors. In 1973 British plants identical to those on the Continent were noticeably less efficient. The British Ford plant needed 67 per cent more labour than its twin in Germany to produce the Escort. Poor work practices reflected badly on British management and workers. There was a steady penetration of the home market by foreign imports. Their share was 5 per cent in 1965, 58 per cent by 1982. The British motorbike industry actually died.

Clearly there were some winners in this economic lottery. Agriculture, depressed since the 1870s boomed in the 1970s. The new oil industry has made an enormous contribution to the economy. The first oil came ashore in 1975 and by 1981 it was meeting all home needs and provided a small export surplus. Many thousands of jobs were created, particularly in Scotland. Despite the loss of her early world lead in computers, their manufacture and development still provided a growth area in the 1970s and 1980s, concentrated in the Thames valley and around Bristol. In Scotland 'Silicon Glen' in Fife was a northern outpost of the high-tech revolution.

Overall the percentage of the population engaged in manufacturing and mining slumped from 39 per cent in 1950 to 24 per cent in 1981. The numbers engaged in the service sector have risen. By 1984 more than twice as many were involved in service industries, 13.4 million, compared to manufacturing, 5.4 million. Much more than when Napoleon made his observation Britain in the late twentieth century was a nation of shop-keepers or to be more accurate a nation of sales assistants. Banking and financial services continued to be important and although by the late twentieth century London had been pushed into third place behind New York and Tokyo it remained one of the great financial centres of the world, earning billions for the country. It was, however, the state and local government not supermarkets and the City which were the major service employers.

Despite relative economic decline and all the changes just outlined almost all Britons in the late twentieth century were massively richer than their grandparents in the inter-war years. The GDP per head almost doubled between 1950 and 1987. Television became universal with 96 per cent of households having one by 1981 and most people spent nearly as much time watching television in the late twentieth century as working. The average female viewer watched 30 hours 38 minutes a week in 1986. Second only to the television in transforming lifestyle, for good or ill, was the car. By 1985 64 per cent of households had one. Both television and the car privatized life compared to the inter-war years. The silver screen was now available in everyone's home rather than at the people's palaces – the cinemas. The private car replaced public transport. The family could be physically isolated as never before but paradoxically less mentally isolated.

If almost all were better off wealth distribution remained very uneven. Admittedly 64 per cent owned their own home by 1987, a staggering transformation in the century as a whole. Even share ownership was more widespread with 20 per cent owning shares in 1987 compared to only 7 per cent in 1950. In general the trend of the twentieth century has been to greater equality: for example, the top 1 per cent owned 60.9 per cent of wealth in 1923 but only 31.7 per cent of it in 1972. The top 10 per cent's share has fallen less dramatically from 89.1 per cent to 70.4 per cent in the same period. The publication *Social Trends* summarizes the situation:

> The late 1970s and early 1980s brought very little change to the pattern of ownership of marketable wealth. The distribution of marketable wealth *plus* occupational and state pension rights saw a movement towards less inequality in the early and mid-1970s, but since 1977 there has been little change.

(1987, p. 99)

There has been a slight evening-out of incomes since the war but the chief redistribution has been from the very rich to the rich. Since 1976 there has been a slight change to greater inequality:

> The distribution of final income shows a similar small increase in inequality between 1976 and 1984, with the share of the bottom 40 per cent of households falling nearly 1 percentage point from 20.1 to 19.2 per cent compared with an increase in the share of the top 20 per cent from 37.9 to 39.0 per cent.
>
> (ibid., p. 98)

Inequalities in wealth are reflected in inequalities in health and education. In 1980 the risk of death before retirement for unskilled workers was 7.5 times greater than for professionals. The professional classes continue to dominate places in higher education. In the sense that there is a smaller percentage of unskilled manual workers Britain is a more equal society but the unskilled continue to be relatively poor. The welfare state has apparently done little to reduce inequalities. One report from the DHSS in 1980, *Inequalities in Health*, under the Chairmanship of Sir Douglas Black argued that health inequality had widened under the National Health Service. The chief beneficiaries have been the middle classes and their professional counterparts although it is clear that many of working-class origin secured a leg-up via the new opportunities of the post-war world.

Education in fact remains one of the areas of relative national failure. Britain continues to educate a small elite well and neglect the broad mass. Despite the vast increase in educational spending a smaller percentage of the age cohort stays on in Britain for post-16 education than in most advanced economies.

> While the United States has 89 per cent of its 16–18 years olds in full-time education, Japan 69 per cent and France 58 per cent, our figure of 33 per cent puts us into a bleak economic position. All political parties now agree on the need for a better educated and skilled workforce.
>
> (*The Independent*, 1990)

The complaint of comparative educational failure depressingly echoes that of the Duke of Devonshire in 1900 (see chapter 3, p. 101).

THE CHANGING POLITICAL STRUCTURE

If the problems facing governments often persist the change in the scale and scope of government itself is truly staggering. The Report of the Kilbrandon Committee on the constitution in 1973 found:

> The cumulative effect of government expansion on people's lives and activities has been considerable. The individual a hundred years ago

hardly needed to know that the central government existed. His birth, marriage and death would be registered, and he might be conscious of the safeguards for his security provided by the forces of law and order and of imperial defence: but, except for the very limited provisions of the poor law and factory legislation, his welfare and progress were matters for which he alone bore the responsibility. By the turn of the century the position was not much changed. Today, however, the individual citizen submits himself to the guidance of the state at all times. His schooling is enforced; his physical well-being can be looked after in a comprehensive health service; he may be helped by government agencies to find and train for a job; he is obliged while in employment to insure against sickness, accident and unemployment; his house may be let to him by a public authority or he may be assisted in its purchase or improvement; he can avail himself of a wide range of government welfare allowances and services; and he draws a state pension on his retirement. In these and many other ways unknown to his counterpart of a century ago, he is brought into close and regular contact with government and its agencies.

(*Kilbrandon Report*, London, HMSO, 1973, pp. 76–8)

The supreme directorate, the Cabinet, has not increased proportionately to the rest of the government machine. Fifteen in Gladstone's day, a late twentieth-century Cabinet will number twenty senior ministers. Outside the Cabinet there has been a considerable expansion with the growing number of junior ministers which has tripled. Supporting these politicians is a vast bureaucracy now exceeding half a million civil servants, ten times the Victorian establishment. Government expenditure reflects its increased role. In 1870 it was £3 per head, by 1970 £400 per head. Since 1970 when total public expenditure was 41 per cent of GNP it has risen to 49 per cent, in 1975, and then fallen back again to around 40 per cent. Although the scope of local government has increased it is relatively much less important today compared to central government. In 1870 over 50 per cent of all public spending was done by local authorities and 80 per cent of this was raised locally through the rates. Local authorities spend less than a third of that which central government spends and even this reduced total depends heavily on central government grants and authorization for borrowing. Thus government is not only more massive but considerably more centralized.

In addition to civil servants a huge army of workers are engaged in the public sector, somewhat in excess of 5 million – over one in four of the national workforce. If the commonest occupation in 1867 was the agricultural labourer, and the miner stands proudly as the symbol of working Edwardian Britain, the public servant fulfils that role today. There are over half a million full-time teachers and nearly another half a million part-timers and support staff who service education. In 1984 1.4

million served in the health and personal social services. These amount to a powerful political lobby both as voters and members of public sector unions. In many ways the Labour Party has, like the French Socialist Party, become the party of the *fonctionnaire* and public employee. Much of the Conservative appeal in 1979 and subsequently has been based on hostility to what was conceived as an over-bloated public sector. The public sector unions were denounced for their behaviour in 1978–9 and it has been argued that the increasing of income tax on the working class converted many C2 voters (better-off manual workers) to Conservatism. Conversely the defence of the Health Service and education has generally been seen as Labour's best electoral cards in the late 1980s. The crude division of the country in the 1860s between agricultural Tory Party and a Liberal industrial interest, an idea in need of some modification, can perhaps be mirrored today by a division between a public sector Labour Party and a Conservative Party based on the defence of the private sector.

The governing elite of the country has clearly changed. Although the Conservatives remain predominantly public school and professional and business background, this is a far cry from the gentry-dominated party of Lord Salisbury and Disraeli. A woman of lower middle-class origins has sat in the position of Robert Gascoigne Cecil. The lower middle classes and even the odd trade unionist surface at party conferences. Etonians are still represented out of all proportion to their numbers but from forming 25 per cent of all Conservative MPs in 1957 they were down to 12 per cent in 1987. The Labour Party has similarly reduced its proportion of the proletarian equivalents to Etonians. Miners formed 15 per cent of Labour MPs in 1951. By 1987 they were 6 per cent. 56 per cent of Labour MPs were graduates in 1987. Both parties were therefore in essence middle class. Forty per cent of Labour MPs were professionals compared to 42 per cent of Conservatives, but they were more likely to be of working-class origins and from state schools. Class differences clearly distinguish the two parliamentary parties but not as obviously as in the inter-war years. Women continue to be massively under-represented in both parties forming only 5 per cent of Conservative MPs and only 9 per cent of Labour MPs. Perhaps in this way more than any other the parliamentary elite remains unrepresentative of late twentieth-century Britain.

THE THATCHER YEARS

The year 1979 marked a milestone in British history with the election of the first woman Prime Minister. Margaret Thatcher, who had taken the Tory Party leadership from Ted Heath in 1975, led the party to victory in 1979 and was to do so again in 1983 and 1987 – thus giving political commentators the handy epithets of 'Thatcherism' and the 'Thatcher era'. The beginnings were, as is so often the case, small. Like Edward Heath, Margaret Roberts, as she was before she married Denis Thatcher, was the product of a small town, an unexciting family and a conventional education. For the second time in the modern era for the Conservatives grammar school won out over public school although the Oxford connection once again remained. In fact, Mrs Thatcher, as a graduate chemist, was also the first scientist to hold the premiership. She also qualified as a barrister and tried to enter politics in both the 1950 and 1951 elections, failing both times in the Labour stronghold of Dartford. Marriage, work and family kept her out of politics until 1957 when she was adopted as Conservative candidate for Finchley which she won in the 1959 election and thus started her long parliamentary career. Ministerial experience, albeit at a junior level, came quickly with an appointment to the Ministry of Pensions and National Insurance in 1961. She acted as Shadow spokeswoman for this, and later Housing and Land, before a substantial promotion made her number two on the opposition benches on Treasury matters. Shadow appointments followed at Fuel and Power, Transport and Education, all of which put her in the Shadow Cabinet. In the 1970 Heath Government Thatcher became Minister for Education (and earned the name 'milk snatcher'), but although she had impressed many party members by her parliamentary adroitness and thorough grasp of political material and issues her stock seemed little higher in 1974 than it had done in 1970. Certainly, the leadership seemed a faint hope for one of such lowly ministerial responsibility. It was therefore odd that within the year Mrs Thatcher would become Tory Party leader and supplant Heath. The explanation for this strange turn of events is not that complex if one remembers that the events of 1975 were not so much the active promotion of Margaret Thatcher but the active demotion of Edward Heath.

By 1975 Heath had an unenviable record as Tory Party leader and even worse than his lack of success in elections was his betrayal of what certain sections of the party would term the Conservatives' best interests. His monumental U-turn in 1972 which had taken a Tory Government into nationalization and interventionist tactics was more than some party activists could stomach. These politicians collected around a number of key personnel and groups, for example, Sir Keith Joseph, the intellectual guru of the so-called 'Libertarians', who favoured a move away from interventionism and collectivism towards freedom and individualism – simply a rejection of the 'ever creeping socialist state'. Joseph set up a body which was soon to become highly influential – the Centre for Policy Studies, just after the February 1974 election defeat. Its adherents were rapidly finding common companions in the Adam Smith Institute, the Institute for Economic Affairs and the Bow Group. All attacked the record of the party under Heath. Running parallel to this campaign was one being organized by the backbencher Airey Neave who simply wanted to get rid of Heath whose brusque manner had offended more than one Tory since he gained the leadership. Neave was sounding out possible candidates to stand against Heath should the opportunity arise. He was able to do this because the Tory Party had recently decided that the way in which its leader was chosen ought to be revamped, and it put the matter into the hands of one of the party's elder statesmen, Lord Home. The Home report came back with the recommendation that the leader should be elected from the Conservative Members of Parliament and more importantly that the leadership should no longer be held in 'perpetuity' as had been the case before. Home suggested that the leader must offer himself for re-election at the beginning of the session of Parliament which followed a general election and at the beginning of annual sessions. A leader would have to gain a majority of 15 per cent of those who were eligible to vote. With the means and the intent the election to challenge Heath's leadership came quickly. Margaret Thatcher was not the natural candidate to bid for the leadership and others more readily presented themselves. However, Neave had already tried to interest William Whitelaw and Edward Du Cann in standing but to no avail, and thus Thatcher was adopted. She won the first ballot defeating Heath by 130 to 119 and thus opened the way for all those who would not stand against Heath but sought the leadership for themselves. William Whitelaw, Geoffrey Howe and James Prior all stood but Thatcher managed to poll more than was necessary for outright victory with 146 votes. A combination of effective campaign management and too many opponents probably explains the result. Certainly, it was a shock to have a woman as party leader but in 1975, despite the Tory faithful's plaudits, Mrs Thatcher was a long way from Number 10.

However, it was during the years 1975–9 that much of the intellectual groundwork for the later attack on the collectivist state and consensus was laid. Most of the credit for this must go to Sir Keith Joseph. With something approaching the zeal of a fundamentalist Joseph explained his vision:

> About twenty years ago I joined the Conservative Party, and later was adopted as Conservative candidate for the then safe seat of Leeds North-East. In 1959 I was given my first ministerial post. But, it was only in April 1974 that I was converted to Conservatism. (I had thought that I was a Conservative but I now see that I was not really one at all.)
>
> (Preston speech quoted in K. Harris, *Thatcher*, London, Weidenfeld & Nicolson, 1988, p. 21)

Joseph was renouncing the years of consensus and especially the policies of Heath. He was calling for a different set of policies and values which would form the basis of the New Right. Chief amongst these were tight control of the money supply, tax cuts, deregulation, attacks on the trade unions and bureaucracy, pruning welfare provision, promoting private education and health, privatization, and espousing of the individualistic ethic – in all distancing the state from its part in welfare and the economy. His own *Reversing the Trend* in 1975 gave way to collective works such as *The Right Approach* in 1976 and the Economic Reconstruction Group's, *The Right Approach to the Economy* in 1977. By 1979 Sir Keith Joseph could attack

> the poisons . . . which wreck a country's prosperity and full employ-
> ment; excessive government spending, high direct taxation, egalitarian-
> ism, excessive nationalisation, a politicised trade union movement
> associated with Luddism, and an anti-enterprise culture (other coun-
> tries had one or two) . . . we are the only country that has all six.

None the less, it would be fallacious to suggest that the Tory Party went into the 1979 election with the basis of what was to become the Thatcher revolution of the 1980s all cut and dried. All they had were intentions and some policy ideas, but the details of policy were not there. The 1979 Conservative manifesto was not markedly different from that of Heath in 1970. Thatcher's party identified the following as the key areas of policy: control of inflation and the trade unions; restoration of incentives; upholding Parliament and the rule of law; extending home ownership; better education and health services; and a strong defence policy. However, the 'winter of discontent' coloured the campaign and resulted in further promises to ensure postal ballots for unions, easing of the closed-shop, and curbing secondary picketing.

One of the main platforms of the Conservative campaign was that Labour had brought the country to industrial chaos exemplified by the growing numbers of unemployed. It is interesting to note that the Conservatives would preside over a huge rise in unemployment during their years in power, intellectually sustainable in the new ideas of the post-Keynesian New Right, but certainly not policy in 1979. All the same, high unemployment made a good campaigning point and was used freely and well in the Conservatives' advertising material which was orchestrated for them by the rising new agency of Saatchi and Saatchi. The poster war allowed for many old scores to be settled and old sores to be opened and the Labour Party, only recently themselves relinquishing the services of the very same Saatchi and Saatchi, made the obvious reference to the last time the country had faced similar difficulties under a Tory Government and ended up with a three-day week and the entire population reading the local press to find out when the lights would go off, and for how long, and stock-piling candles which suddenly became a shortage item.

The lead that the Tories had was, however, too much for Labour to overcome, given its record and the present difficulties, and the Conservatives were victorious. Thus in May 1979, Margaret Thatcher formed her first government and called only men into her Cabinet thus leaving herself not only the first woman Prime Minister but the only woman in government. The Cabinet itself was a mix of the old Heathites, 'One nation Tories' and the 'New Right' Joseph-inspired 'Libertarians' with a fair smattering of party establishment figures. The membership of this first of the Thatcher Cabinets would be an interesting contrast to those that came later and especially those of the later years of her third administration. At this time, however, the Conservatives' priorities were to address those self-same problems that had afflicted Labour since 1976 and ultimately brought down the Callaghan Government.

The first Thatcher Government 1979–83: 'property-owning democracy'

The idea that the first Thatcher Government arrived in power with the intention of breaking the mould of consensus politics is a little far-fetched. The ideology of the New Right was enthusiastically propounded by its proponents but these were few in the government. The great majority of the first Thatcher Cabinet were, as the term was to become used, 'wet'. Significantly, those who were 'dry' were concentrated in the posts most likely to have the biggest say on how government and private money was to be spent. It was vital that the 'dry' element in the Cabinet kept its hands on the purse-strings for it was on this that their position in government, and the eventual success of their proposals, would depend. However, it was still a consensus world outside and the government needed to play by the rules until some semblance of order was established out of the Callaghan chaos. At first the Cabinet was hamstrung by the necessity to settle outstanding wage disputes. There was no question of an incomes policy after Heath and Callaghan's failures in the 1970s. This left little choice. Some sixty different committees at the Centre for Policy Studies were working away on some aspect of the solution and for all their efforts only two options came out of their deliberations. The first was the breaking of the stranglehold of labour and the trade unions which had done so much to make government a difficult task in the 1970s if only by demanding higher wages. The second solution was a more contentious control of the money supply that hit at the root of Keynesian theory. This in itself was not such a departure because the Labour Government of 1976 had admitted as much at the time of the sterling crisis. The old expansionary-contractionary policies, collectively known as demand management, were discredited in the era of 'stop–go' economic policies. By 1976 the Labour Government was publishing targets for monetary growth as the inflation rate and the trade deficit grew. Government cash limits on its own spending were to be incomes policies which would control money in the private and public sectors. Labour's experiment, as we have seen, failed and it was essential that the new Conservative Government come up with something else. There was no way back to the Keynesian era and so the only option was forward with a more radical interpretation of the control of the money supply.

The government's medium-term financial strategy provided the basis of its approach. Relying heavily on the American economist Milton Friedman, financial experts in government accepted that inflation was a monetary phenomenon. If the money supply and its growth was controlled then inflation was controlled too. Unions may well make demands on their employers but unless prices rise, or loans are made, then the wages cannot be paid. If money supply is controlled strongly enough, by constraining bank lending and adopting interest rate controls, then wage demands could be kept lower. There was however the very real danger that this process would also lead to large numbers of firms going out of business and even greater numbers of workers losing their jobs. Two over-riding features operated in this approach to economic policy. It was vital that the government control the rate of growth of the money stock, so that it was broadly in line with the growth in production, and that the government's own Public Sector Borrowing Requirement (PSBR) be kept as low as possible.

The theory may be acceptable, although many economists would question the assumptions, but the practicalities were less than acceptable to many sections of the British population. Even the government seemed to be more than a little in the dark about its own policy. One of the greatest difficulties was that it was basing its actions on precise measurements of such things as money supply when it became abundantly obvious that such measurement was virtually impossible. Moreover, there would be an inevitable time-lag between the implementation of policy and its effects. In the meanwhile the government had to act tough but be flexible. It was in its first budget that the seeds of this economic policy were planted. Top-rate tax on incomes fell from 83 per cent to 60 per cent as did the standard rate from 33 per cent to 30 per cent. VAT was equalized but increased to 15 per cent and it was announced that there would be a reduction of £1.5 billion in PSBR. Government cash limits imposed another £1 billion cut and the proposed sale of public assets raised a further £1 billion. There was no mention of pay and likely limits and the intention was that unions would take their lead from the limits set on spending. Those working in the public sector were already having to do so. Minimum lending rate rose to 14 per cent and would, under inflationary pressure, climb to 17 per cent. The medicine was severe, some claimed it was worse than the disease, but the immediate past performance of the economy demanded some fresh initiative from however unlikely a quarter and at whatever price. The years of managed decline were the real testament to the ills of the British economy and the necessity to try a new approach.

In spite of this thinking one of the very first actions of the Conservative Government was to announce pay increases for the police of 20 per cent and the armed forces of 32 per cent, hardly controlling inflationary wage demands. In part the Tories were constrained by the previous government's action, such as with the Clegg Commission. But, time was needed and often it was bought quickly and expensively in order that the deeper-seated economic policy of money management could work its way through the nation's bloodstream. In the meantime pay settlements were made and a policy of efficiency was pursued. The latter was experienced by large groups of public sector employees and none more so than the civil service. The latter found itself under severe scrutiny, with Sir Derek Raynor of Marks & Spencer appointed to head a Whitehall efficiency drive in May 1979. But this would ultimately appear rather cosmetic when the monetarist medicine began to take hold. The tight fiscal policies and very high interest rates were maintained throughout the period 1979–82 and Britain experienced its fiercest recession since 1931. By 1980 output was falling sharply while unemployment was rising at a steady 100,000 job losses per month. It was the lack of jobs and the threat of redundancy for those in work that moderated pay claims. Certainly inflation fell although the government's opponents would claim as a result of rising unemployment rather than monetary control. The end result was the one required by the government and its success in this area was not lessened by economic arguments about how exactly the result had been attained. The harsh medicine worked and was successful in keeping inflation down to modest levels up to the end of the 1980s. However, there were costs too because unemployment remained high and progressively crashed through the two million and then the three million barriers. In addition there were massive losses of output as firms laid off workers and closed altogether. Not that Mrs Thatcher rode roughshod over trade unions and the working population. Even with the fast growing rate of unemployment trade unionism was strong in its heartlands. The experiences, and successes, of the 1970s had not dimmed the movement's desire to provide for its members and persuade governments that full employment, along with Clause Four, and high wage settlements were necessary targets for all to aim at in the 1980s. The residual strength of the strongest trade unions was sufficient to warn the government off full confrontation until the time was considered more propitious. The February 1981 announcement of proposed pit closures was quickly withdrawn when mining unions organized local strikes. More problems were to come with the election of Arthur Scargill to the Presidency of the Union, with a 70 per cent majority, in 1981. Scargill, a self-confessed Marxist, saw it as the working man's prerogative to attack governments that threatened the unions and working men. He called for two strike ballots in 1982 and 1983 and lost them both indicating that the miners were not yet ready for an all-out assault on the Conservative Government. On the other hand, some would claim that the government was thinking along the same lines and was eager to choose the ground when battle commenced. While the two sides waited so the government turned its attention to other areas of concern.

One such area was local government. There were considerable concerns within the Conservative Party as to the growing influence of the Labour Party's more extreme supporters in certain key urban areas including London and Liverpool. The fact that local authorities were also the largest employers of labour (about one in eight of the total workforce was an employee of the local authorities) also sparked concern. The fear was that 'municipal socialism' would sweep all in its path if the present trends were allowed to continue. Moreover, greater control over local authority spending was also a prime concern. The last reorganization of local government had taken place in 1974 after the implementation of some of the Redcliffe-Maud Commission's recommendations. The Commission's report in 1969 spoke of the need to allow for local autonomy 'within the limits of national policies and local resources'. A similar vein was struck by Mrs Thatcher's Government in 1979 when it was decided that local government activities should use as their yardstick 'the best interests of the nation as a whole'. Once again efficiency and value for money were seen to be the guiding principles in assessing 'the best interests' of the nation. In 1980 the government sought to impose controls on local government borrowing and expenditure. High-spending authorities would have part of the following year's money held back by central government as a penalty. When local authorities responded with raising extra cash by supplementary rates these were also banned in 1982 under the new Local Government Finance Act. The struggle between the local authorities and central government would continue into the next Conservative term of office. However, both tiers of government were concerned by the outbreak of violence in major cities with the Brixton riots in April 1981 and the Toxteth riots in July the same year. Despite the recommendations of the Scarman Report in November 1981 such events would return to the streets of Britain's cities with a depressing regularity.

On the trade-union front the government made progress, in its terms anyway, with the Employment Acts of 1980 and 1982. The latter in particular, which saw the emergence of Norman Tebbit as a political force in the government, gradually ate away at union strengths. With unemployment hitting unions badly and their memberships declining to the tune of 3 million between 1979 and 1983 the government had some room for manoeuvre. In particular the relationship between employee and employer was redressed in negotiations and individual union members were afforded greater protection by the insistence on secret ballots of members. Unions became legally responsible for their actions and both secondary picketing and sympathy strikes were outlawed. In essence the balance was shifted in favour of the employer and towards the traditionally moribund membership which had found itself many times in the past the tool of an over-weighty executive in the unions. These Acts along with later ones became the employers' armoury of legal weapons to break strikes in the second term of the Conservative Government.

One of the main propositions of the Conservative manifesto in 1979 had been the promise of legislation to enable council house tenants to purchase their properties. A large proportion of these tenants wanted to buy their own property but lacked the necessary funds. The government proposed a Bill that would require local authorities, whether they wanted to or not, to make properties available for purchase. In some areas this was already in operation but the proposed legislation would spread the opportunity countrywide. In addition, the Bill suggested that a tenant's length of tenancy ought to be taken into account and that authorities should offer discounts to tenants with the longest occupying gaining most. The Bill became the 1980 Housing Act and it made provision for purchase with local authority mortgages which facilitated tenants becoming owner-occupiers. The Act enjoyed a marked success, and the tenants who used the opportunities it provided joined the growing number of home-owners in the country. The clear decline in the absolute numbers of tenants renting from local authorities was also apparent. In this at least the government's claim that it would help to build a 'property-owning democracy' was in part fulfilled. Some Labour Councils, like Norwich City, tried to oppose such measures, but were forced to comply in the end.

While the Conservatives endeavoured to govern, their opponents made their political task a little simpler by arguing amongst themselves and dividing their forces thus making Mrs Thatcher's job slightly easier for her. The Labour Party entered a new era with the resignation of Jim Callaghan in October 1980 that brought a new leadership to the fore. The traditional division of right and left in the Labour Party revealed itself in the election of the new leader. On the right was Denis Healey, ex-Chancellor of the Exchequer, and on the left was Michael Foot, deputy leader since 1976. Two other candidates, Peter Shore and John Silkin, complicated matters and on the first ballot Healey won but with Foot polling very strongly. With the other contenders out of the way the second ballot gave victory to Foot by ten votes. Healey became deputy leader. It was a distinct victory for the left.

After starting as a journalist, Foot had a chequered parliamentary career, first as MP for Devonport and then as member for Ebbw Vale, Aneurin Bevan's old seat. He was the radical voice of the Labour Party having played a leading role in defending Bevan and attacking Gaitskell initially in the House of Commons and in the period 1955–60, when he was out of Parliament, in his stirring articles in the *Tribune*. Although he suffered at Bevan's hand when the latter turned on CND, Foot maintained a strong policy consistency throughout his career: the pacifist of the 1930s was still actively campaigning for peace and nuclear disarmament in the 1950s, 1960s and again in the 1980s. It was not only in defence policy that Foot's position on the left of the party could be marked. However, along with his election to the leadership came the revival of Tony Benn. The Wembley Conference in January 1981 established an electoral college system for choosing the party leader. In the new amendments voting powers would be split, 40 per cent to the trade unions and affiliated bodies such as co-operative societies, 30 per cent to the parliamentary Labour Party and 30 per cent to the constituency parties. This was the signal for the widening gulf between left and right to broaden to a gaping void. Heated debate followed with plenty of fuel in the party's splits over the EEC, unilateralism, infiltration and entryism tactics by groups such as the Trotskyite Militant Tendency. Labour was not projecting a united front from 1980 onwards and worse was to follow in political and electoral terms.

The growing animosity of some members of the Labour Party to what they saw as more strident calls for action eventually led to a major split in the leadership of the party. David Owen and William Rodgers, along with Roy Jenkins and Shirley Williams, soon to become 'The Gang of Four', published their Limehouse Declaration which announced the establishment of a Council for Social Democracy. It came a week after the Wembley Conference that had marked the upsurge of the left within the Labour Party. By early March twelve Labour MPs had resigned the Party Whip and on 26 March the Social Democratic Party was formed with thirteen Labour MPs and one Conservative. The party immediately opened up negotiations with David Steel, leader of the Liberals, to forge an understanding over electoral management. This was the precursor to the Alliance of Social Democrats and Liberals which would enjoy a large amount of popular support for a brief spell at least.

While part of the Labour Party was splitting away the remaining bulk was involved in yet another tussle. This time Tony Benn, spokesman for the radical left of the parliamentary party, had challenged Denis Healey for the deputy leadership. He came within 1 per cent of victory and in so doing split the party even more in 1983. It was not a propitious time for the Labour Party and the Conservatives knew it. The time was right to consider the possibility of calling a general election. The government's record might be mixed and patchy, and in some areas pretty threadbare, but at least the government could present the appearance of a united front. More importantly the dark days of the Falklands war were over and the country could 'rejoice' in its recent victory, expensive as it may have been, and feel that Britain's prestige had risen slightly under the stern and unyielding leadership of Mrs Thatcher. With a weakened opponent and a new third force in politics which was likely to do more damage to Labour than the Conservatives, 1983 was a good time to go to the country. Mrs Thatcher called an election for 9 June. Conservative

Central Office must have been confident before but the publication of the Labour Party manifesto must have set the seal on victory.

The divisions within the Labour Party made themselves abundantly clear in the manifesto. The severe splits created a document that was an over-lengthy series of checks and balances designed to prevent one faction in the party getting the upper hand over the other. Gerald Kaufman simply claimed that it was 'the longest suicide note in history'. Certainly Labour sealed its own fate. Promises to leave the EEC and maintain a stance of unilateral nuclear disarmament were vote-losers. There was also concern over the party's call for further nationalization and central planning allied to increases in public expenditure. Amidst this bickering the central themes that might have won Labour support seemed to have become lost. The growing tendency for election campaigns to become advertising campaigns allowed both parties plenty of scope for attack. There was certainly no lack of political ammunition for both parties to use but the Conservatives appeared to be able to offer a better leadership. Their manifesto, unimaginatively entitled *The Conservative Manifesto 1983*, stressed the government's achievements and promised further work on the breaking down of the nationalized industries as well as extensive local government reform. With inflation down to low levels and certain areas of the country, significantly the populous south-east, enjoying some prosperity their message fell on ears willing to hear it. The Conservative campaign was well run with few mistakes and the great advantage of being able to play off weakened opponents. The most worrying aspect was the huge rise in Alliance support with it climbing from 14 per cent to 26 per cent in the opinion polls in the last fourteen days of the campaign. On a fairly low turnout of 72.7 per cent the Conservatives held up well and registered some 42.4 per cent. It was the failure of the Labour Party which was the most remarkable thing. With only 27.6 per cent of the popular vote the Labour Party recorded its worst performance since 1918. However, once again the unfairness of the British first-past-the-post system was revealed with the Liberal Alliance only polling 2.2 per cent less than Labour at 25.4 per cent. The disparity in seats was huge, with Labour winning 209 and the Alliance 23. The Conservatives were 188 seats ahead of Labour and had an overall majority of 144. Mrs Thatcher returned to Number 10 in triumph, the first Prime Minister in Conservative colours to win a consecutive term of office since Lord Salisbury.

The second Thatcher Government 1983–7: the share-owning democracy

In the week following the victory Mrs Thatcher restructured her ministerial team. There were key changes not the least being the replacement of Francis Pym by Sir Geoffrey Howe at the Foreign Office. Nigel Lawson replaced Howe at the Exchequer and Leon Brittan became

Home Secretary with William Whitelaw taking a hereditary peerage. The pattern was clear, appointments were made on the basis of adherence to the ideas of the Conservative Party's leader. What was to become a stock phrase in the future, 'One of us', appeared to be the guiding principle of reshuffling the Cabinet. Further changes would take place on a regular basis leading to Mrs Thatcher being accused of using an 'uncertainty' principle as a basis of support from her ministers. The long process of 'drying' out the government had started in earnest. While it went on the government enjoyed the continuing advantage of a divided opposition. In fact, the most ardent criticism of the government could come from its own back benches rather than the shadow front bench. The election defeat had hit Labour very hard and the party resolved that a change of leadership would be necessary in order for it to present itself to the electorate as a viable alternative to the Conservative Government. More pessimistic observers would comment that the immediate task was for Labour to establish itself as the legitimate opposition before it could think in terms of government. The Liberal Alliance's success in the general election, although ultimately disappointing in terms of numbers of seats, had many commentators reaching for their calculators to estimate how close a Liberal Alliance 'breakthrough' might be. In the end it never came but in the despondent years after 1983 the Labour Party was prepared to jump at shadows. Certainly a new leadership would help the party image, unfortunately tarnished by the disastrous Foot era. In the end Michael Foot resigned and left the political stage to a younger generation of politicians. The coming leadership election would be a long and stern one with both factions of the party eager for success. Dispassionate viewers hoped for some compromise with leadership and deputy leadership being split between the left and the right. In the end both sides could feel satisfied. Neil Kinnock, at 41, became leader and thus gave a youthful feel to the leadership. He was the representative of the left and his early political career, as MP for the South Wales mining area, and adherent of the left's articles of faith put him firmly in this faction's mould. He had even refused minor office in Callaghan's Government in 1976. However, Kinnock, as he demonstrated later, was quite capable of feeling at home in the more mainstream democratic socialism of the party's centre turning against the left's Campaign for Labour Democracy of which he had been a founder member. Thus a more flexible leader had appeared and he was matched by the right's choice for leader, Roy Hattersley, who became Kinnock's deputy. With a tendency to gravitate towards each other and being representatives of the party's main factions some saw the new leadership duo as the 'dream ticket'. However, it would take more than a change of personnel to solve many of Labour's problems and make it a viable alternative choice for the British electorate. While Labour started to put its own house in order the Conservatives tackled their second package of legislative reforms.

Sir Derek Raynor's work with the civil service was carried on by Sir Robin Ibbs who produced a further stage of the Thatcher reforms with *The Next Steps*. It was Ibbs who came up with the idea of hiving off various branches of the civil service, notably the Driver and Vehicle Licensing Centre. It was also suggested that different models of civil service operation like those in France and Sweden should be investigated. Another area of reform was in education where the proposed Education Reform Bill became law in 1986. This placed an emphasis on new style examinations and assessments as well as radically restructuring the teaching profession and schools. Under its wings new developments like the GCSE examinations and latterly the National Curriculum and Local Management in Schools have come about, in addition to greater accountability through parent participation in governing bodies and decision-making. These developments were enshrined in the 1988 Education Reform Act.

Local government reform had been an election promise. In the autumn of 1983 the government announced its legislative plans for the abolition of the Greater London Council, and the six metropolitan counties. The struggle with local authorities continued especially over their excess spending. Government attempts to control local authorities led to many bodies trying to increase their income from rates and establishing high rate levels. The government stepped in, in 1984, to impose rates ceilings, or rate-capping, on such authorities. This led to unavoidable confrontations with what became known as big-spending authorities such as Liverpool City Council and the London borough of Newham. Legal tussles resulted with local councillors finding themselves personally responsible for council over-spends in defiance of rate-capping. With the law apparently on the government's side local authorities succumbed to the inevitable with the Abolition Acts for both the Greater London Council and the Metropolitan Councils being passed in 1985. By 1986 these councils had been abolished although residuary bodies were created to wind down such leftovers as property portfolios. Powers locally gravitated to the borough councils and the metropolitan district councils. London became a collection of boroughs with the only extra-borough agency, the Inner London Education Authority, ceasing to exist in 1990. By this stage a system of competitive tendering was also in force which put councils' own DLO (Direct Labour Organisations) under greater threat.

The government also pursued its pledge to privatize a number of national companies and services amongst which were British Telecom, British Airways and British Steel. Effectively this met the New Right's desire to have government withdraw from direct contact with major sectors of the economy and thus allow for the operation of a free market economy. It also hit at the outdated notion of state intervention and support which was still enshrined in the Labour Party's constitution as Clause Four. Here was a government which in Mrs Thatcher's words was prepared 'to roll back the state'. Successive sales of shares in all enterprises were widely oversubscribed by investors and the sales not only created a nation of share-holders but also provided useful short-term revenue for the government. However, opponents of the government were quick to point out that once sold the assets were gone and with them much of the infrastructure of the era of consensus. It was a clear debate between an increasingly costly interventionist government role, as espoused by Labour, and a straightforward withdrawal from direct control pursued by the Conservatives to allow market forces to operate. However, it would be wrong to portray the divide simply in party terms because many Conservatives were as opposed to the sale of national assets as Labour Party supporters. Even Harold Macmillan used his position as elder statesman in the House of Lords to criticize Mrs Thatcher for 'selling off the family silver' and thus denying future generations of Britons the knowledge that they owned collectively the national assets. Criticism or not, the pace of privatization stepped up rather than fell away and the number of share-holders grew sharply in the years 1983 to 1987.

With such huge numbers of new customers the City, already undergoing its own revolution with an entirely new computerized system and open market rules, was about to experience its 'big bang'. But before this shock there was a growth of the money markets and the Stock Exchange in this era, although the effects were not felt nationwide, or certainly not equally across the nation. The prosperous south-east contrasted with the less prosperous north. There is no doubt that the inequitable distributions of the fruits of the era of prosperity under the Conservatives played its part in the party's continuing success. Not only were the old traditional areas of Labour support hardest hit but vital groups in the more open and marginal areas, including C2s or the so-called new working class, certainly gained greatly under the Tories. With such strong support and apparent economic success the government was in a position to try its strength and have a tilt at yet another dragon of the left – the trade unions.

The trade unions had suffered along with Labour under the ministrations of the new economic thought. Membership had declined and unemployment had sapped strength and will. For many ordinary working people and particularly those in the less prosperous north the Thatcher era had not brought any comfort. With unemployment rocketing in certain black spots the advantages of the new home-owning and share-owning democracy seemed a long way off. The clamour for jobs including marches, demonstrations and a repeat of the Jarrow March of the Hungry Thirties graphically reminded the government of lack of success of its policies in certain areas. Nevertheless, the trade-union movement was at its weakest for many years and the government was intent on eradicating yet another of Sir Keith Joseph's 'poisons'. The year 1984 opened up with the government depriving union members of their rights, and ultimately their membership, at GCHQ, intelligence headquarters, at Cheltenham. Soon, however, the government would be met by a much sterner foe in the form of the National Union of Mineworkers.

The government's economic stringencies had kept union activity at a low level since the 'winter of discontent' and the steel strike. Although 1984 was to be another story the government had learned the lessons of the past well while the unions had not. The miners had been instrumental in bringing down the Heath Government in 1974 but their omnipotence had disappeared since then. Twice already they had refused to follow their leader, Arthur Scargill, into direct strike action but by 1984 the government's proposals were clear. A Mergers and Monopolies Commission report into the Coal Board in 1982 stated plainly that it was an uneconomic industry and that pits should close. There had been closures in the past but the miners' strike was more than an argument about the coal industry. As Scargill claimed, 'There is only one response. Faced with legislation we will defy the law.' The trade-union legislation that had hit at secondary picketing, closed-shop traditions and provided for fines of £250,000 had already reduced union support. With numbers declining in the movement as a whole by 14 per cent between 1979 and 1982 the miners were fighting on behalf of the entire trade-union movement. As for the industry itself Scargill's attitude was simple, 'as long as there is coal in the ground then it should be mined'. The logic of this flew in the face of economic sense and the government was determined that 'uneconomic' pits should be closed and the Coal Board announced plans in 1984 to close twenty pits and Cortonwood colliery.

It is hard to avoid the conclusion that the miners fell into a well-laid trap. In 1983 the government appointed Ian MacGregor, a no-nonsense troubleshooter imported on a large salary, to make sectors of British industry efficient. He had already slimmed down British Steel by cutting jobs from 150,000 to 85,000. As the new Chairman of the Coal Board it was his job to do the same to the coal industry and in the process break the union. Plans had been well laid and the number of dual-firing power stations had increased substantially. (These could function on either coal or oil although the latter was massively more expensive.) In addition the power stations' reserves of coal had climbed steadily from 37 million tonnes in 1981 to 57 million tonnes in 1984. The Coal Board was provisioned for a long war of attrition. The strike lasted 362 days from 5 March 1984 to 3 March 1985. It was a physical confrontation from the beginning with no quarter given on either side. The picket lines were not afraid to tackle the police and Orgreave Coke Works became the main battleground of the strike. The confrontation led to severe injuries on both sides and the union's use of 'flying pickets' to reinforce lines anywhere in the country saw the police having to block motorways and delay traffic to prevent them getting to their target areas.

Inevitably, in such a long strike there were many who were forced back to work out of sheer economic necessity although most communities tried to organize some kind of basic relief for families. In the north-east and Wales many families found themselves rapidly going into debt and communities were devastated by hardship and rivalries as many men returned to work. Communities became divided and many remained so even into the next decade after the events of the miners' strike. With a government determined to win even though it was costing an extra £20 million a week to fuel power stations by oil the miners were slowly worn down. Kim Howells of the South Wales Mine Union Executive, and later MP for Pontypridd, may well have been right when he claimed that the miners' strike of 1984 was 'the last great industrial strike', but more germane for the government, and the unions, is his comment that 'the miners defeat knocked the guts out of the Trade Union movement'. The government had used its extensive employment legislation to the full and had imposed fines on the union and then eventually sequestered all £8 million of its assets ensuring a belated apology from the union to the courts in 1986 when they were released. The decision to return to work, when it came, was not overwhelming, ninety-eight votes to ninety-one, but by this time the union was split and terribly weakened, with a rival Union of Democratic Miners enjoying fair support. In the end the government got its way and from 1984 to 1987 the number of colliery workers fell from 181,000 to 108,000 and the number of NCB works fell from 234 to 143 with 42 pits being closed. In addition the tonnes per man shift of 2.59 before the strike rose to 3.96 by 1987.

The further powers granted the government under the 1984 Trade Union Act which supplemented those of the 1980 and 1982 Employment Acts were also deployed against other sectors of the trade-union movement. Another year-long dispute started in January 1986 with the print-workers of News International at Wapping. Likewise strengthened by the new legislation, the owner, Rupert Murdoch, led a successful campaign against SOGAT 82 and the strike, once more acrimonious and violent, ended just over a year later in February 1987 in a victory for the employer. During its second term the government appeared to have fulfilled its promise of taming union activity and allowing the operation of the free market in labour relations.

Amongst the great victories there were battles lost and more particularly a series of embarrassments for the government. The handling of the Falklands war had come under some scrutiny and the Franks Commission had been appointed to investigate claims of negligence although its report found in favour of the government. However, allegations against the government refused to die a natural death and much coverage was given to the incident of the sinking of the Argentinian ship the *General Belgrano*. Leaked documents suggested that the government had not kept to its strict 'rules of engagement' guidelines in this instance.

The claims were made all the more damaging as they came from 'official' sources and were compounded when it was found that vital documents and ships' logs could not be located. In the end Clive Ponting, a civil servant at the Ministry of Defence, made public his suspicions and was charged with leaking the documents made available to the press in August 1984. Ponting subsequently stood trial and, accused of transgressing the 1911 Official Secrets Act, relied on his defence that it was his duty to act in 'the public interest'. Despite being directed otherwise the jury agreed with Ponting and he was cleared. The government was seriously embarrassed and immediately fell into another minefield.

The Defence Secretary, Michael Heseltine, became embroiled in a cabinet controversy over the rival merits of deals to rescue Westland. Westland was a helicopter company that ran into financial difficulties and needed a rescue bid putting together in order to save it. Leon Brittan and Michael Heseltine initially both agreed on the merits of a European Consortium, which included British Aerospace, to mount the rescue bid. However, Brittan changed his mind and opted for a Sikorski (US) bid which also happened to be in line with Mrs Thatcher's thinking. The two ministers then did battle over their respective 'pet' schemes. However, Heseltine believed that the whole issue was getting rail-roaded through Cabinet and complained about the lack of opportunity to put his case. In the end Heseltine resigned over this, storming out of Cabinet into Downing Street in January 1986. Brittan also resigned at the end of January when it was revealed that letters had been leaked which were designed to put pressure on the Chairman of British Aerospace so that the latter would withdraw from the European Consortium thus making the European bid untenable. Mrs Thatcher had already faced criticism that accused her of being President Reagan's 'poodle' and this seemed, like the basing of American missiles at Greenham Common and the use of British bases for American airstrikes on Libya, another example of kowtowing to the United States. Heseltine decided to fight over the issue and the debate that ensued was a potentially very serious threat to Mrs Thatcher and her style of leadership. However, not for the first time, the opposition missed its opportunity and the Prime Minister was allowed to force Heseltine's resignation without having her actions in the affair too closely scrutinized. Further embarrassment came in the same year with the opening of the Peter Wright *Spycatcher* trial in Australia in November. Wright was an ex-intelligence officer, and his memoirs, supposedly highly revealing, were written against the guidelines governing privileged information. The government tried desperately to prevent publication but their case was thrown out of court and the 1911 Official Secrets Act once again was proved to be too limited for government purposes. These events persuaded the government to start work on drafting a new Secrets Bill which was designed to prevent the recurrence of similar events in the future. It came into force in 1989.

On a more personal level there were damaging revelations about key political figures. Cecil Parkinson felt it necessary to resign on 14 October 1983 after revelations about his affair with Sarah Keays. Two years later Jeffrey Archer also resigned as Conservative deputy chairman after allegations about him in the tabloid press concerning the so-called Monica Coglan sex scandal. Archer furiously denied the allegations but resigned none the less. However, not all the publicity was poor for the Conservatives and it is certain that the IRA bombing of the Grand Hotel in Brighton during the Conservative Party Conference in October 1984 stirred much sympathy for the government. Four people died and several were injured very seriously including Norman Tebbit and his wife. The Prime Minister however escaped injury saved in part by her tendency to work very late and she was at government and party business when the bomb exploded in the early hours of the morning. The leavening provided by such an event reminded many Tories that government was not all about confrontation and change but also could embrace compassion and continuity. Certainly there were many who believed that the Tory Party had become hard-bitten in this second term and it was Peter Walker, a wet, who reminded the party in October 1985, the day before the anniversary of the bombing, that the government was becoming 'remote, perhaps uncaring'.

The 1987 election

Despite the warnings 1987 opened up as a possible election year and as the months passed the possibility became a certainty. The stock market was enjoying a boom (it would feel the after-effects of this with the crash on 'Black Monday' in the autumn but that would be after the election), and the budget in March cut income tax by 2 per cent. Throughout spring the government enjoyed consistent leads in the opinion polls and in April Mrs Thatcher made a triumphant visit to Russia thereby appearing to reinforce her global position as a world leader. The local elections in May demonstrated Labour weaknesses and showed up Conservative strengths in the key electoral areas like the West Midlands. The Alliance also appeared to have run its course and made few gains of significance. Within four days of the results the general election was announced for 11 June. While the campaign was running the government benefited from useful government figures showing drops in unemployment and good trade balances. The two main parties each had something with which to attack the other. Labour could point the finger at the Conservatives' continued onslaught on the welfare services noting the moves made in the National Health Service with the recommendations of the Griffiths Report in 1983 and Norman Fowler's Green Paper in 1984 on social security reform. On the other side of the House the Conservatives could still use the old ammunition albeit in a very effective way. Neil Kinnock had made changes in the party slowly reducing the influence of the left on the national executive, bringing in new and loyal talent such as Larry Whitty as General Secretary and Peter Mandelson as Director of Communications, expelling Militant from the movement, and generally instilling ambition and confidence back into the party leadership. However, in the age of the increasingly presidential confrontation in British general elections personality alone, ironically, is not enough. Certainly the Tories made much of Labour policy and none more so than the old albatross of unilateral disarmament. It was a gift to the Conservatives' publicity machine and did much to undermine the good work that brought positive advantages elsewhere for Labour.

The Alliance appeared to suffer with its dual-leadership and it had had its own problems over policy, including defence, in the years running up to the general election. In fact there was little change over the previous contest with the Conservatives polling 42.2 per cent, Labour 32 per cent and the Alliance 22.6 per cent. The result was another victory for Mrs Thatcher thus equalling Lord Liverpool's record in the 1812–27 ministries. The overall majority had fallen but it was still a massive 102 seats and the third Conservative Government in succession could approach office with great confidence.

Mrs Thatcher has enjoyed some measure of good fortune in her political career with the comfortable cushion created by North Sea oil and a fortuitous victory over a Third World country in the Falklands war. However, as many of her defenders are quick to point out, politicians, along with many others, in part create their own luck. Certainly Mrs Thatcher has been good at choosing polling days and her election strategies have been in part dictated by the likely effects of economic indicators and performances. One such piece of creative luck is the close relationship between marked falls in interest rates and the calling of elections. Moreover, of course, the Conservatives have also gained substantially from Labour's own weaknesses which were exposed even more cruelly from 1983 to 1987 by the existence of the Liberal Alliance which made its task very difficult indeed. Certainly, there are those who would claim that much of Mrs Thatcher's importance relates not just to her achievements in the decade of the 1980s and giving politics an alternative to the 'capitalist welfare consensus' but also to the effect she had on her opponents while she held the premiership.

The Labour Party has been as much part of the so-called Thatcher revolution as any institution in British society. It was the third election defeat which allowed an already flexible leadership to make some of the changes that would not have been possible even five years before. Having the right leadership is part of the battle but the right message must also go along with it. Mrs Thatcher had demonstrated in the 1980s that she had a clear message for large portions of the voting population who found her words far from strident – there is no other way to explain her success. But in this success there was a message for Labour, and one that many found totally unpalatable:

> Labour fought a brilliant campaign in 1987 but its policy base was weak and the product kept on showing through . . . much in Labour's manifesto was merely negative resistance to Tory measures or the half-apologetic playing of ancient tunes. Gone were the acute embarrassments of 1983. In their place there was a designer-socialist blandness.
>
> (Ben Pimlott, writing in *The Sunday Times*, 5 July 1987)

However, the leadership of the party heard the message and immediately set in motion the most extensive review of Labour Party policies since the constitution was drawn up in 1918. The Labour Party Policy Review started in 1987 and, directed by Tom Sawyer, has seen off the most electorally damaging policies which had in part cost Labour the last three general elections. Defence has moved away from unilateral to multilateral disarmament and the Labour Party finds itself, with the new wave of optimism sweeping Europe in the opening years of the 1990s, with a possibly more attractive approach than the Conservatives to this important vote winning area of policy. As for the EC the Labour Party was now willing to embrace wholeheartedly Britain's membership and support such initiatives as a single European currency and the Social Charter. As for taxation Labour have adopted a more open approach and predict tax bands in the range of 20 per cent for the lowest and only 50 per cent for the highest. Privatization has also forced the Labour Party to move ground and from a renationalize spirit of 1983 the party now talks in terms of 'some form of public ownership' and hints at 'golden shares' of key utilities rather than total buy-backs. Trade-union legislation has also seen a shift of ground with some Tory Acts to be repealed but secret ballots for strikes and union elections to be retained along with some limits on secondary action. The party is still committed to full employment but has stopped giving a timetable for reductions in the levels of unemployment. Such policy changes, along with a redressing of the balance on the national executive via the mechanism of individual rather than constituency balloting has seen the party shift significantly to the right and into the central ground of the social democratic heritage. Some have found the move more than a step too far and point out that the Labour Party has moved, albeit at its own pace, with the times, and that the times have been the creation of Mrs Thatcher and her three successive governments up to 1990. A new realism, not to speak of revisionism, has been created in the Labour Party and its leader, Neil Kinnock, speaking at the 1988 Party Conference, is the first to defend it:

> When we make these arguments about individuals and about consumers and about competitiveness it is not long before we get the

accusation that we are 'proposing to run the capitalist economy better than the Tories'. Comrades, the day may come when this movement is actually presented with two forms of socialist economy about which it can debate, between which it can choose. But until that day does come the fact is that the kind of economy we are faced with is a market economy. . . . And we have got to run it better than the Tories.

(Quoted by Peter Kellner, in *Contemporary Record*, vol. 3, no. 2 (November 1989), p. 14)

In a sense then we have in the 1990s a new consensus, in Tony Benn's words a 'monetarist consensus', where both parties have some element of agreement. The ground has been shifted, that was Mrs Thatcher's doing, but the Labour Party has responded and appears to be willing to meet the Conservative challenge on a new field of battle, that has been Mr Kinnock's doing. As with other periods of consensus before this one, there are enough differences of opinion to allow for changes of government as issues such as the Community Charge have suggested, but ultimately it will be the British electorate that chooses and judges between the merits of the rival claimants for the ultimate prize in politics.

POSTSCRIPT

As if to reinforce the comments made about the difficulties of assessing recent history which are raised in the controversy section that follows the events of the autumn of 1990 brought the Thatcher era to an abrupt close. Although Mrs Thatcher's leadership had been challenged the previous year by Sir Anthony Meyer her victory seemed merely to confirm her position whilst highlighting some dissatisfaction amongst some sections of the back benches. As befits a history text this book answers some questions concerning events of the past but as we move closer to the present all it can do is to begin to analyse major ideas and issues. The thoroughgoing historical analysis of these more recent events will require a greater perspective which time alone will allow. Certainly, political analysts have already made snap judgements concerning Mrs Thatcher's resignation and the events surrounding this decision. How far these judgements approximate to the truth remains to be seen but some general themes have already clearly emerged.

First, any party that is in office for an extended period and a number of successive terms is bound to falter at some stage. For the Conservatives this faltering has become apparent in their third term of office. Inevitably there is a tendency to look to the leadership when the barrage of criticism rises. One cannot help feeling that it is also true that sacrifice of a leader for the greater benefit of the party becomes tempting. This, of course, enables much criticism to be deflected and at the same time can provide for a useful scapegoat for past mistakes and errors. Second, Mrs Thatcher's style of leadership came in for greater criticism and especially from ministers. This was not new and one is tempted to go back to the resignation of Michael Heseltine over the so-called Westland Affair in 1986 and see this merely as one of a series of serious disagreements between the Prime Minister and leading Secretaries of State. Nigel Lawson's resignation in 1989 was another major political setback and the final resignation, that of Sir Geoffrey Howe after what one newspaper described as 'fifteen months in the political wilderness' was the vital one. Style of leadership and growing criticism of Mrs Thatcher's abuse of Cabinet and shortcircuiting of the cabinet form of government was one major theme in the growing internal and party revolt. Another was the albatross of unpopular policy of which the Community Charge was a prime example – some might say the prime example. An unpopular measure apparently forced on an unwilling population gave opponents a hefty stick with which to beat the government and the Prime Minister. Intransigence in the face of mounting criticism, including mass demonstrations and violence on the streets of the capital in March 1990, suggested a rethink might be judicious. Mrs Thatcher's refusal to rethink, perhaps in her mind associated with that greatest of all evils, the U-turn, was not possible. The issue itself was badly handled by a party that had become slick in presentation of policy but also perhaps too complacent in its approach. With a real issue to berate the government with and a further revamp of party policy in a second Labour Party Policy Review the opposition presented a united critical front to the government. Third, for the first time, at least in public, there were growing signs of real rifts in the government. The Community Charge may well have been the issue preoccupying the population but in the council chambers of state other issues, especially those related to Europe were also dominant. European unification in all its manifestations was an issue that Mrs Thatcher was very suspicious of and the dual themes of political and monetary union saw her adopt her traditional 'Little Englander' role in the face of mounting European, and in some quarters, national pressure.

It was over this unification issue that Sir Geoffrey Howe emerged as the man who could do most damage. His televised resignation speech, to a packed House, on 13 November 1990 was as damning a condemnation of a political leader as a gentle and principled politician could give. Howe had been outraged at the way the Prime Minister, or at least her Office, had treated his letter of resignation and suggested that all that stood between them were 'questions of style'. Caustically Howe remarked that, 'I must be the first Minister in history who has resigned because he was in full agreement with Government policy.' He went on to note that he and Thatcher had shared 700 meetings of Cabinet over eighteen years and that 'something more than simple matters of style would be necessary to rupture such a well-tried relationship'.

Finally, and most telling for any political party, the question of the forthcoming election began to dominate party managers' thoughts. A fourth successive victory was the aim but the query raised was, could Mrs Thatcher deliver such a victory? There were obviously serious doubts within the party and for the second successive time Mrs Thatcher faced a leadership contest. This time the stalking horse would be more of a thoroughbred stallion in the shape of Michael Heseltine. The ex-defence and ex-environment minister who had spent the last five years in the political wilderness had not been wasting his time. He was the most sought-after and easily available after-dinner speaker at local constituency party dinners up and down the country. His personal stature was considerable and his popular acclaim great. However, within the party there were severe doubts and reservations about Michael Heseltine as a potential leader and Prime Minister. His function appeared to be that of the traditional stalking horse preparing a way for the real candidates in a second ballot. The arcane leadership election mechanism of the Tory Party had served Mrs Thatcher well enough in the past. After all she had benefited from it in the 1975 contest with Ted Heath and succeeded in seeing off her other rivals in the second ballot. The system had been devised by Humphrey Berkeley in 1964–5 while he was Conservative MP for Lancaster. (One of the ironies of the situation is that after this he left the Conservatives and crossed the floor of the House to join the Labour Party in 1970.) The rules specified an overall majority for victory on the first ballot, thus 187 was the key figure but the rules also demanded a clear 15 per cent lead over the rival – in this case 56 votes. If no clear victor emerged then there was provision for a second ballot where a simple majority, 187, would be sufficient for victory. Again, if no clear winner emerged at this stage then a third ballot consisting of the leading three contenders but operating a preferential vote, for first and second choices, would take place and by a system of redistribution of the third candidate's votes a leader would emerge. Mrs Thatcher confidently expected a first-round ballot victory and was in Paris when the result was announced. Of the 'promised' 238 votes only 204 were cast and Mrs Thatcher's rival received not the expected 80 votes but 152. The combative response, without (so some felt) due consideration and consultation, was 'I fight on. I fight to win.'

The run of events from that point onwards appears straightforward. Mrs Thatcher, after consultations, decided that her position, especially in Cabinet was now untenable. In an emotive series of interviews with each cabinet colleague Mrs Thatcher found that only two told her she could win. The other nineteen were doubtful of victory or insistent that she stand down. On Thursday 22 November Mrs Thatcher's resignation letter was on its way to Buckingham Palace. The second round of balloting brought forth Douglas Hurd and John Major to challenge Michael Heseltine. The frenetic activity between Thursday and Tuesday, when the second vote took place, saw a major change of fortunes with John Major emerging as a clear favourite to challenge Heseltine with Hurd a poor third. In the final analysis Major failed to get the simple majority required. The result was Major 185, Heseltine 131 and Hurd 56. Although there was some speculation about the third ballot, in the event both of Major's opponents conceded defeat and John Major became the youngest Prime Minister for nearly a century at the age of 47 and after only just eleven years in Parliament. The Thatcher era had come to a close in the sense that Margaret Thatcher was no longer at the helm of the ship but the changes wrought by her will ensure that the effects of the momentous era that bears her name will continue for many years to come. Already there has been speculation about the so-called Treasury Conspiracy and secret meetings in London houses but such conspiracy theorists will need more than meetings and rumour to confirm their suspicions. One way forward might be the next round of political biographies and memoirs and, of course, Mrs Thatcher's own side of the story. However, such analyses lay well beyond the scope of this book and sometime in the future but as always with history and historical study as one chapter closes another is ready to be opened.

CONTROVERSY

With this penultimate chapter this book has come up to date. Certainly its last pages have been concerned with 'contemporary' history but there is no single controversy to finish off the sequence that started some one hundred and twenty years before. There is however a long-standing debate surrounding the investigation of such events, and this concentrates on whether it is possible to have a historical view on such recent events. The very nature of contemporary history mitigates against it and as Geoffrey Barraclough has pointed in his *Introduction to Contemporary History* (1964): 'Much that claims to be contemporary history – whether written in Peking or Moscow, or in London or New York – turns out too often to be little more than propaganda or desultory comment on "current affairs".' This argument is straightforward in that for some contemporary history is a contradiction in terms. The essence of historical analysis and appreciation demands that there is distance between the observer and the events observed. Without this 'disengagement' then criticism becomes impossible and any approximation to being dispassionate simply disappears. Others would claim that such distance serves no purpose because analysis will always suffer from some form of prejudice, either personal or historical, and thus historical investigation gains nothing from distance. Presumably, such writers would be content with Sir Robert Armstrong's view on Mrs Thatcher:

Historians will look back on this decade as the period when, thanks in part to the leadership of a very unusual person, we stopped trying to manage decline and began to look forward: to a different role in the world and a process of economic recovery.

(*The Sunday Times*, 3 December 1989)

However, even Sir Robert has suggested that some distance is necessary by noting that historians will have to look back to the 1980s even though they will find that some contemporaries of Mrs Thatcher will have already done their assessment and interpretations for them. More realistic of today's commentators is Ben Pimlott who, in a recent article, found it impossible to make such sweeping judgements about the Thatcher years and most so of the economic changes that had been wrought:

I will say least about the economy. I was interested by some of the points made by Peter Jay in the 'trial of Thatcherism' on television on 30 April which revealed the extent to which the jury is still very much out on the economy; it will be a long time before one can assess the extent to which economic changes of the 10 years are a product of government action and the extent to which, *mutatis mutandis*, they would have taken place in any case.

(*Contemporary Record*, vol. 3, no. 1 Autumn 1989, p. 14)

He is suggesting that only with the key element of distance and perspective will the 1980s be analysed in context and for that analysis we may have to wait some time yet. Those who choose not to may well find themselves falling into the same trap that Kenneth Harris did in 1988 when he wrote in his concluding chapter on Margaret Thatcher:

Judged by the criteria she set herself in 1979, Mrs Thatcher's achievements deserve to become historic. Her economic targets have all been reached and in many cases surpassed. Inflation, identified as the main economic problem of the 1970s, rising to 25 per cent in 1975, has been reduced to an annual average of little over 4 per cent, and this figure has been coupled during the past six years with a steady growth rate of 3 per cent in the British economy as a whole – a performance equalled in recent years only by Japan. This combination of high growth and low inflation is a task that *every* post-war government has set itself since the 1950s and only Mrs Thatcher's Governments have consistently managed it. The public finances are now in better shape than at any time since the war. The bane of post-war governments, the Public Sector Borrowing Requirement, has been entirely eliminated; Nigel Lawson announced in his 1988 budget that it is now in surplus to the tune of £3 billion.

Manufacturing output is now rising at a higher level than at any time since 1973 and industrial productivity for the year 1987–8 is the highest in Europe. Mrs Thatcher has fulfilled her pledge to reduce direct taxation; the buoyant state of the economy allowed Nigel Lawson to take the most radical step so far in this direction, in his 1988 budget, by reducing the standard rate once 33 per cent to 25 per cent and the top (and now the only other) rate from 83 per cent in 1979 to 40 per cent. 'The 1988 budget', Mrs Thatcher said, '[was] a humdinger. . . . It represented the defeat of everything Labour thought was permanent in political life. It was the epitaph of Socialism.' The trade union problem, the 'British Disease' that seemed to plague industry in the 1960s and 1970s, has been eradicated from the body politic, and the annual rate of industrial stoppages in the late 1980s is running at its lowest level since the late 1930s. It is a remarkable economic transformation when seen against the seemingly irreversible economic decline to which the British people appeared to be resigned in the 1970s.

(Harris, op.cit., pp. 214–15)

A week may be a long time in politics but a decade, or to be precise eleven years, is very brief in historical terms and Harris's assessment of the Thatcher era is open to the vagaries of history but some of his basic assertions are questionable. Simply the jury has not even been selected let alone heard the full case and begun its deliberations. The historical judgement it eventually delivers will lie some way in the future and as always will be open to interpretation and reinterpretation as the years pass.

BIBLIOGRAPHY

For an explanation of the grading system, see the preface p. xiii.

The only political figure of the Thatcher years to have been written about extensively is Margaret Thatcher herself. A number of books of variable quality have appeared and all suffer from the same problem noted in the controversy section of this chapter:

3   Abse, L., *Margaret, Daughter of Beatrice: A Politician's Psychobiography of Margaret Thatcher*, London, Cape, 1989
2/3   Cole, J., *The Thatcher Years*, London, BBC, 1987
2/3   Cosgrave, P., *Thatcher: The First Term*, London, Bodley Head, 1985
2   Gardner, G., *Margaret Thatcher: From Childhood to Leadership*, London, Kimber, 1975
3   Harris, K., *Thatcher*, London, Weidenfeld & Nicolson, 1988
2   Holmes, M., *The First Thatcher Government 1979–1983*, Sussex, Wheatsheaf, 1985
2   Jenkin, J. (ed.), *John Major: Prime Minister*, London, Bloomsbury, 1990
3   Jenkins, P., *Mrs Thatcher's Revolution: The Ending of the Socialist Era*, London, Cape, 1987
2   Kavanagh, D., *Thatcherism and British Politics*, Oxford, Oxford University Press, 1987

3   Kavanagh, D. and Seldon, A., *The Thatcher Effect: A Decade of Change*, Oxford, Oxford University Press, 1989

2   Lewis, R., *Margaret Thatcher: A Personal and Political Biography*, London, Routledge & Kegan Paul, 1975

2/3   Riddell, P., *The Thatcher Decade: How Britain has Changed During the 1980s*, Oxford, Blackwell, 1989

3/4   Young, H., *One of Us*, London, Macmillan, 1989

2   Young, H. and Sloman, A., *The Thatcher Phenomenon*, London, BBC, 1985

On retirement, many leading politicians publish a record of their careers or their diaries and memoirs. Already new books are emerging on the post-Thatcher era, such as:

2   Fowler, N., *Ministers Decide*, London, Chapman, 1991

2/3   Hailsham, Lord, *A Sparrow's Flight*, London, Collins, 1990

2/3   Heseltine, M., *Where there's a Will*, London, Hutchinson, 1987

2   Ingham, B., *Kill the Messenger*, London, Harper Collins, 1991

2/3   Pym, F., *The Politics of Consent*, London, Hamish Hamilton, 1984

2/3   Ridley, N., *My Style of Government: The Thatcher Years*, London, Hutchinson, 1991

2   Tebbit, Norman, *Upwardly Mobile*, London, Weidenfeld & Nicolson, 1988

2/3   Whitelaw, W., *The Whitelaw Memoirs*, London, Aurum Press, 1989

2/3   Young, Lord, *The Enterprise Years*, London, Headline, 1990

For political balance, one might consult the following:

2/3   Callaghan, J., *Time and Chance*, Collins, 1987

2   Harris, R., *The Making of Neil Kinnock*, London, Faber, 1984

2/3   Healey, D., *Time of My Life*, London, Michael Joseph, 1989

2/3   Jenkins, R., *A Life at the Centre*, London, Macmillan, 1991

2   Kavanagh, D. (ed.), *The Politics of the Labour Party*, London, Allen & Unwin, 1982

2   Leapman, M., *Kinnock*, London, Unwin Hyman, 1987

2   Lindley, C. (ed.), *Partnership of Principle: Writings and Speeches on the Making of the Alliance by Roy Jenkins*, London, Secker & Warburg, 1985

2   Owen, D. and Steel, D., *The Time has Come: Partnership for Progress*, London, Weidenfeld & Nicolson, 1987

2/3   Owen, D., *Time to Declare*, London, Michael Joseph, 1991

2/3   Watkins, A., *A Conservative Coup: The Fall of Mrs Thatcher*, London, Duckworth, 1991

2   Williams, G. L. and A. L., *The Rise and Fall of the Social Democratic Party*, London, Macmillan, 1988

For general texts, the following are most useful:

Blake, R., *The Conservative Party from Peel to Thatcher*, London, Methuen, 1985

Boyce, D., *The Irish Question and British Politics 1968–1986*, London, Macmillan, 1988

Butler, D., *General Elections Since 1945*, Oxford, Blackwell, 1989

Hennessey, P. and Seldon, A., *Ruling Performance*, Oxford, Blackwell, 1989

Kavanagh, D. and Morris, P., *Consensus Politics from Attlee to Thatcher*, Oxford, Blackwell, 1989

Sources for coursework

There are a number of texts that concentrate on single events in the Thatcher era such as the Falklands war and the miners' strike, as well as individual election campaigns. Some secondary texts exist for:

2   Adeney, M. and Lloyd, J., *The Miners' Strike: Loss without Limit*, London, Routledge & Kegan Paul, 1985

2   Crick, M., *Scargill and the Miners*, Harmondsworth, Penguin, 1985

2   Freedman, L. and Gamba-Stonehouse, V., *Signals of War: The Falklands Conflict of 1982*, London, Faber, 1990

2   Hastings, M. and Jenkins, S., *The Battle for the Falklands*, London, Michael Joseph, 1983

2   MacGregor, I. and Tyler, R., *The Enemies Within: The Story of the Miners' Strike*, London, Collins, 1986

For individual research, newspapers held in reference libraries will be the most accessible source of information. Obviously it will be many years before official documents, such as cabinet minutes, become available, and then there is always the chance that they will be incomplete for security reasons. There is a mass of current statistical information available through official publications such as *Social Trends* and the Central Office of Information's *Key Data* (both HMSO). Retrospectives in newspapers and on television, such as those that greeted Mrs Thatcher's tenth anniversary in power, provide some form of interim assessment.

14 Britain and the world 1945–90: the 'new Elizabethan age'

INTRODUCTION

The accession of the second Elizabeth in 1952 produced much talk of a renewed national greatness; in the jargon of the time a 'new Elizabethan age' approached. Britain exploded her own nuclear bomb in October of that year and the conquest of Mount Everest by Sir Edmund Hilary in the year of the coronation seemed a fitting symbol of renewed greatness. It was to be 'A new Elizabethan age', but not in the sense anticipated. Britain, under Elizabeth II, was to return to being what she had been in the sixteenth century, an island off the Continent of Europe, a middle-ranked power of local influence. In 1985 she was, for the first time since the first Elizabeth's reign, to become a net importer of manufactured goods. If her navies did not now 'melt away', as Kipling had foreseen in 1897, at least they retreated, by the 1980s, to guarding their island home as in the 1580s. The worldwide Empire had disintegrated. Victorian imperial greatness was to be a fading memory. Empire Day itself was forgotten. The pattern of trade was to return increasingly to what it had been in the sixteenth century; West Germany and the rest of Europe, not India or America, were to be the key commercial partners. Eastern England was to thrive, Liverpool to decline. Perhaps in one sense it was a return to even earlier in the sixteenth century, for not since the reign of Mary had Britain been so dependent and so tied in to the needs of another power. Just as the England of Mary Tudor was an honorary part of the Habsburg Empire so under the second Elizabeth Britain was a key component of the American empire, her countryside covered with US bases even in peace-time. Britain, it seemed, could no longer defend herself. There was a retreat in 1973 to a position not seen since 1534. In that year the Act of Supremacy had cut England off from Rome, sundering her from the ghostly Roman imperium of papal power. In 1973 Britain's accession to the Treaty of Rome marked an end to that absolute national sovereignty proclaimed by Henry VIII. Christendom and a new Roman Empire were being re-created in the shape of the European Economic Community and some would say the province of

Britannia replaced the sovereign British state of the United Kingdom. Both her dependence on America and her growing integration into Europe eroded national sovereignty, but balancing between the two developments helped to preserve the illusion of independence and even greatness.

The most important factor in explaining Britain's international position in this forty-five year period was the continued relative decline of the British economy. By 1953 she possessed 8.6 per cent of the world's manufacturing production, only slightly less than in 1939. The temporary devastation of Germany and Japan had given her a respite, but in relation to the USA Britain was further behind than ever. Her giant ally possessed 44.7 per cent of world manufacture – a position which Britain, even at her most dominant in the nineteenth century, had never held. The average Briton had a living standard half that of the North American. As the other European economies recovered in the 1950s Britain's weakness became manifest and she slid remorselessly down the league table of world economies (see Table 14.1). By the early 1960s West Germany had passed her, and by the 1970s she was trailing France and Japan. By 1980 she held only 4 per cent of world manufacture and had fallen to sixth place. By the late 1980s Italy had pushed her down to number seven despite the so-called Thatcher 'economic miracle' of the decade. On 21 March 1990 *The Independent* produced a forecast of GDP for 1990, based on figures from the OECD and the UK Treasury, which is shown here. In terms of living standards most other West European countries were ahead. Britain's share of world trade showed the same remorseless decline. Standing at 19.8 per cent in 1955 it had fallen to 8.7 per cent in 1976. In the mid-1970s there was much academic debate about Britain ceasing to count as a developed country. It was

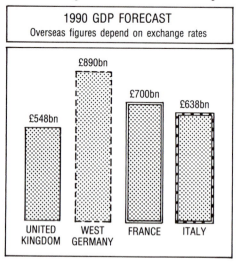

From *The Independent*, 21 March 1990

an interesting topic of discussion whether the once world leader would deindustrialize. A new category would presumably have had to have been invented, a 'retro-veloping' economy. The changes of the 1980s seemed to have ended such speculation and if there has been no economic miracle of recovery, the relative slide has been slowed or even stopped.

Table 14.1 Comparison of the world powers ($ billion)

	USA	Japan	West Germany	France	Britain
1952	350	16	32	29	44
1962	560	59	89	74	81
1972	1152	317	229	224	128
1977	1890	677	508	374	263

Source: After P. Kennedy, *The Realities behind Diplomacy*, London, Fontana, 1981, p. 34.

The problems posed by the mismatch of extensive world commitments and a shrinking industrial base could have been the recipe for repeated national humiliation and extensive human misery. The decline of other great empires did not give much encouragement that either of these fates could be avoided. In practice, decline was managed with much skill by both parties whenever they formed the government. Labour retreated from India and Palestine in 1948 and the Tories left most of Africa by 1964. Labour, as a result of renewed financial crisis, pulled out of Aden and an East of Suez role. By the 1970s little was left to retreat from. The Conservatives precipitated one of the few international conflicts when their enthusiasm for economy encouraged Argentina to seize the Falklands before Britain was ready to give the islands to them. A neat, and on the whole successful, war resulted and helped to conceal reality. The reality was, however, made explicit by the same Thatcher Government which negotiated withdrawal from Hong Kong. The almost universal adoption of Liberal values acted as an anaesthetic to the pain of decline. Empire was wrong; therefore its loss was a moral gain for the country. Few societies have had such success in self-induced pain-killing. Former opponents like Gandhi could be placed in the national pantheon of moral greatness. Churchill's 'half-naked fakir' was after all a slightly eccentric Middle Temple lawyer, as much British as Indian.

Throughout most of the forty-five years covered here, the two parties adopted a broad consensus on Britain's relations with the rest of the world. It was a Labour Government which embraced the American alliance and entered NATO, and also adopted nuclear weapons as a totem of continued national importance. Conservative reaction to the loss of the Suez Canal in 1956 produced a brief breakdown in inter-party agreement but there was no real argument over fundamentals. NATO and the American alliance would go hand in hand with the imperial retreat. On this both parties were agreed. Labour was marginally less keen than the Tories on entry into Europe but both Labour and Tory dissidents opposed it and in both parties the leadership came to endorse it with great hesitancy. In the early 1980s, as the Labour Party seemed to capitulate to CND, there was the possibility of a genuine breakdown in consensus. Labour, in 1983, wanted to abandon nuclear weapons and remove US nuclear bases from Britain. By the late 1980s this could be seen as an aberration and the traditional bi-partisan approach had been restored. Labour was now marginally keener than the Conservatives on Europe and the Conservatives marginally more suspicious of the Soviet Union, and therefore inclined to place greater emphasis on the continued importance of NATO. Genuine differences were, however, slight.

LABOUR IN POWER 1945–51

In 1945 Britain had not slid to the position she was to hold forty-five years later. She was still the undisputed number three in the world and a great power. She still had over one thousand warships with bases around the globe; a huge and powerful airforce second only to the USA; and troops not only back in all the old imperial possessions like Hong Kong and Singapore but now in new territories like Greece, Libya and, of course, Germany. Much of Africa and most of the Middle East were British and her allies the USA and the USSR still looked on her with some jealousy. Britain sat with the other two victors as the 'Big Three' at the Potsdam Conference in July 1945 and assumed one of the permanent seats on the Security Council of the new United Nations. The Chiefs of Staff put their view of Britain clearly in a report of May 1947:

> The United Kingdom, as the senior member of the British Commonwealth and a Great Power, must be prepared at all times to fulfil her responsibilities not only to the United Nations but also to herself as a Great Power. To fulfil her obligations, she must achieve a strong and sound economy which will give her the ability to expand industry and the armed forces immediately on to a war basis.

The same passage of course also points out the weakness of Britain's position. The end of the Second World War found the country more over-extended than in 1918 and economically far weaker. The war had cost Britain one quarter of her national wealth. Over £1 billion of her overseas investments had been sold and £3.3 billion of sterling debts were outstanding. Property and shipping losses came to over £2 billion and much industrial and transport equipment was shattered and in dire need of replacement. The balance of payments was the most pressing problem that arose from all this. Exports had fallen by two-thirds and without US assistance Britain faced possible starvation. Yet the ending of the war in the Far East, much earlier than anticipated, led to the abrupt ending of Lend-Lease. The country in Keynes's famous words faced a 'financial Dunkirk'.

Churchill had gone to the Potsdam Conference in July but, at the end of a three-day adjournment for the British election, Truman and Stalin found themselves facing the new management team of the British Empire, Attlee and the new Foreign Secretary Ernest Bevin. Bevin was both literally and metaphorically a heavyweight and his surprise appointment in preference to Hugh Dalton pleased the civil servants at the Foreign Office:

> I think we may do better with Bevin than with any other of the Labourites. I think he's broad-minded and sensible, honest and courageous. But whether he's an inspired Foreign Minister or not I don't know. He's the heavyweight of the Cabinet and will get his own way with them, so if he can be put on the right line, that may be all right.
> (Quoted in A. Bullock, *Ernest Bevin*, London, Heinemann, 1983, p. 776)

He was a formidable man, the most powerful figure in the Attlee Cabinet, and the key prop to Attlee himself. He lacked any formal education, spoke no foreign languages and uttered his native tongue with a soft Somerset burr. He lacked pomposity and treated everyone from the King and Joseph Stalin to his own secretary in the same way. The King liked him but Stalin did not, claiming simply that Bevin 'is no gentleman'. The French Foreign Minister, Bidault, tended to become 'Bidet' and Molotov, 'Mowlotov', much to the prissy Soviet politician's irritation. Bevin's prejudices were legendary. Top amongst these were Communists, intellectuals and Germans. As he said of the latter to General Sir Brian Robertson, 'I tries 'ard, Brian, but I 'ates them.' His was a giant colourful personality to rival Churchill's. Like Churchill he had the aptitude for hard work wedded to a capacity for imaginative leaps in understanding. His Foreign Office staff, the most exclusive in the civil service, came really to appreciate him, and he them. His years as a trade-union negotiator stood him in good stead and his close personal relations with Attlee meant that he really could make policy. He stands comparison with Salisbury whom he much admired: 'I was reading some papers of old Salisbury, y'now 'e had a lot of sense.' Like Salisbury he took a cool rational view of Britain's interests and like a good trade unionist he was determined to defend his country's interests in the world just as for years he had defended the interests of the Transport and General Workers' Union.

Bevin fully appreciated the difficulties of Britain's position, but like most men of his age he did not doubt her importance. He had no time for the morally magnificent but largely meaningless phrases of left-wingers like Michael Foot, or clever intellectuals like Richard Crossman. He embodied British interests and saw early on that these would have to be stubbornly defended with few weapons. A close working relationship with America was vital but in 1945 that did not look like being too easy to achieve. Isolationism was again a distinct possibility and withdrawal from Europe dangerously likely. The ending of Lend-Lease was an ominous portent. Bevin was deeply suspicious of Russian ambitions and his years in the Labour movement struggling with Communists gave him a very jaundiced view of the 'comrades'. He hoped to achieve a *modus vivendi* with Stalin but quickly came to appreciate the Russian's unwillingness to concede when there appeared to be so much to play for. If the USA were to withdraw from Europe a weakened Britain and a shattered western Europe, with large Communist parties in France and Italy, provided Russia with plenty of opportunities. What Stalin intended was, and is, unclear, but Bevin did not give him the benefit of the doubt. A man with ten million Russian corpses to his credit probably did not deserve it.

Relations with the USA were vital both for Britain's financial position and the security of her worldwide interests. Bevin never forgot this and firmly resisted the anti-Americanism of many of his backbenchers. He was never, however, an American pawn. His firmness often irritated them yet they came to respect him as a friend. There was a very real danger of an Anglo-American rift in the immediate aftermath of the war. Various US politicians, amongst them Henry Wallace, the Secretary of Commerce, had a naive faith in Russian good intentions, and large numbers particularly of Mid-West Republicans looked forward to a return to American isolationism. Lend-Lease was ended abruptly and rapid demobilization and the withdrawal of US troops from Europe looked like being the first step in leaving it defenceless against the massive Red Army. The ending of US co-operation on atomic weapons, breaking the war-time agreement of 1943, was a further straw in the wind indicating a renewed isolation. Keynes succeeded in negotiating a loan to cover the dollar gap but the terms were tougher than expected and reflected US suspicions of British imperial power and the Sterling Area (the trading area based on the Empire accepting sterling as international currency) as a powerful economic block. The problem of Palestine also exacerbated Anglo-American tensions as the powerful Jewish lobby in the ruling Democratic Party resented Britain's resistance to renewed Jewish immigration.

If the Americans were cooler than hoped then the Russians were positively frigid. The meeting of the Council of Ministers of the 'Big Three' showed increasing acrimony. Molotov seemed intent on taking a ruthlessly tough stance and the installation of several puppet regimes throughout eastern Europe could be interpreted as part of a Soviet bid for European hegemony. Talks on the ex-Italian territory in Africa stalemated as did those on the future of Germany. Communist guerrillas in Greece were only contained by expensive British intervention. Soviet moves in northern Persia and against Turkey revived ancient fears of a Russian bid for domination of the Middle East. How serious the threat was is difficult to gauge. It may be, as the British Ambassador, Sir Archibald Clark-Kerr, in Moscow was to write in October 1946:

> They are a very difficult and bad-mannered people; like a pup which is not house-trained, they bounce about and bark and knock things over and misbehave themselves generally, and then next day are puzzled if one is still resentful. They still have a terrible sense of inferiority. They like, therefore, to be treated very nicely in public and it does nothing but harm to shout at them in public; on the other hand shouting in private often does good.
>
> (Quoted in D. Dilks, *Retreat from Power*, vol. II, London, Macmillan, 1981, p. 21)

Certainly there was probably no plan for world, or even European, domination but a determination to safeguard the Soviet Union after a devastating war and make the most of a favourable situation. Bevin was determined not to yield and throughout 1945 and 1946 almost alone stood against Molotov and resisted cabinet pressure to trim Britain's military capacity. He talked as toughly to Molotov as to any employer in his days as a union negotiator:

> Do you want to get Austria behind your Iron Curtain? You can't do that. Do you want Turkey and the Straits? You can't have them. Do you want Korea? You can't have that. You are putting your neck out too far, and one day you will have it chopped off. We know much more about you than you imagine. We know that you cannot stand a war. But you are behaving in such a way that one day there will be a showdown.
>
> (ibid., p. 23)

In March 1946, Churchill, enjoying the leisure of a leader of the opposition, made his famous speech in Fulton, Missouri:

> From Stettin in the Baltic . . . to Trieste in the Adriatic an iron curtain has descended across the Continent. Behind that line lie all the capitals of the ancient States of Central and Eastern Europe. . . . The Communist parties which were very small . . . have been raised to preeminence and power far beyond their numbers and are seeking everywhere to obtain totalitarian control.

Publicly Bevin did not endorse it but privately he fully approved. Slowly US opinion and that on the Labour back benches came round to the idea of firm resistance to the USSR and a realization that the high hopes of a world without great power confrontation, when the new UN would settle everything, was utopian. Bevin played his cards masterfully. He announced the ending of British support to Greece and Turkey in February 1947 which she could no longer afford, and thus 'bounced' the USA into the 'Truman Doctrine' of March 1947. Truman proposed cash for those countries fighting for their freedom and $400 million was forth-coming in May for Greece and Turkey. The replacement of the US Secretary of State, Byrnes, by General Marshall in January 1947 helped relations with Britain and in that same month the British and the US zones in Germany were united into Bizonia, the basis of the future West German state. As early as May 1946 Bevin had been telling the Cabinet: 'the danger of Russia has become certainly as great, and possibly even greater, than a revived Germany.'

Soviet behaviour seemed to confirm this impression and enabled Bevin to carry the Labour Party with him. The 'Keep Left' Group urged a more sympathetic view of Russia but were effectively answered by a forceful pamphlet of the young Denis Healey, entitled *Cards on the Table*. Healey, a one-time Communist, was appalled by Russian treat-ment of social democrats in eastern Europe. Free elections had been held in Hungary in 1946 which gave the Communists 16 per cent of the vote. The leaders of the winning party were all arrested. No free elections were then held until 1990. The year 1947 was the make or break point. Most of the war-time preconceptions had been exposed as irrelevant. The war-time alliance had fragmented and the United Nations became merely an alternative forum for disagreement. Bevin was ill and depressed in the winter of 1946–7 and the renewed financial crisis of 1947 strengthened the hand of all those in the Cabinet urging withdrawal from the Middle East. There was withdrawal from Greece and Turkey, as indicated, and from Palestine but Bevin was intent on involving the US as much as possible while retaining Britain's position as a great power. Over the next two years he appeared to have at least achieved the former and possibly the latter. His greatest success was his response to the Marshall Plan:

> When Marshall made his Harvard speech on June 5th, 1947, offering to provide American support if the Europeans themselves would take the initiative in devising a recovery programme, it is doubtful if he personally realised how fast events would move. Dean Acheson, then his deputy, who played a key role in drafting the speech, briefed a few selected British correspondents on its potential importance, and asked them to make sure Bevin was aware of his views. In fact Bevin was ahead of him. The moment he heard a report of the speech on his bedside radio, Bevin decided to act, without even, as his officials suggested, trying to find out what Marshall meant.
>
> (D. Healey, *The Time of My Life*, London, Michael Joseph, 1989, p. 114)

Bevin translated a vague gesture of goodwill into practical assistance, taking the lead in organizing the European powers and developing the detailed programme of co-operation required by the USA. By September Marshall was presented with a four-year plan of European economic reconstruction and the formal body, the Organization for European Economic Construction (OEEC), was set up in Paris in April 1948. The result was a staggering triumph. A total of $12 billion was used to revive the European economy. By January 1951 the British government could announce it no longer needed its quota of aid. It had had the lion's share. Germany had also recovered and western Europe as a whole was well on the way to wealth and prosperity. It was also as a result much less vulnerable to internal Communist subversion or external threat by 1950.

The provision of military resistance to this subversion was Bevin's other great achievement in the two years after 1947. Already in 1947 Britain had signed a fifty-year treaty of alliance with France. Ostensibly aimed at Germany it was to be the first move in a defensive network which reached its climax in 1949. Bevin was helped in this by Soviet behaviour. In February 1948 democracy in Czechoslovakia was snuffed out. It helped to silence left-wing critics in the party. Bevin had already launched his campaign for a 'Western Union' in a speech to the Commons in January. The Brussels Treaty of March joined Britain and France with the Benelux countries in a mutual defence pact. It was an end to the nineteenth-century isolation and stood in marked contrast to Britain's behaviour in the 1920s. Soviet pressure in Norway and then the crisis over Berlin kept tension high. In June 1948 the Soviet Union blocked road access by the Allies to Berlin, a breach of all previous agreements. The USA with enthusiastic support from Britain airlifted between 5,000 and 8,000 tons a day of food as well as medical supplies into beleaguered Berlin for 324 days. It was made quite clear to the Soviet Union that interference with this airlift would mean war. Ominously B29 long-range bombers arrived in East Anglia. The USA had a monopoly of atomic weapons, a fact the Soviets could not forget. At the same time America resolved to join the West European defence arrangements when Senator Vandenberg's resolution passed the Senate on 11 June by 64 votes to 2. The result was the formal inauguration of NATO in April 1949.

The USSR conceded defeat over Berlin in the next two months and that same year West Germany was created. Soviet intransigence, whether the result of wide-ranging aggression or merely as Clark-Kerr implied the bouncy behaviour of an ill-trained pup, had been disastrous for her interests. A prosperous and armed western Europe was in existence and in forty years it was to destroy the Soviet Empire by peacefully, yet firmly, eye-balling her.

As a corollary to this confrontation with the Soviet Union Bevin and Attlee maintained a defence posture surprising for any peace-time British government and doubly surprising for a Labour one. A worldwide network of military bases was retained and conscription, despite a back-bench revolt, during peace-time was accepted in April 1947. Even more controversial since, but not at the time because the decision was taken in secret, on 18 October 1946 Britain took the first steps in developing her own nuclear weapons. Dalton and Cripps fought the proposal fiercely on financial grounds. The matter was decided when Bevin returned from a lengthy lunch and threw his considerable weight against the two opponents of a British bomb. Once again he was determined Britain should be a great power.

It was this same notion that led Bevin to a certain coolness on moves to greater European integration which began in 1948. Britain had to fall much lower before she humbled herself before the European partners and saw herself merely as a European power. She still had an Empire to guard and a world role to uphold.

India and Palestine – retreat

'The jewel in the crown' of the Empire was rapidly abandoned despite the pretensions of Britain's greatness. Liberals and Liberal Conservatives had for long moved hesitatingly to this goal. The financial cost of holding India was increasingly too great and the moral costs of real repression unacceptable to Liberal England as the response to Dyer's massacre at Amritsar in 1919 showed. Perhaps more important still it had ceased to be a vital economic interest. As chapter 9 indicates British exports of cloth to India had declined rapidly since the First World War, to be replaced by native production or Japanese imports. 'The jewel in the crown' had become an expensive luxury. Only imperial romantics like Churchill opposed the granting of dominion status. The Second World War had provided further blows to British India. The prestige of the Raj found it hard to recover from the rout in Malaya and Burma and the supreme humiliation at Singapore in 1942.

The new Labour Government sympathized with the ideal of Indian independence. Attlee himself had been a member of the Simon Commission of 1930 and self-government now became largely a question of timing. The chief problem remained religious rivalries between Hindus and Muslims. The Muslim League's leader Mohammed Ali Jinnah demanded partition and an independent state of Pakistan. The Hindus looked to the leadership of the Congress Party under Gandhi and Nehru. They hoped, as did the Labour Government, to preserve the unity of an independent India. Regional elections in 1946 produced clear-cut divisions on religious lines and a cabinet mission under the respected old socialist Lord Pethick Lawrence found deadlock between the two sides.

Jinnah called for direct action to create Pakistan and communal violence began on a terrifying scale on 16 August 1946. Thousands died in Calcutta and the army found the restoration of order difficult. Civil war seemed possible with the British caught in the middle. It hastened the decision to withdraw. Attlee decided to fix a deadline for withdrawal – June 1948 – with Lord Louis Mountbatten appointed as Viceroy to supervise the transfer of power. Mountbatten arrived in March 1947 and accepted that partition was inevitable and that independence had to come that year. The 15th of August 1947 was to see the ending of the Raj. The Bill passed the Commons rapidly with muted Tory opposition, Churchill being kept away. Partition and independence were accompanied by the most ghastly atrocities as refugees struggled from one side to the other of the new states. Somewhere between 250,000 and one million died. Lapping quotes an eye-witness, Sardar Shan Kabbhyat Khan:

> We were taking these trains to the Walton railway station because otherwise people were getting worked up in Lahore. There you saw bodies of women, some suckling their babies, and lances straight through the babies and the mothers. Bloated bodies; pulling them out, you couldn't get to those compartments on account of the smell. And then to look at the bodies – no human being could stand the sight of women in such a condition.
>
> (B. Lapping, *The End of Empire*, London, Granada/Paladin, 1985, p. 134)

Given the religious tension, which still continues to this day, some violence was inevitable but whether it would have been less if Britain had withdrawn earlier is open to dispute. Certainly, the new India and Pakistan got off to a better start than the French Indo-Chinese colonies where the colonial power chose to hang on. Attlee and Mountbatten probably did the best possible in the circumstances. There was no legacy of bitterness in India towards Britain and uniquely amongst Third World countries India became and remained a democracy. The first President of the Republic of India, Dr Rajenda Praed, expressed a certain thanks to the ex-colonial power:

> While our achievement is in no small measure due to our sufferings and sacrifices, it is also the result of world forces and events, and last, though not least, it is the consummation and fulfilment of the historic traditions and democratic ideals of the British.
>
> (Quoted in W. D. McIntyre, *Colonies into Commonwealth*, London, Blandford, p. 206)

Despite the atrocities that marked Britain's departure from India, the whole episode was seen largely as a skilled success by the Labour Government. The withdrawal from Palestine was anything but a success and the consequences have cursed the world for over forty years. The bitter conflict between Arab and Jew proved too much and ignominious retreat was enforced. Already by the late 1930s increased Jewish immigration to the British Mandate of Palestine had created a massive problem of law and order. Britain faced an impossible situation. She was anxious to be fair to Arab and Jew. Continued Jewish immigration could only be at the expense of the native Palestinians and acceptance of such immigration would upset the whole Arab world which Britain was anxious to placate. During the war two Jewish terrorist organizations had been founded: the Irgun, under Menachem Begin and the Stern Gang, one of whose leaders was, like Begin, to be another future Prime Minister of Israel, Yitzhak Shamir. Both set about murdering British officials. One was Lord Moyne, killed in 1944 to the personal horror of his close friend Churchill, hitherto a keen ally of the Jews. The Foreign Office was anxious to retain the friendship of Arab regimes in Iraq, Saudi Arabia and Egypt, and to retain the use of Palestine as a military base in the Middle East. US pressure tended to favour the Jews. Truman was very conscious of the powerful Jewish vote in New York and against the advice of the State Department, who like the experts in the British Foreign Office were well aware of broader world interests, put pressure on Britain to admit more immigrants.

Bevin like most Labour Party members was initially very supportive of the Zionist cause but the advice of his experts and the Jewish terrorist tactics persuaded him otherwise: 'Clem, about Palestine, according to my lads in the Office we've got it wrong, we've got to think again.' Britain attempted over the next two years to stem the tide of Jewish immigration and maintain law and order. Jewish atrocities grew, reaching a climax in 1946 with the bombing of the King David Hotel in Jerusalem, which killed ninety-one. One hundred thousand British security personnel were drafted into Palestine and in the year 1945–6 £100 million was spent. Two young British sergeants captured by Irgun were hanged in July 1947. This action produced anti-semitic riots in British cities. The government decided that holding on was not worth it and under the added pressure of the 1947 economic crisis decided to quit in September 1947. The problem was handed over to the United Nations who voted for partition. Britain abstained and refused to co-operate in the process. On 15 May 1948 the British mandate ended and the Jews proclaimed the state of Israel. It was the signal for the first Arab–Israeli war.

Despite withdrawal from India and Palestine there was no intention of running down the whole Empire. Bevin insisted on Britain's continued role in the Middle East. In a paper circulated to the Cabinet in August 1949 this was made quite clear:

> In peace and war, the Middle East is an area of cardinal importance to the U.K., second only to the UK itself. Strategically the Middle East is a focal point of communications, a source of oil, a shield to Africa and the Indian Ocean, and an irreplaceable offensive base. Economically it is, owing to oil and cotton, essential to United Kingdom recovery.
>
> (Quoted in Bullock, op. cit., p. 113)

The Empire as a whole, and Africa in particular, had never been so important to Britain. It was not obvious that Britain's future lay with

Europe. In 1938 the Empire provided 39.5 per cent of British imports and 49 per cent of her exports. In the immediate post-war world both these figures rose:

	Imports	*Exports*
1946–9	48%	57.5%
1950–4	49%	54.0%

In the early 1950s 65 per cent of Britain's capital exports went to the Empire. The Labour Government acknowledged its importance to the British economy with its Colonial Development and Welfare Acts of 1945, 1949 and 1950. It notoriously wasted £36 million trying to make groundnuts grow in Tanganyika in 1948. Britain therefore still remained an imperial power with vast worldwide interests to safeguard. India, Burma and Ceylon were abandoned in the Far East but in Malaya a long and ultimately successful campaign was fought against Communist guerrillas. By 1957 100,000 troops were involved. If Palestine was abandoned and the majority of troops withdrawn from most of Egypt, a large garrison was kept in the Canal Zone and scattered in small bases throughout the rest of the region. The sun had not yet set on the Empire but it was early evening.

The last year of the Labour Government 1950–1

All the problems facing post-war Britain seemed to be present in one form or another during the last months of Attlee's Labour Government. Attlee was tired and Bevin exhausted with deteriorating health finally forcing his resignation in March 1951. Six weeks later he was dead. His successor Herbert Morrison was not a success. Britain continued to show her hostility to closer integration in Europe. The NATO structure that finally emerged was a triumph of a sort for Bevin. He had secured the commitment of American troops to Europe with a command structure remarkably similar to that of the war-time Allies. A US general was to be supreme commander but Britons figured prominently. There was no European army as was favoured by the Frenchman Jean Monnet. If Bevin got the transatlantic structure he wanted Britain was left out of the first moves towards European integration. Britain was not consulted in the setting up of the European Coal and Steel Community which essentially came into being in April 1951. She attempted to obstruct it, but was ignored.

In the Middle East fresh problems multiplied. In Egypt the giant British base in the Canal Zone came under attack and growing Egyptian nationalistic fervour made its continuing viability doubtful. In Iran the Prime Minister Dr Mussadeq challenged British power when he nationalized the Anglo-Iranian Oil Company. Morrison, the new Foreign Secretary, was furious and favoured a Palmerstonian stroke but was informed of its impossibility without massive US support. All Britain could do was send naval forces to the Persian Gulf as an impotent gesture of protest.

The greatest problem of all was posed in the Far East with the outbreak in June 1950 of the Korean War. The attack on South Korea by the North was seen in Britain and America as a Soviet-inspired act of aggression. Baulked in Europe, the Bear in its red outfit was lashing out elsewhere. Britain sent large naval forces to assist the US-dominated United Nations expedition. A small British land contingent was also dispatched. The outbreak of the war forced a much enlarged rearmament programme which was divisive for the Labour Party and harmful to the economy. The threat of the USA extending the war against mainland China when Chinese volunteers intervened also produced strains and stresses in the Atlantic alliance. Korea and the Far East were not so vital an interest to Britain as they were to America. America was annoyed by British recognition of the new Communist China and Britain was deeply concerned at the prospect of the USA using nuclear weapons against China.

Despite this final flurry of problems before the government's expiry in October 1951, the achievements of Bevin and Attlee in the field of foreign affairs had been extensive. US aid had been gained for Britain's economic recovery which was well in hand by 1951. The Soviet threat in Europe, such as it was, had been contained and the seeds of a prosperous western Europe had been sown. Furthermore, in contrast to 1919, US involvement in European affairs had been retained and strengthened. NATO was Bevin's supreme achievement and it gave the Continent of Europe forty years of peace. Outside Europe retreat was the order of the day, but except in Palestine, it was not a rout and Britain was still to be taken seriously as a world power. Her worldwide interests could and would still be defended for a little time longer.

THE CONSERVATIVE VERSION OF MANAGED DECLINE 1951–64

The return of Churchill as Prime Minister with Eden as Foreign Secretary marked no clear break in policy. The party of imperialism and patriotism might sing 'Land of Hope and Glory' at the party conferences and decorate their platforms with Union flags, but the retreat from Empire was to continue at an accelerated pace in the late 1950s. By the time that Labour returned to office, the Empire had contracted to a few scattered territories. As with Bevin, the Atlantic relationship was considered paramount and both Churchill (1951–5) and Macmillan (1957–63) prided themselves on their special relationship with the occupants of the White House. Under Eden (1955–7) the relationship cooled somewhat but did not affect the centrality of NATO to British thinking. There was continuity in nuclear policy and the Conservatives demanded to follow the Americans in manufacturing an H-Bomb, many times more destructive than the A-Bomb, that had devastated Hiroshima and Nagasaki. As with the Labour Government Parliament was not initially informed of the decision. Attitudes to Europe remained essentially the same. There was a suspicion of any moves towards federalism and many would argue that the most vital mistake in the post-war world was made in 1957 when Britain refused to participate in the establishment of the Common Market by the Treaty of Rome. Leadership of the new Europe passed to Paris and Bonn. London was marginalized. At the time there was more concern with the Middle East than Europe and it was here that Britain was to face humiliation and the most obvious public exposure of the hollowness of her claim to great power status.

The Churchill Government 1951–5

Initially the position in the Middle East improved. With the help of the CIA, Iran's Dr Mussadeq was toppled and a pro-western government under the Shah restored in 1953. Churchill and MI6 were delighted. They were less delighted with the price of American assistance. The British company which controlled Iran's oil output had its share reduced to 40 per cent, five American companies took 40 per cent and the Dutch Shell and a French company took the remaining 20 per cent. It was the last time a Middle Eastern government would be toppled from London, but the new regime in Tehran would rely on Washington henceforth rather than the old imperial power. Eden and the Foreign Office adopted a much more realistic view of British power than Churchill and Number 10, as Eden's Private Secretary, Sir Evelyn Shuckburgh, wrote:

> Eden was, from the time I came to know him in 1951, constantly preoccupied with the problem of how to get this country into a tenable position, because we were stretched all over the world in places which we had no possibility of continuing to dominate. It was a question of persuading not only his own party but the nation. He was not helped and he was really rather frightened by the opposite view in the party, rather under the umbrella of the great war leader. Churchill realized the crucial importance of the Suez canal zone, the strong point for the navy, the airforce and the army, linking the Commonwealth as a defence unit. He was therefore very much against the proposed withdrawal. On the other hand he was eighty, Eden his crown prince was for it, and the Americans were for it, so he was in a difficult position.
> (Quoted in Lapping, op. cit., p. 308)

Churchill and many Tory traditionalists felt that the policy of 'scuttle' was triumphant when Eden converted the Cabinet to total withdrawal from Egypt and the Sudan. The great base in the Canal Zone would be abandoned and Egypt, occupied since 1882, would be left to its new military leader Colonel Nasser unencumbered with British troops. Cyprus would be the new centre of British power in the Middle East.

If the Foreign Office believed in reducing commitments there was no intention of abandoning a world role. Britain might now be the junior to America in the containment of Communism but she was not yet a mere European power. A defence paper of 1952 could still be entitled 'A Global Strategy Paper', and the acceleration of the Valiant Bomber programme was intended to give real teeth to this role. The first V-Bomber squadron became operational in 1955. The announcement of the decision to manufacture the H-Bomb that year gave the bombers special significance and together the weapon system seemed to keep Britain in the first division of powers along with the USSR and the USA. Britain's membership of two anti-Soviet defence organizations outside Europe pointed to her continuing world role. In 1955 she joined the South-East Asia Treaty Organization. The presence of two divisions in Malaya, successfully fighting communist guerrillas, and the giant base at Singapore were evidence of real commitment in the region. In the Middle East troops were in Aden and the Persian Gulf and Britain's membership of the new anti-Soviet pact, CENTO (the Central Treaty Organization, or Baghdad Treaty), in April 1955 explained her continued Middle East-ern role despite the withdrawal from Egypt.

Britain's great power status was not merely confined to the military confrontation with Communism. Eden secured an important diplomatic success in 1954 at the Geneva Conference on Indo-China. The long-running battle of the French, with increasing US military assistance, to cling on to their former colonies against the communist organization Viet Minh was finally ended with a compromise. The US Secretary of State, John Foster Dulles disliked and distrusted Eden, whose manner seemed effete and affected to the plain-speaking communist-hating American. Eden's habit of addressing people as 'Dear' or 'My Dear' grated on many. The Canadian Foreign Minister had already remarked to an American friend how much he preferred 'Old Ernie Bevin's "My boy"'. Effete or not, Eden scored a triumph at Geneva in getting far more from the Vietnam Communists and their Chinese and Russian backers than Dulles had anticipated. French withdrawal was facilitated and the division of Vietnam along the 17th parallel agreed upon. The North would be under a communist rule, the South a pro-western one. Laos and Cambodia, the two remaining provinces of French Indo-China, would be independent and neutral. Dulles was irritated by Eden's success and regarded it as a sell-out.

Eden gained a less controversial success in the same year when the integration of West Germany into the Western Alliance was settled. NATO may have been established in 1949 but when the Conservatives came to power 14 NATO divisions faced an estimated 200 under Soviet control. The USA was pressing for the creation of a West German army inside NATO. Failure to respond could have produced US withdrawal yet France was nervous of German rearmament and instead floated the idea of an integrated European army to which Britain herself was hostile. Eden settled the impasse by a rapid tour of European capitals and a skilfully managed conference at Lancaster House in September 1954. The USA and Canada promised to maintain their forces in Europe and Germany and Italy were admitted to full membership of NATO. To quieten France's fears Britain promised to keep four divisions in Germany for fifty years. Russia set up the Warsaw Pact in retaliation but also signalled her desire for an easing of tension by withdrawing from Austria.

Eden and the Suez Crisis

Eden succeeded Churchill without controversy in April 1955. He was heir apparent as Chamberlain had been to Baldwin. Eden's reputation had never stood higher at home and he swept to a comfortable victory in the ensuing general election, with the slogan, 'Working for Peace'. Yet few prime ministers can have fallen so far, so fast. The supreme irony in Eden's case was that his fall came in his own chosen area of expertise, foreign policy. There were ominous signs of weakness in his and Britain's international position. Churchill had a very special place in American affections yet of him the American President, Eisenhower, had already written in his diary in 1953:

> Winston is trying to relive the days of World War II.
>
> In those days he had the enjoyable feeling that he and our President were sitting on some rather Olympian platform with respect to the rest of the world, and directing world affairs from that point of vantage. Even if this picture were an accurate one of those days, it would have no application to the present. But it was only partially true, even then, as many of us who, in various corners of the world, had to work out the solutions for nasty local problems, are well aware.
>
> In the present international complexities, any hope of establishing such a relationship is completely fatuous.
>
> (Quoted in D. Carlton, *A. Eden*, London, Allen Lane, 1981, p. 333)

Eden did not have Churchill's advantages. As indicated already he irritated many Americans with his patronizing mannerisms. More important than any such personality problems, however, was the economic decline of Britain which showed itself in 1955 with the vulnerability of sterling. Butler, the Chancellor, introduced the convertibility of the pound producing speculative runs against it. Britain would be clearly susceptible to the slightest US pressure on her currency.

Egypt and its new ruler Colonel Gamal Abdel Nasser were the occasion of Eden's clash with the USA and the cause of his downfall.

The 37-year-old Egyptian was one of the new breed of Arab nationalists, resentful of the old imperial power and its continued claims to paramountcy in the Middle East. Nasser refused to join the new CENTO and encouraged other Arab states not to join. Cairo radio put out a stream of propaganda against the pro-British Iraqi regime of King Feisal and Nuri es Said and against King Hussein in Jordan. Eden paid a visit to Egypt in February 1955 just before becoming premier and tried to persuade Nasser to join the British defence pact. He lectured the Egyptian soldier much to the latter's irritation. Nasser's holding of Eden's hand in a press picture irritated the future Prime Minister. The visit was not a success and Nasser was intent upon independence and playing the anti-colonial card. He bought arms from Czechoslovakia and Russia and aimed to play off Egypt against the West. Eden's initial reaction was gentle wooing with promises to provide large sums of western aid and to build the Aswan Dam, but this approach changed rapidly when King Hussein of Jordan dismissed his army commander, Sir John Glubb. Eden wrongly put this down to Nasser's doing. Anthony Nutting, Minister of State at the Foreign Office, described Eden's reaction:

> Eden's reaction to Glubb's dismissal was violent. He blamed Nasser and he decided that the world just wasn't big enough to hold both of them. One had to go. He declared that night a personal war on Abdel Nasser. I spent most of that night with him, first in the Cabinet room and then, when he retired to bed, I sat with him and we went on arguing until five o'clock in the morning. He simply would not accept that the dismissal of Glubb was not Nasser's doing. He called me nothing but a Foreign Office clerk and said I didn't understand anything about politics and the implications of this dismissal for Britain and her Prime Minister. At one point he said, 'You won't accept any arguments against Nasser, you are in love with Nasser.' He was becoming irrational.
>
> (Quoted in Lapping, op. cit., p. 316)

Eden decided to apply pressure by dropping the loan, and the USA, infuriated by Nasser's recognition of communist China, went along with Britain. It was felt that Russia could not step in and Nasser would be humiliated and probably toppled. In response the Egyptian leader, on 16 July, announced the nationalization of the Suez Canal. It was simply cocking a snook at Britain and the west. Eden was urged by friendly Arabs like Nuri of Iraq 'to hit Nasser hard', and immediately the first plans were drawn up for military intervention. Operation Musketeer, as it became known, was quickly drafted, but it was found that it would take at least six weeks to get off the ground. It was also decided to approach France, similarly angered by the nationalization of the Canal, which was a French company, despite the British government's major shareholding. France was also angered by Nasser's support for terrorism in French Algeria. France agreed to provide 35,000 troops and 200 planes. Britain would provide 45,000 men and 300 planes including the vital bombers to destroy the Egyptian airforce. Dulles and the Americans exerted all their influence to avoid conflict. A presidential election was due in November and peace in the Middle East was thought to be desirable by Eisenhower to secure his re-election. Early in August Eden wrote to Eisenhower describing his objectives:

> The removal of Nasser, and the installation in Egypt of a regime less hostile to the West, must therefore also rank high among our objectives. We must hope, as you say in your message, that the forthcoming conference will bring such pressures upon Nasser that the efficient operation of the Canal can be assured for the future. If so, everyone will be relieved and there will be no need of force. Moreover, if Nasser is compelled to disgorge his spoils, it is improbable that he will be able to maintain his internal position. We should thus have achieved our secondary objective . . .
>
> Our people here are neither excited nor eager to use force. They are, however, grimly determined that Nasser shall not get away with it this time, because they are convinced that if he does their existence will be at his mercy. So am I.
>
> (Quoted in Carlton, op. cit., p. 416)

A month later Eisenhower was still urging caution:

> The use of military force against Egypt under present circumstances might have consequences even more serious than causing the Arabs to support Nasser. It might cause a serious misunderstanding between our two countries because I must say frankly that there is as yet no public opinion in this country which is prepared to support such a move, and the most significant public opinion that there is seems to think that the United Nations was formed to prevent this very thing . . .
>
> Nasser thrives on drama. If we let some of the drama go out of the situation and concentrate upon the task of deflating him through slower but sure processes . . . I believe the desired results can more probably be obtained. Gradually it seems to me we could isolate Nasser and gain a victory which would not only be bloodless, but would be more far reaching in its ultimate consequences than could be anything brought about by force of arms.
>
> (ibid., p. 419)

British military plans were chopped and changed and necessary equipment was found to be defective. France urged Britain on and to hasten the operation made contact with Israel as a potential assistant. Dulles and the Americans did their best to hold Eden back and proposed a Canal Users' Association. For Dulles this was a device to postpone the use of force and to keep all parties talking. To Eden and the French it was a device likely to provide an excuse for the use of force when Nasser refused to co-operate. Each party in a sense deceived the other. Eden was also being pulled in both directions by forces in Britain. A powerful lobby in the Tory Party was determined that there should be no appeasement and Eden's vanity was wounded by suggestions of parallels with Chamberlain. Macmillan within the Cabinet identified with the 'fire-eaters'. There was also a group anxious to keep within the spirit of the UN. The young Iain Macleod and the influential R. A. Butler could be said to have favoured caution within the Cabinet. The Labour Party was increasingly hostile to force and made it clear that there could be no national consensus if war came. Eden became convinced that he had been deceived by Dulles and despite, or because of, increasing ill health, resolved in October to act. A Franco-Israeli plan looked like providing the moral cover that Eden needed. The Israelis had offered to attack Egypt and race into Sinai. Britain and France could then intervene to seize the canal on the grounds of protecting it from war. Secret meetings were held in France. Eden dragged along an unwilling Foreign Secretary, Selwyn Lloyd, and a deal was struck with the French and the Israelis. The pro-Arab Foreign Office was rightly doubtful of the effects such collusion would have on Britain's relations with the rest of the Arab world. Nevertheless on 22 October Selwyn Lloyd met the Israeli Prime Minister David Ben-Gurion in a villa at Sèvres near Paris. Israel wanted a pre-emptive British strike on the Egyptian bomber force to safeguard Israel's cities. Britain required a moral fig-leaf to justify intervention and refused to move until twelve hours after an Israeli attack. Israel reluctantly agreed. It was an example of the British at their hypocritical worst. The French position was simple and honest. Nasser was an enemy threatening France – they would topple him. The shades of Mr Gladstone hung heavy over the conduct of British foreign policy. As with the first invasion in 1882 Britain needed a moral cover. Then it was defence of the Concert of Europe, now it was international law and the free passage through the Suez Canal. The naked pursuit of national self-interest would not do in Britain's case. The attempt to find a fig-leaf was to add to the humiliation of defeat.

On 29 October the Israelis struck into Sinai. Egypt and Israel each received a twelve-hour ultimatum to withdraw from the Canal. No Israeli forces were within 75 miles of the places they were to withdraw from, and for Egypt it would mean the abandonment of their whole military position. Egypt refused and was promptly hit. The troops set out on their 900-mile voyage from Malta. Eisenhower was outraged. He had timed the Geneva Summit in 1955 to help Eden's election chances in 1955. Eden was not now reciprocating. Britain faced almost universal world condemnation. On 5 November British and French troops seized Port Said and began to advance south to Ismailia. The diplomatic situation rapidly turned into a nightmare. The UN demanded a ceasefire which Israel and Egypt accepted thus removing the moral fig-leaf. There was a run on the pound and dollars were desperately needed to prop it up and pay for oil imports. Harold Macmillan, the Chancellor, and a keen supporter of tough action in September, now insisted on a ceasefire. It was the price of a US loan. A day after they had landed British troops were told it was over.

The whole episode was a disaster internationally. Nasser, far from being toppled, was turned into a Third World celebrity. Britain's friends throughout the Middle East were disheartened, her enemies encouraged. Russia posed as a friend of Egypt by threatening a nuclear strike on Britain and rapidly built up her influence in Egypt. Britain's alignment with Israel, contrary to Foreign Office pro-Arab prejudices, did harm to Britain's position throughout the whole Middle East. Relations with the USA were strained as they were with the French who were filled with contempt for the behaviour of their British partners. Perhaps more than any other episode it symbolized Britain's decline. Eden resigned on 9 January 1957 to be succeeded by Harold Macmillan who had urged invasion and then withdrawal.

Macmillan: the illusion of power

Harold Macmillan proved well equipped to continue the march downhill yet preserve the mystique of great power status. Foreign affairs figures much more prominently in his memoirs than do the more humdrum domestic matters. He became an inveterate traveller often leaving Butler in charge in his absence. He knew Eisenhower well from war-time days and rapidly repaired the breach opened by the Suez Crisis. They met in Bermuda in March 1957 and relations of friendly candour were on display for all to see. This bore fruit in 1958 when a fresh crisis in the Middle East saw close US–British co-operation in sharp contrast to the events of 1956. The friendly regime in Iraq fell in July in a bloody army coup. The bodies of Feisal and Nuri were dragged through the streets of Baghdad. In many ways it was a consequence of Suez and the undermining of British authority to the benefit of Nasser and the radicals. This time the US decided to safeguard western interests in the region and US troops were flown into Lebanon to stabilize that country and to ward off a possible Syrian strike. British troops at the same time moved into Jordan to prop up King Hussein. Both displays of force succeeded in preserving regimes which were felt to be friendly. In the same month Congress repealed the McMahon Act, which had prevented US nuclear co-operation with Britain. This was later to bear much fruit when Macmillan convinced the Americans to provide Britain with Polaris and make possible a credible British nuclear deterrent for the next two decades. Macmillan capitalized on the restored Atlantic partnership when

Eisenhower visited Britain just before the 1959 general election. Macmillan was able to establish a warm personal relationship with the new young Democrat who succeeded Eisenhower as President in 1961. John Kennedy came to have a genuine regard for the much older British statesman and Macmillan was able to pretend to the role of Greek tutor to the Roman Emperor. During the Cuban missile crisis Kennedy consulted with Macmillan almost as one of his Cabinet.

The Prime Minister was also able to maintain a high profile in his relations with Russia. The Khrushchev era was amongst the most dangerous of the Cold War. Nikita Khrushchev had emerged by 1958 as the successor to Stalin. In many respects he was a precursor of Gorbachev – revisionist at home and denouncing Stalinism, but with enough courage and capacity for risk-taking to make him an unpredictable quantity on the international scene. There was less caution than in the days of Stalin and Molotov and a new willingness to gamble and bluff. Fortified by the success of the Sputnik in 1957 the Soviet Union seemed willing to challenge again American world hegemony. There was a renewed confrontation over Berlin and, most serious of all, conflict over the Russian intention to install missiles in Cuba, alarmingly near to the United States. Macmillan was anxious to mediate and extend understanding. He visited Moscow in February 1959 attracting the media's attention with his Finnish fur hat. He played some part in bringing about the summit in 1960 which admittedly achieved little. More importantly he worked hard for the atmospheric nuclear test ban treaty which was finally agreed in August 1963. Such a presence at the tables of the mighty seemed to justify Britain's possession of nuclear weapons.

The whole Macmillan period saw a revolution in defence thinking and an increased reliance on nuclear weapons. Far from being the expensive luxury imagined by CND and the left-wing of the Labour Party they were embraced with enthusiasm as being a cheap means of retaining great power status. Macmillan appointed Duncan Sandys as Minister of Defence to slash conventional defence. The defence paper of 1957 emphasized the high cost of Britain's post-war defence policy:

Demands on Economic Resources

Over the last five years, defence has on average absorbed 10 per cent of Britain's gross national product. Some 7 per cent of the working population are either in the Services or supporting them. One-eighth of the output of the metal-using industries, upon which the export trade so largely depends, is devoted to defence. An undue proportion of qualified scientists and engineers are engaged on military work. In addition, the retention of such large forces abroad gives rise to heavy charges which place a severe strain upon the balance of payments.

(Quoted in M. Dockrill, *British Defence since 1945*, Oxford, Blackwell, 1988, p. 140)

Sandys proposed to abolish conscription and devoted himself to the job of reducing expenditure with an enthusiasm which appalled the service chiefs. The Hull Committee on army manpower needs recommended 200,000 as the minimum number consistent with British defence commitments. Sandys published the figure of 165,000, the total considered possible under voluntary recruiting. Sir Gerald Templer, Chief of the Defence Staff, was not pleased: 'Duncan you're so bloody crooked that if you swallowed a nail you'd shit a corkscrew' (quoted in Healey, op. cit., p. 257). Conscription was abolished in 1960 and increased reliance placed on the deterrent effect of nuclear weapons. Britain had exploded her own hydrogen bomb in May 1957 but possession of the bomb was increasingly not enough. Delivery systems were what separated the men from the boys and it became increasingly clear that Britain could not compete in this area with the USA and the Soviet Union. After spending £60 million the Cabinet decided to cancel 'Blue Streak' in 1960 after it became clear that a further £500 million would be needed. To prolong the nuclear capability of the bombers the US 'Sky Bolt' missiles were to be purchased and Eisenhower agreed to the deal. Unfortunately in November 1962 the USA decided to cancel 'Sky Bolt' leaving Britain with no serious delivery system. Macmillan exerted all his charm and persuasive powers on Kennedy to get him to agree to sell Britain the new Polaris submarine missile. Kennedy reluctantly agreed and the British deterrent was safe for another twenty years but, as many asked, was it still British?

In February 1960 Macmillan made a series of visits in Africa. At Cape Town he intoned the last rites over the British Empire in that continent:

We have seen the awakening of national consciousness in peoples who have for centuries lived in dependence upon some other power. Fifteen years ago this movement spread through Asia. Many countries there of different races and civilisations pressed their claim to an independent national life. Today the same thing is happening in Africa, and the most striking of all the impressions I have formed since I left London a month ago is of the strength of this African national consciousness. In different places it takes different forms, but it is happening everywhere. The wind of change is blowing through this continent, and, whether we like it or not, this growth of national consciousness is a political fact. We must all accept it as a fact, and our national policies must take account of it.

His audience not surprisingly was not enthusiastic but the venue ensured maximum media coverage. Already Ghana had been given independence in 1957. Nigeria, bedevilled by tribal rivalries, was delayed until 1960, but the British had decided to scuttle (see Map 14.1). Suez and the spread of nationalism, especially the militant variety, made the cost of holding colonies against their will insupportable. Only where the issue of departure was complicated by the pressure of white settlers did decolonization become really difficult. Kenya with its white farmers in the highlands proved particularly troublesome. The outbreak of the Kenyan Mau Mau resistance movement and rising in the early 1950s had been largely crushed by 1956, but not before 10,000 had been killed by security forces and nearly ten times that number arrested. The murder of eleven detainees in Hola Camp in 1959 led to a national scandal. Britain, unlike France in Indo-China and Algeria was particularly susceptible to charges of illiberality. The Empire could only be tolerated if profit and decency could be combined, or at least the appearance of decency be given. In October 1959 Macmillan appointed Iain Macleod as Colonial Secretary. Macleod later wrote in *The Spectator*:

> It has been said that after I became Colonial Secretary there was a deliberate speeding-up of the movement towards independence. I agree. There was. And in my view any other policy would have led to terrible bloodshed in Africa. This is the heart of the argument.
> (Quoted in N. Fisher, *I. Macleod*, London, Deutsch, 1973, p. 142)

Macleod's biggest headache was posed by the Central African Federation which was eventually to become Zambia, Malawi and Zimbabwe. The three territories had been federated in 1953 under the leadership of the large white settler minority in Southern Rhodesia (Zimbabwe). The other two territories wanted to go their separate ways and after much argument Britain agreed to dissolve the Federation. Malawi and Zambia were then given their independence under black majority rule. Southern Rhodesia regarded itself as a separate white dominion and the problem of what to do with it was left unresolved when Labour under Harold Wilson replaced the Conservatives in October 1964. With this one exception the British Empire in Africa had been abolished by Macmillan's Government.

In 1962 Dean Acheson, an ex-American Secretary of State, delivered what he hoped was a sympathetic platitude on Britain's position in the world: 'Britain has lost an Empire and not yet found a role.' The role was to be found in Europe but not yet. Under both Eden and Macmillan, Britain distanced herself from the negotiations which led to the setting up of the European Community in January 1958. All Britain could do was attempt to establish a wider and looser European Free Trade Area which would still enable her to have access to the cheap food of her old Empire. The EEC refused to join with the British EFTA and it remained an insubstantial and ultimately sterile organization. By 1961 the Cabinet realized that it had made a mistake in not joining and decided to apply for membership of the EEC. This triggered a violent debate in Britain with vigorous opposition from some Conservatives and much of the Labour Party. Their concern was unnecessary. The ruler of France since 1958, General De Gaulle, saw Britain as a Trojan horse for American influence and was determined to veto her entry. On 29 January 1963 he did just that with a majestic '*Non*'. Britain had truly lost an Empire but

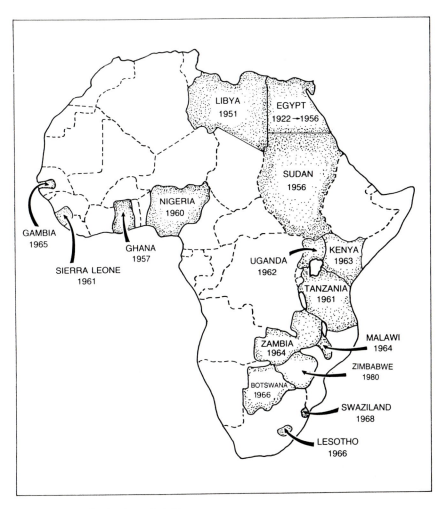

14.1 The decolonization of Africa

not yet found her European niche. That would take another ten years
and two more tries.

THE GOVERNMENT OF WILSON 1964–70

During the six years of Wilson the pretence of great power status became
threadbare. Macmillan's portrayal of the role of world statesman might
evoke satirical comment as in 'Beyond the Fringe', but 'SuperMac' and
his Britain were sufficiently close to the recent reality of world power to
give an edge to the portrayal. Wilson as world statesman was simply
ludicrous in view of the continuing relative economic decline. By 1970
France, West Germany and Japan had overtaken Britain in world econ-

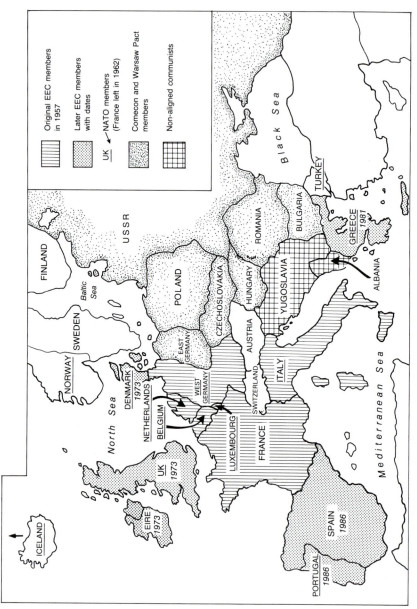

14.2 Europe 1945–89

Original EEC members in 1957

Later EEC members with dates

UK ← NATO members (France left in 1962)

Comecon and Warsaw Pact members

Non-aligned communists

ICELAND

NORWAY

SWEDEN

FINLAND

USSR

DENMARK 1973

EIRE 1973

UK 1973

NETHERLANDS

BELGIUM

WEST GERMANY

EAST GERMANY

POLAND

CZECHOSLOVAKIA

LUXEMBOURG

FRANCE

SWITZERLAND

AUSTRIA

HUNGARY

ROMANIA

YUGOSLAVIA

BULGARIA

ITALY

PORTUGAL 1986

SPAIN 1986

ALBANIA

GREECE 1981

TURKEY

Black Sea

North Sea

Baltic Sea

Mediterranean Sea

omic importance and Britain was sliding rapidly down the standard of living charts of western Europe. The devaluation of the pound in 1967, from $2.80 to $2.40, was another marker of the same directional slide. There was little difference between the new Labour Government and its Tory predecessor in terms of foreign policy. The degree of continuity would have pleased Lord Rosebery just as it sickened the Labour left. The remaining colonies in Africa were rapidly abandoned in 1964–5 with the exception of the difficult problem of Southern Rhodesia. NATO and the nuclear deterrent were quite safe in Labour hands. Harold Wilson had had some sympathy with CND in the 1950s but he rapidly made it clear that Britain would keep Polaris. The rather lame excuse offered was the possible need to defend India against China, a scenario which did not convince either the Indians or the Chinese. CND suffered from exactly the same sort of inflated view of British importance as the extreme Tory right. To the nuclear disarmers Britain's gesture of renunci-ation would give an important moral lead to the world which others would follow. This was clearly nonsense but reality has always been soluble in idealism. The only sop the Labour left received was the cancellation of a fifth submarine. This meant that Britain would only have one at sea at any one time. Wilson clearly intended Britain to maintain her world role. In December 1964 he said: 'I want to make it quite clear that . . . we cannot afford to relinquish our world role.' Denis Healey, the new Defence Secretary, as late as 1966, assured Britain's Far Eastern allies that there would be 'no ratting'. To be fair to both Wilson and Healey it was not obvious that Britain's interests did lie in abandoning her role East of Suez. Her oil supplies from the Middle East, investments, and sources of other raw materials like rubber from Malaysia all seemed to point to a continuing defence posture outside Europe. In 1961 British forces had successfully defended oil-rich Kuwait from General Kasim of Iraq and from 1963 to 1967 successfully aided Malaysian Borneo against an Indonesian threat. There were thus large British forces outside Europe, notably in Aden and Singapore, and to Conservatives and Labour alike it seemed in Britain's best interests to keep them there.

It required another major economic crisis to emphasize the over-exten-sion of British foreign and defence policy commitments. Throughout most of the 1930s when faced with the Nazi menace in close proximity, Britain had not spent more than 3 per cent of her GNP on defence. Since 1945 she had spent more than double this. The drain on her balance of payments of much expenditure abroad was becoming increasingly burdensome and the new Labour Cabinet resolved to cut expenditure to 6 per cent of GNP. This involved the abandonment in 1965 of the projected TSR2 low-level bomber and various other cuts in equipment including a new aircraft carrier. In place of TSR2 it was decided to buy the American FB111A. The days when Britain could produce world-class planes like the Lancaster or even the V-bomber seemed passed. Even these cuts however were clearly insufficient in the light of the crisis of 1967. The devaluation of the pound increased the costs of overseas defence establishments. It was resolved to make dramatic cuts in both equipment and commitments. All British forces would be withdrawn from Malaysia and Singapore by 1971. Aden was to be evacuated immediately. The navy's great fleet carriers were to go in the 1970s and even the American FB111s were to be cancelled. The world role seemed to have vanished as the defence review of 1967 concluded:

> 2 Substantial savings will be made in the demands of defence on the nation's manpower and financial resources. More of our forces will be based in Britain. We plan no major change in the size of our contribution to NATO. The savings will be chiefly obtained from a significant reduction in our military presence outside Europe, and from some changes in its deployment.
>
> (Quoted in Dockrill, op. cit., p. 150)

Europe was to be the new focus of attention as the revived application to join the Common Market indicated. Both the Cabinet and the party was divided on the subject. Wilson maintained a safe position of 'entry when the terms were right'. George Brown, possibly the most dynamic figure in the Cabinet, became Foreign Secretary in August 1966 and was a keen advocate of entry. Wilson himself seems to have been gradually persuaded of the need to make renewed application and a cabinet meeting in October 1966 gave the go-ahead for a Brown–Wilson tour of the European capitals early in 1967. A cabinet meeting on 30 April discussed the pros and cons:

> Eventually we reached the real debate. It took place on a paper by Harold and George listing the alternatives open to us and coming down flatly in favour of an application for entry right away. In the meantime Harold had disposed of the difficulties. Most of the EFTA partners were just waiting our say-so to apply. The Austrian application was hanging fire because of the Russian bar on it, but this was likely to be removed if we went in. As for the Commonwealth, he had been very disappointed at the failure to develop economic links. (This I can believe: Harold has tried very hard to develop them and has had Tommy trying to do so too, without success.) As for political links, the African members had been very difficult whereas Australia and New Zealand had gone Asian. And so, after lunch (during which he had been particularly abstemious), George made the great opening speech for entry. The debate then ran pretty true to form – the big surprises being Dick Marsh's unqualified opposition and Wedgie's passionate speech in favour of a technologically united Europe. Cledwyn Hughes, who has been moaning to me privately about his

fears for the development areas, toed the Wilson line predictably, while Willie Ross stood his ground grimly against. I felt more and more conscious that, however much we might protest, the issue was decided.

(B. Castle, *The Castle Diaries*, 30 April 1967, London, Weidenfeld & Nicolson, p. 249)

Two days later it was resolved to seek 'unconditional application for negotiations about conditions for entry'. Thirty-five Labour MPs voted against entry on 10 May and fifty abstained. They need not have worried as on 16 May General De Gaulle vetoed Britain's entry yet again. He feared Britain was still not sufficiently European, still too inclined to look to Washington and serve as a Trojan horse for turning the EEC into an Atlantic community. To a France which had just left NATO this was an unacceptable vision of the future.

De Gaulle was right in assuming the centrality of Anglo-American relations in British thinking. Wilson and his foreign secretaries, Michael Stewart and George Brown, were anxious to retain their ties with Washington, but increasing US involvement with the war in Vietnam imposed strains on the relationship. The Americans would have liked a symbolic contribution from Britain to the struggle against Viet Cong, the communist-led guerrilla force of South Vietnam. Wilson offered soothing words and gestures of mediation but no men. Direct involvement was totally unacceptable to broad sections of the Labour Party. Britain's refusal to make any sort of physical commitment plus the announced withdrawal from South-East Asia undermined any special relationship which might have existed before. The US failure to consult Britain and her other European allies about her decision to enter strategic arms limitation talks with the USSR in November 1969 thus confirmed suspicions of a cooling relationship.

Britain's declining importance to the USA was a direct reflection, of course, of her declining world importance. Despite Wilson's talk of nuclear guarantees to India it was to Russia that both India and Pakistan turned for help in ending their war over Kashmir in 1965. Britain could also do little in the bitter civil war that broke out in Nigeria as the province of Biafra started to secede. The Labour left criticized Britain's continued support for the unity of the country. The problem of Southern Rhodesia seemed to expose British impotence the most cruelly. Ian Smith, the leader of the Rhodesia Front Party had become Prime Minister of Southern Rhodesia before Labour took office and there had been talk of a unilateral declaration of independence by the 220,000 whites. This would hardly seem acceptable when the overwhelming black majority were left completely unenfranchised. The rest of black Africa found such a course repugnant and both the Tory Government and Wilson's Labour Government sought to head off unilateral declaration of independence. Wilson himself flew to Salisbury (now Harare) in October 1965 to talk Smith out of a drastic breach with Britain. Wilson's public ruling-out of force probably persuaded Smith to go for UDI in November 1965. Britain responded with piecemeal sanctions and Wilson assured his fellow Commonwealth Prime Ministers that they would work in weeks rather than in months. They did not and Britain paid for this as French, German and Japanese cars found a market in Southern Rhodesia in place of British imports. More negotiations with Smith were tried aboard the cruiser *Tiger* in 1966. To many the terms on offer seemed a British climbdown but the Rhodesians rejected them as they did the more modest British proposals in 1968 in talks, this time aboard HMS *Fearless*. Had Smith accepted the terms Wilson would have had considerable difficulty selling them to the Labour Party and the other Commonwealth leaders. Luckily the Rhodesian rejection enabled Wilson to hand the problem on to his Tory successor in 1970. The whole long-running saga showed up Britain's weakness which was not only of material but also of nerve.

THE 1970S: INTO EUROPE

The Conservatives under Edward Heath had attacked the Labour withdrawals from East of Suez and promised to restore some of these commitments. In practice this amounted to no great reversal of policy. The few changes that were made added up to a clinging on to a world role by the fingernails. The old aircraft carrier *Ark Royal* was kept on until 1978 and three mini-carriers ordered, from which Sea Harriers could operate. They were a far cry from the mighty nuclear carriers the US deployed to maintain its world role. The Conservatives, like Labour, accepted that Britain's primary role must be with NATO in Europe. The brutal crushing of the Prague Spring in 1968 when Soviet tanks destroyed the Czech experiment of trying to combine communism and democracy was a frightening reminder of Soviet presence and power. The western democracies perched on the edge of the Asian-European land mass were reminded of the slumbering totalitarian dinosaur that was such an uncomfortable neighbour. It served to reinvigorate NATO defence expenditure. Healey under Labour had promised more money to re-equip BAOR (the British Army of the Rhine) and the new Tory Defence Secretary, Lord Carrington, put up an extra £400 million.

The new Prime Minister was a European in more ways than just being a believer in NATO. Two of his associates commented on this:

> He was always struck by the speed at which Europe was modernising and everywhere we went he pointed out the way in which Europe was investing in new transport, in new facilities and generally higher standards in many ways, and he felt Britain was falling behind.

For Heath, it was never a matter of as it were making Britain's role in Europe that of a lesser power. He saw Britain in Europe as the way back to being a great power again.

(Quoted in P. Whitehead, *The Writing on the Wall: Britain in the Seventies*, London, Michael Joseph, 1985, p. 53)

Europe was not an issue in the 1970 election. The Labour Government was prepared to make another bid for entry, and, with De Gaulle gone, there was high hope of success. Wilson, however, was a European of the head; Heath of the heart. Even with De Gaulle removed, entry was not automatic. The Common Agricultural Policy which had evolved in the 1960s was clearly inimical to British interests. The CAP involved tariffs on food from outside the EEC, the traditional source of Britain's cheap food, and high prices were paid to European farmers to support their income. It was a system designed to protect the interests of France's peasant farmers and it produced mountains and lakes of unwanted and overpriced food and drink. Britain would have to accept this. Difficult negotiations about transitional arrangements safeguarding New Zealand's interests and West Indian sugar producers, the position of the London money market and the sterling balances all dragged on throughout the early part of 1971. The possibility of a French veto still loomed. On 19 May Heath flew to Paris and in long detailed conversations with the French President, Georges Pompidou, convinced the French leader of Britain's good European intentions. Thereafter the chief obstacles were at home. A small band of Tory MPs, with Enoch Powell in the forefront, denounced entry and, more seriously, the Labour Party swung round to oppose Europe. On 28 July the party's national executive condemned Britain's application and the Party Conference voted by a substantial majority in October to stay out. Roy Jenkins, the deputy leader, resigned from the Shadow Cabinet and he and other pro-Market rebels were enough to see Heath home and dry with his European Community Bill, and Britain entered the EEC on 1 January 1973, with Heath signing the treaty of accession in Brussels. The lengthy transitional arrangements softened the cost of the CAP over the next few years. The impact on the direction of British trade was clear.

Entry did not end the debate on the EEC. The return of Labour in 1974 reopened the question of membership. Labour had promised renegotiation or withdrawal. To solve the problem of division within the Party the new government resolved on a referendum in which part of the Cabinet, sixteen, urged a 'Yes' vote and part, seven, urged a 'No' vote. The campaign produced strange alliances. The majority of the Labour Cabinet found itself supported by the bulk of the Tory Party and the CBI. Eventually, 67 per cent confirmed the government's recommendation to stay in. The issue seemed settled but bitter arguments have continued over the question of Britain's payments to the EEC. By 1977 the Treasury was forecasting net out-payments of £880 million, largely arising from the CAP. Only Britain and Germany made such payments and as one of the poorer members of the community this seemed increasingly unfair on Britain. The CAP was to be the source of much ill feeling and friction.

It was the state of the economy that was to dominate Britain's foreign policy in a very overt fashion during the rest of the 1970s, and a devaluation was to symbolize a new British slide. Much of the pressure was outside the British government's control. The world's post-war currency arrangements had already broken down before the oil-price crisis of 1973. The USA abandoned the gold standard in August 1971 and the world entered the age of floating currencies. The sudden hike-up in oil prices in 1973 had a massive depressive effect on the western world transferring $300 billion to the oil producers which they found difficult to spend and thus return to the world economic system. The British economy was particularly vulnerable to shifts in volatile oil funds placed on short-term deposits in New York and London. By 1976 it was generally accepted that sterling was overvalued. In March it fell through the $2.00 barrier and by June it had reached $1.70. Stand-by loans were negotiated and eventually $3.9 billion was borrowed from the IMF with conditions attached. A Labour Government embraced monetarist restraint. It appeared that Britain was now the weakest of the world's major economies. Her economic performance in the 1970s certainly seemed to indicate as much (see Table 14.2). Britain had become the 'sick man' of Europe. In line with economic decline which threatened at times in the 1970s to become absolute rather than relative, Britain's role in the world declined further. Her defence expenditure was reduced to 4.6 per cent of GNP by 1978. The Simonstown Agreement with South Africa was cancelled ending naval facilities at the Cape and the air staging base in the Indian Ocean closed in 1976. Despite decline the governments of both parties proved themselves anxious to retain Britain's nuclear status and the Wilson–Callaghan governments of 1974–9 carried through the Chevaline–Polaris modernization programme in secret. It was concealed from Parliament by charging the £1 billion cost to the maintenance budget.

THE THATCHER YEARS 1979–90

On the surface the new Conservative Government of Margaret Thatcher seemed to heighten Britain's world role and prestige in the 1980s. She found in the new Republican President of the USA, Ronald Reagan, an ideological soul-mate and established an Anglo-American rapport that had not existed since the days of Macmillan. The USA had agreed in 1979 to sell Britain the Trident missile and in 1980 the new government decided to buy this much enhanced nuclear delivery system and thereby

Table 14.2 Annual growth rates of world powers 1950–80

	UK	France	Germany	Italy	Japan	USA
Real domestic product						
1950–5	2.9	4.4	9.1	6.3*	7.1	4.2
1955–60	2.5	4.8	6.4	5.4	9.0	2.4
1960–4	3.4	6.0	5.1	5.5	11.7	2.4
1964–9	2.5	5.9	4.6	5.6	10.6	4.3
1969–73	2.8	6.1	4.5	4.1	9.3	3.4
1970–80	1.9	3.6	2.8	3.0	4.9	3.0
Output per person-hour in manufacturing						
1963–73	4.5	6.7	5.7	7.0	11.2	3.7
1973–6	1.3	3.9	4.5	2.3	2.0	3.4
1976–9	1.2	3.9	3.7	3.0	7.7	2.1
GDP per man-year						
1951–73	2.4	4.4	4.8	5.5	7.9	2.3

* 1952–5

Source: After S. Pollard, *The Wasting of the British Economy*, London, Croom Helm, 1982, p. 346.

maintain Britain's nuclear status into the next century. The Trident system would, in fact, give Britain a much enlarged nuclear capability. In response to the Soviet deployment of medium-range SS20 nuclear missiles in central Europe, Britain invited the deployment of 96 US Cruise missiles at Greenham Common and Molesworth. This elicited noisy but quite ineffective protests from CND groups which suddenly once more grew as the nuclear arms race appeared to be accelerating. Thatcher appeared to enjoy a popularity in the USA unmatched by any British leader since Churchill. This served Britain well during the Falklands war when US aid was invaluable. The government was able to repay the favour in 1986 when alone of America's European allies Britain permitted US jets to operate from British territory against Libya. Britain clearly appeared to the USA to be her most loyal and congenial ally. Possibly as a result of her close working relationship with Washington, the new Soviet administration of Gorbachev decided to court Mrs Thatcher and a surprisingly good relationship developed between the two leaders. The very longevity of her leadership inevitably heightened her world profile and at times Britain seemed to play a vital link role between Europe and the USA and even Soviet Russia. It was almost a return to the days of Ernie Bevin.

The ghosts of Empire even conspired to enhance the Thatcher role of world leader. Early in her administration her first Foreign Secretary, Lord Carrington, was able to secure a triumph in the settlement of the long-running Rhodesian situation. Sanctions had continued since the 1960s but to minimal effect. It was the growing black guerrilla groups of Robert Mugabe and Joshua Nkomo which finally brought the Smith regime to the negotiating table. Under constant guerrilla pressure Smith introduced a new constitution which on the surface appeared to concede the chief British and Commonwealth demand of black majority rule. In April 1979 Bishop Muzorewa became Prime Minister with Smith and other whites in the Cabinet. Real power remained in the hands of the whites and Mugabe's and Nkomo's guerrillas refused to accept the legitimacy of the constitution. The instincts of Mrs Thatcher, like that of the right of the Conservative Party were to recognize Muzorewa and drop sanctions. Lord Carrington and the Foreign Office disagreed:

> Our recognizing the Muzorewa regime would have led to the most appalling problems, starting with the isolation of Britain from the rest of the world, including the United States. It would have settled nothing and intensified the war, leading to much more bloodshed. It would probably have brought the thing everyone had been most anxious to avoid, Soviet and Cuban involvement.
>
> (Quoted in Lapping, op. cit., p. 608)

Carrington got all the parties to a conference at Lancaster House and after skilfully isolating Smith from Muzorewa persuaded the three black rivals to accept a constitution and supervised elections. An ex-Cabinet minister, Lord Soames, was sent out to be the last British Governor and with much tact and considerable bravery on the part of his military and civilian assistants made a success of the mission. The election was won by the Marxist Mugabe who expressed his trust of and fondness for the last British Governor of an African territory. The whole episode was a triumph for the Foreign Office and the tradition, well practised since 1945, of conceding the inevitable with grace and skill. The triumph was essentially Carrington's not Thatcher's.

Two years later roles and tactics were reversed in another imperial issue 8,000 miles to the south of Britain, in the wind-battered South Atlantic: the Falkland Islands. They were inhabited by some 1,800 souls of British descent living largely by sheep-rearing and were in every sense a forgotten, unloved relic. For years the Foreign Office had sought an amicable settlement of their future with nearby Argentina who had claimed the islands since Palmerston had asserted British sovereignty in the 1830s. Had the islanders agreed, transfer to Argentina would willingly have been effected by London. In 1980 Nicholas Ridley, then a junior Foreign Office minister, explained that Britain was exploring a lease-back scheme by which Argentina would acquire the islands with nominal sovereignty but then lease them back to Britain. The idea was howled down in the Commons by MPs on all sides. In December 1981 General Leopoldi Galtieri took over the leadership of a brutal military junta that had ruled Argentina since 1975. The seizure of the Falklands would consolidate the junta's popularity and all the signs were that Britain would not seriously resist. The Thatcher Government's defence review of 1981 proposed to withdraw the one British naval unit in the South Atlantic – the ice-patrol vessel *Endurance*. It seemed a clear signal confirming British indifference.

On Friday 2 April 1982 a large Argentinian invasion force occupied the islands overwhelming the small garrison of Marines. On the same day the Cabinet ordered the preparation of a naval task force. Initially this was probably to strengthen Britain's bargaining position but it received such an assault of criticism in a special session of the Commons on Saturday the 3rd that the Prime Minister declared that all necessary steps would be taken to restore the islands to British rule. Carrington insisted on resigning and carrying the blame for misreading Argentinian intentions. The Prime Minister now really earned her nickname of the 'Iron Lady' with a display of firmness which surprised many of her ministers who still anticipated a compromise settlement. The British government handled the situation with some skill securing the vital support of the USA and the EEC and having Argentina condemned in the Security Council of the UN. The naval task force of 44 ships and 28,000 men was dispatched with an efficiency which compared well with Suez, twenty-six years earlier. It involved frightful risks in view of the lack of adequate air-cover and air-warning. The lack of a major fleet carrier was sadly missed and only the old *Hermes*, scheduled for scrapping, and the mini-carrier *Invincible*, were available with a small force of Harriers. Six ships were sunk and ten damaged. Many more would have been lost had the timing fuses in Argentinian bombs been correctly adjusted. A successful Exocet strike on one of the carriers would have put paid to the expedition and the government. The Prime Minister's nerve and luck held and by 14 June 11,313 Argentinians had surrendered and the Union flag was flying once again over Port Stanley. The cost was approximately £1,500 million with 225 men dead with a further 777 wounded. National honour and international law had been upheld. Whether these were vital British interests must be the subject of continuing debate. The British people clearly felt so and in a democratic country a government should not be pilloried for fulfilling national will. Mrs Thatcher may have reaped the electoral benefits the following year with a landslide victory. Galtieri paid the price of failure. The Fates could easily have reversed their fortunes.

Britain's and Thatcher's world status was raised by this minor colonial conflict conducted in the full glare of media coverage. Britain's response was perhaps puzzling to some but induced a grudging respect from most. The apparent recovery of the British economy also added to this new position. Between 1982 and 1987 Britain's growth seemed the strongest in Europe reversing the pattern of the previous decade and much was made of this in the 1987 election. The reality of decline had not been altered. By the late 1980s Italy had pushed Britain one more place down the league table of the great. She was now seventh in world importance, rich and powerful still, compared to most, but the least important of the leading western economies. Her rate of growth sank by 1989, once again below West Germany and France, and the huge balance of payments deficit indicated continuing economic weakness. The pound also slid once again to the level of the mid-1970s at $1.60 and this in spite of North Sea oil. Hong Kong was dealt with in the traditional Foreign Office fashion, a skilful retreat. Mrs Thatcher was talked into dropping her demands for continued sovereignty over the island of Hong Kong by her flexible men at the Foreign Office. Within Europe the Prime Minister made few friends by her inflexibility and, if she secured victories by reducing Britain's contribution to the EEC budget, her determined opposition to European Monetary Union and the Social Charter seemed increasingly to marginalize her country, making politically explicit the facts of geography. The important changes of 1989 all added up to this process of marginalization. The new American President George Bush was far less inclined than Ronald Reagan to play up to the special relationship. The break-up of the Soviet Empire in eastern Europe shifted the focus of attention to Germany. The German Chancellor, Helmut Kohl, was not one of Mrs Thatcher's fans and the prospect of reunification made Germany's importance all the greater. Bush and the Americans were inevitably forced to shift their gaze to Central Europe. As in the 1950s, a period which Mrs Thatcher had seemed anxious to relive, America was frustrated by Britain's half-heartedness in Europe and Europe was increasingly irritated and inclined to press ahead without their uncomfortable island neighbour. Triumphs like the Falklands and the presence of Ronald Reagan in the White House had made it momentarily possible to believe in a return to Britain's role of the late 1940s and early 1950s. Cinderella had gone to the ball but 1989 broke the spell. Britain was once again seen for what she was, a middle-ranking European state forced by her geographic position and her economic problems to sit on the sidelines.

By 1990 Britain occupied a position in the world very different from that in 1945. Her Empire had gone, she had accepted the inevitable and entered Europe but still seemed the least enthusiastic member of the Community. The direction of her trade and her economic links reflected this change, but still vast investment went into the USA who remained a close economic and diplomatic partner. Britain's overseas investments had been rebuilt and increased many times beyond their 1939 level. Japanese investment in Britain was sought and welcomed in a way unimaginable in 1945. Yet in some very important ways 1990 saw the wheel return to where it had been in 1945. For nearly half a century the Cold War had provided the essential strategic parameters of all Britain's defence and foreign policy planning. The collapse of the Soviet Empire in eastern Europe in 1989 and the prospect of Soviet communism dismantling itself inside the Union ended the Cold War. The great glacier which had covered eastern Europe in 1945 melted with a suddenness quite unlooked for. All at once problems buried since the 1930s resurfaced. Balkan rivalries were still there to plague the Continent and, most ominous of all, a reunited Germany. The 1990s present us with a new Europe with old problems.

CONTROVERSY

One of the major problems for the student of very recent history lies in the 'thirty year rule' which prevents the publication of official records, cabinet minutes for example, until thirty years after the event. In some cases like the abdication crisis of 1936 even then the official records are not released. Despite this handicap the tendency of ministers to rush into print with memoirs, and even to publish full and detailed diaries, has opened up the secrets of cabinet government in a way unthinkable before the war. The Labour Government of 1964 to 1970 has been particularly well, or badly, served in this respect. The Prime Minister himself published in record time, in 1971. Denis Healey, the forceful Minister of Defence, took rather longer and devotes less space to the same period in his *The Time of My Life* (1989). Most important of all have been three diaries – those of Richard Crossman, Barbara Castle and most recently Tony Benn. It is perhaps useful and salutary to take one incident and compare some of these sources on that issue.

A minor theme running through British foreign policy since the 1950s has been Britain's relations with South Africa. From time to time it has received major media coverage when some fresh atrocity has been perpetrated like the murder of Steve Biko or some group of British sportsmen have offended liberal sentiment in Britain by seeking to play there. South Africa has at all times had close economic relations with Britain and trade and investments have been of considerable importance. The system of apartheid and the general treatment of the black majority has always given a moral dimension to the relationship between the two countries. To many groups in Britain, South Africa's white regime has more often than not topped the world's demonology charts.

In December 1967 Anglo-South African relations produced a minor cabinet crisis on the specific issue of selling arms to the Republic. Wilson himself makes an important disclaimer in his book on p. 473: 'In writing this book I have not felt it appropriate in general to draw back the veil which rightly covers the detailed transactions of a cabinet.' Even allowing for this his passage referring to the vital meeting on Friday 15 December 1967 is surely misleading in its glossing over of the issues:

The Cabinet met on the Friday morning with George Brown there, and confirmed the OPD decision that all matters considered relevant to exports and economic policy should be considered in the review which the Defence Committee had decided to make over the next month. It was agreed that the House should be so informed when I announced the expenditure review the following week, making clear that this did not in any sense mean that a decision was already taken in principle.

That afternoon, the most blatant and inaccurate briefing of the press I have ever known was organised, damaging alike to the coherence of the Cabinet and to our standing in the party. The line was that the South African arms policy was to be reversed, and that I had been defeated on the issue in Cabinet. I was in no doubt who was responsible; there were fingerprints all over the place. In any case, George was good enough to write to me defending his action.

(H. Wilson, *The Labour Government 1964–1970*, London, Weidenfeld & Nicolson, 1977, p. 473)

It can be compared with Denis Healey's recollections written many years later:

The resumed Cabinet took place on Friday December 15th. It was the most unpleasant meeting I have ever attended. George Brown was thunderous in denouncing Wilson's campaign of character assassination, and his manipulation of the press. Besides Brown and me, Jim Callaghan, Tony Crosland, Gordon Walker, and Ray Gunter proposed selling the arms immediately. Roy Jenkins, George Thomson, Dick Crossman, Fred Peart, Willie Ross, Dick Marsh and Frank Longford also favoured selling the arms, but after some delay. This made a total of thirteen. The Prime Minister's opposition was supported only by Michael Stewart, Barbara Castle, Peter Shore, Tony Benn, Tony Greenwood, Gerald Gardner and Cledwyn Hughes – a total of eight. George Brown threatened to read out the letter the Prime Minister had sent him in July, asking that he should raise the matter with South Africa. I did read out the Prime Minister's summing up of the committee meeting a week earlier, which agreed in principle to sell the arms. In fact a good time was had by all.

(Healey, op. cit., pp. 335–6)

These two accounts can then be weighed against the diarists mentioned above. Barbara Castle ends a fairly lengthy entry on the meeting with the following:

Harold summed up by first expressing his own point of view: he was against changing our policy. He then said he thought the feeling was eleven to seven against change, but George said tartly, 'Some of us can count and we don't make it out that way.' He, Jim, Healey and

Crosland argued fiercely for Dick's proposal. Peart and Marsh backed it, and suddenly Harold switched. It couldn't be done quite in the way Dick suggested: the proposition that we should solve our problems by selling arms all over the world wasn't on. But we could say there was going to be a comprehensive economic statement in the New Year. In the meantime the policy remained unchanged. Our group was furious and went out utterly disconsolate. My only hope is that Harold intends to use the breathing space to do some more mobilizing. And it is true that there wasn't a majority in Cabinet for making no change. Nonetheless I think we could have got away with it if Dick hadn't put his oar in.

(*The Castle Diaries*, op. cit., p. 340)

Crossman uses the episode to criticize Wilson's style of cabinet management:

'I propose that everything, including South African arms, should be decided in one single package decision.' That, I said, was the line the P.M. should take because it would keep the Cabinet together. As soon as I put this forward Harold's unqualified supporters burst into shouts of fury and said it would be fatal. At this point James Callaghan observed, 'That's far worse than anything.' But, apart from Callaghan, George's supporters came out in favour and so did Frank Longford. At this point Harold also accepted it, adding, 'If that is really wanted by Cabinet I'll accept it, but is it really wanted?' I said, 'Please, Prime Minister, don't count the votes again, make up your own mind, decide for yourself.' He said, 'Well, as for what I want personally I would rather not accept your mediating proposal.' 'Very well,' I said, 'don't accept it,' and he replied, 'No, if it's the wish of Cabinet I will.' So he got himself into this curious situation of forcing Cabinet to decide for him. But I wouldn't take it and said, 'No, I can't accept that. This mediating proposal will be useless unless the Prime Minister really believes in it himself.'

(*The Crossman Diaries*, London, Methuen, 1967, p. 424)

In fact, Wilson got his way, the ban stayed and he kept his Cabinet together. It was a political triumph of sorts. It will, however, be fascinating to read the official record in 1997.

BIBLIOGRAPHY

For an explanation of the grading system, see the preface p. xiii.

Biographies

Ernest Bevin

3   Bullock, A., London, Heinemann, 1983

Winston Churchill

4   Gilbert, M., Vol. 2, Oxford, Heinemann, 1988

Anthony Eden

3   Carlton, D., London, Allen Lane, 1981
2/3 James, R. R., London, Weidenfeld & Nicolson, 1986

Denis Healey

3   *The Time of My Life*, London, Michael Joseph, 1989

I. Macleod

3   Fisher, N., London, Deutsch, 1973

Harold Macmillan

3   Horne, A., 2 vols, London, Macmillan, 1988 and 1989
2   Sampson, A., London, Allen Lane, 1967

Harold Wilson

3   *Memoirs 1916–1964: The Making of a Prime Minister*, London, Weidenfeld & Nicolson, 1986
3   *The Labour Government 1964–1970: A Personal Memoir*, London, Weidenfeld & Nicolson, 1986
3   *Final Term: The Labour Government 1974–1976*, London, Weidenfeld & Nicolson, 1979

General works

4   Barker, E., *Britain and Divided Europe*, London, Weidenfeld & Nicolson, 1971
1/2 Brown, C. and Mooney, P., *Cold War to Detente*, London, Heinemann, 1976
3   Carlton, D., *Britain and the Suez Crisis*, Oxford, Blackwell, 1988

1	Chamberlain, M. E., *Decolonisation*, Oxford, Blackwell, 1985
2/3	Darwin, J., *The End of the British Empire*, Oxford, Blackwell, 1991
	Dilks, D. (ed.), *Retreat from Power*, Vol. II, London, Macmillan, 1981
3	Dockrill, M., *British Defence since 1945*, Oxford, Blackwell, 1988
3	Freedman, L., *Britain and the Falklands War*, Oxford, Blackwell, 1988
2	Hastings, M. and Jenkins, S., *The Battle for the Falklands*, London, Michael Joseph, 1983
2	Kennedy, P., *The Realities Behind Diplomacy*, London, Fontana, 1981
2	Lapping, B., *The End of Empire*, London, Granada/Paladin, 1985
2/3	McIntyre, W. D., *Colonies into Commonwealth*, London, Blandford, 1966
3	Panday, B. N., *The Breakup of British India*, London, Macmillan, 1969
3/4	Thomas, H., *Armed Truce: The Beginnings of the Cold War*, London, Hamish Hamilton, 1986
2/3	Thomas, H., *The Suez Affair*, London, Pelican, 1970

Sources for coursework

There has been a welter of published primary sources which the student can readily obtain and use to make illuminating comparisons. The most obvious are relating to the Labour Government of 1964 and 1970 and these have already been mentioned in the controversy section. The Castle and Benn diaries extend into the 1970s as do Healey's memoirs. The 1950s are well served by memoirs and the Suez Crisis can be looked at with profit through different eyes:

Eden, A., *The Memoirs of Sir Anthony Eden: Full Circle*, London, Cassell, 1960
Lloyd, S., *A Personal Account*, London, Cape, 1978
Macmillan, H., *Harold Macmillan: Memoirs 1914–1963*, 6 vols, London, Macmillan, 1966–73
Nutting, A., *No End of a Lesson*, London, Constable, 1967
Shuckburgh, E., *Diaries of Evelyn Shuckburgh: The Descent to Suez*, London, Weidenfeld & Nicolson, 1986
Memoirs and diaries regularly appear in print, and can be easily found.

Finally, students should be prepared to use and analyse the wealth of statistical data available which has a vital bearing on foreign and colonial policy. Books like *Britain in Context* by John D. Hey (Oxford, Blackwell, 1979) present statistics in a readily available form, but the more adventurous can turn to the annual *Abstract of Statistics* published by HMSO and to the UN and World Bank statistical publications.

Index